Successful Proposal Strategies for Small Businesses

Using Knowledge Management to Win Government, Private-Sector, and International Contracts

Sixth Edition

For a complete listing of the *Artech House Technology Management and Professional Development Series,* turn to the back of this book.

Successful Proposal Strategies for Small Businesses

Using Knowledge Management to Win Government, Private-Sector, and International Contracts

Sixth Edition

Robert S. Frey

ARTECH HOUSE

BOSTON | LONDON
artechhouse.com

Library of Congress Cataloging-in-Publication Data
A catalog record for this book is available from the U.S. Library of Congress.

British Library Cataloguing in Publication Data
A catalogue record for this book is available from the British Library.

ISBN-13: 978-1-60807-474-7

Cover design by Vicki Kane

© **2012 ARTECH HOUSE**
685 Canton Street
Norwood, MA 02062

10 9 8 7 6 5 4 3 2 1

For
my friend and colleague,
Mike McDermott,
whose energy and 'be-there-whenever'
dedication are exemplary

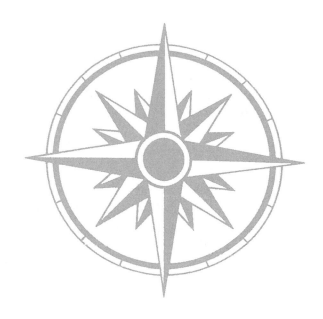

Contents

Chapter 6

Chapter 7

Chapter 8

Chapter 9

Chapter 10

Appendix D

Selected list of acronyms and abbreviations   599

Selected bibliography   645

About the author   669

Index   673

Acknowledgments

THE SIXTH EDITION OF THIS BOOK HAS BEEN DEVELOPED, EXPANDED, and refined during the past 25 years. I would like to express my appreciation once again to Mr. Bruce Elbert, series editor of the Artech House Technology Management and Professional Development Series. He must also be recognized and thanked for relentlessly yet good-naturedly stretching the book into new areas. This work has been enhanced greatly through his efforts, and I am genuinely appreciative. Artech's acquisition editor, Ms. Deirdre Byrne, has ably orchestrated and supported the development of this new edition.

The graphic-arts talent and sustained responsiveness of Ms. Lisa Richard must also be recognized. Lisa generated the graphics for all six editions of this book. She can be contacted at lotslr@austin.rr.com.

Finally, the business and editorial acumen of Mrs. Terry Raezer Frey contributed significantly to the value, consistency, and readability of this work. For her love and unconditional day-to-day support, I am both a better author and a better person.

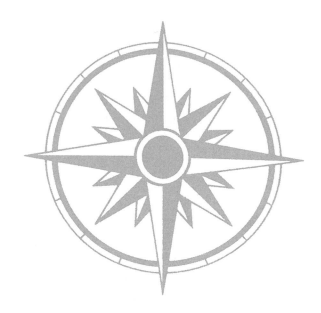

Introduction

BUSINESS OWNERS, leaders, and marketing professionals all pursue economic success. Conveying the strengths of your organization in terms that are meaningful to your customers' technical requirements, business objectives, and mission goals is critical to that success. Directly applicable for both small and large businesses, *Successful Proposal Strategies for Small Businesses, Sixth Edition*, provides extensive context, field-proven approaches, and in-depth techniques for business success with the federal government, the largest buyer of services and products in the world. The deep value of this book is found in its *practicality*—it functions immediately as an essential guide to winning new business. Fundamentally, the book will serve as an insightful "partner" in your firm. It will help you to plan, organize, and execute effectively and efficiently across the many dimensions of proposal development and business development. Using this book, small companies with a viable service or product can learn how to gain and keep a customer's attention, even when working with only a few employees. The book will assist you in avoiding many of the pitfalls associated with pursuing government, private-sector, and international business and, in the process, save valuable bid-and-proposal money and contribute to your organization's confidence and success as a competitor in the high-velocity global marketplace.

Fundamentally, *Successful Proposal Strategies for Small Businesses*: *Using Knowledge Management to Win Government, Private-Sector, and International Contracts, Sixth Edition,* and its companion DVD are highly accessible, self-contained desktop references developed to be informative, practical, and easy to use. They help small and mid-sized businesses, as well as nonprofit organizations and public-sector agencies, achieve effective, efficient, and disciplined business development, capture management, proposal development, and knowledge management (KM) processes. These, in turn, contribute to increased contract and grant awards, bookings, and enhanced levels of revenue. Using this book, any small company or organization with a viable product or service can learn how to gain and keep a client's attention, even when working with only a few employees. Entrepreneurs can use the book to assist in establishing best-of-breed business development, capture management, proposal development, knowledge management (KM), and publications infrastructures and processes within their organizations. In many ways, a small company's future performance in the marketplace will be a direct result of how effectively it chooses to implement disciplined business development, proposal development, and KM processes and methodologies, as well as the modes of thinking presented in this work.

Reviews of previous editions of this book have been published in such prestigious forums as *Business Week* (New York); *USAToday.com*; *Minorities and Women in Business* (Washington, D.C.); *Turning Point* magazine (Los Angeles); *Canada One Magazine* (on the Web); *E-merging Business* magazine (Pacific Palisades, California); *Small Business Advisor* (Los Angeles); and *Women's Business of South Florida* (Hollywood, Florida). In addition, Amazon.com lists exemplary reviews of the book's various editions.

Successful Proposal Strategies for Small Businesses, Sixth Edition, provides effective, field-tested guidance for small businesses (SB), disadvantaged business enterprises (DBEs), minority business enterprises (MBEs), women-owned business enterprises (WBEs), service-disabled, veteran-owned (SDVO) firms, and other organizations to plan, organize, manage, and develop effective, highly competitive responses to federal, state, and local government requests for proposals (RFPs) or requests for solution (RFSs), private-sector solicitations, and international tenders. Entrepreneurs, business development staff, capture managers, proposal managers, proposal writers, proposal specialists, and coordinators will benefit from applying the structured processes illustrated in this work.

Specific focus is on small and midsized business enterprises and exploring the important human and organizational dynamics related to the proposal life cycle that contribute directly to winning new contracts. Step by step, *Successful Proposal Strategies for Small Businesses, Sixth Edition,* clearly maps and details every stage of the contractor proposal response life cycle. This work shows how to maximize small business strengths and leverage knowledge and intellectual capital in order to conduct client-centered marketing and produce benefits-focused, requirements-driven proposals and oral presentations that respond fully to client success criteria and critical issues. This new edition discusses the proposal solution development process, the critical elements of and differences between understanding and approach, proven approaches for building the cost/price volume, and the criticality of business culture and investments in proposal success. Importantly, careful consideration is given to the overall reduction in discretionary spending in the federal marketspace in 2012 and beyond[1]. The sixth edition is also valuable for educators in preparing grant proposals and in teaching proposal development courses in business curricula in colleges, universities, and distance-learning programs. Importantly, a full section is devoted to successful grant proposal management. Furthermore, as the U.S. federal government evolves and sells its services to other branches of government, government staff can also leverage the proven and agile marketing, knowledge management, proposal development, and communications strategies presented in this edition.

Salient among the new edition's contributions to this field is its focus on the proposal as a sales document and on demonstrating how structured and repeatable KM processes, approaches, and automated tools directly benefit companies' proposal and oral presentation development efforts. The book places the proposal response process within the larger context of small companies' overall strategic and mission planning, as well as business development and corporate communication and image management activities. An extremely comprehensive and expanded listing of small business Web-based resources, as well as business and proposal-related acronyms, is also provided both in the book and on the accompanying DVD. The DVD also includes fully updated, useful, and timesaving proposal- and marketing-related templates, along with planning and review tools.

---

1   In FY2010, the federal government spent less on goods and services through contracts than it did in FY2009 across both defense and civilian agencies. See David Hubler, "Federal Contract Spending Slowdown Just Beginning, OMB Official Says," *Washington Technology,* February 18, 2011.

Among the highly beneficial aspects of this book's sixth edition are significant additions and expanded treatment of topics that include: (1) proven processes and tools for building a competitive cost/price volume, (2) approaches for developing key conceptual graphics very early in the proposal process, (3) differences between and key structural elements of understanding and approach, (4) step-by-step guidance through the proposal solution development process, and (5) linkages between business culture and investments in driving proposal success.

Successful Proposal Strategies for Small Businesses, Sixth Edition, gives both the big picture and the down-in-the-trenches perspective about marketing and proposal development, management, production, and infrastructure support in a rapidly evolving global economy. The book discusses how marketing and proposal life cycles can and should mesh with operational, management, and infrastructure support activities within a small company and shows how human and organizational dynamics drive successful marketing and proposal processes.

Unlike most books, e-books, DVDs, and training seminars on developing proposals, *Successful Proposal Strategies for Small Businesses, Sixth Edition,* focuses on the special constraints and strengths of small businesses as they relate to the proposal process. Many of the best-known proposal seminars, for example, are designed for large businesses competing on massive defense and aerospace hardware and systems procurements. Marketing and proposal development in a small business environment—particularly in the support services arena—presents special challenges in terms of support infrastructure, staffing levels, depth of expertise, bid and proposal resources, and business culture. Meeting these distinctive challenges is the purpose of this new edition.

The late Vince Lombardi, legendary coach of the Green Bay Packers, is reputed to have said that he longed to "lie exhausted in victory." That is, to expend the very best effort, to harness the talent and spirit within, and to channel that immense power toward a very specific goal. In Lombardi's thoughts, that goal was victory in the early Super Bowl competitions of the National Football League. In my own thoughts, that goal is to bring all the knowledge, experience, initiative, and positive emotion—the passion—I can into producing a winning proposal.

Unlike many other professions, proposal preparation in the contractor arena for federal, state, local, private-sector, and international opportunities occurs in very discrete and often overlapping bundles of intense activity. There is a clear beginning, middle, and end to the preparation process. Often in a mere span of 5 to 45 days and nights, a host of technical and programmatic information, cost strategies, and marketing intelligence must be condensed, distilled, and fitted together into a set of polished documents. Considering the length of time required to bring journals and books to press, it is astounding that such a choreographed process of information retrieval and management, assembly, and packaging must unfold in the space of only a week or several weeks! And yet for those small and large businesses that compete in the contracting marketplace, it is a matter of survival.

Successful proposal preparation is built largely upon a winning attitude, commitment, attention to detail, teamwork at all levels, communication, emotional and physical endurance, and adequate and well-timed allocation of company human and material resources. To be sure, success also depends upon marketing intelligence about the customer and your competition, informed and timely bid–no bid decisions, planning, scheduling, and superior information management. But my experience has suggested that what makes the difference once a company decides to respond to an RFP or SF330 synopsis lies in the area of human and organizational dynamics rather than in technical and strategic excellence alone. Can a diverse group of technical, management, and support people work together effectively for protracted periods of time—including nights, weekends, and holidays—to produce a winning document? Will company management commit the best technical talent, contract with proven proposal development consultants, lease or acquire adequate computer or publishing equipment, make dedicated work space available for the proposal team, or allocate bonus monies to reward the above-and-beyond efforts of particular people?

To lie exhausted in victory. Plans and milestone schedules, bullet drafts and storyboards, writing and editorial guidelines, action item lists, internal review cycles, and document configuration management schemas all come down to one thing—getting a winning proposal assembled, out the door or uploaded, and delivered before the established due date. While I was coordinating a $100 million Air Force proposal for a Virginia-based contractor, the entire marketing and proposal life cycle came down to one overcast Saturday in December, not long before the holidays. Thoughts were not on marketing target identification, intelligence gathering, teaming arrangements, RFP analysis, outline development, program pricing, or Red Team review comments. Rather, there were 150 copies of various volumes that had to be photoreproduced and put into three-ring notebooks, with multiple foldout pages inserted in each one, and an overnight carrier office nearby that was scheduled to close promptly at 5 P.M. Just the night before, several members of the proposal team had worked into the early morning hours. People were exhausted from several weeks of grueling schedules, missed meals, and no recreation, taping boxes shut at breakneck speed, loading them into several cars, and making multiple trips to the shipping office. When that effort was over, I, along with several members of my staff, felt too tired to move. And yet, there was a palpable feeling of accomplishment, a feeling of victory.

For those full-time professionals in the proposal development business, proposals must become a way of life if we are to survive and grow in our careers. Alternative strategies for time management, stress management, family life, and personal pursuits must be developed and nurtured. In ways analogous to military service, the proposal professional must adjust quickly despite tiredness, personal and family concerns, time of day or night, and level of pressure. But the possibility of personal satisfaction from performing proposal work well can be second to none.

Chapter 1

Competitive proposals and small business

S*uccessful Proposal Strategies for Small Businesses: Using Knowledge Management to Win Government, Private-Sector, and International Contracts, Sixth Edition,* is designed to provide entrepreneurs, as well as beginner and experienced proposal managers, capture managers, proposal writers, proposal specialists and coordinators, and business development staff with a useful resource for planning, organizing, managing, and preparing effective responses to U.S. federal government requests for proposals (RFPs), requests for solutions (RFSs), and architect-engineer (A-E) standard form (SF) 330s. (Architectural and engineering firms submit SF330s routinely to establish their credentials with client organizations.) There is also significant attention devoted to responding to U.S. private-sector solicitations and international tenders.

This book illustrates the close relationship between the federal acquisition process and the response life cycle that unfolds within the contractor community. The specialized statutory and regulatory structure that currently governs and dominates the federal acquisition process and the contractor proposal process is summarized. Important directions and challenges in the federal acquisition process are highlighted. Ethical business acquisition practices are emphasized, and effective long-term marketing and customer-relationship building approaches are presented.

Small businesses are confronted with distinctive opportunities and constraints in the federal marketplace. *Successful Proposal Strategies for Small Businesses* focuses specifically on small business enterprises, exploring the important human and organizational dynamics related to the proposal life cycle that can facilitate success in acquiring new business. Thinking to win is a crucial aspect in the world of federal, private-sector, and international procurement.

Salient points in the contractor proposal response life cycle are discussed in detail, as are the major components of the proposal documents and the client's RFPs. The role of a small company's proposal manager is explored at length, and valuable knowledge management (KM) activities in support of the proposal process are described. Effective proposal-writing techniques are provided along with successful proposal publication and production scenarios. Proposal and marketing cost-tracking, control, and recovery strategies are reviewed; and select client and competitor information and intelligence sources for the U.S. government, U.S. private-sector, and international opportunities are enumerated (Appendix C). Guidance for planning and producing compliant and responsive SF330s is presented. And structuring proposals for international and U.S. private-sector clients is discussed as well. Finally, to support the users of *Successful Proposal Strategies for Small Businesses*, a comprehensive and expanded listing of proposal, business, and acquisition-related acronyms is provided as are definitions of select terminology (Appendix D).

No one person or methodology can offer absolutely definitive step-by-step instructions to win federal, private-sector, or international proposals. There are no shortcuts to building and growing an entire business development infrastructure to market clients, develop long-term professional relationships, and win new business. In recognition of the hard work, right thinking, informed decisions, careful planning, and exacting execution of proper proposal techniques, this book is offered as a starting point in proposal literacy. We hope that it serves as a users' manual, consulted frequently for suggestions and guidance throughout the proposal planning and response process. Best wishes for successful proposals in your company's future!

1.1 Overview

Winning. The federal competitive procurement process [1] is absolutely binary—contractors either win or lose with their proposals. With the exception of multiple-award situations, there are no rewards for coming in second. To allocate your company's bid and proposal (B&P), marketing, and internal research and development (IR&D) funds to pursue procurements for which there is only a marginal probability of winning is, at best, questionable business planning. Your small business will grow best when you maximize your proposal win rate. Federal agencies often have a variety of domestic, as well as overseas,[1] contractor or vendor firms from which to select a specific supplier of goods or services. At a minimum, you have to know your potential client and his or her requirements and critical success factors, as well as hopes, fears, and biases; and, in turn, your client must be made aware of your company's particular technical capabilities and solutions, relevant contractual experience, managerial experience, available human talent, and financial stability in the context of an ongoing marketing relationship. One or two briefings from your company to top-level government agency administrators will most likely be insufficient to secure new business in the highly competitive federal marketplace. This applies to the state, municipality, and U.S. private-sector marketplaces as well. Organizations, in general, procure goods and services from companies that they have come to know and trust and that have demonstrated an ongoing interest in an organization's mission as well as technical, operational, programmatic, and profitability (budgetary) issues. Increasingly, client organizations expect your company to share both technological and cost risks for a given program.

Many small contracting firms that provide goods and services to the federal government are primarily or even solely dependent upon federal contracts for their survival and growth. Consequently, proposal development, management, design, and preparation are the most important business activities that your company performs. Proposal development and writing are more than just full-time jobs. It can be a 12- to 16-hour-a-day, 6- or 7-day-a-week effort just to keep from falling hopelessly behind [2]. Proper, intelligent planning and preparation will

---

1   Competition is growing from Japanese, Chinese, Taiwanese, South Korean, Singaporean, Australian, and Canadian as well as Western European and Eastern European companies and government organizations for U.S. government contracts. By way of specific example, the British corporation, VT Group, has contracts with the Department of Defense, U.S. Coast Guard, and NASA. The British-Italian company Agusta-Westland, Inc., and Eurocopter compete on U.S. Air Force contracts. BAE Systems PLC in the United Kingdom is the largest foreign player in the U.S. defense marketspace (www.usaspending.gov).

certainly make proposal development more manageable. Your company should not start developing a proposal unless it intends to win. An exception to this guideline is if your company wants to submit a proposal on a particular procurement in order to gain experience in assembling proposals or to gain recognition from the government as a potential supplier [3]. The American Graduate University suggests that as many as three-quarters of the proposals received by government procuring agencies are deemed to be nonresponsive or inadequate [4]. If your company competes heavily in the federal marketplace, then proposals are your most important product.

It does not matter how large your company is. For example, let us assume that yours is a company with $12 million posted in revenue during the last fiscal year. To simply maintain revenues at that level during the next fiscal year, you will burn $1 million each month in contract backlog, as shown in Figure 1.1. That means that you must win $1 million each month in new or recompete business just to keep the revenue pipeline full. Yet winning $1 million per month in new or recompete business will not allow your company to grow revenuewise at all! To put that $1 million of business per month in appropriate context—your company would have to bid $3 million per month in proposals and have a win ratio of 33% to bring in that level of revenue. And $3 million worth of proposals translates into identifying two to three times that amount in potential marketing opportunities that then have to be qualified and pursued. Many times, release schedules for procurement opportunities slip, or funding is withheld, or the specific requirements get rolled into a larger procurement. As a result, what appears to be a solid lead in January has evaporated by June. See Figure 1.2 for an illustration of this pipeline process. Note that

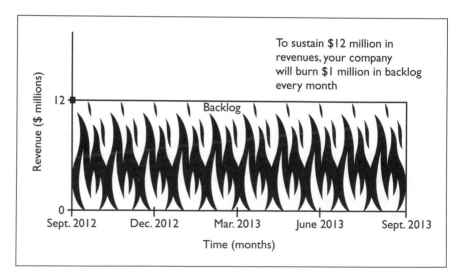

Figure 1.1
Contract backlog
burn rate.

Figure 1.2
Your business opportunity pipeline must remain full to maintain and grow your revenue base and meet bookings goals.

The figure contains the following labels:

$72 million in opportunities must be identified

Lack of program funding
Slippage of RFP/RFS release date
Delay in contract award
Delay in proposal evaluation
Cancellation of program

$36 million in proposals must be bid

Win rate of 33%

$12 million in contract awards

Yield

To maintain $12 million revenue per year

business development has *bookings* goals; operating groups have *revenue* goals. The same applies for a company with $1.2 billion of posted revenue.

"Without a plan, the proposal process will be chaotic and the product, at best, will be inferior" [5]. Gone is the time of last-minute, haphazard proposal preparation by a few individuals working in isolation from senior management, in-house review, such resources as a proposal knowledge base, and other corporate or divisional guidance. Your company simply cannot compete effectively with the many U.S.-based and overseas contracting firms if every proposal you submit is not your finest effort. Your company will, of course, not win every procurement—25% to 40% is a reasonable win ratio, although certain firms have been documented to win 60% or more of their proposals consistently—but you must strive to have each and every proposal be in the competitive range [6] from a technical, management, past performance, and cost standpoint.

It is important to note that a technically sound, programmatically effective, and competitively priced proposal is not enough. With content and cost must come readability, appearance, and format. And these elements require dedicated time to accomplish. Cover design, page formatting, editing, generating graphics, word processing and desktop publishing, proofreading, and photoreproducing, as well as collating, assembling, and electronic uploading to client Web sites are all vital steps in the overall proposal preparation cycle. Put yourself in the role of a government evaluator. That person, along with his or her colleagues, has to look at many proposals for each procurement. Why should I do business with you? is the question they are asking themselves. Would you enjoy struggling through a poorly written, amateurishly prepared document in the evening or on the weekend? Indeed, there are increasing numbers of small and large businesses chasing a limited number of federal dollars. Even relatively minor procurements are resulting in 50 or more proposals that are submitted. For major procurements, the competition is even more intense. In late 2011, the federal government received approximately 600 proposals from industry in response to one high-profile Department of Homeland Security services (including maintenance and upgrade of individual pieces of hardware and software for full managed services solutions[2]) bid opportunity. Two hundred of those proposals were from large businesses, and 400 were from small businesses. Debriefings across a wide variety of agencies suggest that evaluators are spending 15 to 30 minutes on each company's proposal during the preliminary round of evaluation. There simply is no more time available to them.

As a result, it is more imperative than ever that your company's proposal stand out in a positive way. Create difference! Section 52.215-7 of the Federal Acquisition Regulations (FAR), "Unnecessarily Elaborate Proposals or Quotations" (April 1984), cautions contractors not to submit

---

2   Services included software design and development, operations and maintenance, IT program support, and independent test, verification, validation, and evaluation.

proposals that contain elaborate artwork, expensive paper and bindings, and expensive visual and other presentation aids. To be sure, certain federal agencies, as well as some state and local organizations that follow the FAR, will look unfavorably on any proposal documents that go beyond basic typewriter-level presentation values. Yet your competitors are spending tens of thousands of dollars both in-house and through professional proposal consulting firms to prepare full-color, graphics-intensive, high-impact proposal documents and multimedia oral presentations. The challenge is to know your client well enough to sense what level of proposal media and presentation style they will respond to favorably. Some clients stipulate that proposals should demonstrate the quality of deliverable document that your company is capable of producing. You will have to balance the perception of cost consciousness in your proposal documents and electronic submittals with the genuine need to make your volumes establish the standard of presentation excellence among those submitted for a particular procurement.

1.2 From set-asides to full-and-open competition

There are no "bluebirds" in full-and-open competition. The gravy train—to the extent that it still persists in the business world—is over! A reorientation and fundamental transformation of your company's collective thinking and attitude will be required to begin the challenging shift from 8(a) [7] set-aside procurement to competitive and ultimately full and open (F&O) federal business acquisition. The term *8(a)* refers to the U.S. Small Business Administration's (SBA; http://www.sba.gov) program to assist qualified small and woman- and minority-owned businesses during their early years of operation. Program participation is divided into two stages: developmental and transitional. The developmental stage lasts 4 years and the transitional stage spans 5 years. Established in July 1953 under the Eisenhower administration, the SBA provides financial, technical, and programmatic assistance to help Americans start, operate, and grow their businesses. The 8(a) program, named for Section 8(a) of the Small Business Act (Public Law 85-536), is the most well-known element of the Minority Enterprise Development (MED) program. Since 1953, the SBA has provided assistance to more than 20 million small business owners. The SBA provides financial assistance through its participating lenders in the form of loan guarantees, not direct loans. In 2011, the SBA had a portfolio of more than $90 billion in loan guarantees to small businesses. The SBA's FY2012 budget request stands at $985 million [8].

Currently, Karen Gordon Mills administers the SBA. A previous SBA administrator, former investor and owner Aida Alvarez, suggested that diversity, technology, and globalization were critical to small business success in the twenty-first century.

Today, the SBA has a leadership role in implementing advocacy and loan programs as well as support services to the benefit of all 27.67 million small businesses nationwide [9]. The Obama administration launched the "Startup America" public/private initiative to accelerate high-growth entrepreneurship throughout the United States. The SBA will commit $2 billion as a match to private-sector investments over the next 5 years in promising high-growth companies. The SBA's purpose is to "promote small business development and entrepreneurship through business financing, government contracting, and technical assistance programs," as presented in the FY2007 *SBA Budget Request and Performance Plan* [10]. The statutory goals for government-wide procurement preferences that were established in 1996 and still pertain today stipulate that fully 23% of federal prime contracts will go to small businesses. In fact, in FY2009 (the most recent year for which data are available), 21.89% of all federal dollars was awarded to small businesses [11]. Small businesses were awarded $96.8 billion in federal prime contracts in 2009 [11]. The Performance Scorecard is based on the goal hierarchy established by the Government Performance Results Act (GPRA). In accordance with GPRA, SBA identifies its overarching strategic goals, the outcome goals associated with each general goal, and the specific performance goals and performance indicators that are used to measure how programs contribute toward outcome goals [12].

The SBA took concrete steps to increase opportunities for small businesses to receive federal contracts with its regulations of June 30, 2007. These regulations stipulate that companies with federal contracts must recertify their size status as small businesses on long-term contracts when they merge with or are purchased by another business, when a contract option is exercised, or at the end of the first 5 years of the period of performance of the contract [13]. As published in the *Federal Register* on February 10, 2012, SBA increased 37 small business size standards for 34 industries in North American Industry Classification System (NAICS) Sector 54, Professional, Technical, and Scientific Services.

In 2007, the SBA created the Patriot Express program to assist all veterans with small business ownership. There are 4 million U.S. veterans who are also small business owners. Visit http://www.sba.gov/patriot-express to learn more about the services of this initiative [14].

In late 2006, the SBA—in cooperation with the Office of Federal Procurement Policy (OFPP)—launched a Small Business Procurement

Scorecard for 24 federal agencies. Patterned after former President George W. Bush's President's Management Agenda (PMA), the Scorecard helps aggressively track and monitor the status of each agency's small business goal achievement. Among the federal agencies that met their small business contracting goals in FY2008 (the most recent year for which these specific data are available) were SBA, Department of Energy (DOE), General Services Administration (GSA), and the Department of Homeland Security (DHS).

The SBA's national Small Business Week honors the contributions of the nation's small business owners. Winners are selected on their record of stability, growth in employment and sales, sound financial reports, innovation, and the company's response to adversity, as well as community service.

Changing attitudes can be a difficult and lengthy process. The process of change must begin and be fostered on an ongoing basis by senior management, through such forums as marketing meetings, acquisition team meetings, proposal kickoff meetings, your company's internal newsletter or communications vehicle (intranet-based or hard copy), and project management mentoring programs. The thinking and processes that proved so successful and comfortable during the early developmental 8(a) years of your company's history are often precisely the very things that thwart your company's potential for growth in the competitive arena. Many entrepreneurial companies are characterized by informal business organizations and cultures that are functional and effective for small companies only.

However, if companies are successful and grow in terms of revenue, equity, Earnings Before Interest, Taxes, Depreciation, and Amortization (EBITDA), positive cash flow, human resources, and client and technical knowledge, they will reach a point at which an informal culture and organization are thoroughly inadequate. This is particularly apparent in the areas of planning, management structure and processes, internal and external communications, and support infrastructure. Successful, growing companies should reorganize, bring in new senior operations and business development executives as appropriate, and develop and implement a strategic planning process [15]. Management responsibilities should be delegated downward and outward so that a small company's organizational structure is not so "sharply hierarchical" [16]. Empowerment is critical to the most junior level possible within your organization. Senior management should actively encourage all staff to identify and understand problems and then propose positive, team-oriented solutions. When implemented, this approach helps to leverage everyone's talents and domain-specific expertise and contributes to the collective knowledge base of the company.

Dedicated effort in accordance with a well-defined, yet flexible, plan, broad-based and in-depth knowledge of your clients and competitors, superlative performance on past and present projects, and a formalized company organization and communication network all contribute to successful proposals. In an extremely important quantitative study conducted by Price Waterhouse in the 1990s, it was determined that companies that exhibit superior performance as measured by competitive contract awards managed "their business acquisition as a formal, disciplined process. These companies view business acquisition as a structured set of interrelated activities to win contract awards. The superior performers continuously improve the methods they use to pursue opportunities" [17]. For example, small businesses with a Project Management Office (PMO) can leverage this organization to share business development and proposal development information and best practices across the operations staff. The PMO can also train and assist staff in collecting quality, schedule, cost, and risk mitigation metrics and success stories from the contracts on which they are working.

In an effort to help ensure the long-term success of participants in the 8(a) program, the SBA has established goals for the percentage of 8(a) and non-8(a) contracts that a company should pursue, with the number of non-8(a) contracts increasing each year. A company is put on a schedule during its final 5 transition years in the 8(a) program, with non-8(a) business targeted to be 55% to 75% of company revenues by the final year prior to graduation into the arena of full and open competition [18]. Your company will need to develop an exit strategy from the 8(a) program if you are to survive and prosper. That strategy might include developing a balanced albeit aggressive mix of government (across civilian, defense, law enforcement, and intelligence agencies) and commercial contracts, establishing long-term business partnerships with major prime contractors, and mergers and acquisitions. Small businesses that have been successful in leveraging partnerships with major prime contractors into increased revenue point to their flexible pricing strategies, solid past performance record, and sufficient financial backing [19]. The important point is to begin a structured, ongoing planning process to envision business life beyond the 8(a) program several years prior to graduation. One extremely valuable approach is to conduct semiannual focused planning sessions, during which specific actions required for successful 8(a) exit are identified, documented, communicated, and acted upon. You will want to assess and clarify such business parameters as your firm's:

- Contractual performance monitoring and measurement program;
- Bookings, revenue, and profitability goals;

- Core technical competencies and areas of excellence;
- Required certifications and accreditations (e.g., SEI CMMI®, ISO, ITIL, IEEE);
- Business development staffing, structure, and processes;
- Accounting system and cost accounting practices;
- Project management approaches, processes, and tools;
- Quality management system;
- Procurement systems and practices;
- Knowledge management and knowledge-sharing practices;
- Training requirements and schedules;
- Delegation of authority process;
- Internal lines of communication;
- Recruitment capacity and processes.

From a business development perspective, it is also important to pursue non-8(a) contract opportunities *several years* in advance of graduation from the program. Winning full-and-open (F&O) competitions is critical to your company's own confidence, as well as the confidence of teaming partners and banking institutions in your company. Strongly consider investing in, developing, and honing the competitive business skills necessary for your success in the F&O competitive arena. Building business development and proposal development infrastructures—and staffing them with seasoned, proven performers who are incentivized in both the short and long term to win—are pivotal steps in the direction of successful graduation from the 8(a) program and sustained business growth beyond the protection offered by the 8(a) program.

Critical to your success beyond the 8(a) program is working closely with federal government staff to communicate and explore acquisition strategies and contractual vehicles that allow your small company to bid on your current work as the prime contractor. This strategy will allow you to retain more of your financial business base than if you were limited to a subcontractor role only.

Most importantly, however, is for your firm's executives to reinvent themselves and the company. *What do we mean by "reinvent"?* Shortly, you will no longer be classified as an 8(a) firm, able to enjoy a certain degree of protection from the broader forces of full market competition. So you cannot *think* "small" or "8(a)." For example, contracts for $750,000 should *not* be in your business development opportunity pipeline any longer. If you are a $20 million, 100-person company, you should be identifying, qualifying, and pursuing—as the prime—federal government contracts greater than $5 million and 50 people. Note that these contract opportunities should align closely with your strategic plan and core competencies. You have to build a business culture of people, processes, knowledge, and supporting technologies that is focused on the future and focused on success at a higher level of achievement. And the future is characterized by high-velocity competition that demands passion and commitment from every member of your organization. *There is no looking back!*

It is important to point out cogent examples of companies that have successfully migrated out of the 8(a) program and flourished in the open competitive arena.

For example, RS Information Systems, Inc. (RSIS; now Wyle Information Systems) in McLean, Virginia, graduated from the SBA's 8(a) program in 2003 as one of the largest support services companies measured by number of employees (1,600 staff) and level of revenue ($259 million). In early 2007, RSIS stood as the largest privately held federal IT prime contractor. The company emerged as a recognized mission-support leader in consolidated IT services and enterprise managed services, voice telecommunications, cybersecurity, and scientific support services. RSIS was sold to Wyle in 2008.

Santa Barbara Applied Research, Inc., (SBAR) received the prestigious 8(a) Graduate of the Year Award from the U.S. Small Business Administration in January 2004. SBAR is an information technology and engineering firm that supports NASA, the U.S. Navy and Air Force, and the U.S. Coast Guard as well as commercial clients. Led by Grace Vaswani, SBAR's president and CEO, the company was certified into the 8(a) program in 1991 and graduated in 2000. It is still doing business at the time of this writing.

A third 8(a) success story is Byles Janitorial, under the leadership of Army veteran and president, William L. Byles, Sr. This African-American-owned, Nashville, Tennessee–based firm received the National 8(a) Graduate of the Year Award in 2006 [20]. Byles Janitorial was still going strong as a minority business at the time of this writing.

Other examples of successful graduates of the SBA's 8(a) Program include CMI Management headquartered in Alexandria, Virginia; Nobis Engineering, Inc., in Concord, New Hampshire; Kelly's Cleaning Service, Inc., of St. Croix, U.S. Virgin Islands; Data Systems & Technology, Inc., headquartered in Reston, Virginia; and J.M. Waller & Associates, Inc., in Burke, Virginia; as well as Omega Technologies, Inc., in Fairfax, Virginia; ICS Telecom in Rochester, New York; Naughton Energy Corporation in Pocono Pines, Pennsylvania; and LS Gallegos & Associates, Inc., in Englewood, Colorado.

Companies that do in fact emerge successfully from the 8(a) program enter a very challenging business landscape in which they no longer qualify for contractual preferences offered under Federal Acquisition Regulations (FAR)-mandated small business size criteria (e.g., 1,500-person employee threshold or the $25.5 million revenue standard). In addition, these emergent businesses do not have the human resources, financial assets, process maturity, and market footprint to compete effectively on a sustained basis in the full and open space with such giant corporations as Northrop Grumman, General Dynamics (GD), Computer Sciences Corporation (CSC), HP, Boeing, Lockheed Martin, and the like. As Rodney P. Hunt, president and CEO of RS Information Systems, noted in an article that appeared in *Washington Technology* magazine [21], "This pattern of activity undoes the hard work of so many in government and industry to cultivate small businesses and move them into the mainstream marketplace. It also diminishes the benefits to government and taxpayers of a category of companies that have critical experience and past performance rarely found among small companies, as well as the flexibility and niche experience often unavailable at large companies." Of note is that the General Services Administration (GSA) invited industry comments on this very issue immediately prior to the high-profile GSA Alliant full and open GWAC procurement.

1.3 Small business constraints

In terms directly relevant to proposal design, development, and preparation, many small businesses must navigate effectively amidst a narrow opportunity pipeline, very limited B&P funds, a lack of depth in human resources, a small business base and market presence, a contract backlog deficit, a low level of contractual experience, a lack of name recognition in the marketplace, and line of credit and other financial challenges. A small business base, for example, can lead to higher indirect costs, which in turn can place a company at a competitive disadvantage during procurement efforts. An insufficient staff can translate to few or no people dedicated to the tasks of advanced and strategic planning, ongoing marketing and relationship building with particular client organizations, proposal operations, proposal reviews, proposal editing and proofreading, proposal publication, oral-presentation preparation and delivery, and postproposal marketing so important with GWAC and ID/IQ contract vehicles. Staffing challenges emerge quickly as full-time project managers and technical subject matter experts (SMEs) work 40 billable hours each week for their client and then additional time to serve as proposal managers, proposal reviewers, or presentation team members. (In predominately service-oriented contracting firms, the company's overall profitability is affected by the degree to which its personnel are fully billable. Transfer ratios, that is, billable time versus total time worked, must remain very high.) And thin contractual experience can lead to low or marginal scores received for "Past Performance" or "Relevant Experience" sections of the RFP, RFS, and the SF330.

1.4 Maximizing small business strengths

America's nearly 27 million small businesses employ more than 50% of the country's private workforce. According to the SBA, 552,600 new small businesses recorded initial employment in 2009. And women are creating new businesses and new jobs at more than double the national rate and represent more than one-third of all people involved in entrepreneurial activity, according to the *Global Entrepreneurship Monitor (GEM) 2005 Report on Women and Entrepreneurship* [22].

Small businesses (corporations that employ 500 people or less) constitute 99.7% of U.S. employers [22, 23]. "These companies have certain competitive advantages: They are lean in terms of administration, they can position themselves in a market niche that large corporations cannot fill, and they can offer superior service to customers" [24]. On June 24, 1998, the White House announced new federal rules to give minority firms an edge when bidding for federal government contracts while respecting a 1995 U.S. Supreme Court ruling that limited affirmative action programs. Under these new rules, small firms that are certified to be socially and economically disadvantaged by the U.S. SBA will receive a "price evaluation preference" (price break) of 10% in calculating the lowest bidder for government contracts [25].

It is the policy of the United States, as stated in the Small Business Act, that all small businesses have the maximum practicable opportunity to participate in providing goods and services to the government. To ensure that small businesses get their fair share, the SBA negotiates annual procurement preference goals with each federal agency and reviews each agency's results. The SBA is responsible for ensuring that the statutory government- wide goals are met in the aggregate. The current statutory goals are as follows [26]:

- 23% of prime contracts for small businesses;
- 5% of prime and subcontracts for small disadvantaged businesses;
- 5% of prime and subcontracts for women-owned small businesses;

- 3% of prime contracts for Historically Underutilized Business Zone (HUBZone; see Appendix D) small businesses;
- 3% of prime and subcontracts for service-disabled veteran-owned small businesses.

Small businesses have the potential to respond rapidly to emerging business opportunities because they have fewer layers of management approval in the decision-making chain. Company policies can be modified quickly to meet client requests and requirements [27]. Small businesses can carefully control their growth in terms of acquiring technical talent (subject matter experts) and penetrating new market sectors. The opportunity for excellent in-house communications throughout the network of authority exists with small businesses. Small companies are ideally positioned to develop, right from the start, open-architecture internal automated KM systems for maintaining and searching staff résumés, project summaries, proposal modules, lessons learned, success stories, and marketing opportunities. And because of the staffing deficit, people tend to become cross-trained and proficient in a wide variety of tasks. More people are given the opportunity to understand the big picture of the proposal life cycle and of specific business targets. Conversely, in large, multidivision corporations, very few staff fully understand the multidimensional complexities of massive procurement targets. On large procurements, for example, some major firms devote one or more staff exclusively to handling subcontractor résumés. In a small firm, that level of work breakdown is simply not possible.

1.5 SBIR and STTR programs

Important mechanisms for generating revenue in the small business community for those firms with strong scientific or engineering capabilities include the three-phase Small Business Innovation Research (SBIR) program (see http://www.sba.gov/about/index.htm) and the Small Business Technology Transfer (STTR) pilot program (see http://www.sba.gov/content/small-business-technology-transfer-program-sttr). Enacted on July 22, 1982, as part of the Small Business Innovation Development Act (P.L. 97-219), the SBIR program encourages small businesses with fewer than 500 employees to explore their technological potential and provides the incentive to profit from its commercialization. This legislation requires federal agencies to set aside special funding for relevant small business research and development (R&D). Worldwide commercial rights to any patents normally will go to the small company. President Obama signed a bill into law (P. L. 111-214) that reauthorized the SBIR program through September 2011. The SBIR program is highly competitive and merit based—it is in no way an assistance program for small businesses. It is, however, open only to small American-owned and independently operated businesses (at least 51% owned by one or more U.S. citizens or lawfully admitted permanent resident aliens) and is not intended for nonprofit organizations.

The risks associated with conducting significant R&D efforts are often beyond the economic and resource capabilities of small businesses. SBIR, in effect, protects small businesses and enables them to compete on the same level as larger businesses. In FY2007, the SBIR program produced 3,814 Phase I awards and 1,542 Phase II awards for $1.644 billion. Since its beginning, the SBIR program has awarded more than $22.3 billion to various companies, thus allowing them to test high-risk theories and develop innovative technologies. Of note is that companies with 10 or fewer employees have won more than one-third of all SBIR awards to date, and the SBIR program has consistently awarded more than 10% of its funds to minority-owned firms. Five of the 11 SBIR federal agencies required to participate in the SBIR program based on their R&D budgets make more than 90% of the awards annually—Department of Defense (DoD), Department of Homeland Security (DHS), Department of Health and Human Services (DHHS), Department of Energy (DOE), NASA, and the National Science Foundation (NSF). Other agencies include the Department of Agriculture (USDA), Department of Education, Department of Transportation (DOT), EPA, and the Department of Commerce.

The Small Business Administration's Office of Technology has the responsibility for coordinating the SBIR and STTR programs. SBA prepares a quarterly online Presolicitation Announcement (PSA) that lists the agencies that will make SBIR offerings in the next fiscal quarter, along with the release, closing, and award announcement dates. The quarterly PSA also provides a one-line statement for each SBIR topic. However, this PSA is not a substitute for the agency SBIR solicitations themselves. DoD will automatically send its solicitations to all companies on the SBA PSA mailing list, but no other agency does. You will have to research SBIR solicitations online from each agency in which your company is interested each year. Some agencies, such as DoD and DHHS, issue more than one pamphlet or bulletin each year in which SBIR solicitations are published. Each participating federal agency publishes an extremely helpful volume of abstracts that summarizes the SBIR proposals that it funds each year. To obtain a copy, you can contact the SBIR program manager in each agency in which your company has interest.

The SBIR program has three phases: Phase I, Feasibility Study; Phase II, Full-scale Research; and Phase III, Commercialization. More than 15,000 small businesses have received at least one Phase I SBIR award. Funding at Phase I extends up to $100,000, and finances up to 6 months of research. Phase II funding can reach $750,000, and research can span 2 years. Only Phase I winners are considered for Phase II. With the DOE, for example, success ratios have been about 12% in Phase I and 45% in Phase II. Some states, such as Kentucky through its SBIR Bridge Grant program established in 1988, as well as Alaska and Delaware, assist small firms to continue product development research projects begun under federal Phase I SBIR awards.

As a result of the Small Business Innovation Research Program Reauthorization Act of 2000, the SBA's Office of Technology established the *Federal and State Technology Partnership* program, or FAST. FAST was designed to strengthen the technological competitiveness of small businesses in all 50 states as well as the District of Columbia and U.S. territories. FAST is a competitive grants program that allows each state to receive funding that can be used to provide an array of services in support of the SBIR program.

In most cases, Phases I and II provide full allowable costs and a negotiated fee or profit for the small company. Phase III involves no SBIR funding, although the SBA has developed the Commercialization Matching System to help SBIR awardees locate funding sources for finalizing their innovations. The small business might procure funding for Phase III of the SBIR process from commercial banks (e.g., the Small Business Investment Corporation, the equity investment arm of the Bank of America Community Development Banking Group); venture capitalists; private-sector nonprofit small business lending groups; large companies; or other non-SBIR federal agency funding. Other help is available for companies entering the commercialization phase of the SBIR program. For example, Dawnbreaker (http://www.dawnbreaker.com), a professional services firm located in Rochester, New York, has assisted more than 3,400 SBIR and STTR awardees since 1990. Dawnbreaker staff work with SBIR Phase II grantees to develop a strategic business plan and to prepare the firm for commercialization. Dawnbreaker then hosts two Commercialization Opportunity Forums in Washington, D.C., each year to showcase firms that are ready to enter the third SBIR phase [28].

More than 39% of Phase II SBIR projects will result in a commercialized product. Successfully commercialized SBIR projects include DR-LINK, a natural language retrieval system based on linguistic technology that processes ongoing news streams or information from databases. Patent examiners at the U.S. Patent and Trademark Office now use the DR-LINK system daily to search for prior art in more than 4,000 published databases. This SBIR effort was funded through DARPA, the Defense Advanced Research Projects Agency. SBIR support from the National Science Foundation, DOE, and DoD allowed AstroPower of Newark, Delaware, to develop superior thin-layer silicon- and gallium-arsenide techno logy with optical and speed advantages in photovoltaic devices. With funding provided by EPA's SBIR program, Atlanta-based EnerTech Environmental successfully developed a process to generate clean energy from municipal solid waste. The NSF and National Institutes of Health (NIH) have made major SBIR contributions to research conducted by Martek Corporation in Columbia, Maryland. This biotechnology firm discovered how to make a critical ingredient needed by infants that is normally found in mothers' milk. Medical and health organizations in Europe and the World Health Organization (WHO) have recommended that this critical ingredient be added to infant formulas to offset nutrient deficiencies in babies that are not breast-fed. And Scientific Computing Components, in New Haven, Connecticut, has leveraged SBIR funds to produce a number of breakthroughs in commercial software related to high-performance computing.

Finally, Montana-based Resodyn Corporation developed a commercial-scale biodiesel plant that converts animal fat and recycled cooking oil to biodiesel at costs competitive with traditional diesel fuel. This innovation built upon a SBIR award from the USDA.

Although the format for SBIR Phase I proposals varies across the participating federal agencies, a typical format is as follows:

- Cover sheet;
- Project abstract, anticipated benefits, and key words;
- Identification and significance of the problem or opportunity;
- Background information;
- Phase I technical objectives (measurable, specific objectives to be accomplished during Phase I);
- Phase I research work plan;
- Related work;
- Relationship to future research and development;
- Potential postapplications (commercialization strategy);
- Key personnel (principal investigator/project directors);
- Facilities and equipment;
- Subcontractors/consultants;

- Prior, current, or pending support of similiar proposals or awards;
- Budget;
- Previous SBIR awards (company commercialization history).

The STTR pilot program's role is to foster the innovation necessary to meet America's scientific and technical challenges in the twenty-first century. Central to the program is the expansion of the public- and private-sector partnership to include joint venture opportunities for small businesses. Each year because their R&D budgets exceed $1 billion, DoD, DOE, DHHS, NASA, and NSF are required under the STTR to reserve a portion of their R&D funds for award to small businesses and nonprofit research institution (e.g., colleges and universities) partnerships. At least 40% of the work must be performed by the small business. The nonprofit research institution must be based in the United States, and can be a non-profit college or university, domestic nonprofit research organization, or Federally Funded R&D Center (FFRDC). Like SBIR, STTR is a competitive, three-phase program coordinated by the SBA and announced through the PSA process. Award thresholds are $100,000 for Phase I and $750,000 for Phase II. In FY2007, the STTR program distributed $242.9 million across 634 Phase I awards and 213 Phase II awards.

1.6 Organizing your company to acquire new business

To support your company's efforts to acquire, that is, win new and follow-on business, strongly consider forming, and then actively supporting, a dedicated business development or advanced planning group.[3] In many smaller firms, marketing and proposal efforts are handled exclusively through each division or line organization. One division may or may not be aware of duplication of marketing efforts with other divisions, related contractual experience performed by another division, or human talent and subject-matter expertise in another division, for example. The formation of a centralized corporate BDG should not preclude a given division's involvement in its own business planning and proposal development. Rather, the BDG can serve to focus, channel, and support divisional

---

3   The name of these business and planning groups varies from company to company. Some are called business development groups (BDGs), advanced planning groups, strategic planning and business development groups (SP&BDGs), special programs groups, and marketing departments, for example.

business-related activities in accordance with your company's formalized mission statement [29] and strategic plan. Because of its enterprise-wide vantage, the BDG can help identify and make available the appropriate human talent, material resources, and information resident throughout your entire company in order to pursue a business opportunity. The functional charter of the BDG can also extend to include the following closely related activities:

- Strategic, business, and marketing planning;
- Business opportunity/Federal Business Opportunities (FBO) and other opportunity tracking and reporting;
- Intelligence gathering: marketing support and client contacts[4];
- Formalizing the process of establishing business objectives, gathering data, analyzing and synthesizing data, prioritizing, and action planning;
- Acquisition team formation and guidance;
- Bid–no bid decision-making coordination[4];
- Teaming agreement negotiation and coordination[4];
- Cost strategizing for proposals[4];
- Company information management, distribution, and archiving (including proposal data center, or automated knowledge base);
- Proposal and documentation standards development and dissemination;
- Proposal coordination and production[4];
- Oral presentation development and coaching;
- Company image development (branding) and public relations;
- Corporate communications (such as newsletters, trade shows, and advertising);
- Marketing and proposal management training.

To ensure adequate connection with and visibility from senior management, a full-scale BDG should be under the leadership of a vice president (VP) for business development. The most appropriate candidate for this pivotal position is an individual with an advanced and relevant technical degree coupled with at least 7 years of clearly demonstrated competitive business development experience and success with "closing the deal" in the federal government arena. Ensure that the candidates you consider can

---

4   These elements are essential for all firms, even very small ones, to enter the federal marketspace.

bring a successful track record of identifying, qualifying, and winning major-impact programs. Contacts alone are a necessary but insufficient gauge of a business developer's successful performance. This individual must also possess or develop a solid knowledge of your company's internal operations, assets, and capabilities, as well as the buying habits and specific sell points of your clients.

Even under the constraints faced by very small companies (less than $5 million in annual revenues), this VP functions most effectively when he or she is not obligated to be an on-the-road company marketeer as well as an internal business-development planner, organizer, and administrator. (In addition, a high-energy, well-organized administrative assistant seems absolutely essential to enhance the functionality of the VP position.) Under this VP's guidance would be two primary functional groups: external and internal sales support (see Figure 1.3). The external sales support element might include a full-time corporate marketeer(s) as well as a key division manager(s). External sales efforts would involve direct client contact and interaction at multiple technical and administrative levels. It would also extend to relationship building with potential major teaming partners and specialty subcontractors appropriate to your company's lines of business (LOBs) or product lines.

The internal sales support element might be subdivided further into proposal development and production, KM, and corporate communications, as depicted in Figure 1.4. Proposal development and production should logically include publication of the proposal documents. Proposal design and development become extremely challenging if they do not include oversight of the priorities and resources of the publications group. The function and focus of both the external, as well as internal, sales support elements are to project a professional,

Figure 1.3
A cooperative sales approach ensures effective information exchange and increases win probability.

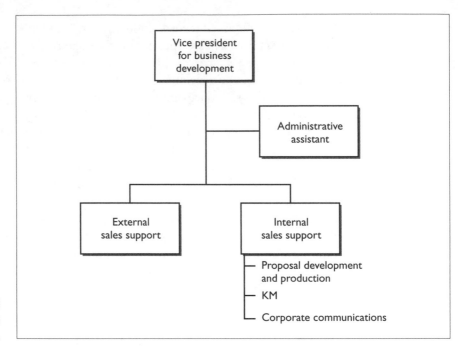

Figure 1.4
Suggested BDG
organization.

client-oriented corporate image or brand. Understanding your client's business and mission, technical requirements, hopes, fears, and biases and demonstrating that understanding in every proposal you prepare is absolutely critical to your success in the federal marketplace in 2012 and beyond (see Figure 1.5). Superior proposals should complement the public relations and advertising activities of your firm.

Effective interaction and cooperative information exchange and knowledge transfer between the external and internal sales support staff are absolutely critical to proposal success and an increased win probability. Neither group succeeds on its own. Marketing intelligence learned from client and competitor interaction must be infused into the proposal during the important bid–no bid decision-making process, prekickoff meeting planning sessions, the kickoff meeting itself, the formal internal review steps, and postproposal activities, such as preparation for oral presentations and Final Proposal Revision (FPR). Clear, formalized, well-supported internal sales support processes contribute to winning new business. Too many times, companies view the identification of marketing opportunities as paramount to their success. As important as these leads can be, unless there is a well-defined, structured set of processes and methodologies internal to your company that harness the necessary human talent, information technology resources, dedicated space, and B&P

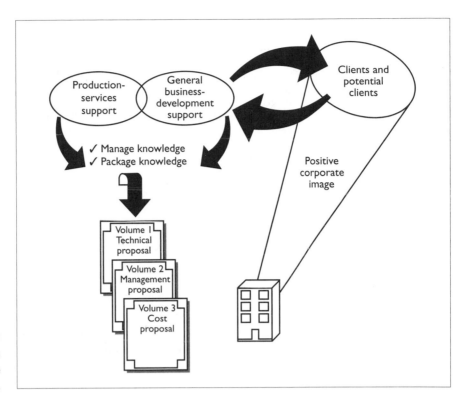

Figure 1.5
Projecting an
appropriate
corporate image.

monies, the leads do not result in contract awards. They result in also-rans (proposals submitted that do not win).

It has been this author's observation that small companies tend to undergo oscillations, and even convulsions, between centralized business development and control, and decentralized divisional or regional business activities. Instead of using the BDG as a vital corporate support structure, some companies prefer to dissolve or descope the BDG, despite the 1- to 2-year extraordinary level of effort generally required to establish the BDG in the first place. Full-time corporate business development staff can be significantly more effective than employees assigned to BDG support on a part-time basis only. A certain level of centralized oversight and control is highly beneficial and cost-effective. Continual restructuring and refocusing of marketing activities result in the diversion of valuable time and energy into counterproductive internal organizational challenges. Building an effective and responsive business development infrastructure takes time—on the order of 2 or 3 years. Senior management must be attentive to, yet patient with, this dynamic process.

Figure 1.6 illustrates a proven growth paradigm for small businesses that contract with the U.S. federal government. Several key areas associated with thriving within the federal market space require additional

- Diversify customer base—early!
- Win every GWAC, ID/IQ, and GSA schedule possible!
- Maintain an aggressive customer satisfaction program.
- Stretch your entire organization— pursue and bid at least twice as many opportunities as you can comfortably support.
- Attract and retain really good people—don't get stuck on the wrong side of the 80/20 rule!

Figure 1.6
Proven growth
paradigm.

exploration, including business culture, management, planning, marketing, and financial/infrastructure.

- *Business culture.* Your small company's business culture must be simultaneously employee-centric and customer-focused. Leveraging a corporate value system that builds on trust within the executive leaders, your organization should be driven to performance excellence and the advancement of your customer's mission.

- *Management.* Accountability and decisiveness are two critical ingredients for successful management of your organization. There must be a system for total accountability. Along with accountability must come authority and genuine "skin in the game." Key people, who should be seasoned performers, must feel emotionally and financially engaged with the business outcomes of your organization. Decisiveness includes the willingness and capacity to take measured risks.

- *Planning.* Every organization functions best with a strategic plan (see Section 1.7) that derives from a corporate vision and mission statement. It is vital to review actual progress against goals, objectives, strategies, and action plans on a regular basis. Goals generally have 3- to 5-year time horizons, whereas objectives have 1-year time frames. All goals and objectives should be meaningful, measurable, and achievable.

- *Marketing.* The keys in the marketing area are staff and focus. You must stay focused on your company's core competencies when pursuing bid opportunities. Avoid the "shotgun approach" that leads to dilution of B&P funds and human resources. In addition, ensure that there is a business development leader as well as a proposal development leader. The proposal development leader should have a strong command of proposal processes as well as knowledge management practices.

- *Financial/infrastructure.* Your organization must develop excellent banking relationships. Invest in robust accounting systems because timely and accurate financial status reporting is essential. Integrate systems, including a human resources information system (HRIS), recruitment, accounting, and procurement. Pursue external quality assurance certification and assessment [e.g., ISO 9001:2008, SEI CMMI®, ITIL, Six Sigma, Agile project management, ISO 20000 (codification of ITIL in a measurable standard), ISO 27000, and Control Objectives for Information Technology (COBIT)]. Consider hiring a chief administrative officer (CAO) to integrate and manage the infrastructure people and processes.

1.7 Effective strategic and mission planning

Strategic and mission planning are crucial considerations to ensure a planned pattern of growth for your company and to focus your bid–no bid decision making. According to Thompson and Strickland, a strategic plan is "a comprehensive statement about the organization's mission and future direction, near-term and long-term performance targets, and how management intends to produce the desired results and fulfill the mission, given the organization's overall situation" [30]. Strategic planning works best (that is, is more widely accepted and more easily implemented) when it is interactive to a certain extent, not merely formulated by a separate group who creates the plan with everyone else then told to follow it. The starting point for the strategic planning process is understanding the fundamental goal of your company. No matter how small your company may be, this goal should be identified, understood, developed, communicated, and revisited. Important questions to keep in mind when formulating a strategic plan for your company are listed next [31]:

- Where is your company now (the "as-is" state) in terms of market sector or LOB (that is, defining your business)?
- What is your company's mission in the marketplace?
- What is your company's distinctive (core) competence?
- Who are your company's principal clients (i.e., market segmentation)?
- What are your principal services, products, or knowledge lines?
- What is your company's brand?

- Where does your company want to be businesswise in 5 years (the "to-be" state)? Develop a vision of the future state of your business.

- What are your company's internal strengths and weaknesses (for example, business, technical, knowledge base, internal business processes, public relations, and fiscal capability)?

- What external business or economic opportunities, threats, or challenges (e.g., the entry of new competitors into the marketplace, adverse government policies, adverse demographic changes, and global security issues) face your company now [32]? These are often referred to as SWOTs, for strengths, weaknesses, opportunities, and threats.

- Who are your primary competitors? Understanding how your competition thinks and acts is critical to your success (competitor analysis) [33].

- How are your company's knowledge assets being monitored, developed, and applied?

- How do you identify the domains of knowledge that matter to the competitive strategy of your company? In effect, how do you find the seeds of innovation and sustained competitive advantage in a dynamic global marketplace?

Strategic planning is not a static process; rather, it should be a dynamic, living activity. Business conditions and priorities change over time and technologies refresh constantly, and your strategic plan should reflect this evolution. Provide the necessary resources and steering mechanisms to implement your strategic plan, and revisit and revise the plan regularly. The mission statement is a close adjunct of the strategic plan.

Formulating, articulating, and implementing a meaningful strategic plan is critical for obtaining lines of credit through banking institutions and demonstrating to government auditing agencies that planned business growth over a period of time justifies an expansion in business base and therefore a long-term reduction in company overhead costs. Strategic planning also serves as the overarching guidance for your company's marketing activities, which is the focus of our next chapter. In addition, strategic planning provides formalized, informed guidance for making bid–no bid decisions on specific proposal opportunities. If responding to an RFP and winning that piece of business does not mesh with your company's principal lines of business and mission in the marketplace, then submitting a proposal is not appropriate. Just because your company has the technical capability to perform most of the scope of work does not mean that you should invest the time, energy, and resources into preparing a proposal.

1.8 Converting knowledge into proposal success

The question becomes not whether, but how quickly companies will move to embrace the knowledge model of the corporation.
—Richard C. Huseman and Jon P. Goodman "Realm of the Red Queen," The Corporate Knowledge Center @ EC², p. 15 [34]

A Baldrige Foundation survey of 700 *Fortune* 500 chief executive officers (CEOs) determined that knowledge management came in second as the top challenge facing companies—right behind globalization. Dr. Karl E. Sveiby—former executive chairman and co-owner of Ekonomi+Teknik Förlag, one of Scandinavia's biggest publishing companies in the trade press and business press sector, and now a professor of knowledge management in Finland—defines the term *knowledge management* as the art of creating value by leveraging an organization's intangible assets, or intellectual capital [35]. "Intellectual capital is the most important source for sustainable competitive advantages in companies," suggests Professor Johan Roos of the Imagination Lab Foundation in Lausanne, Switzerland, and formerly of the International Institute for Management Development (IMD) in Switzerland [36]. "The knowledge of any organization is found in its people, substantiated in its business processes, products, customer interactions, and lastly its information systems" [37]. In *Working Knowledge: How Organizations Manage What They Know* (Harvard Business School Press, 1997), Tom Davenport and Laurence Prusak emphasize that "[k]nowledge is as much an act or process as an artifact or thing" [38]. Knowledge is an asset that flows [39].

At the most fundamental level—that of a mathematical equation—KM is a dynamic combination of structured processes and automated tools multiplied by executive-level leadership and vision—and leveraged exponentially by passionate people and communities of practice (CoPs) (see Figure 1.7):

$$KM = [(Processes + Tools) \times Vision]^{People}$$

For practical purposes, KM is a holistic cluster of sustainable, proactive, conscious, and comprehensive organizational and business

Figure 1.7
Developing a sustainable KM solution.

activities that encompasses enterprisewide processes, techniques, and professional practices and interactions. These dynamic activities are directed toward enhanced decision support throughout the entire organization, informed business actions, and rapid prototyping of technical solutions, as well as rapid prototyping of proposal documents, improved client support, and product innovations. Specific process elements in KM span: (1) creating, (2) identifying, (3) collecting, (4) indexing, (5) codifying, (6) organizing, (7) evaluating, (8) making visible and actionable, (9) accessing, (10) leveraging, and (11) optimizing institutional knowledge for conservation, distribution, and reuse. When actively supported and valued by forward- looking senior management, a culture of mutual trust, the passion of people at all levels, and technology-based user-driven solutions and tools, KM encourages your organization's people to create, share, and benefit from their own, as well as your stakeholders' and clients', knowledge. KM also encapsulates individual and project team (e.g., CoPs) knowledge into transferable corporate assets that offer potential market value and provide valuable decision support. Data must be converted into information, which is transformed into knowledge, which, in turn, must grow into authentic understanding and action. Practical business benefits of KM are presented in Figure 1.8.

Implementing business processes that actively promote knowledge valuation, development, transfer, management, and congealment will help American companies maximize both intellectual and structural capital. Traditional command-and-control management functions must now give

Figure 1.8
KM provides the
ability to anticipate
and adapt to
change.

Enterprisewide, ongoing application of intellectual capital to
achieve organizational mission and goals

Benefits
• Improves decision support through just-in-time intelligence
• Enhances mission performance
• Facilitates informed business actions
• Fosters rapid prototyping of proposals and technical solutions
• Encourages improved client support
• Supports risk-mitigation initiatives

way to mapping and acquiring intellectual capital, communicating a clear
vision for the firm, developing and implementing a business lexicon with
shared meanings and nuances to foster generalized understanding of
strategic goals, and facilitating the rapid assessment and multidirectional
flow of knowledge throughout the organization. Caveats and
pronouncements issued from senior management will not be dispersed and
internalized throughout the knowledge organization or knowledge
enterprise.

Since 1991, major international corporations and organizations have
proactively established executive-level positions in knowledge
management. These firms include PricewaterhouseCoopers, Booz Allen
Hamilton, Canadian Imperial Bank of Commerce (CIBC), Dow Chemical,
and IBM Corporation, as well as Monsanto, Skandia AFS, Texas
Instruments, and Xerox [40]. Other companies and organizations at the
vanguard of recognizing and acting upon the reality, and the value, of
intellectual capital and intangible assets (e.g., corporate brain power,
organizational knowledge, client relationships, innovation ability, and
employee morale) include General Electric and Altria Group, Inc., which
have launched considerable efforts to understand and enhance intellectual
capital management.

In addition, Buckman Laboratories International, a U.S.-based
biotechnology firm and manufacturer of specialty chemicals for water
treatment, pulp and paper, and leather industries, has created a Knowledge
Sharing Department. Buckman Labs provides incentives in the form of
financial rewards and management positions to those employees who
contribute to its knowledge-sharing culture. Chevron has engineered a best
practice database to capture and make available the company's collective
experience with drilling conditions and innovative solutions to technical
problems on site. And Sweden's Celemì company published the world's
first audit of intangible assets in its 1995 annual report. Celemì's Intangible
Assets Monitor focuses on its customers (image-enhancing customers,

from whom testimonials are valuable; brand names; trademarks); their internal organization (patents, computer systems, management infrastructure); and their staff (competencies, flexibility). Skandia published the first-ever annual report supplement on intellectual capital. Pfizer of Switzerland has created competence models for recruiting executives that include knowledge building and sharing as important criteria. WM-data of Sweden (now part of Logica plc), an information technology (IT) company links nonfinancial indicators to strategy, and considers financial ratios of little use for management. And Sweden's

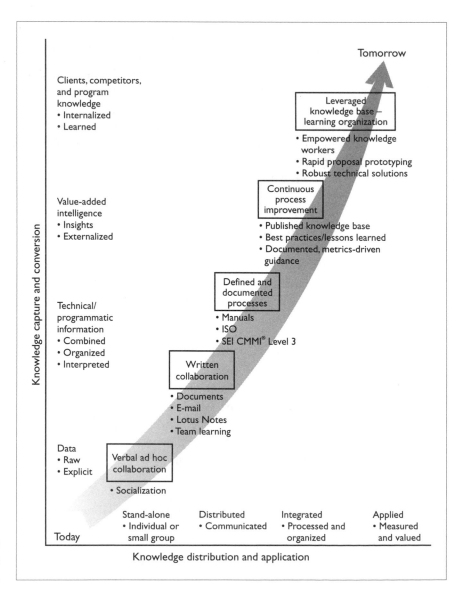

Figure 1.9
Knowledge maturity model.

leading telecommunications company, TeliaSonera, has published an annual Statement of Human Resources for each year of the past decade. This statement includes a profit-and-loss account that visualizes human resources costs and a balance sheet that shows investments in human resources [41].

"The business problem that knowledge management is designed to solve is that knowledge acquired through experience doesn't get reused because it isn't shared in a formal way.... But the ultimate goal isn't creating a departmental island of success recycling. It's giving the organization the capacity to be more effective every passing day with the gathering of institutional memory the way human beings have the capacity to become more effective and mature every day with the accumulation of thoughts and memories" [42]. A representative knowledge maturity model is presented in Figure 1.9. From direct experience in a small information technology business, we know this to be the case. KM processes such as a grassroots birds-of-a-feather program and corporate-level centers for excellence built around core competencies, have been implemented not merely to create internal hubs of institutional contract-related experience and technical know-how, but rather to facilitate the cost-effective, time-efficient rapid prototyping of proposals and presentations related to business development with a minimum of full-time staff. Until recently, most companies and organizations—large and small—knew how to produce goods or services only. Now they must learn how to apply the right knowledge within appropriate infrastructures, processes, technologies, and geographies. The U.S. federal government's Federal Acquisition Regulations (FAR) still employ only the terms supplies and services (FAR Part 8) in reference to contracting. There is no mention of knowledge as a value-added product or service. On the other hand, International Accounting Standard (IAS) 38 specifically recognizes intangible assets, such as brand names, patents, rights, customer lists, supplier relationships, designs, and computer software.

During a speech before the American Accounting Association's annual meeting held in Dallas, Texas, in August 1997, Michael Sutton—chief accountant of the U.S. Securities and Exchange Commission (SEC)—noted that "historically, accounting has been strongly influenced by the reporting needs of a manufacturing-based economy" [43]. In April 1996, the SEC had convened a symposium on intangible assets in Washington, D.C., during which invited participants from prestigious business, academic, and government organizations discussed issues related to the measurement of intangible assets by preparers of financial reports, concerns about disclosures related to intangible assets, and the experience of U.S. and overseas trendsetters with regard to the accounting and disclosure of intangible assets. The SEC, however, has not yet provided any guidelines or issued any directives vis-à-vis intangible assets for direct application in American corporations. Baruch Lev, professor of accounting and finance at New York University's Stern School of Business, concludes that "[n]early 40% of the market valuation of the average company is missing from its balance sheet" [44]. Clearly, your company's success will depend increasingly upon the quality of your people in terms of the level of knowledge, information, know-how, and know-why at their fingertips as well as your management's ability to systematically foster highly adaptive and openly collaborative business processes that leverage this collective knowledge and enable intelligent decision making (see Figure 1.10).

KM has become a significant enterprisewide initiative within a growing number of civilian and defense agencies in the U.S. federal government. The General Services Administration (GSA) appointed the federal government's first chief knowledge officer (CKO), Dr. Shereen Remez, in mid-1999. Major KM initiatives are also under way within NASA, the Department of the Navy (DoN), U.S. Army and Army Corps of Engineers

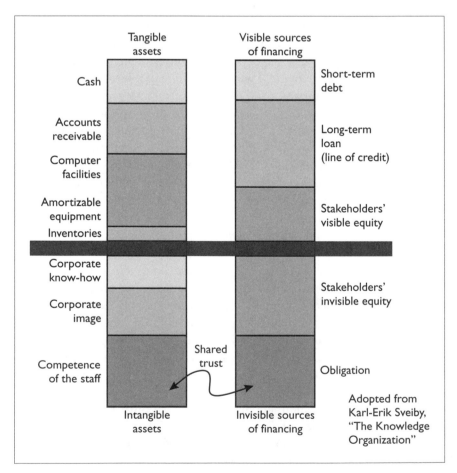

Figure 1.10
Balance sheet of the knowledge organization.

(USACE), the Federal Aviation Administration (FAA), Federal Highway Administration (FHWA), Government Accountability Office (GAO), Department of State (DOS), Department of Homeland Security, and many others. According to a study published by the Input (Deltek) research firm, the "U.S. Government spending on Knowledge Management (KM) products and services will increase at a compound annual growth rate of 9 percent, from $820 million in GFY 2003 to nearly 1.3 billion by GFY 2008." Many agencies are expected to make significant investments in KM in the next 5 years, including the Departments of Homeland Security, State, and Justice. The Federal Chief Information Officers Council (the CIO Council) established the Knowledge Management Working Group as an interagency body to bring the benefits of the government's intellectual assets to all federal organizations, customers, and partners (see http://www.km.gov). Comprised of the CIOs of 30 federal agencies and departments and representatives from the Office of Management and Budget (OMB), the CIO Council works to improve agency practices related to the modernization, sharing, and performance of federal government information assets and resources. The CIO Council, whose charter was codified formally through the E-Government Act of 2002, also is responsible for implementing elements of the Government Paperwork Elimination Act (GPEA), Government Performance and Results Act (GPRA), Federal Information Security Management Act of 2002 (FISMA), and the Information Technology Management Reform Act of 1996 (Clinger-Cohen Act). Importantly, the federal government sponsored the first major 4-day KM e-government (e-Gov) conference in Alexandria, Virginia, in April 2000 and again in April 2001. The second conference was titled *The Catalyst for Electronic Government*. In 2008, its ninth year, the conference focused on actionable strategies and innovative approaches.

1.8.1 KM benefits proposal development

Now, how does KM relate to proposals and proposal management? Just as knowledge management is concerned with which knowledge should be available where, when, and in which form within an organization, proposal management—at its core—is concerned with assembling, synthesizing, and packaging knowledge into a fact-based story that articulates benefits and validates strengths to the client within a very limited time frame. With small companies in particular, leveraging the collective intellect and institutional knowledge is integral to business development achievement and superlative, long-term client support. Improving the processes and systems used to transfer and manage knowledge is an ongoing, critical function.

Proposals are, first and foremost, knowledge products that include a host of marketing, technical, programmatic, institutional, pricing, and certification information. Through a choreographed process of knowledge generation, transfer, and congealment, a proposal is designed to sell both technical and programmatic capabilities of a company to accomplish all required activities (or provide specified products) on time and at a reasonable cost to meet client needs and requirements (see Figure 1.11). In addition, your proposal must often convey more intangible values and benefits such as peace of mind, problem-solving acumen, fiscal stability, risk mitigation, and so forth. Consider, for example, Verizon's "Rule the Air" and Corona's "Find Your Beach". The same goes for books. When you purchase a paperback or hardcopy book, you are not buying wood pulp and soy inks. And when you buy an e-book, you are not purchasing electrons. You are buying insight, a romantic escape, or guidance.

Your company's proposal document(s) is scored, literally, by the client's evaluators against formalized, specific standards in a process analogous to pattern recognition. A proposal is the tangible result of knowledge- building processes, supported in turn by hard and directed work and buoyed by a positive collective attitude within your company's proposal team of knowledge workers, as world-renowned management consultant Peter Drucker in 1998 termed employees in the new American economy.

In actuality, résumés and project summaries reflect in one form a significant percentage of intellectual capital of an organization, small or large. Relevant knowledge resident in the employees of the company as

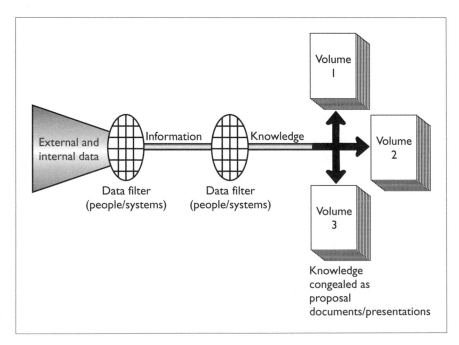

Figure 1.11
The knowledge transfer process.

gained through education, training, and professional experience coupled with initiative, dedication, and innovation is highlighted in each résumé. Similarly, effective project summaries reflect the organizational knowledge of the firm from technical, managerial, and geographic perspectives.

Crucial to proposal success is the transfer of relevant marketing information, lessons learned from current and past contracts, and technically and programmatically relevant best practices to appropriate members of the proposal team. And from there, that information must be interpreted, assigned value, and translated into knowledge that will ultimately be congealed into the actual proposal documents—into "elevator speeches," narrative, theme statements, graphics, captions, compliance matrices, presentation slides, tabs, and so forth. If marketing and other data and information do not find their way into the knowledge product called a proposal, then a company's proposal will not receive maximal point score. Therefore, the marketing data are valueless. In effect, if intellectual capital measured in client, project, competitor, technology, and political knowledge is not transferred to appropriate staff (knowledge workers) and converted efficiently into hardcopy or electronic proposal documents via established, articulated business processes, your company's proposal win ratios in terms of dollars (x dollars of contracts awarded for every $100 of contract value pursued) and number (x number of proposals won) will be suboptimal.

In your own company, evaluate critical decision points in your business processes. The bid–no bid or downselect decision point in the marketing or proposal life cycle is one salient example within the private sector. Decision quality improves—as measured by leveraged B&P dollars, increased proposal win rates, heightened staff morale, and enhanced revenue stream—when the right knowledge is available and applied when and where it is required. That right knowledge may take the form of customer understanding, knowledge of incumbent staff compensation packages, competitor intelligence, relevant political insight, innovative technical solution, current resource allocation, and so forth. See Table 1.1 for a list of the types of knowledge assets that your organization should identify, assess, archive, and disseminate internally—in effect, value.

With information and knowledge becoming the currency of American business in the twenty-first century, the organizations that can share this new currency ecologically in an effort to arrive at effective and appropriate solutions for both their external and internal clients in the shortest possible time and with the least amount of resources expended will be those firms that occupy favorable positions, or *optima*, above the knowledge landscape. From these vantage points, companies will be less likely to be displaced by new or "disruptive" technologies, reconfigured marketing

Company Assets

Company core competencies (technical discussion)

Company bonding, registrations, and certifications

Licenses

Maps (e.g., office locations, project locations, number of projects by state or region)

Customer base

Patents

Trademarks

Company organizational charts

Company best practices

Industry certifications and accreditations [e.g., Software Engineering Institute (SEI) Capability Maturity Model Integration$^®$ (CMMI$^®$), ITIL v3, ISO 9001:2008, ISO 20000, ISO 27000, and IEEE]

Facility and personnel security clearances

Industry and business community awards, commendations, and recognitions (e.g., SBA Entrepreneur of the Year, Ernst & Young)

Customer endorsements and commendations

Small/minority business involvement; HUBZone involvement

Corporate-sponsored community service and outreach activities

Company videos

Facilities diagrams

Best management practices (BMPs)

Technical and business articles and books authored by company staff

Interview guides

Vendor manuals

Contractual Resources

Project or product descriptions or summaries

Project performance metrics

Award-fee statistics per project/overarching trends

Project success stories

Customer survey results

Table 1.1
Cross Section of Company Knowledge and Information Assets

Human Resources

Résumés

Personnel diversity data (minorities, women, veterans, handicapped individuals)

Incumbent capture rates

Employee turnover rates (at the corporate and individual project levels)

Employee recruitment plan and metrics

Employee retention metrics (at the corporate and individual project levels)

Staff by project, office, technical discipline, and degree

Business Development and Proposal Development Assets

Strategic plans and benchmarking data

Market segmentation analyses

Competitor information

B&P spending patterns

Winning proposals

Multimedia presentations to clients

Teaming agreements

Teaming-agreement statements of work (SOWs) and service level agreements (SLAs)

Proposal templates (e.g., executive summaries, cover letters)

Freedom of Information Act (FOIA) documents

Proposal lessons learned (from client debriefings)

Sales volumes by client sector, line of business (LOB), and geographic area

Tactical business plans

Corporate Infrastructure and Process Assets

Documentation capabilities

Business processes (e.g., procurement systems and mechanisms, financial systems, invoicing procedures, cost accounting, scheduling, automated tracking tools)

Table 1.1
(continued)

Project-Specific Assets

Customer evaluation reports (i.e., PPIRS, ACASS, CPARS, PPAIS, and PPIMS ratings)
Award-fee determinations

Contract deliverables

Service-level agreements (SLAs)

Earned value analysis (EVA) results by project

Work breakdown structures (WBSs)

Project management plans

Computer-Related Assets

Software development capabilities and practices

Software source code for proprietary applications

Nonoperational hardware and software test-bed environments

Computer equipment and resources
Corporate innovation centers

Financial Assets

Budget forecasts

Capital expenses

Annual revenues

Relationship Assets

Cooperative agreements with colleges and universities, particularly HBCUs

Strategic business alliances (with such organizations as Microsoft, IBM, Dell, and Oracle as well as Northrop Grumman, Lockheed Martin, Boeing, and Intel)

Public Relations Assets

Ads placed in professional and trade journals

Table 1.1 Trade-show modules (text and graphics)
(continued)
External news releases

Engineering/Manufacturing Assets
Engineering white papers (position papers)
Manufacturing defect-rate data
Engineering drawings
Engineering change proposals (ECPs)
Test procedures
Requirements data
Policies and Plans
Make-or-buy policy
Management plans
Health and safety plans
Technology transfer plans
Professional compensation plans
Design control plans
Software quality assurance (SQA) plans
Phase in–phase out and transition plans
Subcontractor management plans
Configuration management (CM) plans
IR&D

Table 1.1
(continued)

paradigms, social and demographic shifts, fluctuations in consumer confidence, global tensions, and political and legislative climate changes.

1.8.2 Internal and external clients: looking at clients in a whole new way

Let us reconsider the notion of clients. Within a traditional company, clients are perceived as the buyers or procurers of the products or services being offered by that company. In a knowledge-oriented company, clients include both external elements, such as buyers; key subcontractors and hardware, software, and equipment vendors along the entire supply chain; national recruiting firms; regulatory agencies; local colleges and universities; and government institutions, as well as internal clients. The latter might include professional, project management, and support staff;

operational and consulting units; sales and marketing elements; procurement; contract administration; financial and accounting resources; human resources and recruiting; quality assurance project management office (PMO); senior management; and so forth (see Figure 1.12). The currency of knowledge must flow in meaningful, multidirectional pathways among all of these clients. For example, effective and efficient linkages among your company's procurement, recruiting, PMO, quality assurance, operational units, sales and marketing, and senior management staff (*internal clients*) and your key subcontractors, vendors, and suppliers, and national as well

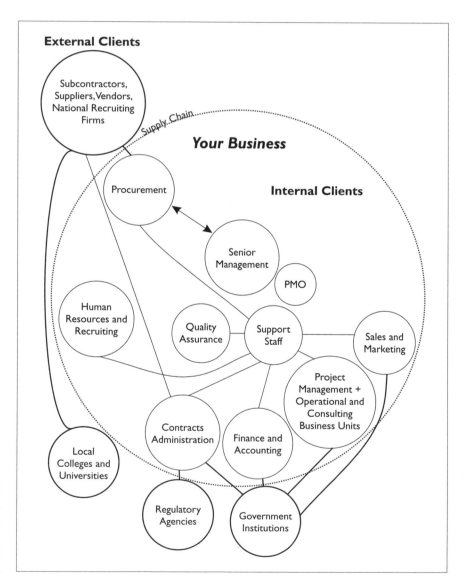

Figure 1.12
Ensure that knowledge flows among your internal and external clients.

as local recruiting firms (*external clients*) enable high-confidence supply chain management, agile hiring of key personnel in accordance with government operational requirements, and rapid procurment of equipment from original and reseller equipment manufacturers (OEMs). Each client is critical to the sustainability and performance (i.e., positive energetics) of the company, and each requires, and in turn provides, vital information and knowledge to the other, much as enzymes are shared within a living cell to perform a host of vital maintenance, replicative, and growth functions.

ENDNOTES

1. See Federal Acquisition Regulation (FAR) Part 6.

2. "Do-It-Yourself Proposal Plan," TRW Space and Defense Proposal Operations, Rev. 3, February 1989, p. iii.

3. Stewart, Rodney D., and Ann L. Stewart, *Proposal Preparation*, New York: John Wiley & Sons, 1984.

4. *Proposal Preparation Manual*, Vol. II, Covina, CA: Procurement Associates, Inc., 1989, pp. 1–2.

5. "Do-It-Yourself Proposal Plan," TRW Space and Defense Proposal Operations, Rev. 3, February 1989, p. ii.

6. See FAR 15.609. Competitive range consists of those proposals that have a reasonable chance of being selected for contract award. Win percentages can be presented in two very distinct ways: in terms of numbers of proposals won versus total number submitted and also in terms of dollars awarded versus total potential dollars for all procurements on which your company proposed. For example, if your company has won 35% of its proposals in terms of number and only 12% in terms of dollars, that means that you are winning proposals of low dollar value.

7. 8(a) refers to Section 8(a) of the Small Business Act [15 U.S.C. 637(a)], which established a program that authorizes the SBA to enter into all types of contracts with other agencies and let subcontracts for performing those contracts to firms eligible for program participation based upon the criteria established in 13 CFR 124.101-113. The SBA's subcontractors are referred to as "8(a) contractors." (See FAR Subpart 19.8.) Eligibility in the program focuses on those groups that have historically been denied access to capital, educational resources, and markets.

   In 1998, the SBA listed 6,100 8(a) firms throughout the United States. Of those firms, 45.7% were owned by African-Americans, 22.9% were owned by Spanish-speaking people, and 20.7% were owned by

Asians. The remaining companies were owned by Puerto Ricans, Native Americans, and Aleuts. Slightly more than 20% of the 8(a) companies are currently based in the Washington, D.C., area. The SBA allocated $5.2 billion in 1995 in set-aside contracts for minority-owned businesses. [See Munro, Neil, "Clinton Set-Aside Plan Becomes Election-Year Pawn," *Washington Technology*, April 11, 1996, pp. 5, 93; and Munro, Neil, "8(a) Program Survives Republican Attack," *Washington Technology's 8(a) and Small Business Report*, September 12, 1996, p. S-6.]

8. http://www.sba.gov/content/fiscal-year-2012-budget-summary.

9. Statistics about business size (including small business) from the U.S. Census Bureau, http://www.census.gov/econ.smallbus.html.

10. Small Business Administration—FY2007 Budget Request and Performance Plan, p. 40, http://www.sba.gov/idc/groups/public/documents/sba_homepage/serv_abt_budget_1.pdf.

11. *The Small Business Economy: A Report to the President,* U.S. Small Business Administration, Office of Advocacy, 2010, p. 46.

12. *SBA Budget Request & Performance Plan*, FY2004 Congressional Submission, Fourth Printing, February 10, 2003, p. 2.

13. Higgins, Sally, "Feds Update Recertification Regulations," *Kansas City Small Business Monthly*, September 2007, p. 24.

14. Moore, Dennis, "Patriot Express Assistance," *Kansas City Small Business Monthly*, September 2007, p. 9.

15. Cranston, H. S., and Eric G. Flamholtz, "The Problems of Success," *Management Decision*, Vol. 26, September 1988, p. 17.

16. Hartman, Curtis, and Steven Pearlstein, "The Joy of Working," *INC.*, November 1987, p. 62.

17. O'Guin, Michael, "Competitive Intelligence and Superior Business Performance: A Strategic Benchmarking Study," *Competitive Intelligence Review*, Vol. 5, 1994, p. 8.

18. Murray, Bill, "Looking Beyond Graduation," *Washington Technology's 8(a) and Small Business Report*, March 7, 1996, p. S-4.

19. Anderson, Tania, "8(a) Companies Learn the Secret of Partnering," *Washington Technology*, October 10, 1996, p. 22.

20. Small Business Notes, Release Number 06-52, September 1, 2006, http://www.smallbusinessnotes.com/federalgovernment/sba/sbanews/sbanews090106.html.

21. Hunt, Rodney, "8(a) Grads Face a Daunting Future," *Washington Technology*, Vol. 21, No. 17, September 4, 2006.

22. SBA Office of Advocacy, Frequently Asked Questions, updated January 2011, http://www.sba.gov/sites/default/files/files/sbfaq.pdf, and Minniti, Maria, I. Elaine Allen, and Nan Langowitz, *Global Entrepreneurship Monitor 2005 Report on Women and Entrepreneurship*, The Center for Women's Leadership at Babson College and London Business School, 2006.

23. http://www.score.org/small_biz_stats.html.

24. Fox, Harold W., "Strategic Superiorities of Small Size," *Advanced Management Journal*, Vol. 51, 1986, p. 14.

25. "Disadvantaged Firms to Get Edge in Bids for Federal Contracts," *Baltimore Sun*, June 25, 1998, p. 2A. See also Dale, Charles V., *Minority Contracting and Affirmative Action for Disadvantaged Small Businesses: Legal Issues*, CRS Report for Congress, February 24, 2006 [Order Code RL33284].

26. http://www.sba.gov/content/small-business-goaling.

27. Hartman, Curtis, and Steven Pearlstein, "The Joy of Working," *INC.*, November 1987, p. 67.

28. Frank, C., "Uncle Sam Helps Small Business Get High Tech to Market," *Missouri TechNet News*, November 4, 1997; http://www.umr.edu/~tscsbdc/sbirsumm.html.

29. A mission statement is a concise, written expression of a company's long-term business, technical, and programmatic goals. It is a narrative outline of "who we are, what we do, and where we are headed" (Thompson, Arthur A., and A. J. Strickland, *Strategy Formulation and Implementation: Tasks of the General Manager*, 4th ed., Homewood, IL and Boston, MA: BPI/IRWIN, 1989, p. 23.). Once formulated, this statement should be communicated publicly to employees, clients, and vendors, among others. One effective mechanism is to add a "pull quote" from your company's mission statement to your marketing brochures, annual reports, company letterhead, or newsletter. Some companies have poster- sized copies of their mission statement displayed prominently in their facilities to clearly convey their identity.

30. Thompson, Arthur S., and A. J. Strickland, *Strategy Formulation and Implementation: Tasks of the General Manager,* 4th ed., Homewood, IL: Irwin, 1989, p. 19.

31. Certain elements in this listing were adapted and modified from Piper, Thomas S., "A Corporate Strategic Plan for General Sciences Corporation," Spring 1989, p. 1 (unpublished).

32. For additional business challenges, as well as opportunities, strengths, and weaknesses, see Thompson, Arthur S., and A. J. Strickland, *Strategy Formulation and Implementation: Tasks of the General Manager,* 4th ed., Homewood, IL: Irwin, 1989, pp. 109–111.

33. Benchmarking is a rigorous process for linking competitive analysis to your company's strategy development. Benchmarking is a method that measures the performance of your best-in-class competitors relative to your industry's key success factors. It also is a mechanism for identifying, learning, and adapting the business processes by which the best-in-class achieve those performance levels to your company.

    "Benchmarking results should provide insight into how well we are doing and specific process changes that will improve our operations." See Leibfried, Kate H. J., and Joe Oebbecke, "Benchmarking: Gaining a New Perspective on How You Are Doing," *Enterprise Integration Services Supplement,* October 1994, pp. 8–9.

34. Huseman, Richard C., and Jon P. Goodman, "Realm of the Red Queen: The Impact of Change on Corporate Structure, Corporate Education, and the Emergence of Knowledge Organizations," The Corporate Knowledge Center @ EC^2, Annenberg Center for Communication, University of Southern California, 1998, p. 15.

35. Angus, Jeff, Jeetu Patel, and Jennifer Harty, "Knowledge Management: Great Concept . . . But What Is It?" *InformationWeek*, No. 673, March 16, 1998.

36. "Community KM Glossary," http://knowledgecreators.com/km/kes/glossary.htm and Karl E. Sveiby, "What Is Knowledge Management?" p. 2; http://www.sveiby.com/articles/KnowledgeManagement.html, April 2001.

    The term *intellectual capital* is attributed to economist John Kenneth Galbraith (1969). Intellectual capital includes individual talents and knowledge as well as documented knowledge that spans reports, research papers, patents, software source code, books, articles, and manuscripts. See also Touraj Nasseri, "Knowledge Leverage: The Ultimate Advantage," *Kognos: The E-Journal of Knowledge Issues,* Summer 1996.

37. Roos, Johan, "Intellectual Performance: Exploring an Intellectual Capital System in Small Companies," October 30, 1996.

38. Hoyt, Brad, "What Is KM?" *Knowledge Management News,* 1998; http://www.kmnews.com/Editorial/whatmk.htm.

39. Davenport, Tom, and Larry Prusak, "Know What You Know," http://www.brint.com/km/davenport/cio/know.htm, 2000.

   Tom Davenport holds the president's chair in information technology and management at Babson College in Wellesley, Massachusetts. Larry Prusak is a Distinguished Scholar in Residence at Babson College.

40. "Knowledge Management: Collaborating on the Competitive Edge," *CIO White Paper Library*, 2000; http://www.cio.com/sponsors/ 0600_km.

41. Grundstein, Michel, "Companies & Executives in Knowledge Management," http://www.brint.com/km/cko.htm.

42. Information in this paragraph was drawn from Karl E. Svieby, "What Is Knowledge Management?" pp. 5–6; http://www.sveiby.com/ articles/KnowledgeManagement.html, April 2001.

   See also Karl E. Sveiby, "The Intangible Assets Monitor," http://www.sveiby.com/articles/IntangAss/CompanyMonitor.html, December 20, 1997. Celemì employs metrics such as efficiency (sales per customer, staff turnover), stability (repeat orders, growth in sales per administrative staff), and growth/ renewal (average years of professional competence). Celemì is headquartered in Malmö, Sweden, and is dedicated to creating processes that help companies leverage the power of learning.

43. Sutton, Michael H., "Dangerous Ideas: A Sequel," p. 3; http://www. corpforms99.com/83.html. (Remarks delivered during the American Accounting Association 1997 Annual Meeting in Dallas, Texas, on August 18, 1997.)

44. http://www.martech.co.nz/kbl.html#intro.

   Professor Lev notes, "How ironic that accounting is the last vestige of those who believe that things are assets and that ideas are expendable." See Baruch Lev, "Accounting Needs New Standards for Capitalizing Intangibles," *ASAP: Forbes Supplement on the Information Age*, April 7, 1997; http://www.forbes.com/asap/97/ 0407/034.htm.

Chapter 2

Strategic partnering and subcontracting opportunities

S TRATEGIC ALLIANCES can contribute synergy that results in sustained competitive advantage in a rapidly changing global business environment. The stakes are high and the opportunities are real. Many major corporations now maintain their own internal procurement and small business centers or agencies. For example, the Bethesda, Maryland–based space and aeronautics megacorporation, Lockheed Martin, staffs five internal procurement agencies nationwide. "Twenty-two to 28 percent of the company's contracting dollars go to small, disadvantaged and women-owned businesses." Computer manufacturer Gateway, based in Irvine, California, has awarded several million dollars worth of contracts to more than 1,000 small businesses [1].

Hamilton Standard, a division of United Technologies in Connecticut; The National Renewable Energy Laboratory (NREL) in Golden, Colorado; and the Jet Propulsion Laboratory (JPL) in Pasadena, California, were all winners of the Dwight D. Eisenhower Award for Excellence from the U.S. Small Business Administration. Science Applications International Corporation (SAIC) of McLean, Virginia, won this honor in 2011. The Eisenhower Award is a national program for large prime contractors in the manufacturing, service, R&D, and construction arenas that have excelled in their use of small businesses as subcontractors and suppliers. Divisions of Lockheed Martin in Orlando, Florida, and Cherry Hill, New Jersey, have been among the winners of the Eisenhower Award in the manufacturing and service categories [2].

2.1 Subcontracting opportunities and pathways to success

Evidence of new directions in subcontracting is seen in the public/private partnership among the SBA, General Motors, Ford Motor Company, and Chrysler that was designed to improve opportunities for minority-owned small businesses in a major industry. This landmark memorandum of understanding (MOU) marked the first time that a private-sector industrial group of this magnitude and importance has engaged in partnership with the SBA. The MOU represented a sharp increase in the contract dollars flowing to small disadvantaged businesses (SDBs) [3].

In general, proactive small business entrepreneurs are significantly leveraging their limited marketing, financial, and technical resources as well as augmenting their revenue stream by attracting and forming strategic partnerships, as subcontractors and protégés, with large prime contracting companies to pursue new business opportunities and expand work with existing clients. Many procurements let by the U.S. federal government, as well as by the public sector at the state and local levels, stipulate small, small disadvantaged, minority-owned, women-owned, HUBZone, or veteran-owned business target thresholds for the resulting contracts. For example, a procurement related to the Everglades by the state of Florida required that a minimum of 16% of the contract revenue be allocated to minority-/women-owned business enterprises (M/WBE).

The opportunities for small business success have never been better! As of February 2012, the federal government's subcontracting goals were as follows:

- 23% for small businesses;
- 5% for women-owned businesses;
- 3% for HUBZone small businesses;

- 3% for service-disabled veteran-owned businesses.

These guidelines are of direct benefit to small businesses of all types because they require large federal contractors to proactively team with small businesses to pursue U.S. government contracts.

2.2 Critical success factors

Critical to a small firm's subcontracting success are the following elements: (1) superlative contractual performance on existing or past projects (being the best-in-class); (2) flexible, audited, and approved pricing strategies and structures; (3) the allocation of top-flight, dedicated professional staff to proposal teams with the prime contractor; (4) fiscal strength as measured by such parameters as operating profit, net income, EBITDA, positive cash flow, operating history, and future business assumptions; (5) well-defined and articulated value proposition for a specific opportunity, core competencies, and product lines; and (6) fair, equitable, and ethical teaming agreements that are always honored. Strategic alliances or partnerships must be managed as enduring business relationships—with mutually compatible objectives, shared risks and resources, real-time knowledge transfer, and mutual trust.

Understand that the prime contractor will have to sell your small company's human talent and knowledge, contractual experience, and fiscal solvency in their proposal to a given public- or private-sector client. Make that task extremely easy for them by having a customer-focused, fact-based story to tell, and make that information available to them in a timely manner during the subcontractor selection and proposal response life cycle. Be responsive! Far too many small businesses submit poorly written, incomplete materials to the prime contractor for integration into the prime's proposal. This inappropriate practice adds to the prime contractor's B&P costs, and detracts from your working relationship with that prime in the future. It may also lead to the dissolution of your relationship with the prime contractor, as I witnessed personally in 2011. You may need to contract freelance or temporary staff to prepare required proposal modules and other materials in an electronic form compatible with the prime contractor's publishing systems. Above all, adhere to the proposal schedule as developed by the prime contractor. These aspects of working with prime contractors are reviewed in Chapter 7. With significantly tightened federal budgets for contracting, your small business *must amplify* your efforts to satisfy your prime contractor partners.

Whenever possible, small businesses should strive to forge and negotiate exclusive teaming agreements with prime contractors which are active and successful within your company's major LOBs. Cultivate successful contractual experience within the prime's and your target client's technical areas of interest. Understand how to conduct contractual business with the prime and the ultimate client. Demonstrate your company's ability to staff the project with stellar professional staff (through incumbent capture, for example) who are committed to the life of the project and not merely senior staff whose résumés help to win the job, but who leave the project after a minimal amount of time. Build camaraderie in the relationship, and establish a mutually beneficial strategic partnership for the long term.

2.3 Specific strategies for achieving subcontracts

The following strategies can help you achieve subcontracts with prime contractors:

- *Register your small business with the Central Contractor Registration (CCR) portal (http://www.ccr.gov) right away.* In 2004, the U.S. Small Business Administration's PRO-*Net* database was combined with the Department of Defense's (DoD) Central Contractor Registration (CCR) database. *The result?* One Web portal for vendor registration and for searching for small business sources—and an integrated, more efficient mechanism that small businesses can use to market their products and services to the federal government. The "Dynamic Small Business Search" (DSBS) site facilitates in-depth searching for teaming partners throughout the small business community. Categories span location, certification, NAICS code, and company size. The CCR is the primary vendor database for the U.S. federal government. This system collects, validates, stores, and disseminates data in support of agency acquisition missions. Both current and potential federal government vendors are required to register with CCR in order to be awarded contracts by the U.S. government. The CCR Web portal is also valuable for searching for small business sources. [PRO-*Net* and the Procurement Automated Source System (PASS) database are now defunct.]

  Prime contractors and other nonfederal agencies use SUB-*Net* (http://web.sba.gov/subnet) to post subcontracting opportunities.

These may or may not be reserved for small business, and they may include either solicitations or other notices—for example, notices of sources sought for teaming partners and subcontractors on future contracts. American Recovery and Reinvestment Act (ARRA) subcontracts solicitations are posted here. Small businesses can review this Web site to identify opportunities in their areas of expertise. While the Web site is designed primarily as a place for large businesses to post solicitations and notices, it is also used for the same purpose by nonfederal agencies, state and local governments, nonprofit organizations, colleges and universities, and even foreign governments. This Web site has shifted the traditional marketing strategy from the shotgun approach to one that is more focused and sophisticated. Instead of marketing blindly to many prime contractors, with no certainty that any given company has a need for their product or service, small businesses can use their limited resources to identify concrete, tangible opportunities and then bid on them.

- *General Services Administration (GSA) Subcontracting Directory* (http://w3.gsa.gov/web/i/subs_dir.nsf/). This directory is published as an aid to small businesses seeking subcontrator opportunities with GSA prime contractors.

- If appropriate, list your firm with the Worldwide Minority Business Network (http://www.mbnet.com/).

- *Participate in private-sector supplier diversity programs.* According to DiversityBusiness.com, major corporations and organizations ranging from Cisco Systems, AT&T, Raytheon, Lockheed Martin, Verizon, and Xerox Corporation to Apple, IBM, Accenture, Deloitte, and Mircosoft maintain and staff robust supplier diversity programs. These programs actively seek, certify, qualify, develop, and use M/WBEs and Disabled Veteran Business Enterprises (DVBEs). For example, AT&T spent $9.2 billion with diverse suppliers in 2010, representing 18.8% of its procurement base.

- *Register and prequalify your small business with the SADBUS, or Small and Disadvantaged Business Utilization Specialist, in specific federal agencies.* At the state level, the analogous office may be called the "Office of Supplier Diversity and Outreach." And many large corporations now have small business centers, staffed with Small Business Liaison Officers (SBLOs). Every federal contracting agency and prime contractor doing substantial business with the federal government is obliged to designate an SBLO or SADBUS within the agency or firm. This person is the first point of contact for your small business wishing to make your products and services known to the contracting entity.

- *Create, maintain, and register an easily accessible Web site for your small company.* Prime contractors often perform Internet searches to locate potential teaming partners. Registration refers to listing your site with various Internet-based promotion resources, such as 123 Submit PRO, AddMe, Submit Away!, and Submit All.

- *Interact with Small Business Development Centers (SBDCs) in your state (http://www.sba.gov/sbdc/).* The 63 SBDCs with 1,100 service locations nationwide are educational and research resources for small businesses. The Association of Small Business Development Centers (ASBDC; http://www.asbdc-us.org) links each SBDC program into a national network. In addition, some states maintain Regional Minority Supplier Development Councils and Regional Minority Purchasing Councils. There is also a National Minority Supplier Development Council, Inc. (NMSDC) (http://www.nmsdc.org).

- *As fiscally appropriate for your small business, employ reputable consulting firms to open the door to strategic partnership discussions.* Reputable consulting firms include INPUT Deltek Information Solutions (http://www.input. com), Deltek, Federal Sources, Inc. (FSI) (http://www.fedsources. com), and Centurion Research Solutions (http://www.centurionresearch.com), all located in Virginia.

- *Register your company in the Diversity Information Resources (DIR) online M/WBE sourcing portal.* This portal includes more than 8,500 certified M/WBEs, veteran, and HUBZone businesses. It provides exposure to major corporations that are seeking opportunities with M/WBE, veteran, service-disabled veteran-owned, and HUBZone-certified suppliers. In addition to access to the M/WBE portal, the supplier registration link allows your corporation to establish a supplier registration link from your corporate Web site. (http://www.diversityinforesources.com/)

- *Attend and participate in appropriate conferences and trade shows for your industry.* Small businesses are strongly encouraged to attend and participate in relevant federal government conferences. NASA's small business conference is one such forum.

At the Ninth Annual NASA Mentor-Protégé Program Conference held for 2 days in December 2004 in Washington, D.C., more than 200 NASA protégés and other attendees learned about the fundamentals of the NASA Mentor-Protégé Program, principles of effective teaming agreements, and proven approaches for winning new business within the Mentor-Protégé relationship. As a presenter at this particular NASA conference, I know firsthand how much knowledge is shared and learned in this particular forum.

- Visit prime contractor directories, such as those maintained by the U.S. Department of Commerce (http://www.osc.doc.gov/osdbu/ Primes.htm), U.S. Census Bureau (http://www.census.gov/ procur/www/subcontract.html), and the Department of Defense (http://www.acq.osd.mil/osbp/ doing_business/subcontracting_ directory_0908.pdf).

- *Secure your company's membership and participate in trade and business associations.* This includes interaction with such associations as the Institute for Supply Management (ISM). With more than 34,000 members, ISM is a not-for-profit association based in Tempe, Arizona, that provides national and international leadership in purchasing and supply management research and education. ISM meetings offer forums for developing important business relationships with procurement representatives of large corporations. ISM can be contacted on the Web at http://www.ism.ws or by calling (800)888-6276.

- *Consider listing your company in the Thomas Register of American Manufacturers.* Major corporations and government agencies often consult this resource for suppliers that operate nationally. Visit http://www.thomasnet.com.

- *Visit Internet sites to learn more about potential prime contractors.* For example, Hoovers, a D&B comapny, (http://www.hoovers.com) provides detailed business and financial information about major corporations.

2.4 Becoming part of a governmentwide acquisition contract (GWAC) team

Governmentwide acquisition contracts (GWACs) are multiple award task order or delivery order contractual vehicles for various resources and services hosted, or "owned," by one agency of the federal government, but which other specified federal agencies can use as well. GWACs are ID/IQ contracts that help federal agencies meet their technology requirements through a customizable solution. Hardware, software, and services can be purchased as a total technology solution. Phacil, Inc., in Arlington, Virgina, is one example of a small firm that has generated significant business success through the GSA Alliant Small Business GWAC in 2011.

GWACs were given statutory weight through the Federal Acquisition Streaming Act (FASA) of 1994 and are defined in FAR 2.101. The government can realize economies of scale by centralizing the purchase of certain types of services or products through these ID/IQ GWAC vehicles. There is a limitation on the total percentage of the GWAC that one agency can use, and each GWAC has its own specific terms and conditions. Despite a small administrative and contracting fee levied by the host federal agency, the direct benefit is that other government agencies do not need to incur major acquisition and procurement costs when using the GWAC vehicle. As part of a GWAC team, your small business can proactively sell the fiscal and efficiency benefits of GWACs to a broad group of constituencies, including government agency chief information officers (CIOs), as well as establish government-funded venture capital programs to support R&D within the IT sector.

GWACs are critical federal contractual vehicles for small, midsized, and large businesses. They have become the vehicle of choice for many government agencies. *Why?* Because much of the procurement paperwork, price justifications, and contractor selections can be done up front in the GWAC procurement process. Individual purchases can then be made from a small cadre of qualified vendors quickly through the use of a task order competition or purchase order. Your company should prime as many GWACs as possible and, as an alternative, be an integral part of as many GWAC teams as you can. Increasingly, these are the key pathways for doing long-term work in the federal market space. Examples of important current and upcoming GWAC vehicles include GSA Streamlined Technology Acquisition Resources for Services (STARS II), GSA Alliant Small Business, GSA Connections II (CNX II), NIH Chief Information Officer–Solutions and Partners 3 (CIO-SP3), COMMITS NexGen, NASA Solutions for Enterprise-Wide Procurement (SEWP) IV, and DHS EAGLE II (Enterprise Acquisition Gateway for Leading Edge solutions).

GSA's nationwide *8(a) Streamlined Technology Acquisition Resources for Services (STARS) GWAC* is a small business set-aside contract for technology solutions with a ceiling of $15 billion. This contract vehicle is the replacement contract for the 8(a) FAST small business contract. STARS is a multiple-award, ID/IQ contract vehicle with a 3-year base and two 2-year option periods. GSA extended the ordering period through November 30, 2011; order performance must be completed by May 31, 2014. The contract spans eight distinct functional areas (FAs) designated by NAICS codes, including Customer Computer Programming Services; Computer Systems Design Services; Computer Facilities Management Services; Data Processing, Hosting and Related Services; Other Computer Related Services; Internet Publishing and Broadcasting; All Other

Information Services; and Wired Telecommunications Carriers. Directed task orders up to $4 million each for federal civilian agencies are allowable pursuant to 41 U.S.C. 253(c)(5). Directed task orders up to $4 million each for DoD activities are compliant with Section 843 of the 2008 National Defense Authorization Act (NDAA). Importantly, 8(a) credit can be transferred back to the client agency via the Federal Procurement Data System (FPDS) Program ceiling.

Specific benefits of the STARS GWAC vehicle are: (1) hardware, software, and services can be procured as part of an integrated solution; (2) it supports small businesses and meets procurement preference goals; (3) it provides availability and access to proven small business and 8(a) technology providers; (4) procurement lead times are short; and (5) it has low user fees (0.75%). Fundamentally, the 8(a) STARS GWAC provides solutions for a wide spectrum of information technology solutions, including cybersecurity, information assurance, virtualization, sustainability, health IT, cloud computing, IPv6, Voice over Internet Protocol (VoIP), and Web 2.0.

GSA became the first executive agency to offer a contract vehicle set-aside exclusively for HUBZone firms in 2003. Contracts enable federal agencies to fulfill their information technology (IT) requirements through the utilization of small businesses that are located in HUBZones. Agencies have a statutory goal to spend 3% of their federal procurement dollars with HUBZone small business firms.

The GSA HUBZone IT GWAC was designed to provide federal agencies with access to qualified HUBZone contractors. The 36 qualified technology firms under this contract are primarily engaged in providing electronic data processing services including the processing and preparation of reports and automated data entry. Keylogic Systems, Inc., of Morgantown, West Virginia, was issued a task order worth $4 million over 3 years by the EPA, Washington, D.C. TELESIS Corporation of Rockville, Maryland, received a task order for data processing services valued at $150 million over 5 years.

NASA's Solutions for Enterprise-Wide Procurement (SEWP) IV GWAC vehicle is geared to provide the latest in IT products for all federal agencies. SEWP has a total of 38 prime contractors, 21 of which are small businesses, which offer a vast selection and wide range of advanced technology to all federal agencies including the Department of Defense. These technologies span software products including software as service (SaaS), IT hardware, and network and telecommunications products. Running through 2014, SEWP offers low prices (generally below GSA Schedule prices) and the lowest surcharge (0.45%).

The National Institutes of Health Chief Information Officer—Solutions & Partners 2 (NIH CIO-SP2*i*) GWAC contract provides information technology hardware, software, systems, and services in support of IT solutions within NIH and other government agencies. This vehicle was let by the National Information Technology Acquisitions and Assessment Center (NITAAC), and was extended through December 2011. The follow-on NIH CIO-SP3 $20 billion opportunity was let in 2010, with award decisions pending as of February 2012.

The U.S. Department of Commerce created the COMMerce Information Technology Solutions (COMMITS) Next Generation (COMMITS NexGen) as the follow-on to the extremely successful COMMITS GWAC contract awarded in 1999. This GWAC, which was awarded in late 2004 and now under the direction of GSA, has an $8 billion ceiling and a 10-year period of performance. It is available for use governmentwide. Task orders were awarded through July 2011, and task order life cycles may extend to January 20, 2016

Alliant is a GWAC offered through GSA to consolidate and replace Millennia, ANSWER, ITOP II, Safeguard, Virtual Data Center, and other GWACs. GSA made 58 awards under this $50 billion, 10-year vehicle. Functional areas include cyber security, information assurance, vituraliztion, sustainability, health IT, cloud computing, IPv6, and Web 2.0. The GSA Millennia GWAC had done more than $6 billion worth of business, ANSWER more than $2 billion, and ITOP II about $2 billion.

Awarded as a small business set-aside to a total group of contract holders that stood at 69 small business primes in December 2011, the Alliant Small Business (SB) GWAC provides a $15 billion ceiling and period of performance through February 2, 2014, with one 5-year option. Solutions provided under Alliant SB mirror those under Alliant listed above. Finally, the Veterans Technology Services (VETS) GWAC was awarded as a smal business set-aside contract for Service-Disabled Veteran-Owned (SDVO) small technology firms. Its period of performance extended to February 1, 2012, with one 5-year option with $5 billion ceiling. VETS provides system operations and maintenance and information systems engineering solutions.

2.5 How mentor-protégé programs can help your business

Created by Congress in 1990 (P.L. 101-510), the DoD Mentor-Protégé Program (MPP) (http://www.acq.osd.mil/osbp/mentor_protege/) is a socioeconomic initiative that encourages major DoD prime contractors (mentors) to develop the technical and business capabilities of small disadvantaged businesses, qualified organizations that employ people with severe disabilities, and women-owned small businesses (protégés) in the context of long-term business relationships. Through credit toward subcontracting goals or some direct reimbursement of costs, the MPP provides tangible incentives for the major prime contractors to establish and implement a developmental assistance plan designed to enable the small business to compete more successfully for DoD prime contract and subcontract awards. Mentors represented in the MPP encompass a broad range of industries: environmental remediation, engineering services and information technology, manufacturing, telecommunications, and health care. These include Booz Allen Hamilton, Northrop Grumman, Lockheed Martin, IBM Business Consulting Services, Science Applications International Corporation (SAIC), and Raytheon Company. Protégés receive assistance in marketing and business planning, management, training, needs assessment, bid and proposal preparation, human resources practices, quality assurance (including ISO certification), environmental protection, emerging technologies, and health and safety procedures.

Protégé firms participating in the program benefit by receiving training in the latest technology pertinent to their business niche. Like their mentor, protégé firms also enjoy the benefit of a long-term stable relationship, which helps create a stable business base. Also included in the benefits are expanded subcontracting opportunities throughout the mentor corporation for the protégé and the protégé's ability to pursue the larger, sometimes bundled requirements by bringing along the mentor as its partner. Another benefit whose value is not as easily quantifiable is the guidance and vision a mentor firm provides to its protégé on the particular industry's direction and trends.

The Air Force Mentor-Protégé Program (http://www.airforcesmallbiz. org/small-business-programs/support/mentor-protege.php) involves competition rather than application. The Air Force requires meaningful participation by Historically Black Colleges and Universities and/or Minority Institutions (HBCU/MIs). Program oversight and monitoring are provided through the Air Force Outreach Program Office (AFOPO) located in San Antonio, Texas.

The Mentor-Protégé Program as set forth in legislative and regulatory coverage has two major goals:

1.   Have mentor companies provide developmental assistance and technology transfer to their protégés.

2.   Have protégés establish relationships with major Air Force contractors, develop necessary business and technical

capabilities to perform significant work for Air Force and other DoD contracts, and expand and diversify their customer base.

The Department of Homeland Security's (DHS) Mentor-Protégé Program (http://www.dhs.gov/xopnbiz/smallbusiness/editorial_0716.shtm) is designed to motivate and encourage large business prime contractor firms to provide mutually beneficial developmental assistance to small business, veteran-owned small business, service-disabled veteran-owned small business, HUBZone small business, small disadvantaged business, and women-owned small business concerns. The program is also designed to improve the performance of DHS contracts and subcontracts, foster the establishment of long-term business relationships between DHS large prime contractors and small business subcontractors, and strengthen subcontracting opportunities and accomplishments at DHS. Through self-identification, DHS small business outreach events, networking, and marketing, the mentor-protégé team jointly submits an agreement to the DHS OSDBU for review and approval demonstrating the mutually beneficial relationship of the two parties.

The Federal Aviation Administration (FAA) also maintains an active mentor-protégé program (http://www.sbo.faa.gov/sbo/MentorProtege.cfm). The FAA's program is designed to motivate and encourage larger businesses to assist Small Socially and Economically Disadvantaged Businesses (SEDB), Service-Disabled Veteran-Owned, HBCUs, MIs, and Women-Owned (WO) Small Businesses. The goal is to enhancing the capabilities of these protégé organizations to perform FAA prime contracts and subcontracts, foster the establishment of long-term business relationships between these entities and mentor corporations, and increase the overall number of protégés receiving FAA prime contract and subcontract awards.

Other federal government agencies that sponsor a Mentor-Protégé Program include the Department of Energy (DOE) (http://diversity.energy.gov/business/mentor-protege.htm), DOE's Oak Ridge National Laboratory (ORNL) (http://www.ornl.gov/adm/smallbusiness/mentor.shtml), NASA (http://osbp.nasa.gov/mentor.html), the SBA (http://www.sba.gov/content/ mentor-prot%C3%A9g%C3%A9-program), the Department of State (http://www.state.gov/m/a/sdbu/c14690.htm), and the EPA (http://www.epa.gov/osdbu/ pdfs/protege.pdf).

The U.S. Small Business Administration's Mentor-Protégé Program enhances the capability of 8(a) participants to compete more successfully for federal government contracts. The program encourages private-sector relationships and expands SBA's efforts to identify and respond to the developmental needs of 8(a) clients. Mentors provide technical and management assistance, financial assistance in the form of equity investments or loans, subcontract support, and assistance in performing prime contracts through joint venture arrangements with 8(a) firms.

Recent data suggest that small firms participating in the mentor-protégé programs have experienced significant growth. Specifically, among 226 agreements reviewed there was a net gain of 3,342 jobs within protégé firms; there was a net revenue gain in excess of $276 million within the protégé firms; and mentors reported an additional $695 million in subcontract awards to small disadvantaged business firms. Mentor firms reported value accrued to them as the direct result of developing a technically qualified and more competitively priced supplier base for DoD requirements. As mentor firms restructured and right-sized, they often formed strategic alliances with protégé firms for the specific purpose of outsourcing functions previously performed in-house. Similarly, the DoD gained by having an increased number of cost-effective, technically qualified small business sources for defense prime contracting as well as subcontracting requirements.

Your reasons to enter and participate in mentor-protégé programs should extend far beyond subcontracting dollars alone. Your company should be willing to invest its nonreimbursable funds and your employees' billable time for training in order to develop a long-term teaming relationship premised upon mutual trust, respect, communication, and flexibility. The process of being selected by a mentor corporation can take up to 1 year. The mentor-protégé programs present opportunities for realizing diverse technical capabilities, efficient contract management, exposure to new technologies and business practices, expanded work potential, and exposure to new federal clients. The CEO of one protégé firm stated "We measured success by what we learned rather than what was earned."

AMEC, an international engineering and project management company, won the Dwight D. Eisenhower Award for Excellence in Services contracting from the U.S. SBA in 2011. Named for the U.S. President whose administration the SBA was founded, the award honors large federal prime contractors that have excelled in using small businesses as subcontractors and suppliers. Within DoD in 2011, SAIC received the prestigious Nunn-Perry Award, named in honor of former Senator Sam Nunn and former Secretary of Defense William Perry. SAIC's protégé was Engineering/Remediation Resource Group, Inc. in Martinez, California. Check out the Nunn-Perry mentor awardees–perhaps you can forge a partnership that makes business sense to both parties.

A great number of small businesses are eager to engage in Mentor-Protégé programs—both formally through NASA, the Air Force, or Small Business Administration, for example, or informally with a larger, more established company that does business within a similar marketspace. Eagerness to partner with a larger firm in an effort to grow and mature one's small business shows excellent initiative. However, the small-business protégé must be willing to be a very proactive participant in this special relationship. Importantly, the protégé should provide the larger company with a solid "business case" for serving in a mentorship role. Approaching a large business and simply petitioning that firm for a subcontract with several billable, full-time equivalent (FTE) staff is to do two things: (1) alienate and irritate the large company and (2) significantly reduce your small company's chances to forge a genuine, long-term Mentor-Protégé partnership with that specific large business.

So how does your small company establish and communicate a "business case" for an informal Mentor-Protégé relationship with a specific large company? Here are some very practical, field-tested ideas and approaches.

Building upon your own small company's existing contractual work, *identify* and *qualify* a new marketing opportunity within that same government agency or private-sector client. Perhaps this new opportunity is one that your company can prime as a small business, small disadvantaged business, HUBZone, woman-owned business, or veteran-owned business, but you do not have all of the competencies or qualifications in house to perform all functional areas in the Statement of Work (SOW) or Statement of Objectives (SOO) alone. Or perhaps this new marketing opportunity is one that is beyond the size, scope, and complexity that your small business can realistically prime, but if you teamed with a large company as its principal subcontractor, that large firm could meet its subcontracting goals required by the contract.

Then, take this new marketing opportunity to the specific large company with which you want to partner and present it to that company's key decision makers. Prepare for this meeting well in advance. Take the time to craft a tailored, targeted, and professional-looking presentation that highlights the "business case." This briefing should be 10 slides or less. Indicate the tangible benefits associated with doing business with you and your small company's desire to establish a long-term, professional working relationship with them. Benefits that you can highlight might include:

- Your established relationships throughout the customer organization at technical, programmatic, contractual, and leadership levels;

- Your small business's in-depth knowledge of the customer and his or her hopes, fears, biases, success factors, and critical issues associated with the new marketing opportunity;

- Your exemplary and verifiable past performance experience, replete with high award fee scores and customer commendation letters;

- Subject matter experts (SMEs) within your small business who will make themselves available to assist in proposal development, writing, and review;

- SMEs within your small business who would be available for participation in oral presentations to the customer, both as part of the marketing intelligence-gathering process (Call Plan execution) and the proposal development life cycle;

- Partial fulfillment of small business subcontracting goals for the large company;

- Your track record of superlative proposal development and support;

- Your commitment to respond quickly and comprehensively to proposal-related and contractual/administrative "data calls" from the large company, should it be the prime contractor.

You might also volunteer to help the large business prepare a white paper or position paper that defines viable technical and programmatic solutions to the customer agency or organization for this particular marketing opportunity.

When the proposal process is underway, be willing to share an appropriate percentage of the proposal production costs. Do not expect the large business to shoulder all of the production responsibility and costs. Pay whatever amount you commit to promptly.

Any effective relationship is a two-way street. The Mentor-Protégé partnership is absolutely no exception.

ENDNOTES

1. Mulhern, Charlotte, "Round 'Em Up," *Entrepreneur*, Vol. 28, No. 8, August 1998, p. 120.

2. "Lockheed Martin Division, Nova Group Earn SBA's Top Awards for Subcontracting," SBA Number 98-43, June 4, 1998; http://www.sba.gov/news/current/98-43.html.

3. U.S. Small Business Administration, "Vice President and SBA Administrator Announce Pact with Big Three Automakers," Press Release Number 98-09, February 19, 1998; http://www.sba.gov/news/current/98-09.html.

Chapter 3

Marketing to and with your clients

[G]et in the path of their judgment ... to make your product part of an already existing code.
—Adcult USA

3.1 More than just selling

Demonstrate how you can help meet your client's requirements and performance thresholds, provide solutions, and minimize associated technical, contractual, schedule, and fiscal risks.

Marketing involves far more than just short-term or one-time selling in response to immediate issues and needs. It is a long-term process of dedicated commitment to and cultivation of your client's success as well as your specific business and product lines as defined in your strategic plan. Your client wants to know that you'll be around next year, and 5 years down the road, to offer him high-quality products and superior services at competitive costs. Marketing means learning about your client's technical requirements, contractual and fiscal constraints, and programmatic as well as regulatory concerns. It involves developing an in-depth understanding of your client's business strategy and culture, organizational structure and dynamics, and procurement decision-making processes and buying influences. You will want to help your client appreciate the value of not just buying a product or service, but rather buying a solution [1]. Effective marketing takes time.

Functionally, marketing is about understanding your client and his or her users and stakeholders, your competition, your potential teaming partners, and the specific technical and programmatic benefits (strengths) your company can provide (see Figure 3.1).

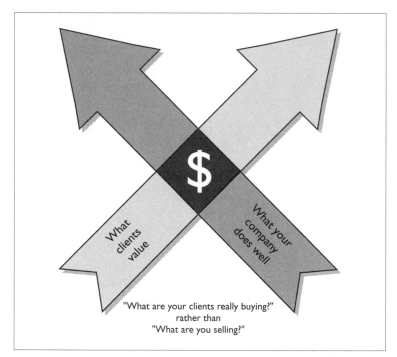

Figure 3.1
The point of intersection.

(Within figure:)

What clients value

What your company does well

$

"What are your clients really buying?"
rather than
"What are you selling?"

- What other companies have provided goods and services to your client?

- How are those companies and their respective staff perceived by your client?

- Because potential teaming partners are part of the knowledge equation as well, does your client favor the formation of teams? How are your potential teaming partners perceived by your client?

- How can your company contribute in positive ways to your client's bottom line (private sector), program budget (federal and state), or hard currency deficit (international clients)?

Fundamentally, marketing means championing the customer [2]. It begins with target identification and proceeds through the qualification phase. The goals of qualification are validating that you can win the opportunity, building a business case to demonstrate that the opportunity warrants bidding, gathering customer intelligence through relationship building, and jump-starting the capture team.

Within the federal government market space, the business developer or marketer's role is to gain robust insight into the customer and the customer's stakeholder community in an ethical and professional manner. The overall business development life cycle is depicted in Figures 3.2 and 3.3. This insight, or marketing intelligence, then becomes the basis on which a superior proposal solution is built. Figure 3.4 shows the key categories of marketing intelligence that will ultimately become part of the proposal solution. Notice that these categories mirror sections of most proposals.

Major areas of focus for the business developer span target identification and qualification. These include:

- Identifying marketing leads and maintaining the leads list for assigned market segments (e.g., science and engineering, civilian programs);

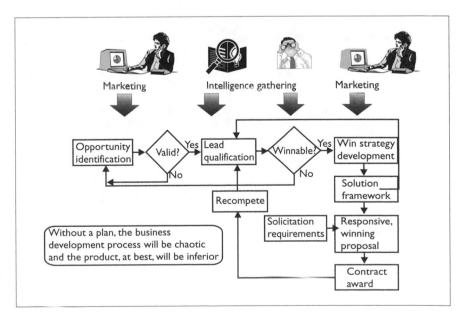

Figure 3.2 Overall business development life cycle.

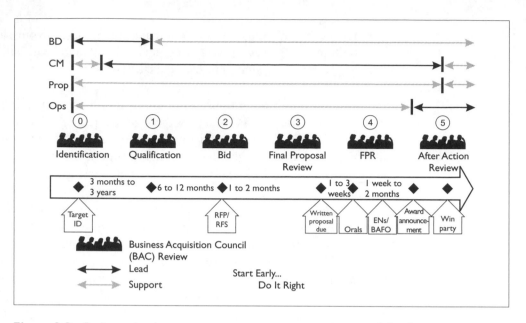

Figure 3.3 Business development, capture management, and proposal development time line.

Figure 3.4 Marketing intelligence categories.

- Marketing the customer—helping the customer understand "Why you?" or "Why your team and not your competitors' teams?";
- Knowing the customer's buying habits and sell points;
- Legitimately influencing the acquisition strategy and RFP (e.g., educating the customer about the potential GWAC vehicles under which a procurement might be released);
- Developing and executing the call plan (see Section 3.6);
- Drafting the initial win strategy and solution framework;
- Building the *business case* for pursuing the specific procurement (i.e., business case for investing B&P dollars and human resources for developing and submitting a proposal and oral presentation, as required);
- Serving as an integral member of the capture team through phase-in of the contract and after-action review of the proposal.

Specific factors that must be considered when building the business case for pursuing a given procurement are presented in Figure 3.5. Ensuring, for example, that the procurement aligns with your company's core competencies and the annual business plan are two of the most critical

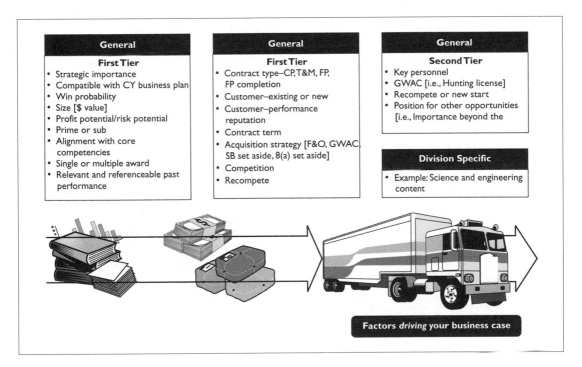

Figure 3.5   Important business case factors.

parameters to consider when generating a defensible business case—one that can be presented to and approved by executive management.

In the case of federal procurements, your company must also determine the following when building your business case:

- That the particular target program is real and will be funded;
- That the RFP or request for solution (RFS) will indeed be issued;
- That political and procurement conditions within the specific government agency will allow for genuine competition in the case of a recompetition;
- That you understand who the customer is;
- That you have identified the customer's *unstated* criteria for the award (*stated* criteria are given in the RFP and amendments).

Figure 3.6 defines winning proposals in the context of stated and unstated criteria. It is around these stated and unstated criteria that you will want to develop and validate the benefits and strengths that your company offers.

Learn the superset of civil servants who will serve on the evaluation or selection board for your procurement. Does the client expect to get the most cost-effective solution? In effect, is price the real driver of the acquisition? Or is best value important to your client [3]?

Over time and in a variety of ways, inform the client about your company's distinctive human talents, technical capabilities and knowledge

- It's all about winning:
    Winner is the prime, as evaluated by the customer, whose approach (proposal) is demonstrably different and superior when evaluated against stated and unstated criteria

- Questions:
    1. Who is the customer?
    2. What are the unstated criteria?

Figure 3.6
Stated and unstated criteria.

base, past and present contractual experience, management and subcontractor approaches, and financial stability and approved financial and accounting systems in ways that demonstrate how you can help meet his or her requirements and minimize, as well as share[1] associated technical, contractual, and fiscal risks. Be sure to meet your client's emotional or intangible needs as well—help them feel secure knowing you are looking out for them. Provide them with peace of mind [4].

If your potential client does not know your firm, he or she is less likely to buy from you. You must differentiate your company from every other company in a positive, credible way. Marketing is the process of persistently helping your client understand and believe that your brand of product or service will contribute substantively to his or her mission, program, and career success. Build your differentiated suite of solutions into the decision pathway of your client's infrastructure and buying influences. Know and cultivate ongoing relationships with the "sell points" within your customer's organization, that is, the people in the decision-making chain.

3.2 Transactions are personal—people buy from people

Face time with your client is critical. Why? Because people buy from people they know and trust, and they buy emotionally. Interaction with your client should be conducted in a concerted manner by a variety of levels within your company— from marketing and senior management staff to mid-level technical personnel and project managers. Client visits by your marketing staff are necessary to open doors and establish new relationships with a potential client. These visits should be ongoing and augmented by additional information-sharing visits by members of your senior management as well as appropriate, select staff from among your technical and programmatic ranks. For your company's president to invest energy and time in focused direct client contact is essential to demonstrate and authenticate your corporate commitment to a given program or project. The only way to develop a robust, contextual understanding of your client and his mission, overall program goals and objectives, funding processes, and technical concerns both now and going forward is to personally interact with him and his staff as well as cognizant contracting, procurement, and management decision-making personnel (sell points).

---

1   Increasingly, risk sharing is a stipulated expectation of federal clients. The Department of Veterans' Affairs' (VA) $650 million Austin Automation Enterprise System contract was a major case in point. See Appendix D for additional details.

Given the decentralized marketing activities of many firms—both small and large, technical and line managers are often in a position to make their own decisions about pursuing marketing opportunities. In my experience, this has resulted frequently in the pursuit of marginal targets that may have been appropriate from a technical standpoint but were not considered thoroughly from programmatic, cost, strategic planning, or proposaling perspectives. In fact, many times no marketing has taken place—the announcement on FedBizOpps (http://www.fedbizopps.gov) or government agency procurement Web sites is the first time that the project has been identified and considered for a bid–no bid decision. If your company does not market the client, you cannot expect to win contracts. There are, at minimum, several firms that qualify technically for most any government opportunity. Unless you can set your company apart in a positive way from your competition, you will not acquire new business consistently.

Paul V. Lombardi, former president and chief operating officer of DynCorp, has noted that "[u]ltimately, the government is buying people. The transactions are personal" [5]. A sales representative for a mid-Atlantic analytical chemistry laboratory remarked to me that a proposal that he had submitted received extremely high marks from the prime contractor and the ultimate government client. Why? Because this rep had marketed the client and was able to answer all of his relevant questions and concerns in the context of responding to the RFP. And in competitions between experienced contracting firms, relationships assume an even larger role in the final decision-making process. Plan on attending professional and trade association gatherings; meeting and talking with your clients at conferences, trade shows, and expositions; participating in sporting events; and going out to lunch (with each party paying his or her own check), for example.

3.3 Listen to your client

First and foremost, listen to your client—and listen to understand, not to reply [6]. Take every opportunity to learn about his or her requirements, budget concerns and trends, technical problems both now and over the horizon, staffing goals, scheduling issues, experiences with your competitors, professional and personal likes and dislikes, and career goals. Importantly, learn who are your client's mentors, champions, advocates, and adversaries. Too many times, a company attempts to force-fit its clients into the company's own technical or programmatic compartments. Give your prospective client a chance to participate in your marketing presentations. Get your technical people in front of your client to have meaningful discussions on a variety of important technical, programmatic, and financial issues well in advance of the release of the RFP, RFS, or SF330 synopsis. Your company should be marketing an existing federal opportunity for the life of the current contract. Introduce and reinforce innovative, solution-oriented technical, management, and staffing approaches that will appear later in your own proposal. Indeed, a compelling case can be made that the sale is made pre-RFP and that the proposal only closes the deal. A reasonably well-constructed proposal will not make up for inferior technical homework, poor management plans, or high costs [7]. And inferior and outdated marketing intelligence about your client, teaming partners, and competitors will most certainly result in a proposal loss.

3.4 Infuse marketing intelligence into your proposal

To be useful at all, the marketing information that your company collects must be documented, analyzed, distributed, and archived so that it can be retrieved and updated easily. There is no point in marketing your client if you do not apply what has been learned into conceptualizing, designing, and producing your proposal. All information gathered that is relevant to a given procurement should be provided to the specific capture manager and proposal manager. Appropriate marketing information must shape and also be fitted directly into your proposal at several critical stages, as illustrated in Figure 3.7. During the proposal response life cycle, there is a minimum of three critical inflection points at which marketing information should be infused into the process. These include: (1) prekickoff activities, (2) the formal kickoff meeting, and (3) the formal review processes such as the Red Team review. These topics are discussed in Chapters 7 and 12, respectively. Current marketing information should shape postproposal activities as well. Procurement-specific, client-specific, and competition-specific information collected and analyzed by your company's external sales staff must be shared (as appropriate from a competition sensitivity and need-to-know standpoint) with the capture manager, proposal manager, and the proposal team and internal sales staff at these times. During the prekickoff phase, accurate, current marketing intelligence helps drive (in addition to the RFP requirements found in Sections L, M, C, H, and others) the architecture of the proposal outline, the benefits-oriented thematic structure of the proposal narrative (story that articulates the strengths of your solutions), the project management approach, and the costing and staffing

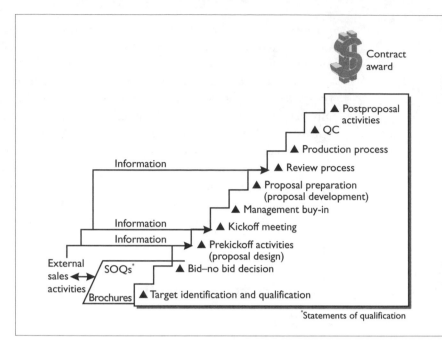

Figure 3.7
Marketing
information is
critical to proposal
success.

strategies. Without this marketing intelligence, your company would be like any other firm that was responding to the RFP only, with no further guidance from the client than the words on the pages (or bytes in the electronic file) of the RFP.

At the formal kickoff meeting, in-depth marketing intelligence as shared by a member of your company's external sales group will assist members of the proposal team—particularly those charged with writing significant sections of the proposal narrative—with a reasonably full-life big picture of the procurement opportunity, the client's sentiments and concerns and hot buttons, and the competition.

Again, during the formal review cycles, marketing intelligence should be used as a benchmark against which to measure the thematic success of the proposal documents at that stage in the response life cycle. In the terminology of satellite remote sensing, marketing should supply the "ground truth" that authenticates your company's proposal for the particular client and project at hand.

As depicted in Figure 3.7, the flow of information and support moves in both directions between the internal sales staff to the external sales staff. For example, the internal sales staff will assist their external sales counterparts in the development of effective marketing brochures, briefings, and statements of qualification (SOQs) that are valuable tools in helping your client to better understand and remember your company's capabilities and talents—in effect, your corporate brand.

3.5 Intelligence gathering and analysis techniques

One potentially effective technique of intelligence gathering and analysis is for your company's external sales support staff and division managers to visit the contracting offices of your primary federal client agencies in order to obtain specific information on existing contracts. Learn the contract title and numbers of existing contracts, the incumbent contractor(s), the projected contract renewal date, and the nature of the work, as well as the staffing size, contract dollar amount, contract duration, and contract type and vehicle (e.g., GWAC). Ask for the names and telephone numbers of the contracting officer's technical representative (COTR) and contracting officer (CO) for each contract. Supplemental information can be gathered by visiting specific federal agencies' Web sites and downloading copies of their acquisition forecast lists. You can also go to Acquisition Central at https://www.acquisition.gov/comp/procurement_forecasts/index.html. Public Law 100-656, the Business Opportunity Development Reform Act of 1988, amended the Small Business Act to emphasize acquisition planning. The law requires federal agencies to compile and make available projections of contracting opportunities that small businesses (including minority, women-owned, HUBZone, veteran-owned, and service-disabled veteran-owned) may be able to perform. These lists are called different names by various agencies, for example, procurement forecast, active contracts list, advanced procurement plan, and active contracts register-contractor sequence.

The Department of Transportation (DOT) procurement forecast includes contracting opportunities from DOT's participating operating administrations, available sorted by operating administration and procurement category (http://osdbu. dot.gov/Procurement/index.cfm). The FAA posts its procurement forecast at http://www.sbo.faa.gov/sbo/procurementforecast.cfm. The Air Force provides a Long Range Acquisition Estimate (LRAE) that is designed to help firms identify procurements that offer opportunities for their participation early in the acquisition process and to help them improve the timeliness and responsiveness of their proposals (http://www.airforcesmallbiz.org/opportunities/index.php). You can also have the LRAE send you notifications and updates on specific contract opportunities for the Air Force.

Other federal agencies that provide procurement or acquisition forecasts on line include the following:

- Department of Veterans Affairs (http://www.vendorportal. ecms.va.gov/eVP/fco/EntireVA.aspx?Type=complete);
- U.S. Department of Agriculture (http://www.pforecast.net/);
- NASA (http://prod.nais.nasa.gov/cgi-bin/nais/forecast.cgi);
- Department of Homeland Security (http://www.fido.gov/dhs/aap/ publicviewsb.asp);
- Department of Energy (http://hqlnc.doe.gov/forecast) (procurement searches are available by such parameters as NAICS code, solicitation method, release quarter, award quarter, and incumbent contractor);
- General Services Administration (http://www.gsa.gov/portal/ext/html/site/fco/category/25544/hostUri/portal);
- Department of the Interior's Interior Department Electronic Acquisition System-Electronic Commerce (IDEAS-EC) (https://ideasec.nbc.gov/j2ee/forecast).

When you obtain this marketing intelligence from in-person contacts, agency procurement briefings, and budget documents, Web sites, and published sources, record it carefully in a table, such as the one presented in Table 3.1. Someone within your organization must be responsible for maintaining the tracking tables and keeping them secure. It is critical that the information is accurate, current, and relevant. Try to collect information on both short- and long-term opportunities. One to two years is not too long a lead time for advanced business planning (see Figure 3.8). Once client target tracking tables are compiled for a given federal agency, preliminary bid–no bid decisions, proposal resource allocation, bookings goals, and revenue stream projections can be made in a planned and rational manner. These potential marketing targets comprise your company's opportunity pipeline. This initial downselecting process, if done in a structured way, will allow your company to focus scarce resources in the direction of viable targets and prevent your internal sales group and publications staff from becoming totally overburdened. There is nothing more debilitating to morale companywide than to produce losing proposal after losing proposal because of too few resources chasing too many targets. Be selective, and then produce a stellar proposal every time you submit one to your client.

Automated tools are available to support business opportunity tracking and decision making. The WinAward marketing management system from

#	Project Title	Acquisition Manager	Incumbent(s)	Contract #	RFP Release Date	Duration of Contract	Prime/Sub	Estimated Level of Effort per Year	Potential Contract Dollar Value
1	A-E Services to perform Hazardous Toxic & Radioactive Waste (HTRW) & environmental compliance services USACE-Mobile District	Ms. Jennifer Brothers	AABC Corp.	DACA01-07-R-0115	7/12	1 base year + 4 option years	Prime	35 full-time equivalents (FTEs)	
2	Investigation and design for remediation of misc. HTRW sites USACE-Omaha District	Mr. Tim Grayson	AAAC Corp.	DACA45-07-R-0011	10/12	Indefinite delivery	Sub	8 FTEs	
3	Environmental contract for Ft. George G. Meade, Maryland	Mr. Greg Yost	AACB Corp.	DACA31-08-R-0039	4/13	Indefinite delivery	Sub	5 FTEs	
4									
5									

Table 3.1 Sample Client Tracking Table (U.S. Army Corps of Engineers)

Figure 3.8
Formalized
business
acquisition
processes produce
tangible results.

The superior performers manage their business acquisition as a formal, disciplined process.
These companies view business acquisition as a structured set of interrelated activities to win contract awards.

Competitive Intelligence Review

Bayesian Systems (http://bayes.com/winaward.html) in Gaithersburg, Maryland, is one example of a Windows-based, robust software product for bid life-cycle management. WinAward retains and manages data characterizing specific marketing leads, retains costs associated with the bid process, determines award probabilities, and supports a rigorous bid decision process.

Once a preliminary downselecting procedure has been completed, capture plans and associated call plans (direct customer contact plans) can then be generated to pursue the qualified list of targets. Your company will want to collect and continually validate in its capture plans the following type of information:

- Project name (according to government sources, that is, use the client's name for this project);

- Client name (to the level of the line organization) and organizational chart;

- Client mission and vision statement and recent developments in the client's operational environment;

- Incumbent contractor(s), if applicable;

- Potential competitors;

- Specific services or products being procured;

- Key evaluation factors for award and client success criteria;

- Anticipated RFP or RFS release date (include anticipated dates for the preproposal conference, release of any prequalification questions, and oral presentations);

- Anticipated contract award date;

- Projected phase-in period;

- Anticipated contract dollar value to your company;

- Superset of source evaluation board membership;

- Relevant contractual experience (for your company);

- Proposed project manager (for your company);

- Other proposed key staff (from your company);

- Potential teaming partners.

Take the time to know your teaming partners, their technical expertise, human talent, cost strategies, contractual performance, financial stability, business processes, industry best practices (e.g., ISO, ITIL, SEI CMMI®), contract-performance liabilities and conflicts of interest (COI), and any pending litigation or government inspector general (IG) investigations. Ask your client what they think of your prospective teaming partner. Consider the benefits and disadvantages of exclusive versus nonexclusive teaming arrangements. (See Chapter 21 for more discussion regarding teaming agreements.)

3.6 Call plans

A call plan should be designed to clearly indicate whom within your company will be visiting the client, as well as when, why, and at what level of the client organization. An overview of the call plan process is presented in Figure 3.9. Note the importance of electronically archiving call plan results.

Information gathered from direct client contact should include the following.

Government or commercial buying organization and key personnel.

Obtain the official organizational charts for the client organization, and learn the full names and functions of the important technical and contractual decision makers (sell points).

Currently, what is the client doing technically and programmatically?

Is the client planning to migrate their automated process from one computer platform or operating system to another? Have regulatory or

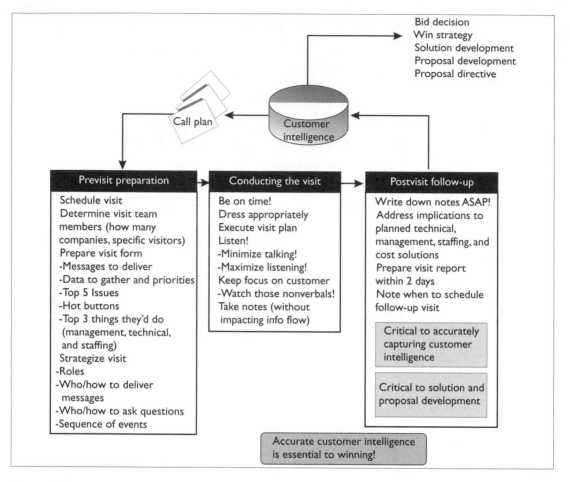

Figure 3.9 Call plan process.

policy changes imposed new demands on the client's programs? Will service-to-the-customer-style e-government necessitate a telecommunications center capable of handling significantly more queries per unit time? How do the requirements associated with Office of Management and Budget (OMB) Exhibit 300s drive your client's technical requirements? Bottom line: Learn the technical and managerial issues that are important to your client now and over the life of the upcoming contract.

What is planned for the future?

Through interaction with the client's staff, understand the evolutionary changes anticipated and planned for the period of performance of the contract.

What relevant documents or articles have the client and incumbent contractor personnel published?

Has the client established a public-access reading room, library, or Web site that archives documents and articles relevant to the particular contract? If so, plan to visit or browse and copy, download, or take notes from appropriate materials. Sometimes photocopying of hardcopy materials has to be scheduled in advance, so call ahead. In other cases, copying is not permitted—only note taking.

Strengths and weaknesses of the incumbent contractor.

Incumbent contractor refers to the company performing on the current contract.

Can your company hire incumbent personnel?

Incumbent personnel refer to those staff members employed by the incumbent contractor on the specific project that is being recompeted. Placing these people under contingent hiring agreements and including their résumés in your proposal can be highly beneficial to your prospects of winning the contract. Incumbent personnel are known quantities to the client. Those staff are knowledgeable about and familiar with such elements as the client's current and future technical directions, organizational and reporting structures, and procedures and protocol. There is a reduced learning curve and thereby reduced risk associated with contract phase-in and start-up given a staffing mix that includes a significant number of key incumbent staff. *Contingent hiring* refers to the establishment of a signed agreement between an individual and a company that stipulates, upon contract award, the person will be hired to perform certain duties on the particular contract. Ensure that the client holds any incumbent staff to whom your company extends a contingent hiring agreement in high regard professionally and personally. Very importantly, interact with incumbent staff during noncore business hours away from their job site, if at all possible. You might also host an open house or technical interchange meeting combined with an open house at a local hotel or conference center to introduce your firm to the incumbent staff. Publicize the open house through print ads, radio spots, social media such as Facebook and LinkedIn, and word of mouth. Dynamics Research Inc.'s (DRI) LinkedIn site is an excellent example of a corporate social media interchange point because it clearly presents the core technical competencies/business service areas, provides major client sectors, and offers a concise company history. Plan to have members of business development, executive management, recruiting, and human resources participate. Develop a take-away flier for attendees and deploy a Web site for prospective new hires through which they can post their résumés in confidence and receive current information about the status of the procurement.

One proven approach to incumbent capture is to identify one or several key incumbent staff professionals, build a rapport with them to win their hearts and minds to your company's cause, and then leverage their strong working relationships and leadership skills to bring other incumbent staff into the fold—in effect, into a formal, written commitment with your company. This Pied Piper technique requires absolute confidentiality and honoring of all agreements, commitments, and promises that were made during the incumbent capture and proposal phases. And it must be done in full recognition that the incumbent staff is, in many cases, putting their careers and reputations on the line for your company.

Which client personnel will sit on the source evaluation board?

Attempt to learn who the probable key candidates are for the SEB, including technical, contracting, legal, and administrative staff. Learning their sentiments, concerns, goals, and professional backgrounds can be very advantageous when composing your proposal narrative and developing benefits-oriented graphics.

Who is the competition? What does your company know about them?

The client's contracts office will tell you the name of the incumbent contractor, as will published and Web-based agency acquisition forecast lists. Advance knowledge of the identity and technical competence of additional competitors can be gleaned from conversations with other companies in the same industry; watching newspaper, professional-journal, social media, and Web-based job-site classified ads,[2] preproposal conference attendance lists, and Freedom of Information Act (FOIA) requests for previously submitted proposals to the client and monthly technical progress reports for the specific program or project.

Is your company qualified to bid alone, or must you team as the prime contractor or as a subcontractor?

There are circumstances under which teaming to win a contract is very appropriate. Talk with the client about his or her predispositions about and experiences with teaming arrangements. And sometimes your company may

---

2 This practice can be very beneficial to learn what projects your competition is pursuing as well as their staffing deficits. Regularly check monster.com, Yahoo! careers, careerbuilder.com, clearancejobs.com, dice.com, and other job-searching sites.

be too small to prepare a credible management plan as the prime contractor. For example, the contract staffing requirement may be 35 full-time equivalents (FTEs) per year. If yours is a 60-person company, you may want to consider establishing a teaming relationship with a larger qualified prime.

What are your company's technical, programmatic, costing, and staffing strengths and weaknesses regarding the particular opportunity? Can you overcome your shortcomings in time?

After preparing a realistic inventory of your strengths and weaknesses, your Acquisition Team will have to determine if ongoing marketing efforts combined with hiring success (to address staffing deficits), cost restructuring [in accordance with Defense Contract Audit Agency (DCAA) stipulations], and exploring specialty subcontracting arrangements (to mitigate technical deficits and programmatic risks) will result in a favorable bid position for your company.

It is critical that the information collected during interaction with your client be recorded electronically and then distributed on a need-to-know basis within your company. You may want to develop client contact reports, which include such information as the following:

- Client;
- Contact name and title;
- Contact date;
- Company representatives in attendance;
- Contact type (such as visit, call, or conference);
- Mission (your company's objectives for the contact);
- Summary of results, broken down into technical, management, staffing, phase-in, and cost categories or "buckets";
- Next action.

These reports might be made accessible to your staff via a password-protected, firewalled company intranet or vitural private network (VPN).

Support services contracts are often characterized by very diverse, sometimes even conflicting, requirements, because they frequently take the form of umbrella task-order, level-of-effort (LOE) contracts serving multiple government representatives. The challenges associated with marketing and preparing the proposal for such bids center on creating as complete and detailed a picture as possible of various decision makers' needs within the client's infrastructure. To this end, it is very useful to build a detailed technical-marketing activity into the proposal development life cycle, using domain experts to interview as many of the cognizant

Preproposal Interview Form

Date: _____

Interviewer(s): _____   _____

Interviewee(s): _____   _____

1. Please provide a brief description of the work that you expect contractors to perform under this contract.

   Note to interviewer: This should be a ½- to 1-page description. Attach a separate write-up to accommodate it. It is very helpful to get important reprints and other documents from the interviewee, though not to the extent that it becomes impossible to assimilate them. Concentrate on the main points! Also, be on the lookout for material for graphics.

2. What are the most critical areas of the work (i.e., the technical or management issues that are driving the contract)?

   Provide some key sentences or bullets. This is very critical as these points will drive the proposal themes and technical and management responses.

3. How many contractors are currently supporting this work? Do you expect this level to change?

4. Are there any particularly important contractor personnel whose names you can give us, who are key to your effort?

5. What kind of skill mix do you require for this work?

   Does the client want more high-level people ("partners" and thought leaders) or lower-level support? On technical jobs, what kind of proportion (labor mix) of senior programmers, analysts, junior programmers, scientists, and engineers is desired?

6. What kind of management structure best supports this work?

   How does the client think management would best support him or her (e.g., what kind of organizational structure and processes)?

7. Are there any areas in which you think substantial change or innovation is required? "Innovation" could be either technical or managerial.

   Probe for areas where you can suggest innovation! Examples: Does the client feel that he or she needs short-term support with highly specialized skills? Is the client looking for some particular kind of management structure?

8. If you had the chance, are there any changes you would make in the nature of your contractor support?

   Tie this to the previous question. Get the client to tell you how you can look like a hero!

9. How do you see your contractor support requirements evolving in the future?

   Get information about future skill mix and staffing levels. What are the client's hopes, fears, or biases about budgeting, and how does he or she see these affecting the need for support? For example, does the client see a larger or smaller role for the support contractor in the areas of science, operations, and instrument engineering?

10. What do you think your future critical issues are likely to be?

    This is an extremely critical question! Get as much information as possible regarding projected future problems and drivers, and the directions from which the client thinks solutions might emerge. This will be a dominant part of the proposal!

11. What would you be looking for in a winning proposal for this effort? In particular, what do you see as the highest priorities that would be given the most attention in a winning proposal?

    Try to draw the client out about his or her hot buttons and likely selection criteria. That is, what could distinguish you from your competitors in a strong, positive way?

12. Can you suggest anyone else to whom we might talk to get more information on these topics?

Figure 3.10   Preproposal interview form. (Adapted with permission from Dr. Richard Isaacman.)

government staff as possible. The purpose of this activity is to bring your company's understanding of the requirements to the next level of technical detail after the initial round of marketing visits. The preproposal interview form presented in Figure 3.10 is very useful for this purpose. Armed with it, your company's technical marketers—usually working-level support services staff—can hold technical discussions with many government task leaders and monitors in a manner that yields fruitful management approaches and proposal themes. Note that the questions center on three areas: (1) hot buttons, that is, critical issues and their likely evolution; (2) ghosts, that is, possible problems with the current support (if there is an incumbent); and (3) discriminators, that is, approaches that allow you to propose a superior solution well-tailored to your client's requirements that

	A	B	C	D	E	F
1	**Name of Customer "Sell Point"**	**Title and Role in Government Agency**	**Potential Source Evaluation Board Member**	**Dates Visited / Company Interview Participants**	**Technical**	**Management / Subcontractor Management**
2	Mr. Bill Sullivan	Deputy Branch Chief, Code 20x	Yes	3/12/12 and 4/11/12; Maria Gallagher and Josh Fellows	Significant proponent of ITIL v3 best practices; favors Remedy 7.5 over 7.3	Hopes to have direct access to subject matter experts; expects all contractor Task Leads to serve in a "player-coach" role
3						

	G	H	I	J	K
1	**Phase-In / Phase-Out**	**Staffing / Key Personnel**	**Potential Teaming Partners and Team Configurations**	**Past Performance**	**Cost / Price**
2	Very concerned that operational schedules are maintained during transition, particularly relating to the three software development tasks under the new contract	Wants all contractor managers to hold PMP certification	Anticipates that single-vendor solutions will not be feasible; does not want a large contractor team	Record of performance-based success with multiple SLAs is critical	This will be a "best-value" procurement; however, price very close to the Independent Government Cost Estimate is important in 2012 and beyond with constricting agency discretionary funds.
3					

Figure 3.11   Use this spreadsheet to support proposal writing and review.

Client:_____ **Address:**_____ **Telephone No.: (__)_____**

1. Are you meeting with a representative of corporate management or facility management?

2. What are the specific types of needs or activities of the client?

3. Are these needs managed through an in-house technical organization, professional service contracts, or both?

4. What is the total company or facility budget for all goods and services for the current and upcoming year? (Is the budget published and can we have a copy?)

5. How much of this budget will be spent on professional services or consulting?

6. Who is responsible for management and procurement of services in each specific requirement area?

7. Is there an organizational chart available that can help us understand the client? Can we have a copy?

8. Which of our competitors are under contract or have recently performed work for the client? Are any of the competitors under term or national service contracts? When are these contracts up for rebid?

9. Are there any opportunities evident from the discussions for our company to benefit the client? What is the time line for these opportunities?

10. Is there a requirement that our company be listed as an approved firm on a procurement list? Are we on it? Who in the client's organization is responsible for maintaining the list?

11. Does the client have Minority Business Enterprise/Woman-Owned Business Enterprise (MBE/WBE) goals for their procurements? Are there specific MBE/WBE firms that the client recommends?

12. How does the client conduct the procurement of service contracts? Who is (are) the decision maker(s)?

Figure 3.12
Private-sector client information interviewing tool.

your competitors cannot. In effect, your proposal will tell a more compelling, client-focused story that conveys benefits and strengths.

As a practical matter, it is not a good idea to walk into a client interview and start reading from a list of questions; the form should be completed by the interviewer as soon as possible after the interview (preferably within 24 hours). When feasible, it is useful to send two company staff members to the interview; they can alternate asking questions and taking notes, and address any gaps in each other's recollections when completing the interview form later. The completed interview write-ups should be

Questions

Day-to-Day Operations

1. What are your specific responsibilities and organizational requirements?

2. What are the most significant challenges to meeting your performance goals today?

3. How are effectiveness and efficiency measured in your organization?

4. How is success measured within your organization?

5. What performance metrics have been established and documented? How well do they support your organization's measures for effectiveness, efficiency, and success? How would you improve these?

6. Please describe the level of importance that cost control and financial management occupy within your day-to-day operations.

7. Currently, how is your organization working to retain and leverage intellectual capital?

8. Can you suggest anyone else to whom we might talk to get more information on these topics?

Management for Moving Forward

1. Where do you believe there is substantial room for change or innovation? Innovation could either be technical or managerial.

2. Are there any "sacred cows" (protected structures or functions) within the organization?

3. Explain how important organizational change management—changing culture, attitudes, and policies—is for your organization.

4. What are the critical things that need to be fixed or enhanced within your area of operation? What changes in agency policies will impact your work directly and why? What do you consider to be your primary future challenges? (What are the things that keep you up at night?)

5. What kinds of management structure, staffing plan, and skill mix best support your work?

6. What are the key challenges perceived from a federal management standpoint? What would you recommend as a path forward?

Customer and Contractor Assessment

1. Who are your current support contractors? How many contractor staff from each company support your operations?

2. How are your current contractors performing from both a technical and a management perspective?

3. What do you see as their specific strengths and weaknesses?

4. Please describe your contractors' level and type of support.

Figure 3.13
Client information interviewing tool.

5. Are there contractors that possess a great deal of institutional knowledge and would be considered key personnel?

6. Help me to understand your specific concerns regarding contract phase-in periods.

7. Have service-level baselines been established for your area of support?

8. How are your business processes now aligned with your IT portfolio? How will that alignment change over time?

Figure 3.13
(continued)

reviewed by the capture manager, proposal manager, and key proposal writers before actual writing begins in order to identify common issues out of which proposal themes can emerge. These write-ups also represent a wealth of technical and programmatic knowledge that can be mined by the proposal writers in order to address client concerns in depth. Building an Excel spreadsheet to capture the results of customer meetings and how those results are applicable across various sections of your proposal is a proven technique to aid in this process (see Figure 3.11) Figures 3.12 and 3.13 provide additional potential interviewing tools when interacting with your private-sector client or potential federal government client.

3.7 Maintain management visibility on your contracts

A very practical and relatively easy marketing technique applicable to contracts on which your company is the incumbent (contractor performing on the current contract) is for members of your company's executive and division-level management to visit the client staff as well as your on-site personnel on a regular basis. Executives from one highly successful small business visit their clients nationwide at least once every business quarter. Their actions validate commitment! Build and continue to cultivate communication networks with client staff at both professional and appropriate social levels, including professional association meetings and government-industry council meetings and symposia, such as the Maryland Space Business Roundtable in Greenbelt, Maryland, and the National Space Symposium in Colorado Springs, Colorado. Let your client know that his contract is important to your company by showing a real physical presence at his job site during the entire contract life cycle and not merely at contract renewal. A discussion of your management's commitment to a particular project in the proposal narrative is far more persuasive when it has been substantiated by regular site visits by your senior managers over time. Quantify those visits.

Senior management can communicate on an ongoing basis with, for example, on-site company staff through e-mail, company newsletter and e-newsletter, intranet, informal briefings, video teleconferencing (VTC) friendly on-site luncheons (brown bag, bring-your-own lunches are fine), and performance recognition meetings and award ceremonies on site. There is an enhanced sense of loyalty among your on-site staff to your company that can follow from ongoing management presence and genuine interest. Too often, on-site staff, due to sheer proximity to the client and isolation from contact with your company's management, develop greater loyalty to the project and to their government counterparts than to your company. When recompetition comes around, your staff may not be so concerned as to which company they work for but rather that they stay associated with the project. And your competition may find them easy targets to lure away with contingent hire agreements.

It is critical that senior management take an active role in client interaction, relationship building, and other marketing activities. "A senior executive's instinctive capacity to empathize with and gain insights from customers is the single most important skill he or she can use to direct a company's strategic posture" [8]. Know when to have your senior management visit your client, and make sure that your management knows what is necessary to convey as well as to learn.

3.8 Project managers as client managers

Your company's project managers (PMs) should develop self-recognition as client managers and first-tier marketing generalists. These managers are in the enviable position of being in day-to-day contact with your clients. PMs should be taught and mentored on how to cross-sell your company's services and products. They can help your client better understand and appreciate the direct benefits of your firm's core competencies and solutions. PMs can appropriately, yet persistently, inquire as to what additional services your company can provide to this client. Expanding services to existing clients is the most cost-effective form of marketing activity. You need to recognize your PMs as an integral part of your public relations, or reputation management, initiatives. PMs put a face on your company; they need to be your local advocate. Your project managers can also be instrumental in obtaining letters of commendation from your clients, which in turn can be used in proposals to authenticate your technical and programmatic expertise. Letters of commendation should be filed in your

Please rate how we are doing for the following activities:

	(Not doing well at all)			(Doing very well)		
	1	2	3	4	5	N/A
Clear and Effective Planning (schedules, updates)						
Support for Client Decision Making						
Regular Communication and Feedback						
Innovative Ideas						
Appropriate Experienced Staffing Applied						
Appropriate Technical Support Provided						
Cost-Effective Project Performance						
Issues Resolved Appropriately						
General Client Satisfaction						
Meeting Project or Task Objectives						
On-Time Deliverables						

Other comments:

Thank you.

Figure 3.14   Performance scorecard.

Figure 3.15
Automated
performance
questionnaire.

Question	Score
Quality of Delivered Service—Degree to which products/services meet technical performance standards.	4.00
Cost Control—Extent to which company accurately estimates and controls cost to complete work.	4.00
Timeliness of Performance—Effectiveness in completion of major tasks, milestones, or deliverables on schedule.	4.00
Program Management—Overall performance in planning, scheduling, and monitoring task.	4.00

Edit Survey Results

company's proposal library, and scanned into electronic format in your automated knowledge base for rapid retrieval and easy placement into a proposal document.

Your company should also regularly assess performance levels on each of your current contracts. That assessment must necessarily include an evaluation of your performance by your client. Figure 3.14 offers one such performance scorecard that might be used. Figure 3.15 presents an automated performance questionnaire.

3.9 Commercial off-the-shelf acquisition

There is a clearly discernible migration toward commercial off-the-shelf (COTS) procurement within the federal arena, particularly in the area of software products. COTS products represent industry's best—they are tested and piloted before deployment in the marketplace. They are also readily available off of the GSA schedule. Congress and the Office of Management and Budget (OMB) within the Executive Office of the President have indicated a preference for COTS solutions, which constitutes an important consideration in obtaining funding for a federal agency.

Significantly, the goal of the E-Government Act of 2002 is to maximize return on investment (ROI) of government IT assets and portfolios. Tomorrow's enterprise success factors have changed from technology-centric ones to those premised on "business + security," "business + enterprise architecture," and "business + capital planning." COTS tools play a key role in addressing enterprise IT asset management issues as well as developing and deploying integrated enterprise technical solutions. Importantly, COTS products tend to drive down the total cost of ownership (TCO) of IT portfolios.

On March 26, 2004, the Department of Energy (DOE) deputy secretary issued a memorandum for developing a single, integrated IT infrastructure within that federal department. One of the key elements specified by the deputy secretary was to reduce operational costs and increase security by moving to a single, integrated IT infrastructure. Specific future challenges for DOE span providing a common operating environment (COE) of secure and easily accessible core applications, enhancing service performance levels across a broad range of diverse government customers; implementing a practice to build once, and then use many times; implementing an enterprisewide information cybersecurity governance, management, and architecture in accordance with the Federal Information Security Management Act (FISMA); and aligning IT direction with DOE's business strategies and mission.

Also, as the Department of Defense (DoD) pushes toward more COTS solutions, it is facing a greater need to integrate those solutions with each other and with existing systems. The requirement for defense suppliers to use commercial off-the-shelf components, subsystems, software, and solutions extends back to 1994 and then-U.S. Secretary of Defense William Perry. The COTS directive foresaw the following benefits: (1) reduced development costs, (2) diminished equipment costs as the DoD migrated away from MIL-SPECs and competition among suppliers, and (3) lower life-cycle costs as technology insertion mitigated the impact of obsolescence. Standard architectures and components would translate to "maximum compatibility, cost-effective upgrade, and the widest range of continuing options" [9]. More than 15 years following Secretary Perry's caveat, a number of key benefits have indeed accrued. Complex requests for quotation (RFQs) with fine-grained specifications down to the component level are now rare. Systems integrators (SI)[3] will accept COTS specifications as well as standard qualification reports [9]. Technology insertion has proven to be a major benefit of COTS implementation, with programs developed on one generation of processors, qualified on the successive generation, and now deployed on the third generation hardware [9]. COTS open-systems hardware and software products have become the foundation of both military and aerospace electronic and opto-electronic integrated systems [10]. In an interview with the Army's Chief Information Officer (CIO)/G6 that appeared in *Military Information Technology* magazine [11], the CIO reported that the Army is leveraging what the commercial sector does in areas such as the Global Information Grid (GIG) and the Defense Information Systems Network (DISN). However, a countertrend is the movement toward "modified COTS," with "program-specific modifications to functionality or input/output" [9].

This extensive use of COTS software components in system construction presents new hurdles to system architects and designers. Some federal agencies are discovering, however, that a practice that was intended to streamline acquisition—and that does so in many cases—also raises some challenging issues associated with data conversion and systems integration. For example, government requirements may have to be shoehorned to fit the features of COTS products. In specific cases, software bridges and interfaces can be designed and developed to address this issue. There are also the matters of intellectual property and licensing that must be addressed. When COTS products are modified, ownership of the new product becomes open to question. And "[f]ormerly, government

---

3   Representative leading system integrators include Capgemini, Ernst & Young, Computer Sciences Corporation (CSC), Deloitte LLP, HP, PwC, and Science Applications International Corporation (SAIC).

officials who were in a hurry to buy off-the-shelf equipment such as personal computers could sidestep the normal, time-consuming bidding practices by awarding a sole-source contract directly to a minority-owned firm that could fill the order" [5]. According to the National Federation of 8(a) Companies based in Arlington, Virginia, the longstanding federal acquisition reform legislation allows "agency officials to make purchases of selected equipment from a large list of preapproved contractors, large and small" [5].

A broad cross-section of federal agencies has recently examined their high-end computing (supercomputing) requirements. These agencies include the Defense Advanced Research Projects Agency (DARPA), DOE, NASA, NIH, the National Oceanic and Atmospheric Administration (NOAA), the National Science Foundation (NSF), and the National Security Agency (NSA). In general, these agencies are using COTS-based high-end computing solutions. Examples of high-end computing applications areas with federal government involvement and interest include nuclear stockpile stewardship, global climate modeling, ocean state prediction, geophysical phenomena such as earthquakes, aeronautics, weapon systems design, signal processing, and materials modeling.

The Federal Acquisition Streamlining Act (FASA) of 1994 stipulated that a commercial item can still be a commercial item if it has one of two modifications. The first is a modification, any kind of modification, that is customarily available in the marketplace. This is a type of modification that the contractor has done in the commercial marketplace. But the other kind of modification allowed under FASA is a modification for government use. Even if it has a modification for government use, it is still considered to be a commercial product. Commercial item services are services that are customarily sold in the marketplace for a set price for a particular task. This is a great opportunity for small business.

3.10 Pursuing firm-fixed-price and invitation-for-bid opportunities

In negotiated services contracts, relationship building through marketing is paramount to success. However, selling computers or reprographic paper—in effect, products—under firm-fixed-price (FFP) contracts often involves less in the way of personal interaction. FFP contracts require that "the contractor delivers the product or performs the services at a specific time at a price that is not subject to any adjustment of actual costs incurred during contract performance. It places 100% of the risk on the contractor and places the least amount of administrative burden on the government"

[12]. Maximum profit can be earned by managing FFP contracts aggressively and identifying, understanding, and controlling risk. During business planning and when marketing, your company will want to establish an appropriate mix of targets between cost-reimbursement and FFP types of opportunities.

Invitations for bid (IFBs), or sealed bids, result in an FFP contract. Bids are opened publicly, and the award is made immediately to the lowest priced, responsible, responsive bidder. No discussions are allowed, and no exceptions may be taken by the contractor. IFBs are suitable for COTS purchases as well as for small support services contracts. Understanding your company's cost structure and your vendors' costs as well as being able to operate at maximum efficiency during contract performance are critical to making profit on IFB/FFP opportunities. Profit on cost-reimbursement type contracts is termed *fee*.

3.11 Using the request for information and the request for comment as valuable marketing tools

In circumstances under which the government is seeking to establish that adequate competition exists within industry to release a solicitation or to determine if industry has developed specific technologies that the government requires (assess project feasibility), an agency will issue a request for information (RFI), sources sought, screening information request (SIR), or request for comment (RFC) on a statement of work (SOW). In fact, the Federal Acquisition Regulations encourage government agencies to promote early exchanges of information about future acquisitions (see FAR, Part 15.201). This practice is intended to identify and resolve concerns regarding such things as proposed contract type and vehicle, requirement feasibility, suitability of evaluation criteria, business size standards [determined by North American Industry Classification System (NAICS) codes[4]], and availability of reference documents.

Your company's response to an RFI, sources sought, SIR, or RFC should be prepared in the same professional manner as a proposal. Too many times in the case of an RFI, companies will submit marketing brochures or other prepared, canned materials rather than develop a customized, client-oriented package that provides specific benefits you can offer to your client. Responding to an RFI presents a significant

---

4   NAICS codes replaced SIC codes that had been developed in the 1930s. "NAICS" is pronounced like "nakes."

opportunity for your company to demonstrate in writing that you are interested in supporting the client and in developing solutions for your client's issues and challenges. Also, you will learn about the client and possibly the competition. As with an RFP, respond specifically to the client's requests. Authenticate your technical capabilities with references to specific contractual experience. Help your client to better understand your company's particular strengths and how they will be of benefit to him. Submit the RFI on time and to the correct location. Hand delivery can also be beneficial, although, increasingly, electronic submittal is required and hard copies are expressly disallowed.

Fundamentally, your response to an RFI is *not* about your company, but rather about how your company can benefit the client.

3.12 Contractor prequalification statements

Certain client organizations require that a company be prequalified or pre-approved prior to the company being able to receive RFPs, RFSs, RFQs, RFIs, and other solicitation documents. Such registration data are now collected online via the Web site https://www.bpn.gov/ccr/. Prior to 2003, the federal Standard Form 129 (Revised 12-96), "Solicitation Mailing List Application," served as one prequalification vehicle. The SF129 is no longer used.

State and local governments as well as private-sector clients and educational institutions may issue contractor prequalification applications or contractor qualification questionnaires[5] in order to prequalify a listing of potential contractors. Examples of the wide-ranging list of clients that request such information are the Colorado Department of Transportation; the City of San Fernando, California; and the University of Pennsylvania. The information required can be broad-ranging in scope but often includes such information as the names of principals of the company, financial information, years of contractual experience, project list, debarment status (has your company currently been debarred from submitting bids?), minority business status, professional registrations by state, and equipment lists. Again, timely and accurate completion is important.

---

5   These questionnaires can be called bidder's list applications, general subcontractor surveys, potential supplier profile questionnaires (PSPQs), preliminary qualification questionnaires, qualified suppliers lists (QSLs), and vendor forms.

3.13 Ethics in marketing and business development

Ethical conduct in all business activities, whether domestic or international, should be your company's corporate standard at all times [13]. The development and implementation of a formal set of ethics rules that prohibits any type of procurement fraud by employees, agents, consultants, or subcontractors, coupled with ongoing training and reinforcement, would be a prudent step to align your organization with DoD FAR Supplement (DFARS) 203.10, titled *Contractor Code of Business Ethics and Conduct.* A contractor's management system should include a written code of business ethics and conduct as well as an ethics training program for all employees. According to an article published in the *Harvard Business Review*, new federal guidelines now recognize the organizational and managerial roots of unlawful conduct and base fines partly on the extent to which companies have taken steps to prevent misconduct [14].

In their important work titled *Formation of Government Contracts*, George Washington University law professors John Cibinic, Jr., and Ralph Nash, Jr., discuss standards of conduct in two broad categories, namely, "those dealing with improper influence on Government decisions and those requiring honesty and disclosure of relevant facts in dealing with the Government" [15].

FAR subpart 9.5 addresses the organizational conflict of interest. Part 3 of the FAR presents guidance regarding "Improper Business Practices and Personal Conflicts of Interest." One example, the Anti-Kickback Act of 1986 [codified at 41 U.S.C. §§ 51–58 (1988)] discussed in FAR 3.502-2, is legislation designed to deter subcontractors from making payments and contractors from accepting payments for the purpose of improperly obtaining or rewarding favorable treatment [16] in connection with a prime contract or a subcontract relating to a prime contract. The term kickback means any money, fee, commission, credit, gift, gratuity, thing of value (for example, promise of employment), or compensation of any kind. Unlike its precursor in 1946, the 1986 act includes all types of government contracts. Finally, the 1986 act places new reporting requirements on prime contractors and subcontractors. Possible violations of kickback laws must be reported in writing to the Inspector General (IG) of the appropriate federal agency, the head of the contracting agency if the agency has no IG, or the U.S. Department of Justice.

The Procurement Integrity Act (41 USC § 423), about which there is considerable confusion on the part of both civil servants and contractors, prohibits the release of source selection information (e.g., technical evaluation plans, competitive range determinations, ranking of proposals or competitors) and contractor bid or proposal information. The Act, which was implemented in FAR 3.104, provides that the government cannot impart information to one bidder or proposer without making that information public to all potential bidders or proposers. And the False Claims Act Amendment of 1986 facilitated prosecution of complex defense procurement fraud cases.

Many private-sector corporations—your potential prime contractors or clients—have enacted written policy codes that govern gifts and entertainment. One major East Coast manufacturing firm stipulates that its employees are forbidden to accept any incentives in exchange for increased purchases through a given supplier or subcontractor. Gifts are defined very strictly, to include dinners (unless incidental to a business meeting), money, discounts on personal purchases, holiday presents, tickets to theaters and sporting events, airline tickets, hotel accommodations, and repairs or improvements at prices other than for fair market value.

Finally, the nonpartisan, nonprofit Defense Industry Initiative on Business Ethics and Conduct (DII) (http://www.dii.org/) was established in June 1986 by 18 major defense contractors (now 85). These contractors pledged to adopt and implement a set of principles of business ethics and conduct that acknowledge and express their federal procurement-related corporate responsibilities to the Department of Defense as well as to the public and to each other. The defense industry signatories are united in their commitment to adopt and implement principles of business ethics and conduct that acknowledge and address their organizational responsibilities. Further, they each accept the responsibility to create an organizational culture in which ethics is paramount and compliance with federal procurement laws is a strict obligation. The DII's essential strength lies in sharing best practices to maintain the highest ethical standards, encouraging employees to ethical conduct, and requiring compliance in the course of its business activities.

DII and its signatories offer a broad range of training tools, including a DII Toolkit online to help you start an effective ethics program at your own small business.

3.14 Advertising, trade shows, and high-impact public relations

As with brand name recognition in consumer advertising and marketing, increasing the baseline level of name recognition for your company is important to your overall business development success. Well-targeted public relations (PR), trade show, and advertising efforts will probably

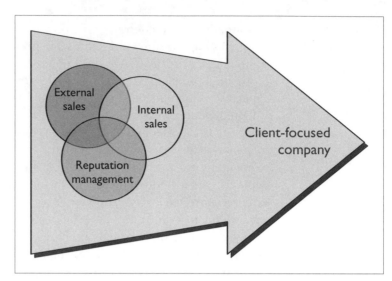

Figure 3.16
One common
vision.

not result directly in sales or contracts but will help to build an image of legitimacy and solid foundation for your company that can and should be leveraged by your external and internal sales teams and public relations or reputation management efforts (see Figure 3.16).

There are many freelance graphics artists, for example, who can develop high-impact ads on a cost-per-ad basis for placement in key business and trade publications without the significant fees associated with retaining an advertising and design agency. Figure 3.17 provides an example of an ad developed for a small company. Watch for special issues of publications important to your lines of business that may focus directly on market segments that are part of your strategic plan. Cases in point are *Washington Technology; World Dredging, Mining, and Construction;* and *Chemical Week.* The latter publication, for instance, ran a special supplement devoted to the state of New Jersey. Companies that did chemical or environmental business or were positioning themselves to do such business in New Jersey could then place ads in that particular supplement.

Increasing the baseline of name recognition for your company is important to your overall business development success.

Appearance at and participation in selective trade shows will increase your company's visibility in the specific business community you serve. Professional-looking tabletop trade show booths can be designed and populated with attractive, powerful photographs and other imagery for only a few thousand dollars total. If your company does work for the Department of Defense, for example, that agency maintains public domain photographs

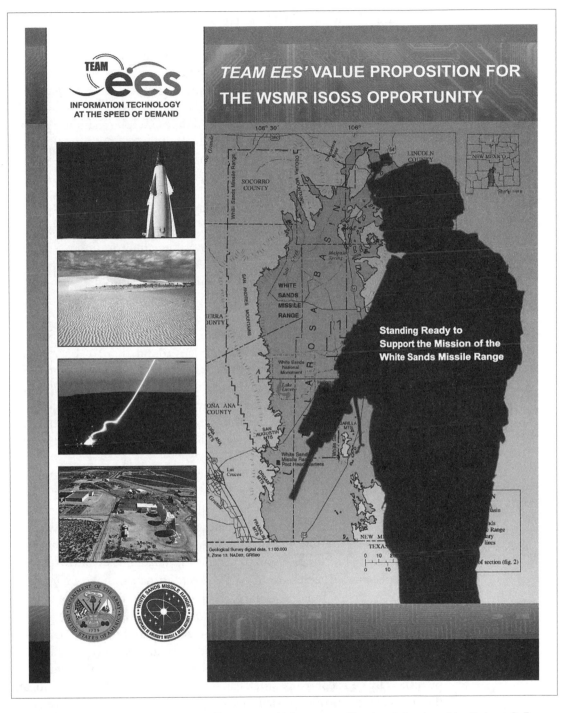

Figure 3.17 Advertisement for a small company. (Ad conceptualized and developed by Robert S. Frey and Sung Hong for EES, LLC, Germantown, Maryland. Reprinted with permission from Matt Collins, Chief Administrative Officer (CAO), EES.)

that are available for nominal fees at its Anacostia Naval Air Station near Washington, D.C. NOAA has a Web-based photo library at http://www.photolib.noaa.gov/. NASA also maintains an extensive Web-based image and multimedia library at http://nix.nasa.gov/. An outstanding Web site that points to a host of public domain image galleries spanning the USDA, Air Force, Navy, and U.S. Geological Survey (USGS) is located at http://www.usa.gov/Topics/Graphics.shtml. Professional stock imagery may be procured from photo houses or from the Internet (e.g., http://www.fotosearch.com/photodisc) for limited usage instead of taking your own photographs.

Other public relations efforts can take the form of news releases to appropriate business, financial, and professional and trade journals. News releases will, of course, need some kind of news hook; that is, you will need to provide a financial or business editor with something around which to build a headline and weave a story line.

Your company's credibility depends in part upon the efficient distribution of news about your success. You might consider employing the services of a media relations firm, such as BusinessWire (http://www.businesswire.com/portal/site/home). BusinessWire, a San Francisco–based "bricks-and-clicks" company founded in 1961 and now a wholly owned subsidiary of Berkshire Hathaway, is used by public relations and marketing professionals to disseminate news releases, photos, multimedia, regulatory filings, and other information. News release subjects include breaking news, earnings results, product announcements, mergers and acquisitions, public policy, legal issues, Webcasts, and press conference advisories.

Importantly, BusinessWire's news wire circuits enable organizations to target their news to select audiences based on specific geographic and industry market needs. BusinessWire's delivery network is comprised of 60 news agencies, financial and information providers, and Web-based news services around the world. Your news releases will also be delivered automatically to hundreds of online services and databases worldwide, including Reuters Business Alert, Wall Street Journal.com, *New York Times Online,* Dow Jones & Company, MSNBC.com, Bloomberg Financial Markets, USA Today.com, Yahoo! Finance, and AOL.

Another effective PR technique related to trade and professional journals is to generate and place articles in these publications [17]. This process is highly cost-effective, and reprints of articles that have been published by your company's staff can be used in proposals to authenticate the firm's and the proposed staff's expertise. It is advantageous to contact the editorial staff of appropriate trade journals to obtain the agendas and editorial themes of upcoming issues as well as submission guidelines.

In addition, your company should definitely create and maintain its own Web page on the Internet, replete with logo, easy-to-use icons, and engaging content, and accessible for data mining with well-known search engines, such as http://www.google.com (metasearch engine), http://www.dogpile.com (metasearch engine), http://www.hotbot.com, http://www.metacrawler. com, http://www.yahoo.com, http://www.altavista.com, http://www.surfwax.com, http://www.webcrawler.com, http://www.lycos.com, and http://go.com, as well as http:// www.excite.com. Register your URL name with http://www.register.com. Your Web page should clearly identify your company's lines of business up front, and provide user-friendly, quick-loading access to information about how your firm can support clients successfully. Include an electronic fill-in form that Web site visitors can complete and e-mail or mail to your marketing staff. You might build in the text from recent external news releases, information about your office or project locations and client base, corporate awards, core competencies, GSA Schedule, qualifying NAICS codes, and upcoming trade show appearances. Add your Web site address to business cards, marketing brochures and fliers, and promotional items such as golf balls, key rings, or calculators. Finally, include electronic point-and-click hyperlinks on your Web pages to other pertinent Web sites that provide additional regulatory, technological, business, or contractual information. Register your Web site with appropriate search engine providers on an ongoing basis.

In developing your company's Web site, three key elements will require significant attention: (1) design, (2) functionality, and (3) audience appeal (see Figure 3.18). Under the design element, important factors include readability, clear purpose of the site, and site architecture. Within the element of functionality, considerations include navigability, intuitive search capacity, order management/e-commerce, actionability [18], and download speed. Under audience appeal, you need to consider such key parameters as visitor retention, consistent Web site mood, and brand name recognition.

Remember that whatever the level of funding that can be allocated for these types of important activities, the critical thing is to do them on a consistent basis. Clients are more likely to buy goods and services from companies they know or have heard about in the press or trade literature. Public relations helps bring your company and its capabilities to life and keeps your company's name embedded in decision makers' minds.

For very select major-impact proposal efforts, your company might consider a full-scale corporate communication campaign that uses the following media and tools:

- Newspaper and trade magazine ads;

Figure 3.18
Important
Web-site
parameters.

- Web sites;
- Selective radio ads for key events (e.g., open houses and trade shows);
- Attendance at industry or customer events;

- Billboards;
- Signage within appropriate offices, airport terminals, and conference centers;
- Social media outreach.

The key to this type of expanded campaign is advanced planning and *consistency of message*—both in the written text and in the graphical images.

We have now introduced the federal competitive proposal environment and the strengths and constraints of small businesses operating in that arena. A company organizational scenario was offered, along with a presentation of strategic and mission planning. Specific, effective marketing techniques, as well as ethical conduct for business development, were discussed.

We will now examine the RFP, the solicitation document issued by both government and private-sector client organizations. The RFP should not be a call to action, as it many times is, but rather a continuation of the ongoing process of marketing your client. As a former fighter pilot and business executive observed during a major Air Force Space Command procurement, "The proposal is a terrible place to educate the client."

ENDNOTES

1. Graham, John R., "Getting to the Top, And Staying There," *The New Daily Record,* Baltimore, MD, July 26, 1997, p. 7B.

2. This metaphor was borrowed from Prokesch, Steven E., "Competing on Customer Service: An Interview with British Airways' Sir Colin Marshall," *Harvard Business Review*, Vol. 73, November/December 1995.

3. "Any time the government makes an award to a contractor who is neither the highest technical offeror nor the lowest price offeror, then the government has made a best-value determination; it has made a trade-off between technical and cost features." See Hackeman, Calvin L., "Best Value Procurements: Hitting the Moving Target," McLean, VA: Grant Thornton, 1993, p. 3 (a white paper prepared in connection with Grant Thornton's Government Contractor Industry Roundtables).

4. Ray, Dana, "Filling Your Funnel: Six Steps to Effective Prospecting and Customer Retention," *Selling Power*, July/August 1998, p. 44.

5. As quoted by Behr, Peter, "Just Say Know," *Washington Post*, April 1, 1996.

6. Goldberg, Mim, "Listen to Me," *Selling Power*, July/August 1998, p. 58.

7. "Selected Viewgraphs from Judson LaFlash Seminars on Government Marketing and Proposals," *Government Marketing Consultants,* July 1980.

8. Gouillart, Francis J., and Frederick D. Sturdivant, "Spend a Day in the Life of Your Customers," *Harvard Business Review,* January/February 1994.

9. Cavill, Peter, "COTS: The Reality," *Military & Aerospace Electronics,* June 2005, p. 13.

10. Keller, John, "Could RoHS Mean the End of COTS as We Know It?" *Military & Aerospace Electronics,* Vol. 17, No. 7, July 2006, p. 1.

11. "Information Warfighter: Leveraging Commercial Internet Protocol Technology," *Military Information Technology,* Vol. 10, Issue 7, August 2006, pp. 33–34.

12. McVay, Barry L., *Proposals That Win Federal Contracts: How to Plan, Price, Write, and Negotiate to Get Your Fair Share of Government Business,* Woodbridge, VA: Panoptic Enterprises, 1989, p. 29.

13. For a variety of articles that all focus on business and professional ethics (including international marketing ethics), see *BRIDGES: An Interdisciplinary Journal of Theology, Philosophy, History, and Science,* Vol. 2, 1990.

14. See Paine, Lynn Sharp, "Managing for Organizational Integrity," *Harvard Business Review,* March/April 1994.

15. Cibinic, John, and Ralph C. Nash, *Formation of Government Contracts,* 2nd ed., Washington, D.C.: George Washington University, 1986, p. 107.

16. According to Ropes and Gray, examples of favorable treatment that are illegal include receiving confidential information on competitors' bids, obtaining placement on a bidders' list without meeting requisite qualifications, obtaining unwarranted waivers of deadlines, obtaining unwarranted price increases, and recovering improper expenses. Contractors should also be aware of the Fraud Awareness Letter issued in September 1987 by the DoD Council on Integrity and Management Improvements, which identified "indicators of potential subcontractor kickbacks." See "Complying with the Anti-Kickback Act: Guidelines and Procedures," *Developments in Government Contract Law,* No. 10, September 1990.

17. Schillaci, William C., "A Management Approach to Placing Articles in Engineering Trade Journals," *Journal of Management in Engineering,* September/October 1995, pp. 17–20.

18. Smith, P. R., and D. Chaffey, *eMarketing eXcellence: The Heart of eBusiness*, Oxford, England: Butterworth-Heinemann, 2003, p. 164.

Chapter 4

Requests for proposals

4.1 Overview

In addition to federal government RFPs, there are RFPs released by state, county, municipality, and city governments, as well as by private-sector companies and international governments.

The federal government RFP or performance-based Request for Solution (RFS) that your company requests and receives or downloads from the Web is the culmination of a lengthy planning, budgeting, and approval process. It is a solicitation document issued to obtain offers from contractors who propose to provide products or services under a contract to be awarded using the process of negotiation. Federal procurement is governed by strict statutory and regulatory frameworks that are intended to reduce the risk of fraud, favoritism, and undue influence. In addition, and very importantly, these frameworks are designed to reassure taxpayers that their tax dollars are being spent appropriately [1]. The federal procurement process is highly structured to ensure that the award of a contract is made fairly (see Figure 4.1).

The RFP is a complex document, often prepared under proposal-like conditions. That is to say, it is written and reviewed by a variety of civil servants under tight schedule constraints and is subject to delay caused by, for example, late inputs, protracted legal reviews, program modifications, funding issues, or changes in contractor support of the SOW development.[1] RFPs often contain conflicting or ambiguous requirements, as well as incorrect cross-references, particularly in Section L, "Instructions, Conditions, and Notices to Offerors." (An offeror is any company or organization that responds with a proposal to the RFP.) This may result in part because RFP documents are often assembled using

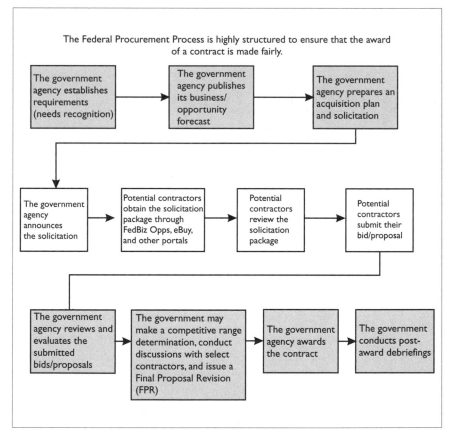

Figure 4.1
Structured federal
procurement
process.

---

1   Many SOWs, specifications, Performance Work Statements (PWS), and Statements of Objectives (SOO) are researched, written, and prepared by contractor personnel under separate contract to the government procuring agency. Because of conflict-of-interest issues, companies that have contracts to prepare SOWs cannot legally compete on particular procurements for which they have prepared the SOW or PWS.

boilerplate materials from previous or similar RFPs. When there are conflicting guidelines, submit questions for clarification in writing to the appropriate government point of contact by the date specified in the RFP. Your questions,[2] along with those from other firms, may result in the government issuing an amendment to the RFP. Within the DoD, Integrated Product Teams (IPTs) have been employed to ensure the proper integration of the various parts of the RFP.

Contractors should not assume that the RFP reveals the full intent of the client's preferences, sentiments, or requirements. There are the *unstated* criteria to address, as discussed in Chapter 3. By the same token, care must be exercised to respond precisely to the RFP requirements in the order in which they are provided. For example, if the RFP calls for a discussion of technical understanding and approach, past performance, and key personnel in that order, your proposal should be structured to respond in exactly that order. Do not build in additional levels of quality or unrequested services that will inflate your company's costs when compared with your competitors. Do not propose a Mercedes when the client wants a Buick! A general rule is to take no deviations or exceptions to the stated RFP requirements, and do not submit alternate proposals, even though they may be allowed. The government has spent considerable time, energy, and resources in performing functional and data requirements analyses; conceptualizing measurable evaluation factors (e.g., past performance), subfactors (e.g., project profiles), elements (e.g., management of complex contracts), and standards (e.g., meeting specific performance metrics); and developing the RFP and its SOW[3] to reflect its concept of a technical solution for a given project or program. It can, therefore, be perceived as presumptuous on a company's part to propose an alternative. Your pre-RFP marketing efforts should have provided intelligence as to the feasibility and acceptability of alternate proposals.

RFPs can range from a few pages to thousands of pages, replete with attachments, for major aerospace and defense procurements. Most RFPs are now being distributed via electronic media (Internet, DVD, agency portals) instead of in hardcopy form.

Importantly, when an RFP is posted on the Web (e.g., FedBizOps, eBuy), assign a member of the proposal team to check and recheck that Web site several times each day during the entire proposal life cycle.

---

2   Because they will become public record, be certain that your questions do not reveal a weakness or lack of understanding about the project on the part of your company.

3   A statement of objectives (SOO) and/or Performance Work Statement are used increasingly instead of a government-written SOW to maximize the flexibility afforded to offerors to propose innovative and cost-effective approaches and solutions.

Amendments or other modifications can appear there only minutes before proposal due date and time. This was, in fact, the case with a $180 million DOE–National Nuclear Security Administration (NNSA) solicitation. With some government Web sites, such as Wright-Patterson Air Force Base (AFB), you can register to be notified of changes to the specific procurement via e-mail message. Other Web sites do not have or allow this function.

When hardcopy RFP documents are mailed or picked up at the client site (as is the case with classified solicitations from intelligence agencies, for example), some contractors elect to scan the RFP into electronic files using some type of optical character recognition (OCR) or intelligent character recognition (ICR) technology. Scanning can facilitate electronic searches for RFP requirements, which in turn can be transferred to electronically stored storyboard templates. It also facilitates searches for hard-to-locate requirements or duplications. A word of caution regarding scanning—time must be allotted to spell check electronically, review, and correct the scanned file. Scanning accuracy levels vary widely depending upon the scanner technology itself and the physical quality of the hardcopy document.

In accordance with the Uniform Contract Format established at FAR 15.406-1, government COs must prepare and assemble RFPs in a specific manner as enumerated in the following sections.

4.2 Part I—the schedule

Section A: Solicitation/Contract Form (Standard Form 33);

Section B: Supplies or Services and Prices/Costs;

Section C: Description/Specifications/Work Statement (The SOW may include system specifications, contractor tasks and services, products, contract end items, data requirements, and schedules, for example. It is an essential part of the RFP.)

Section D: Packaging and Marking;

Section E: Inspection and Acceptance;

Section F: Deliveries or Performance;

Section G: Contract Administration Data;

Section H: Special Contract Requirements.

4.3 Part II—contract clauses

Section I: Contract Clauses.

4.4 Part III—list of documents, exhibits, and other attachments

Section J: List of Attachments.

4.5 Part IV—representations and certifications

Section K: Representations, Certifications, and Other Statements of Offerors ("Reps and Certs");

Section L: Instructions, Conditions, and Notices to Offerors;

Section M: Evaluation Factors for Award (used to determine proposal page allocations, writing emphases, and thematic structure).

Presented a slightly different way, the RFP does the following:

- Describes the requirement in Sections B, C, D, E, F, and J;
- States the government agency's terms in Sections A, B, G, H, I, K, and J;
- Describes the evaluation criteria in Section M;
- Prescribes the proposal format and content in Section L;
- Provides process information in Sections A and L.

Figure 4.2 presents the table of contents (Section 11) from an RFP issued by NASA Headquarters for the Headquarters Information Technology Support Services (HITSS) contract in 2011. This form is a Standard Form 33, "Solicitation, Offer and Award," which appears in federal RFP documents.

The contractor's response to the government's RFP is called the proposal, the focus of Chapters 7 and 8 of this book.

SOLICITATION, OFFER AND AWARD	1. THIS CONTRACT IS A RATED ORDER UNDER DPAS (15 CFR 700)		RATING NONE		PAGE OF PAGES 1	92

2. CONTRACT NUMBER	3. SOLICITATION NUMBER NNH11351229R	4. TYPE OF SOLICITATION ☐ SEALED BID (IFB) ☒ NEGOTIATED (RFP)	5. DATE ISSUED 04/08/2011	6. REQUISITION/PURCHASE NUMBER 4200351229

7. ISSUED BY CODE HQ	8. ADDRESS OFFER TO (If other than Item 7)

NASA/Goddard Space Flight Center
Headquarters Procurement Office
Greenbelt MD 20771

NOTE: In sealed bid solicitations "offer" and "offeror" mean "bid" and "bidder".

SOLICITATION

9. Sealed offers in original and _____ copies for furnishing the supplies or services in the Schedule will be received at the place specified in Item 8, or if hand carried, in the depository located in _____ until **1400 ET** local time _____ **05/09/2011**
(Hour)   (Date)

CAUTION: LATE Submissions, Modifications, and Withdrawals: See Section L, Provision No. 52.214-7 or 52.215-1. All offers are subject to all terms and conditions contained in this solicitation.

10. FOR INFORMATION CALL:	A. NAME Ricarda Mason	B. TELEPHONE (NO COLLECT CALLS)			C. E-MAIL ADDRESS Ricarda.E.Mason@nasa.gov
		AREA CODE 301	NUMBER 286-6718	EXT.	

11. TABLE OF CONTENTS

(X)	SEC.	DESCRIPTION	PAGE(S)	(X)	SEC.	DESCRIPTION	PAGE(S)
		PART I - THE SCHEDULE				PART II - CONTRACT CLAUSES	
X	A	SOLICITATION/CONTRACT FORM	1	X	I	CONTRACT CLAUSES	39
X	B	SUPPLIES OR SERVICES AND PRICES/COSTS	9			PART III - LIST OF DOCUMENTS, EXHIBITS AND OTHER ATTACH.	
X	C	DESCRIPTION/SPECS./WORK STATEMENT	18	X	J	LIST OF ATTACHMENTS	51
X	D	PACKAGING AND MARKING	19			PART IV - REPRESENTATIONS AND INSTRUCTIONS	
X	E	INSPECTION AND ACCEPTANCE	20	X	K	REPRESENTATIONS, CERTIFICATIONS AND OTHER STATEMENTS OF OFFERORS	52
X	F	DELIVERIES OR PERFORMANCE	22				
X	G	CONTRACT ADMINISTRATION DATA	23	X	L	INSTRS., CONDS., AND NOTICES TO OFFERORS	57
X	H	SPECIAL CONTRACT REQUIREMENTS	33	X	M	EVALUATION FACTORS FOR AWARD	84

OFFER (Must be fully completed by offeror)

NOTE: Item 12 does not apply if the solicitation includes the provisions at 52.214-16, Minimum Bid Acceptance Period.

12. In compliance with the above, the undersigned agrees, if this offer is accepted within _____ calendar days (60 calendar days unless a different period is inserted by the offeror) from the date for receipt of offers specified above, to furnish any or all items upon which prices are offered at the price set opposite each item, delivered at the designated point(s), within the time specified in the schedule.

13. DISCOUNT FOR PROMPT PAYMENT (See Section I, Clause No. 52.232.8)	10 CALENDAR DAYS (%)	20 CALENDAR DAYS (%)	30 CALENDAR DAYS (%)	CALENDAR DAYS (%)

14. ACKNOWLEDGEMENT OF AMENDMENTS (The offeror acknowledges receipt of amendments to the SOLICITATION for offerors and related documents numbered and dated):	AMENDMENT NO.	DATE	AMENDMENT NO.	DATE

15A. NAME AND ADDRESS OF OFFEROR	CODE	FACILITY	16. NAME AND TITLE OF PERSON AUTHORIZED TO SIGN OFFER (Type or print)

15B. TELEPHONE NUMBER			15C. CHECK IF REMITTANCE ADDRESS ☐ IS DIFFERENT FROM ABOVE - ENTER SUCH ADDRESS IN SCHEDULE.	17. SIGNATURE	18. OFFER DATE
AREA CODE	NUMBER	EXT.			

AWARD (To be completed by government)

19. ACCEPTED AS TO ITEMS NUMBERED	20. AMOUNT	21. ACCOUNTING AND APPROPRIATION

22. AUTHORITY FOR USING OTHER THAN FULL AND OPEN COMPETITION: ☐ 10 U.S.C. 2304 (c) ( ) ☐ 41 U.S.C. 253 (c) ( )	23. SUBMIT INVOICES TO ADDRESS SHOWN IN (4 copies unless otherwise specified)	ITEM

24. ADMINISTERED BY (If other than Item 7) CODE	25. PAYMENT WILL BE MADE BY CODE

26. NAME OF CONTRACTING OFFICER (Type or print) Ricarda Mason	27. UNITED STATES OF AMERICA (Signature of Contracting Officer)	28. AWARD DATE

IMPORTANT - Award will be made on this Form, or on Standard Form 26, or by other authorized official written notice.

AUTHORIZED FOR LOCAL REPRODUCTION
Previous edition is unusable

STANDARD FORM 33 (Rev. 9-97)
Prescribed by GSA - FAR (48 CFR) 53.214(c)

Figure 4.2 Table of contents from an RFP.

4.6 The importance of Section L (instructions to offerors)

Section L of the RFP or RFS provides specific instructions for preparing and structuring the proposal document. (Note, however, that on occasion these instructions are found in Section M. RFPs from the Sacramento District of the U.S. Army Corps of Engineers' are cases in point.)

Turn to Section L as one of the first steps when evaluating a new RFP. Section L drives the structure and form of your company's proposal response. Together with Sections C (SOW or PWS), M (Evaluation Criteria), and H (Special Contracts Requirements), Section L provides the basis for the architecture of the proposal documents. Of note is that recent versions of Section L within the U.S. Department of Transportation and National Institutes of Health (NIH) include an element titled "Why Should We Contract with You?"

Margin requirements, font family and size, number of foldout (11 × 17-inch) pages permitted, page count, double-sided photocopying, binding and packaging specifications, résumé formats, project experience (past performance) formats, number of copies of each volume, and oral presentation slide specifications are among the publication parameters that may be addressed in this important section of the RFP. In addition, software application, version, and compatibility for electronic upload or DVD submittal may be stipulated. Here, you may also find specific guidance as to how your proposal should be structured in terms of the outline and numbering conventions. For example, you may see that your technical volume should consist of six major sections, each numbered according to the convention I.A, I.B, I.C. Outlining the proposal volumes should take into account guidance from Section L, as well as Sections M and C and other parts of the RFP or RFS as appropriate. Remember to use the verbiage from the RFP itself, particularly Section C, to build your proposal outline. Evaluators, their administrative support staffs, and government-hired consultants or evaluators[4] will be looking for those same words to ensure that you have a compliant submittal.

The proposal manager for a given RFP should ensure that your internal publication group receives a copy of all of the instructions from Section L during the prekickoff planning activities. Your publication group can then develop RFP-specific page templates and provide the

---

4   Certain government agencies use consultants from industry (e.g., Noblis [http://www.noblis.org]) or academia to verify past performance client references and validate technical discussions or proposed solutions.

technical writers and subject matter experts (SMEs) with estimated word counts per page. Words-per-page guidelines are important so that the writers adhere to the page allocations established either within the RFP itself or by the proposal manager. Vague instructions, such as, Write 10 pages of text on systems engineering, could result in 2,500 words or 7,500 words, depending upon font, margin, and linespacing settings. Instead, provide written instructions to each writer, indicating that one should provide, for example, 1,500 words for Section 2.2, "Effective Software Engineering Approaches."

4.7 Section M (evaluation criteria): toward maximizing your score

The general criteria by which the government will evaluate your proposal are presented in Section M of each RFP. The Competition in Contracting Act (CICA), as implemented in the FAR, requires that price or cost to the government be included as an evaluation factor in every source selection. In some cases [such as National Aeronautics and Space Administration (NASA) RFPs], points are clearly allocated for each scored portion of the proposal, such as mission suitability and personnel management; however, many times the evaluation criteria must be derived from a somewhat vague narrative, as in Table 4.1.

Table 4.1
Example of Nebulous Evaluation Weightings

Criteria	Weight
1. Offeror's understanding the problem and proposed technical approach	Most important
2. Offeror's applications-related experience	Less important
3. Experience and training of individuals who will work under the contract	Same importance as 2
4. Offeror's general experience in developing software of comparable size, complexity, and content to this project	Same importance as 2
5. Offeror's general experience in maintaining and operating (M&O) a computer-based system of comparable size, complexity, and content to this project	Less important than 2
6. Offeror's proposed management plan	Less important than 5

4.8 Greatest or best-value approach

Although it can increase the cost of acquisitions, federal agencies have been encouraged proactively by the U.S. General Services Administration (GSA) to develop and issue source selection procedures that include the greatest or best-value approach, especially as it applies to the acquisition of Federal Information Processing (FIP) resources. Approximately half of the states employ some type of best-value procurement [1]. In states that permit best-value procurement, the specific method may be called "performance-based procurement," "competitive best value bidding," or "innovative procurements," among other terms. Among the strengths of the best-value approach from the federal government's perspective are that it: (1) allows greater flexibility to balance technical and total cost factors on the basis of the proposals actually received rather than on the basis of a pre-defined formula that combines technical and total cost ratings or rankings; (2) leverages the experience and personal judgment of senior governmental decision makers; and (3) permits the evaluation to take place just before the start of actual contract performance [2]. Ultimately, the goal of best-value procurement at both the federal and state levels is to combine the twin goals of efficient contracting and enhanced taxpayer trust in the procurement process [1].

According to the Federal Acquisition Regulations at FAR 2.101, "best value" means the expected outcome of an acquisition that, in the government's estimation, provides the greatest overall benefit in response to the requirement. The FAR Part 15 allows the use of several best-value competitive source selection techniques. Within the best-value continuum, government agencies may choose an approach that ranges from lowest price technically acceptable (LPTA) to the trade-off proces, wherein trade-offs between cost/price and noncost factors are permitted. The result is that technical capabilities or past performance may play a dominant role in the source selection, and the government may accept an offer other than the lowest price proposal. DoD relies heavily on the use of the best-value process to evaluate offers from potential contractors. In FY09, DoD chose a best-value process for approximately 95% on its new, competitively awarded contracts of $25 million or more.

In practice, however, "best value" means different things to different federal agencies. Best value for NASA is not equivalent to best value for the United States Air Force. Up-front marketing intelligence gathering will be required to ascertain how the specific agency interprets best-value procurement.

4.9 Emphasis on performance-based acquisition (PBA)

Performance-based acquisition is a major trend within federal procurement.[5] In FY2002, for example, the Department of Defense awarded more than 20% of its service requirements using performance-based specifications [3]. According to an Office of Management and Budget (OMB) report on "Bush Administration Priorities" issued in April 2004, the federal government as a whole had as a goal of achieving 40% performance-based contracts for 2005 [4]. In July 2006, OMB's Office of Federal Procurement Policy (OFPP) set a goal of having 40% of all contracts being performance based [5]. The Bush Administration reenergized PBA as a key initiative by emphasizing the importance of *contracting for results.* This emphasis was also an integral message in the President's Management Agenda (PMA), which called for creating a better government that is citizen-centered, results-oriented, and market-based. As a direct result of the Bush Administration's re-energizing of the PBA approach, the OMB in 2001 issued a mandate (OMB Memorandum M-01-11 [2/14/01 memo] and M-01-15 [3/19/01 memo]) that explicitly directs agencies to write performance-based techniques on a specific percentage of the total eligible service contracting dollars worth more than $25,000. The Services Acquisition Reform Act (SARA), which was included in the National Defense Authorization Act of 2004 (P.L. 108-136), provides incentives for performance-based services acquisitions in a manner similar to what the Federal Acquisition Streamlining Act (FASA) and the Clinger-Cohen Act did with regard to federal hardware procurement.

The principal objective of PBA is to express government needs in terms of required and measurable performance objectives, outcomes, and/or results, rather than the method of performance. This approach is to encourage industry-driven, competitive solutions and commercial best practices. The overarching focus is on the *results,* not the processes used to deliver those results. Either a performance work statement (PWS) or statement of objectives (SOO) may be used for performance-based service acquisition (PBSA). Performance-based RFSs describe how the contractor's performance will be evaluated in a quality assurance surveillance plan (QASP). Positive and negative incentives are identified as appropriate.

There are a number of important government acquisition tools available to encourage responsive contract performance. One such tool is

---

5   Note that the term *performance-based acquisition* (PBA) has replaced *performance-based contracting* (PBC).

the use of an award fee (AF) provision that provides, in appropriate situations, an incentive for superior contractor performance. The AF provision is the acquisition strategy that integrates the government customer's needs with the level of performance desired/required into the contract performance criteria provided in the award fee plan. Fundamentally, the objective of an award fee is to motivate the contractor to excel.

The award fee contract is an incentive contract designed to obtain specific acquisition objectives by relating the amount of award fee payable under the contract to the contractor's performance. The Award Fee Evaluation Board (as in the case of the U.S. Army) or Performance Evaluation Board (as in the case of NASA) provides critical oversight to the process, thus ensuring the evaluation of the contractor's performance is fair and provides an incentive for superior performance. This process is outlined in the award fee plan that directs all major activities to be performed by the government during the AF determination process.

Award fee contracts are a type of incentive contract, as described at FAR Subpart 16.4. Incentives are embedded within the contract type itself [e.g., fixed price incentive fee (FPIF), fixed price award fee (FPAF), cost plus incentive fee (CPIF), and cost plus award fee (CPAF)]. Many incentive contracts include only cost incentives, which take the form of a profit or fee adjustment formula and are intended to motivate the contractor to effectively manage costs. The amount of the award fee to be paid during each evaluation period of contract performance is determined by the government's evaluation of the contractor's performance in terms of the criteria stated in the contract, such as quality, timeliness, technical ingenuity, and cost-effective management. This determination and the methodology for determining the award fee are unilateral decisions made solely at the discretion of the government.

To facilitate effective contract surveillance, federal procurement regulations require agencies to develop quality assurance surveillance plans (QASPs) for all service contracts. A QASP, which directly corresponds to a contract's specified performance standards, is used to measure contractor performance and to ensure that the government receives the quality of services [acceptable quality level (AQL)] called for under the contract and pays only for the acceptable level of services received. An AQL is the variance from a performance standard that a contractor is allowed, before the government rejects its services. Generally speaking, a contractor will be given an opportunity to correct nonconforming services if it can be accomplished within the required delivery schedule.

Contract surveillance is a function of contract administration that involves using a variety of insight and oversight methods to gauge contractor performance. The extent of contract surveillance is based on risk management. Contract surveillance, including the use of QASPs, is a critical element in the effective administration of performance-based service contracts.

The PWS is a statement within the solicitation that identifies the technical, functional, and performance characteristics of the agency's requirements. The SOO is an alternative to the PWS. It is a summary of key agency goals and outcomes. The QASP is a plan for assessing contractor performance in order to ensure accomplishment of the government's objectives. The level of surveillance is linked to contract dollar amount, risk, and complexity of the requirement.

Executive Order 12931, issued on October 13, 1994, directed executive agencies of the U.S. government to "place more emphasis on past per- formance and promote best value rather than simply low cost in selecting sources for supplies and services." Additionally, in accordance with the Office of Federal Procurement Policy Best Practices Guide of May 1995, "the use of past performance as an evaluation factor in the contract award process makes the award (de facto) 'best value' selections." The U.S. Navy led the way in this acquisition innovation in 1989 when it employed a methodology for "greatest value source selection" of firm-fixed-price supplies in which cost and past performance were the only factors for award.

It is a central principle of acquisition reform in the federal arena that source selections must place greater weight on past performance empirical data and commensurably less on the technical and management proposal writing skills in determining best value. A performance-based SOW focuses on contractor accountability for required outcomes and results rather than on the details of how the contractor is expected to accomplish the tasks. Performance-based SOWs include methods and standards that will be used for performance measurement, clearly established deliverables and other reporting requirements, and well-defined task completion criteria. Performance metrics may take the form of automated system availability (uptime), resolution times for user issues, and time to hire and place qualified, cleared, technical personnel.

Contract data requirements lists (CDRLs) have also migrated toward a performance-based structure within Department of Defense procurements. Performance-based specification of contract data requirements defines the government's need for data (in hardcopy, electronic, e-mail, or other format) and gives the contractor latitude to propose the content and format of data to be provided to meet the requirement.

Because severe competitive pressure has encouraged some contractors to promise more than they can deliver, the government has found that it is particularly useful to compare actual performance with promised or bid performance on earlier or similar contracts. Did the contractor deliver the quality of work promised? Was the contract executed in a timely manner with major milestones met consistently? Was cost adequately controlled? With respect to the proposed effort, are proposed costs realistically estimated? Are salaries consistent with experience for the area? Do they raise questions about the ability of the contractor to perform as proposed and, thus, put the government at risk in terms of continuity of operations? Using a best value approach, these criteria can be compared and contrasted for each offeror to determine the overall greatest value for the government.

Your company's strategy for responding to an RFP should definitely take into account the evaluation criteria. For example, if "Key and Other Résuméd Personnel" are stipulated to count 50 out of 100 total points, then carefully tailored résumés and biographies should receive significant emphasis in your proposal response. Keep in mind, however, that every evaluation point is critical. Do not overlook sections that count 100 points, and only focus on those that count 250 points. *A point is a point is a point.* Evaluation criteria should also serve as a guide for page allocations. Heavily weighted items should have an appropriately high number of pages allocated to them. Use Section M as a guide in your company's final bid–no bid decision for the particular procurement. Let us suppose that the evaluation criteria place significant scoring weight (50%) on past performance with the particular agency. Your firm, although it has marketed the client well, has only performed on one or two small contracts for this client. When you evaluate Section M and determine this, you may want to rethink the decision to expend the time, resources, and money to prepare a credible proposal as the prime contractor. Subcontracting or teaming may be a more appropriate and cost-effective solution.

4.10 Influencing the content of an RFP—legitimately

RFPs are generated by client (government or private sector) staff who have problems to solve and needs to meet within certain budgetary and time constraints. Your company's marketing efforts should be directed toward understanding those problems and constraints and introducing the government staff to innovative solutions that can be applied better, faster, more cost-effectively, and with less performance risk than your competition. By talking with your client's staff at a variety of technical, programmatic, and contractual levels well in advance of the release of an RFP, your company may be successful in helping to shape the requirements of that RFP. Help your client understand his or her problem or issue in terms that your company can meet. Consider the following: a government agency has a need to archive important hardcopy documents. Your company supplies storage space, file boxes, and warehousing staff. Your goal is to help the government staff understand their requirements in terms of physical warehousing and rapid, just-in-time access and retrieval. Now let's say that your company specializes in microfilming services. Your goal is to help that same government agency understand their requirement in terms of microfiche and microfilm processing. Finally, let us consider that your company's focus is on high-resolution document-scanning technologies and long-term electronic storage media. Your marketing goal is to define the requirement in terms of leading-edge image processing, digitization, image indexing, and mass storage. Then when the RFP is written, the requirements stipulated will reflect the industry or technology that the government believes will provide the best solution. Influencing the RFP legitimately is a skillful craft, but it can be and is accomplished all the time. You will often hear of RFPs being "wired" for this or that company. A case could be made that with effective marketing, every RFP is predisposed in terms of technical requirements and position descriptions, for example, for one vendor or another, or at least one class of vendor over another. It is your company's task to predispose RFPs in your direction!

Influencing the RFP legitimately is the product of relationship building, careful listening, and idea sharing. Let us suppose that your company employs Ph.D.-level scientists with combined specialties in water resources management and advanced software design. Convincing your client that his problem requires the analytical depth that sophisticated computer models can provide might very well result in RFP position descriptions that require dual training in scientific disciplines and computer modeling for key staff. And this capability may be one that your competition does not have and cannot get easily.

In the course of marketing your client, you may determine that rapid, on-site response to task orders is perceived to be critical to the upcoming contract's success. You may be able to convince the client to stipulate a geographic distance requirement in the RFP. That stipulation might require all offerors to have offices within 15 miles of the client's site—something which you have but which will cost your competition time and money to establish.

Another pathway by which to legitimately influence RFPs is to assist the government in seeing the value of a specific contract vehicle (e.g., Alliant SB) on which your company is a prime contractor. Be proactive in offering specific language from previous RFPs or contracts that your new customers may be able to employ in the forthcoming solicitation that will align with your strengths as a company. Performance-based, metrics-driven past performance is one example. If you have strengths in that regard, try to have that requirement embedded in the new solicitation.

If a draft RFP is released, provide a meaningful critique that includes ideas for enhancement. In a respectful manner, identify any inconsistencies with industry best practices.

4.11 Other types of solicitation documents

In addition to federal government RFPs, there are RFPs released by state, county, municipality, and city governments as well as by private-sector companies and international governments (see Chapter 22).[6] Many of the marketing and proposal planning, designing, scheduling, writing, and publication guidelines and processes, as well as KM approaches, that apply to federal procurements can be used effectively with these other important types of proposals. Central to any proposal effort is developing a response that carefully, concisely, and completely meets your client's needs—whether that client is the U.S. Air Force Space Command, Princeton University, PEMEX (Petróleos Mexicanos) in Mexico (petroleum organization), the Environmental Protection Administration in Taiwan, Ford Motor Company, or the Port Authority of New York and New Jersey.

Because private-sector companies are not obligated to adhere to the federal Uniform Contract Format, their solicitation documents can vary substantially. General Electric's or Public Service Electric and Gas's RFPs, for example, can be quite different than DuPont's or BT's (British Telecommunications plc) RFPs. Many private-sector solicitations, however, address the following major elements:

- Understanding the problem/requirements;
- Technical approach/solution;
- Project organization and management approach;
- Project schedule;
- Health and safety;
- Qualifications and experience: résumés, key competencies, project summaries, and business references;
- Terms and conditions as well as contract compliance schedules;
- Potential conflicts of interest;

---

6   International RFPs may be called tenders or terms of reference.

- Subcontractors;
- Cost and other financial terms (supplier financing, countertrade, and letters of credit).

In addition, some companies require the completion of a complex set of forms as an addendum to the proposal itself. These forms can request a variety of institutional, financial, and contractual information and can be very time-consuming to prepare.

With international proposals, efforts must be made to remove references to U.S.-centric references and regulations from project summaries and the main proposal narrative. In many cases, time must be allocated in the proposal response milestone schedule to have the proposal and its associated documents (such as corporate certifications and articles of incorporation) translated into another language, such as Spanish or Mandarin Chinese. Your company's ranking by prestigious business journals or organizations is often important to include in international proposals.

Let's take a closer look now at private-sector solicitations.

Endnotes

1. Heisse, John R., " 'Best Value' Procurement: How Federal and State Governments Are Changing the Bidding Process," April 29, 2002; http://www.constructionweblinks.com/Resources/Industry_Reports__N ewsletters/April_29_2002/best_value_procurement.htm.

2. See *Source Selection: Greatest Value Approach*, Document #KMP-92-5-P, U.S. General Services Administration, May 1995.

3. *BMRA Procurement Alert Notice*, Fairfax, VA: Business Management Research Associates, Inc. Vol. 8, No. 3, Fall 2003.

4. Muzio, David, "Bush Administration Priorities," Office of Management and Budget, April 8, 2004; http://www.amciweb.com/con301_oe/ppt_pres/HHS/2004%20CON%20301%20-%20April%208.ppt.

5. Miller, Jason, "OMB Puts Pressure on Agencies to Boost Use of Performance-Based Acquisitions," *Government Leader,* August 11, 2006.

Chapter 5

Private-sector solicitation requests

Ｉ N ADDITION TO FAR-driven RFP- or RFS-based proposals submitted in
response to federal government procurement solicitations, companies
should consider other important types of proposal documents such
as private-sector proposals, product proposals, R&D internal proposals,
grant proposals for education, international proposals, and health care
proposals. Many times, nongovernment proposals are most analogous to
bids in that price is the primary determinant for award. In the commercial
sector, communication with the client organization during the proposal
process is not precluded by FAR-type regulations, so your company's
marketing efforts can be more aggressive and protracted. In private-sector
solicitation documents, there may be no instructions to offerors (i.e.,
Section L) or published evaluation criteria (i.e., Section M).

A product proposal tends to be built upon a point-by-point format.
There is no management plan or other response required wherein you
have to take into consideration client preferences that go well beyond what
is explicitly in the RFP. Health care proposals are similar to product

proposals, and lend themselves to boilerplate or "templatized" response far more easily than solution-driven RFP-based proposal responses.

Private-sector solicitation requests may be issued in hardcopy form as RFPs or Inquiries documents, and might also be presented as an informal telephone call or FAX from the client organization. Whatever the form or format of the request from the client, the response on the part of your company or organization must be customized and targeted, reflect the relevant marketing intelligence you have obtained, and concisely convey the benefits of doing business with your firm. Private-sector proposal documents that you will prepare can range from a very focused letter (1 to 5 pages) to volumes that are well in excess of 100 pages. In many instances, private-sector clients will include specific vendor qualification and data questionnaires, bid forms, and professional services agreement (PSAs) that must be completed fully and accurately and included with your proposal submittal package.

Most private-sector proposals must be submitted to a named location and point of contact by a specific date and time. Although corporations and other private entities are not bound by the stringent proposal acceptance parameters of the Federal Acquisition Regulations (FAR 52.215-1) when conducting business with other companies for private projects, timely submittals are becoming increasingly important. Plan to have your private-sector proposal arrive on time and with the appropriate number of copies in your submittal package. And be sensitive to your client: Refrain from sending a proposal to United Parcel Service (UPS) via Federal Express (FedEx), for example.

The following listing represents the variety of elements that may be required in a private-sector proposal. Note the similarity to federal proposal responses. Boldface items are among the ones encountered most frequently. Some elements may be presented as appendixes in your proposal document.

- **Introduction or Executive Summary**
- **Scope of Work**
- Understanding of the Project/Nature of the Required Services
- **Technical Approach/Solution**
  - Alternative approaches
  - Bibliographic references
- **Experience and Qualifications**
  - Corporate contractual experience
  - Experience of key personnel
- **Team Organizational Structure**

- **Project Management Approach**
  - Roles and responsibilities
  - Project control
  - Ongoing communications with client
  - Availability of staff
- **Proposed Project and Task Milestone Schedules**
- **Task Subcontracting Approach**
- **Project Deliverables**
  - Quality control and quality assurance programs
  - Future action plans
- **Client References**
- **Résumés**
- **Project Summaries**
- **Sample Work Products and Deliverables**
- **Annual Reports, 10Ks, Financial Statements, and Dun & Bradstreet (D&B) Reports**
  - Equal Opportunity Employer Program and goals
  - Training certificates
  - Licenses, registrations, and certifications
- **Certificates of Liability and Unemployment Insurance**
- Affirmative Action Plan
  - Existing contract disclosure
  - Complete list of contractor affiliates and their locations
- **Representations and Certifications**
  - Type of business organization
  - Taxpayer identification number (TIN)
  - Corporate status [sole proprietorship, partnership, limited liability company (LLC)]
  - Certification of Independent Price Determination (Noncollusive Bidding and Code of Ethics Certification)
  - Preference for labor surplus area (LSA)
  - Certification of nonsegregated facilities
  - Certification regarding a drug-free workplace
  - Cost accounting practices and certifications
  - Certification of no investigation (criminal or civil antitrust)

- **Indemnification** (protection for the client against the risk of legal claims)
  - Damage to persons or property
  - Negligence on the part of the contractor
- **Nonconflict of Interest Statement**
- **Confidentiality Agreement**
  - Health and safety plan
  - Commercial terms and conditions
  - Equipment billing rate schedules
- **Project Costs**
  - Names, titles, and hourly rates for specific job classifications
  - Sample Invoice
  - Bid Bond
  - Comprehensive General Liability Insurance and Worker's Compensation Insurance
  - Intellectual property rights and design ownership

As part of your proposal library or automated proposal knowledge base, your company should have a collection (in both hardcopy and electronic form as applicable) of various licenses, certifications, insurance coverage, TIN numbers, training certificates, and so forth. Ready, albeit secure and controlled, access to this information will make building your responses to private-sector solicitations much easier and quicker.

5.1 Grant proposals—winning what you bid

As with federal government proposals, the focus of the grant proposal is on selling. Grant proposals are, fundamentally, sales documents. Nevada-based grants and fund-raising expert David G. Bauer speaks of two distinct types of grantsmanship. One is *reactive* and the other is *proactive*. Reactive grantsmanship involves developing the project first, looking for funders, and then scrambling to meet a deadline. On the other hand, proactive grantsmanship begins with researching funding sources and then expands to cultivating professional relationships with relevant grantmakers. Your organization should definitely practice *proactive* grants development.

5.1.1 **Letters of inquiry**

In many cases, organizations must first prepare a brief letter of inquiry (LOI) before receiving an invitation to submit a full grant proposal. The letter of inquiry provides a valuable forum for vetting project ideas with potential funding sources. It allows you to build a connection between your project's goals and the grantmaking foundation's or agency's mission, philosophy, and interests. Be concise in this letter of inquiry—three pages is adequate. The first paragraph should provide a synopsis of the project and the requested funding amount. Include such elements as the project title, name of your organization, qualifications of key project staff, competencies of your organization, notional schedule, and "statement of need" along with a clear, logical, and achievable methodology to the stated need. Focus on the tangible and intangible benefits of your proposal, and convey a passionate dedication to your project.

Before you start writing your grant proposal, invest the time to plan your approach and develop a realistic schedule for completing the grant application (see Figure 5.1). Importantly, build in time for internal reviews by principal investigators (PIs) and other colleagues.

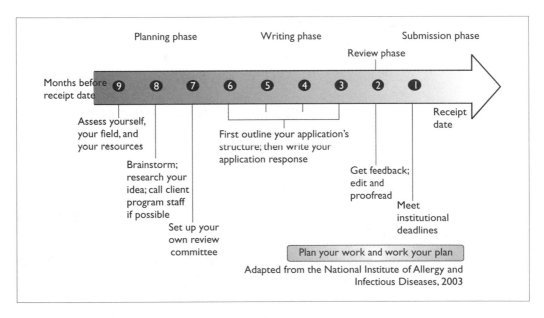

Figure 5.1   Forward-looking preparation time line.

5.1.2 **Balancing the technical and the nontechnical**

Place yourself in the peer reviewers' shoes and, thus, balance the technical and the nontechnical throughout your grant proposal (see Figure 5.2). To begin, develop a title for your project that invites reviewers to read your proposal. Most grantmaking staffs are generalists. Therefore, you should include both technical and nontechnical information throughout your proposal. Begin each paragraph simply, and then progress to more complex information. You might use *Scientific American* as a model for the level of writing to use in the nontechnical paragraphs.

5.1.3 **Standard grant proposal components**

The 11 components of most grant proposal applications are presented in Figure 5.3. Tell your overall story in nontechnical terms up front in 1—Proposal Summary. Grab positive attention and build trust quickly. Convey what you want to do and what preliminary work you have accomplished. Clearly identify why your project is important. What is the intellectual merit of the proposed activity? What are the broader impacts of the proposed activity? Articulate the tangible benefits to industry and government as well as to the grantmaking organization. Explain why you will succeed. Identify how much your project will cost, and how your budget is cost-effective. Show how your project is related to other research in the field. Keep the proposal summary to one page in length. It serves as the foundation of your grant proposal. Importantly, it may be the only section reviewed by all evaluators.

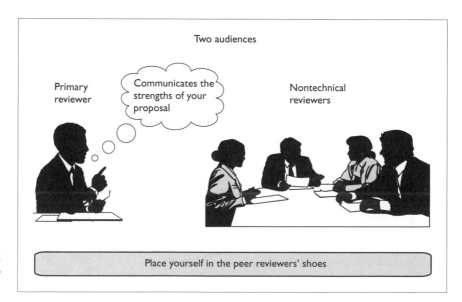

Figure 5.2
Writing to your
audiences.

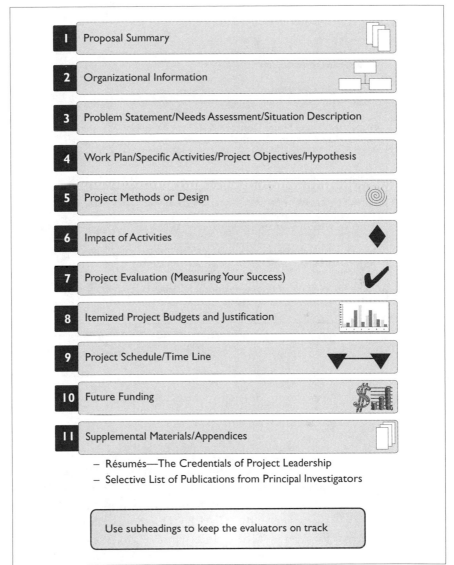

Figure 5.3
Grant proposal
components.

Web-based grants development resources are provided in Figure 5.4.

5.2 Nongovernmental organizations (NGOs)

Nongovernmental organizations (NGOs), international nongovernmental organizations (INGOs), and local nongovernmental organizations (LNGOs) are nonprofit, voluntary associations of citizens organized on a

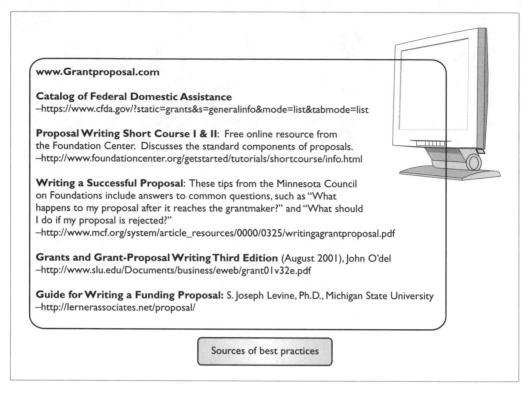

www.Grantproposal.com

Catalog of Federal Domestic Assistance
–https://www.cfda.gov/?static=grants&s=generalinfo&mode=list&tabmode=list

Proposal Writing Short Course I & II: Free online resource from
the Foundation Center. Discusses the standard components of proposals.
–http://www.foundationcenter.org/getstarted/tutorials/shortcourse/info.html

Writing a Successful Proposal: These tips from the Minnesota Council
on Foundations include answers to common questions, such as "What
happens to my proposal after it reaches the grantmaker?" and "What should
I do if my proposal is rejected?"
–http://www.mcf.org/system/article_resources/0000/0325/writingagrantproposal.pdf

Grants and Grant-Proposal Writing Third Edition (August 2001), John O'del
–http://www.slu.edu/Documents/business/eweb/grant01v32e.pdf

Guide for Writing a Funding Proposal: S. Joseph Levine, Ph.D., Michigan State University
–http://lernerassociates.net/proposal/

Sources of best practices

Figure 5.4   Resources for developing compelling grant proposals.

local, national, or international level that operate independently of government or business structures and have noncommercial objectives. NGOs include the Canadian Red Cross, Cooperative for Assistance and Relief Everywhere, Inc. (CARE), Doctors Without Borders [Medecins Sans Frontieres (MSF)], International Medical Corps (IMC), and Catholic Relief Services (CRS). Task-oriented and driven by people with a common interest, NGOs perform a variety of services and humanitarian functions, bring citizens' concerns to the attention of governments, monitor policies, and encourage political participation at the community level. They provide analysis and expertise, serve as early-warning mechanisms, and help monitor and implement international agreements. Some are organized around specific issues, such as human rights, the environment, or health care.

NGOs must often compete for funding sources via a proposal process. An example of an RFP open to select NGOs was issued through Border Partners in Action (Border PACT), an extensive network of U.S.–Mexico-border higher education institutions dedicated to building human capacity through education and training. Based at the University of

Arizona, Border PACT is coconvened by the Consortium for North American Higher Education Collaboration (CONAHEC), the American Council on Education (ACE), and the Asociación Nacional de Universidades e Instituciones de Educación Superior (ANUIES). Working in smaller regional groups, as well as within the larger Border PACT network, 65 member institutions have joined forces across the border to serve as agents of change in solving the many challenges they face as borderlands communities. Border PACT's goal is to provide a means for higher education institutions, researchers, student groups, NGOs, and American-Indian and Mexican indigenous border communities on both sides of the U.S.–Mexico border to develop joint programs in conjunction with their communities intended to derive shared solutions to common problems.

Border PACT issued an RFP for its grants program. In order to apply, a brief proposal of five pages maximum, 1.5-spaced, in no smaller than 10-point font size (12-point preferred) was required that addressed the following points:

- Names of the two lead binational participating institutions, including the primary contacts at each institution, their positions or titles, physical addresses, post office box, phone numbers, faxes, and e-mail addresses.
- Description of the proposed activity, including purpose, persons involved, and a timetable of activities. (Note: it would be advisable to include a schedule with major milestones in Gantt chart format.)
- Description of how the proposed project will benefit the borderland community or communities involved.
- Discussion of how the project will be publicized and promoted, along with identification of the targeted audience for the project and the number of people impacted.
- Resources, capabilities, and infrastructure to implement the project.
- Description of how the activity will be sustained beyond the life of the seed grant.
- Proposed budget, including matching or in-kind resources.

The required format for the proposal included a hardcopy of the proposal and supporting documents, as well as a copy of the proposal on an electronic medium, IBM Windows version, in document Microsoft Word format, or rich text format (RTF). The proposal was stipulated to include both a time line and work scope for the proposed projects spanning August to December. All proposals required discussion of concrete outcomes, evaluation mechanisms, and funding strategies for continuing the project beyond its initial stages.

The specific submission process for this particular RFP involved the following:

- Submissions of proposals must include a letter of endorsement by the president of each of the institutions, or the president of the board of directors for NGOs, or chief executive officer of an agency.
- A hardcopy of the proposal and supporting documents.
- A copy of the proposal in Microsoft Word.
- Submission of all materials by 5:00 P.M. Tucson time.

Next we will examine the dynamic arena of federal government acquisition in an era of e-government. There are many new dimensions to consider. We will begin by focusing on how RFPs emerge from the federal acquisition process.

Chapter 6

The federal acquisition process: emerging directions

6.1 Major trends going forward

What has changed in federal government acquisition and proposaling, and what are the major trends going forward into 2012, 2013, and beyond?

On February 2, 2011, the administrator for the Office of Federal Procurement Policy (OFPP), Daniel I. Gordon, issued a formal memorandum entitled "Myth-Busting: Addressing Misconceptions to Improve Communication with Industry During the Acquisition Process." The document was distributed to chief acquisition officers, senior procurement executives, and chief information officers throughout the federal government. This memorandum recognized that early, frequent, and constructive engagement with industry (both small and large businesses) is important for the successful acquisition and execution of complex, high-risk procurements, including those for large information technology (IT) projects. Increasing communication in the form of a "myth-busters" educational campaign is one of the key tenets of the Office of Management and Budget's (OMB) "25 Point Implementation Plan to Reform Federal IT Management." Importantly, this OFPP memorandum identifies 10 pervasive myths or misconceptions about the interaction between government and industry. Two examples suffice to illustrate the direction in which OFPP wants acquisition to proceed in the future. The first example is particularly noteworthy for small businesses.

- *Misconception*—"Getting broad participation by many different vendors is too difficult; we're better off dealing with the established companies we know."
- *Fact*—The government loses when we limit ourselves to the companies with which we already work. Instead, we need to look for opportunities to increase competition and ensure that all vendors, including small businesses, get fair consideration.
- *Misconception*—"We can't meet one-on-one with a potential offeror."
- *Fact*—Government officials can generally meet one-on-one with potential offerors as long as no vendor receives preferential treatment.

Some federal agencies have developed policies for communicating with industry while others have not, resulting in disparate practices and confusion on the part of both industry and government. To provide better direction to the federal acquisition workforce and to clarify the nature and schedule of engagement opportunities for industry, the 24 Chief Financial Officer (CFO) Act agencies (e.g., Department of Defense, Department of Energy, NASA, Department of Education, Department of Health and Human Services, and Department of Veterans Affairs) are now required to develop a vendor communication plan, to make these plans available to their acquisition workforce and the public, and to update their plans at least once every year. At a minimum, acquisition plans for high-risk, large-dollar, and complex programs, such as those for major IT systems and for recompetitions that need to attract new entrants to ensure adequate competition, will include a comprehensive vendor engagement strategy. This strategy includes convening at least one "industry day" or a presolicitation or preproposal conference and allows for a reasonable amount of one-on-one engagement. A case in point is the Department of State Vanguard 2.1 opportunity, which was issued in 2011 and included both a group and a one-on-one due diligence session for those contractors that opted in by submitting a Statement of Qualifications. In addition, the vendor engagement strategy allows time for discussions, as needed and in accordance with FAR Part 15, during the proposal evaluation process—or requires written justification as to why those steps are unnecessary. OFPP will be working with the Federal Acquisition Institute (FAI), Defense Acquisition University (DAU), and agency training practitioners to conduct an awareness campaign among government acquisition staff to eliminate unnecessary barriers to engagement with industry.

The "25 Point Implementation Plan to Reform Federal IT Management" was issued on December 9, 2010, by then United States chief information officer, Mr. Vivek Kundra.[1] A key focus of this critical plan was the alignment of the federal acquisition cycle with the technology cycle. The current federal acquisition process can require government program managers to specify their agency or organization's requirements up-front, which can be years in advance of program initiation. Given the pace of technological change, the lag between when the government defines its requirements and when the contractor begins to deliver support is enough time for the technology to fundamentally change, which means that the program may be outdated on the day it starts.

The procurement reforms enacted in the 1990s provided tools to speed up the acquisition process, but, according to the "25 Point Implementation Plan," the government failed to take full advantage of those tools, so programs continue to be delayed longer than the life of the associated technology. In particular, the use of multiple-award indefinite-delivery, indefinite-quantity (ID/IQ) contracts, called for in the 1994 Federal Acquisition Streamlining Act (FASA), was intended to allow quicker issuance of task orders to be competed through streamlined "fair opportunity" mini-competitions among the multiple contract holders. The creation of government-wide acquisition contracts (GWACs) for purchasing IT goods and services was also intended to provide a limited number of specialized vehicles open to the entire government that could quickly respond to individual agency needs.

While the innovations in FASA have produced benefits, Mr. Kundra continued, too often those tools are not used or not used effectively. IT acquisition, particularly for large projects, continues to move slowly. In addition, requirements are often developed without adequate input from industry and without enough communication between an agency's IT staff

---

1   Mr. Kundra, who was appointed by the Obama Administration as the first federal CIO in 2009, departed this position in August 2011 to become a Fellow at Harvard University. He then joined Salesforce.com as executive vice president of Emerging Marketings. The current federal CIO is Mr. Steven Van Roekel, who had served as the director of the Federal Communications Commission (FCC).

and the program employees who will actually be using the hardware and software. Moreover, agencies often believe that they need to develop a cost estimate that is low in order to have the project approved. As a result, requirements are too often unrealistic (as to performance, schedule, and cost estimates), or the requirements that the IT professionals develop may not provide what the government program staff and stakeholders expect—or both. If the "25 Point Implementation Plan" is indeed implemented and executed over time, small business should expect more, and more frequent, communication opportunities with government agencies with regard to procurement requirements. You will want to be fully prepared to present and discuss the specific ways in which your organization and its solutions will benefit the government in terms of quality, schedule, cost, and risk mitigation.

Under OMB's leadership, there is a move underway to migrate from individual department-defined standards to federally defined standards [United States Government Configuration Baseline (USGCB), Federal Desktop Core Configuration (FDDC), and NIST Special Publication (SP), *Recommended Security Controls for Federal Information Systems*]. The purpose of the USGCB initiative is to create security configuration baselines for information technology products widely deployed across the federal agencies. The USGCB baseline evolved from the FDDC mandate. The USGCB is a federal government-wide initiative that provides guidance to agencies on what should be done to improve and maintain effective configuration of settings focusing primarily on security.

As noted in the "25 Point Implementation Plan to Reform Federal IT Management" (2010), part of a broader IT transformation within the federal government involves the fundamental shift from building custom systems to adopting light technologies and shared solutions. The former federal CIO asserted that the shift to light technologies, that is, cloud services, which can be deployed rapidly, and to shared solutions will result in substantial cost savings, allowing agencies to optimize spending and allowing agencies to reinvest in their most critical mission needs. For example, the General Services Administration (GSA) recently entered into a contract to shift e-mail services to the cloud, resulting in a 50% cost reduction over 5 years—a savings of about $15 million. In the "25 Point Implementation Plan," Mr. Kundra contended that agencies must focus on consolidating existing data centers, reducing the need for infrastructure growth by implementing a "Cloud First" policy for services and increasing their use of available cloud and shared services.

In February 2010, the Obama Administration launched the Federal Data Center Consolidation Initiative (FDCCI) and issued guidance for Federal CIO Council agencies. The guidance called for agencies to inventory their data center assets, develop consolidation plans throughout fiscal year 2010, and integrate those plans into agency fiscal year 2012 budget submissions.

The FDCCI was aimed at assisting agencies in identifying their existing data center assets and formulating detailed consolidation plans that included a technical road map and clear consolidation of targets. The FDCCI will cut down the number of data centers across the government and assist agencies in applying best practices from the public and private sector, with goals to: (1) promote the use of green IT by reducing the overall energy and real estate footprint of government data centers; (2) reduce the cost of data center hardware, software, and operations; (3) increase the overall IT security posture of the government; and (4) shift IT investments to more efficient computing platforms and technologies.

Another major federal initiative involves the natural environment and sustainability. EPA created the Environmentally Preferable Purchasing Program in 1993 to help federal officials meet these requirements. Most recently, these requirements have included Executive Order 13514, Federal Leadership in Environmental, Energy and Economic Performance (October 5, 2009), which ordered federal agencies to use sustainable practices when buying products and services. Environmentally preferable means "products or services that have a lesser or reduced effect on human health and the environment when compared with competing products or services that serve the same purpose," according to the Instructions for Implementing Executive Order 13423. This comparison applied to raw materials, manufacturing, packaging, distribution, use, reuse, operation, maintenance, and disposal.

Applicability of EPP principles in specific acquisitions will vary depending on a variety of factors, such as the type and complexity of the product or service being purchased, whether or not the product or service is commercially available, the type of procurement method used (e.g., negotiated contract or sealed bid), the timeframe for the requirement, and the dollar amount of the requirement. The important point here is to be aware of the growing requirement for Environmentally Preferable Purchasing, and the need to demonstrate this awareness insofar as procurement practices and methodologies in your proposals.

Building on an initiative launched by the Under Secretary of Defense (Acquisition, Technology and Logistics), the Department of Defense (DoD) has developed and promulgated a set of procedures now used throughout the department when conducting negotiated, competitive acquisitions using FAR Part 15 procedures. The new DoD Source Selection Procedures—referred to as the "Shay Memo" from Mr. Shay D. Assad, director of Defense Procurement and Acquisition Policy—became mandatory for all competitive acquisitions under FAR Part 15. All RFPs issued after July 1, 2011, have been subject to these new standardized procedures for both technical and past performance evaluation factors for award. The goal of these procedures is to ensure that the DoD's source selection process delivers quality and timely services and products to United States warfighters and to the nation at the best value for our taxpayers.

A contractor's technical ratings will include an evaluation of the quality of the contractor's technical solution for meeting the government's requirements. Additionally, and very importantly, the technical rating process will also include an assessment of the risk associated with the contractor's specific technical approach in meeting the government's requirements. Technical rating and risk rating may be combined or considered separately. Note that proposal risk is separate and distinct from the program-level risk. Proposal risk involves an assessment of the risks inherent in the very choices and elements that comprise a particular solution. Is "Solution XYZ" likely to cause significant disruption of schedule, increased cost, or degradation of performance? If so, the risk rating will be high. Conversely, the program-level risk focuses on potential risks that may occur once a program is being executed.

Under the new source selection procedures, DoD Past Performance Evaluation Teams can use any or all of the following sources of past performance information for evaluation of a contractor's information: (1) past performance information provided by the offeror (e.g., past performance volume or section of a proposal); (2) past performance questionnaires completed by other government staff regarding a given contractor's performance on a specific program or project; and (3) Past Performance Information Retrieval System (PPIRS), Federal Awardee Performance and Integrity Information System (FAPIIS), Electronic Subcontract Reporting System (eSRS), as well as other databases, and interviews with contracting officers, government program managers, fee determination officials, and the Defense Contract Management Agency (DCMA). Past Performance Evaluation Teams will use the above-mentioned information to determine how it applies to generating a performance confidence assessment. In the case of "Substantial Confidence," the government has a high expectation that the offeror will successfully perform the required effort based on the offeror's recent and relevant performance record.

Governmentwide Acquisition Contracts (GWACs) and Indefinite Delivery/Indefinite Quantity (ID/IQ) contract vehicles have been with us for a number of years now, and that trend certainly continues. However, the *rapidity* with which Task Order Requests for Proposal (TORFPs) are released to industry under various GWAC and ID/IQ vehicles has increased to the point of becoming somewhat overwhelming. Many small businesses simply do not have the proposal development infrastructures in place to respond effectively and efficiently to these TORFPs. Yet being the prime or a major subcontractor on agency GWACs and ID/IQs is critical to small business success. Many procurements are just not available to those firms that are not part of a GWAC team. The General Services Administration's Alliant Small Business GWAC contract is a case in point. Once it was awarded in December 2007, Alliant became an important contractual vehicle for defense and civilian agencies. The small business winners have to market potential client agencies and also stand up internal task order proposal development engines. In effect, winning isn't winning anymore—in the world of GWACs and ID/IQs, it's merely a first step toward actually booking new business. Importantly, it is often unclear exactly which GWAC or ID/IQ contracts will emerge as the "vehicle of choice" for the government. The original Department of Commerce COMMITS master contract is an example of a GWAC that proved to be extremely popular, and was used across such agencies as the National Oceanic and Atmospheric Administration (NOAA) and the Department of Energy. The Department of Transportation's (later GSA administered this GWAC) Information Technology Omnibus Procurement (ITOP) II contract was also used for a broad range of agencies, including NASA and the U.S. Coast Guard.

Another major trend in federal proposaling is the expanded importance of *certifications* for both organizations and individuals. Such certifications include Software Engineering Institute (SEI) CMMI®, ISO 9000 (ISO 9000:2000, ISO 9001:2008, and ISO 9004:2000), ITIL (ISO 20000), and the Project Management Professional (PMP). These certifications identify "an adherence to a standardized set of professional guidelines and an understanding of best practices" [1]. Companies who achieve CMMI® certification significantly improve their performance across multiple dimensions. Carnegie Mellon University's (CMU) SEI released an important report entitled *Performance Results of CMMI®-Based Process Improvement* (CMU/SEI-2006-TR-004). This report presented quantitative evidence from 35 organizations of measurable improvement across five relevant performance categories: customer satisfaction, quality, productivity, schedule, and cost. The median improvement over time (from pages *xi* and 7 of CMU/SEI-2006-TR-004) is presented in Table 6.1.

Conferred by the Project Management Institute (PMI), the PMP certification offers individual certification for project and program managers to demonstrate their advanced knowledge of and experience with key project management concepts [2]. Of note is that PMI has earned ISO

Performance Category	Median Improvement Percentage
Cost (e.g., reductions in cost of delivery, cost of quality, and cost of rework; improved budget estimation accuracy)	34%
Schedule (e.g., reductions in schedule variation and days variance from plan; improved proportion of milestones met and estimation accuracy)	50%
Productivity (e.g., software production)	61%
Quality	48%
Customer Satisfaction	14%

Table 6.1
Applying SEI CMMI® Processes Drives Measurable Process Improvement

17024 accreditation for its PMP credential program. In addition, a certified earned value management system (EVMS) and a Defense Contract Audit Agency (DCAA)-certified accounting system (e.g., Deltek) on the part of industry have taken on increasing importance in federal procurement decisions. Fundamentally, these certifications provide the government with enhanced confidence in a contractor's baseline key practices and the contractor's ability to meet the government's requirement for operational excellence [3].

The importance value of *risk mitigation* has climbed as well. Potential risk associated with capital investment, enterprise architecture (EA), cyber and physical security, technical performance, schedule adherence, cost control, safety, and environmental impact is undergoing an increasing level of scrutiny. Significantly, contractors are being required to discuss the possible risks associated with their proposed technical, management, staffing, and phase-in (transition) solutions directly in their proposals. These are separate and distinct from risks that may arise during the contract itself.

Past performance as an evaluation factor for award is now weighted more highly than in past years. I have personally seen as high as 40% of the total score devoted to past performance. Furthermore, the government is routinely querying the PPIRS and CPARS databases to learn more about a given contractor or contractor team's performance across a wide spectrum of contracts. This practice is reflected in recent solicitation documents and proposal debriefing documents. For example, a 2011 civilian agency solicitation stated that "The Government will access and review data from the Contractor Performance Assessment Reporting System (CPARS) or similar systems to obtain up-to-date documentation on the offerer's ability to meet the requirements of this solicitation." Gone are the days when government evaluators only reviewed the past performance citations that the contractor provided within the proposal response itself. In addition, past performance questionnaires that must be completed by other government agencies on behalf of the contractor and then sent to the procuring government agency are increasingly common. The questionnaires themselves are now including an item called "business relations." Clearly, the government evaluators want to ascertain from fellow government managers that a given contractor conducts its day-to-day business in a courteous and professional manner that does not require significant government oversight.

In order to limit the number of full proposals received for a given procurement opportunity and therefore the associated proposal evaluation resource and time requirements, the government is increasingly employing a two-step or *two-phase procurement approach*. Step One often involves submittal of a 5- to 10-page response on the part of industry to a series of specific questions. These questions span relevant past performance experience, established structured processes, financial stability, and so forth. A subset of the total respondents is then invited to submit a proposal in response to the final RFP or RFS. An $80 million Army procurement at White Sands Missile Range (WSMR) followed this exact process. Some federal agencies are also using a two-part opt-in/opt-out process. A statement of qualifications may be required to demonstrate that a given contractor is indeed committed to pursing work on a specific project opportunity.

6.2 Rapid order task response

Increasingly, the U.S. federal government is letting contracts, which, upon award, require the winning contractor(s) to respond to Task Order Requests for Proposal (TORFPs). These solicitations are also called Task Order Requests (TORs). The types of contracts include Blanket Purchase Agreements (BPA), Indefinite Delivery/Indefinite Quantity (ID/IQ) contracts, Multiple Award Contracts (MACs), and Governmentwide Acquisition Contracts (GWACs). Representative examples of these contracts include the $24 billion, 7-year Air Force Network-Centric Solutions-2 (NETCENTS) vehicle; General Services Administration (GSA) Alliant Small Business (SB) vehicle; Department of Veterans Affairs (VA) Transformation Twenty-One Total Technology (T4); Navy SeaPort Enhanced (SeaPort-e) vehicle; the North American Aerospace Defense

Command/Northern Command (NORAD/NORTHCOM) Advisory and Assistance Services (N2A2S) contract; and the Department of Homeland Security (DHS) Enterprise Acquisition Gateway for Leading Edge Solutions (EAGLE) contract. EAGLE II will follow a similar framework.

As important as these contracts awards are to the winning companies and their teammates, from a day-to-day operational standpoint, these BPAs, ID/IQs, MACs, and GWACs can place significant strain on an organization's proposal development and pricing infrastructures from a number of key perspectives. First, the sheer volume of potential opportunities in any given timeframe can be high—25 in a day are not uncommon for some of these contract vehicles. These notices, which may arrive via e-mail or be accessible through a Web portal, must be evaluated as to their applicability to the company and its strategic direction and core competencies. A firm and final bid/no-bid decision must be made rapidly by an appropriate combination of Business Development and Operations staff. *Why so fast?* Because in many cases, the task order proposal is due back to the government in final form—replete with technical solution, staffing, and pricing—within 15 days or less from the date of TORFP or TOR release. Responding to multiple TORFPs can stretch even large corporations' proposal development capabilities. Whereas large businesses have the resources to maintain task order proposal teams distinct from strategic proposal teams that focus on major-impact bids,[2] small businesses can find themselves quickly overwhelmed by TORFP responses coupled with RFPs and RFSs with more traditional 30- to 45-day response life cycles.

Several field-proven key practices can be applied to mitigate some of the challenges associated with rapid-response, task order-type proposals.

- First and foremost, whenever possible, market to the customer before the TORFP is released. This will facilitate learning the customer's hopes, fears, biases, success factors, and critical issues that can then be addressed in your proposal. Second, define, document, communicate, and follow a structured and repeatable process for tracking, evaluating, responding to, reviewing, and submitting task order proposals (see Figure 6.1 for a sample process).

- In addition, develop proposal templates that contain as much information as possible that is repeated from proposal to proposal. In many cases, the structure or architecture of task-order proposals

---

2 One specific billion-dollar, Virginia-based corporation maintains three separate and distinct proposal teams—one for rapid task-order responses, a second for traditional RFP responses, and a third for major-impact, extremely strategic bids.

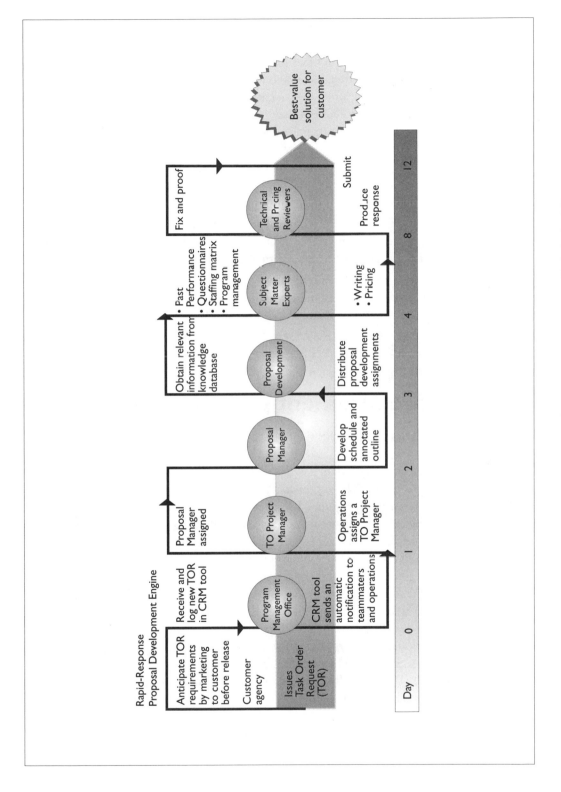

Figure 6.1 Implementing a streamlined, disciplined proposal engine facilitates rapid response to Task Order RFPs.

associated with a given ID/IQ contract is very similar from one to the next. Many sections repeat from proposal to proposal, such as an introduction of your company and your relevant capabilities and your overall management approach. The more elements of the proposal that can be prepackaged in advance of the release and bid of a TORFP, the more time you will have to construct the best team from among your partners, tailor the technical and staffing solutions, generate the pricing, and review the document for both compliance and customer-focused content.

- From a resource allocation perspective, ensure that there is adequate subject matter expertise available from operations staff to develop tailored technical solutions for each task-order RFP that your company elects to bid. In general, proposal development staff do not possess the domain-specific knowledge and experience to perform this function.

- Finally, a small business will have to carefully balance the mix of task-order RFPs to which it responds with the more traditional longer lead-time RFPs and RFSs. One proposal manager cannot handle both types of proposals on a sustained basis.

6.3 Federal procurement process overview

How do RFPs and RFSs originate? The answer is that they are extraordinarily complex contractual documents prepared by a variety of government employees in accordance with an intricate, formalized sequence of regulated procedures. It was during World War II that the federal government began to carefully regulate its procurement processes. From that time until the mid-1990s, U.S. procurement law evolved toward increased complexity (multiphased contracts and elaborate evaluation methods) and increased competition, even in subcontracting. The focus was on accountability, that is, objective and defensible acquisition decisions [4]. Contracting officials and technical staff alike were extremely concerned that the competitive efforts for which they had oversight responsibility were conducted in full accordance with appropriate agency-specific procurement regulations. However, federal acquisition streamlining and reform legislation enacted in 1994 and 1996 along with the President's Management Agenda (PMA) of 2001 placed more decision-making and discretionary authority back in the hands of government contracting officials.

6.4 Statutory and regulatory requirements for competition

The FAR system is part of the Code of Federal Regulations (CFR) [5]. It is the FAR that is the primary source of procurement regulations used by all federal agencies in their acquisition of supplies [6], construction, services [7], and research and development with appropriated funds. All of the provisions and clauses that are used in government contracting are found in the FAR, which is interpreted and applied in areas of dispute through a complex process of litigation and court and special governmental board decisions [8]. The DoD FAR Supplement, NASA FAR Supplement, Air Force Supplement, and Department of Energy Supplement all augment and amplify the FAR and should be used in conjunction with the FAR when determining acquisition regulations relevant to DoD and Air Force contracts, and NASA and DOE policies and procedures. Your company can review and download the FAR in HTML, PDF, and other formats from the Web at http://www.acquisition.gov/far. Agency supplements to the FAR and services regulations complement the FAR but do not contradict it.

The FAR is the primary source of procurement regulations used by all federal agencies in their acquisition of goods and services.

The FAR system, which became effective on April 1, 1984, replaced the Federal Procurement Regulation (FPR) used by civilian agencies of the federal government, the Defense Acquisition Regulation (DAR) used by DoD, and the National Aeronautics and Space Administration Procurement Regulation (NASAPR) used by NASA. The Commission on Government Procurement, established on November 26, 1969, by P.L. 91-129, was given the charter of studying the statutes, policies, regulations, and practices affecting government procurement and recommending improvements. Following years of effort, the FAR was announced in the *Federal Register* on September 19, 1983 [9]. You can locate the important standard forms (SFs) included in RFPs in FAR Part 53 Forms.

The Federal Acquisition Regulations System was established to codify and publish uniform policies and procedures for the acquisition of goods and services by all executive agencies. The FAR record is divided into Subchapters a through h, and Parts 1 through 52 (plus Part 53-Forms). Give particular attention to Subchapter c, "Contracting Methods and Contract Types." The opportunity for your company to submit written comments on proposed significant revisions to the FAR is provided through notification of proposed changes in the *Federal Register*. The

Federal Register is the official daily publication for rules, proposed rules, and notices of federal agencies and organizations, as well as executive orders and other presidential documents. The current volume of the *Federal Register* (Volume 76, 2011) can be found online at http://www.gpoaccess.gov/fr/index.html. In addition, you can search the *Federal Register* from 1994 to present at this Web site.

FAR Part 15—Contracting by Negotiation, establishes that in negotiated procurements the bidder must be responsible; evaluation criteria are flexible, that is, tailored to the procurement; and the acquisition process may be competitive or noncompetitive. Unlike sealed bidding (IFBs), negotiated procurement is not merely a series of steps. Every federal government agency has a somewhat unique pattern of procurement activity. Be sure to visit the contracting offices of your company's target client agencies and obtain copies of the handbooks that govern procurement practices for that particular agency.

6.5 The source selection process

Competitive negotiation is formally called *source selection*. This process, which is regulated by the FAR at Subpart 15.3 and designed to select the proposal that represents the best value to the government, normally involves the following steps.

First, an RFP is prepared and publicized by the government. Federal government RFPs all look essentially the same in terms of major sections (A through M) as a result of the application of the Uniform Contract Format (UCF), established at FAR Subpart 15.204.1 (see Table 15-1 in the FAR).

Second, technical and cost proposals are submitted to the client organization by offerors in the contractor community.

Third, proposals are analyzed, evaluated, and rated by a team of client staff against documented, weighted criteria and unstated standards.

An award can be made at this stage without discussions, based on the decision of the Source Selection Authority (SSA).

Fourth, potentially successful proposals are identified and included in the competitive range (shortlisted, see FAR Subpart 15.306) based on price and other factors; all others are eliminated from further competition and the offerors notified in writing of such.

Fifth, oral and written discussions are conducted with those offerors in the competitive range for the principal purpose of eliminating deficiencies in their proposals.

Sixth, those offerors are given an opportunity to submit BAFOs or Final Proposal Revisions (FPR) (see FAR 15.306).

Seventh, BAFOs are evaluated and a contract award is made to the offeror whose proposal is most advantageous to the client, as determined on the basis of stated evaluation criteria.

Eighth, unsuccessful offerors are notified promptly in writing (per FAR 15.503).

Finally, debriefings are held with unsuccessful offerors.

According to FAR 2.101, *acquisition* means the acquiring by contract with appropriated funds of supplies or services by and for the use of the federal government. There are four primary phases in the acquisition process used by the U.S. government: (1) needs assessment and determination; (2) acquisition planning; (3) solicitation release, proposal evaluation, contractor selection, and contract award (source selection phase); and (4) contract administration. Within NASA, for example, there are the following major steps in the acquisition process: (1) selection of a candidate project; (2) commitment to project planning; (3) project planning review; (4) project approval by Deputy Administrator; (5) RFPs; and (6) system design, development, and operation (see Figure 6.2). The federal government fiscal year (FY) begins on October 1 of each year.

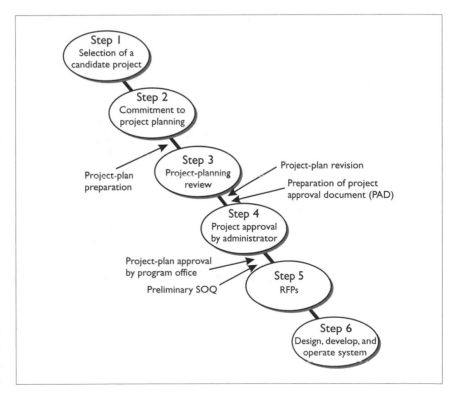

Figure 6.2
NASA acquisition process. (*Source: Statements of Work Handbook* NHB 5600.2., p. 3.)

Fundamentally, source selection involves two processes:

1. Selection of a contractor;

2. Formation of a contract.

The federal government uses a hierarchical source selection organization, the size of which depends upon the complexity, size, and importance of the procurement [10]. The source selection process has traditionally been dominated by weapons procurement. The formal source selection procedures of the U.S. Air Force serve as a frequent model for other federal agencies as well as international governments. As of July 2011, the Air Force has followed the source selection framework presented in the Shay Memo (Department of Defense Source Selection Procedures) that will govern all DoD competitive procurements. All formal U.S. government source selection systems are structured for objectivity, legality, and thoroughness. Most systems use successively weighted levels of evaluation, which allow the government to assign relative importance to each evaluation criterion. In the new DoD system, a Souce Selection Authority (SSA) is supported by a Source Selection Advisory Council (SSAC), which in turn is supported by a Source Selection Evaluation Board (SSEB).[3] The SSEB is actually groups of teams that evaluate the proposal. The SSEB teams are further divided into subpanels, areas, items, factors, and subfactors. It is at the level of subfactor that the actual scoring (evaluation) occurs. The overall evaluation is then a compilation of subscores. Scoring can take the form of numbers; a plus, check, minus scheme; colors; or adjectives (pass/fail; outstanding to unsatisfactory). Scoring of proposal responses is weighed against the prescriptions (standards) [11] set forth in the government's highly proprietary *Source Evaluation Guide* (or *Handbook*). The NASA system includes a Source Selection Official (SSO), an SEB, committees, panels, and subpanels. Again, evaluation occurs at the subpanel level. Of note is the fact that evaluation scores are not binding on source selection officials "as long as the official has a rational basis for the differing evaluation" [12].

In accordance with FAR 1.602-1(a), COs have the authority to enter into, administer, or terminate contracts and make related determinations and findings (D&F). The D&F detail the proposals that will be included in the competitive range and the reasons for those decisions. The

---

3   The U.S. Army Corps of Engineers' (USACE) source selection organization is the SSEB. In this agency, the SSEB is comprised of separate technical-evaluation and cost-evaluation teams. This organization is designed to ensure active, ongoing involvement of appropriate contracting, technical, logistical, legal, cost analysis, small business, and other functional staff management experience in the procurement process.

determination is the conclusion or decision supported by the findings. The findings are statements of fact or rationales essential to support the determination and must cover each requirement of the statute or regulation (FAR 1.701).

6.6 Full-and-open competition

Full-and-open competition means all responsible sources are permitted to compete. The major requirement of the Competition in Contracting Act (CICA) of 1984[4] was that full-and-open competition is the required standard for awarding contracts. CICA '84 established the civil service position of competition advocate to promote and ensure the use of full and open competition whenever feasible [13]. "The Office of Federal Procurement Policy Act (41 U.S.C. § 404) requires that each executive agency of the Federal Government designate an advocate for competition for the agency and for each procuring activity within the agency" [14]. The fact that cost and technical volumes are evaluated separately is not a statute or part of the FAR but is simply part of traditional practice. In full-and-open competitively negotiated bids, the CO is not bound by the Source Selection Board's decision. He or she can, in fact, override the conclusions and recommendations of the selection board. And no Final Proposal Revision is required.

No matter how objectively the RFP and the proposal evaluation process are structured, or how much the client's contracts office enforces competition in contracting protocol, in the final analysis the evaluation is one of human judgment. Remember that the proposal must address both *stated* and *unstated* criteria. Human judgment certainly pertains to the unstated criteria.

6.7 Major contract types

There are two basic types of contracts that result from the negotiated bid process: fixed price and cost reimbursement. A firm-fixed-price contract provides for a price that is not subject to any adjustment on the basis of your company's cost experience in performing the contract. This contract type places full responsibility and maximum risk on your company for all costs and resulting loss or profit. The latter calls for paying the contractor all incurred direct and indirect costs, as defined and specified in the contract, plus some profit [15]. When bidding fixed-price opportunities, your

---

4   The CICA '84 was implemented in the FAR through Federal Acquisition Circulars (FACs) 84-5 and 84-6.

company must ensure that it fully understands the scope of work and terms and conditions of the contract in order to ensure an acceptable profit.

In addition, there are several unusual combinations of fixed-price and incentive-type contracts. These include Fixed-Price Incentive Fee (FPIF) (FAR 16.403, http://www.acquisition.gov/far/) and Fixed-Price Award Fee (FPAF) (FAR 16.404, http://www.acquisition.gov/far/).

The fixed-price incentive (FPI) contract provides for an adjustment of profit and the establishment of the final contract price by means of a formula based on the relationship of final costs to a negotiated target cost. Under this type of contract, the following elements are negotiated at the outset: a target cost, a target profit, a ceiling price, and a formula for establishing final price and profit.

When costs are less than the target cost, the contractor's profit is increased in accordance with the formula negotiated. When costs exceed the target, the contractor's profit is reduced. Therefore, both the government and the contractor share in the risk. However, the contractor still shoulders significant risk, because if actual costs far exceed the target, the formula for adjustment of profit may yield a negative figure or a net loss.

The government's assumption of risk is limited also by the ceiling price negotiated, as that is the maximum amount the contractor can be paid. To provide an incentive consistent with the circumstances, the formula should reflect the relative risks involved in contract performance.

Under FPAF contract vehicles, award-fee provisions may be used in fixed-price contracts when the government wishes to motivate a contractor and other incentives cannot be used because contractor performance cannot be measured objectively. Such contracts shall establish a fixed price, including normal profit, for the effort. This price will be paid for satisfactory contract performance. Award fees earned (if any) will be paid in addition to that fixed price. FPAF contracts provide for periodic evaluation of the contractor's performance against an award-fee plan.

6.8 Significant recent paradigm shifts in federal government acquisition

Change has been *the* constant in the federal government acquisition arena since the mid-1980s. Two decades ago, a gradual shift began in *what* the federal government was buying [16]. Specifically, in FY1985, supplies and equipment accounted for 56% or $145 billion (in 1999 constant dollars) of the contracting dollars, compared with services, construction, and R&D [17]. By FY1999, however, the largest acquisition category was services, standing at $78 billion, or 43% of total spending [17]. Among the top items in the services category was professional, administrative, and management support [16]. That trend continues in 2012.

In addition to the changes in *what* the federal government was buying, there have also been significant changes in *how* the government has been buying goods and services [16]. The decade of the 1990s saw such landmark legislation as the Federal Acquisition Streamlining Act (FASA) of 1994 and the Federal Acquisition Reform Act (FARA) of 1996. Congress had enacted these important pieces of procurement reform legislation to enable the government to take full advantage of the commercial marketplace and to allow contracting officers to exercise sound business judgment, initiative, and creativity in satisfying the needs of their agency customers [18].

This paradigm of procurement change continued into this century with the President's Management Agenda (PMA) of 2001. And the trajectory of change continues to this day, with the goals of *increased accountability* from both the federal government and the contractor communities; *streamlined acquisition processes;* procurement that focuses on *measurable results,* service quality, and customer satisfaction (performance-based contracting and acquisition); and *expanded confidence* on the part of the American people in their federal government and the disposition of their tax dollars. Today's acquisition environment is one that emphasizes increased transparency, competition, and savings.

Further, federal agencies are making increased use of contracts awarded by other agencies as well as Federal Supply Schedule (FSS) contracts awarded by the General Services Administration (GSA) [19]. Ordering procedures for FSS are governed by FAR Subpart 8.4. Use of the FSA FSS grew from $4.5 billion in 1993 to $10.5 billion in 1999 [20]. Most of this growth was in the area of information technology. Of note is that GSA studies have shown that acquisition time is reduced significantly under schedule buys [20].

Congress passed the FY09 Duncan Hunter National Defense Authorization Act that enhances competition under multiple-award contracts, including FSS, by requiring that "fair notice" be given to all contractors for orders expected to exceed the simplified acquisition threshold (SAT).

Collectively, these acquisition changes tell us that the federal acquisition environment is now characterized by a greater reliance on services and information technology [20]. Additionally, electronic commerce (EC) is being used as the preferred approach to accomplish a variety of procurement tasks and to streamline and improve federal buying practices [20]. Of note, however, is that electronic procurement carries with it associated cybersecurity, personal privacy, reliability, and data integrity issues. Because the U.S. government is one of many players in the global services- and information-driven economy, it will have to continue to become a more savvy, commercial-oriented buyer [20].

Figure 6.3 presents in sequential order some of the critical legislation, executive orders, and other federal guidance that have been instrumental in shaping U.S. government procurement decisions and actions as well as contractor proposal responses during the past two decades.

Competition in Contracting Act (CICA) of 1984 (P.L. 98-369): This act amended the Armed Services Procurement Act and the Federal Property and Administrative Services Act of 1949 to enhance competition in federal

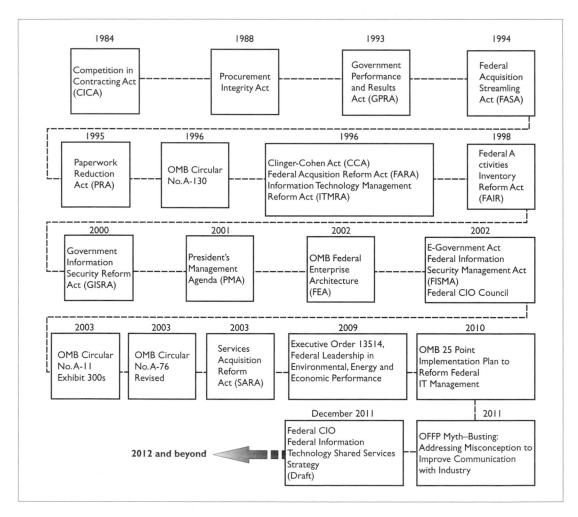

Figure 6.3 Critical legislation, regulations, and policy guidance that have driven federal procurement actions and contractor proposal responses.

contracting by requiring a justification for any procurement in which full-and-open competition would not be obtained. This public law was enacted for the purpose of increasing the number of government procurements conducted under the principles of full-and-fair competition, as opposed to contracts that are issued under noncompetitive arrangements such as "sole source" or "set-aside" awards. Contracting officers are required to promote and provide for full-and-open competition in soliciting offers and awarding U.S. government contracts over and above the simplified acquisition procedures (SAP) threshold. Maximum competition is desirable from a public citizen perspective because it results in the timely delivery to the U.S. government of quantity products and services at reasonable cost.

Procurement Integrity Act (1988): This act prohibits the disclosure of "contractor bid or proposal information" and "source selection information."

Government Performance and Results Act (GPRA) of 1993: This act established strategic planning and performance measurement in the federal government to improve the efficiency and effectiveness of federal programs. Under the GPRA, the director of the Office of Management and Budget (OMB) requires each federal agency to prepare an annual performance plan covering each program activity set forth in the budget of the agency. OMB must establish performance goals to define the level of performance to be achieved by a program activity, and express such goals in an objective, quantifiable, and measurable form.

Federal Acquisition Streamlining Act (FASA) of 1994 (Title V, FASA VP.L. 103-355; signed into law October 13, 1994): This act required federal agencies to establish cost, schedule, and measurable performance goals for all major acquisition programs, and to achieve on average 90% of those goals. FASA focused largely on the purchase of commercial items and smaller dollar buys (those under $100,000). Importantly, the act exempted commercial items from many unique government requirements. Acquisitions over the micro-purchase limit ($2,500) but not exceeding $100,000 were reserved for small businesses. Under FASA, contracting officers were encouraged to use approaches in awarding contracts that leveraged SAP. In addition, FASA gave agencies statutory authority to access computer records of contractors doing business with the federal government. The act also placed a greater emphasis on the use of past performance when selecting a contractor [21]. FASA "repeals or substantially modifies more than 225 provisions of law to reduce paperwork burdens, facilitate the acquisition of commercial products, enhance the use of simplified procedures for small purchases, transform the acquisition process to electronic commerce, and improve the efficiency of the laws governing the procurement of goods and services" [22]. "The bill strongly encourages the acquisition by federal agencies of commercial end-items and components, including the acquisition of commercial products that are modified to meet government needs " [23]. Instrumental in the generation of this specific legislation was Executive Order 12862, the Government Performance and Results Act (1993), and the Chief Financial Officers Act of 1990.

Finally, FASA encouraged the use of electronic commerce, and established the statutory framework for task and delivery order contracting [24].

Paperwork Reduction Act (PRA) of 1995: The Paperwork Reduction Act established a broad mandate for agencies to perform their information resources management (IRM) activities in an efficient, effective, and economical manner.

OMB Circular No. A-130, "Management of Federal Information Resources": This circular provides uniform governmentwide information resources management policies as required by the Paperwork Reduction Act of 1980, as amended by the Paperwork Reduction Act of 1995.

Clinger-Cohen Act of 1996 (P.L. 104-106, signed into law on February 10, 1996): Enactment of the Clinger-Cohen Act was driven by the federal government's growing reliance on information technology (IT) and the resulting increased attention and oversight on its acquisition, management, and use. Building on FASA, Clinger-Cohen provided the statutory foundation to streamline IT acquisitions and minimize layered approvals. The act emphasized accountability, outcomes-based performance, and results-based IT management. It promoted the improved performance of the civilian agency acquisition workforce, and it allowed contracting officers to select competitive contractors more efficiently. In addition, Clinger-Cohen required federal agencies to use a disciplined, business case-driven capital planning and investment control (CPIC) process to acquire, use, maintain, and dispose of information technology. The use of commercial-off-the-shelf (COTS) products was to be maximized.

The Clinger-Cohen Act rescinded the *Brooks Act* (P.L. 92-582), also known as Qualifications Based Selection (QBS), which was enacted on October 18, 1972. This 1972 act had established the procurement process by which architects and engineers (AEs) were selected for design contracts with federal design and construction agencies. The Brooks Act had also established a qualifications-based selection process, in which contracts for AEs were negotiated on the basis of demonstrated competence and qualification for the type of professional services required at a fair and reasonable price.

Federal Acquisition Reform Act (FARA) of 1996 (Division D of P.L. 104-106; 40 U.S.C. 1401; signed into law on February 10, 1996): This act enables the federal procurement system to emulate many of the most successful buying practices used in the commercial marketplace. Focused on reforming how the federal government makes larger dollar purchases and acquires IT, FARA increased the discretion of federal contracting officers in making competitive range determinations and lowered the approval levels for justification and approvals resulting in efficient competition. FARA also permitted the use of SAP in the acquisition of commercial items up to $5 million.

Information Technology Management Reform Act (ITMRA) (Division E of P.L. 104-106, signed into law on February 10, 1996): This act enables the federal procurement system to emulate many of the most successful buying practices used in the commercial marketplace. It is focused on reforming how the federal government makes larger dollar purchases and acquires IT. Establishes the role, duties, and qualifications of the CIO within federal agencies.

Federal Activities Inventory Reform Act (FAIR) of 1998: This is legislation that requires agencies to identify functions that could be performed by the private sector [20].

Government Information Security Reform Act (GISRA) of 2000: This act brought together existing IT security requirements from the Paperwork Reduction Act of 1995 and the Clinger-Cohen Act of 1996. GISRA also codified existing OMB IT security policies found in OMB Circular A-130 and IT security budget guidance in OMB Circular A-11, "Preparation, Submission, and Execution of the Budget." Specifically, GISRA directed agency CIOs to conduct annual IT security reviews of their systems and programs. Review results are to be reported to OMB. After GISRA expired in November 2002, the *Federal Information Security Management Act* (FISMA) was signed into law as Title III by President George W. Bush as part of the Electronic Government Act of 2002. FISMA permanently reauthorized the framework established by GISRA.

President's Management Agenda (PMA) (launched in August 2001): President George W. Bush's vision for government reform is guided by three important principles: (1) citizen centered, (2) results oriented, and (3) market based. In the PMA, Mr. Bush identified five governmentwide initiatives and nine program initiatives. Governmentwide initiatives include Strategic Management of Human Capital, Competitive Sourcing, Improved Financial Performance, Expanded Electronic Government, and Budget and Performance Integration. The PMA was launched as a strategy for improving the management and the performance of the U.S. federal government. Importantly, federal agencies have been held publicly accountable for adopting the disciplined approaches of the PMA through a governmentwide colorimetric scorecard system (GREEN—YELLOW—

RED). GREEN indicates that a given agency has met all of the established standards of success under the PMA, or that the agency's implementation is proceeding according to plan. The PMA continues unofficially under the Obama Administration.

Federal Enterprise Architecture (FEA): To facilitate efforts to transform the federal government into one that is citizen centered, results oriented, and market based, the OMB is developing the Federal Enterprise Architecture (FEA), a business-driven and performance-based framework to support cross-agency collaboration, transformation, and governmentwide improvement. Begun on February 6, 2002, the FEA is being constructed through a collection of interrelated "reference models" designed to facilitate cross-agency analysis and the identification of duplicative investments, gaps, and opportunities for collaboration within and across federal agencies. FEA provides OMB and other federal agencies with a new way of describing, analyzing, and improving the federal government and its ability to serve the American citizen. The outcome of this effort will be a more citizen-centered, customer-focused government that maximizes technology investments to better achieve mission outcomes.

Electronic Government (E-Government) Act of 2002 (P.L. 107-347, 44 U.S.C. Ch. 36; signed into law December 17, 2002): This act, which advocates a more citizen-focused approach to current governmentwide IT policies and programs, was designed in part to institutionalize the PMA. This law requires federal agencies to develop performance measures for implementing e-government. This act also requires agencies to conduct governmentwide e-government initiatives and to leverage cross-agency opportunities to leverage e-government. The federal CIO Council, originally established in 1996 by Executive Order 13011, was codified under the E-Government Act. This Council is comprised of the CIOs of 29 federal agencies as well as representatives from OMB. Its charter is to implement elements of GPRA, FISMA, and ITMRA. The federal CIO Council is the principal interagency forum to assist CIOs in meeting the goals of the PMA.

In addition, the E-Government Act established an Office of Electronic Government within the Office of Management and Budget to improve federal management of information resources.

OMB Circular No. A-11: The Office of Management and Budget uses the information reported in Circular A-11, Exhibits 53 and 300, to assist with budget decisions. Federal agencies must map their IT investments to the FEA reference models to help OMB and other federal organizations identify potential opportunities to collaborate and eliminate redundant spending.

OMB Circular A-76 (revised May 29, 2003): Circular A-76 is a set of policies and procedures to help determine whether public or private sources will undertake the federal government's commercial activities and services, ranging from software consulting and research and lab work to facilities management. The roots of Circular A-76 can be traced from the former Bureau of the Budget's Bulletin 55-4 (issued January 15, 1955), which stated that the federal government would "not start or carry on any commercial activity" that the private sector could do. Revisions have been made periodically ever since. A-76 is a federal government management tool. The A-76 competition provides an opportunity for government managers to streamline organization, implement best business practices, increase productivity, enhance quality, increase efficiency of operations, lower operational costs, and adjust IT initiatives to new regulatory drivers such as the PMA. The A-76 study process focuses on:

- Government/customer requirements;
- Organizational structure;
- Work processes;
- Defined outcomes;
- Competition.

Historically, the government wins 50% to 84% of competitions. But regardless of who wins, 30% to more than 40% savings are achieved.

Although there had been a governmentwide moratorium on the competitive outsourcing practice for a time, there have been efforts in Congress to again allow competitions between companies and federal employees for government work. For example, competitive sourcing provisions were included in the FY2011 Full-Year Continuing Appropriations Act. No approval has been given yet.

Services Acquisition Reform Act (SARA) of 2003 (P.L. 108-136; Title 14 of the FY2004 National Defense Authorization Act): This legislation provides additional incentive for use of performance-based contracting for services. The Services Acquisition Reform Act authorized the formation of an Acquisition Advisory Panel, whose members were announced by the OMB on February 1, 2005. The panel's statutory charter was to review and recommend any necessary changes to acquisition laws and regulations as well as government-wide acquisition policies. The objective of these activities was to ensure the effective and appropriate use of commercial practices and performance-based contracting. The panel, which was formed by former Representative Tom Davis (R-VA), issued its Final Working Draft in December 2006—a 448-page document divided into

seven chapters of findings and recommendations
(http://www.acquisition.gov/comp/aap/documents/DraftFinalReport.pdf).
Reviews of the panel's recommendations by the federal contracting
community have been mixed, and the ultimate impact of the
recommendations on federal procurement practice is unknown [25].

The federal government spent $3.456 trillion in FY2010, according to
the Congressional Research Service. Managing and modifying the complex
set of processes by which the government procures goods and services has
proven to be daunting, but progress is definitely underway.

6.9 Understanding the Federal Acquisition Streamlining Act (FASA)

*The trend in federal acquisition is toward electronic commerce,
purchase of commercial products, and streamlining the procedural
framework.*

As illustrated in Figure 6.4, the federal procurement landscape is very
dynamic and vectored in part toward faster, better, cheaper (FBC).[5]
Emerging trends span fast-track e-business procurement, electronic proposal submittal, best-value source selection, and performance-based
acquisition with associated technical, schedule, and cost control metrics, as
well as award fees. In addition, federal procurement since 1999 has followed much more of a partnership model wherein the government expects
contracting firms to not only mitigate but share both technical and cost
risks. In a major Department of State solicitation let in draft form in
mid-2011, the government stipulated to industry to assume "a reasonable

---

5   In 1992, then NASA Administrator Daniel S. Goldin challenged all of NASA, including the aerospace industry and
     academia, to use an FBC approach to project management. By initiating FBC project management, NASA
     intended to maximize the overall amount of scientific results obtained on a mission while minimizing the impact of
     a failed spacecraft. From 1996 to 2000, there were 6 mission failures out of 25 total missions flown, which,
     according to a March 13, 2001, audit report issued by the NASA Office of Inspector General (IG-01-009) "were
     clearly associated with exploring the boundaries stimulated by FBC." A Department of Defense review of five
     rocket failures between August 1998 and May 1999 found that government contractors were trying to do too much
     with too little resources and needed more training for mission-critical technical staff. Today, there seems to be two
     distinct management philosophies within NASA and the aerospace industry. One philosophy adheres to the value
     of faster, better, cheaper, if organized and configured properly. Proponents of the FBC approach point to
     Microsoft, which, during the past 20 years, has shortened schedules, cut costs, and enhanced performance.
     Conversely, the other philosophy says faster, better, cheaper—pick any two. Cheaper spacecraft are equated with
     lower performance, according to this approach.

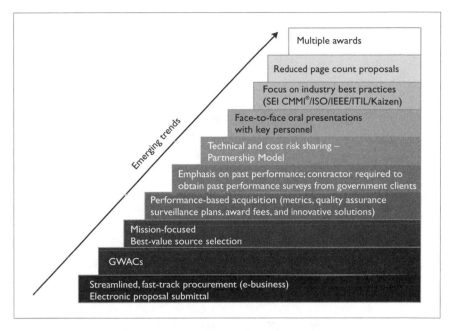

Figure 6.4
Federal
procurement
environment—
market-based and
results-oriented.

share of financial and business risk associated with the contract ... that enhances service quality, provides cost effective solution, and consistently meets Department of State goals and Service Level Agreements." Important resources for information about e-government, electronic commerce, and federal acquisition reform are presented in Table 6.2.

The focus now is on innovative solutions, presented in proposal documents and oral presentations in concise form, that infuse industry and commerical best practices, such as the Software Engineering Institute (SEI) Capability Maturity Model Integration® (CMMI®) structured software engineering methodologies, ISO 9001:2008 and 9002:2008 standards, Institute of Electrical and Electronics Engineers (IEEE), Kaizen, and IT Infrastructure Library (ITIL) v3 disciplined approaches. ITIL provides the foundation for quality IT service management. This series of documents was developed originally by the British government. The Kaizen method is a Japanese management concept focused on continuous incremental improvements.

Many procurements require face-to-face oral presentations between your proposed program staff and government technical, programmatic, and contractual leadership. Multiple, rather than single, awards are very common. And GWAC vehicles are now established critical contractual gateways to priming contracts with a variety of federal agencies.

Centralized contractor registration is required to inform the government that your company is ready to do business with the government. Register your small business with the CCR portal (https://www.bpn.gov/ccr/default.aspx) right away. As of January 1, 2004,

USA.gov
http://www.USA.gov Official portal that offers easy and comprehensive access to all online U.S. government resources. USA.gov is an interagency initiative administered by the U.S. General Services Administration's Office of Citizen Services and Innovative Technologies. Formerly FirstGov.gov, changing names in December 2006.
U.S. Small Business Administration (SBA)
http://www.sba.gov
Central Contractor Registration (CCR)
https://www.bpn.gov/ccr/default.aspx
Federal Business Opportunities (FedBizOpps)
http://www.fbo.gov You can also follow FedBizOpps on Twitter. Formerly the Electronic Posting System (EPS), FedBizOpps is the single governmentwide point of entry (GPE) for federal government procurement opportunities that are expected to exceed $25,000 (see FAR 5.1).
E-Government Web Site
http://www.whitehouse.gov/omb/egov Official Web site of the Office of E-Government & Information Technology within the Office of Management and Budget.
Army Single Face to Industry (ASFI)
https://acquisition.army.mil/asfi/ Portal to U.S. Army business opportunities. Includes an acquisition tool set and procurement notification mechanism.

Table 6.2
EC, e-Gov, eB,
and Acquisition
Reform Resources

Minority Business Development Agency (MBDA)
http://www.mbda.gov The Minority Business Development Agency (MBDA) is part of the U.S. Department of Commerce. MBDA is the only federal agency created specifically to foster the creation, growth and expansion of minority-owned businesses in America. MBDA focuses on assisting minority-owned firms to increase their export activity in support of President Obama's National Export Initiative (NEI). MBDA's Web site contains useful information related to business development for start-up firms, including strategic planning and marketing. Headquartered in Washington, D.C., with regional offices in Atlanta, Chicago, Dallas, New York, and San Francisco, MBDA provides assistance to socially or economically disadvantaged individuals who own or wish to start a business. Such persons include: Asian-Pacific Americans, Asian Indians, black Americans, Eskimos/Aleuts, Hasidic Jews, Native Americans, Spanish-speaking Americans, and Puerto Ricans. In addition, MBDA provides funding for Minority Business Development Centers (MBDC), Native American Business Development Centers (NABDC), Business Resource Centers (BRC), and Minority Business Opportunity Committees (MBOC) located throughout the United States.
DoD EMALL (Electronic Mall)
http://www.dscc.dla.mil/programs/emall/ Operated by the Defense Logistics Information Service (DLIS), the DoD EMALL is the single entry point for DoD and other federal, state, and local agency customers to find and acquire more than 39 million off-the-shelf, finished good items and services from the commercial marketplace and government sources. EMALL is designed to provide an e-commerce, enterprise-wide, Web-based solution for one-stop shopping, searching, ordering, and shipment. The DoD EMALL offers cross-catalog shopping for the purpose of comparison pricing and best-value decision making. All vendors meet FAR and DFAR requirements and statutory requirements and have a federal government contract in place. The DoD EMALL now hosts more than 1,400 commercial catalogs with more than 1,000 of those being from SBA-designated businesses.
Defense, Procurement, and Acquisition Policy (DPAP) Business Transformation Agency
http://www.bta.mil

Table 6.2
(continued)

the U.S. Small Business Administration's PRO-*Net* database had been combined with the DoD's Central Contractor Registration (CCR) database. *The result?* One Web portal for vendor registration and for searching small business sources—and an integrated, more efficient mechanism for small businesses to market their products and services to

Federal Acquisition Institute (FAI)
http://www.fai.gov Since 1976, FAI has been working to promote the development of a professional acquisition workforce within the federal government.
Procurement Technical Assistance Centers (PTACs)
http://www.dla.mil/db/procurem.htm The Defense Logistics Agency, on behalf of the Secretary of Defense, administers the DoD Procurement Technical Assistance Program. PTACs are a local resource that can provide assistance to businesses in marketing products and services to federal, state, and local governments.
WomenBiz.gov
http://www.womenbiz.gov Portal for women-owned businesses selling to the government. Established by the Interagency Committee on Women's Business Enterprises (IACWBE).
Small Business Innovation Research (SBIR) and Small Business Technology Transfer (STTR) Program Information
Department of Energy (DOE): http://energy.gov/oe/technology-development/small-business-innovation-research-sbir Department of Defense (DoD): http://www.acq.osd.mil/osbp/sbir/ Navy: http://www.navysbir.com/ Air Force Research Laboratory (AFRL): http://www.afsbirsttr.com/portal.aspx NASA: http://sbir.gsfc.nasa.gov/SBIR/SBIR.html National Science Foundation (NSF): http://www.nsf.gov/eng.iip/sbir/ Defense Advanced Research Projects Agency (DARPA): http://www.darpa.mil/opportunities/SBIR_STTR/SBIR_STTR.aspx/ U.S. Small Business Administration: http://www.sba.gov/content/small-business-innovation-research-program-sbir-0

Table 6.2
(continued)

the federal government. All of the search options and company information that existed in PRO-*Net* are found at the CCR's "Dynamic Small Business Search" site. The CCR portal is part of the Integrated Acquisition Environment (IAE), one of the 24 important e-government initiatives under the President's Management Agenda (http://www.whitehouse.gov/omb/ budget/fy2002/ mgmt.pdf).

FedWorld Information Network

http://www.fedworld.gov
Established in 1992 by the Department of Commerce to serve as an online locator service for a comprehensive inventory of information disseminated by the federal government. The site is now managed by the National Technical Information Service (NTIS).

Navy Electronic Commerce Online (NECO)

https://www.neco.navy.mil
This interactive Web site provides direct, online access to Navy electronic business opportunities.

FedMarket

http://www.fedmarket.com
The site's free content provides a significant number of helpful, easily understood, brief articles on selling to the federal government, proposal writing, GSA schedules, and federal compliance issues. The company also offers federal sales training, proposal training, and contracting seminars.

NASA Acquisition Internet Service (NAIS)

http://prod.nais.nasa.gov/cgi-bin/nais/index.cgi
The NASA Acquisition Internet Service (NAIS) provides easy access to procurement forecasts across the NASA centers. NAIS business opportunities are posted by date and classification. One can also use the NAIS "Search" function to find business opportunities by date, classification, NASA center, or keyword. NASA's Procurement Reference Library provides tools such as a search of the FAR and the NASA FAR Supplement (NFS).

Assistant Secretary of the Air Force/Acquisition (SAF/AQ)

Table 6.2
(continued)

http://ww3.safaq.hq.af.mil/
Provides information on Air Force-specific acquisition reform initiatives and success stories.

It was Federal Acquisition Circular (FAC) 2001-16, dated October 1, 2003, that amended the Federal Acquisition Regulations (FARs) to require contractor registration in the CCR database. This same circular also eliminated the Federal Acquisition Computer Network (FACNET) and

Department of Transportation (DOT) Office of Small and Disadvantaged Business Utilization (OSDBU)
http://osdbu.dot.gov Includes the agency procurement forecast (under Procurement Assistance) as well as tips for marketing to the DOT.
Acquisition Central
http://www.acquisition.gov Maintained by the Integrated Acquisition Environment (IAE), e-Gov initiative, Acquisition Central fosters a secure business environment that facilitates and supports cost-effective acquisition of goods and services in support of mission performance. Good site to begin the process of doing business with the federal government.
VetBiz.gov
http://www.vetbiz.gov Web site operated by the Department of Veterans Affairs designed to assist veteran entrepreneurs start and expand their businesses in the federal and private marketspace. Site includes a veteran business database.
National Women Business Owners Corporation (NWBOC; formerly the Women Business Owners Corporation), Washington, D.C.
http://www.nwboc.org The National Women Business Owners Corporation, a national 501(c)(3) nonprofit corporation, was established to expand competition for corporate and government contracts through implementation of a pioneering economic development strategy for women business owners. NWBOC seeks to provide more corporations with the opportunity to enhance their procurement practices and to provide to women suppliers the opportunity to compete. In July 2011, NWBOC was approved by the U.S. SBA to be a third-party certifier for the new purchasing programs: "Woman-Owned Small Business (WOSB) Program" and the "Economically Disadvantaged Woman-Owned Small Business Program" (EDWOSB).
Government Executive **Magazine**
http://www.govexec.com/management GovExec.com is a government business news daily. This site has a specific focus on Homeland Security, defense, technology, and management.

Table 6.2
(continued)

Service Corps of Retired Executives (SCORE)
http://www.score.org Founded in 1964, SCORE is a nonprofit association of more than 13,000 volunteer business counselors serving 364 chapters in urban, suburban, and rural communities throughout the United States and Puerto Rico. SCORE is a resource partner with the U.S. SBA. SCORE members are trained to serve as counselors, advisers, and mentors to aspiring entrepreneurs and business owners. These services are offered at no fee, as a community service.
Federal Register
http://www.gpoaccess.gov/fr/ Published by the Office of the Federal Register, National Archives and Records Administration (NARA), the *Federal Register* is the official daily publication for rules, proposed rules, and notices of federal agencies and organizations, as well as executive orders and other presidential documents.

Table 6.2
(continued)

designated a single governmentwide point of entry on the Internet called FedBizOpps (http://www.fedbizopps.gov) where federal agencies are to provide universal and convenient access to information about their procurement opportunities. In addition, FedBizOpps replaced both the paper and electronic *Commerce Business Daily.*

Now that we have an understanding of RFPs and how they originate in the federal acquisition process, we will examine the contracting community's proposal response life cycle and its critical components.

ENDNOTES

1. Gibson, Diane, L., Dennis R. Goldenson, and Keith Kost, "Performance Results of CMMI®-Based Process Improvement," Carnegie Mellon Software Engineering Institute, CMU/SEI-2006-TR-004, August 2006.

2. Flading, Jeffrey L., "Certifications and the Contracting Community," *Contract Management,* Vol. 47, No. 7, July 2007, pp. 18–22.

3. Flading, Jeffrey L., "Certifications and the Contracting Community," *Contract Management,* Vol. 47, No. 7, July 2007, p. 20.

4. *Writing Winning Proposals,* Farmington, UT: Shipley Associates, 1988, p. 3-3. The phenomenon of increased competition is also noted by Cibinic, John, and Ralph C. Nash, *Formation of Government Contracts,*

2nd ed., Washington, D.C.: George Washington University, 1986, p. 522.

5. The National Archives has published the CFR annually since 1938. This compilation of executive orders, proclamations, and rules and regulations for departments and agencies does for administrative law what the U.S.C. does for statute law. Material for the CFR is drawn from the calendar year entries in the *Federal Register*, a daily publication of Executive Branch documents and notices of public applicability and legal effect. [*History at NASA* (NASA HHR-50), Washington, D.C.: NASA Headquarters, 1986, p. 11.]

6. Per FAR 2.101, *supplies* means all property except land or interest in land.

7. Per FAR 37.101, *services contract* means a contract that directly engages the time and effort of a contractor whose primary purpose is to perform an identifiable task rather than to furnish an end item of supply.

8. The Comptroller General of the United States and the Government Accountability Office (GAO) that he heads "have been given a prominent role in the oversight of Government procurement and procurement related functions" (Cibinic, John, and Ralph C. Nash, *Formation of Government Contracts*, 2nd ed., Washington, D.C.: George Washington University, 1986, p. 53).

9. *Introduction to the Federal Acquisition Regulation Training Course*, Vienna, VA: Management Concepts, pp. 1–3.

10. *Writing Winning Proposals*, Farmington, UT: Shipley Associates, 1988, pp. 3–11.

11. Standards assist the government evaluators in determining how well a proposal meets the requirements. Several standards might be developed for one evaluation factor. Depending upon the evaluation factor, standards may be qualitative or quantitative. Standards are necessary because evaluators are not supposed to compare proposals. They must, therefore, have some standard against which to determine if a proposal satisfies the RFP. See *Writing Winning Proposals*, Farmington, UT: Shipley Associates, 1988, pp. 3–23.

12. Cibinic, John, and Ralph C. Nash, *Formation of Government Contracts*, 2nd ed., Washington, D.C.: George Washington University, 1986, pp. 644–645.

13. McVay, Barry L., *Proposals That Win Federal Contracts: How to Plan, Price, Write, and Negotiate to Get Your Fair Share of Government Business*, Woodbridge, VA: Panoptic Enterprises, 1989, p. 11.

14. Cibinic, John, and Ralph C. Nash, *Formation of Government Contracts*, 2nd ed., Washington, D.C.: George Washington University, p. 311.

15. Holtz, Herman, and Terry Schmidt, *The Winning Proposal: How to Write It*, New York: McGraw-Hill, 1981.

16. Hinton, Henry L., *Federal Acquisition: Trends, Reforms, and Challenges*, Washington, D.C.: United States General Accounting Office (GAO), March 16, 2000, p. 6. Testimony before the Subcommittee on Government Management, Information, and Technology, House Committee on Government Reform, GAO/T-OCG-00-7.

17. Hinton, Henry L., *Federal Acquisition: Trends, Reforms, and Challenges*, Washington, D.C.: United States General Accounting Office (GAO), March 16, 2000, p. 4.

18. Hinton, Henry L., *Federal Acquisition: Trends, Reforms, and Challenges*, Washington, D.C.: United States General Accounting Office (GAO), March 16, 2000, p. 8.

19. Hinton, Henry L., *Federal Acquisition: Trends, Reforms, and Challenges*, Washington, D.C.: United States General Accounting Office (GAO), March 16, 2000, pp. 6–7.

20. Hinton, Henry L., *Federal Acquisition: Trends, Reforms, and Challenges*, Washington, D.C.: United States General Accounting Office (GAO), March 16, 2000, p. 7.

21. Hinton, Henry L., *Federal Acquisition: Trends, Reforms, and Challenges*, Washington, D.C.: United States General Accounting Office (GAO), March 16, 2000, p. 9.

22. Brockmeier, Dave, "Help Shape Federal Acquisition Regulations," *Business Credit*, Vol. 97, No. 3, March 1995, p. 40.

23. Brockmeier, Dave, "Help Shape Federal Acquisition Regulations," *Business Credit*, Vol. 97, No. 3, March 1995, p. 42.

24. Hinton, Henry L., *Federal Acquisition: Trends, Reforms, and Challenges*, Washington, D.C.: United States General Accounting Office (GAO), March 16, 2000, p. 18.

25. Hardy, Michael, David Hubler, and Matthew Weigelt, "Experts Nitpick SARA Panel Proposals," *Federal Computer Week.com*, January 8, 2007, http://www.fcw.com/article97283-01-08-07-Print.

Chapter 7

The proposal life cycle

You can't close the sale when you have not made the sale.

L ET'S NOW TAKE A CLOSER look at what proposals really are, how they fit into a small business's total marketing life cycle, and the important planning, decisions, knowledge products, organization, and reviews required to prepare a successful proposal.

7.1 What is a proposal in the competitive federal and commercial marketplace?

Technically, a proposal is an offer prepared by a contractor (such as your company) to perform a service, supply a product, or a combination of both in response to an RFP or RFS document posted at FedBizOpps or an SF330 synopsis issued by a procuring agency. Proposals are legal documents, often incorporated by reference into the final contract that the government establishes with your company upon award. That means that they must be factual and accurate—including information provided in résumés and project summaries.

A proposal is designed to sell both technical and managerial capabilities of a company to accomplish all required activities on time and at a reasonable cost. Your company's proposal document(s) is scored, literally,[1] by the client's evaluators against formalized, specific standards. A proposal is the written, electronic, or oral (or any combination of the three) result of informed thinking, knowledge assimilation, and marketing processes, supported in turn by hard and directed work and buoyed by a positive collective attitude and commitment within your company's proposal team. A proposal is, first and foremost, a sales document. To be sure, it includes a host of technical, programmatic, institutional, pricing, and certification information, but it must remain sales oriented. The sales target is to convey as many strengths to the client as possible in terms that are meaningful to them. In the federal government marketspace, those items are quality, schedule, cost, and risk mitigation (as well as safety, security, and other elements[2]).

A proposal involves marketing your company to a government, private-sector, or international client. It is a closing sales presentation, supported concretely by traceable and auditable credentials and tailored to persuade your client to select your company for the award because you are best-qualified to achieve the results your client wants to achieve [1]. In the words of a senior U.S. DOT official, write your proposal from the government COTR's perspective. Help him or her to feel comfortable that your company will meet schedules, budgets, and other performance parameters. Demonstrate that you understand and can function well in the COTR's world. Make the COTR want to link his professional future with your company. A proposal is, necessarily, continued dialogue with your client. Proposals are, in fact, the primary vehicle for winning new federal government business in the competitive arena.

---

1   Scoring can take the form of numeric scores, color-coded scores, pluses and minuses, or qualitative (adjectival) narrative comments, such as "very good" and "good" or "low risk."

2   Strengths may also have a federal or political "flavor", such as job sustainment. Leveraging local resources—vendors, suppliers, individual professionals—on the "Space Coast" of Flordia plays well in NASA Kennedy Space Center proposals.

A proposal is a closing sales presentation, presented persuasively in story form and supported concretely by traceable and auditable credentials and solutions.

To reiterate, a proposal (as well as a bid, that is, a response to an IFB) is an offer or response [2]. A proposal is not necessarily a contractual document. But under specific circumstances, an offer can be made into a contract by the government. The client uses your proposal and those of your competitors as the primary sources of information upon which to base their selection of a winning contractor. Government evaluators are in no way obligated or encouraged to review publicly available material about your company (with the exception of past performance history) that is not included within your proposal. That means that you have to ensure that all relevant and salient materials are included along with your proposal within the parameters of any page, font, or other administrative or documentation limitations.

To continue, a proposal is a package of carefully orchestrated and documented arguments woven into a compelling story. Nothing should be put into your proposal by accident! Each section of a proposal should present carefully constructed discussion and meaningful evidence to convince your client that you should be awarded the contract because of the superiority of what you are proposing. To do this, you have to support the following messages in writing:

- You understand your client's project requirements, critical issues, and success criteria as well as *business* and *mission* goals and objectives.

- Your innovative, solutions-oriented approach satisfies all requirements. (Be careful not to imply that your approach exceeds requirements unless you can confirm that such enhancements can be delivered for no additional cost; this can result in the client thinking that you are proposing and charging more than that for which they are asking.) Conversely, your proposal must offer more than merely performing the required work in order to be scored highly during the evaluation process.

- Your approach offers tangible and intangible benefits to the client in terms the client sees as meaningful now and over the life of the contract.

- Your approach minimizes schedule, cost, and technical performance risk and maximizes opportunities for mission success.

- You are better (that is, more reliable, more experienced, and less expensive) than your competitors.

Why us? Why not our competitors? These are the simple yet profound questions that the late internationally known and respected proposal consultant Hyman Silver[3] insisted proposals must answer effectively. Through the vehicle of your proposal, your company must finish the process of convincing your client to select you over your competition.

Proposals are important deliverable products. One carelessly written and poorly presented proposal can damage your company's reputation with your client or potential client. Experience suggests that clients tend to remember contractors that have submitted inferior proposal responses. I have heard many senior managers say that they want to submit a proposal to "introduce the company to the client." If this is not a waste of B&P funds, nothing is. Introduce your company through marketing calls, leave-behind brochures, carefully tailored letters, social media, or at industry trade shows and conferences. But do not expend the human, time, and financial resources to respond to a solicitation document unless you intend to win.

7.2 Where does the proposal fit into the total marketing life cycle?

The proposal life cycle (in particular, for procurement efforts on which your company is the prime contractor) begins well before the actual writing and production of a response to an RFP or RFS. Figure 7.1 presents an overview of the entire marketing and proposal life cycle.

There are a number of salient elements in the overall contractor marketing and proposal process. The proposal process may include additional color team reviews (Blue, Pink, Red, and Gold, for example). Please note

---

3   This phrase was coined in 1975 by Hyman Silver, former president of H. Silver and Associates (HSA; http://hsilver.com) based in Los Angeles, California. Mr. Silver held senior engineer and marketing positions with McDonnell Douglas and Rockwell International before founding HSA. He passed away in 2011. Having been to courses that Hy Silver taught personally, I can attest directly that his expertise in the federal contracting community will be missed. Among his key proposal aphorisms were: "The road to the customer's judgment that you are the winner of a specific competition is very, very long." (Hy Silver's Executive Proposal Management School, Washington, D.C., April 1989.)

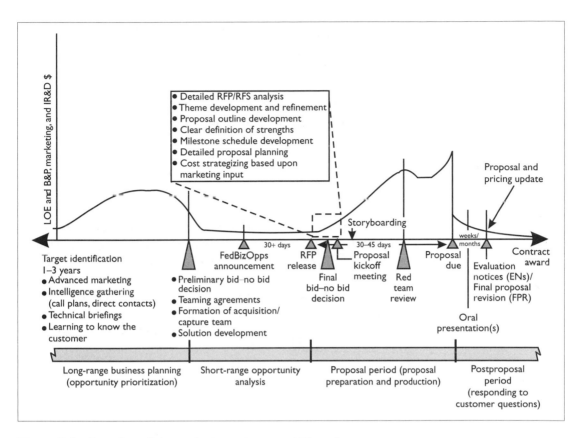

Figure 7.1 Overview of the marketing and proposal life cycle.

that the concepts and processes introduced in the following items will be expanded in subsequent chapters of this book.

Long-term, preliminary marketing intelligence collection and direct client contact

- Presell the client on your company's qualifications and commitment to complete the job successfully. Create customer sentiment[4] favorable to your company through technical briefings and discussions at various levels of the client's organization. Learn about such concerns as your client's technical requirements, business and mission goals, financial concerns, scheduling issues, and decision-making processes. Verify that the project is a real, funded target.

---

4   Hyman Silver coined the phrase.

For companies that provide support services, solutions built upon well-managed human talent and applicable contractual expertise are precisely what they are selling.

Formation of your company's acquisition/capture team for a particular qualified procurement opportunity

- Assemble a small team of management, marketing, and technical staff that will meet on a regular basis to develop a capture plan and share information gleaned from client contacts conducted in accordance with the call plan. Themes, or sales messages, for your proposal should begin to emerge—all focused on delivering *strengths* to the government in terms they see as being important. Identify your company's competitive strengths and weaknesses through a SWOT analysis. Identify staff and relevant project experience to be used in your upcoming proposal. For companies that provide support services, solutions built upon well-managed human talent and applicable contractual expertise are precisely what they are selling.

- Résumés and project descriptions (project citations or contract summaries) can be tailored and fine-tuned well in advance of the release of the final RFP. Take the time to gather the kinds of detailed educational, certification, technical, and programmatic experience information that your clients normally require in their RFPs. Because staffing and past performance are critical evaluation factors for award in many RFPs, and because collecting specific information on staff and projects can require so much time, it is highly advisable to get started early. Build this information into your automated proposal knowledge base.

Government's announcement of the procurement online at FedBizOpps (http://www.fedbizopps.gov)

Most RFPs are downloadable from government Web sites and portals such as Fed BizOpps. In some cases, your company must provide a written request to the appropriate government procuring agency for each particular RFP. However, telephone or facsimile requests are generally not accepted. E-mail requests are often acceptable.

- The time to market your client for a particular project is now closed. Once the RFP or RFS has "hit the street," agencies will not allow any marketing relevant to the project under competitive bid.

Release of the RFP by the specific government procuring agency or through a particular Web portal

- For select procurements, your company will have to register with your client to obtain password access to the specific RFP. In other cases, solicitation documents are posted on such sites as GSA eBuy (http://www.ebuy.gsa.gov/) and FedConnect (https://www.fedconnect.net/FedConnect)

Government preproposal (bidders) conference

- Plan to attend the preproposal conference. If allowed, prepare questions for the client and submit them in writing in advance of the conference.

- Pay attention to client requirements that may be mentioned at the conference but not written in the RFP. Some conferences might include facility or site visits. Check in advance to see if photography is permitted and, if so, take relevant photos or video.

Final internal bid–no bid decision

- All such decisions should be made according to defined, structured business criteria and include (at a minimum) a member of senior management, the business development or advanced planning staff, the appropriate division manager, a contracts/pricing representative, and the proposal manager.

- Good marketing intelligence will help to facilitate an appropriate business-based bid decision.

- What is the probability of winning?

- Favorable financial return is an important consideration.

- Does your company have the people and facilities necessary to prepare a superior proposal and perform the project successfully?

- Does the project have potential strategic business advantages to your company and is it in alignment with your strategic plan?

- Teaming arrangements must be considered by performing a gap analysis (see Figure 7.2) that identifies the "gap" between your competencies and experience and the government's requirements.

- Is your company the incumbent; if not, can you unseat the incumbent realistically?

Areas of Required Support in DRAFT Statement of Work (SOW)	DRAFT SOW/Industry Day Briefing/Vendor Q&A *Page Numbers*	Your Company's Competencies	Past Performance Validation/Comments
Enterprise-wide IT infrastructure and support services	SOW p. 1	High	
Seat management (Managed services contract)	SOW p. 1; Vendor Q&A, p. 1	High	
Server support for shared applications	SOW p.1	High	
IT research, development, and test	SOW p. 1	**GAP**	
ITIL-based service-oriented model (ITIL v3)	SOW p. 2	High	
Record of cost savings	SOW p. 2	High	
Performance-based contracting excellence	SOW p. 2	High	
Secure computing environment -IT Security Program Management -Network Security Center Management -IT Security Monitoring -Security Compliance Planning and Management	SOW pp. 3, 33	High	
LAN/WAN support	SOW p. 5	High	
Tier 2 Help Desk Support	SOW p. 5	High	
Geographically dispersed support	SOW p. 5	**Moderate**	
File Management	SOW p. 13		
Print Management	SOW p. 14		
FISMA, HSPD -12, FIPS 140 -2, Federal Desktop Core Configuration (FDDC)	SOW p. 15	High	
Life Cycle Management of Personal Computing	SOW p. 16	High	
Software License Management	SOW p. 17	High	
PC Risk Management	SOW p. 117	High	
Network Management	SOW p. 18	High	
Network Asset Management	SOW p. 18	High	
Systems Administration	SOW p. 18	High	
Maintenance and Patching Management	SOW p. 19	High	
Network Monitoring	SOW p. 119	High	
Remote Access Support	SOW p. 120		
Project Management	SOW p. 121	High	
High -Performance Computing (HPC)	SOW p. 126	**GAP**	
Service Catalog Management	SOW p. 128	**GAP**	
Capacity Management	SOW p. 129		
IT Service Continuity	SOW p. 1	High	

Figure 7.2 Use a detailed "gap analysis" to build your team in a structured and disciplined manner.

Refer to Figure 7.3 for a representative bid–no bid decision matrix. Your company might use a total score of 75 or higher to pursue a project.

Prekickoff planning meeting (conducted by the proposal manager)

It is often helpful for your small company's project managers (PMs) or program managers—the people who most likely will be called upon to serve as proposal managers—to envision the up-front proposal planning process in terms of deliverable products. These are very much analogous to the types of products that are integral to every program, project, task, and delivery order in your company's contractual experience base. Just as every PM develops

Date: _____

Client: _____
Project: _____
Prepared by: _____
Approved by: _____

GO: _____
NO GO: _____

	10	9	8	7	6	5	4	3	2	1	0	Ranking	Comments
Strategic relevance (how well does project fit company marketing strategy?)			Fits well with marketing strategy		Fits somewhat into the marketing strategy				Does not fit into marketing strategy				
Relationship with client			Close and excellent relationship with no problem projects		Fair or good relationship with some project problems				Strained relationship; problem project; selection questionable				
Knowledge of project			Strategic project/prior knowledge and marketing		Prior knowledge; no prior marketing				No prior knowledge or marketing				
Company staffing capabilities			Staff can perform all project requirements		Staff can perform most of the project requirements				Minimal or no staff capabilities				
Project competition			Competition manageable		Face formidable competition				Project wired for competition				
Company qualifications relative to competition			Technically superior; can demonstrate experience on similar contracts		Equivalent to competition; may have slight edge				Inferior to competition				
Potential for future work			Project will lead to future work		Possible future work				One-time project; no future work				
Profitability of project			Good profit potential		Moderate profit				Little profit				
Project schedule			More than adequate		Adequate				Not adequate				
Time, B&P costs, and resources to compete effectively for project			Favorable		Reasonable				Excessive				

Figure 7.3 A formalized bid–no bid decision matrix facilitates rational, business-based decision making.

and adjusts staffing levels to meet changing requirements, generates project milestone schedules in accordance with the client's requirements, and tracks project budgets to ensure cost control, so too must your proposal manager work with the capture manager and other staff in your company to develop a series of discrete products early in the proposal response life cycle, as shown in Figure 7.4. Particularly in very small companies, there may be insufficient overhead resources (nonbillable staff) available to maintain a proposal library or cybrary, provide proposal coordination support, assist with résumé and project summary development, and solidify teaming agreements. Those critical tasks must be accomplished by the proposal manager, and in a very limited time frame. The specific work products should be assembled in a document called the Proposal Directive (also called a Capture Plan).

The Proposal Directive is a carefully structured "living document" that serves as the "encyclopedia" of a win for a given procurement opportunity. During the course of the acquisition/capture and proposal process, the Proposal Directive may undergo 10 or more iterations as new intelligence about the competition, for example, is uncovered and other information (e.g., win themes) is further refined. The Proposal Directive is the repository that contains all of the relevant information about the customer organization, competition, specific program/project, and relevant processes and technologies (e.g., ITIL v3, SEI CMMI Maturity Level 3,

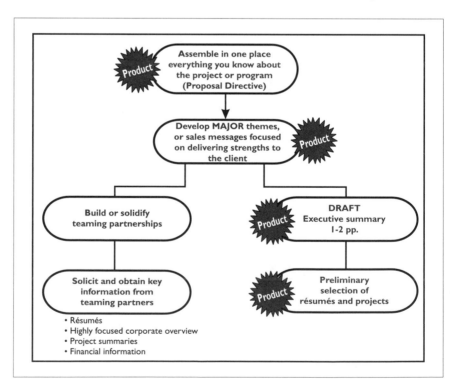

Figure 7.4
Critical prekickoff
proposal products.

ISO 9001:2008, and so forth). It contains the call plan reports from customer visits; a synopsis of the hopes, fears, biases, success criteria, and critical issues of key government decision makers; the win strategy white paper for your company along with the proposal outlines for each volume; win themes and discriminators; proposal response milestone schedule; and specific proposal-related action items. Thus, the *marketing intelligence* that Business Development staff gather is collected in the Proposal Directive. The *solution sets*[5] for the technical, management, staffing and key personnel, phase-in/phase-out, past performance, and pricing areas of the proposal that the Acquisition/Capture Team develop based on the marketing intelligence and research are documented in the Proposal Directive. And the *proposal development work products*—schedules, outlines, action items, and so forth—are also included within the Proposal Directive. It is important to note that the Proposal Directive is a highly competition-sensitive document and, therefore, must be safeguarded very carefully, through permission-based access to proposal portals and/or minimal hardcopies.

The following critical tasks are part of the prekickoff planning process.

- Develop a detailed outline for each proposal volume, using RFP Sections L, M, C, and H, as well as the Contract Data Requirements List (CDRL), Data Item Descriptions (DIDs), and RFP attachments as appropriate. Take the time to assign responsible parties to each section. Allocate pages to each section in accordance with the relative weighting of Section M evaluation criteria. For example, if past performance will count for 20% of the total score and there is a 50-page limit to the proposal, plan on approximately 10 pages for the past performance section.

- Develop a workable proposal response milestone schedule that includes adequate writing, review, recovery, production, QC, and shipping or uploading time.

- Develop and modify existing proposal themes. Themes are conclusive and compelling reasons why the client should select your company over and above your competitors.

- Select résumés and project summaries for the proposal.

- Generate a draft executive summary based upon your marketing intelligence win strategy white paper, and the evaluation factors found in Section M of the RFP. This will help to guide your writers

---

5   Think of a "solution" as a "choice"—a specific project organizational configuration, particular key personnel, one technical tool versus another, and so forth.

to produce consistent, well-integrated narrative and graphics. Include graphics in your executive summary if at all possible. A full-color foldout page (11 × 17 inches) that captures the technical and programmatic essence of your proposal is one high-impact way to sell the benefits of doing business with your company early in the proposal.

- Develop a preliminary design concept for the proposal volume covers.

- Identify critical supplies so that they can be ordered in advance (such as three-ring notebooks, special colored paper, customized tabbed divider pages, and specialized software[6]).

Proposal kickoff meeting [with subcontractor(s), if any] directed by the proposal manager

This meeting should be attended by senior management, appropriate marketing staff, the proposal manager, the proposal coordinator, all key technical staff who will be engaged in writing major sections of the proposal, key reviewers, a representative from contracts/pricing, and if necessary, a representative from human resources and a representative from publications.

- Emphasize team spirit, a winning attitude, and the support, commitment, and interest of senior management.

- Distribute detailed technical, management, and cost volume outlines as part of the Proposal Directive.

- Distribute DRAFT executive summary. Having a draft of the executive summary at this stage will help everyone involved in the proposal-writing process to better understand what the client expects. It will also help to establish the major strategic themes your company wants to integrate throughout the proposal.

- Share critical marketing intelligence about your client, and discuss key win strategies.

- Technical and management writing assignments are made, along with page limits (give writers an estimate of the number of words per page) and allocations (in accordance with Sections M and L of the RFP) and writing conventions (such as capitalization, hyphenation, and punctuation). Themes, critical issues of the project, and

---

6   Certain RFPs require that cost and technical volumes be submitted in specific software applications (e.g., Microsoft Word, Excel, Corel WordPerfect) and versions of those applications that your company may have to purchase.

success criteria are explained to the writers. Clear responsibilities for action items will be assigned.

- Stipulate electronic file formats, software application and version, and file configuration control procedures.

- Assignments are made to contracts/pricing and human resources staff.

- Items that require the approval of senior management should be presented and finalized.

- Address the criticality of proposal security for both electronic and hardcopy versions of the resulting proposal documents.

Storyboarding, to include the development of "elevator speeches," annotated outlines, and populated "pain tables"

Storyboarding (the associated work products are also referred to as "scenarios" and "scribble sheets") is a critical management process that focuses on building a coherent, consistent, and compelling proposal story. Building on the marketing intelligence and solution sets for a given procurement, key stakeholders in the proposal process (your capture manager, proposal manager, business development staff, subject matter experts, and so forth) meet in a series of brainstorming sessions and generate the following critical work products: (1) annotated outline for each major section of the proposal that provides an expanded architecture for each proposal section; (2) "elevator speeches" that tell the overarching story for each section; and (3) populated "pain tables" that illustrate your company's understanding of the customer's "pain points" and major issues, your approach/solution, and your company's value proposition (see Figures 7.5 through 7.8). Your value proposition includes the tangible and intangible benefits that your solution will bring to the customer organization.

Storyboarding allows your company and your proposal and capture teams to achieve the "right dive angle off the board." Just as a championship diver cannot adjust her position relative to the water when she's a mere foot above the surface, neither can a proposal team move in a fundamentally different direction when it is deep into the proposal response life cycle—at least not without a lot of depleted morale, extremely long hours, wasted resources, and interpersonal challenges across the team.

Coming out of the storyboarding process, one should be able to review the elevator speeches from end to end and grasp the entire fact-based storyline of the proposal response. Significantly, all of these work products that are developed during storyboarding are directly importable into your proposal. In addition, these can be augmented with "success stories," past

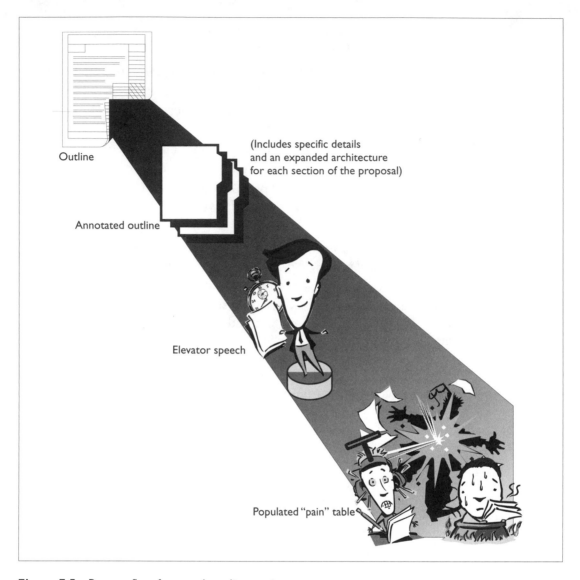

Outline

(Includes specific details
and an expanded architecture
for each section of the proposal)

Annotated outline

Elevator speech

Populated "pain" table

Figure 7.5 Process flow for storyboarding sessions.

performance validation, and features/benefits tables. Success stories might follow the "SAR Model"—Situation, Action, Results.

- *Situation* refers to the challenge or issue that the government was facing;
- *Action* combines the steps, people, processes, and tools your company used to address the issue;

Major work products

- Annotated outline
- Elevator speech
- Populated "pain table"

Sample elevator speech

Our team will employ a systems engineering life-cycle process to ensure effective IT infrastructure management at DOE HQ. Our team has collected and documented many best practices and lessons learned from our past systems design and engineering support activities. As recognized industry leaders in the provision of engineering support services, our team will provide exceptional support for DOE's Systems Engineering Environment. We are working together today within the DOE complex—at field sites, at operations offices, and at headquarters. We have a low-risk plan to ensure continuity of operations from Day One. Our approach is based on the Global Services Methodology (GSM), which recognizes the importance of corporate business drivers as the basis for technology change and complies with Federal Enterprise Architecture guidance throughout the systems engineering life cycle. GSM delivers consistent, repeatable processes to the management of systems design, engineering, installation, and maintenance activities.

Sample pain table

Understanding the Environment			Approach/Solution		Value Proposition
Major Issues	Contractor Challenges	Critical Success Factors	Process	Schedule	Measurable Outcomes
Improved Service Delivery	• Continuously maintaining high levels of service availability	• Measurable increased customer and stakeholder satisfaction	• Enhanced tools tied to TIVOLI to deliver near real-time network performance information	• Day 1-forward	• Exceed the current availability SLA metric • Increase network infrastructure MTBF
Reducing support costs incurred today because of redundant system solutions operating at HQ	• Overcome system engineering implementation inefficiencies and security vulnerabilities due to lack of central planning and coordination	• Successful network consolidation that centralizes systems engineering planning and operations currently performed in several HQ organizations	• Systems engineering planning is centralized using consolidated resources, configuration management processes, and a consistent, structured planning methodology	• Day 1-forward	• Better leverage valuable technical resources across HQ • Reduce redundant solutions • Minimize security vulnerabilities • Provide better incident response from the Help Desk • Improve unified solution ROI
Validating DOE Enterprise Architecture compliance	• Systems design and engineering must be driven by DOE Enterprise Architecture	• Architecture guidance and CPIC governance process are applied to technology and engineering projects consistently	• Integrate Architecture guidance and CPIC governance in the FOCUS Phase of project planning	• Day 1-180	• Exhibit 300 rationale for technical and engineering projects accepted by OMB on initial submission

Figure 7.6 Major work products emerging out of the storyboarding process.

- *Results* are the benefits that your firm provided in terms they see as important.

2.0	Management plan
2.1	Phase-in plan
2.2	Personnel management
2.2.1	Staffing plan
2.2.2	Cultural diversity plan
2.2.3	Training plan
2.2.4	Total compensation plan
2.3	Business management
2.3.1	Organization
2.3.1.1	Logistics
2.3.1.2	Imaging technology
2.3.1.3	Publishing
2.3.1.4	Metrology
2.3.1.5	Library
2.3.1.6	Administrative programs
2.3.1.7	Clerical support
2.3.2	Subcontract management
2.3.3	Management of government furnished property
2.3.4	Financial tracking database
2.4	Cost control plan
2.4.1	Cost-effectiveness
2.4.2	Cost fluctuation

Figure 7.7
Basic outline.

- *Features* refer to the assets, characteristics and attributes of your company's solution and competencies.
- *Benefits* are quantitatively and qualitatively robust strengths and advantages that your firm offers the government in support of a particular program, project, or task as well as their overarching business and missions goals.

Timely submission of first draft technical and management input to proposal manager. Graphics should be prepared and produced in close association with the text.

- Ongoing interaction and feedback between the capture manager, proposal manager, and the proposal writers are critical for developing a viable draft document quickly and efficiently.
- It is frequently beneficial to conceptualize key graphics before writing the associated narrative.

2.0	**Management plan**
2.1	Phase-in plan Preaward activities Establish transition "Tiger" team Conduct open house Prepare continuity of operations plan (COOP) Prepare security plan Prepare staffing plan Define subcontraction plan and IPT approach Identify transition challenges; define corrective action plan Postaward activities Kickoff meeting Deliver COOP, security, and staffing plans Advise and recruit Observe operation; collect intellectual knowledge Define invoice format
2.2	Personnel management Management tools and techniques Program management plan Task order management systems Performance measurements and metrics Personnel retention Resolution of personnel problems
2.2.1	Staffing plan General staffing plan and incumbent capture Key personnel, qualifications, certifications, security clearances, and commitment Other staff qualifications, certifications, clearances, and commitment Surge protection planning Staffing risks
2.2.2	Cultural diversity plan Company professional staff Community contributions
2.2.3	Training plan Comprehensive cross-training program Technical refresh training Speciality and mandatory training programs Security CBT awareness training
2.2.4	Total compensation plan Incentize employees Semiannual performance bonus program Spot "bonus" program Employee-of-the-month awards President's Award

Figure 7.8
Corresponding
annotated outline.

	Company benefits plan Prepaid tuition plan PC-buy program

2.3	Business management
	Process optimization
	    Use of industry's best practices
	    Incorporate lessons learned
	    Continuous communication improvements

2.3.1	Organization

2.3.1.1	Logistic
	Seat management
	Procurement management
	    Spares depot
	    Equipment repair and return services
	    Hardware and software purchasing
	Vendor management

2.3.1.2	Imaging technology
	Image tools
	    Access and viewing
	Image storage
	    Database management
	Image analysis

2.3.1.3	Publishing
	Content management and guidelines
	    Web development
	    Database management
	    Section 508 compliance
	    Export control compliance
	    Security

2.3.1.4	Metrology Measurement technology Calibration methods Metrology equipment and tools Metrology laboratories Standards

2.3.1.5	Library
	Organizational transformations
	    Information database
	    Search and browse tools
	    Change management

2.3.1.6	Administrative programs
	Content management
	    Program description storage
	    Accessing and viewing program information
	    Database security

Figure 7.8
(continued)

2.3.1.7	Clerical support Resource management Task order management Performance measurements Reporting and communication process
2.3.2	Subcontract management Finalize teaming agreement Define work assignments Establish performance monitoring, metrics, and measurements Define deliverables Implement cost control
2.3.3	Management of government-furnished property Property tracking and accountability GFE inventory Maintain software licenses Hardware and software upgrades
2.3.4	Financial tracking database
2.4	Cost control plan Collecting and aggregating labor hours and costs Controlling indirect rates and costs Using automated program management tools Deltek
2.4.1	Cost-effectiveness
2.4.2	Cost fluctuation Tracking and analyzing variances Establishing and documenting cost savings

Figure 7.8
(continued)

Editing and review of technical and management input

Submission of technical and management input to publication group

- Ensure that electronic files are compatible.
- A virtual private network (VPN), secure extranet, or firewalled File Transfer Protocol (FTP) site can be used for rapid file transfer from remote sites or teaming partners in other geographic locations. Mircosoft SharePoint 2010 and Privia by Spring CM are two options for collaborative workflow and document management.

The key is to use the Internet to transact business while simultaneously employing security technologies to ensure full confidentiality.

Submittal of cost and staffing information to contracts

- It is critical to conceptualize and develop the cost volume in close association with the technical and management volumes (see Figure 7.9). Staffing selections, technical solutions, facilities and information technology resources proposed, and your proposed management plan and organizational structure all can have profound cost impacts. Proposal costing is sophisticated business, not mere number crunching. The key is to have financial staff involved with direct program or project experience who can interact appropriately and effectively with the technical proposal team.

Preparation of complete first technical or management draft with one master copy only

Proofing and review of first draft

- Entire document frozen 24 hours prior to Red Team review.

Red Team review of technical, management, and cost volumes (1 to 2 days only)

Integration of all Red Team review comments (1 to 2 days) by proposal manager, selected technical staff, and the proposal coordinator (if needed)

Quality check of format and content by publication group

Preparation of second complete technical or management draft

Figure 7.9
Develop the cost volume in close association with the technical and management volumes.

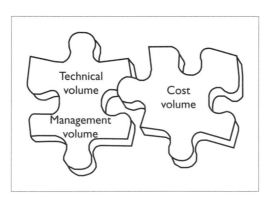

Proofing and review of draft

Preparation of revised cost volume

Gold Team final review of technical, management, and cost volumes

- Entire document frozen 72 hours prior to final delivery to client.

Final production, integration of text and graphics, quality check, photoreproduction, collation, assembly, and preparation for delivery (3 days)

Signatures on cover letter and cost proposal forms (it is suggested that you purchase a stamp that reads ORIGINAL)

Final delivery

- Late proposals cannot be accepted by the government (see FAR 14.304). Even 1 minute past due is still late! And with electronic uploads, 1/100th of a second past the due time on the government's server clock is too late. Request, obtain, and archive a time- and date-stamped receipt.

Archiving of hard and electronic copy of proposal text and graphics in your corporate library

- These materials should be stored along with all of the marketing intelligence documents, Freedom of Information Act (FOIA) requests, competitor information, the original RFP and amendments, and other materials relevant to this procurement. Being able to easily retrieve this material, even months or years later, is critical if you are required to respond to Evaluation Notices (ENs), submit a Final Proposal Revision (FPR), or deliver an oral presentation. This material should form the core of your proposal knowledge base for the recompetition.

Oral presentation defense, FPR, and facilities inspection

- Certain agencies require that FPR submittals or ENs be submitted as change pages to your original proposal submittal. Being able to retrieve your original submittal easily is a vital time saver.

- Take time to strategize and develop a powerful, well-rehearsed presentation.

Attend government debriefing when your company is an unsuccessful offeror and also when you win (see FAR 15.1003). Learn why you won.

Develop lessons learned (also called an after-action review) and discuss with key proposal staff. Share lessons learned with other proposal managers. Archive and review these lessons, looking for patterns.

7.3 Bid-no bid decision-making process

Being very selective with the procurements your company decides to pursue is a first step toward long-term proposal and general business development success. Careful selection of bid opportunities improves your proposal win probability and maximizes the return on general and administrative (G&A) dollars your company has invested in the proposal effort (see Figure 7.10). Identifying sufficient high-dollar, high-probability opportunities for which your company is qualified is a necessary step prior to selection of particular targets. The essence of the bid–no bid downselection process relates to four primary factors.

- *The probability of winning.* Does the client know your company and does your company know the client? Is there an incumbent contractor? Is that contractor performing satisfactorily? What is the nature of the relationship between the incumbent and the client? Does marketing intelligence indicate that your company is in a favorable competitive position to win?

- *The reality of the procurement.* Will the program or project receive funding and will the competition be genuine, or does the government really intend to retain the incumbent?

- *The desirability of obtaining the contract.* What are the profit expectations? Will the contract result in a strategic business advantage for your company, such as a foothold in a new geographic location or market sector? Importantly, will the procurement align with and support your company's stated objectives as presented in your strategic plan and mission statement? What are the inherent risks and liabilities? What is the add-on or follow-on potential? Does the

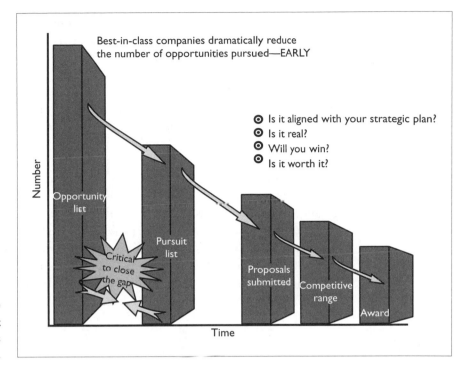

Figure 7.10
Downselect
opportunities
early.

procurement require any up-front capital expenditure or cost sharing by your company? Will new staff with specific subject matter
expertise have to be recruited and hired?

- *The necessary facilities, resources, and human talent to perform the
work on schedule and within budget, as well as to prepare a compliant and credible proposal that also tells a compelling, client-focused
story.* Are the very best staff available to write and review the proposal documents? Are there other key competing proposal priorities
that will dilute the effectiveness of the proposal development group?
Is there secure floor and wall space available in your facilities to
house and support a proposal team? Are there sufficient computers
and high-output printers that will be able to be dedicated to the proposal publication effort?

The bid–no bid process must balance the cost of responding; the
availability of human, material, and other resources; and the magnitude of
the business opportunity. The availability of in-house or consultant staff,
facilities, and equipment resources to provide effective proposal support
cannot alone drive the decision-making process but certainly must be
considered. If your company cannot commit the best resources to prepare
the proposal, then you should strongly reconsider any decision to bid the

procurement, at least as the prime contractor. For the small business, the vice president of business development must perform this downselection process, working with a multidisciplinary team. The company's owners should get involved as well.

The major objective of the bid–no bid process is to arrive at a rational, business-based consensus within your company to pursue or not pursue a given procurement opportunity. It is advisable to conduct both a preliminary (pre-RFP release) and final (post-RFP release) bid–no bid decision. This applies to small as well as large companies.

Poor bid–no bid decision making is arguably the most common cause of business development failure in the federal contracting marketplace. Many U.S. small businesses fail within their first 5 years of operation[7]. Merely because your company has related technical expertise does not mean that you have a high probability of winning the business or that the business fits strategically with your goals and direction. The shotgun approach to business development and proposal development will be unsuccessful in the long term. Laser-like focus will serve you much better.

7.4 Planning and organizing

Once you receive an RFP or RFS, your acquisition/capture team for that procurement should conduct an audit of the document, carefully mapping and accounting for all requirements, including the CDRL and DIDs. Review the staffing level requirements and position descriptions in the RFP. Formulate appropriate questions to be submitted in writing to the government for clarification. Be prudent in asking questions because your competitors will be given or see posted copies of those questions along with the government's response.

Various automated tools are available to support the RFP analysis and proposal development processes. These software products include RFPMaster, Qvidian (formerly Sant and Kadient) (http://www.qvidian.com), Meridian for RFP Analysis (XRSolutions; http://xrsolutions.com), and GovWin CRM (Deltek; http://www.deltek.com).

---

7   Economic survival is a very real challenge for small business leaders. Data from the U.S. Small Business Administration's *Small Business Economy Report to the President* [3] indicate that in the period 1995–2006, there were more than 500,000 small business "deaths" *each* year.

7.4.1 Draft executive summary

Prior to your company's formal kickoff meeting for each procurement effort, an individual appointed by the capture manager should prepare a one- to two-page executive summary that introduces high-level themes, demonstrates your company's understanding of the importance of the client's project or program, indicates that your company has the credentials and talent to do the project, provides an overview of your company's approach, as well as its direct benefits to the client and his mission, and highlights key project staff and past performance.

Your executive summary should applaud your client and your client's achievements. It should honor—and demonstrate your alignment with—your client's mission and vision. In addition, it should be structured to address in summary form the evaluation factors found in Section M of the RFP. Help your client understand exactly how your company will enhance their mission achievements, funding, business processes, congressional notoriety, technical excellence, and so forth.

7.4.2 Theme development

A theme is a substantiated sales message, a point of emphasis, an advantage, a unique or superior benefit, or a supported claim. Themes reappear, woven inextricably throughout the proposal volumes and serve to focus and unify the entire presentation (see Figure 7.11). A good theme is direct,

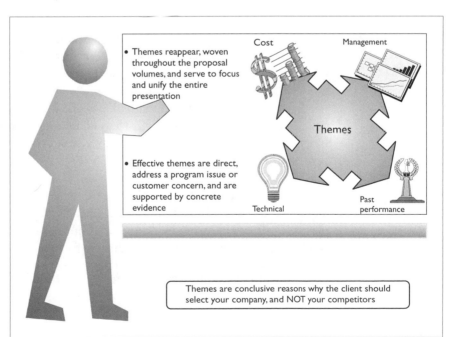

Figure 7.11
Themes are major story elements in your proposal.

addresses a program issue or customer concern, and is supported by concrete evidence. Your company's strengths and the competition's weaknesses can be the bases for themes. Themes are highly sensitive material and should always be marked as competition-sensitive materials when distributed to staff throughout your company and extended team for review and comment. It is suggested that your company purchase ink stamps that read Competition-Sensitive.

There are two types of themes: (1) common themes and (2) unique themes, or discriminators. Common themes, although obvious and unprofound, are still important to incorporate into your proposal. Your company, being located within 5 miles of the front gate of NASA Goddard Space Flight Center (GSFC) and thus available to support customer needs quickly, is an example of a common theme because many times this is an expectation on the part of NASA GSFC. Unique themes, or discriminators, are based upon particular advantages your company can offer and upon distinct disadvantages of your competition. Discriminators are vital, credible points that are meaningful to your client (i.e, *strengths* to your client) and constitute the real sales hooks. You need to do your marketing intelligence-gathering homework to identify these discriminators and then locate them at appropriate points in the proposal documents. Perhaps your company is the only known proposer that has developed personal-computer-based air-traffic-controller instructional materials for a particular office of the FAA. A discriminator that you would certainly include in your proposal is a statement that highlights this unique contractual experience and the value that this brings to the government. It should appear, as appropriate, in section headings, the narrative, graphics, and captions. This message can also be conveyed via photographs or your proposal volume cover design. You can even reinforce this important unique theme in your compliance matrix.

In small proposals (fewer than 50 pages), your company may wish to develop 8 to 10 major themes and 15 to 20 minor (or subsection) themes. In larger proposal efforts, there may be 25 or more major themes and several hundred minor themes.

The following are select examples of themes. The particular procurement situation dictates whether these may be common or unique, major or minor. In all cases, thematic statements must be tailored for the particular client and program or project. Importantly, each theme must be validated by quantitative and/or qualitative facts.

- Best practices and lessons learned from our phase-ins with ONR, NAVAIR, and DOE will be applied to ensure a smooth transition from day one of this important contract.

- Our real-time supervision and automated performance assessment methods have proven to be responsive and timely for other USACE clients.

- Our competitive benefits have proven to be a powerful tool for motivating and retaining key personnel, thus ensuring full continuity of operations.

- Our exemplary past performance with the U.S. Navy is the credibility base for this procurement.

- Our innovative technical approach based upon SEI CMMI®–structured methodologies allows for cost effective software engineering with a focus on your stakeholders' requirements.

- We offer established relationships with world-class computer science departments at universities such as George Washington University to ensure an ongoing, accessible base of talent.

- We understand and have direct experience with the Clinger-Cohen Act and the Department of Energy's IT capital planning requirements and financial planning.

- We will ensure continuity of operations (COOP) through industry-trend-setting employee retention rates made possible by superlative, yet cost-competitive fringe benefits.

- We will use specific, mutually agreed-upon metrics to quantify and monitor customer perceptions of and satisfaction with our level of technical proficiency and interpersonal skill.

- As extensions of the Air Combat Command's staff in Europe, much of our energy will be dedicated to developing and supporting solutions-based decision making consistent with the external and internal drivers that impact day-to-day operational activities.

- We will address problem resolution proactively and positively in the context of partners working toward common goals.

- We will conduct business at the operational level in strict accordance with FIP, commercial leasing, and software licensing procedures and protocols.

- The ABC team: superlative service built upon knowledge, common sense, and that intangible personal touch.

- We have a high level of competence demonstrated by NASA customer-approval ratings of 97.0% in the last quarterly review period.

- The accuracy of our cost and labor projections, as well as our accountability, are illustrated by costs being within 2% of budget each month.

- We will prove to be highly capable representatives as we honor the daily and big-picture needs of an agency whose work and mission are critical to the economic health of America within the global marketplace.

- Our management and procurement structures have been specifically designed to support accelerated schedules, immediate mobilization, and midcourse changes.

- We will support DOE's Strategic Action Plan and the Department's innovative e-government initiatives to help achieve alignment with the Federal CIO's "25 Point Implementation Plan to Reform Federal Information Technology."

- Our cost-effective approach to environmental solutions meshes closely with the USACE's nationwide initiative to improve business practices and to produce quality results.

- Our well-established advocacy, mentoring, and practice of process control and checking also links with the Navy's emphasis on process improvements directed toward revolutionizing effectiveness, being more responsive to customer needs, and being more accountable to taxpayers.

- We transitioned the contract in Savannah River with 100% retention of qualified, incumbent personnel, while maintaining 99.89% system availability at all levels.

- Our networked environment, business culture of technical resource and knowledge sharing, proactive administrative support, and ongoing project communication facilitated by our Web portal will ensure that staff and resources are on the job when and where they are needed to support the U.S. Postal Service.

- We are able to propose proven leadership that allows program continuity while preserving program institutional knowledge.

- ABC Company has crafted a very effective, successful, and proven recruitment process. We have cultivated a companywide business culture that attracts and retains highly talented professionals.

- This single-vendor management approach will eliminate program accountability complexities, reduce costs, and minimize overall management risks and personnel issues and concerns to the Department of Health and Human Services.

- We bring an established track record of competing and submitting 96% of deliverables to the Department of Transportation ahead of schedule.

- Our demonstrated record of careful cost controls will result in best-value support to NOAA throughout the life of the contract.

- In-house IR&D on interactive software is directly applicable to the technical solution for this important NASA/MSFC project, thereby saving you money.

- The total Washington, D.C.–based data management resources of our company will be available for application to specific needs of this important EPA program through our program manager.

- COTS hardware that we have proven in similar situations will minimize start-up time requirements, development costs, and reduce the phase-in period.

- Dedicated, hand-picked software engineer offers 18 years of documented success in developing and managing automated systems for the DoD.

- All our proposed professional staff are currently working successfully on the existing contract and hold active secret clearances.

- We will leverage our automated trend analysis database to support risk mitigation.

- Proximity of our company's headquarters to Fort Bliss will ensure effective, real-time communications with the COTR and CO.

- We are a progressive minority-owned firm with an established $3 million line of credit to ensure financial flexibility and stability.

- Our company staffs and maintains an office within 5 miles of the IRS work site.

- Our company was the incumbent on the last modeling and simulation project, which successfully formed the basis for this one.

- Our company has served the Air Force Center for Environmental Excellence (AFCEE) successfully for the past 2 years. Our legacy of field-tested performance...

- State-of-the-art technology meets the EPA's current and projected requirements; that is, no new technology is needed.

- An excellent team of well-qualified, well-integrated subcontractors reduces program risk. We know how to work together successfully.

- Our company's organizational structure has a one-to-one correlation with the Air Force's project organization for ease of interface and communication.

- Our QA-QC program, already implemented at McClellan AFB, will ensure rapid problem isolation and resolution.

- Our integrated project team (IPT) approach will focus upon the formulation of small, agile teams to evaluate emerging technologies and offer informed, context-based business and technical recommendations.

Your company's Acquisition/Capture Team members should convey appropriate themes to your client during the client contact and marketing phases of the proposal life cycle. Then, when those themes reappear in the proposal, the client will tend to view them as natural outcomes of previous conversations and meetings rather than unvarnished marketeering tactics. And once again, themes should be woven into the proposal body, carefully integrated into headings, text, captions, figures and tables, and even compliance matrices (under a comments section).

7.4.3 Storyboards

Proposals are choreographed exercises in knowledge and information management, assembly, and packaging.

Storyboards, bullet drafts, scenarios, mock-ups, and scribble sheets[8] are proposal tools designed to break the proposal planning, control, and tracking process into bite-sized pieces. Proposal choreography provides the proposal manager with a mechanism designed to develop a coherent, consistent document from multiple authors with varying degrees of writing skill in a limited time frame. Storyboards help to ensure that all RFP or RFS requirements are addressed. They also assist in linking text with graphics and help technical authors overcome any initial writer's block. Many times these tools prove vital for coordinating subcontractor input. Choreographic techniques are most effective and appropriate for the technical volume of a proposal, but can certainly be applied to other volumes as well.

Select proposal choreographic guidelines include the following:

- Identify the scope and context of the section or subsection to be choreographed.

---

8   Proposal choreography, that is, the manner by which a proposal response is planned, controlled, and tracked section-by-section, can be referred to by a variety of names: storyboards (a term borrowed from Hollywood moviemaking), bullet drafts, scenarios (the method of Hyman Silver and Associates), mock-ups (a process used by Shipley Associates), and scribble sheets (a method employed by the former TRW, now part of Northrop Grumman). Choreography will be used herein to refer interchangeably to storyboards, bullet drafts, scenarios, mock-ups, and scribble sheets.

- Identify appropriate sections of the RFP or RFS that correspond to that particular proposal section or subsection.
- Develop an introductory paragraph called an "elevator speech" (see Figure 7.12) that sets the tone and provides the emphasis and focus for the narrative of the section or subsection. The elevator speech should convey the "essence of your offer" in a given proposal section.
- Prepare major and minor theme statements for the section or subsection.
- Prepare five to eight statements that clarify and direct your writing approach for the section or subsection. These short statements are to include the major and minor points to address in the narrative. The bullet statements are to build upon and resonate with the thematic statements.
- Generate key graphic concepts and compose a thematically meaningful caption, one that focuses on benefits to the client.

Figure 7.12
Building your
elevator speech.

- Prepare a concluding or summation sentence for the section or sub-section that focuses on the evidence for the government concluding that your company offers significant strengths to them.

The number of storyboards, bullet drafts, or scenarios to be developed for any given proposal depends upon the complexity of the RFP. Small procurement efforts, for example, might only require 10 to 15 storyboard sheets. A sample bullet draft worksheet is shown in Figure 7.13 and a representative storyboard form is presented in Figure 7.14.

Proprietary Bullet Draft Worksheet

Proposal volume:	Subsection number:	Writer:	
Subsection author:		Page limit:	Due date:
RFP requirement:			
Discriminator:			
Themes:			
Features:		**Benefits:**	

Introductory paragraph or elevator speech (verbatim):

Major points (bullet format):

Concluding sentence (verbatim):

Approved by: _____   Date: _____

Figure 7.13
Sample bullet draft worksheet.

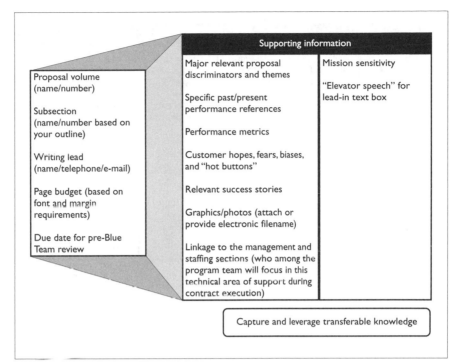

Figure 7.14
Storyboard
template.

7.5 Kickoff meeting

The formal kickoff meeting is your capture manager's and proposal manager's best opportunity to inspire and imbue their team with a winning attitude. The proposal manager can do this most effectively if he can demonstrate that he has planned carefully, organized a workable proposal response schedule, and made the best use of company resources. The attendance of your company's senior management during the kickoff meeting is highly desirable in order to ensure that the importance of the procurement to your firm's future is communicated in person.

7.6 Writing

The goal of each proposal author is to obtain the maximum score for each subsection. This is accomplished most effectively when writers follow the storyboards or bullet drafts carefully. Proposal writing is not recording as much as one knows about a given technical or programmatic topic. Too often, technical staff who are assigned to write proposal sections merely provide a voluminous quantity of material that does not address the specific elements contained within the RFP, nor does it mesh effectively with

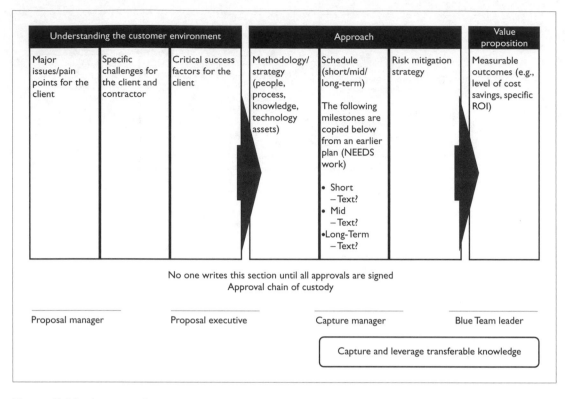

Figure 7.14 (continued)

the narrative and graphics prepared by the other authors. Quantity alone is totally inadequate to yield a winning response. Crisp, distilled writing focused on the benefits to the customer that follows the RFP precisely and is complemented by appropriate graphics and photographs is a major step in the right direction.

One goal of preproposal intelligence gathering is to have assembled a hardcopy or electronic technical library of documents relevant to the procurement at hand. Your proposal writers should consult this resource material in advance of the release of the RFP. In addition, the government often provides contractors with access to a technical library of project documents once the RFP is released. These resources can provide the basis for the detailed, client- and program-specific narrative that is a requirement for successful proposals. Papers and technical documents will help illuminate the types of technical issues of interest and concern to your client. You will want to demonstrate a strong understanding of these issues.

Writers should also keep in mind that in the case of multiyear projects, they must prepare a response that factors in evolutionary program growth and change, as well as *technology insertion*, the addition of advanced technological modules or elements into an existing infrastructure.

Metrics—explicitly *quantitative* measures of success—are an important means of validating the themes and the storylines of your proposals. As illustrated in Figure 7.15, metrics may encompass both *technical* (e.g., business system availability) and *programmatic* (e.g., schedule compression by X days) parameters. These metrics should be integrated into the text and graphics of your proposals, as appropriate.

Oftentimes, proposal writers need additional insights into the customer's mission, vision, leadership, business goals, strategic plan, and programmatic organization. This is where the Web is so valuable in today's proposal process. Each federal government organization maintains an extensive repository of such information at its agency Web site (see Figure 7.16), and many agencies publish and make public important and insightful publications, such as the Navy's *Mayport Mirror* (Mayport, Florida; http://www. mayportmirror.com), the *Army Times* (http://www.armytimes.com/) and the *Missile Ranger* at White Sands Missile Range in Las Cruces, New Mexico (http://www.missileranger.com).

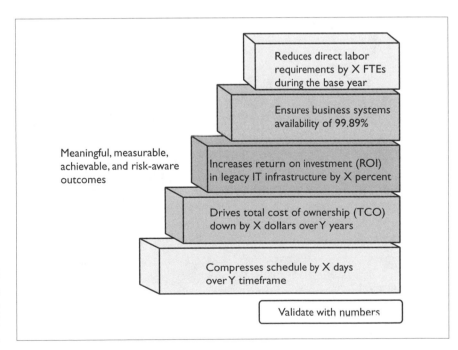

Figure 7.15
Metrics are essential for telling your fact-based story.

Figure 7.16
Web-based
research is valuable
for proposal
success.

What can you learn and use from such Web-based information? In particular, you can begin to see patterns in your customer's *presentation of itself* and its actions—patterns that include repeated keywords, images, icons, color schemes, phrases, and priorities. Then, as appropriate, based on specific marketing insight into this customer, these patterns can be driven into your proposal across several key areas such as the Executive Summary and oral presentation, as shown in Figure 7.17. *Your goal?* To let your customers see themselves in your proposal. When an evaluator reviews your submittal, she should be able to look at it and say, "Yes, I can

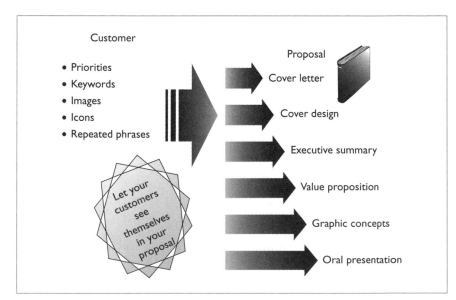

Figure 7.17
Driving mission
sensitivity into
your proposal.

see my program in here. And this company really understands the issues that are important to me and offers meaningful solutions in words and graphics that I recognize."

To continue, the Web offers additional important resources for proposal writers. Frequently, writers need some help getting started with their sections that goes above and beyond the "elevator speech," annotated outline, and populated "pain table." Figure 7.18 offers a number of extremely beneficial Web sites that can be leveraged to provide key jumping-off points for initial paragraphs as well as insight into the most recent industry best practices. I find the Gartner site (http://www.gartner.com) of particular benefit. The white papers or position papers offered at that site for a modest charge are invaluable as sources from which to glean sound ideas for writing.

7.7 Major contractor review cycles

Proposals are important vehicles for bringing bookings, and ultimately revenue, into your company. To maximize your win probability, all proposals

Figure 7.18
Web sites you
should use and
bookmark.

that your company produces should be subject to careful internal review before delivery to your client. Senior management endorsement of and participation in the review cycles is strongly encouraged. The purpose of the color team reviews is to determine if the *strengths* that your company offers the government are clear, validated, and very apparent. In addition, reviews assess the responsiveness of the proposal to the given RFP or RFS; ensure that your company's themes are apparent throughout the entire proposal; identify any statements that could be misrepresentative of your company or of the potential client; and provide concrete suggestions for improvement in such areas as structure, strategy, technical approach, risk management, benefits to the government, and pricing. Reviews are not exercises in fault-finding, but rather are the objective, solutions-oriented critique of vital company documents. Figure 7.19 shows a flow diagram of the internal review process. Note the close link between technical/

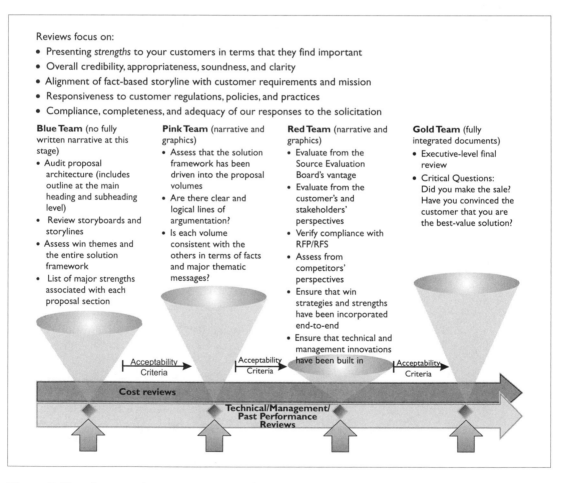

Reviews focus on:
- Presenting *strengths* to your customers in terms that they find important
- Overall credibility, appropriateness, soundness, and clarity
- Alignment of fact-based storyline with customer requirements and mission
- Responsiveness to customer regulations, policies, and practices
- Compliance, completeness, and adequacy of our responses to the solicitation

Blue Team (no fully written narrative at this stage)
- Audit proposal architecture (includes outline at the main heading and subheading level)
- Review storyboards and storylines
- Assess win themes and the entire solution framework
- List of major strengths associated with each proposal section

Pink Team (narrative and graphics)
- Assess that the solution framework has been driven into the proposal volumes
- Are there clear and logical lines of argumentation?
- Is each volume consistent with the others in terms of facts and major thematic messages?

Red Team (narrative and graphics)
- Evaluate from the Source Evaluation Board's vantage
- Evaluate from the customer's and stakeholders' perspectives
- Verify compliance with RFP/RFS
- Assess from competitors' perspectives
- Ensure that win strategies and strengths have been incorporated end-to-end
- Ensure that technical and management innovations have been built in

Gold Team (fully integrated documents)
- Executive-level final review
- Critical Questions: Did you make the sale? Have you convinced the customer that you are the best-value solution?

Acceptability Criteria

Acceptability Criteria

Acceptability Criteria

Acceptability Criteria

Cost reviews

Technical/Management/ Past Performance Reviews

Figure 7.19   Structured review process results in excellent end products.

management and cost volume reviews. Additional insight into the goals of internal proposal meetings and reviews is presented in Figure 7.20.

In organizations that do a significant percentage of their business with the federal government, the proposal review process is generally associated with a series of formalized color reviews, such as Blue, Green, Pink, Red, and Gold. However, regardless of the level of structure or formality of your internal review process, there are several key elements to keep in mind.

Put yourself in the shoes of your customer's evaluators when performing your internal review. These are the people who grade your proposal "test." Your proposal is *not* about your organization. Rather, it is about how your organization will be of direct benefit to your customer and your customer's career, program, stakeholders, business, and mission. You will certainly need to ensure that your proposal is fully compliant with the requirements set forth in your customer's formal solicitation document, such as the RFP or RFS. However, compliance is a necessary but insufficient condition to win. To win with a high level of consistency (greater than 60%), every section and subsection of your proposal documents—for example, Technical, Management, Staffing, Phase-In, and Past Performance—must be focused on how your people, approaches, solutions, technologies, and past performance will add substantive value to your customer in terms they find meaningful (e.g., quality, schedule, cost, and risk management).

In addition, you will want to ensure that the marketing intelligence that you gained about your *customer's* hopes, fears, biases, and critical issues; your *competitors'* strengths and weaknesses; applicable *technologies and key practices* such as Software Engineering Institute (SEI) Capability Maturity Model Integration® (CMMI®) and Information Technology Infrastructure Library (ITIL); and relevant *political conditions* and developments are woven into your proposal in such a way as to support your overarching proposal "story." Customer intelligence and insight are the direct result of multiple face-to-face meetings over time with key customer decision makers—also known as "sell points."

7.7.1 Blue or Pink Team

The Blue or Pink Team evaluations are generally early course correction reviews. Front-end load your proposal response schedule to ensure that solution development is completed and work products reviewed *before* the actual writing begins. The fundamental technical architecture and pro-grammatic direction of your company's proposal should be evaluated at this stage, defi- ciencies identified and articulated, and corrective actions and specific solutions offered. Avoid focusing on formatting, aesthetic, edi-torial, or page-count aspects of the proposal documents at this early stage.

Kickoff Meeting

Ensure that all participants fully understand the team's goals and plans for developing the proposal.

Goal

Communicate the proposal development process, including themes, writing assignments, and mile-stones.

Storyboard Session

The storyboarding session is a roll-up-the-sleeves working session to develop the main thematic structure, technical and management solutions, and graphics for the technical and management volumes and oral presentation. Representatives must process the depth of technical and program-matic expertise necessary to develop a winning solution.

Goal

Develop the proposed solutions and the main thematic and graphics structure for technical and management volumes.

Pink Team Review

The purpose of Pink Team is to provide an early architectural assessment of the proposal—to answer the question, Is the proposal structured appropriately? Managers with a good under-standing of this customer and this RFP should attend to provide an objective, fresh look at the proposal. Each attendee should read and be familiar with the final RFP as well as the latest proposal directive, before the meeting. The Pink Team attendees should be prepared to support the Red Team— continuity is critical.

Goal

Develop a clear consensus for required structural changes, modified staffing solution, and any revisions to the technical approach. The important objective is for reviewers to provide actionable guidance.

Pink Team Debrief

Directly following the Pink Team Review, reviewers will explain their Pink Team review findings to the proposal writers. Proposal writers are expected to join the reviewers for this debriefing.

Goal

Communicate the consensus of the review to the writers. Provide priorities and direction for continuing proposal development efforts.

Figure 7.20 Internal proposal meeting and review process goals.

Red Team Review

The purpose of Red Team is to serve as a mock government source evaluation board. Evaluations must be guided primarily by Section M of the RFP or RFS as well as the Statement of Work (SOW) or the Performance Work Statement (PWS) and Sections L, H, etc. Reviewers must develop a consensus on the findings and recommendations. Red Team attendees have participated in the Pink Team review and understand the direction and guidance defined at Pink Team review.

Goal

Assess the responsiveness of the entire proposal to the evaluation factors for award. Answer the question, Is this a winning proposal?

Red Team Debrief

Directly following the Red Team Review, reviewers will explain their findings to the proposal writers. Proposal writers are again expected to join the reviewers for this debrief.

Goal

Communicate the consensus of the review to the writers. Provide priorities, direction, and actionable guidance for continuing proposal development efforts.

Gold Team Review

The Gold Team Review is limited to executive management staff. The purpose is to perform a high-level review of the final proposal.

Goal

Ensure adequate integration of Red Team comments and direction.

Oral-Presentation Practice Sessions

The purpose of these practice sessions is to evaluate the presentation slides, key messages, and presenters under simulated presentation conditions. The presentation will be timed. The speakers will practice and receive actionable guidance on the presentation.

Goal

Ensure Team provides an effective, compelling, and winning presentation.

Figure 7.20 (continued)

If possible, electronic configuration control of the proposal documents should remain in the hands of the proposal technical writing team up through the response to and integration of Pink or Blue Team comments. An interactive meeting should take place between the reviewers and the proposal writing team once the review is complete in order to clearly communicate the strengths and weaknesses of the proposal effectively. The focus is on substantive corrective solutions. Such comments as "beef up this section," "weak," "needs work," or "rewrite this part" are not helpful. Comments beneficial to the proposal writers include "Enhance Section 4.6 by discussing specific automated cost and schedule control applications, particularly as they are compatible with …" or "Augment your discussion of technical and contractual interfaces with the Navy by including a graphic that clearly indicates points of contact. A rough sketch of this graphic is attached." Reviewers should attempt to provide specific guidance, direction, and solutions, as well as encouragement.

7.7.2 Red Team

The Red Team functions as an internal SEB, critiquing the proposal for compliance with RFP instructions and evaluation criteria (as found in Sections L and M, respectively, of the RFP). The Red Team looks for consistency and continuity among sections and volumes (intervolume compatibility), inclusion of sales messages and win strategies, presence and substantiation of strengths to the government, themes, clarity of text and artwork, and overall believability and persuasiveness. The capture manager and proposal manager will determine how to respond to the Red Team comments, particularly when there is disagreement among reviewers. Figure 7.21 presents a sample proposal reviewer's comment sheet.

The Red Team serves as a recommending group. Logistically, the Red Team reviewers should be fully dedicated to the effort, preferably colocated and isolated from the day-to-day demands of business during the course of their review. Red Team reviewers should include a number of people with appropriate technical competence and persons with high degrees of marketing and management competence. No reviewer should have participated in the proposal writing effort for sections they are assigned to review. Red Teaming is not merely an editorial exercise. Make available a copy of the full RFP to Red Team members, along with any amendments and a full kickoff meeting package (proposal directive) that includes your major and minor themes and completed storyboards or bullet drafts. The proposal manager should provide written instructions to the Red Team reviewers explaining what the expectations of the review process are and asking that comments be detailed and explicit so that the proposal team can respond effectively to those comments. The Red Team

Red Team Evaluation Report

Proposal Title _____   Reviewer _____
Volume No./Title _____   Date _____
Section or Block No./Title _____

Criteria	Evaluation				
	Good	Average	Inadequate	Not Applicable	Cannot Judge
1. Overall impact (scoring potential)	❏	❏	❏	❏	❏
2. Readability and understandability	❏	❏	❏	❏	❏
3. Responsiveness to RFP requirements	❏	❏	❏	❏	❏
4. Responsiveness to evaluation criteria	❏	❏	❏	❏	❏
5. Theme inclusion	❏	❏	❏	❏	❏
6. Presentation format (including graphics)	❏	❏	❏	❏	❏
7. Technical content quality	❏	❏	❏	❏	❏
8. Believability and persuasiveness	❏	❏	❏	❏	❏

Specific suggestions for improvement:

Figure 7.21   Sample proposal reviewer's comment sheet.

proposal draft should include a table of contents, compliance matrix, and list of acronyms.

The Red Team review is designed to assess the following:

- Overall impact and competitiveness of proposal;
- Readability and understandability;
- Compliance with RFP or RFS requirements—both overt and hidden;
- Inclusion of major and minor themes;
- Effectiveness of the presentation, including graphics and photographs;
- Quality of technical and programmatic content;

- Believability and persuasiveness of the story (are the specific benefits and strengths to the client very apparent?).

Because compliance with the RFP or RFS is *necessary but not sufficient* for proposal success, it is important that your Red Team review process take several additional steps beyond compliance verification. As portrayed in Figure 7.22, assign specific Red Team members to also assess whether your win strategies have been woven throughout your proposal, or do they appear on page 2 and not again until the end of the document? Another Red Team member could validate that your company's proposed innovations and forward-looking solutions indeed appear throughout the sections of the proposal. As an insightful DOE contracting officer once told me and my company's capture and proposal team at the postproposal debriefing, "Compliance + validated storyline + comprehensible presentation = high win probability." We had attended this particular debriefing following a $425 million contract award!

When conducting Red Team reviews, most organizations employ a "vertical" type process that focuses on specific parts of the proposal. Unfortunately, these types of section- or volume-specific reviews are essentially "stovepiped" exercises that do not consider continuity and alignment of messaging and storyline throughout the entire proposal. Instead, primary attention is given to proposal *compliance* and *structure*.

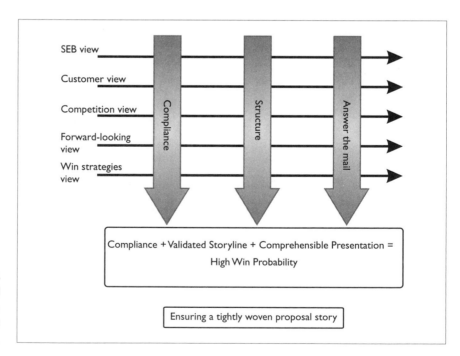

Figure 7.22
Red Team should conduct both vertical and horizontal reviews.

One often hears the expression—"We have to answer the mail." And, yes, you do, but that's not enough.

The winning proposal is the one which, as evaluated by the customer, is demonstrably different and superior when evaluated against *stated* and *unstated* criteria. The stated criteria are those requirements found in the RFP or RFS documents as well as amendments and other publicly available materials. These are the requirements to which every bidder has access. That is why merely answering the mail—in effect, responding to the stated requirements—is not good enough to win.

Here's where the "horizontal" type of internal proposal review comes into play. Conducted in close conjunction with the vertical, section-specific review, the horizontal review ensures that your proposal "story" built on the hard-won marketing intelligence about your customer and competitors appears throughout your proposal. It's the marketing intelligence gained from the customer set that provides the unstated criteria—details about what they are really looking for but will not put in writing in the solicitation. The horizontal review helps to ascertain that your major sales messages (known in proposal parlance as "themes") and overarching proposal storyline carry through from page 1 of your proposal to the final page. Far too often, a company's proposal starts off rich in sales messages, and after page 3 or 4, these important messages are never seen again in the entire document.

So take the time to conduct an integrated set of vertical and horizontal proposal reviews, and then take action to respond to the substantive comments that emerge from the review processes. Your proposal win probability will most certainly increase, which in turn means more bookings and increased revenues for your organization. And that translates to sustained business growth.

The recommendations and comments that emerge from the Red Team review should be presented to the proposal writing team in a briefing and weighed and integrated (as appropriate) into the proposal volumes under the direction of the capture manager and proposal manager. Specific people should be assigned to completing all action items identified as essential.

Red Team reviews should be scheduled early enough in the proposal response cycle to allow sufficient time for the proposal manager and proposal writers to implement an adequate recovery. Typically, on a 30-day response cycle, this is 8 days prior to the final production and delivery of the proposal documents.

7.7.3 **Gold Team**

In some companies, the Gold Team is a final review of the proposal volumes by members of senior management. Other firms use the Gold Team as a final proofreading and quality assurance stage. Figure references, pagination, and table of contents should be verified at this point. Participants include your proposal manager and your senior executives. The fundamental question to answer is: Have we made the sale? Actually go through your proposal and pull out the specific points that contribute to justifying selection of your company in accordance with the Evaluation Factors for Award (Section M). Make a list of these points and confirm that there is sufficient evidence for the evaluators to select you.

7.7.4 **Black Team**

Black teaming is a low-profile, highly confidential activity designed to assess the strengths, weaknesses, and current business activities of the competition. A document known as a competitor assessment might be generated from black teaming. Black teams generally report to a member of senior management of the prime contractor. Black teams may include an outside legal firm or marketing intelligence consulting group who can investigate the competition without involving your company directly.

7.7.5 **Black hat review**

Black hat reviews of your proposal strategy and approach can be conducted by leveraging the knowledge and experience of recent hires within your company who came from your competitors. Check your résumé database for the names of these people. Then interview them regarding your competitors' (their former employers') business approaches and cultural biases. Document this information for future use. Black hat reviewers attempt to identify gaps in your proposed solution set so that it can be strengthened with respect to the competition.

Black hat reviews can also be conducted successfully by outside consulting firms or individuals. These outside resources "pretend" that they are your competitors ("the bad guys" and hence the name "Black Hat") and look for ways to defeat your proposal. In effect, they predict how your competitors can win as a way to test and improve your win strategies. An appropriate time for the black hat review is after the Pink Team process but before the Red Team process.

Black hat reviews also can include an in-depth analysis of your known competitors, their strengths and weakenesses, why they want to pursue the given program (business case), their probable past performance citations, potential technical and their management approaches, and their possible teaming configurations. Effort can be directed toward developing candidate themes and overarching elevator speeches for the competitors. You can then make modifications, as appropriate, to your own technical and management approaches.

7.8 Preparing for orals and Final Proposal Revision (FPR)

Proposal team activity does not stop following submittal of the volumes to the client. Once a company's proposal is determined to be within the competitive range based upon the evaluation factors, the client may elect to have the company deliver an oral presentation to the evaluation panel or to submit a Final Proposal Revision (FPR), or both. The FPR is, in effect, the opportunity to enhance your proposal. Generating an effective presentation and planning and rehearsing for orals are very important and require significant time and focus. Many times, FPRs involve providing the client organization with a revised cost volume that reflects the lowest possible cost for which your company can successfully perform the statement of work.

Increasingly important in the federal procurement process, oral presentations provide an excellent opportunity to reaffirm your company's distinctive capabilities, innovative technical solutions and their benefits, and risk-aware program management approach. Capabilities include qualified personnel (proposed project manager and key staff), phase-in experience, cost-effectiveness of your approach, and records of outstanding contractual experience, among others. The oral presentation cannot exceed the government-assigned time limit, which can range from 15 minutes to several hours. Multiple rehearsals or dry runs are crucial to help your company's staff gain confidence as presenters and to acquaint them with public speaking, tight time limitations for presentation, and smooth computer and audiovisual equipment operation. Some government agencies and private-sector clients require multimedia presentations, replete with color, sound, and highly professional imagery. Clients want to meet and interact with the proposed project team face to face. They want to be comfortable with the people they will work with during the contract life cycle. Consider the oral presentation forum as a group interview process.

7.9 Debriefings (refer to FAR 15.1003)

Contractors that have submitted proposals to the U.S. government for a particular procurement are legally entitled to debriefings. Debriefings may take the form of a face-to-face meeting, teleconference, fax, or letter. Meetings and teleconferences are generally attended by representatives of the government's contracting office, project technical staff, and financial and legal offices. Request a debriefing in writing through the client's contracts offices. Lessons and information that your company can learn from a debriefing experience include the following:

- Breakdown of your technical score by proposal section (this is provided in very general terms);
- Process by which the scores were derived by the government evaluators;
- Strengths, weaknesses, and deficiencies points of your proposal;
- How best to proceed with the next proposal to the same procuring agency; What specifically is important to that agency, for example, a reluctance to accept complex teaming arrangements, close and effective control of subcontractors and consultants that may be proposed, an emphasis upon a particular project management configuration, and incumbent capture strategy;
- Advisability of making further offers to the particular client.

Certain federal organizations such as the Air Force, NASA, and Army provide detailed written debriefing documents and/or slide presentations.

Do not expect to have your proposal compared with your competitors' proposals during a formal debriefing process. Additionally, there is no page-by-page analysis of your propsal, or debate about or defense of the Source Selection Authority's (SSA) decision. Further, competitor proposal performance and cost strategies are strictly off limits. You may, of course, request a copy of the winning proposal volumes under the FOIA. Company-sensitive trade secrets and commercial or financial information contained in the competitor's proposal will not be released indiscriminately by the government. Instead, the proposal documents will undergo review both by the competitor (preliminary) and the government to ensure that only information in accordance with the FOIA is released.

We are now ready to take a closer look at the major parts of a proposal submitted in response to a formal RFP or RFS.

ENDNOTES

1. Holtz, Herman, and Terry Schmidt, *The Winning Proposal: How to Write It*, New York: McGraw-Hill, 1981.

2. The federal IFB, or sealed bid procedure, should result in a firm-fixed-price contract. This procedure is especially well-suited for government purchases of COTS items. Bids are opened publicly and the award is made immediately to the lowest priced, responsible, responsive bidder. No discussions are allowed, and no exceptions may be taken by the contractor.

   The federal government has been moving in the direction of procuring dual-use, COTS, and nondevelopmental items (NDI). An example of this procurement trajectory is in the purchase of intelligence and electronic warfare (IEW) equipment for the U.S. Army. (See "DOD's Airborne Recon Plan Pushes Sensors, Image Recognition," *Sensor Business News*, May 8, 1996.) In FY1997, DoD seeks a $250M *Dual-Use Applications Program* (DUAP). With COTS/dual-use embedded in DoD acquisition, MIL SPECS no longer provide giant defense firms with an artificial edge over agile new defense entrants into the marketplace. (See "DOD Acquisition Chief Pushes COTS/Dual-Use, Wants More Suppliers," *Technology Transfer Week*, Vol. 30, April 1996.)

   The concept of responsiveness was developed in sealed bidding, wherein a Contracting Officer is prohibited from considering any bid that deviates from the IFB. This prohibition does not apply to negotiated procurements. (See Cibinic, John, and Ralph C. Nash, *Formation of Government Contracts*, 2nd ed., Washington, D.C.: George Washington University, 1986, pp. 523–524.)

   An RFP, which results in competitive proposals for competitive acquisitions under P.L. 98-369 (Competition in Contracting Act of 1984) is a more flexible approach used in sole source or competitive situations. Any contract type from fixed-price to cost-reimbursement can be used. The government opens and reviews proposals privately. The number and identity of offerors are not revealed (immediately), and award may be based upon considerations other than price. Considerable discussion between the government and the offeror may or may not take place. The offeror may take exception to the solicitation terms or may submit alternate proposals. And modifications to proposals by the offerors are permitted. Upon acceptance, the proposal or offer becomes a contract in some government procurements wherein the technical and contractual requirements are tightly specified.

3. U.S. Small Business Administration, *Small Business Economy Report to the President*, 2009, p. 108.

Chapter 8

Major proposal components

8.1 Overview

YOUR COMPANY'S response to a competitive RFP or RFS will generally consist of a set of volumes: technical, management, and cost. These volumes may be called different names in different RFPs; technical approach, business management, and cost or price are several variations. In addition, there will probably be a transmittal, or cover, letter; an executive summary, which is often part of the technical volume but may be a stand-alone volume and should also appear in the cost volume; and various supporting volumes such as quality assurance plan, program management plan, quality assurance, configuration management plan, and health and safety plan. Sometimes, the technical and management volumes are contained in one single document. A U.S. government RFP may require that SF 33s, "Solicitation Offer and Award," and SF 1411s, "Contract Pricing Cover Sheet," be submitted as separate volumes. Technical volume page counts for federal proposals can range from 10 to 15 sheets to hundreds or even thousands of pages, although certainly there is a migration toward fewer rather than more pages. And certain major aerospace and defense proposals can contain more than 70 individual volumes, considering executive summary, technical volume, management volume, cost volume, make or buy policy, quality assurance plan, recruitment plan, health and safety plan, subcontractor plan, and so forth. The trend, however, even with billion-dollar procurements, is to require proposals on the order of 100 to 200 total pages. Focused, highly refined graphics and text are required to convey your messages, tell a fact-based, compelling story, and meet all of the RFP requirements in a concise manner. In a growing number of instances, you will not "write your way" to success, but must use graphics.

8.2 Transmittal letter

The transmittal, or cover, letter should do more than simply transmit your proposal documents to the government or private-sector client. (Note, however, that there are occasions wherein a client will strictly preclude any letter other than a brief transmittal. The U.S. Coast Guard Operations Support Center in Martinsburg, West Virginia, is a case in point.) The letter should be viewed as one more opportunity to call your client's attention to the advantages to be gained from doing business with your company. This letter should be prepared on your company's letterhead with the appropriate office location address and be signed by your company's president or executive vice president. It should emphasize your president's personal commitment to the successful completion of the particular project or timely delivery of the specified product or service. It is advisable to attach a copy of the transmittal letter with each volume of the proposal because the volumes are often distributed to a committee of client evaluators.

Since the transmittal letter requires the signature of a member of senior management, the proposal manager should plan to have the letter completed for signature several days in advance of the proposal due date. The fluctuating schedule of business executives could result in their being out of the office at the very time their signature is required on the letter and cost volume forms.

Definitely avoid the following hackneyed wording in your transmittal letters:

We are pleased to submit this proposal in response to Air Force Solicitation No. FA890311R8002.

Be creative and inventive, yet to the point and in accord with any specific RFP instructions. Briefly convey your company's enthusiasm to contribute to your client's technical, programmatic, and budgetary success on this important project. Consider the following example:

> *When DOT partners with our company, you are harnessing the talents and focused energies of business people who are also information technology specialists. Four years of outstanding IT service provide the technical matrix in which fiscally prudent and market-driven business decisions are made every day. We very much appreciate that you and other DOT staff members have invested your time and effort in reviewing our submittal. From the vantage of our knowledge and experience base, we certainly see the challenges—and the genuine mutual successes—that are possible under this important program.*

8.3 Technical volume

From a client evaluation perspective, the technical volume of your proposal is frequently weighted most heavily. This means that this volume is absolutely crucial to the success of any proposal effort. Sometimes, however, contractor technical staff and senior management place too much attention on responding to this volume, to the detriment of the remainder of the effort. Proposals are not only technical approaches and solutions, though to be sure, these items are critical. As noted previously, proposals are fundamentally sales documents—and every point counts toward your overall score.

The technical volume is the volume most often storyboarded, that is, broken down into logical subparts and "choreographed" to encourage written responses from the proposal team that are consistent thematically and compliant with the RFP requirements (see Figure 8.1). From a big picture vantage, the technical volume presents the following:

- What your company is selling;
- What the specific benefits to the client are;
- Why you are selling it;
- How your company will perform its function(s);
- How it is better than the competition.

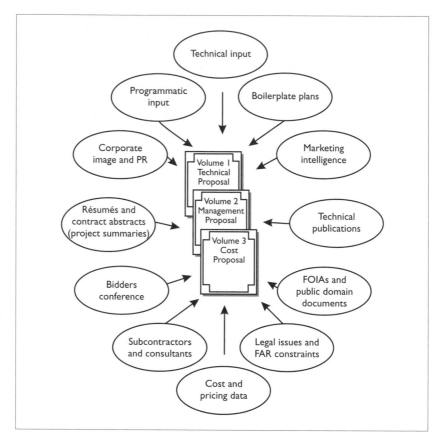

Figure 8.1
Proposals are choreographed exercises in information and knowledge management, assembly, and packaging.

8.3.1 **Front cover**

Your company's image,[1] or collective identity, should be conveyed in the cover design of your proposal documents, provided that the RFP does not stipulate otherwise. The cover should attempt to: (1) attract positive attention with an appropriate high-impact presentation, (2) identify the RFP and the offeror (your company) in words and images, and (3) convey the most significant benefits or themes of your proposal. Almost every RFP states somewhere in the preparation instructions that attractive, colorful covers, diagrams, and such are uncalled for and, if used, show that the offeror is unresponsive and not very cost-conscious. Real-world surveys indicate, however, that attractive covers are noted positively by government evaluators. They are, after all, human beings who respond more

---

1   Company image should be conveyed uniformly throughout all of your externally distributed materials, including business cards, letterhead, envelopes, marketing brochures, annual reports, marketing fliers, advertising, trade show booth, displays, social media sites, and signage.

favorably to attractive images than bland cover stock. In addition, some clients will assess your proposal as indicative of the caliber of deliverable your company would produce during the contract life cycle.

Your company's logo (and those of your teaming partners, if appropriate), photographs and artwork, and meaningful text can be combined to create a stunning cover design using CorelDRAW Graphic Suite X5, Adobe Illustrator Creative Suite (CS) 5 or Adobe Photoshop CS5, for example. Numerous companies offer royalty-free stock photographs as electronic images (e.g., .jpeg, .gif, .tif, and .bmp formats) that are legally usable in your proposals from a copyright and intellectual property standpoint. Royalty-free images are generally acquired for a one-time-only fee. To avoid unwanted and potentially costly litigation, never use photographs or artwork scanned from published books or magazines without the written consent of the photographer, artist, or publisher. Modifying a photograph is insufficient to reproduce it without permission. Useful repositories of public domain photographs include, http://www.usa.gov/Topics/Graphics.shtml (case sensitive), http://www.af.mil/photos/, http://nix.nasa.gov, and http://www.photolib.noaa.gov. The company called One Mile Up, Inc., (http://onemileup.com/), which is located in northern Virginia, sells all major federal government agency logos on a CD called "The Book of Seals" for approximately $695. These high-resolution logos are in Encapsulated Postscript (.eps) format and can be enlarged to poster size for trade show booths and other displays.

Royalty-free images and clip art of specific technology areas such as information technology and business settings and tools can be purchased through the following Web sites:

- Jupiterimages (http://www.jupiterimages.com/RoyaltyFreePhotos);
- Dynamic Graphics (http://www.dynamicgraphics.co.nz/);
- iStockphoto (http://www.istockphoto.com/photo);
- Getty Images (http://gettyimages.com/CreativeImages/RoyaltyFree);
- Thinkstock (http://www.thinkstockphotos.com/);
- Clipart.com (http://www.clipart.com/en/);
- Photos.com (http://www.photos.com/en/).

You may require the support of an outside printing vendor to generate multiple copies of two- or four-color covers. If you elect to use three-ring notebooks to package your proposal volumes, be sure to have spines and back covers designed and produced, too.

8.3.2 Nondisclosure statement on the title page

The nondisclosure statement should appear on the title page of each proposal volume. Designed to protect your company's proprietary information from illegal disclosure (see Figure 8.2), it serves notice that the content of your proposal documents is sensitive. Reference to the nondisclosure statement should be stamped or printed onto each page of each volume (e.g., Use or disclosure of data on this page is subject to the restriction on the title page of this document). The nondisclosure statement will not, however, prevent the government from releasing information from your submitted proposal in accordance with the FOIA. Sometimes an RFP or RFS will stipulate the exact verbiage for the nondisclosure statement.

Similarly, for commercial proposals, the nondisclosure statement identifies the document as containing proprietary information not to be disclosed outside of the client organization, unless authorized by the proposer. This obtains less protection than is desirable, but it at least puts the reader on notice.

8.3.3 Executive summary

The executive summary should be written so that even an uninformed reader will absorb and understand the principal ideas and major storylines expressed in each of your proposal volumes. The executive summary, which in many proposals is only one to two pages in length, should be structured to do the following:

- Introduce high-level themes that will reappear throughout the proposal volumes (technical, management, past performance, and cost).

Figure 8.2
Sample nondisclosure statement for the title page.

The information contained in this proposal shall not be disclosed outside the government (or client organization, as appropriate) and shall not be duplicated, used or disclosed, in whole or in part, for any purpose other than to evaluate this proposal. If a contract is awarded to this offeror as a result of or in connection with the submission of the data herein, the government shall have the right to duplicate, use, or disclose the data to the extent provided by the contract. This restriction does not limit the government's right to use information contained in the data if it is obtained from another source without restriction. The data subject to this restriction comprise the whole of this proposal.

- Enumerate your company's applicable credentials and applicable contractual track record.

- Demonstrate that your company understands the mission-level and business importance, as well as the technical requirements, of the project or product deliverable.

- Indicate that your company can perform the project successfully or provide the product or service on schedule and within budget.

- Provide an overview of your technical and management approaches/solutions and their benefits for this project in accordance with Section M of the RFP. This might be done in table form.

- Highlight your key project staff for service contracts in particular (by name if your client knows them).

- Focus on the primary reasons why the client should select your company as its partner on this important contract. How will the client's selection of your firm benefit them from a technical, programmatic, risk mitigation, and cost perspective? What specifically makes your company the best-value solution for this client?

- Demonstrate your local, established presence in the applicable geographic area that ensures your preparedness to meet client requirements in a timely manner and comprehend the local political and regulatory decision-making environment.

- Convey your firm's successful consulting work and your proven ability to manage multiple tasks simultaneously.

- Highlight your successful performance history with the client. Provide one or two success stories, as well as key lessons learned and best practices.

- Point to your solid knowledge base in applicable technical areas that will provide value-added technical support and direct benefit to the client.

- Outline your highly effective management strategies that ensure schedule adherence, cost control, and superior-quality deliverables. Introduce your project management leadership to the client, and demonstrate their pivotal programmatic, technical, and teamwork strengths.

- Bring to life your company's corporate commitment to partnership with the client to support its mission and business goals.

The benefits of your company must be sold right here.

Use photographs of related projects, equipment, and systems and installations to help authenticate your contractual experience and technical approach. A busy government decision-maker or private-sector executive should be able to scan your executive summary in about 5 minutes and understand at least the high points of what it is you are selling and why you are the company to be selected.

If at all possible and in accordance with RFP instructions, develop a full-page (8.5 × 11 inches) or foldout page (11 × 17 inches) graphic as part of the executive summary that conveys the primary benefits to the client of your company's approach. Tell your proposal story in one graphic image through the judicious use of photos, line art, clip art, and carefully selected words. If prepared well, this can be a powerful tool for capturing reviewer attention and interest in the remainder of your proposal.

8.3.4 Building a compliance (cross-reference) matrix

Compliance, cross-reference, or traceability matrices are all terms for tables that clearly map the RFP requirements (from Sections C, L, M, and H as well as the CDRL, DIDs, and RFP attachments as appropriate) to the specific sections within your proposal in which your company responded to a given RFP requirement. These matrices often appear in the front matter of your proposal volumes but may be placed at the very end of each proposal volume as an 11 × 17–inch foldout page that will allow the government evaluators to be able to refer constantly and easily to the matrix. Table 8.1(a–c) illustrates sample compliance matrices. Table 8.1(a) is a common, straightforward approach. Its format was dictated by the RFP. Table 8.1(b) includes reference to both text sections or paragraphs and figures contained in the proposal response. Table 8.1(c) presents a detailed mapping of elements from Sections C, L, and M of the RFP to proposal response sections and subsections. Note that in certain cases, the response to specific RFP elements is found in more than one proposal section or subsection. The number of columns in a compliance matrix varies depending upon whether you elect to delineate your responses by text sections and graphics. You might also consider adding a comments column in which important themes can be introduced, as shown in Table 8.1(c).

8.3.5 Narrative body of the technical volume

Translate your company's features into benefits to and strengths for your client.

If Section L of the RFP allows, each section (and major subsection) should be written to include an introduction, body, and summation. The body, or main narrative portion, might include a discussion of: (1) your company's understanding of the client's requirements, including how these

SOW Element	Proposal Section
1	2.1.1.a.
2	2.1.1.b.
3	2.1.1.c.
4	2.1.1.d.
5	2.1.1.e
6	2.1.1.f.
7	2.1.1.g.
8	2.1.1.h.
9	2.1.1.i.
10	2.1.1.j.
11	2.1.1.k.
12	2.1.1.l.
13	2.1.1.m.
14	2.1.1.n.

(a)

Table 8.1 Sample Compliance Matrices: (a) Common, Straightforward Approach; (b) With Reference to Text Sections, Paragraphs, and Figures Contained in the Proposal Response; and (c) Detailed Mapping of Elements from Section C, L, and M, of the RFP to Proposal Response Sections and Subsections

requirements might evolve over the life cycle of the contract along with his operational and business environment; (2) your customer's critical issues associated with the requirements or task performance; (3) your company's innovative approach to addressing the requirements, including lessons learned and quantitative success stories from similar contractual experience; (4) your customer's success criteria for the task or effort; (5) benefits of your approach to the customer; and (6) potential performance, schedule, cost, safety, and environmental risks and how your company will mitigate or avoid these risks. Strive to prepare a solution-oriented proposal—one that offers the least technical, schedule, cost, and political risks to your client. And weave your themes throughout the narrative sections of your proposal. Avoid phraseology like "Our major theme for this section is …" That is not effective proposal writing. I worked with one enthusiastic proposal manager who, upon learning about themes in my proposal training seminar, included "major themes" as a heading in his proposal. We had some restructuring to do!

Table 8.2 is a sample structure for a section of a technical volume in a task-order procurement. In responding to a particular RFP, you should

RFP Number		Proposal	
		Part	**Part**
Section/Paragraph		**Figure**	**Section/Paragraph**
L.2.A.5	Separation of technical and business proposals		Part I, Part II
L.2.B.	Technical proposal instructions	Part I	Part I
L.2.B.1.a(1)	Objectives		I, 2 all
L.2.B.1.a(2)	Approach		I, 3 all
L.2.B.1.a(3)	Methods		I, 5 all
L.2.B.1.b(1)	Experience	6-1, 6-3	I, 6.4; Appendix C
L.2.B.1.b(1)(a)	Pertinent contracts	6-1	I, 1 all; I, 6 all; and I, Foreword supporting materials (attached)
L.2.B.1.b(1)(b)	Principal investigator	6-4	I, Foreword; I, 3 all; I, 4 all
L.2.B.1.b(2)	Personnel	6-3	I, 6.4; I, Appendix C
L.2.B.4	Other considerations		I, Foreword; I, 3 all; I, 4 all
L.2.B.5	Special instructions		I, 5
L.2.C.1	Cost and pricing data	Part II	Part II
L.2.C.1.a(1)	Materials		II, SF 1411, Attachment
L.2.C.1.a(2)	Direct labor		II, SF 1411, Attachment
L.2.C.1.a(3)	Indirect cost		II, SF 1411, Attachment
L.2.C.1.a(4)	Special equipment		II, SF 1411, Attachment
L.2.C.1.a(5)	Travel		II, SF 1411, Attachment
L.2.C.1.a(6)	Other costs		II, SF 1411, Attachment
L.2.C.1.b(1)	Judgmental factors		II, SF 1411, Attachment
L.2.C.1.b(2)	Contingencies		None
L.2.C.2	Total plan compensation		II 4, all

(b)

Table 8.1 (continued)

RFP Element Attachment A (SOW)	Proposal Section	Comments
SOW 1.0	B.1.1	Our team has the specific satellite instrumentation experience, capabilities, and knowledge to support all of the requirements of the SOW.
SOW 2.0	B.1.2	Our staff, including our senior scientist, have a total of 16 years of prior involvement with this project. We understand the mission objectives as well as the system requirements.
SOW 3.0	B.1.3	Our knowledge gained from supporting four launches coupled with our extensive experience supporting scientific projects provides us with an understanding of the critical project elements.
SOW 4.0	B.1.4	Our team has taken an integrated approach to all functions of the development effort to ensure high user engagement and satisfaction.

Table 8.1
(continued)

structure your outlines and proposal volumes in accordance with the numbering scheme and conceptual scenario provided in Section L and Section M. And use the exact wording from Section C as outline headings and subheadings, if possible. When clients ask for ABC, give them ABC, not BCA or XYZ. In other words, focus on and respond directly to the client's requirements. Translate your company's distinctive capabilities and extensive expertise into benefits to your client. This can be done in the narrative, in features and benefits boxes (as shown in Table 8.3), and in figure captions and table legends.

The summation of each major technical section of your proposal might highlight key elements of your approach in the language that your customer uses in the evaluation process. For example, all parts of the Department of Defense (since July 1, 2011) use the term "Performance Confidence" in Section M, Evaluation Factors for Award. NASA speaks in terms of "Significant Strengths." Why not close each major technical section of the proposal with a brief summation entitled "Performance Confidence" or "Significant Strengths," as applicable to the customer's terminology? In four or five sentences, help the evaluators understand

Body	3.3	Technical task #3 • Elevator speech textbox
	3.3.1	Introduction
	3.3.2	Understanding the EPA's requirements for Task #3 (include how requirements may evolve over the contract life cycle) • Pain table
	3.3.3	Critical issues associated with task performance
	3.3.4	Your company's (or team's) innovative technical approach (focus on the "how"—how will you leverage your *people, processes, knowledge,* and *technology* assets to meet your customer's requirements)
	3.3.5	Success criteria for Task #3
	3.3.6	Benefits to EPA (quality, schedule, cost)
	3.3.7	Potential risks and mitigation strategies
	3.3.8	Summation

Table 8.2
Sample Technical
Volume Outline

clearly why the major points in the given technical section contribute directly to a strong sense of confidence that your company's approach will ensure superior contractual performance or why they constitute significant strengths to the customer's organization, goals and objectives, and overall mission. Make it very easy for the customer evaluation team to identify the strengths of each section of your proposal so that they can complete their scorecard with specific examples.

8.4 Management volume

The management volume of a proposal is many times the most overlooked and poorly constructed document in the entire proposal package. Too often, the management volume sections are viewed to be mundane boilerplate, in which each government agency is interchangeable. The management volume is a project- and agency-specific narrative that clearly demonstrates how your company will manage staff and subcontractors, maintain reasonable spans of authority, control schedules and costs, assess and measure technical performance, address technical issues, share knowledge efficiently, meet performance thresholds, and access resources companywide as necessary—all to the benefit of your client. In general, your management volume must describe and illustrate the following clearly:

Features	Benefits
Single-vendor solution with a lean organizational structure	Straightforward lines of authority and communication with the IRS, resulting in more effective and efficient service and problem resolution
Proven approach to transitioning incumbent personnel	Reduced risk through retention of institutional IRS knowledge and smooth contract start-up within 30 days of award
Project structure tailored specifically to the IRS's unique requirements	Responsiveness, flexibility, and value of service results in high customer satisfaction
Project-management team highly experienced and successful in the management of eight similar task order contracts	Proactive approach to meeting IRS needs due to complete familiarity with the contract process; the process functions as a mechanism to facilitate superior service
Three years of experience in facilities management	Effective maintenance of IRS baseline, with associated cost savings estimated to be $200,000 over the life of the contract
Four years of experience in prototyping and implementing advanced application technologies	Ability to plan and execute the IRS's migration to newer technologies within the contract life cycle to support critical business objectives

Table 8.3 Features and Benefits Box

- How your company proposes to organize and marshal its resources to perform on the project or deliver the products or services;
- The roles and span of authority of your proposed project manager;
- How your company's project staff will communicate and interface with the client on an ongoing basis over the life of the contract;
- How you will manage the effort more efficiently and effectively than your competition;
- Your company's identity (through staff résumés and related and past contractual experience);
- That you can accomplish the project successfully, within schedule constraints and under or within budgetary margins (including automated tools and industry-standard best practices);
- The rationale for forming your particular teaming arrangement, if there are subcontractor(s) involved;

- That you have successfully managed projects of similar size, scope, complexity, and contract type, along with relevant examples of such projects.

Here is a suggested outline for the management approach:

- Introduction
- Project Organization (include functional project organizational chart populated with staff from your firm, as well as with subcontractor staff, and clearly indicate reporting relationships).
- Project Leadership
  - Project manager's role and span of authority
  - Accessing corporate resources (discuss your company's commitment of resources to project success, and the specific mechanisms that you employ to make this happen at the level of day-to-day business)
  - Project initiation and task order kickoff strategies
- Ongoing Communication with the Client Organization
  - Client and company technical and contractual interfaces and general topics of communication and interaction
  - Reporting schedules
- Project Execution
  - Staffing Management
    - Recruiting, retention, and turnover metrics
    - Recruiting policies and practices
    - Corporate benefits package (total compensation plan)
    - Capacity to meet workload fluctuations and accelerated schedules
    - Staff training, cross-training, and technical refresh practices and associated funding
    - Security clearances [e.g., secret, top secret, sensitive compartmentalized information (SCI), Q and L (DOE), and C6 (DHS)]
  - Schedule Management—effective schedule control approaches and automated tools
    - Task prioritization methodologies
    - Demonstrated history of meeting interim and final project deadlines

- Proposed schedule of project by task (Gantt charting)
- Task Order Management—approaches and tools
  - Metrics-driven work planning and monitoring
  - Response to evolving project requirements
  - Problem management and escalation processes
- Risk Management—cost, schedule, and technical performance risk avoidance and mitigation approaches
- Quality Management
  - Continuous process improvement (CPI)
  - Application of industry-standard structured processes and methodologies [ISO, Capability Maturity Model Integration® (CMMI®), IEEE, ITIL, Lean Six Sigma, and Kaizen]
  - QA metrics tracking
  - Interim and final deliverables
- Financial Management
  - Industry-standard cost control approaches
  - Automated cost tracking and control tools (e.g., Deltek modules, Oracle's Primavera)
- Efficient and compatible invoicing and reporting mechanisms
- Subcontractor Management
- Rationale for teaming
- Project manager's approval of subcontractor staffing
- Ongoing communication with project team
- Invoice verification
- Integration of subcontractor staff into task activities
- Work assignments
  - Issue escalation and resolution processes

You must demonstrate convincingly how your company will perform the work, manage and control the work, manage and control changes to it, and be responsive to the client's current and evolving needs. You should demonstrate a staffing and facilities capability sufficient to handle a project of the size proposed. Depending upon the requirements set forth in Section L of the RFP, the management volume might include the following sections and subsections.

Introduction   An introduction should highlight the key aspects and associated benefits of your company's management approach. These might include a project organization that accommodates evolution and growth within the contract; assignment of seasoned and qualified personnel who understand the specific needs, goals, and metrics of their particular areas of support; clear definition of roles, responsibilities, and lines of communication; and the engaged support of your senior management for the contract.

Executive summary   An executive summary is similar to that used in the technical volume.

Project organization   Project organization addresses such items as project leadership, spans of authority and control of your proposed supervisory staff, and the clear lines of communication between your project manager and his or her technical and support staff. Emphasize your project manager's access to required company resources and this particular project's visibility and importance to your senior management. Demonstrate that your project organization can accommodate evolution and growth (or workload fluctuations) within the contract.

Corporate organization   The corporate organization section presents an organizational chart in graphic form, highlighting how the specific project under consideration is linked managerially and structurally to the company as a whole. Demonstrate a streamlined managerial structure with direct access to senior-level support and resources companywide.

Client-contractor interfaces   A section on client-contractor interfaces presents your company's proposed working relationship with the client at technical, programmatic, and contractual levels. Answer the question: If I am the client, whom do I contact within your company for project status in terms of technical accomplishment, schedule, cost, and deliverables, and so forth? Demonstrate clearly in narrative and graphic form the lines of interaction between your company's technical, programmatic, and contractual staff and the client's counterparts[2]. Discuss the clearly defined reporting pathways within your company.

---

2   It is very effective to develop a graphic that illustrates your company's contracts group interacting with the client's contracts office, and your proposed project manager (and task leaders or delivery order managers) interacting directly with, for example, the client's contracting officer's technical representative (COTR), assistant technical representative (ATR), and technical monitors (TMs).

Management plan   A management plan discusses your proposed project manager's authority, roles and responsibilities, and his or her relevant project management experience. Describe how your project manager will interface with your company's senior management and key government staff to manage the project effectively and efficiently. Demonstrate through reference to lessons learned and best practices from other similar contractual experience that your management approach can accommodate evolving, fluctuating, and unforeseen workloads; multiple task assignments; requirements creep;[3] and unanticipated employee turnover. Discuss work planning and monitoring, allocation of project resources, review of project work, and regular reporting to the client. The management plan may include contract phase-in and phase-out plans.

Cost and time controls   In a section for cost and time controls, describe how your company plans to maintain control over the schedule and cost once the project begins. Illustrate specific and innovative control techniques proposed, emphasizing automated daily cost tracking and accounting, scheduling, and purchasing techniques (e.g., micropurchases), if appropriate. Explain what your company does to correct cost excesses in cost reimbursable contracts. For the U.S. government, clearly indicate that your cost accounting and purchasing systems are approved by the Defense Contract Audit Agency (DCAA) and that your company complies with cost accounting standards (CAS) and FAR cost principles. If a management information system (MIS) or "digital dashboard" is used to forecast resources and track task progress and performance metrics, articulate how it will be employed on this particular contract. State that your firm has the ability to control its workload through prudent and structured bid–no bid decisions.

Scheduling   Demonstrate in graphic form the major schedule milestones and contract deliverables. Discuss automated scheduling tools that your company has employed successfully on other contracts of similar size, scope, complexity, and contract type.

Staffing plan   Describe staffing levels required in each labor category over the life of the contract. Discuss your company's successful recruitment policies, ongoing staff training and technical refreshment programs, and internal programs to ensure employee motivation and retention (compensation plan).

---

3   *Requirements creep* refers to the gradual expansion of the scope and complexity of the tasks or project.

Key and other résuméd personnel   Present short biosketches that highlight experience relevant to the procurement.

Résumés   Present résumés in the proper format as specified by the RFP, tailored to the specific requirements of the procurement. Map or link the individual's expertise and experience to the position description found in the RFP. Be certain that the government evaluators will understand precisely the benefits that each proposed staff member will bring to the particular project.

For program, project, or task manager résumés, consider the following key elements:

- Maximum number of staff managed at one time;
- Type of staff (labor category) managed;
- Success stories managing projects of similar size, scope, and complexity;
- PMP certification;
- Clearances;
- Year of management experience;
- Experience with schedule management and earned value management (EVM) tools;
- Subcontractor management experience [number of subs, types of subs (large business, small business)];
- Success meeting performance-based service level agreements (SLAs);
- Phase-in/transition experience and success;
- Knowledge-sharing and communication skills and techniques;
- ISO, ITIL, CMMI, Six-Sigma, Lean experience;
- Personal management-related awards, commendations, and/or emails from government customers;
- Education and training.

Company capabilities and experience   Describe your company's quality, reliability, and timeliness record on projects of similar scope, schedule, budget, and contract type.

Clients often use past performance as the single most important, reliable predictor of future performance.

Related experience   Bring your company's relevant contractual experience to life. Focus on project successes such as cost savings (tell how many dollars), schedule adherence (tell how much time saved), repeat business from a client, value-added service, fulfillment of performance-based metrics and service level agreements (SLAs), and the application of innovative technologies and processes. Highlight lessons learned from previous and existing experience that can be applied quickly and transparently to the contract under consideration. Pay particular attention to preparing and tailoring the narrative of past and related experience because of the increasing importance of this area as an evaluation factor for award.

Subcontracting plan   For major subcontractors, include a letter of commitment from the president of the subcontracting firm(s). This is in addition to a formal teaming agreement. Provide evidence of sufficient subcontractor control and your full accountability as the prime contractor. Discuss your project manager's oversight of the subcontractor(s)' staffing and invoices; issuance of subcontractor work assignments in accordance with performance metrics; planned methods for evaluating subcontractor performance; clear definition of subcontractor tasks and responsibilities; communicating and reporting practices and procedures between your company and the subs; meeting times and schedules; and problem identification, escalation, and resolution strategies. Ensure that your company's interactions with your subcontractor team are transparent to your client. Demonstrate that you will hold your subcontractors to the same rigorous quality standards and metrics for technical performance as you do your own company.

Company facilities and special resources   Describe the mechanism in your company to make resources and facilities available as necessary to support the project successfully. Indicate any government-furnished equipment (GFE) or contractor-furnished equipment (CFE) required. Describe how your facilities and equipment are applicable to the SOW or Statement of Objectives (SOO), and how you will use them in meeting critical project requirements. If you maintain a secure facility, mention that, as appropriate.

Risk management   Think of risk as *uncertainty surrounding a desired outcome*. Within the U.S. federal government space, risk is *not* a good thing at all. Conversely, it is something to be anticipated, avoided, and if and when it does occur, be mitigated. Risk can adversely impact mission success, which in turn can jeopardize American lives, property, and national security and interests. In government parlance, risk has two critical dimensions: (1) the *probability* (qualitative or quantitative) or likelihood that a program or project will experience an undesired event or consequence such as cost overrun, schedule slippage, safety mishap, compromise of security, or failure to achieve a needed technological breakthrough; and (2) the *consequences,* impact, or severity of the undesired event were it to occur.

Effective risk management strategies are becoming an increasingly important evaluation factor for award (Section M criterion) within federal government competitive proposals. This is due in part to the growth of performance-based acquisition (PBA), which focuses on specific results and outcomes in support of federal agency missions. Risk management refers to the systematic and disciplined application of management policies, procedures, and approaches to the task of identifying, analyzing, evaluating, addressing, and monitoring/evaluating risk. Importantly, risk management must be coupled tightly with key project management processes. NASA recognized this, for example, when it included "Risk Management" as a key element under the "Business Management Approach Subfactor" in a major engineering procurement for Glenn Research Center in Cleveland, Ohio. The NASA Procedural Requirements (NPR) 8000.4A (expiration date 12/16/13) discusses this particular federal agency's understanding of and expectations regarding risk management.

As a contractor responding to federal Requests for Proposal (RFPs) and Requests for Solutions (RFSs), you will want to ensure that each element of your proposed technical, management, staffing, and phase-in approach is assessed in terms of its potential for: (1) disruption of schedule; (2) increased cost; (3) degradation of technical performance; (4) the need for increased government oversight; and (5) the likelihood of unsuccessful contract performance. Perform this assessment of your proposal *before* you submit the documents (or upload the electronic files) to your government customer. When evaluating its contractors' proposals, DoD assigns Proposal Risk ratings to each Mission Capability subfactor in accordance with Shay memo, dated March 4, 2011[4]. To be sure, risk is a significant component of any large, technically complex, performance-critical operating environment that a contractor will face. An organization cannot eliminate all risks, so some acceptable level of risk must be assumed to meet contract objectives, provide the best value, and arrive at a realistic cost solution.

Within the management section or volume of your proposal, you will want to present an organized, systematic, and continuous decision-making process that seeks to mitigate risks and increase the likelihood of achieving all contract and task goals.

---

4   Shay D. Assad is the director of the Defense Procurement and Acquisition Policy, Department of Defense.

- *Identify.* Discover and describe the risk in terms of an undesirable event.
- *Analyze.* Evaluate the probability and consequences of the risk and assign priority.
- *Plan.* Determine the best approach to mitigate the risk and assign responsibility.
- *Track.* Monitor and measure the efficiency and progress of the mitigation plan.
- *Control.* Assess mitigated risk level and determine risk disposition.

Underlying all of these process elements should be a strong emphasis upon open and ongoing communication and documentation within the project team to ensure that risk mitigation goals are established, understood, implemented, and maintained. The documentation also serves as an audit trail to establish the origin and rationale for all risk-related decisions. You will want to demonstrate how you will build a risk-smart workforce and operational environment. Specific steps toward that goal span the following:

- Encouraging a culture wherein learning from experience is valued and lessons are shared;
- Evaluating risk management results to support innovation and support continuous improvement;
- Capturing and sharing key practices internally and with the government customer organization.

Two other critical aspects of risk management discussions in proposals to the federal government are *leadership* and *action*. Your government customer will want to see that there is a single point of contact in your project organization who is empowered to be ultimately accountable for risk-related issues. In addition, you must illustrate the process by which demonstrable and timely action will be taken to address performance, schedule, and/or cost risks.

Federal government proposal evaluators are, in general, extremely risk averse. That means that your proposal will have to offer people, processes, and tools focused on risk mitigation throughout the project life cycle.

Based upon marketing intelligence about your client's concerns and goals, demonstrate that your company will keep the project on schedule, control costs, retain key technical staff, maintain more efficient allocation of staff resources, respond to fluctuating workloads, conduct cross training, and so forth. You must convince your client that your company will make them look good in the eyes of their superiors, including possibly the U.S. Congress. Demonstrate that you are fully capable of risk identification, analysis, and mitigation. Given the growing emphasis on performance-based acquisition (defined at FAR subpart 37.6), this is a critical element in the management proposal.

Risk Radar is one example of an automated risk management tool used by both government and industry. Produced by American Systems (Chesapeake, Virginia), this Microsoft Access database application uses standard risk management terminology and supports industry-accepted risk management processes prescribed by the Software Engineering Institute's Capability Maturity Model® (SEI CMM®) Level 3, the *IEEE Standard 1540 for Software Life Cycle Processes–Risk Management*, and the Software Program Manager's Network (SPMN) "16 Critical Software Practices for Performance-Based Management." Risk Radar is a comprehensive risk management application that serves as a centralized warehouse for archiving, tracking, and managing project risk data. Risk Radar supports continuous and proactive risk management by helping project managers categorize, prioritize, track, report, and mitigate project risk while keeping the highest priority risks clearly in management's sight. This enables managers to make sound risk decisions before they have a chance to transition into costly problems affecting project cost, schedule, or performance. Importantly, Risk Radar encourages open risk communication across all project levels and provides managers the risk visibility they need to make timely and informed risk management decisions. Risk Radar includes 22 standardized reports that enable project managers to view and track important risk data. It provides the ability to establish standard values for categorizing and prioritizing project risks according to *Probability of Occurrence, Risk Impact,* and *Risk Exposure.* Another risk management tool from American Systems is called Risk Radar Enterprise. This is a Web-based application designed to facilitate proactive risk management and communication within an Enterprise Risk Management system.

Oracle's Primavera Risk Analysis is another risk analytics solution that integrates cost and schedule risk management.

Configuration management   Depending upon the technical scope of work, and particularly for software and hardware systems design, development, and maintenance, discuss how your company will address configuration control, design, development, and implementation.

Data and information management   Depending upon the SOW or SOO, discuss how you will apply automated tools to assist in data and information collection, analysis, archival, and retrieval. Also describe your techniques for ensuring data integrity and information assurance (IA) and for controlling data access. Indicate if your management information systems are compliant with government standards.

Work breakdown structure   The work breakdown structure (WBS), which is most often included in the management volume, is an organizational resource-allocation tool that can be used to assist with project management structuring, cost estimates, and cost substantiation. (See Figure 8.3.) Sometimes referred to as a work element structure, the WBS helps to "interrelate the technical, management, and cost aspects of the work" [1]. Specifically, the WBS is developed to ensure that all required work elements are included in your company's technical approach and management plan without duplication. Lower-level tasks and subtasks that can be more easily scheduled and estimated in terms of staffing are identified and arranged in hierarchical fashion to assist in the overall accumulation (or roll up) of resource requirements. During actual project performance, the WBS serves as a tool for cost control,

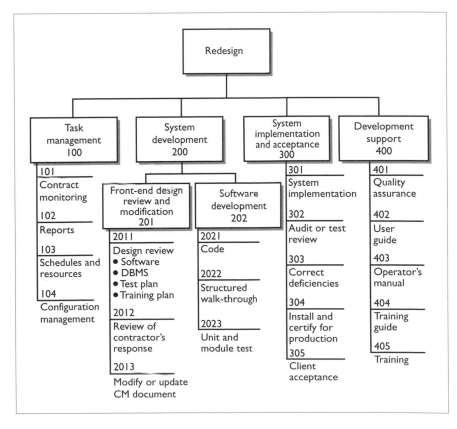

Figure 8.3
Sample WBS.

along with a monthly estimate-to-complete (ETC) analysis. WBSs can be developed using MS-Project and MS-Visio in combination.

Technical performance measurement system   Highlight any performance metrics that your company may employ to estimate, monitor, assess, and report project performance in an effort to identify potential problems before they devolve into major issues. Discuss performance metrics that this client will apply on the contract. Metrics might include system availability, time to fill technical position openings, and response time to user help requests. NASA, the Air Force, and DOE have moved proactively toward PBA.

Deliverable production and quality assurance   Demonstrate through reference to other successful project execution that delivering superior-quality deliverables which have undergone internal quality review prior to submittal to the client is a top priority to your company. Discuss formalized QA-QC procedures and proactive process planning and review mechanisms that have been established within your company. For example, perhaps you have implemented a program that includes document design meetings and senior technical review (STR) for all contract deliverables. Describe this program and how it will benefit your client on the particular contract at hand. You might also discuss your deficiency tracking program and include a sample deficiency tracking form.

Summation   Reinforce your primary management theme statements in a set of strong closing paragraphs. Present significant strengths that your customers will quickly recognize as important to their business and mission success.

8.5 Cost volume

Cost is always pivotal in competitive procurements. It is, therefore, important for your company to develop an early technical design and management approach upon which cost strategies and preliminary bottom-line prices (bogeys) can be built. The costing effort will also be facilitated by generating a staffing plan as soon as possible after RFP release. Develop your cost volume in close association with the technical and management volumes. The technical solution and staffing plan must be integrally linked with the pricing strategy.

The cost volume must contain resource estimates, costing methodology, and a rationale sufficient to allow the client to establish the fact that the product or service to be provided will be cost-effective and that the cost estimates are realistic to perform the contract work successfully [1]. Resource estimates include direct costs (primarily labor[5]), other direct costs (ODCs) (for example, material, travel, computer costs, and consultants), and indirect costs [overhead and general and administrative (G&A)]. Credibility is essential in deriving the optimal balance of performance and cost. Cost volumes also include terms and conditions and responses to representations and certifications (Section K of the RFP). Provide sufficient detail to satisfy the client. Ensure that your marketing efforts have provided this kind of detailed guidance from the client.

There are automated tools available on the market to assist your company in the preparation of various costing estimates. ProPricer Standard Edition and Estimator Editon, produced by Executive Business Services, Inc. [(951)693-0440; http://www.propricer.com] in Temecula, California, are examples of a COTS application.

Cost proposals are analyzed by the government to assess realism and the probable cost to the government. Cost realism is the process of independently reviewing and evaluating specific elements of each offeror's cost estimate to determine if the estimated proposed cost elements are realistic for the work to be performed, reflect a clear understanding of the requirements, and are consistent with the methods of performance described in the offeror's technical proposal.

If total or cost element ceilings are included, the evaluation will also assess the maximum probable cost based upon such ceilings. The client is interested in proposed methods to control costs that do not have a negative impact on contract performance. Cost and pricing data must be current, accurate, and complete.

To expand further regarding cost realism, this analysis refers to the government's evaluation of the system of logic, assumptions about the future, and reasonableness of the historical basis of your cost estimate. That is, cost realism focuses on the elements that make up the foundation of the estimate.

Cost realism analysis answers questions such as the following:

- Are the assumptions used in your estimating process reasonable?
- Has the historical database used been normalized to account for environmental parameters such as inflation?
- Is the cost estimate logical? Does it make sense in the context of the hardware or software product or service being estimated?

---

5   Because of holidays, vacation, and sick leave, the total number of labor hours in one staff year equals approximately 1,860.

- Does the estimate display a bias toward being too low or too high? If so, how is this bias displayed in the estimate?

- Is the cost estimating organization motivated to produce an inordinately high or low estimate in order to serve the contractor's own purposes?

- If the product is fixed-price sole source, has the historical basis data been hand-selected and therefore skewed to ensure the cost estimate obtained is unreasonably high or unreasonably low?

- If the program is competitive, has the contractor or government program office created program expectations that are far too optimistic?

A forward pricing rate agreement (FPRA), as defined in FAR 15.801, is a written agreement negotiated between a contractor and the government to ensure that certain rates and factors are available during a specified period for use in pricing contracts or contract modifications. Such rates and factors represent reasonable projections of specific costs that are not easily estimated for, identified with, or generated by a specific contract, contract end item, or task.

The trend in cost volumes is to make that document more sales-oriented—with more narrative, themes, graphics, and attractive formatting. They too should contain a copy of the executive summary.

The cost volume has a higher level of confidentiality than the other proposal volumes. Fewer copies should be made, and they should be distributed for internal company review on a need-to-know basis; however, build in time for thorough review and quality checking. Clients often require that the cost volume be submitted separately from technical and management. Many companies produce their cost volumes within the contracts or procurement departments rather than through a publications group.

8.6 Price to win

Price-to-win analysis is a process or methodology that companies use to increase the probability of their winning critical proposal opportunities. You can have a third-party organization develop the price-to-win, and compare to your company's cost and profit. Ideally, this analysis process evolves over a period of time, thus allowing for the integration of new competitive and customer intelligence as well as the company's capture team's maturing perspectives on the particular opportunity. Market-driven business intelligence gleaned from documented, publicly accessible customer purchasing patterns should be assessed. Several key questions that should be considered during the iterative price-to-win process are: (1) What is your government customer willing to pay and what is he or she expecting to receive for that amount of dollars given the particular contract type? (2) What are your known competitors likely to offer to the government in their proposals, including technical, programmatic, and staffing solutions as well as pricing? (3) What are the specific linkages between your price and your proposed solution set? In the process of price-to-win, key goals are to determine the "minimum cost solution" and the best-value solution among a range of alternatives, as well as to identify major cost and risk drivers.

8.7 Government contract requirements

The federal government imposes standards, procedures, guarantees, and documentation requirements on companies with which it does business; and it exacts significant penalties for noncompliance [2]. The Truth in Negotiations Act (TINA) was enacted in 1962 to protect the government from unscrupulous DoD contractors who supported their cost proposals with erroneous information. Congress extended the Act in 1984 to include all government contracts. On all negotiated contracts and subcontracts in excess of $500,000, your company will be required to furnish certified cost or pricing data. The government will include a "Price Reduction for Defective Cost or Pricing Data" in any resulting contract.

Small businesses must also be aware and knowledgeable about federal CAS. Created by Congress in 1970, the CAS was designed to "promote uniformity and consistency in the way defense contractors measure, assign, and allocate contract costs" [3]. The applicability of the CAS was extended in 1988 to include all negotiated government contracts in excess of $500,000. The "contract clauses involving CAS also restrict changes in company accounting practices.... Cases exist where a company has made an accounting change only to learn later that it owed the government money" [3]. As an entrepreneur, you will be well served to implement and energize a well-organized, highly trained, and watchful contract administration group.

ENDNOTES

1. Stewart, Rodney D., and Ann L. Stewart, *Proposal Preparation*, New York: John Wiley & Sons, 1984, p. 126.

2. Wall, Richard J., and Carolyn M. Jones, "Navigating the Rugged Terrain of Government Contracts," *Internal Auditor*, April 1995, p. 32. This section draws upon Mr. Wall and Ms. Jones's article.

3. Wall, Richard J., and Carolyn M. Jones, "Navigating the Rugged Terrain of Government Contracts," *Internal Auditor*, April 1995, p. 33.

Chapter 9

The proposal solution development process

9.1 Solution development overview

Solutions are the essence of the final, written proposal. A winning proposal requires carefully constructed winning solutions. Every element in a well-crafted proposal involves a *choice*, and each choice results in a part of your overall *solution*. A *solution set* constitutes all of the choices your company makes with regard to its teaming strategy, technical approach, management and subcontractor management approach, key personnel and staffing selections, phase-in/phase out (transition) timeline and processes, quality management methodology, and risk management approach, as well as past performance references and cost/price strategy. Critically, *develop your solution set early* in the capture process—*prior* to the release of the final solicitation documents so that you can validate the key elements of your solution with the customer. Refine your solutions through customer feedback as well as ongoing market research and meaningful insights provided by companies with which you are teamed on the specific marketing opportunity.

Early solution development streamlines the entire proposal process; it saves time, precludes significant rework after formal color review cycles, and reduces overall bid and proposal (B&P) costs—all of which are vital to small businesses in this era of hypercompetitiveness and reduced discretionary federal government spending. A case in point is the September 2011 recommendation to the congressional Joint Select Committee on Deficit Reduction of cutting the federal contractor workforce by 15%. Your goal should be to begin solution development at the draft RFP stage of the federal acquisition cycle for a specific opportunity. You do not need a final RFP to construct and refine many of the elements in your solution. For example, your overall corporate-level approach to risk management, including your risk officer or lead staff person, risk planning methodology, specific quantitative (e.g., composite risk index) and qualitative risk assessment and estimation processes, "critical chain"–based project management, and risk tracking and analytical tools, along with knowledge-based risk management and risk mitigation and avoidance success stories are not directly dependent upon the requirements in a government solicitation document. To be sure, there will need to be connections drawn between your overall risk management approach and the potential project-specific risks that may occur during contract execution. However, the essentials of your approach can be established and refined well in advance. The same is valid for your company's total compensation plan (TCP), subcontractor management approach, phase-in (transition) plan, and cost and schedule control processes and tools, as well as many other proposal sections, including your plan for recovering from unanticipated problems and corporate training/cross-training programs.

9.2 Solution development tools

Solution development tools include a Win Strategy white paper, which should document the essence of your offer across all major sections of your proposal. It is the precursor to the Executive Summary, and it serves to force your company and your team to think through and architect solutions in advance of the actual proposal response. We know that in any given proposal, there are a number of fundamental and predictable sections, even though there may be permutations in the exact titles across various solicitations [e.g., management approach (used in some Department of Energy

solicitations), management plan (used in some Department of Justice proposals), management organization and management systems (used in some
Environmental Protection Agency proposals)], and program management
approach (used in some Intelligence Community proposals). Importantly,
we do not need a draft or final RFP to know this. These sections include:

- *Technical approach:* Understanding the requirements, approach,
  and tangible and intangible (e.g., attention to detail, peace of mind)
  benefits to the customer;
- *Management approach:* Including organizational structure, performance and quality management, schedule management, and cost
  management, as well as resource management, staff develop-
  ment/training, communications plan, knowledge-sharing plan, and
  specific mechanisms to access corporate assets;
- *Staffing plan:* Key personnel, recruiting and retention approach,
  total compensation plan (TCP);
- *Phase-in/phase-out:* Transition approach for both incumbent capture and an alternative to incumbent capture, in effect, a Plan B;
- Subcontractor management, subcontractor interfaces, and subcontractor utilization along with teaming configuration and rationale for
  teaming;
- Quality management plan;
- Risk management and Mitigation;
- Past/present performance;
- Cost/price and bases of estimates (BOEs).

Structure your Win Strategy white paper to articulate and document
your key solutions (choices) for each of these major sections; collectively,
these constitute your solution set. In the case of past performance, for
example, identify the highly relevant projects that you will cite that are
similar in size, scope, complexity, and contract type, as well as the
government staff (e.g., contracting officer, contracting officer's technical
representative, and technical monitor) who will be listed as key points of
contact and references for these same projects. For your management
approach, discuss whether you will implement an integrated project team
(IPT) or an organizational framework that is constructed with specific
teammates focused on particular functional or task areas (or a hybrid
management configuration). When developed with enough lead time prior
to the release of the final solicitation document from the government, key
solutions that are captured in your Win Strategy white paper can then be
vetted with appropriate government staff and modified and refined

accordingly. Your goal needs to be to make the government aware—informally, not in writing—of your solution set across all of the aforementioned sections before they read about it in your proposal. Remember that the proposal is the final exam in the overall business development process—your solutions must be presold. The content of the Win Strategy white paper should be based on many of the key elements of your proposal directive, including strengths, weaknesses, opportunities, threats (SWOTs); call reports; and customer hopes, fears, biases, critical issues, and success factors. This white paper is a narrative that integrates the various components of the Directive into a cohesive "story" to be used by proposal writers and contributors in the event that there is a final *go* bid decision made. The business development and capture management functions in your company should work on this deliverable collaboratively to ensure that there is effective communication and inclusion of all of the details learned during the course of the business development process. The Win Strategy white paper should be approximately two to three pages in length and can be leveraged by executive management for multiple decision-making purposes, including adding niche subcontractors or unpriced vendors, final bid/no-bid, and investments in staff, hardware, software applications, facilities, and/or training that may offer significant strengths and thus improve the overall value of your offering to the government.

Other important solution development tools encompass "pain tables," in which are captured customer "pain points" and other key elements of understanding such as the as-is and to-be operational environment, your approach, and benefits to the government of your approach in terms of enhanced quality, timeliness, cost control and avoidance, and risk mitigation. Innovation tables, risk tables, and elevator speeches, as well as process flow diagrams, features/benefits tables, success stories and proof points, and a listing of key strengths that your company brings to the specific customer represent other valuable and field-proven tools through which to capture and illustrate your solutions.

9.3 Solution development process

One of the most effective and efficient ways by which to extract key information that will contribute to the overall solution set of your proposal is to conduct and facilitate a series of highly interactive solution development strategy sessions. These sessions should include representatives from within your own company, as well as from across your entire team. Participants in these meetings should come fully prepared, having read and studied the solicitation documents in detail, and should be knowledgeable in one or more of the following areas: (1) the customer's as-is and to-be operational environment; (2) the customer's hopes, fears, biases, critical issues, and success factors; (3) the project-specific technologies and tools, along with particular technical and programmatic processes; (4) major business and governance drivers, including statutes, regulations, directives, policies, and standards for this specific government customer; and (5) relevant corporate past performance and key resources such as centers of excellence and corporate innovation centers that can be applied directly to the specific contract. Additionally, people who attend these solution-generating sessions must be fully engaged and interactive. One key rule of engagement is no cell phones or personal digital assistant (PDA) of any kind. An experienced meeting facilitator is critical to obtaining meaningful and substantive outcomes that can then be used to develop sections of the proposal effectively. That individual must be able to draw ideas and information out of the heads of a broad spectrum of technical subject matter experts (SMEs), executive leaders, project managers, and business development staff. Figures 9.1 and 9.2 provide real-world examples of a subset of vital information that was collected for a Department of Homeland Security (DHS) proposal through the efforts of approximately 15 people during the course of 3 days of intensive, face-to-face interaction. Every one of the solution sets for the 13 tasks was addressed and documented in a consistent manner using the same categories, or "buckets," of information as a standard framework. This framework is built from Sections, C, H, L, and M of the solicitation document, as well as the Past Performance Questionnaire (PPQ). The PPQ is always a rich source of information as to the elements the government deems to be important, such as quality of service, timeliness, efficiency and effectiveness, key personnel management, and cost control, along with minimizing government oversight of the project. This practice greatly facilitates the next step in the proposal development process, namely, the actual writing of the elevator speeches, generating process flow diagrams as real artwork, refining features/benefits tables, and crafting full-scale narrative for the understanding and approach sections of your proposal. The more relevant big-picture insights as well as quantitative and qualitative details that you capture during the solution development process, the more powerful and highly rated by the government evaluators that your proposal sections are likely to be. Importantly, technical details alone are insufficient to win proposals. Make certain that the solution development strategy sessions focus significant attention on the relationship across technical task areas. Is one or more task subordinate to another? Are several tasks the logical extension of another task? Are certain tasks—such as those relating to project management,

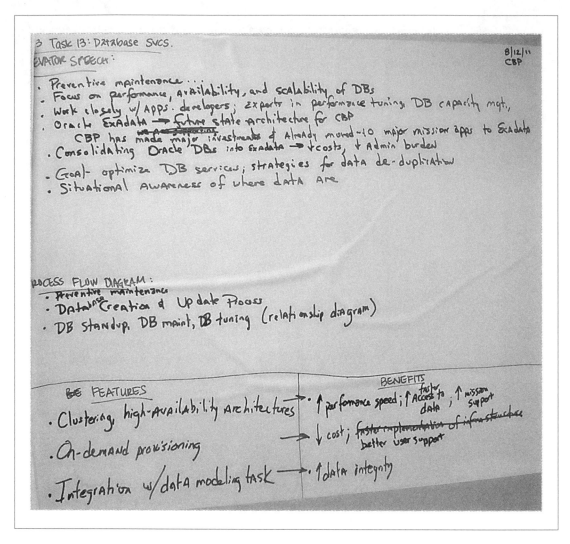

Figure 9.1 Capture the key elements that will be communicated in your elevator speech during the solution development strategy sessions.

quality control, and configuration management—cross-cutting, in that they relate across multiple other task areas?

As you conduct your solution development strategy sessions, it is necessary that participants fully grasp the key differences as well as the connections between understanding and approach, the topic of Chapter 10.

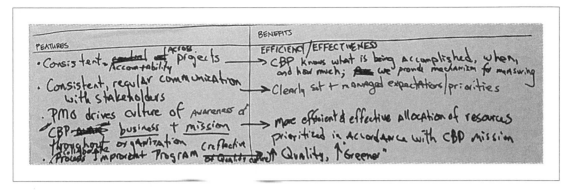

Figure 9.2 Ensure that all features of your solution have associated benefits that are meaningful to your customer.

Chapter 10

Customer understanding and program approach— they are that important

O F THE NONPRICE REASONS that companies—both small and large—lose competitive proposals, lack of understanding of the customer and lack of a clearly articulated approach stand at the forefront. Although both of these critical aspects seem to be straightforward and intuitive, this is certainly not the case, as has been demonstrated numerous times with tier-one corporations, mid-tier companies, and small firms alike. In a proposal context, understanding is all about the customer—their mission and objectives, the fusion of their business needs and technical requirements, their governance framework, and their stakeholders—in terms that make sense to that customer. Compelling understanding sections articulate clearly how the customer envisions success, all within the confines of the framework and page limitations that the RFP or RFS requires.

Although very much related to and building directly upon understanding, approach in a proposal must convey precisely how your company will perform the specific work for the customer on a particular contract over the full life cycle of the engagement, whether that timeframe is measured in months, years, or even decades. Contracts, technologies, staffing levels, and best practices are not static; your approach should not be, either. One major reason for finishing the business development life cycle outside the winner's circle relates to the strong tendency to substitute past performance for approach. To be sure, past performance can and should be leveraged as validation for the approach that your organization will apply on the new (or recompete) program or project. However, the entire battery of journalistic questions—*who, what, where, when, why, how, and how many*—should be asked and answered in the graphics and supporting narrative that you develop. It is not enough to indicate that your organization has successfully applied Lean Six Sigma principles on a project for the Department of the Army. You must also show how, specifically, your firm will apply both Lean and Six Sigma principles on the new work for the Air Force, and how this approach will be of direct, tangible benefit to the Air Force in terms of enhanced quality of product or service, schedule adherence, cost control and avoidance, and risk mitigation.

When crafting high-impact understanding and approach sections in a proposal, it is critical to add value, insight, and specificity beyond a mere

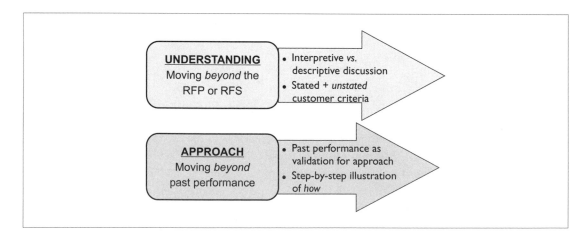

Figure 10.1 You earn significant strengths by developing a proposal that contributes significantly toward exceeding the contract requirements in a manner that provides additional value to the government. [Language appeared in a NASA Request for Quotation (RFQ), September 30, 2011.]

> Understanding must anchor the work to be performed within the
> *broader context* of the customer's mission, goals, and objectives, while
> simultaneously the approach must be *highly focused* on how this
> particular work will be done on this program or project to the benefit
> of the customer.

baseline level (see Figure 10.1). For example, in the case of understanding, merely repeating the stated requirements found in the government solicitation documents and associated amendments adds no value to your proposal and therefore will result in lower evaluated scores. The government knows what their requirements are; providing a slightly reworded version of those same requirements back to them in your proposal document indicates only that you have read the RFP or Request for Solution (RFS). It also consumes valuable "proposal real estate" (i.e., page count) that can be far better employed to demonstrate understanding of the overall and specific stated and unstated requirements of the proposed contract that you have gained through business development and research activities, and to convey your company's ability for transforming that understanding into accomplishment. Invest the space to discuss the inherent problems associated with the operational aspect of the given procurement. Then in your approach section, present how you will overcome those potential risks and challenges.

10.1 Digging more deeply into understanding

Fundamentally, understanding emerges from a combination of sources, the most relevant and vital being direct, face-to-face interaction over time with the superset of appropriate sell points in the customer agency or organization for a given marketing opportunity. A single meeting with the contracting officer, Small and Disadvantaged Business Utilization (SADBU) officer, or chief information officer (CIO) is far from sufficient to glean the hopes, fears, biases,[1] critical issues, and success factors necessary for

---

1   Mr. Ron Trowbridge, a former owner of RS Information Systems, Inc. (RSIS) and a current owner of Energy Enterprise Solutions, LLC (EES), in Germantown, Maryland, introduced the hopes, fears, and biases concept in 1998.

proposal understanding sections that stand head and shoulders above your competition.

Your proposal must move beyond the merely descriptive toward being far more interpretive and connective. Let's use a metal stop sign that we see at many street corners in the United States as a concrete example. A descriptive discussion might be as follows: "The stop sign has a red background and white lettering. It is eight-sided, and generally manufactured using reflective paint or stripping. The octagon measures 30 inches in width, and *yy* inches in height. It is often mounted on a metal or wooden post, which in turn is embedded into the ground *zz* feet. The first stop signs in the United States were posted in Michigan. The stop sign conveys that drivers must bring their vehicles to a complete halt before proceeding with caution. Conversely, an interpretative or connective discussion might include the following: "Stop signs are symbolic of our system of laws to provide for a structured and ordered society, which has its foundations in the Enlightenment-era thought of writers such as Englishman John Locke. These signs contribute to driver and pedestrian safety. Stop signs are part of a spectrum of roadway signage that includes 'yield,' 'railroad crossing,' 'speed limit,' and 'pedestrian crossing.' As a driver, one's decisions regarding a stop sign are subject to resulting actions by police officers as well as local courts. Court interpretations have associated with them a body of case law." And so forth. The point here is to build context into your proposal understanding sections.

One way to think of context in a proposal is to use a professional football analogy. For example, the Washington Redskins football team is part of the National Football Conference (NFC) East Division. In turn, the NFC East is an integral part of the overall NFC, along with the NFC North, South, and West. Together, the NFC and American Football Conference constitute the National Football League, or NFL. The NFL is part of the larger universe of professional sports leagues in North America, which includes Major League Baseball, the National Basketball Association and Women's NBA, and the National Hockey League. To bring context back into the proposal world, consider a specific government agency requirement for the delivery of information technology (IT) services. When you put together the understanding section, think in terms of the overall framework into which this particular set of IT services fits. Remember that IT is an *enabler*, not an end in and of itself. There are governance parameters, business dimensions, and mission-level goals and objectives that guide the overall technical IT requirements. Therefore, you might consider the following:

- How this specific set of IT services fits within the particular government agency's strategic plan and information resources management plan;
- Federal and agency-specific statutes, regulations, policies, procedures, directives, and standards that will govern the IT work to be performed; for example, Homeland Security Presidential Directive (HSPD)12;
- Budget justification and reporting requirements (OMB Exhibit 300s);
- Relevant NIST Special Publication (SP) 800-xx series standards that address computer security;
- Impact of meeting relevant Federal Information Security Management Act (FISMA) requirements;
- How these IT services mesh with the Federal CIO's "25 Point Plan";
- Relevant business drivers associated with these particular IT service requirements.

To provide some grounding for the concept of business drivers, consider a recent IT services requirement for the Department of Homeland Security Customs and Border Protection (CBP) organization. Task 11, Statement of Work element 6.11, focused on support for CBP's Automated Commercial Environment (ACE). ACE is a complex, large-scale Java EE-based system using SAP and DB2 as its backend that supports the tracking and movement of cargo throughout the United States. As important as the technical details of automated failover, clustering, and rolling recycles are, these take a distant second place to the core business driver of maximum up-time of CBP's ACE system, which, in turn, is critical for the efficient flow of legitimate truck traffic across U.S. borders, as well as for the increased adoption of ACE by commercial organizations that is so important for revenue generation by the government.

Understanding in your proposal can also be conveyed very effectively by developing relationship diagrams, such as the one depicted in Figure 10.2. Look for how various tasks align with and/or follow from others. Identify tasks such as IT policy development or task order project management that cross-cut the entire project and depict them in a graphic accordingly. One word of caution—do not overengineer the relationships among the various tasks of a project. That knowledge should emerge from your business development efforts with the particular customer.

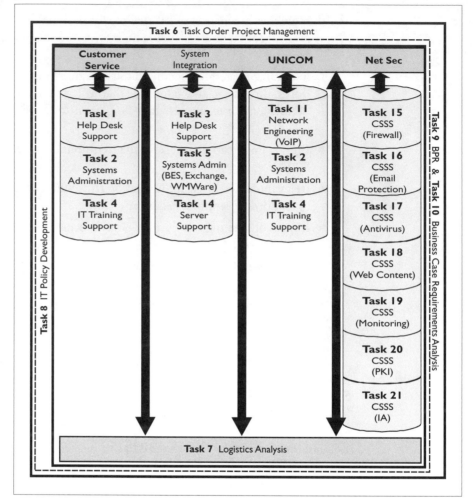

Figure 10.2
Insightful relationship diagrams demonstrate to the customer that you understand and have carefully considered the connections across seemingly disparate tasks.

Your advance business development efforts should definitely include the execution of the customer call plan for each contract opportunity. Face-to-face interaction with the superset of customers who might be involved in a given source selection is critical to increase the probability of winning (P_{win}). This superset most likely includes department or center leadership, contracting officer, and contracting officer's technical representative (COTR), as well as cognizant branch chiefs, division directors, and technical monitors. Candidate questions to ask include the following:

- What business processes within the government agency does this task (or functional area) enable and support?

- What are the technical critical issues and challenges associated with this task currently? How will those issues and challenges change in the future?

- How might innovation be introduced to this particular task (in close collaboration with the government)? What would these innovations include?

- To what other task does this specific task relate, and how? Describe the connections (this information can then be applied in building a relationship diagram). How does this specific task, in combination with other tasks, support the agency's overall mission?

- What particular federal mandates, policies, and procedures are related to the governance of this task?

- How would the government envision success on this task now and going forward?

- What are the managerial critical issues and challenges associated with this task currently? How will those issues and challenges change in the future?

By applying an interview-style approach to both business development staff and technical subject matter experts, proposal professionals can help to extract critical "tacit" information learned during the call plan execution process and then document it to ensure that it is in an "explicit" format. This information can be leveraged to sell your organization's knowledge of the customer and their project.

10.2 Building a powerful approach section

We have seen that understanding sections in a proposal focus on the customer. The approach section, in turn, illustrates and describes the people, processes, knowledge, and tools that your company will apply to meet and exceed the requirements, acceptable quality levels (AQLs), and service level agreements (SLAs) established by the government (Figure 10.3).

The kinds of questions to pose as you strategize the development of your approach sections include:

- Who on our team will get up every morning and care about the level of performance on this task or functional area?

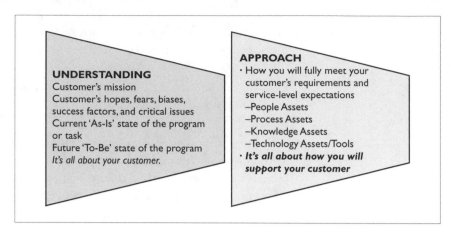

Figure 10.3
Understanding informed by in-depth customer insights drives a detailed approach that delivers meaningful benefits to that customer.

- What structured key processes will our organization apply to the success of this task? What performance metrics will be used to assess our work?

- Where will our project team be located to be serve this customer? Where is any reachback capability located, and how specifically will it be accessed for this project?

- When do we expect that process improvements will result in tangible cost savings to the government?

- Why will our solution deliver exemplary performance, ensure schedule adherence, and contribute to cost reduction or stabilization over time?

- How will our team integrate a specific suite of software applications into the customer's current operational environment?

- How many staff and what skill mix are required to successfully perform this task or functional area?

You will find that some proposal and capture team members will think in "written" or "tabular" form (see Table 10.1). Other people will envision similar information graphically (see Figure 10.4). The important point is to capture and document information in ways that contribute to the development of compelling approach sections that are aligned meticulously with customer insight and knowledge. Importantly, Table 10.1 can also be used to support the construction of a work breakdown structure (WBS), staffing matrix, and bases of estimate (BOEs).

Fundamentally, apply a disciplined and repeatable methodology to developing the understanding and approach sections of your proposal. Use concrete models such as those presented in Table 10.1 and Figure 10.4 to assist team members in recognizing the kinds of questions they should

Sequential Steps	Industry Best/Key Practices	Tools and Technologies	Relevant Government Regulations, Policies, and Guidelines	Skill Sets/Labor Categories	Number of Each Type of Staff Professional	Post Performance Validation	Results or Benefits to the Government
	(Processes)	*(Technologies)*		*(People)*	*(People)*		
I. Fill in the series of steps associated with each element in your Approach	**Examples:** • ISO 9001:2008 • SEI CMMI Maturity Level 3 • ITIL v3 • PMBOK 5th Edition • Lean Six Sigma	**Examples:** • Microsoft Office Sharepoint Server (MOSS) 2010 • MS Project 2010	**Examples:** • FISMA • NIST SP 800 series • FEAF • DoDAF	**Examples:** • Program Manager • Systems Engineer II • Security Specialist		On what projects has this specific step been used successfully and for what Government customer?	• Enhance Performance Quality • Ensure Schedule Adherence • Control and Monitor Costs • Reduce Program Risks

Table 10.1 Importantly, this table can also be used to support the construction of a Work Breakdown Structure (WBS), staffing matrix, and Bases of Estimate (BOEs).

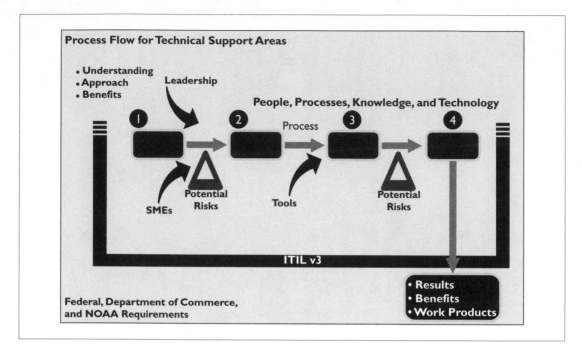

Figure 10.4 Your approach must be clear, straightforward, and linked directly with benefits to the customer in terms they understand.

consider. Be fully aware that descriptive writing alone is not sufficient to convey genuine understanding. One technique for moving well beyond mere descriptive writing is explored in Chapter 11.

Chapter 11

Developing key conceptual graphics first

"**V**ISION DOMINATES our sensory landscape," wrote Stephen Few [1]. Indeed, people get most of their information about the world through visual perception. A well-designed data graphic, for example, can help someone understand the underlying data much better than a simple table of numbers. Effective design presents information in an organized manner, making it easy for the viewer to understand the roles and the relationships between the elements, as Maureen Stone noted [2].

Graphics, figures, illustrations, and tables are taking on an increasing level of significance in today's era of the 118-page Statement of Work (SOW) and the corresponding 30-page limitation for your company's technical approach section. There are now many situations in which you literally cannot write your way to proposal success. The old proposal adage of simply "answering the mail" has little applicability in 2012 and beyond. In general, attempting to meticulously address every Statement of Work, Statement of Objectives (SOO), or Performance Work Statement (PWS) element, subelement, and sub-subelement is not the pathway to success. Even if it were still the 1980s when proposals were often greater than 100 pages and frequently more than 500 or even 1,000 pages in length with more than 10 separate volumes, graphics would be vital to convey your company's understanding, approach, and benefits to the customer. In fact, literally drawing out what you understand about a project and how you will approach delivering exemplary support to the government is a technique that has proven to be invaluable in my direct experience during the past 14 years. You can quickly see relationships and connections, as well as gaps in your company's knowledge that must be addressed through additional business development activity and research.

Let's consider several diverse examples. In a 2011 Department of Energy (DOE) Sandia National Laboratories (SNL) Request for Quotation (RFQ), Criteria I, A. Company Experience and Past Performance, required offerors to "[r]elate your experience and past performance to elements in the SOW in sufficient detail to demonstrate understanding of the requirements and a capability to deliver. The Offeror's experience and past performance should demonstrate proficiency in the following areas in the SOW: II, III, IV and V." So how might this set of requirements be rendered into graphical form? Build a three-column table that illustrates the direct technical correlation (i.e., relevance) between your team's past performance and the SNL SOW elements and that also demonstrates the proficiencies you bring to SNL across SOW areas II, III, IV, and V. In this same RFQ, there was a requirement for offerors to "discuss methods used for the prevention, detection and resolution of performance difficulties." "Method" or "methodology" should be trigger words that signal *use a graphic*, such as a flow diagram.

The Mission Suitability Subfactors, Subfactor A—Technical Approach, a $200 million NASA Headquarters solicitation from 2011, included the following statement: "The government will evaluate the depth and thoroughness of the Offeror's understanding of project management life cycle processes and best practices in a NASA IT environment." Using a graphic would be a very sound way to illustrate understanding of any life cycle. In the same NASA solicitation, it was stated that "[t]he Government will evaluate the effectiveness of the Offeror's approach to manage and maintain the HQ Data Center to ensure availability, reliability, and uninterrupted services at all times." "Approach" is another pivotal solicitation word that should elicit the thought to generate a graphical concept on your part.

The United States Department of State (DoS) Bureau of Information Resources Management (IRM) issued a major Phase I RFP in 2011. It included the following language under "Proposal Requirement Instructions"—all within a single paragraph:

- "clear and complete description of ... approach"
- "comprehensive and innovative"
- "compliant with all applicable statutes, regulations, policy and guidance"
- "results and outputs needed by IRM, its customers and other external entities"
- "sound technical approach that clearly demonstrates how implementation of the proposed solutions will deliver timely, standard, reliable, secure, flexible, responsive, compliant and cost effective services to meet the needs of DoS"
- "understanding and approach"

Rather than launch into writing narrative as a first step, what we developed was a graphic (Figure 11.1) that was then used to capture information during the solution development strategy sessions (see Chapter 9). Importantly, this same graphic was then built right into the actual proposal response. That is a critical point—develop graphics that can serve as the centerpiece for specific proposal sections.

Figure 11.1
Presenting complex narrative requirements as a carefully integrated and meaningful graphic assists government evaluators in quickly discerning the essence of your offer.

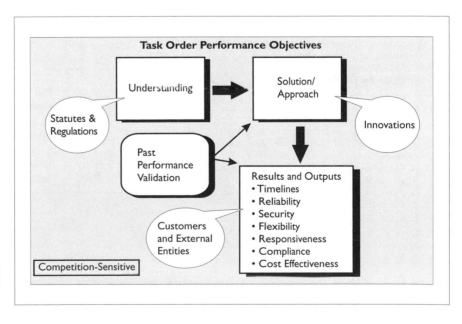

In Figures 11.2 and 11.3, slides that were developed by leaders within NASA for an IT Summit held in San Francisco, California, in 2011 reflect the type of integrated graphic that effectively brings together technical elements, business and financial drivers, statutes/policies/standards, and performance-based risk management. These are outstanding models for your company to use in modified form and format to demonstrate your big-picture understanding of a given program, project, or task.

Another technique for both the capture of information and ideas, as well as to include as part of the proposal design, is a Who, What, Where, When, How, and Why diagram. Additional graphical tools encompass cause and effect diagrams, compare and contrast diagrams, Ishikawa or fishbone diagrams, life-cycle diagrams, affinity diagrams (see http://www.doh.state.fl.us/hpi/pdf/AffinityDiagram.pdf), and use-case diagrams, which present a graphical overview of the functionality provided

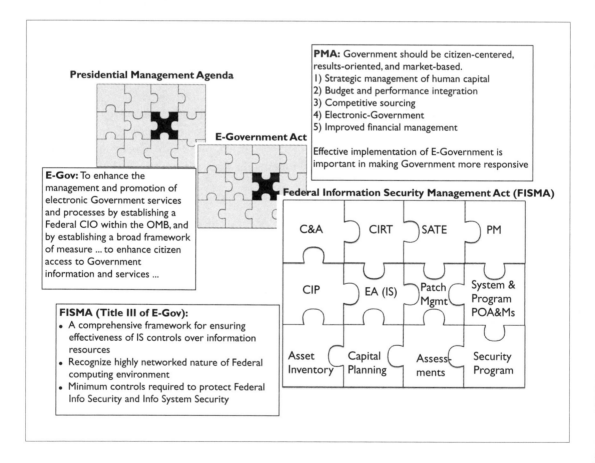

Figure 11.2 Clearly, the government values illustrating how governance, management, and technical pieces fit into an integrated whole.

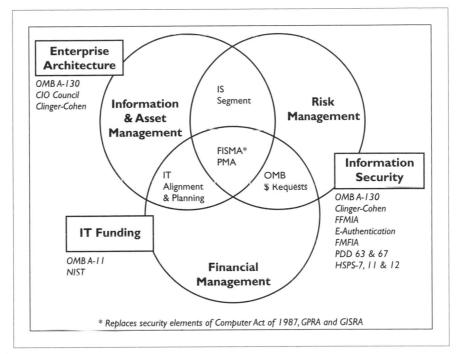

Figure 11.3 Using a Venn diagram to depict the dependencies across business and technical parameters.

by a system in terms of actors, their goals represented as use cases, and any dependencies among those use cases. Yet other ways to present ideas and concepts graphically include a Boston Consulting Group (BCG) matrix, layer charts, and radar or cobweb charts. A genuinely excellent reference for a wide variety of visualization techniques is found at "A Periodic Table of Visualization Methods" (http://www.visual-literacy.org/periodic_table/periodic_table.html). Consult this URL often!

You might also consider the following references and resources to transform ideas into high-impact graphics.

- Börner, Kay, *Atlas of Science: Visualizing What We Know,* Cambridge, MA: Massachusetts Institute of Technology, 2010.
- Few, Stephen, *Show Me the Numbers: Designing Tables and Graphs to Enlighten,* Oakland, CA: Analytics Press, 2004.
- Mike Parkinson's Billion Dollar Graphics Web site, http://www.billiondollargraphics.com/index.html.
- Parkinson, Mike, *Do-It-Yourself Billion Dollar Business Graphics: 3 Fast and Easy Steps to Turn Your Text and Ideas into Graphics That Sell,* Annandale, VA: Pepper Lip Press, 2007.
- Reynolds, Gary, *Presentation Zen: Simple Ideas on Presentation Design and Delivery,* Berkeley, CA: New Riders, 2008.

- Roam, Dan, *The Back of the Napkin: Solving Problems and Selling Ideas with Pictures*, expanded edition, New York: Portfolio (Penguin Group), 2009.
- Tufte, Edward R., *Envisioning Information*, Cheshire, CT: Graphics Press, 1990.[1]
- Tufte, Edward R., *The Visual Display of Quantitative Information*, Cheshire, CT: Graphics Press, 2001.
- Tufte, Edward R., *Visual Explanations: Images and Quantities, Evidence and Narrative*, Cheshire, CT: Graphics Press, 1997.

Generating "word clouds" of the RFP or RFS using Wordle (http://www.wordle.net/) has proven to be a useful technique to get people thinking. The clouds give greater prominence to words that appear more frequently in the source text, and can serve as the basis for conceptualizing graphics and proposal cover designs. Figure 11.4 is a Wordle creation based upon this chapter.

The cloud-based Software-as-a-Service (SaaS) called Prezi (http://prezi.com/), cofounded by Hungarian architect Adam Somlai-Fischer, is a presentation software and storytelling tool for exploring and sharing ideas using a virtual canvas. Prezi is distinguished by its Zooming User Interface (ZUI), which enables users to zoom in and out of their presentation media. Text, images, videos, and other presentation media are placed upon the canvas and can be grouped together in frames. Users then designate the relative size and position between all presentation objects and may pan and zoom in and between these objects. Prezi's stated mission is to "make sharing ideas more interesting," and it is intended to be an intuitive tool to develop and share ideas as a visual narrative. A proven proposal best practice is to express key solutions as graphics during the solution-development process. When you have drawn out your solutions as graphics, they become much more streamlined, elegant, and aligned.

---

1   Edward R. Tufte, Ph.D., characterized by the *New York Times* as a famous theorist of information presentation, is Professor Emeritus of political science, statistics, and computer science at Yale University.

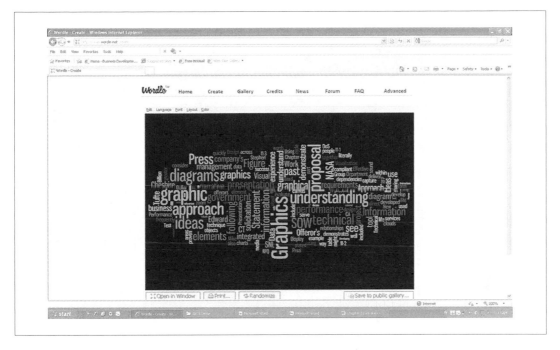

Figure 11.4 Prominent words in this chapter stand out quickly in this Wordle creation.

ENDNOTES

1. Few, Stephen, *Information Dashboard Design: The Effective Visual Display of Data,* Sebastopol, CA: O'Reilly Media, Inc., 2006.

2. Stone, Maureen, "Choosing Colors for Data Visualization," January 17, 2006, http://www.perceptualedge.com/articles/b-eye/choosing_colors.pdf.

Chapter **12**

Acquisition/capture and proposal team activities

W HEN A COMPANY is tracking a particular marketing opportunity, advanced planning and strategizing are crucial to its ultimate success. One mechanism that companies use in this up-front marketing planning is the concept of an acquisition/capture team.

12.1 Formation and function of acquisition/ capture teams

The acquisition/capture team is formed in advance of the release of the formal RFP or RFS by the client organization. Under the direction and guidance of an acquisition manager, capture manager, or campaign manager, team members (usually three to five people) participate in preproposal intelligence gathering (including FOIA requests), strategizing, briefing the potential client in a structured manner through your call plan process, interviewing incumbent staff and facilitating open houses or technical interchange meetings to attract qualified staff, developing strategic proposal themes, and generating bullet drafts or storyboards to use as storyline planning and compliance-verification tools during the proposal process. Fundamentally, the capture or campaign manager "owns" the successful pursuit and award of the particular program or project. He or she must focus every day on doing what it takes to win. The essence of capture management is "the winning solution" and resource management. Capture management is the logical extension of the business development process. The capture manager shoulders full ownership for capture of the opportunity. He or she is accountable for: (1) leading the solution development effort across all elements of the proposal, including technical, management, subcontractor management, phase-in/phase-out, staffing/key personnel, past performance, and cost/price; and (2) marshaling and managing all of the internal and external resources (including writers and operations staff) necessary for successful development and delivery of the proposal and all of its associated deliverables, including opt-ins, oral presentations, final proposal revisions (FPRs), and evaluation notices (ENs). The proposal manager functionally "reports" to the capture manager for a given proposal engagement. Specific capture or campaign manager responsibilities include the following:

- Shouldering overall responsibility for the successful pursuit of selected programs or proposal efforts for the business development group.

- Maintaining the highest level of program accountability of all capture team members. The capture manager is the holder of the vision and the winning solution for the program.

- Working with the business development lead to negotiate teaming agreements and Exhibit As, and identifying workshare and staffing based on business case analyses, gap analyses, and the capabilities of potential teammates.

- Developing and maintaining the overall capture plan (proposal directive) for the specific opportunity, in close coordination with the proposal manager.

- Responsible for writing the Win Strategy white paper, which is the precursor to the executive summary. The focus of the Win Strategy White Paper is the clear articulation of the technical management and subcontractor management, staffing/key personnel, phase-in/phase-out, past performance, and cost/price solutions for a given proposal in concise narrative form in advance of the actual writing of the proposal to assist in the final bid/no bid decision-making as well as to guide the writing team in developing a carefully integrated proposal response.

- Leading solution development strategy sessions to "extract" and document technical understanding, approach, benefits to the government, success stories, and so forth, and ensuring that the right internal and teammate resources are in attendance and actively participating.

- Orchestrating meetings associated with identifying, developing, and documenting the management solution set [i.e., the choices that must be made regarding project organizational structure, key personnel, role of the project management office (PMO), and programmatic tools such as Risk Radar Enterprise and Deltek CostPoint].

- Preparing the proposal calendar and detailed annotated outline, in close coordination with the proposal manager, and monitoring due dates for each element of the proposal.

- Ensuring that the final proposal and all interim work products are of superior quality and are delivered to the cognizant government procuring organization in full compliance with all requirements and amendments and by the date and time designated by the government.

- Working closely with business development in structuring the overall approach and win strategies and managing the capture plan, which is an action-oriented, structured plan that defines how the company will win a given marketing opportunity.

- Coordinating Freedom of Information Act (FOIA) requests for past contracts, monthly technical progress reports, and so forth. Ensuring the dissemination of that information to appropriate proposal team members.

- Participating in incumbent capture initiatives (open houses, job fairs, technincal interchange meetings, face-to-face meetings with incumbent staff).

- Developing and monitoring B&P budgets, in conjunction with the proposal manager.

- Attending the preproposal conference or industry day.

- Communicating with executive management regarding proposal status and resource requirements.

- Facilitating communication across the technical, programmatic, and cost elements of the proposal team, both within the company and across subcontractors.

- Leading the pricing strategy process and participating in developing the cost model.

- Attending government debriefing.

The acquisition/capture team is joined by and augmented by the proposal team when the RFP is released.

Crucial to proposal success is the transfer of relevant marketing knowledge and intelligence to appropriate members of the proposal team. And from there, that knowledge must be translated and driven into the actual proposal documents—into narrative, theme statements, graphics, captions, and the compliance matrix. If your marketing intelligence does not find its way into the proposal, then it cannot be evaluated and point scored. Therefore, it is valueless.

12.2 Prekickoff activities

Time spent in effective planning and strategizing will be critical to the success of the overall proposal effort.

Once an RFP or RFS to which your company will be responding is released, the proposal manager and key members of the Proposal Team should dedicate at least one if not more days to detailed analysis of that RFP along with in-depth proposal planning. Don't panic or become overly anxious, because the time spent in effective planning and strategizing will be critical to the success of the overall proposal effort. Too many times, proposal drafts emerge from review cycles with the recommendation for fundamental restructuring of the overall outline, proposed staffing solution, related contractual experience, primary strategic themes, and so forth. Building concurrence, based on the validated marketing intelligence you have collected, early in the proposal planning process will save innumerable hours later in the proposal life cycle.

The goal of prekickoff planning is to ensure that the formal kickoff meeting is an efficient and effective forum of information exchange and assignment making. During the prekickoff planning phase of the proposal response life cycle, you should do the following.

Perform a detailed RFP analysis.

Deduce probable weighting of evaluation criteria from Section M of the RFP. The goals of RFP analysis are to: (1) become familiar with the proposal structure and format (Section L), (2) understand each technical and programmatic requirement in detail, (3) understand the source evaluation criteria and client success criteria (Section M), (4) evaluate your company's pre-RFP assumptions about the procurement and the client, and (5) develop written questions for submission to the client.

Prepare a draft executive summary.

The draft executive summary will be invaluable in assisting writers to fully understand the scope of the procurement and your company's primary sales messages. The executive summary should be one to two pages in length. It should be built directly from the Win Strategy white paper.

Develop and hone your strategic win themes, with a focus on articulating the elements that will constitute strengths and significant strengths.

Review the proposal debriefings files, related proposals, project descriptions, and résumés in your company's proposal data center or library (knowledge base).

Learn what you did right on previous proposals, and where your company missed the mark.

Plan to get the right people to write proposal sections at the right time; obtain senior management's support to make them available.

Prepare the Proposal Directive or kickoff package.

Appendix A presents a modified example of an actual completed package. The outline for the proposal does not follow the standard A, B, C format; rather it was mapped directly to the numbering scheme in the client's RFP. In this particular case, technical and financial information was included in one volume.

When the Proposal Directive has been prepared, it is then appropriate to convene the formal kickoff meeting.

Another example of a technical volume outline is presented in Table 12.1. Again, this outline was built using the numbering scheme presented in the client's RFP. This type of outlining configuration effectively serves multiple purposes and is highly recommended. First, it assists in the generation of a cross-reference or compliance matrix for the proposal volume. Second, it links themes, critical issues, and strengths with specific proposal sections and subsections so that your company's proposal writers know what to infuse into their narrative. Clearly defined points of contact

Technical Volume Outline Procurement Name						
Company Outline Number	RFP Section	Technical Item	Person Responsible	Page Allocation	Themes/ Critical Issues/ Strengths	Status
—	—	Executive summary	John Smith	2		Closed
1.	L.5.1	Mission suitability factors	Jane Jones	0.5 (Intro)		Open
A.	L.5.1.A	Key personnel	James Goodfellow	0.5 (Intro)		Open
A.1		Project factors	Sally Bates	1.5		Open
A.2		Deputy project manager	John Smith	1.5		Open
B.1	L.5.1.B.1	Overall understanding	James Goodfellow	0.5		Open
B.1.1	SOW 1	Data center operations	Sally Bates	3		Open

Table 12.1 Effective Outline Configuration Tracks Status and Ensures Compliance

for each section and subsection are noted, and the status of each can be tracked. This overview provides an excellent starting point for the proposal kickoff meeting discussion.

12.3 Proposal kickoff meeting

The kickoff meeting for a proposal activity is cochaired by your company's capture manager and proposal manager. This is the opportunity to build upon the successful activities of the capture team.

Invite all members of the proposal team, including major subcontractors[1] if appropriate.

- Principal writers and contributors;
- Representative of senior management to demonstrate personally corporate commitment to the proposal and the project;
- Representative from contracts department;
- Publications group manager;
- Human resources manager;
- Key reviewers (Red Team participants).

Distribute key materials (Proposal Directive or kickoff package).

- Full RFPs, not only Section C, the SOW or statement of objectives (now is not the time to save money on photocopying costs);
- Complete listing of the proposal team membership and their specific roles;
- Evaluation factors for award;
- Hopes, fears, biases; success criteria; and critical issues (see Figure 12.1);
- SWOTs (see Figure 12.2);
- Competitive analysis (see Figures 12.3 and 12.4);
- Proposal summary sheet (see Figure 12.5);
- Milestone schedules in calendar format for each proposal volume;
- Proposal volume outlines and writing assignments (see Table 12.1), including page and word allocations;
- Validated win themes, discriminators, and strengths;
- Thematic and writing guidelines;
- Draft executive summary;
- Program organizational chart;
- Résumé format requirements;
- Documentation and production requirements;

---

1   You may want to hold a separate meeting with the subcontractors since they may not have exclusive teaming agreements with your company. You do not want anyone with divided loyalties gaining access to competition-sensitive proposal information.

HOPES

➢ Integrate air-war fighting lessons into space warfare
➢ Enterprise information management
➢ Vision for innovation to go forward
➢ Successes to help expand budget

FEARS

➢ Competition with Army
➢ Staffing continuity
➢ Budget constraints

BIASES

➢
➢

SUCCESS CRITERIA

➢ Single point of contact, integrated management team
➢ Visibility into tasks, cost, performance
➢ Continuity of operations—overall system uptime and availability
➢ Immediate filling of secure positions (security clearance and staffing processes)

CRITICAL ISSUES

➢ High-quality training programs
➢ Local decision making
➢ Security clearances

Figure 12.1
Hope, fears, biases; success criteria and critical issues.

STRENGTHS

➢ Integrated product team (IPT)
➢ Major Air Force small-business contractor
➢ Proven low-risk transition
➢ Highly successful incumbent capture history
➢ Key personnel have in-depth subject-matter expertise
➢ Subcontractors bring extensive technical knowledge base
➢ Outstanding past performance on mission-support contracts
➢ Consulting arrangement in place with former senior Space Command officer

OPPORTUNITIES

➢ Economies of scale—cross-utilization of staff
➢ Partnerships and technical alliances
➢ Preservation of institutional knowledge
➢ Application of structured process
➢ Most competitors have no Colorado presence

WEAKNESSES

➢ Prime has USAF but no Air Force Space Command contract experience
➢ Lack of current major Colorado presence by the prime
➢ Engineering not among prime's core competencies
➢ Lack of geographically close facility
➢ Limited commitments from current incumbent staff

THREATS

➢ Incumbent real-time progam knowledge
➢ Level playing field encourages low-ball bid
➢ Current incumbent has 90% award fees

Figure 12.2
SWOT analysis results.

Figure 12.3
Competitive
analysis.

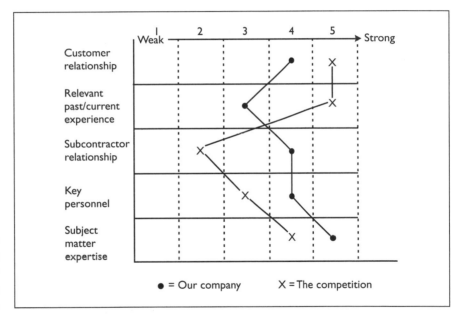

Figure 12.4
Competitive
analysis, another
approach (snake
diagram).

- Action items sheet;
- Telephone and e-mail contact list.

Emphasize senior management commitment to this important project. This is the reason for the member of senior management to be in attendance.

Proposal Summary Sheet
Proposal title: Internal B&P charge code: Proposal manager:

1. Solicitation or RFP #:
2. Proposal due date and time:
3. Client name (point of contact):
      Telephone:
      E-mail:

4. Dollar value 5. Level of effort (FTEs) 6. Type of contract: 7. Period of performance: 8. Place of performance: 9. Contract start date:

10. Proposal copies required
      Technical:
      Management:
      Past performance:
      Cost/price:
11. Page limitations:

12. Overview of scope of work: 13. Offer acceptance period (proposal validity period): 14. Packing label delivery address:
15. NAICS code:
16. Subcontractors/teammates: Specialty vendors: 17. Key personnel: 18. Other résuméd personnel:
19. Project summaries your company will use:
20. Defense Priorities and Allocation (DPAS) rating:
21. Security clearances required (staff and faculty):
22. Oral presentations:
23. Source evaluation process and staff:

Figure 12.5
Proposal summary sheet is an integral part of the proposal directive package.

Build motivation. Emphasize your company's proposal win bonus policy.

Highlight the nature of the procurement and what marketing intelligence your company has collected regarding the opportunity.

Review your competitors' as well as your own company's strengths and weaknesses (SWOT analysis).

Discuss the concrete reasons for bidding on this procurement (i.e., sales hooks).

Highlight the strategies for winning (technical, management, past performance, cost). Why your company and not your competition?

Discuss any major or unexpected changes in the RFP from what had been expected during your intelligence-gathering efforts (capture plan activities).

Discuss the respective strengths and roles of your teaming partners and subcontractors.

Review the proposal outlines.

Review the proposal milestone schedules. Emphasize the importance of adhering to the schedule from start to finish.

Make well-defined writing assignments; assign specific action items for tracking to appropriate staff.

Discuss writing guidelines (such as style, page limitations, and words per page).

Review your major validated sales messages (themes) and storyline for this proposal, along with significant strengths you offer the customer.

Discuss the résumés and related contractual experience that will be included with your proposal.

Obtain approval of the concept for the cover design of the proposal volumes.

Review the staffing plan and WBS.

Identify special needs (such as binders, tabs, photography, and colored paper, DVDs, and specialty software applications).

Determine who will deliver the proposal to the client and by what means (for example, driving and air travel).

12.4 Postkickoff activities

Prepare storyboards

- They are vital for subcontractors.
- They help technical authors overcome their initial writer's block.
- They ensure that all RFP or RFS requirements are addressed in your outline.
- They foster the smooth integration of writing from various authors.
- They link text and graphics or photographs.
- They are primarily associated with technical proposal volume.

In the several days following the storyboarding sessions, the proposal manager should spend sufficient time either face to face or virtually with members of the proposal writing team in order to do the following:

- Make certain they understand precisely what is expected from them during the proposal effort;
- Help the writers understand how their input relates to and fits with the entire proposal;
- Reinforce the need to incorporate appropriate proposal themes throughout their writing;
- Impress upon them the importance of adherence to the milestone schedule.

Keep in mind that all of these activities are designed and intended to assist your company and your staff to remain on track over the entire course of the proposal response life cycle.

We will now turn our attention to the role of the proposal manager, the individual charged and empowered with the responsibility and authority to oversee and orchestrate the entire proposal and postproposal response life cycle. Her principal task is to drive the solutions developed by the capture team into the proposal volumes.

Chapter 13

The role of the proposal manager

The job of leaders is to paint an actionable vision ...
—Roger N. Nagel, *Industry Week*

13.1 Overview

The proposal manager appointed to plan, organize, schedule, manage, arbitrate, and execute a given procurement response for a small business is the pivotal individual in the entire proposal process. He or she must skillfully balance the business opportunity against severely limited B&P monies and scarce human and material resources. And if those elements were not enough, the entire proposal response cycle unfolds in a matter of a few weeks—indeed, most smaller procurements have only 15- or 30-day response fuses. Certain state and local RFPs have response times measured in several days, as do task order proposals under certain GWAC vehicles, such as, Air Force NETCENTS, Navy Seaport-e, and DHS EAGLE.[1] Amazingly, some responses are due in 24 hours from time of RFP or Task Order RFP (TORFP) receipt by industry!

Your company needs several people (in very small firms, two people may be sufficient) to be well trained in the art and science of proposal management and development. Candidate staff need to possess (and ultimately enhance) the ability to plan and organize their own activities as well as those of a wide variety of other staff. Proposal managers should be effective leaders and positive motivators; exercise tact and diplomacy; display drive and enthusiasm; and practice thoroughness, organization, and attention to detail. Most importantly, they must take full ownership of the proposal development process.

Specific knowledge required for proposal manager candidates includes: (1) a broad understanding of your company, including its history, core competencies, products, services, personnel and human talent, facilities, technologies, and pricing policies; (2) demonstrated capability and experience with interviewing subject matter experts and management staff to extract and then document key information relevant to a given proposal effort; (3) broad exposure to the operations of the particular marketplace, such as the federal regulatory and statutory structure; (4) awareness of the potential competitors in your company's marketspace; (5) knowledge of public relations and marketing techniques; and (6) appreciation of documentation and computer-based publication methods so that the proposal is a well-presented sales document and knowledge product.

Reporting functionally to the capture manager, the proposal manager is charged with driving the solutions into the technical, management, past performance, and cost volumes of a proposal.
In many small companies, the proposal manager for a given procurement is drawn from the technical ranks because of the individual's knowledge of the project. Sometimes, the proposal manager will also be proposed formally as the project or program manager. Because of the lack of depth of human resources in small firms, the proposal manager will likely have to provide the client on an existing contract with 40 hours per week of technical and programmatic support in addition to his proposal management responsibilities and obligations. Midsized and large companies have the comparative luxury of a full-time proposal

---

1   NETCENTS stands for Net-Centric Solutions, Seaport-e is Seaport Enhanced, and DHS EAGLE is the Department of Homeland Security Enterprise Acquisition Gateway for Leading Edge Solutions.

management infrastructure, which can be drawn upon for proposal support as required. The proposal manager will most likely interact directly with the proposal coordinator or specialist within the business development group. The proposal coordinator or specialist can augment and complement the skills, knowledge, and time resources of the proposal manager. Small companies should avoid the very natural tendency of allowing the proposal coordinator or specialist, because that individual is probably a full-time overhead person, to assume too many of the proposal manager's (or capture manager's) functions and obligations. Both individuals should work together closely, but tasks should not merely be transferred from one person to the other. Proposal coordinators often participate in more than one proposal effort at a time. In fact, there are instances in small firms of one person coordinating 10 or more proposals simultaneously.

13.2 Generalized job description

The job description of the proposal manager is extremely open-ended, but in general he or she must provide organizational direction for the entire proposal effort, extended to include the following:

- Organizing, directing, and taking ownership of the internal company proposal team and the overall proposal development processes, which should be structured and repeatable;

- Attending preproposal conference;

- Monitoring B&P budgets, in conjunction with the capture manager;

- Developing proposal directive and orchestrating the proposal kick-off meeting in cooperation with the capture manager;

- Facilitating interactive storyboarding and solution development sessions. Being proactive in developing strategic win themes and discriminators and the overall proposal storyline along with the capture manager;

- Developing and controlling proposal development schedule in close collaboration with the capture manager;

- Developing targeted questions and interviewing in-house and teammate technical and programmatic staff to extract from them critical information to include in the proposal;

- Remaining current on all amendments and modifications to the solicitation;

- Overseeing incorporation of feedback from formal color review teams (Blue, Pink, Red, and Gold);
- Coordinating all aspects of proposal documentation and production;
- Coordinating all Evaluation Notice (EN) responses and Final Proposal Revision (FPR) logistics;
- Orchestrating oral presentation slide development and oral practice sessions;
- Attending government debriefings;
- Conducting postaward debriefings (after-action reviews) internally, regardless of outcome, and revising business development and proposal development strategies as appropriate;
- Developing proposal boilerplate (reuse) material to incorporate in future RFP opportunities through an automated, text-searchable knowledge base;
- Training additional staff on proposal management skills;
- Developing and continuously improving the company's proposal development processes to streamline and improve proposal development.

The proposal manager must also translate purpose into specific actions, as illustrated in Figure 13.1.

A detailed position description for a proposal manager is provided in Figure 13.2. Figure 13.3 shows the sample text for a classified

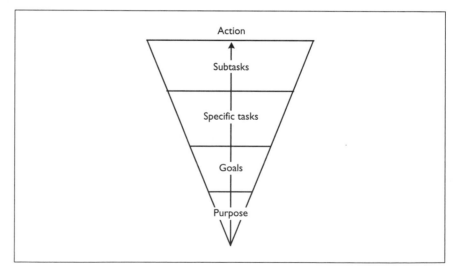

Figure 13.1
Proposal management—translating purpose into action.

Position Description

Title: Proposal Manager
Organization: Proposal Development Group

Nature and Scope of Position
The Proposal Manager organizes, directs, and takes ownership of internal proposal teams and the overall structured and repeatable proposal development processes. The manager develops and updates Proposal Directives [including points of contact (POCs), outlines, schedules, and so forth], orchestrates kickoff meetings, and facilitates storyboarding sessions in close coordination with the capture manager. The manager takes a proactive role in the development of strategic solutions, win themes, and discriminators. The manager is responsible for coordinating all aspects of proposal documentation and production, which may include submission of responses to requests for information, submission of questions to contracting officers, and preparation of material for formal reviews. The manager is expected to contribute to the continuous improvement of proposal development processes and take a hands-on approach to proposal tasks.

Reporting Relationship
The Proposal Manager reports to the Proposal Director/Capture Manager.

Responsibilities
Take end-to-end ownership and command of the proposal process for assigned proposals, including oral presentations, ENs, and FPRs.
Create outline and schedule for proposals; remain current on all proposal amendments and modifications.
Provide detailed guidance to proposal writers and contributors both within the company and among subcontractors; develop targeted questions and interview technical and programmatic staff to extract critical proposal-related information.
Write significant portions of proposal/ marketing narrative (for technical, past performance, and management sections of proposals) in real time.
Edit, organize, and refine entire proposal for final delivery.
Provide requested information for proposal development to companies hiring the company as a subcontractor.
Contribute to knowledge base and stores of "boilerplate" material for effective reuse in proposals.
Lead storyboarding, kickoff, and review meetings; assist proactively in development of strategic win themes and discriminator.
Communicate proposal-related requirements and status to senior management as appropriate.

Critical Attributes
Exceptional communication skills;
Leadership and management skills;
Ability to work independently or as part of a team;
Flexibility;
Ability to multitask on concurrent projects;
Superior organizational skills;
Motivator;
Positive, proactive attitude.

Qualifications
Bachelor's degree in professional writing, journalism, English or communications;
Four to seven years of progressive experience in a fast-paced, high-volume proposal environment;
One to two years of management experience;
Hands-on knowledge of electronic file management;
Good familiarity with standard MS Office software, e-mail applications, and Web browsers.

Physical Requirements (per ADA [1992])
Significant level of repetitive motions, such as fingering/keyboarding;
Ability to differentiate colors on paper and on a computer monitor;
Tasks may involve lifting packages less than 20 pounds;
Majority of tasks performed while sitting in nonadverse environmental conditions.

Figure 13.2   Detailed description of the proposal manager position.

Figure 13.3
Sample classified
ad for proposal
manager
candidates.

We are currently seeking a full-time Proposal Manager to become part of our Corporate Proposal Development Team. Candidate needs to be a solutions-oriented, results-driven, and high-energy individual to serve as a hands-on leader for multiple proposal efforts of varying size. Responsibilities will include participating in development of strategic solutions, win themes, outlines, storyboards, and schedules. Critical attributes include exceptional communications skills, leadership, interviewing skills, teamwork, flexibility, organization, motivational skills, and a "do-whatever-it-takes" attitude. Must have proven ability to write proposal narrative, rapidly and effectively conceptualize graphics, and provide guidance to proposal writers and contributors. Knowledge management and document production experience a plus.

advertisement designed to attract top-flight candidates for a proposal manager position.

Recruit, organize, and direct the proposal team.

Arrange for necessary human, material, and computer resources. Requisition or obtain dedicated, secure floor and wall space to prepare the proposal.

Getting enough of the right resources for a proposal at the right time can be challenging in both small and large businesses. This is one of several points at which senior management's direct involvement is critical. Give every proposal that your company designs and prepare the resources necessary to win, or do not bid.

Attend preproposal (bidders) conference (see FAR 15.409).

- Identify competitors and potential teaming partners;
- Obtain the client's official definition of evaluation criteria;
- Note any last-minute changes to the RFP or RFS;
- Listen for hidden messages from the government (e.g., We are happy with the incumbent);
- Obtain details about the contract job site.

Ensure adequate planning of the proposal effort.

Time spent on planning and strategizing early in the proposal response cycle before the formal kickoff meeting is crucial to the overall success of the proposal team. Participate in RFP analysis, schedule and outline development, page allocation, writing assignments, and storyboard preparation and review. Talk often with key technical writers, reviewers, and your publication staff to ensure that people understand your expectations and your role and responsibilities, as well as theirs.

Prepare and then negotiate B&P budget estimates with senior management; monitor and control B&P and ODC expenditures along with the capture manager.

With the capture manager, prepare B&P projections to ensure select key technical and programmatic staff are available to prepare the best possible proposal.

It is highly advisable that your company develop and implement a method for projecting and tracking B&P-related costs. Direct labor for marketing a potential business target as well as for the proposal writing, cost development, proposal development, and production of the proposal, oral presentation, and FPR should be estimated in detail for the entire proposal life cycle. In addition, ODCs, including travel, communications initiatives (billboards, radio spots, print ads, and Web sites, for example), classified advertising for new hires, subcontractor costs, temporary staff, and proposal consultants should be estimated as well. These estimates should be completed by the assigned proposal manager and capture manager in advance of a proposal tracking number (for time sheets) ever being assigned and approved by a member of senior management. The approved forms (hardcopy or electronic) are then used as an extremely effective tool to manage the cost of the entire proposal process in a manner analogous to managing a project. B&P projections can then be approved or disapproved by senior management based upon what the company had allocated for B&P expenditures for a given fiscal year.

The benefits of this structured, planned approach are that actual costs for proposal development, including marketing and postproposal activities, are more accurately projected as real data are collected and that new estimates are calibrated against these real data. Proposal managers and capture managers should be held accountable for any significant proposal-related cost overruns. Another benefit is that there is an up-front commitment to make select key technical and programmatic staff available to prepare the best possible proposal.

Due to staffing constraints, small companies may need to bring temporary publication staff on board for a portion of the proposal response cycle. In addition, outside professional proposal consultants with technical or proposal development specialties and expertise such as solution facilitation may be required to augment your company's internal resources. There are companies throughout the country that offer end-to-end proposal development services.[2] They will write, review, and produce your proposal for a negotiated fee.

Define and present proposal themes and strategies.

Ensure adherence to proposal themes within the proposal documents. The marketing intelligence that your company's acquisition/capture team has collected for a particular procurement must be translated into the thematic messages that are embedded throughout the proposal volumes. As proposal manager, you will need to set the marketing tone for the entire proposal response. Ensure that the documents are designed to be, and ultimately become, sales documents—authenticated by technical, programmatic, contractual, staffing, institutional, and technological strengths, lessons learned, metrics, and innovations.

Organize and conduct the preproposal activities and proposal kickoff meetings.

The proposal manager should communicate with the acquisition/capture team that has done the direct marketing with the client to ensure that all of the intelligence gathered has been communicated and is understood thoroughly.

Provide needed information to your company's contracts and pricing staff.

Include information regarding direct labor, travel, equipment purchases, property rentals and purchases, government-furnished equipment (GFE) and contractor-furnished equipment (CFE), subcontractors and consultants to be used, documentation requirements for contract deliverables, proposed cost center, recommended fee and profit margin, and pricing strategies. Develop the technical and management volumes in close coordination with the cost volume. Communicate regularly with costing and contracts staff.

Review and critique proposal input from the authors.

Whether received in electronic form through a secure extranet or intranet site, in hardcopy form, on CD-ROM, or via electronic mail, a proposal

---

2   Full-service firms are located coast to coast, including Organizational Communications, Inc. (OCI) in Reston, Virginia (http://www.ociwins.com); SM&A in Newport Beach, California (http://www.smawins.com); The Proposal Group in Towson, Maryland (http://www.lenduffy.com); H. Silver and Associates (HSA) in Los Angeles, California (http://www.hsilver.com); and Shipley Associates in Kaysville, Utah (http://www.shipleywins.com).

manager must review the sections and subsections of the proposal for a myriad of factors including RFP compliance, thematic continuity, storyline integrity, technical accuracy, programmatic appropriateness, risk minimization, and client awareness. Provide writers with interactive, ongoing feedback so that they stay on target from both a technical and schedule standpoint. Help them to understand the importance and value of their contributions.

Plan the project (organization, schedule, and budgets).

One of the most important aspects of proposal planning is selecting the staff whom you will propose to the government as your company's project or program team. Early staffing selection and management approval of this selection will be extremely beneficial to the entire proposal team. Definitive staffing decisions will make many processes easier, from résumé development and organizational chart generation to cost structuring and management plan preparation. Too many times, staffing decisions are delayed so that technical solutions can be developed and technical writing can be accomplished. Gathering detailed information for each résumé can be extremely time-consuming. Every time a staffing change occurs, a new résumé must be developed or tailored. Name changes also present editorial challenges in both text and graphics in the sense of finding every instance in which a person's name had appeared and putting in the new person's name.

The proposal manager and capture manager must ensure that an appropriate project schedule is developed that accounts for all client-required deliverables. This project schedule must be tightly linked with the details of the management plan.

- *Maintain ongoing communication and liaisons with senior management to select subcontractors, identify key project personnel, review the proposal progress, and obtain assistance as needed.* Use every opportunity to brief managers with the proposal status and issues that they can help to resolve.

- *Maintain client contact in conjunction with the business development or advanced planning groups.* Although your company's marketing staff cannot discuss the particular procurement for which a proposal is being prepared with the client, ongoing relationship building, customer relationship management (CRM), and discussions must continue.

- *Coordinate subcontractor liaison with the contracts department.* Ensure that technical information, résumés, project summaries, and cost data are submitted in a timely manner. Many times small disadvantaged businesses (SDBs), disadvantaged business enterprises (DBEs), and small, woman-owned businesses (WOBs) do not have adequate administrative staffs to prepare proposal input for your company (the prime) in electronic format or compatible electronic format. That means additional word processing tasks for your company's publication group.

- *Arbitrate Red Team and other review cycle comments.* Provide written instructions to the Red Team reviewers explaining what the expectations of the review process are and asking that comments be detailed and explicit so that the proposal team can respond effectively. During the recovery period following a review cycle, the proposal manager may have to assign "tiger teams" to ramrod the effort to fix any major deficits identified during the review process. Comprised of a small number of very senior staff and subject matter experts, these teams will need to work quickly and effectively to address these major weaknesses. Senior management support for adequate resources is vital at this stage.

- *Keep the proposal team members motivated.* Attend to such needs as meals and special transportation requirements. Do not forget your support staff. They are the ones called upon to produce proposal after proposal on a regular basis. Demonstrate clear, concrete appreciation for a job well done.

- *Ensure adherence to the proposal response milestone schedule.* As proposal manager, you must be relentless in adhering to the schedule. Time spent in prekickoff strategizing, planning, communicating, and decision making will serve you well downstream in the response cycle. Ensure that even the early proposal response milestones are met. There is no need, indeed it is counterproductive, to take every proposal schedule down to the final hour. Manage the process effectively from beginning to end. It will be exhausting, but everyone will benefit from a well-executed process, and your proposal will have a much better probability of being a winner.

- *Review and respond to all amendments to the RFP or RFS.* The government will often release one or more amendments to the original RFP in response to questions from offerors or to make a correction. (A U.S. Army RFP included eight amendments, including one amendment issued several days before final submittal. The amendments offered no indication through change bars or bold or italic text what the government had changed, which necessitated reviewing literally hundreds of pages for each amendment.) Each of these amendments must be reviewed carefully because they may, but certainly do not have to, extend the due date of the proposal. In some cases, amendments can have significant impact on staffing, technical approach, costing, page count,[3] and font size, for example. Amendments must be acknowledged in the proposal response, sometimes in your company's transmittal letter, as well as in the completed Representations and Certifications (Reps & Certs), Section K.

- *Ensure timely delivery of the requisite number of proposal volumes.* Avoid packaging all of the proposal documents in one box when delivering. Divide the copies among several boxes to minimize the loss if a box is dropped or misplaced.

- *Ensure that the transmittal letter and cost volume forms have all the necessary signatures.*

- *Evaluate the performance of personnel assigned to work on the proposal.* Once the proposal has been submitted to the government, take the time to evaluate the performance of both technical and support staff during the proposal response period. More than likely, you will be serving with these people again. Identifying who requires proposal development mentoring will be beneficial to them and to you. Express your appreciation. Hold a party, recommend people for bonuses, and arrange for proposal team T-shirts or other team-building items to enhance morale.

- *Prepare for orals and FPR.* Ensure that your entire proposal—text, graphics, and cost data and justifications—are archived in a secure manner and easily retrievable. You will have to refer to your submittal frequently as you prepare for an oral presentation in front of the client or a written FPR.

Ensure that your presentation team is reinforcing your company's answer to the question: Why us and not our competition?

Depending on what Evaluation Notices (ENs) have been identified in your original proposal, FPR responses can be involved and time-consuming. Also, there may be more than one FPR, as was the case with an $800 million Air Force Space Command proposal.

In many cases, you as proposal manager will have to gain management support in reassembling the initial proposal team to prepare a solid response. Oral presentations will also require dedicated time to strategize your response and then conduct dry-run practice sessions to hone the public speaking skills and cooperative interaction of the project team. Individuals who critique these practice sessions should ensure that the presentation

---

3   For example, an amendment to a USACE-Sacramento RFP changed the original technical volume page count from 80 to 65. This change had a significant effect on the structure of the final technical volume.

team is reinforcing your company's answer to the question, "Why us and not our competition?" Staff should practice a sufficient number of times to present their material effectively while standing calmly looking at their audience. Make sure that the presentation is timed during the dry runs so that all of your material can be presented well in the time allotted by the government. Verify with the government exactly what audiovisual and computer equipment will be provided for you and also inquire as to the size of the room. Perhaps you could visit the presentation room beforehand and photograph it. If your company is taking its own computer equipment, slide projector, or overhead projector (this was a requirement on a NASA oral presentation not long ago), make sure to take extension cords, spare bulbs, and backup DVDs or flash drives. Test the actual equipment you will be taking before arriving for the presentation.

Many government agencies require presentations as part of the proposal response. NOAA, DOE, the U.S. Coast Guard, Air Force, and Army, and the Federal Deposit Insurance Corporation (FDIC) are several such agencies in which specific organizations often require presentations. Today, with multimedia presentation software, such as Microsoft Power-Point 2010, Prezi, HyperStudio 5.5, CyberLink's Medi@Show 5, Harvard Graphics Advanced Presentations version 3.0, and Harvard Graphics Pro Presentations 3, presentations can be more professional and alive than ever [1, 2].

Request and attend the client debriefing.

A debriefings file within your knowledge base is an excellent training tool for novice proposal managers within your company. It is important to understand exactly why your company was not selected for award of a given procurement. Ask questions of the government contracting and technical staffs in attendance at the debriefing. The most important activity is to document and communicate the lessons learned from the loss to other proposal managers and senior management within your company. Maintain a debriefings file and refer to that file before beginning the next proposal for a given customer.

Guard overall proposal security.

To help ensure confidentiality, proposals should not be discussed outside the office. Proposal-related paper, including graphics, cost tables, and narrative, must be shredded and disposed of when it is no longer needed through a reputable waste management firm. Companies have been known to purchase competitors' trash! And network or PC/Mac-level password protection and encryption are essential to guard the electronic proposal files.

If at all possible, the proposal manager should have no writing assignments. In small firms, however, this is very difficult to avoid. Yet if the proposal manager is to be effective in that capacity, he needs to attend to a myriad of technical details and human and organizational issues and not be burdened with writing proposal sections.

13.3 Changing focus of proposal management

Traditionally, proposal managers—both full-time staff members within a federal contractor organization as well as freelance and agency-based consultants—bring solid experience and a knowledge base that are focused toward compliance, process, and documentation. Both today and in the future, however, compliance- and process-driven proposal management approaches alone cannot and will not produce winning proposal documents and stellar oral presentations on a sustainable basis. Instead, proposal managers must combine these important baseline approaches with solution development and facilitation; idea generation and genuine creativity; and proactive, engaged leadership. In this way, they become more valuable to their organization and also become more sought-after knowledge workers in the marketplace at large. The need for an expanded and renewed focus on solution development competencies within the ranks of proposal management professionals has arisen in large part from the migration toward performance-based acquisition (PBA) within the federal government marketplace.

Solution development refers to the critical activity of building and articulating fact-based *storylines* or *story arcs* that convey a federal contractor's specific approaches to providing meaningful, measurable, achievable, and risk-aware outcomes for its federal government customer. Robust solution sets must encompass such proposal areas as technical, program management, staffing, phase-in, and past performance. The storylines must link together such major elements as "Understanding the Customer Environment," "Approach," and "Measurable Outcomes" in a manner that ensures continuity of major sales messages or themes.

To amplify further, solution sets and their associated storylines are fact-based, quantitatively validated articulations of the framework and spirit in which a federal contractor will approach providing services and/or products to the federal government. These services and products must be designed *to directly benefit the customer* given the contractor's understanding of the government environment, requirements, and mission. The "customer" will most likely include the specific government agency and its users, customers, and stakeholders.

In today's extraordinarily competitive and solution-driven federal marketplace, the *delta,* or difference, between winning and coming in second borders on the microscopic. Proposal managers can provide very tangible value to their organizations as measured by an enhanced proposal win rate by fortifying their skill sets to span all of the key elements presented in Figure 13.4. These important proposal management competencies include detailed compliance with the solicitation document (#1); process flow coordination (#1); documentation and production, editing, and quality control (#2); and configuration control. In addition, and most importantly, proposal managers must develop and hone their skills in solution development and leadership (#3 and #4) to attain proposal management success.

Let's take a closer look at performance-based acquisition, or PBA. PBA is an established element within the federal marketplace. The Request for Solution (RFS) has become as common, if not more prevalent, than the traditional Request for Proposal (RFP). And even many RFPs have performance-based components, including quantitative metrics, performance standards and thresholds, options to propose most efficient organization (MEO) staffing options, and performance-based work statements (PBWSs). Now, the focus is on *innovative, risk-aware solutions.* These must be presented in proposal documents and oral presentations in clear and concise words and illustrations that build on such industry best practices and disciplined approaches as the Software Engineering Institute's Capability Maturity Model Integration® (CMMI®) structured software engineering methodologies, ISO 9001:2008 and 9002:2008 standards, Information Technology Infrastructure Library (ITIL) v3, PMBOK Fifth Edition good practices, Lean Six Sigma, and

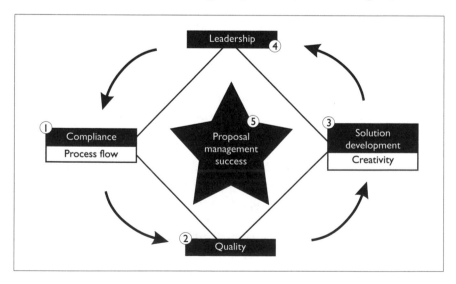

Figure 13.4
Solution development, creativity, and leadership are critical competencies for proposal management professionals now and in the future.

Institute of Electrical and Electronics Engineers (IEEE) guidelines. Importantly, performance-based service contracting which was a major component in President Bush's Management Agenda, and that emphasizes market-based, results-oriented, citizen-centered government is still very much in practice.

Performance-based acquisition is a procurement strategy defined and described at FAR Subpart 37.6 and in the Office of Federal Procurement Policy's (OFPP's) Policy Letter 91-2 (dated April 9, 1991). That strategy structures all aspects of an acquisition around the *purpose* and *results* of the work to be performed, as opposed to either the manner in which the contractor or offeror must perform the work or the processes that must be used. The *WHAT* is emphasized over and above the *HOW*. (In general, if the level of effort, staffing levels, skill mix of staff, or educational levels of staff are specified in the RFP, then the contract is *not* performance based.) The key elements of a PBA performance work statement for *services* are: (1) a statement of the required services in terms of output, and support for the agency's mission; (2) a measurable performance standard for the output; and (3) an acceptable quality level (AQL) or allowable error rate. The government may employ a variety of measurement methods, including a project surveillance plan, quality assurance surveillance plan (QASP), or an award-fee evaluation plan. The primary elements of a PWS for *hardware* or *end-item deliverables* are: (1) a specification of what the end product must do in terms of performance, along with any critical constraints such as weight or footprint, and (2) measures of quality that are related directly to the end product's capacity to perform its intended use.

This innovative federal PBA strategy leverages the ingenuity of industry while providing the government with access to the best commercially available products, services, processes, knowledge, and technologies. From the government's perspective, use of performance-based acquisition strategies reduces acquisition cycle times and costs, because contractors are not compelled to perform to detailed design-type specifications that can inhibit creativity and efficiencies. Most importantly, performance-based contracts help to ensure contractor *accountability for mission-focused results.*

Fundamentally, all federal contractors, including small businesses, must be able to prepare proposals and oral presentations that demonstrate *innovative* performance approaches for managing *risk* proactively while ensuring superior *quality*. In return for performance excellence, contractors earn positive monetary incentives for meeting technical, schedule, and cost standards and thresholds or service level agreements (SLAs).

13.4 Effective solution development

So how can proposal managers become integrally involved in solution and storyline development? Proposal managers can provide significant benefit to their organizations by proactively leveraging diverse resources such as customer strategic plans, technical library documents, Web sites, and call plan results. *Why?* To conceptualize, develop, and produce results-focused storyboards, solution sets, storylines, proposal narrative, and graphics concepts in concert with other capture and proposal staff. In the course of a proposal manager's self-learning process, graphics concepts, background information on government leaders, and other useful information emerge. For example, in researching IT standards that are applicable to a given customer, one might locate a compelling graphic concept that is already known to that customer because it is an integral part of their Web site. That graphic may be used as is, or modified, to convey a key concept in a federal contractor's proposal narrative or oral presentation. Or a listing of critical-path activities that a proposal manager locates through the federal customer's technical library can be built into a table in the proposal that demonstrates understanding of that customer's operational environment.

Web-based research on recent awards by a given customer to competitors can also shed considerable light on that customer's buying habits and preferred technical solutions. Speeches and biosketches or *curricula vitae* of key federal leaders as well as published papers of those individuals can prove to be invaluable in proposing meaningful, on-target solutions to those same customer leaders. Given the level of executive review and approval, customer news releases are excellent sources of knowledge. Specific words and phraseology that are used can be incorporated into the proposal or oral presentation. Customer telephone directories as well as Web sites can help proposal managers understand how the customer's organization is structured and also provide insight into key graphic or word concepts that the customer chooses to use frequently. Documented trip reports that follow from executive call plan execution can be rich reservoirs of direct insight into a customer's hopes, fears, biases, and critical issues and success factors. Federal government publications such as Air Force Base (AFB) papers again can shed light on the latest points of interest to the customer community. Specific examples include the weekly *Missile Ranger* newspaper at the Army's White Sands Missile Range (WSMR) in New Mexico, the *Space Observer* at the 21st Space Wing at Peterson AFB in Colorado, the *Army Space Journal*, the weekly *Fort Carson Mountaineer* in Colorado, the *Army Times*, and the weekly *Redstone Rocket* newspaper in Huntsville, Alabama. These publications are available online. Another important resource for proposal managers is customer briefings to industry.

In the process of researching and thinking and learning about the customer, the program, and the mission, the proposal manager should focus on how the knowledge and information being collected contributes to overall understanding of the customer, the strategy of his or her federal contracting company, the approach and solution that follows from that strategy, and the tangible and intangible benefits or "value proposition" that particular solution set brings to the customer and its program as well as its overall mission (see Figure 13.5). The storylines for the proposal and the oral presentation emerge from the critical thinking and synthesis of ideas that are leveraged to populate such diagrams as that shown in Figure 13.5.

Let's examine a sample storyline:

Our corporation will work together in close partnership with the Department of the Army to enable greater knowledge sharing among Army communities in support of the overall Army Transformation. Collaborative Web-based knowledge portals, e-learning technologies, systems integration,

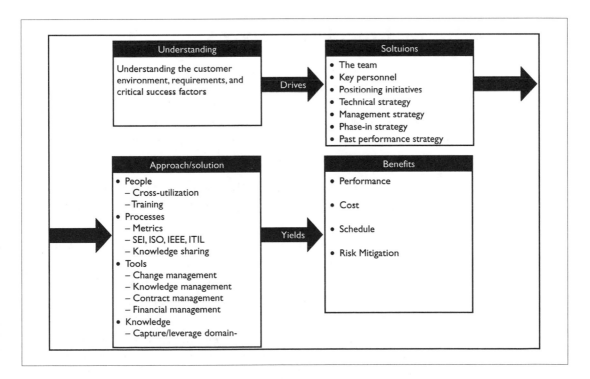

Figure 13.5   Example of customer-focused, benefits-based solution pathway.

intelligent data mining, intelligent agents, and expert systems technologies will be assessed and deployed with an enterprise-wide focus targeted to maximize the Army's investments in its people and knowledge assets. Such knowledge sharing will facilitate improved, fact-based decision dominance by commanders and business stewards in the battlespace, organizations, and Army's mission processes. This decision dominance will contribute directly to the effectiveness and day-to-day safety, security, and quality of life of America's warfighters worldwide.

This sample storyline conveys the tools, technologies, and approaches that the federal contracting firm will employ in delivering significant benefits to the Army mission of transformation and to the men and women warfighters around the globe. Such a storyline would be used at an overarching level (1.0 or 1.1) in a management or technical approach, with much greater qualitative and quantitative detail provided in the subsections that would follow. Of note is that in a recent government debriefing on a major winning proposal, the company I was supporting learned that *Compliance + Validated Storyline + Comprehensible Presentation* translates into a very high probability of winning.

13.5 Useful technical templates

Another value-added action that a proposal manager can take is to build a series of templates or checklists that align with each of his or her company's primary corporate core competencies. These templates might be leveraged in the following ways to support winning new and recompete contracts and to help everyone, including the proposal manager, better understand the business and what the company is selling.

- The business development (BD) staff can use the templates to help prepare for face-to-face meetings with current and/or prospective customers as well as potential teammates.
- The capture management staff can use these templates to assist in generating technical solutions.
- The proposal development staff can use these templates to prepare for interviewing subject matter experts (SMEs) and to assist in the proposal writing process.
- The operations/technical/consulting staff can use these templates as they conceptualize and craft the technical understanding and approach sections of a proposal.

Consider these checklists as: (1) jumping-off points for additional interview questions on a specific technical topic, (2) points to consider in crafting specific understanding sections of a proposal, and (3) foundational elements from which to build particular technical approach sections of a proposal. Resources used in building these checklists included formal DoD, NASA, Help Desk Institute (HDI), and the National Institute of Standards and Technology (NIST) documents as well as Government Accountability Office (GAO) reports and white papers prepared by Gartner. In addition, completed proposals were mined for meaningful information.

An example of a technical template is presented here:

[Provides alternative names by which a given area technical support service is known in the industry]
Help Desk/End-User Support/Service Desk Support

[Characterizes the area of support using a definition formulated by the recognized industry-leading professional organization in that discipline.]

The Help Desk Glossary, published by the Help Desk Institute (HDI), offered the following definition: "The operation that provides technical information to customers and solves technical problems by providing support and information." The handbook continued: "To increase the productivity of people using information technology in a company, you need to provide an efficient and effective means to answer their questions and solve their problems." What lies at the heart of a help desk operation is a sophisticated database that contains all the information necessary to handle call reporting, asset management, and problem resolution.

[Overview of major elements and functions associated with help desks:]

- Problem management—Web-based knowledge management system to track issues. Problem management should include: problem logging, problem identification, call assignments, tracking problems to resolution, alerting personnel if a call is taking too long, elevating a call's status to a higher priority, and problem diagnosis.

- Performance measurement and metrics for uptime, average time to answer, and average handle time [*well-defined* service level agreements (SLAs)]. Key attributes of successful SLAs include: (1) define products and services provided, (2) establish a manner in which they will be delivered, (3) establish quality standards to be achieved, (4) provide measurement criteria, (5) establish reporting criteria, and (6) negotiate and accept cost of delivery. Performance measurement should be supplemented by trend analysis, <u>root cause analysis</u>, and other statistical methodologies.

- <u>Asset management</u>—This is important for two reasons. First, it allows help desk personnel to solve problems by providing accurate, up-to-date information on the caller's environment. Second, it serves as a library of information about the government's asset base.

- <u>Configuration Management</u> (CM)—Updating inventories of assets.

- <u>Change Management</u>—Activity through which any change affecting the information system is made in a controlled way with as little inconvenience as possible. Focus for coordinating changes in hardware and software to ensure a smooth transition for customers.

[Important points of consideration in thinking and writing about help desks]

- ITIL v3 service management methodology—A holistic view of managing IT;

- User-defined levels of service [e.g., power user, very important person (VIP) user];

- Tier 0 self-service support [e.g., self-learning, frequently asked questions (FAQs), Web forms];

- Help Desk Institute (HDI);

- Tools—e.g., Remedy and FrontRange HEAT;

- Ongoing training programs;

- Customer communication;

- Quality management—ongoing customer satisfaction surveys;

- Call reporting;

- Data security;

- Desk-side versus virtual support;

- Support for mobile computing;

- Technology interfaces to other applications that facilitate customer support, such as e-mail, paging, personal digital assistants (PDA) devices, and fax services.

[The potential tangible strengths to consider in demonstrating the value of your help desk solution]

- <u>Benefits to Government</u>: Productivity, continuity of operations, minimized number of unnecessary software licenses, increased return on investment (ROI) on IT portfolio, and providing the government with a way to manage purchases based on real usage figures for hardware, software, peripherals, and networks.

13.6 Complementary roles and responsibilities of proposal and capture managers

Capture managers and technical leads are integrally involved in solution set and storyline development, but it would behoove proposal managers to become deeply immersed in this process as well. Of particular note is that important dovetailing occurs between the capture manager and proposal manager functions. Proposal managers and capture managers are most effective together when: (1) they communicate multiple times each day, (2) brainstorm solution sets and storylines together, (3) use each other as sounding boards for key ideas and concepts, and (4) share what they know about the customer, program, key staff, and applicable technologies openly and in an atmosphere of mutual trust. This author worked steadily for 8 months on a $500 million proposal for the U.S. Air Force Space Command as the proposal manager. Every morning, the capture manager and I met to plan the actions and follow-up issues for the day, identify problem areas in the proposal process, share ideas about pivotal, solution-conveying graphics, and ensure that the major storylines were being articulated throughout each one of the seven proposal volumes.

Contemporary proposal development is about articulating and illustrating a fact-based, validated storyline that provides tangible value (strengths) for the federal government customer as well as its users, customers, and stakeholders. That proposal storyline must be told convincingly, while simultaneously being in full compliance with Sections L and M of the RFS from an infrastructure and requirements standpoint. Current and future proposal management professionals must prepare themselves to be an integral part of the proposal solution set and storyline development process. Compliance is necessary, but certainly not sufficient. Innovative, cost-effective, risk-aware solution sets and storylines that span people, processes, technologies, and knowledge assets that federal contracting firms can provide are what is needed to win proposals now and in the coming years.

13.7 The growing importance of oral presentations

During the past several years, the federal government has used oral presentations to augment and even largely replace written proposals submitted by the contractor community for competitively negotiated procurements.

Since 1994, various agencies of the federal government, including the Department of Energy, Army, Nuclear Regulatory Commission, NASA, Centers for Disease Control, Federal Aviation Administration, Internal Revenue Service, and Bureau of Engraving and Printing, have experimented with selecting contractors on the basis of oral presentations instead of hardcopy or electronic technical and management volumes. And in 1997, the Federal Acquisitions Regulations included—for the first time—coverage of oral presentations.

A major goal for the government is to reduce the level of written materials associated with the procurements process. In addition, oral presentations permit government evaluators to receive relevant information directly from the key members of the contractor's proposed team who will perform the work on the contract. And expect evaluators to address past performance during oral presentations. In this manner, communication and the exchange of information between the government and the contractor can be enhanced. The government is, in effect, conducting job interviews of key staff. Proposal-related costs could be reduced for the government as well as the contractor with the implementation of oral presentations. In addition, procurement lead times can be reduced significantly.

From both a legal or contractual and practical perspective, debate continues over exactly what portions of a contractor's proposal will be integrated into the resultant contract. Various federal agencies have videotaped the oral presentations for later review, although there is no regulatory requirement that prescribes that a record of the oral presentation be maintained. Both video and audio tape may become available through the Freedom of Information Act (FOIA). Time limits on oral presentations, number of participants from each contractor, number of presentation materials, and type of presentation materials all vary from agency to agency.

Although no standards for oral presentations have emerged, there is a distinct movement in the direction of such presentations throughout the federal government. A proven provider of outstanding oral presentation conceptualization and development is The 24 Hour Company in northern Virginia. You can contact them at (703)533-7209 or http://www.24hrco. com.

13.7.1 **Outsourcing oral presentation support**

As a small business, you might consider using the services of an outside oral presentation consultant to assist your own internal presentation team. One proven resource about whom this author has direct working knowledge is Gregory W. Pease. He delivers professional oral presentation coaching and proposal consulting services to customers in all industries. Mr. Pease combines 20 years of technical, management, and proposal experience and graduate education in management to help teams deliver powerful presentations. You can reach Mr. Pease at http://www.tenzing-consulting.com or at (301)237-3727.

13.7.2 **Oral presentation development process**

Your company will benefit by following a structured, repeatable process for developing your oral presentations. As illustrated in Figure 13.6, begin building your oral presentation slides with an outline mapped directly to the RFP or RFS. It is advisable to include specific references to the RFP on each slide of the presentation (e.g., L.2.1), as well as embed frequent road-map slides that let the evaluators know exactly where you are with respect to their RFP during your oral delivery. Be sure to build on and leverage the best-of-breed slides from previously prepared oral presentations. These should be an integral part of your proposal knowledge base.

When populating slides for the new presentation with text and graphics, add an action caption (sometimes called a tag line or bumper sticker) to each one that completes and closes the thought and focuses on direct benefits to the client. Plan to review the slides once they are populated with text, graphics, mapping to the RFP, and action captions several times prior to finalizing and producing them in hardcopy and electronic format on DVD or flash drive. Be sure to review the slides using the actual projection device for the formal presentation. Sometimes color palettes or photos that appear crisp on a computer screen become pixilated and jagged when projected onto a large screen.

When preparing for the oral presentation practice sessions, identify the top two or three major messages found on each slide. This is a vital step because it facilitates the development of scripting and also ensures that each member of your presentation team tells your company's proposal story clearly and consistently. Because most people are not public speakers, it is often helpful to develop basic scripts for them, such as the following:

Sample script for X slide   During the fulfillment of my project management function in support of DOE in Washington, D.C., I have gained an

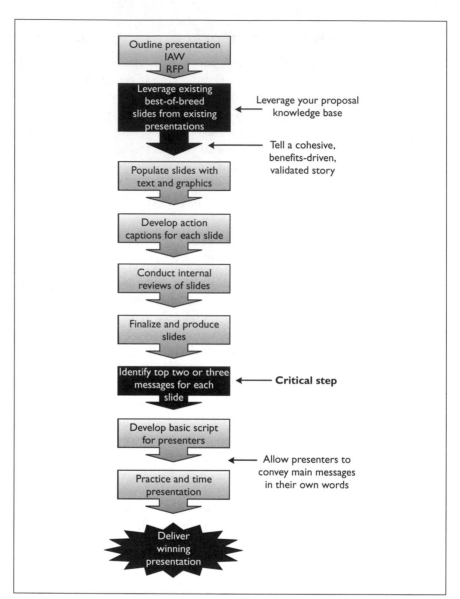

Figure 13.6
Structured oral
presentation
development
process.

in-depth knowledge of your current work and resource requirements. My daily, face-to-face interactions with DOE technical and contractual staff have contributed directly to this understanding. We have designed our site organization to fully support all current DOE requirements. Our proposed organization is flexible to accommodate growth and evolutionary changes in your requirements.

Sample script for Y slide   I previously mentioned our proven automated tool. Now let me tell you how it will help me—and you—every day of this contract. It will be the primary operational management tool. Interactive, secure, and Web-based, this tool has proven itself on our mission-critical contracts with USACE in Baltimore and at the U.S. Coast Guard in West Virginia. We funded the entire development of this automated tool, so it will be available to you at no direct cost.

Sample script for Z slide   To reinforce a major point, we will also retain complete responsibility for performance in each and every task area of this contract. In my role as group manager, I will ensure that prime contract terms, conditions, and performance measures flow down and are followed by both of our subcontractors. The members of our integrated team will all work to the same standards. We will communicate regularly with you through programmatic reviews and with each of our teammates to review their performance. You will benefit directly from our approach with our subcontractors, who are fully accountable to us for their performance. We, in turn, will be fully accountable to you for the contract's overall success.

However, as long as team members communicate the major messages for each of their slides, allow them to speak in their own words rather than memorizing or reading their text. Add real-world examples and anecdotes that validate and bring your major points to life. Conduct several practice sessions, including timed dry runs, to ensure that the physical hand-off from one presenter to another is smooth, that the presentation can be delivered within the allowed time frame, and that each presenter establishes eye contact with his or her audience. In addition, practice manipulating the computer or acetate vugraphs (yes, these can still be required; NASA Ames Research Center is a case in point) to ensure that the right cadence is maintained during the presentation. In most cases, the dress for presentations is formal business attire. Ensure that the team takes several small bottles of water with them into the actual presentation.

Increasingly, oral presentations include an ad hoc response to a sample task or problem, or series of government questions. Your presentation team members may be tasked with developing a follow-up presentation in real time after just having given their formal briefing. The government will assess how the team members interact with each other to solve the issue and develop a credible presentation with the materials at hand. You should know in advance of the oral presentation date whether this step will occur. Prepare accordingly by taking blank acetate slides, colored writing markers, and flip charts, as appropriate.

13.7.3 **Specific oral presentation guidelines for success**

Presentation software involves four distinct communication modes: (1) speech, (2) text, (3) graphics, and (4) electronic. For your audience—the government evaluation team—*meaning* is image-driven and received via their eyes and ears in a group setting, which is subject to group reaction. That meaning is textured by the presenters' body language, gestures, eye contact, tone of voice, voice inflection, pauses in speaking, and choice of words. Note that presenters will speak at about 120 to 180 words per minute. Conversely, people read at rates from 250 to 1,000 words per minute.

Points of emphasis

- Tell a cohesive and fact-based story.
- Think graphically—limit the amount of text on any given slide and make the graphics jump off the page.
- Punctuate the oral presentation with real-world examples—bring it to life!
- Include a benefits-oriented action caption on each slide (e.g., Collaboration Through Clearly Defined Communication Pathways, or Directly Applicable Experience Will Minimize Program Risks).
- Ensure legibility of all text and graphics callouts.
- Personalize the presentation—avoid use of the words "the government," but rather talk in terms of yourself or other individuals' names.
- Convey enthusiasm and positive passion during the presentation.
- Go for the close—ask for the sale.

Internationally acclaimed speaker and executive coach, Andy Bounds of Liverpool in the United Kingdom (http://www.andybounds.com), provides the following beneficial guidance for oral presentations. Concentrate on the "AFTERs," that is, what your customer will come away with *after* your organization provides its services or delivers its products. For example, your company is not really delivering independent verification and validation (IV&V) services, but rather you are providing reduced system problems, enhanced schedule adherence, and lower life-cycle costs. Fundamentally, you are helping to ensure that the end users of the system get the support and functionality that they require. These stand among the important AFTERs of effective IV&V support.

Other guidance that Andy Bounds offers is to use the word "you" frequently, particularly at the beginning of the presentation. Presentations should be structured and sequenced to convey benefits to the customer at the beginning, in the middle, and at the end as well. Various people pay attention more at specific points of a presentation; therefore, it is important to capture the attention of each type of listener. Consider the presenter and the presentation slides as two "individuals"—the human presenter uses words and sentences to convey her messages whereas the slides "speak" largely in graphical form. Thus, it is critical that the presenter and the slides are not trying to "say" the same things. Additionally, this argues strongly *against* mere recitation of the text on the slides. You should consider reading and applying the guidance found in Andy Bounds' book, *The Jelly Effect* (Capstone, 2007). Having seen Andy Bounds present in person in Savannah, Georgia, I can attest to the validity of his key practices.

13.7.4 Field-proven guidance for powerful oral presentations

1. Your number-one job during the oral presentation is to convey trust and teamwork, as well as enthusiasm, for this program. Conveying facts and managerial details is secondary.

2. Help the government to clearly understand what they receive after they sign a contract with us—both the tangible and intangible benefits.

3. Good practices:

   a. Make frequent eye contact with the government evaluation team during your time as a presenter. This helps to build trust.

   b. Speak in a conversational tone and style, as if you were talking across the table with the evaluators.

   c. Keep your messages straightforward and streamlined—do not feel compelled to address every point on a given slide—indeed, this should absolutely not be done. Facts tell, but stories sell. And you are selling.

   d. Never read the slide to the audience.

   e. Avoid using the expression, "This chart shows…"

   f. Several seconds of pause after delivering a key point is a great thing to allow the audience to absorb it. It's okay to say nothing for a few moments to allow a point to hit home.

   g. Keep the old slide on screen when changing presenters and then project the next slide on the screen.

   h. Communicate important messages more than once—some repetition is a very good thing.

   i. Put your most critical, interesting, and relevant messages first, not last. The rest of your communication should reinforce and justify these key messages. Audiences' concentration drops during a presentation.

   j. Vary the inflection of your voice.

4. Avoid weak expressions such as, "I think," "I believe," and "I feel." Rather, use powerful assertions such as "We are confident that ..."

5. Make use of effective phrases, introductory statements, and transition remarks:

   a. "Here's how what I do every day will help you."

   b. "It's been my experience that ..."

   c. "The lesson I've learned from working on ..."

   d. "We understand what it means to ..."

   e. "We overcame that operational challenge by ..."

6. Employ straightforward questions that you as a presenter ask and then immediately answer:

   a. "So what is the benefit of our approach to NASA in terms of schedule adherence and cost control?"

   b. "And what does this mean for the DISA?"

   c. "And how do we get there?"

7. Use appropriate words:

   a. Use "emphasize" or "underscore" or "underline," rather than "stress."

   b. Use "who" when referring to people, rather than "that."

8. Expressions heard during oral presentation practice sessions that should never be used:

   a. "No, our team will basically fail..."

   b. "You have failed..."

    c. "We go downhill…"

9. Dress and mannerisms:

    a. Men should wear a crisply pressed suit and professional tie (no Daffy Duck or Homer Simpson ties, please); women should wear professional business attire.

    b. Shoes need to be polished and be business professional.

    c. All cell phones, PDAs, iPods, and so forth must *not* be brought into the presentation room.

    d. Men—remove loose coins from pockets and keep hands out of pockets.

    e. Stand facing the audience with arms at your side or fingertips together in front of you.

    f. Do not turn your back on the audience to point to a specific element on a given slide.

    g. Each presenter should "close off" his or her final slide with a from-the-heart affirmation of his or her commitment to your team, your project manager, or the government program.

10. Logistics:

    a. If allowed, take a high-quality projection screen.

    b. If allowed, take a high-resolution projector, with a backup bulb and extension cords as well as duct tape to attach the cord safely to the floor.

    c. Take a stopwatch with large, backlit numbers.

    d. Take small bottles of water for the presenters. This is critical!

    e. Take a laser pointer with backup batteries, but use that tool sparingly.

13.8 Attending to the details

Your company may want to consider establishing a petty cash fund to handle unforeseen proposal requirements such as photocopying, color laser copying, photography, graphic enlargements for foldout pages (11 × 17 inches), and small office supplies. The proposal manager should have access to this fund. He or she should also be given keys and access codes to the building and appropriate offices, file cabinets, printers, and have access to this fund. He or she should also be given keys and access codes to the building and appropriate offices, file cabinets, printers, and computers. Evening and weekend proposal work requires ready access to networks, hardcopy materials, external disk drives, and other storage media.

At the formal kickoff meeting, it is advisable to generate and distribute a list of key proposal participants, including subcontractors and consultants. The list should provide names, telephone numbers (office, home, mobile, and Blackberry/iPhone), and e-mail addresses.

The proposal manager must ensure timely delivery of the proposal. Often, the mailing address is different from the hand-carried delivery address. For air carriers, such as FedEx and UPS, military bases will need barracks or building numbers and not simply mail stops. Allow sufficient time for contingencies such as inclement weather, heightened security levels at government installations in our post-9/11 world, automobile breakdowns, construction delays, accidents on the road, and delays in public transportation. Know exactly who will deliver the proposal to the government site. Deliver the required number of copies of the proposal document to the correct address. Avoid the use of couriers for proposal delivery because they do not have a vested interest in making certain your proposal documents are delivered undamaged and on time. Finally, obtain and retain a receipt from the government that is stamped with the time and date of your delivery and signed by an authorized recipient.

13.9 Control of the schedule

Proposals are challenging to complete, because for most of us they are an effort above and beyond our normal contract-related responsibilities. In your small company, you probably do not have a comfortable depth of staff in either the publications department or in the technical ranks. But adhering to the agreed-upon schedule will help to make the process smoother and help to ensure that the finished product is one that your company can be proud to submit. Winning competitive proposals requires a substantial amount of planning and guidance, well before the release of the RFP, during the actual proposal-preparation process, and in the postproposal phase.

Seasoned proposal managers come to realize that, in general, everything about the proposal process will take longer than planned. A novice proposal manager will quickly ascertain that many participants in the process—from the technical writers to the subcontractors to the publications group—feel that they are being pressured unnecessarily. And supporting departments, such as human resources or engineering, may be indifferent to even a well-planned proposal milestone schedule due to their own customer's requirements. Subcontractor technical, staffing, and cost information is often late or due to their own customers' requirements delivered in an electronic format that requires conversion and cleanup.

When generating the schedule for your proposal, be sure to take into account the effects of weekends and holidays, important company social functions, and competing priorities within the publications group. Generating a calendar-type schedule as shown in Figure 13.7 that notes the highlights of the proposal schedule is one effective tool in keeping the overall proposal effort in perspective. A Gantt or bar chart is another tool that indicates the many simultaneous proposal activities. Effective implementation of a proposal milestone schedule is challenging and often thankless work. People tend to procrastinate, or want to keep polishing their writing, or have competing priorities. Frequent but brief proposal status meetings coupled with the full support of senior management will definitely assist a proposal manager to keep his or her proposal effort on schedule. A word about management support. Senior management involvement is critical to ensure adequate resources are committed at the right times throughout the proposal response life cycle. Management buy-in to your technical solution, staffing plan, management approach, and costing strategy is also pivotal early in the response life cycle. However, senior management must also be willing to entrust and empower the appointed proposal manager to orchestrate the proposal response activities. They must allow the proposal manager to take ownership of and responsibility for the entire task. Too many times there is significant micromanagement of the process or senior management gets involved late in the response process and significantly revises the staffing plan, costing strategy, or technical solution.

13.10 Training additional staff in proposal-management skills

Particularly within small companies, the number of experienced proposal managers is very low, sometimes two or less. One way out of the quandary of always using the same people to manage proposals is to have novice proposal managers directly assist their more experienced colleagues. After two or three assists, perhaps the novice could be appointed as the primary proposal manager with full responsibilities and obligations, but with access to the support of the more senior proposal staff. Outside consultants can also be used for just-in-time proposal training and mentoring.

Sunday	Monday	Tuesday	Wednesday	Thursday	Friday	Saturday
	1 — Release of RFP. Copy and distribute RFP to proposal team.	2 — Analyze RFP. Generate kickoff package.	3 — Analyze RFP. Generate kickoff package.	4 — Kickoff meeting. Writing assignments made.	5 — Proposal writing. Ongoing communication between proposal manager and writers.	6 — Proposal writing.
7 — Proposal writing.	8 — Preliminary assessment of writing by proposal manager.	9 — Proposal manager's comments back to writers.	10 — Proposal writing.	11 — All proposal sections delivered to proposal manager by writers in electronic form. Proposal manager reviews all sections and electronic files before sending to Publications Department. Production of Red Team draft.	12 — Production of Red Team draft. Distribution of Red Team draft by close of business.	13 — Red Team review.
14 — Red Team review.	15 — Interactive meeting between Red Team reviewers and entire proposal writing team.	16 — Red Team recovery period (proposal manager prioritizes sections that require reworking).	17 — Red Team recovery period.	18 — Red Team recovery period.	19 — Proposal manager reviews all sections that have been reworked and provides comments back to writers.	20 — Additional writing or modification.

Figure 13.7 Calendar provides the highlights of the proposal schedule for easy review.

Sunday	Monday	Tuesday	Wednesday	Thursday	Friday	Saturday
21 Additional writing or modification.	22 Proposal manager reviews all modified sections again.	23 All materials provided to Publications Department for generation of final Gold Team draft.	24 Production and editing of Gold Team draft.	25 Gold Team review.	26 Final production.	27
28	29 Photore-production and final quality-control, packaging.	30 Deliver proposal volumes to client.				

Figure 13.7 (continued)

In-house proposal management and preparation seminars are another option to be considered. Curricula can be developed in-house, and seminars can be held in the evening or on a weekend. The point is to expand the base of proposal management experience within your company. This helps to prevent personnel burnout and promotes better proposal efforts, which in turn translates to winning more often.

13.11 Finish the job at hand

A proposal manager's duties are not over once the proposal documents have been delivered or uploaded to the government. The proposal manager should either personally review or assign someone to review the entire proposal to identify, for example, any omissions, critical errors, and areas that require improvement. If the procurement cycle includes discussions or an FPR, the proposal manager and his or her team (with direction from the capture manager) need to prepare a meaningful response to written questions as well as rehearse oral responses for the face-to-face meeting with the client.

Finally, the proposal manager should prepare a written lessons learned of the entire proposal effort for senior management. Examples of outstanding commitment by members of the proposal team should definitely be noted along with observations, suggestions, and recommendations to improve your company's proposal process. Senior management should then review and act appropriately on the recommendations. "[L]ess successful performers treat every opportunity as a discrete and unique event. These companies spend little time examining and improving their approach…. The proposal process is left unchanged. Each proposal team must relearn how to put together a proposal and experiences the same problems over and over again" [3]. Take the time as a company to learn from each proposal experience and apply those lessons to improving the process on a continuous basis. If ever there was an application for continuous process improvement, the proposal and oral presentation response life cycle is it!

The successful proposal manager has provided leadership for his or her proposal team throughout the entire proposal response life cycle.

13.12 Successful proposal managers

The most successful proposal managers with whom I have worked and been associated possess a marked ability to motivate and communicate with people of all levels—from company presidents to technical proposal writers to publications staff to financial and administrative personnel. They command and instill confidence in others by their technical knowledge, business development acumen, self-confidence, and encouragement. Often, they hold advanced degrees in a relevant technical discipline and have an intimate working knowledge of the particular client organization and its business processes and sell points. Successful proposal managers know when to push their proposal team, when to empathize, when to encourage, when to be flexible, and when to relax. They have a well-developed sense of humor and can laugh even during the most intense proposal development and production periods. These individuals talk with senior management and are forthright in that communication. Senior management, in turn, better understands the technical, management, staffing, costing, and logistical issues at hand that must be addressed and solved. Finally, successful proposal managers seek work-arounds. They demonstrate a certain proposal agility. If one way does not produce the desired result, they are very willing to try another and another until they achieve a resolution. Fundamentally, they are leaders, facilitators, communicators, and listeners—and owners of the proposal development process to the smallest detail.

ENDNOTES

1. Wodaski, Ron, "Planning and Buying for Multimedia: Effective Multimedia for the Small Office," *Technique: How-To Guide to Business Communication*, October 1995, pp. 16–25.

2. Joss, Molly W., "Authoring Alchemy: Ingredients for Brewing Up a Multimedia Masterpiece," *Desktop Publishers,* January 1996, pp. 56–65.

3. O'Guin, Michael, "Competitive Intelligence and Superior Business Performance: A Strategic Benchmarking Study," *Competitive Intelligence Review*, Vol. 5, 1994, pp. 8–9.

Chapter 14

Proposal production and publication

PUBLICATION OF A SET of superior-quality proposal volumes is a professional-level, time-intensive, dedicated effort. It is not a lower level clerical function that can be accomplished adequately and consistently by marshaling the secretarial and administrative support available within your company. Even small businesses benefit from a dedicated core publications staff of at least one desktop publisher or word processing operator and one graphic artist.

Senior management is well served to recognize and support the publication professionals they have on staff, even if they number only two or three people. Support is most meaningful in the form of senior management's judicious, targeted involvement in assisting the proposal manager to maintain the proposal response schedule at every milestone. Otherwise, publication staff are faced with compensating for schedule slippages along the way. And when schedules are missed on a regular basis and significant levels of night and weekend publication time become routine, publication staff morale can be at risk. Turnover among publication staff can be highly detrimental to your company's ability to prepare outstanding proposal documents every time.

Proposal efforts are not complete when technical, management, and part performance volumes are written and reviewed, and the costing is completed after careful integration with the technical and management approaches and staffing plan. There remain the following critical production-related activities:

- Editing of both text and graphics;
- Creation or generation of tables of contents, lists of figures and tables, and compliance matrices;
- Proofreading of text and graphics (pay extra attention to proposal covers; they make a first impression and you want it to be positive);
- Electronic and hardcopy configuration management and version control;
- Word processing and desktop publishing;
- Generation of graphics and insertion of graphics, figures, and tables into the documents;
- Coordination of outside printing activities (for example, covers, spines, laminated tabs, and specialty color pages);
- Photoreproduction and in-house color printing;
- Collation;
- Assembly and binding (such as three-ring vubinders, Velobinding, GBC or comb binding, and plastic coil), including placing covers, spines, and tabs into binders;
- Preparation of required, virus-free DVD copies;
- Conversion to PDF format for upload to the client's Web site, business opportunity portal, or e-mail as appropriate[1];
- Final quality checking;
- Packaging;
- Completion of specific bid forms and packaging labels; labeling;

---

1   Allow adequate time for uploading. Be certain to retain the time and date report that verifies when your files were accepted by the client's server. Remember, it is your client's time that is the one that counts, not the one on your company's computer system. Being late by 1/100th of a second is still late, and can result in your proposal being rejected. Establish and enforce an internal service level agreement (SLA) that stipulates uploading no later than 4 hours prior to due date and time.

- Shipping and delivery (delivery is more personal in the international and commercial arenas; a senior person from your company should perform this function);
- Obtaining time- and date-stamped receipt.

It is recommended that the proposal publication be a centralized corporate function. Continuity of publication staff promotes uniformity of the image of the proposal documents from proposal to proposal. A core group of staff should become intimately familiar with, and cross trained in, the document preparation process. Disciplined policies and procedures are much more easily implemented and repeated in a centralized working environment. Establishing a secure intranet or extranet will allow your company to leverage subject matter expertise throughout your organization in geographically disparate locations in support of proposal efforts.

14.1 Internal documentation standards

To ensure that your company's proposal and contract deliverable documents have a similar look and feel, it would be highly beneficial to develop a corporate handbook of format and style, publications guide, or analogous guidebook. This handbook might be posted on your company's intranet. The publications group, in conjunction with the business development staff and senior project management staff within your company, should be involved in developing and maintaining the format and style standards that will help to ensure the presentation of a uniform company image for both proposals and contract deliverables. This guidebook should address some or all of the following topic areas:

- Editorial style;
- Technical writing guidance;
- Technical report formats;
- Correspondence (memos, transmittal letters, and so forth);
- Proposals, including résumés and project summaries;
- Marketing presentations and brochures.

Always follow the formatting guidance provided in Section L (instructions to offerors) of the RFP or RFS when preparing your federal proposals. However, in-house written documentation standards will assist technical writers, proposal reviewers, and publication staff to work toward a consistent style and structure of presentation.

A useful technique for each proposal effort is to have someone in your company with editorial capability develop a listing of RFP-specific terms that will appear in your proposal so that writers and publication staff will capitalize, hyphenate, and abbreviate those terms in accordance with the particular government agency's parlance.

14.2 Document configuration management and version control

Once sections of a proposal are written, it is critical to control the internal release of and changes to those sections throughout the proposal life cycle. The centralized publications group should consider maintaining a master hardcopy proposal book for each volume in three-ring binders. Such binders allow for quick page replacements. One set of master proposal books should be made available to the proposal manager, and another should be under the direct control of the publications group. The pages from a third and final master copy may be hung on the cork-lined walls of your secure "war room" facility to allow for comment and review.[2] Then, as new proposal sections are created and existing ones modified with the authorization of the proposal manager, the publications group should be responsible for generating the change pages and inserting them in the master proposal books and hanging them on the walls of the war room. Establishing and maintaining a "living" master proposal document that iterates during the course of the proposal response life cycle will be of valuable assistance to all proposal contributors.

Your company's publications group should maintain electronic and hardcopies of the proposal documents at each review stage. For example, when the publications group produces the Red Team draft, all electronic files should be copied to a storage medium appropriate for the data volume of the proposal. Mass storage devices and removable cartridge drives and media include compact disk (CD), DVD optical disk storage media, USB flash drives (up to 1 terabyte), Iomega REV drives and removable disks, and external hard drives from Western Digital, Seagate, and Toshiba. External hard drives can cost as little as $1 per gigabyte of storage. A universal serial bus (USB) flash drive is a compact USB flash memory drive that acts like a portable hard drive, letting you store and transport computer data. These drives hold large amounts of information and are

---

2   The technique of affixing documents to the walls of the war room is slowly being phased out, in part due to file sharing made possible through computer networks and the Internet. It is still valuable, however, particularly for reviewing oral presentations.

about the size of a pack of chewing gum. Despite the different brands and names—JumpDrives, Pocket drives, Pen drives, and Thumb drives—they are all pluggable and portable. USB flash drives use the USB protocol to interoperate with PCs and Macs with a USB port.

Currently, USB flash drives are available with up to 1 TB of storage capacity. Additionally, USB flash drives act like portable hard drives to which you can add and delete files as many times as you need to do so. With CD-Rs and DVD-Rs, you can only add data once, and you cannot remove data once burned onto the disk. Your firm might also consider tape backup systems, or rewritable Sony or Hewlett-Packard magneto-optical cartridges.

One hardcopy should be retained in the exact form and format of the Red Team draft. Then, if a computer hard drive fails, the network server crashes, or electronic files are corrupted in some way due to power surges or electrical storms, the last major draft version will be available, unmodified, in both electronic and hardcopy forms. It is advisable to back up all electronic proposal files to secure storage media at least once each work day. Make certain to store one set of media at an off-site location as part of your corporate disaster recovery (DR) plan.

A key aspect of proposal document configuration management is the use of time, date, path, and file name on the specific storage medium on all draft proposal pages. Headers can be in a small font and, of course, must be removed prior to submittal to the client. The following is an example of a useful header for a page in the technical volume of a proposal to the Federal Aviation Administration:

14:25 Friday, November 16, 2012 c:\proposal\A-1-3.FAA *CD: Tech-A.1*

Such headers allow easy identification of when a particular page was last modified and on which storage medium the backup file for A-1-3.FAA resides.

Another beneficial configuration technique is the use of colored paper for various proposal drafts—for example, pale blue paper for the Blue Team and pale red for the Red Team.

And finally, do not discard draft proposal sections until after the proposal has been submitted. You can never be sure that you will not want to refer to an earlier version of the proposal. For security of competition-sensitive information, keep all such materials in locked storage and shred them using a cross-cut shredder when the proposal is submitted. A document destruction firm might also be used to destroy all interim draft proposal materials. Many will come to your facility and pick up the paper waste and shred it on your premises. Remember to retain a complete hardcopy and electronic copy of the final version of the proposal submitted to the government for use during FPR and orals preparation—future proposals, and potential protest or FOIA requests.

14.3 Freelance and temporary publication staff

Many companies, including small businesses, respond to fluctuating publication workloads with outside support from freelance, part-time on-call, or temporary staff. Your company's publications group manager will be well served to develop and maintain an active listing of prequalified local freelance graphics artists, word processing operators, desktop publishing specialists, editors, and proofreaders to call upon during peak periods. Freelance staff, if called upon consistently, will be able to develop an understanding of your company's internal documentation standards, proposal development processes, and technical and support staff. In the case of freelance staff, make certain that they sign a nondisclosure agreement (NDA) so that they cannot legally share proposal-sensitive information with any other company or individual.

14.4 Incorporating technical brilliance up to the last minute

One of the most challenging aspects of responding to an RFP or RFS is incorporating the best materials into the final document within a very limited time frame, and still delivering the proposal on time. The balance between process and content is delicate but very important to consider and constantly revisit. Solution sets, technical and programmatic input, tailored boilerplate plans, marketing intelligence, nuances of corporate image, résumés, project descriptions (summaries) of past performance, cost and pricing data, and legal opinion—all of these elements must be brought together quickly and effectively. However, precisely because the proposal preparation cycle must be a controlled, choreographed process of planning, analysis, writing, multiple review, and publication, potentially brilliant technical or programmatic ideas and knowledge might not be incorporated into the final document. There simply may not be enough hours to integrate the change(s) into the text from a publication standpoint. Technical, management, and cost volumes of a proposal are ecological in the sense that a change in a system design concept affects cost, and an alteration in the WBS affects the program plan and cost as well. These wide-ranging changes take time to identify and make consistent across the proposal volumes both in the text and graphics. Unfortunately, the publication staff invariably are caught in the crossfire of last-minute changes. Their task is to generate a well-presented, smooth-reading, consistent, and integrated set of documents, which in final form always takes more time to produce than in draft form. Deciding between structure (generating a polished, final document) and chaos (ongoing freethinking that can result in significant technical and programmatic enhancements) is a challenging pivot point for the proposal manager, but one that can actually work to the benefit of your company's proposal.

The balancing act for the proposal manager is to allow the entire proposal process to remain fluid enough to accommodate evolutionary change (content) while simultaneously maintaining a firm commitment to milestone schedules and completion of action items (process). Regular brainstorming sessions can prove valuable, and building in extra space in the proposal documents will facilitate the easy incorporation of new ideas late into the production process. Human and organizational dynamics come into play in graphic relief during the proposal process. Management commitment of sufficient human and material resources, bonus and incentive programs, effective cross training, and the infusion of a winning attitude all can be brought to bear on the often arduous schedule of responding to federal procurements.

It seems imperative to me for the proposal manager to direct the publications group to generate as complete a document for each volume as possible as early in the proposal response life cycle as they can. Not that final formatting needs to be accomplished, because this can be counterproductive given today's high-end desktop publishing software applications. What is important is seeing and working with a complete rough draft so that technical gaps, RFP compliance issues, and program management inconsistencies are identified early. In addition, flexibility and effective communication across the entire proposal and capture team will facilitate incorporating newly released CPARS information, a photo of a just-received corporate award, and recently learned customer insight into your proposal.

14.5 Graphics are an integral part of your proposal

Appropriate use of graphics, photographs, screen captures, line art, and clip art (noncopyrighted art available on the Web or on DVD, for example) of all kinds will increase the evaluators' interest in and positive response to your company's proposal. It is essential not to submit a boring, lackluster proposal to any potential client organization. Well-designed graphics can convey complex information in an easily understood format. See Figure 14.1 for an example of a graphic appropriate for an executive summary. And in page- or word-limited proposals, graphics can present significant quantities of information in very limited space. Most proposals benefit from and many, in fact, require graphical presentations of staff skills, contractual experience, client-contractor interfaces, company organization, project organization, and project milestone schedules. Photographs might be added to personalize your company's résumés, particularly if your client knows your proposed key staff. Appropriate photographs of your company's facilities, specialized computer equipment, engineering and manufacturing centers, COTS products, and design prototypes can also greatly enhance your proposal's sales value. Photodocumentation brings projects and products to life, and also serves to break up the text for easier reading and fuller comprehension.

In his work, *Seeing Is Believing,* Arthur Berger claims that visual images have the power to generate intense feelings and emotions precisely because they connect with people's beliefs and values [1]. The advertising

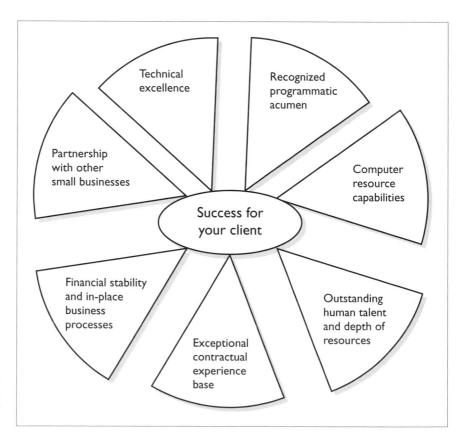

Figure 14.1
Sample graphic that introduces your company's primary thematic story line to your client.

industry understands very well the power of the visual image, specifically in combination with verbal messages [1]. Sandra Moriarty, a professor of journalism and mass communication at the University of Colorado–Boulder, asserts that visual and verbal communication modes are interdependent. Visual communication may be different from language-based communication, but Professor Morarity contends that both are equally important [2]. My own two-and-a-half decades of experience in proposal development for the federal government demonstrate that this is certainly the case. In fact, I strive to include some graphical element on each and every proposal page to add to the visual interest and value, and therefore the comprehension of the ideas expressed. Including graphics that do not connect directly with your proposal messages add little value and indeed may be viewed by government evaluators as gratuitous. For example, adding the silhouette of an American warfighter by itself simply because this is an Army proposal does not strengthen you offering, and in fact detracts from it.

A word of caution about graphics found on the Web. The majority of photos and graphics on the Web are designed to look good on your monitor, which can display a maximum resolution of 72 pixels per inch (ppi). Printed material requires at least 150 dpi, with 300 dpi preferred for high-quality hardcopies. Do not assume that you can capture noncopyrighted photos and graphic images from the Internet and use them in your proposal. Plan ahead and purchase photographic images and clip art from such sources as AbleStock, which offers high-resolution, royalty-free images (http://www.jupiterimages.com/collections/ablestock.com) and Jupiterimages, Inc.'s http://www.jupiterimages.com/, http://www.clipart.com, http://www.dreamstime.com, and http://www.photos.com/. Other excellent photo image sites available online are Seattle-based Getty Images (http://gettyimages.com), http://corbisimages.com, and Fotosearch (http://www.fotosearch.com). Make certain that you only purchase *royalty-free* images, that is, an image that does not require your company to invest additional funds every time the image is used in proposals, marketing materials, trade show signage, annual reports, and so on.

One powerful software tool that can convert, capture, compress, organize, enhance, view, and print graphics files is International Microcomputer Software, Inc.'s HijaakPro Version 5. This application supports more than 115 graphics formats, including raster (e.g., .gif, .jpeg, .bmp, and .psd), vector (e.g., .dxf, .txt, and .pic), and metafile (e.g., .eps, .pict, and .wmf) types. See http://www.imisidesign.com.

14.5.1 Action captions

Fundamentally, proposals are sales documents. In any sales document, whether it is a brochure or mailer or proposal, there are significant messages conveyed through photographs, artwork, and words. In proposals, these messages are called themes. Think of a theme as a statement that you make in a proposal that explains exactly why the client should select your company for contract award and not select your competition. In short, Why you? Themes should always be substantiated and authenticated with facts and metrics. One great place to use theme statements is in the captions for figures, tables, photographs, and other graphic presentations. Let's look at the difference between simply identifying what a graphic or photograph is, and using the caption to convey important sales messages tailored to the specific procurement.

- Instead of "Project Organizational Chart," your caption might read *"Our company's project team is configured to manage multiple USACE work assignments efficiently."*
- Instead of "Map of Local Company Locations," your caption might read *"The proximity of our company's offices to Fort Campbell will afford rapid response to the Army's changing requirements."*
- Instead of "Capabilities Matrix," your caption might read *"Each one of our eight proposed senior technical staff holds an accredited degree in a relevant engineering and scientific discipline."*
- Instead of "Laboratory Staff," your caption might read *"Our well-trained laboratory staff are dedicated to and trained in quality-oriented USEPA procedures that ensure appropriate chain-of-custody handling."*
- Instead of "Appropriate H/S Procedures" your caption might read, *"We actively practice a comprehensive Health and Safety program designed to meet the requirements of 29 CFR 1926.65 for hazardous waste site work."*
- Instead of "Scope of Our Support Services," your caption might read *"We provide cost-effective, innovative support services across a broad spectrum of environmental regulatory acts, including the Clean Air Act."*
- Instead of "Technical Approach Overview," your caption might read *"Our technical approach embraces documented system-availability metrics to ensure performance success today and into the future."*
- Instead of "Understanding of SOW," your caption might read *"Our understanding of Air Force Space Command SOW requirements*

allows us to apply tailored key practices such as ITIL v3 to optimize performance efficiencies."

In each of these examples, we have taken a flat statement and added positive, dynamic sales messages. We have introduced benefits of our approach and capabilities to the client. These sales messages, or themes, should be developed early in the proposal response cycle so that the entire proposal writing team can incorporate them into their narrative and into the captions they develop for their graphics. If a particular RFP stipulates that figure and tables shall be named in a particular manner, you must adhere to that guidance.

14.5.2 Configuration control of graphics

Configuration control of the graphics in your proposal is made difficult because many graphics are submitted to your publications group without captions (for figures) or legends (for tables) and their number within the proposal volumes may change several times depending upon placement within a specific section or subsection. The proposal manager can assist with this configuration management issue by insisting that writers submit graphics concepts with appropriate numbering and clear linkage to specific outline sections. Adding a file path name in a very small font directly into the graphic file (so that the path specifications print with the graphic image) will also help when these graphics iterate or shift within the document. And retain that identifying file name in the final proposal as well. That way, 6 months later, when one of your staff is building a new proposal response, she can quickly reference the specific graphic for ease of electronic retrieval.

14.6 Role and structure of your publications group

A small company's publications group is often tasked with multiple responsibilities, such as proposals, contract deliverables, presentations, Web-site design, and marketing brochures. The core staff of this group should be cross- trained in a variety of operations, software applications, communications protocols, and hardware platforms. And it is critical that the publications group be able to accept, incorporate, and manage outside assistance. The group's policies and procedures, software, and hardware should not be tailored so that temporary or freelance employees or other in-house staff cannot support the group effectively and efficiently during "crunch" (crisis) documentation periods. In addition to an active list of local freelance staff, the manager of your company's publications group should consider maintaining lists of local photography and visual imaging vendors and photoreprographics houses that offer pickup and delivery services as well as rapid turnaround.

The continuity of publications group core personnel is very important for smoothly operating proposal efforts. Proposal managers benefit from seasoned, competent documentation staffers. Having established successful proposal production departments from the ground up for six federal contracting firms, I can testify to the benefits of human continuity within the publications group. Continuity, cross training, and a positive attitude are salient elements in proposal publication success. Loss of skilled and cross-trained staff can cut deeply into productivity and inflate overall proposal publication costs significantly.

In order to facilitate a smooth proposal operation, your company will need to determine the document throughput capacity of the publications group. How many new proposals of average size (for your firm) per month can be handled adequately with the core staff? If your bid–no bid process causes additional proposals to enter the publications "pipeline" each month, will additional staff, computer equipment, and floor space be needed? Keep in mind that an informed, aggressive bid–no bid or down-select process is the checkpoint or gate that controls proposal document flow-through. Your company should avoid overloading your publications group and your business development infrastructure with proposal efforts that have low-win probabilities. That practice wastes B&P money and can be very detrimental to morale. Preparing and submitting proposals on a law-of-averages basis—the more we submit the better the chance of winning—is a devastating and debilitating practice in both human and financial terms.

Keep in mind that editing and proofreading must be integral parts of the proposal publications process, not merely nice-to-have services. The publications group can be a good source of editorial support.

14.7 Software and hardware compatibility, standards, and recommendations

In today's era of desktop publishing—integrating sophisticated text configurations and complex graphics and creating multicolumn page layout designs on a personal workstation—computer platforms, peripherals, and software applications are important considerations for any company that prepares proposals. The ongoing explosive proliferation of third-party hardware compatibles and multiple variations of software applications argues strongly for your company adopting a uniform standard for hardware platforms, software applications and versions, storage media, and peripherals.[3] This standard is best adopted as early in your company's corporate life as possible, and then kept uniform and current. The same version of operating software, such as Microsoft Windows 7 or Mac OS X, should be installed on all your company's computers. As much as possible, the default settings should be consistent from machine to machine, and the printer drivers and fonts should be the same.

In addition to software and hardware compatibility, computer and peripheral redundancy and maintenance should also be considered. Your publications group should be adequately equipped with printers that have expanded random access memory (RAM) to print complex graphic images, 64-bit[4] computers with multiple high-storage hard drives (e.g., 1 TB) and expanded high-speed dynamic RAM (4 GB preferred), and color high-resolution monitors (preferably 23 inches with flat screen and multiple USB 2.0 and soon to be released 3.0 ports). A 4-hour response time maintenance agreement with a local, reputable support vender for all your proposal publication computer equipment is highly recommended.

When establishing hardware and software standards for your company, keep in mind the various external organizations, vendors, and freelance support with which your system at the hardware, software, and storage media levels must interact on a regular basis. For example, perhaps several of your major federal clients require contract documents be delivered in WordPerfect Office X5 rather than Microsoft Word 2007 or 2010, or your top graphics service bureau[5] use Iomega REV cartridges for transferring large files rather than CD-ROM or magneto-optical disk, or two of the firms with which you team most frequently operate in an Apple Mac Pro environment rather than with IBM-compatible PCs, or the majority of the known freelance staff in your immediate area are most competent and proficient in Word 2003 rather than Word 2010.

Significant computer-based experience during the past 25 years suggests strongly that whatever system platforms your company selects should be open architecture—designed for and fully capable of responding to the exponential pace of software and peripheral advancements. Your central processing units (CPUs) should be equipped with as much

---

3   Printers manufactured by the same company, for example, can vary in the number of words printed per page.

4   64-bit refers to the amount of data that a computer chip can process at once. Both Intel and AMD have introduced 64-bit chips and Mac offers the G5 64-bit processor.

5   Service bureaus are for-profit organizations that provide such support as typesetting, electronic file conversions and raster image processing (RIP), 35-mm slide generation, and prepress film generation.

dynamic RAM as is necessary to operate and execute all of your software applications and printing tasks in an efficient manner. Printers should have expanded RAM to accommodate graphics files, as well as integrated text and graphics files. Storage media must be capable of handling ever-increasing data volumes and of rapid random retrieval. Today, an average-sized proposal—replete with full-color cover and integrated text and graphics—can extend to more than 200 MB. One proposal alone could fill some USB flash drives, and only three would fit on a CD-ROM. A single graphics file that contains several scanned photographs can be more than 50 MB [3]. One final note: Back up files regularly. Your proposal process probably cannot sustain major data losses—ever!

From a software applications standpoint, proposals do not generally lend themselves to being prepared with high-end, full-scale desktop publishing packages such as Corel Ventura 10 and Adobe PageMaker 7. This is because of the very tight production time frames. Ventura, for example, is best suited for the publication of books and other lengthy documents that are frozen (approved with no changes) and then have styles (page layout parameters) applied to them. In the IBM-compatible world, MS Word, MS PowerPoint, and Adobe Illustrator Creative Suite (CS) 5 are the primary applications for proposal development. By keeping text in MS Word, which many technical and administrative staff can manipulate, the documentation process can receive more in the way of ad hoc support from throughout your company and the local freelance community. In addition, technical changes can be accommodated until a much later stage in the production life cycle. The high-end packages also have an associated steep learning and proficiency curve.

14.8 Electronic proposal submittal and evaluation

In an effort to streamline the evaluation and source selection processes, certain federal agencies require both hardcopy and electronic copy (such as electronic upload to a Web portal, DVD, and e-mail) proposal submittals. It is commonplace that cost data are submitted on DVD in Excel or Lotus, for example. The technical and management narrative, as well as oral presentations, have migrated to delivery in MS Word, MS PowerPoint, and PDF. Be certain to provide your proposal in the specific version of the particular software application requested on the correct size and storage capacity diskette. Increasingly, proposals are also uploaded to government acquisition Web sites and no hardcopies are involved whatsoever.

Electronic source selection (ESS) integrates communication technology, database applications, and information management systems to reduce risk and increase the productivity and efficiency of source selection evaluations (see Figure 14.2). ESS uses standard, as well as proprietary, software applications and hardware to produce a paperless environment for source selections and to streamline RFP preparation. ESS has already been used in major DoD programs such as Joint Strike Fighter (JSF), Landing Platform Dock (LPD-17), and Global Broadcast System (GBS).

In the electronic source evaluation process, the government harnesses the Internet to distribute and receive RFPs and RFSs. The productivity of the selected ESS tool reduces risk, cost, and time associated with the government's evaluation of proposals. Sensitive information is controlled, while simultaneously being available to key decision makers in diverse locations for streamlined consensus building. Electronic source evaluation facilitates an understanding among all government participants of how each part of the procurement affects the whole. This is key to providing a united front during higher-level review. The electronic process also provides flexibility in linking with other analyses and in quantifying the decisions.

The U.S. Air Force Materiel Command (AFMC) has migrated to electronic evaluation for all major system procurements [4]. Electronic evaluations are already being used for many smaller procurements as well. Each AFMC center is in the process of defining and developing its own methods for electronic evaluation. In addition, the Headquarters Marine

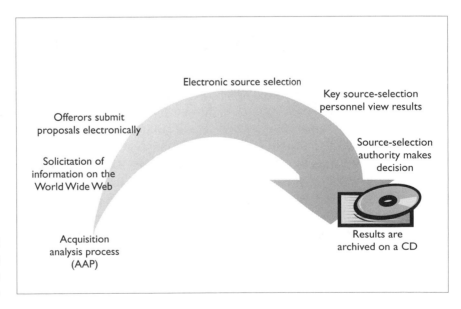

Figure 14.2
Representative
electronic source
selection process.

Corps Electronic Acquisition Team supports the Marine Corps Paperless Acquisition Initiatives.

CACI's FedSelect Windows-based proposal evaluation software (http://www.caci.com/bmd/FedSelect/fedselect.shtml), which is available on the GSA Schedule, is designed to provide a best value source selection process among competing proposals. Version 4.0 of this application uses evaluation factors/areas along with criteria/thresholds. FedSelect provides fully traceable and automatically documented proposal evaluations focused on capturing rating and risk rationales behind the business decision. It is supported by links to proposal strengths and weaknesses. It also has preformatted interim and final reports that can be used to brief decision-making officials. FedSelect has been in use at the Missile Defense Agency (MDA) Defense Advanced Research Projects Agency (DARPA) for 15 years, along with NASA, GSA, and the National Archives.

FedSelect supports source selection/proposal evaluation with Administration, Evaluation, Caucus, and Reports modules. The software uses existing solicitation information and is completely tailorable. FedSelect also does not require the use of a full-time LAN administrator. The software is managed easily by the administrator (contract specialist).

The Electronic Source Selection Tool (ESST) that bd Systems (a subsidiary of SAIC) developed has been in use on all major source selections performed at the Air Force Space and Missile Systems Center at the Los Angeles Air Force Base since 2000.

It is important to note that electronic source selection tools are just that—tools. They are enablers of the source selection process, but people make the final decisions.

14.9 Important documentation tips

Proposal documents are presented very attractively in double-column format, which provides the added bonus of 10% to 15% more text per page, depending on the font selected. Conserving the white space at the end of lines of text is part of the reason why double-column formatting provides for more words per unit of space. This space savings is very important for page-limited proposals. See Figure 14.3 for an example of a double-column proposal page format.

When compiling a list of acronyms, perform a global search for a beginning parenthesis "(". If acronyms have been defined in the text, and they should be, this technique should identify most of them. The acronym list for your proposal can, like the compliance matrix, be put on a foldout page so that the government evaluators can have constant and easy access to the acronym definitions. Ensure that acronym lists stand outside the

1.0 TECHNICAL APPROACH

Proposal documents are presented very attractively in double-column format, which provides the added bonus of 10-15% more text per page, depending upon the font selected. Conserving the "white space" at the end of lines of text is part of the reason why double-column formatting provides for more words per unit of space. This space savings is very important for page-limited proposals.

Proposal documents are presented very attractively in double-column format, which provides the added bonus of 10-15% more text per page, depending upon the font selected. Conserving the "white space" at the

> **This space savings is very important for page-limited proposals.**

end of lines of text is part of the reason why double-column formatting provides for more words per unit of space. This space savings is very important for page-limited proposals.

1.1 Understanding the Technical Requirements

Proposal documents are presented very attractively in double-column format, which provides the added bonus of 10-15% more text per page, depending upon the font selected. Conserving the "white space" at the end of lines of text is part of the reason why double-column formatting provides for more words per unit of space. This space savings is very important for page-limited proposals.

Proposal documents are presented very attractively in double-column format, which

provides the added bonus of 10-15% more text per page, depending upon the font selected. Conserving the "white space" at the end of lines of text is part of the reason why double-column formatting provides for more words per unit of space. This space savings is very important for page-limited proposals.

Proposal documents are presented very attractively in double-column format, which provides the added bonus of 10-15% more text per page, depending upon the font selected, as shown in Figure 1-1. Conserving the "white space" at the end of lines of text is part of the reason why double-column formatting provides for more words per unit of space. This space savings is very important for page-limited proposals.

Figure 1-1.

Proposal documents are presented very attractively in double-column format, which provides the added bonus of 10-15% more text per page, depending upon the font selected. Conserving the "white space" at the end of lines of text is part of the reason why double-column formatting provides for more words per unit of space. This space savings is very important for page-limited proposals.

1.1.1 Software Applications

Proposal documents are presented very attractively in double-column format, which provides the added bonus of 10-15% more text per page, depending upon the font selected. Conserving the "white space" at the end of lines of text is part of the reason why double-column formatting provides for more

Figure 14.3 Sample double-column proposal page format.

core page count, or that they can be accommodated within the page budget and still address all other requirements.

For lengthy proposals, customized tab pages should be prepared to serve as page dividers for ease in locating important sections. Tabs are ordered by the set and by the cut. Ten sets of seven-cut tabs means 10 complete sets of tabs each of which has seven tabbed pages. Many higher end photocopier machines can produce tabs, even laminated ones, right in your office.

The human and organizational dynamics of the proposal process are probably the most important elements of all. Chapter 15 will highlight these very real issues.

14.10 Virtual proposal centers, intranets, and extranets

An *intranet* or private network is an internal information distribution system that uses Web technology (such as hypertext and TCP/IP protocols) to allow an organization to access specific information in a form and format designed just like an Internet home page and accessed over the Internet. However, the general Internet community cannot enter your company's intranet site because it is firewalled. In effect, an intranet is a separate system with limited access[6] using a Web browser identical to Internet Web browsers such as Windows Internet Explorer 9 (IE 9), Google Chrome, Mozilla Firefox, and Maxthon. The organization develops its own internal home page, with links to various sites or locations containing information within the site. Intranets provide services such as data storage, e-mail, and search-and-retrieval functions. On the other hand, an *extranet* incorporates encryption technology to allow secure access to an intranet over the Internet (see Figure 14.4). The FedEx do-it-yourself tracking system represents an example of a sophisticated extranet. Now how are these systems applicable to, and useful for, proposal development—permitting teams to focus on proposal content and quality?

An intranet can be used to create a virtual proposal center (VPC) within your company, which in turn can be used to manage, support, and simplify the proposal development process for the firm. A VPC enables your entire proposal team—even when geographically separated—to have a secure, common electronic work center with access to an expandable

---

6   As opposed to a file server, electronic mail, or collaborative software (groupware) such as IBM Lotus Notes or Microsoft Exchange Server messaging software. Microsoft Exchange Server 2010 now enables confidential communication.

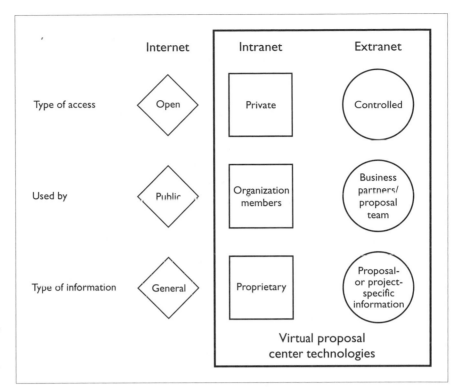

Figure 14.4
Comparison of
electronic
networked data
warehouses.

repository of important automated proposal tools, project- and marketing-related information and knowledge base, and proposal templates required to help develop a successful proposal. A VPC facilitates real-time status checks for every proposal participant, regardless of physical location. Intranet and extranet technologies become invaluable time and B&P cost-savers with geographically dispersed, complex teams. Both travel and administrative time and costs can be reduced. Schedules and action item lists can be shared, and version control can be monitored and maintained more easily. And appropriate levels of security and access control can be built into your system. Companies such as Intravation, Inc., in San Mateo, California (http://www.intravation.com), offer off-the-shelf software applications designed to build virtual proposal centers within your firm.

Intravation's VPC tool is a collaborative, browser-based intranet and Internet application that enables organizations to plan, assemble, review, store, and disseminate proposal information. By reducing the amount of time spent on nonvalue-added tasks, VPC permits teams to focus on proposal solutions, content development, and quality.

Another enterprise document and content management tool of direct benefit to proposal development is infoRouter (http://www.inforouter.

com), produced by Active Innovations, Inc., in East Setauket, New York. Through the robust capacity and intuitive architecture and results of the infoRouter Web-based solution, organizations can save money and time by lowering the cost managing documents. Your company's documents can be accessed securely from anywhere in the world. The only things required are a connection to the infoRouter server and a Web browser. Integrated full-text searching and powerful advanced search features make it simple to locate exactly what you need.

With direct, hands-on experience using both VPC and infoRouter, I can attest to the business value of both tools in terms of serving as a proposal knowledge base.

14.10.1 Useful document management systems (DMS) and other collaborative tools

In general, document management systems (DMSs) are used by individuals, office work groups, and enterprises to store organize, locate, and track the documents being produced as a part of their work. Document management is the automated control of electronic documents—images, spreadsheets, word processing documents, and complex documents—through their entire life cycle within an organization, from initial creation to final archiving. The document management process allows organizations to exert greater control over the production, storage, and distribution of documents. This yields greater efficiencies in the ability to reuse information, reduce duplication of effort, enhance organizational awareness, control a document through a workflow process, reduce document cycle times, and collaborate among geographically dispersed groups and individuals. The full range of functions that a DMS may perform includes document identification, storage and retrieval, tracking, metadata, security, version control, work-flow management, and presentation—across different computer platforms and in asynchronous mode (i.e., at no prescribed time), as well as over a variety of electronic networks, including the Internet.

Document Locator (ColumbiaSoft Corp., Portland, Oregon; http://www.documentlocator.com/features/) and DocuXplorer Software (Archive Power Systems, Inc., New York; http://www.docuxplorer.com) are but two examples of document management systems on the market today. Additional tools are Google Docs and Xerox DocuShare.

In the architectural, engineering, and construction industries, Autodesk's Buzzsaw software-as-service (SaaS) (http://usa.autodesk.com/buzzsaw) allows documents and drawings to be shared with members of your team while being maintained securely. Document revisions and markups are shared in real time among architects, engineers, reprographers, developers, and contractors.

Novell's GroupWise 8 (http://www.novell.com/products/groupwise/) multiplatform business collaboration solution offers full document management through the same interface that users already employ for messaging and scheduling. The planned GroupWise 2012 will integrate with iPad to support mobile computing and also provied Skype presence.

Other useful collaborative tools that have been proven within operational proposal environments include Privia Bid and Proposal Management by SpringCM and Microsoft Office SharePoint 2010. Privia (http://www.springcm.com/solutions/privia-bid-and-proposal-management) facilitates the use of standard desktop applications, including all Microsoft Office applications. It allows you to connect and disengage remote contributors and reviewers as needed without IT assistance. This tool allows a team to simultaneously share, edit, and review documents in real time with version control safeguards. Importantly, Privia's document libraries are open to advanced searches and provide the source for appropriate content for reuse.

Microsoft Office SharePoint Server 2010 (http://sharepoint. microsoft.com/en-us/Pages/default.aspx) provides a platform for sharing information and for working together as proposal teams. Users are able to create and control their own collaborative workspaces. The entire document life cycle can be managed with this tool's integrated Enterprise Content Management (ECM) capabilities.

As with any system for information management, there are a number of complementary and competing standards that describe the architecture of DMSs. Some of the more prominent standards include the following:

1. *Open Document Management (ODMA) application programming interface (API).* ODMA is an industry-standard interface for managing documents that allows users to store, retrieve, and share documents with security and version control. ODMA enables desktop applications to interface with document management systems in a flexible manner without the need of a hard-coded link between the application and the DMS. Thus, ODMA allows multiple applications to access the same DMS. ODMA simplifies integration and interoperability of standard desktop applications with DMSs. Using ODMA, desktop applications access and manipulate documents carried in DMSs as easily as if they are residing in the locally accessible file system.

2. *Object linking and embedding (OLE).* This proprietary standard from Microsoft allows objects in one application to be linked

dynamically to objects in another. For example, a graph in a word processing document can be linked to the original data in a spreadsheet application. When the data in the spreadsheet change, the graph in the document is automatically updated to reflect those changes. OLE allows applications to share data as well as the functionality of the originating applications.

3. *Object Management Group (OMG).* Based in Needham, Massachusetts, OMG, an international, open-membership not-for-profit computer industry consortium, was founded in April 1989 by 11 companies, including 3Com Corporation, American Airlines, Canon, Data General, Hewlett-Packard, Philips Telecommunications N.V., Sun Microsystems, and Unisys Corporation. The organization develops enterprise integration and visual design standards. The OMG established Common Object Request Broker Architecture (CORBA) as the "middleware that's everywhere" through its worldwide standard specifications. CORBA's open, vendor-independent architecture and infrastructure is used by computer applications to work together over networks.

Open Text Corporation's Enterprise Content Management (ECM) Suite 2010 (http://www.opentext.com) is a collaborative application that delivers integrated archiving, metadata management, search, and records management as part of an integrated content management system.

Why use document management systems for proposal development? The benefits of document management for small businesses include: (1) leveraging intellectual capital such that knowledge is created once, then reused many times; (2) managing workflow, controlling the flow of information through all phases of a proposal process; (3) fostering more effective teamwork among a distributed workforce; and (4) allowing rapid response to events such as RFP amendments and extensions to the proposal due date.

14.11 Using freelance proposal writers to maintain technical productivity

Carefully managed freelance writers and interviewers can be of invaluable assistance to your proposal manager at select phases of the proposal response life cycle (see Figure 14.5). If deployed on a just-in-time, as-needed basis, individual assignments should last from 2 or 3 days to

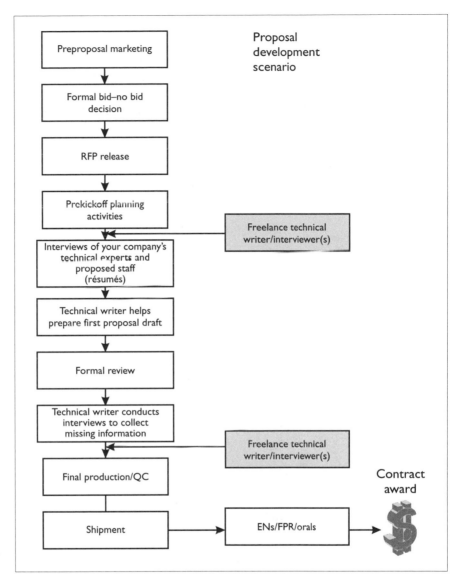

Figure 14.5
Carefully managed freelance writers can help you to control B&P costs.

2 or 3 weeks. The point here is not to add to B&P costs, but rather to maintain your company's technical staff at maximum productivity and billability. The writers and interviewers would be trained by your proposal manager to extract appropriate technical and programmatic information from your firm's professional and managerial staff. Following the interview process, the freelance writers would then translate "technical-ese" into marketing-oriented, high-impact narrative that conveys the benefits and value of your approach and credentials to the client. Interviews can be conducted in person, by telephone, or via carefully constructed e-mail queries,

and can be worked in before and after core business hours or during lunch breaks. The goal is to minimize the time that any billable staff person is diverted from direct client support, while simultaneously controlling the proposal schedule and generating integrated, well-crafted proposal text.

Effective freelance writers and interviewers bring an understanding of the documentation process and possess technical or professional writing or English-language and communications skills. Real-world experience with well-managed and trained freelance specialists serving in this capacity demonstrates an astounding 40% reduction in overall B&P costs!

Sources of freelance writers and interviewers include local colleges and universities as well as the following organizations:

- Association of Proposal Management Professionals (APMP)
  http://www.apmp.org/
- American Independent Writers (AIW)
  7817 Evening Lane
  Alexandria, VA 22306
  Tel. (703)660-9336
  http://www.amerindywriters.org
- Independent Writers of Chicago (IWOC)
  28 East Jackson Building
  Suite 1020 #W686
  Chicago, IL 60604
  Tel. (800)804-4962
  http://www.iwoc.org
- Independent Writers of Southern California (IWOSC)
  P.O. Box 34279
  Los Angeles, CA 90034
  Toll-free phone: (877)79-WRITE
  http://www.iwosc.org
- Cassell Network of Writers (CNW)
  45 Main Street
  P.O. Box A
  North Stratford, NH 03590
  Tel. (603)922-8338
  http://www.writers-editors.com
- World Wide Freelance Writer
  http://www.worldwidefreelance.com
  (comprehensive listing of independent consultants and firms in all areas of expertise)

- Society for Editors and Proofreaders (United Kingdom)
  Harwood House
  53 Harwood Road
  London SW6 4QP
  http://www.sfep.org.uk

ENDNOTES

1. Schultz, Benjamin, "Business Documents Don't Have to Be Boring," *Business Communication Quarterly*, Vol. 69, No. 4, December 2006, p. 409.

2. Schultz, Benjamin, "Business Documents Don't Have to Be Boring," *Business Communication Quarterly*, Vol. 69, No. 4, December 2006, pp. 407–408.

3. In 1994, the average file size was approximately 18 MB. By late 1995, that had grown to an average of 73 MB. See Hevenor, Keith, "Storage Product Buyers Guide," *Electronic Publishing*, August 1, 1996, p. 10.

4. Information about the AFMC's electronic proposal evaluation initiative was obtained from Davidson, Paul, "U.S. Air Force SMC Innovations in Electronic Procurement," *APMP Perspective I*, Vol. I, July/August 1996, pp. 7, 12, 13, 15.

Chapter 15

Human and organizational dynamics of the proposal process

*The classic mechanistic model ... fails to engage to the fullest
extent an organization's most important asset—its people ...*
—The PeopleWise Organization, Kepner-Tregoe

CRITICAL THINKING IN THE WORKPLACE. Several years ago, Kepner-Tregoe, a Princeton, New Jersey–based organizational-management consulting firm and international leader in developing the critical thinking skills of people, conducted an in-depth, audited survey of more than 1,400 managers and hourly employees. What was being examined in this important study was how much an organization's collective thinking is being tapped to resolve the big strategic and operational issues, as well as the day-to-day impediments to competitiveness and profitability. The results? Sixty-two percent of workers surveyed believed that their organizations are operating at half—or less—of the brainpower available to them. These perceptions were reflected in responses by the managers as well. More than 40% of workers said they do not feel valued by their organization. And yet delighting clients and pleasing stakeholders "are the hallmarks of organizations in which people can—and want to—contribute their very best" [1].

15.1 Modifying our thinking to win

Your company's entry into the arena of competitive procurements brought with it the requirement for a fundamental shift in thinking and business-related behavior throughout the ranks of management as well as the professional and support staff. Senior management, for example, must appreciate the significance of proposals and proactively support the development and enhancement of the processes associated with the proposal response infrastructure. In addition, each division of your company must make full use of the collective human and contractual expertise resident throughout the entire firm. Divisions cannot operate effectively in isolation from each other or from corporate direction. The dynamics of genuine teamwork and knowledge sharing take on accentuated meaning in the competitive marketplace. People at all levels within the company must work together with clearly defined objectives, for example, to collect and assess marketing intelligence, develop meaningful, benefits-driven solutions, write proposals, review proposals, and publish proposals. In too many companies, a small cadre of technical and support staff produce the significant bulk of the proposals. That practice does not encourage team building, knowledge sharing, and a wider sense of ownership of and accountability for the company's success.

Proposals do not follow a fully democratic process. Companies must recognize that effective proposal management follows from informed, albeit authoritative decision making at the appropriate time. A proposal effort can become mired if people are not instructed to heed the guidance of the proposal manager. On the other hand, the proposal manager must listen to team members and make informed and balanced judgments. And senior management must clearly and repeatedly reinforce the role and authority of the proposal manager, the criticality of sharing knowledge internally, and the importance of meeting the schedule milestones.

There is no more important corporate activity than proposal development for a contracting firm.

An entrepreneur—the very person(s) who founded the company—can often be an unwitting impediment to the development, implementation, and enforcement of rational, formal, repeatable business development processes. Not because they do not want their company to succeed. Quite the contrary. However, they know that they built their company to its current revenue base and market position within the small business contracting community on savvy, intuition, risk taking, and shoot-from-the-hip decision making. Successful marketing and proposal development in the competitive arena are, on the other hand, built upon a methodically applied and continuously enhanced set of disciplined business practices and processes. And that is an entirely different mind set than that which founded and nurtured the fledgling company.

15.2 Building a competitive work ethic

It is likely that your company's very existence and future growth depends upon winning 25% to 40% of the formal proposals you submit. Proposal development is an absolutely essential corporate activity within your organization. Every resource in your company must be made available to the successful completion of each proposal, and everyone needs to share in a strong sense of accountability for winning new and recompete business. There are many details that must be attended to in the course of preparing a proposal that do not require the direct, hands-on attention of the proposal manager. Such activities include electronic searches of the résumé and project description subdirectories or data bases to determine appropriate staff to meet position descriptions and to ascertain relevant company contractual experience. Technical editing and tailoring of résumés, project descriptions, and the technical and management narrative would be of invaluable assistance. In addition, administrative support in the form of photocopying, meal arrangements for evening and weekend work, and text-entry word processing (yes, this still occurs) are each vital to the overall success of the proposal preparation process.

No one person can address all of the details, for example, of technical content quality, writing consistency, and compliance with the RFP. Therefore, your company would benefit from more people being trained and available on an as-needed basis to assist in the preparation of the proposal in addition to the technical authors, proposal manager, and publications group. The burden of preparing winning proposals must be shared among all professional and support staff. Instill this work ethic among all your staff through regular briefings on new business prospects, competitors, and new technologies. A rotating schedule of administrative support being on call to support proposal activities after core business hours is one mechanism for ensuring broader involvement and appropriate levels of support for the proposal team and publications group. Everyone's future depends upon winning! The acquisition/capture team is an excellent vehicle through which to build a winning attitude for a given proposal effort. And when your company expands, you should hire technical and programmatic staff who possess strong proposal-related backgrounds, either from successful competitors or good business colleges and universities. Successful proposal experience and the mindset that fosters proposal success can be highly synergistic. I have personally witnessed a small company, which had very few people trained in the art and science of proposal development and management, become far more sophisticated and successful with the addition of key technical and programmatic staff who had proposal backgrounds. This knowledge influx helped to underwrite and authenticate the ongoing proposal development training programs that had been initiated in the company previously.

15.3 Strong link between project performance and proposal success

The integral connection between superior project performance and proposal success cannot be overemphasized. Past performance and key staff are two of the most significant evaluation factors in most support services proposals. Your client or potential client wants to ensure that your company has performed to expectation on contracts of similar type, size, technical scope, staffing level, complexity, and geographic area. Solid references from COTRs, COs or KOs (contracting officers in defense organizations) and technical monitors (TMs) are critical to your company being awarded the next contract. Project schedule slippages, low-quality interim and final deliverables, and cost overruns on your current or past contract work translate into hurdles that have to be overcome during the marketing, bid–no bid, and proposal processes. Verify all of your project-related references before your proposal is submitted to ensure that you will receive a very positive reference from the government points of contact. Also ensure that titles, telephone numbers, mailing addresses, and e-mail addresses are current.

Client staff have demonstrated on numerous occasions that they have enduring memories—for superior as well as poor performance. Perceptions are paramount in contracting. Just as your company networks and shares information, so do your client counterparts. If your company has allowed significant schedule slippages or incomplete deliverables to be submitted, you will be remembered for the wrong reasons. Those negative perceptions can take several contract cycles to overcome. They can also seep throughout the client's organization; so that if your performance was below average at a particular Air Force installation in Texas, a potential client at an Air Force location in Colorado Springs may have heard negative comments. The key is to leverage outstanding contractual performance into exceptional project experience in your proposals. Project and proposal processes and successes are closely linked, as shown in Figure 15.1.

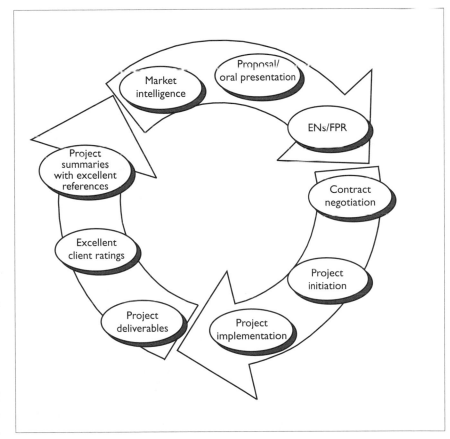

Figure 15.1
Proposals and project deliverables each require planning, technical effort, senior review, contractual involvement, and production expertise.

15.4 Past performance—it's more important than you think!

Confidence in a prospective contractor's (in effect, your company) ability to perform satisfactorily—or better—is an increasingly important factor for the federal government in making a *best value* source selection decision. For more than two decades under the Federal Acquisition Regulations (FARs), federal government acquisition officers have been allowed to consider contractor past performance in their selection criteria for contract award. According to the FAR, "past performance shall be evaluated in all source selections for negotiated competitive acquisitions expected to exceed the simplified acquisition threshold" [FAR 15.304(3)(I)].

In recent years, however, changes fostered by the Federal Acquisition Streamlining Act (FASA) and the Federal Acquisition Reform Act (FARA), also known as the Clinger-Cohen Act, have expanded the role of past performance in the federal acquisition process. In fact, the government's desire to select high-quality contractors has resulted in past performance representing up to 50% of the source selection criteria in certain instances. On a high-profile $800 million Air Force procurement let several years ago, for example, past performance accounted for approximately 30% of the score under the evaluation factors for award (Section M of the RFP).

Past Performance Information (PPI) is the *relevant* data regarding a contractor's actions under previously awarded contracts. It includes the contractor's record of: (1) conforming to specifications and standards of good workmanship, (2) containing and forecasting costs on any previously performed cost reimbursable contracts, (3) administrative aspects of performance, (4) history for reasonable and cooperative behavior, and (5) commitment to customer satisfaction and business-like concern for interests of the customer.

The federal government uses a variety of sources to obtain past performance information regarding contractors, including the following:

- Questionnaires completed by the contractor's federal government customers;
- Web-enabled Contractor Performance Assessment Reporting System (CPARS) via the Past Performance Information Retrieval System (PPIRS) (http://www.ppirs.gov/);
- Past Performance Proposal Volumes supplied by the contractor;
- Telephone interviews;
- Central Contractor Registration (CCR) Program;
- U.S. Army Corps of Engineers Architect/Engineer Contract Administration Support System (ACASS) for unclassified work only (module of CPARS);
- Construction Contractor Appraisal Support System (CCASS) for unclassified work only (module of CPARS);
- Corporate Web sites;
- Internet.

Let's take a closer look at the questionnaires that are completed by a contractor's federal government customers. Frequently, the questionnaire will include requests for specific information about the contractor's quality of service, project management effectiveness, timeliness of performance, and cost-effectiveness. From the contractor's perspective, these questionnaires should be a vital part of the overall proposal response. *Why?* First, because the government's response to these questionnaires carries far more weight than the contractor's own self-appraisal about its past performance excellence. Second, because the questionnaire provides valuable and detailed insight into the performance, schedule, and cost parameters that the government agency letting the new contract deems to be important. Therefore, the key elements found in the past performance questionnaire should be built into your proposal responses, as appropriate.

For instance, a questionnaire may include queries related to accurate and timely deliverables, ability to effectively manage subcontractor performance, timely identification and mitigation of risks, resolution of contract performance problems, ability to fill technical vacancies rapidly, and responsiveness to end-user requirements. Other queries relate to phase-in/transition, management of multiple projects simultaneously, responsiveness to government requirements, ability to work independently of the government's guidance, ability to handle fluctuating workloads, adherence to safety and health procedures, and compliance with quality control plans. These elements can then be woven into the contractor's proposal volumes in such a manner as to demonstrate the processes, tools, and staff resources that will be applied and deployed to meet these subtle requirements that may or may not be stated explicitly elsewhere in the RFP or RFS.

Additionally and very importantly, certain federal government agencies will go beyond the past performance citations of the prime contractor and its subcontractors included in a prime contractor's Past Performance Proposal Volume. For example, the Air Force's Performance Risk Assessment Groups (PRAGs), which are chartered to assess the *performance confidence*[1] each contractor, will also unilaterally consider additional projects and programs not included in a contractor's Past Performance Volume. Performance confidence evaluates a contractor's present and past performance to establish a confidence rating of that company's ability to successfully perform as proposed. What this practice means in very practical terms is that past performance "blemishes" can and

---

1   Rather than *performance confidence,* some federal government organizations use *performance risk* in their assessment of contractor past performance proposal submissions.

will be uncovered by government evaluation teams. For the prime contractor and its subcontractors, this practice on the part of the government underlines further the close connection between *project performance success* and *new business success.* In effect, the business development and proposal development success of a contractor is directly dependent on its operational and contractual success.

Past Performance Information Retrieval System (PPIRS)

The PPIRS database mentioned earlier is available to all source selection officials across the entire federal government. Driven by FAR 42.1502 and 42.1503, its purpose is to assist federal acquisition officials in purchasing goods and services that represent the best value for the federal government. Contractor access to PPIRS is gained through the Central Contractor Registration (CCR) (http://www. bpn.gov/ccr/default.aspx) process. A contractor must be registered with the CCR and must have created a Marketing Partner Identification Number (MPIN) in the CCR profile to access PPIRS information.

Formerly called the Past Performance Automated Information System (PPAIS), PPIRS is currently sponsored by the DoD E-Business Office and administered by the Naval Sea Logistics Center Detachment Portsmouth (NAVSEA). The federal PPIRS database is a Web-enabled application that allows the retrieval of contractor past performance information. In May 2010, the Office of Federal Procurement Policy (OFPP) and the Acquisition Committee for eGovernment (ACE) determined that the Contractor Performance Assessment Reporting System (CPARS) will be used as the single past performance reporting system federal-wide to collect and transmit performance evaluations to PPIRS.

Contractor Performance Assessment Reporting System (CPARS)

CPARS is a Web-enabled Department of Defense enterprise application that collects and manages the library of automated CPARs. CPARS is for unclassified use only. A CPARS report assesses a contractor's performance and provides a record, both positive and negative, on a given systems, services, IT, and operations support contract during a specific period of time (typically one year). Completed CPARS report cards are tranferred to PPIRS on a weekly basis. Each assessment is based on objective facts and supported by program and contract management data, such as cost performance reports, customer comments, quality reviews, technical interchange meetings, financial solvency assessments, construction/production management reviews, contractor operations reviews, functional performance evaluations, and earned contract incentives. Contracts of $1 million and up in the business sectors of service and information technology are required to have an associated CPARS report on the contractor. Because contractors are vital partners in the performance assessment process, contractor senior management representatives may request access to all records pertinent to their corporate entity.

DoD policy states that past performance evaluation information (e.g., CPARS report) is privileged source selection information and is not releasable under the Freedom of Information Act (FOIA). Further, FAR Subpart 42.1503 (b) states: "The completed evaluation shall not be released to other than Government personnel and the contractor whose performance is being evaluated during the period the information may be used to provide source selection information." What this means is that your company cannot make a FOIA request for a competitor's CPARS information.

Architect-Engineer Contract Administration Support System (ACASS)

ACASS is a database of selected sensitive but unclassified (SBU) information on architect-engineering (A-E) firms. ACASS provides required information for DoD and federal government selection committees to aid them in their process of awarding A-E contracts. It is maintained by the Portland District of the Contractor Appraisal Information Center. It contains detailed Standard Form 254 and now SF330 data on contractors, DoD awards, and past performance evaluations for the last 6 years of A-E services contracts. For more information on ACASS, go to http://cpars.csd.disa.mil/ acassmain.htm.

ACASS provides an efficient and economical automated database system by which to adhere to these requirements. The use of ACASS for past performance history is mandated for all DoD agencies in the Defense Federal Acquisition Regulation Supplement (DFARS). For the Corps of Engineers, ACASS eliminated the need for 43 district offices to disseminate performance evaluations among each other and to maintain copies of SF254s. ACASS is a catalyst for overall improvement in performance of the A-E community. If the performance evaluation is to be rated "below average" or "poor," the A-E firm will receive notification of such prior to the evaluation being signed by the reviewing official. The firm then has 15 days to appeal the proposed rating.

Construction Contractor Appraisal Support System (CCASS)

CCASS is an automated database of performance evaluations on construction contractors. CCASS provides sensitive but unclassified PPI for DoD and federal government contracting officers to aid them in their process of evaluating construction contractors' past performance. As with ACASS, it is maintained by the Portland District of the Contractor Appraisal Information Center. For more information on CCASS, go to http://www.cpars. csd.dsa.miccassmain.html.

Acquisition reform legislation, policies, and guides are intended to move source selections into increasingly greater use of "best value" procedures, in which considerations of noncost factors (such as technical, management, and PPI) might justify award to other than the apparent low-cost offeror. In particular, these reforms require source selection officials to consider relevant past performance as a measure of performance risk for future contract awards. *Make certain you know what the grades are on your company's report card!*

15.5 Proposals can be fun!

Successful proposal efforts can be fun, in addition to being a lot of hard work. The level of fun is directly dependent upon how well a variety of people can interact during the arduous proposal response life cycle. Publications staff, for example, must interact effectively and courteously with technical and other content contributors. A graphics artist might need to spend some time talking with one of the technical writers in order to understand fully what that author wanted to convey through a particular graphic concept or to help that author conceptualize a graphic. That interaction need not be confrontational in either direction. The writer should want to ensure that his graphic is well presented and be pleased that another professional is attending to that detail. And the artist should want every graphic to be accurate and convincing and not become overly frustrated with the back-of-the-envelope stick figures that the writer may have submitted originally. Communication and cross-fertilization of ideas within the Proposal Team should be actively encouraged by the proposal manager.

Fun can take the form of some office-appropriate humor injected into the proposal process in liberal proportion. And a special meal involving the proposal team members is a nice perk, too. The proposal manager should help make the proposal team members feel appreciated and good about what they are doing for the company. As the days and weeks of the proposal response life cycle unfold and the proposal team becomes more tired and worn, pleasant humor, nice meals, meaningful professional and gender-appropriate compliments, and effective communication assume even larger importance. And gift certificates distributed by senior management to the team on a late night or weekend can lift everyone's spirits and contribute to even more productivity.

15.6 Maximizing human intellect

[U]nlike traditional raw material—which is inspected, warehoused, bar-coded, and audited—corporate knowledge is scattered, hard to find, and prone to disappear without a trace.
—Thomas A. Stewart, *Fortune* magazine

Converting human intellect into useful products and services, including proposals, is becoming increasingly critical to any business's success [2]. "We now know where productivity—real and limitless productivity—comes from. It comes from challenged, empowered, excited, rewarded teams of people. It comes from engaging every mind in the organization" [3]. There is an accelerating recognition among corporations that their future profitability depends upon intangible assets such as "creativity, flexibility and the speed with which they can share new ideas and information. In a literal sense, modern corporations *are what they know*" [4]. Major international corporations such as PwC, Skandia Life (Sweden), Xerox, Hewlett-Packard, BP, SAIC, and Dow Chemical are spending significant resources on knowledge identification and management. And the U.S. Securities and Exchange Commission (SEC) hosted a conference that focused on accounting for and reporting intangible assets. Alan Webber, a founding editor of the Boston-based business magazine *Fast Company*, has noted that "[t]he world of business is realizing that ultimately, what matters is the quality of the people in the organization, and how they treat their customers and how creative they are in coming up with new products and new services" [5].

Another significant transition among such major corporations such as Microsoft, Compaq, Sun Microsystems, and Hewlett-Packard is the paradigm shift away from business as a battlefield to that of business as a "complex ecosystem in which the company that wins is the one that is quickest to adapt. Employee individuality and diversity are honored and encouraged" [6]. To adapt to new market circumstances and translate them quickly into meaningful opportunities, your employees simply cannot be viewed and treated as mere mindless troops, crank-turners, or line items on an accounting spreadsheet. The originators of business process reengineering (BPR)—Michael Hammer, James Champy, and Thomas Davenport—have come to recognize the real-world failure of their concept of "fundamental rethinking and radical redesign of business processes to achieve dramatic improvements in critical, contemporary measures of performance, such as cost, quality, service, and speed." In essence, they forgot the people [7]. As Michael Verespej cautions, "We must remember that knowledge workers keep their tool kits in their heads. We must learn to lead people, not contain them. We must learn to listen" [8].

With small companies in particular, leveraging the collective intellect and knowledge is integral to business acquisition achievement. Providing work environments that are conducive to the generation, exchange, respect, and appropriate application of ideas will pay dividends in morale, employee retention, and revenue. Pleasant physical facilities, progressive human resources policies, an open-door management culture, and concrete incentive programs, for example, all participate in inspiring and harnessing the best in and from your employees.

Dr. Douglas Soat, a psychologist who consults to businesses regarding human resources issues, has identified two critical motivators for both technical and nontechnical staff that result in excellence on the job. The first is "setting challenging but realistic expectations," and the second is "demonstrating a true concern for employees" [9]. I can certainly attest to the validity of the latter. I have seen my role in proposal development during the past 25 years to be that of facilitator—a person to grease the wheels of the proposal response process as well as the management decision-making mechanism. How can I help staff do their jobs more effectively and efficiently? What training and additional equipment do they require? Do they need a ride to public transportation after working very late at night? I have arranged for and purchased meals for my staff and have had special breakfasts at which I have brought in the food from home. I have talked with employees, at their request, about personal issues, not offering any solutions, but simply providing an attentive ear. In addition, I have also pursued and received out-of-cycle raises, spot bonuses, and gift certificates for staff in an effort to demonstrate in a tangible way their value to the proposal process.

Your company will be well served to recognize the value of competent, dedicated, team-oriented, and solution-oriented support and technical staff in maximizing performance and engineering business development success.

On a regular basis, I have worked hand-in-hand with my staff when we had to stay 26 hours straight (with breaks and meals) to finish a proposal or provide support over a weekend or on a holiday. Staff know that I will be there with them to the end to get the job done. The concern for quality is lived each day. They also know that I will share their accomplishments on and contributions to proposals and contract deliverables with senior management. Their successes are documented and reappear in detail in the narrative of their performance appraisals. I have extremely high standards for quality and productivity, and these are communicated to staff regularly and in a variety of forms. When I managed staff on a full-time basis, I asked a lot of them and attempted to give a lot back to them as well. In every employee relationship, I have attempted to foster trust in the person by trusting him or her and treating the person with dignity and respect. I recognize the value of competent, dedicated, team- and solution-oriented support and technical staff in maximizing performance and fostering business development success.

15.7 Proposal professionals as change agents

Professional proposal staff can become integral participants in the positive transformation of an organization and its business processes [10]. The detailed analysis and articulation of a company's identity as well as its business processes, operational functions, relationships with clients and vendors, success stories and best practices, and internal resource- and knowledge-sharing mechanisms—the very activities that proposal staff do on a day-to-day basis—can be of direct benefit to the company in ways that extend far beyond proposal development and production. Your professional proposal staff can be among the most effective facilitators of knowledge exchange across your organization's divisional, geographical, and hierarchical boundaries. The "excellent ideas, streamlined operations, cost efficiencies, and technical superiority" [11] that are shared internally with and by your proposal staff can be of immense benefit, not only for the next contractual competition, but also to each element of the company.

15.8 Wellness in your proposal process

Fundamental health and wellness involve nutrition, exercise, sleep, and mind-body interrelationships. Employees who manage stress well tend to be more healthy, productive, cooperative, and creative. By supporting employee stress resilience, proposal managers may improve the quality of the work environment and reduce their own stress.

Senior management should investigate ways to apply flex time realistically in order to allow employees to participate in wellness programs that help them recharge during the work day. Proposal managers should actively encourage staff to take breaks away from their workstations, during which they might read, walk, or exercise in some other way. Supply fresh fruits, vegetables, other low-fat, low-sodium nutritious foods, and spring water to the proposal team on a regular basis. Ensure that staff are given some dedicated time during the height of the proposal life cycle to get out of the office physically and mentally and share time with family and friends. The proverbial all-nighter is not only counterproductive to the overall proposal process and product, but physically and mentally detrimental to the people who are the proposal team.

Proposal managers must make every effort to support the proposal team in a proactive manner with words and actions of encouragement and reliable guidance. Provide a private forum for staff to express their feelings in appropriate ways rather than letting those feelings fester and build to the point of an inappropriate emotional outburst sometime later. Help everyone know and feel that they are appreciated and respected, and are an integral part of an exciting proposal process.

During the marketing life cycle, your company will want to control costs very carefully. Monitoring and managing bid and proposal costs are discussed in Chapter 16.

ENDNOTES

1. *Minds at Work: How Much Brainpower Are We Really Using? A Research Report,* Princeton, NJ: Kepner-Tregoe, 1997.

2. Quinn, James Brian, Philip Anderson, and Sydney Finkelstein, "Managing Professional Intellect: Making the Most of the Best," *Harvard Business Review*, March/April 1996.

3. Quinn, Judy, "The Welch Way: General Electric CEO Jack Welch Brings Employee Empowerment to Light," *Incentive*, September 1994, p. 50.

4. Hamilton, Martha A., "Managing the Company Mind: Firms Try New Ways to Tap Intangible Assets Such as Creativity, Knowledge," *Washington Post*, August 18, 1996, p. H1.

5. Hamilton, Martha A., "Managing the Company Mind: Firms Try New Ways to Tap Intangible Assets Such as Creativity, Knowledge," *Washington Post*, August 18, 1996, p. H5.

6. James, Geoffrey, "It's Time to Free Dilbert," *New York Times*, September 1, 1996, p. F-11.

7. Mariotti, John, "Nursery-Rhyme Management," *Industry Week*, May 5, 1997, p. 19.

8. Verespej, Michael A., "Only the CEO Can Make Employees King," *Industry Week*, November 16, 1998, p. 22.

9. Soat, Douglas M., *Managing Engineers and Technical Employees: How to Attract, Motivate, and Retain Excellent People*, Norwood, MA: Artech House, 1996, p. 119.

10. McVey, Thomas W., "The Proposal Specialist as Change Agent," *APMP Perspective*, May/June 1997, p. 13.

11. McVey, Thomas W., "The Proposal Specialist as Change Agent," *APMP Perspective*, May/June 1997, p. 3.

Chapter 16

Controlling bid and proposal costs

SMALL BUSINESSES SPEND on the order of $1,000 to $2,000 for every $1 million of total contract value. This might expand to a range of $30,000 to $50,000 for a $5 million procurement, or approximately 1%. The late proposal consultant Hyman Silver and many others have suggested that 5% of total contract value be spent on marketing, B&P, and IR&D. Decision drivers regarding marketing, B&P, and IR&D expenditures will, of course, vary according to strategic importance, contract type (cost-reimbursement or fixed-price), fee and profit margins, and your company's incumbency status regarding the particular business opportunity. Small businesses often cannot spend 5% of total contract value due to cash flow, line of credit, and contract backlog parameters. It certainly does require money to win proposals, but the careful application and control of that money can be leveraged into contract award.

What does it cost to get new business, and how are those costs recovered?

If a company wants to capture $5 million of new business during fiscal year (FY) 2012 and it has a win percentage on proposals of 30%, then it has to estimate the costs associated with pursuing $15 million of new business.

All companies, including those competing in the federal marketplace, need to develop strategies for becoming knowledgeable about and then capturing new business. Within the small business contracting community that serves the federal government, a relatively narrow subset of professional staff is involved in identifying, tracking, qualifying, and capturing new business. This staff may include business development and marketing, proposal development, and division-level management professionals. Coordinating short- and long-range opportunity tracking can be challenging in small businesses because of staffing limitations and also because centralized control of business development in such firms is often an evolutionary development rather than a fact of life present from the point of the company's founding. Many times, division managers are primarily responsible for "growing" their respective divisions and have been accustomed to overseeing their own business acquisition activities. Corporate marketing staff may then assist division managers with particular marketing activities.

Marketing and B&P costs can only be projected, monitored, and controlled once a company has determined the extent to which it wants to expand each operating division in accordance with an agreed-upon mission statement and strategic plan. Extending the mission statement and strategic plan down to the competitive procurement level is the key to success. Procurements within the appropriate dollar range and contractual type must be ascertained to be available before growth projections can be made realistically. In-depth knowledge of specific client organization planning, programming, budgeting, and procuring processes, acquisition cycles, and decision-making pathways is imperative to make this determination. If, for example, a company wants to capture $5 million of new business during its FY2012 and it has a win percentage on proposals of 30%, then it has to estimate the costs associated with pursuing $15 million of new business. (Start by listing the potential marketing opportunities, identifying the best opportunities, calculating associated B&P costs, and totaling the numbers.) Fifteen million dollars of viable marketing opportunities in this company's specific LOBs must then be available during FY2012. This small company should plan to spend $150,000 during FY2012 in marketing and B&P costs. These cost estimates should be tracked, monitored, evaluated, and modified on an ongoing basis.

Marketing, B&P, and IR&D costs are recoverable through G&A charges to the federal government. Upon invoicing the government for services rendered, a contractor will typically collect G&A and other indirect costs associated with operating a business.

16.2 Tracking B&P expenditures

Analyzing direct labor and ODCs associated with preparing a proposal as well as the associated postproposal activities in advance of a bid–no bid decision, and then tracking these costs carefully during the entire proposal life cycle, will be beneficial to your company for several reasons. First, accumulating real B&P data over time will allow for increasingly accurate B&P projections as new estimates are calibrated against these real data. Early B&P analysis and estimation will help ensure that adequate resources are made available to prepare an outstanding proposal. Figure 16.1 provides a representative B&P initiation form. Tables 16.1 and 16.2 present templates that can be used to capture and track B&P data. These data should be entered electronically into a spreadsheet application such as Microsoft Excel or data base software application such as Microsoft Access to access easily and prepare comparative graphics for trend evaluation and future projections.

16.3 Business development bonus policy

B&P expenditures increase the indirect rates that your company must submit in response to competitive procurement solicitations. Capture managers or proposal managers are the individuals charged with developing, defending, monitoring, and controlling B&P budgets. In effect, they are fully accountable. Success in the increasingly cost-competitive federal marketplace of 2012 and beyond demands that acquisition and proposal development costs be kept to a minimum. Therefore, to the fullest extent possible and keeping within Department of Labor guidelines, proposal development efforts must be accomplished during nights and weekends. And the reality, as I have observed it and lived it on both coasts, is that many major U.S. contracting and consulting firms nationwide also minimize B&P costs by unpaid night and weekend work. As a small company, your professional, exempt employees should keep B&P charges to an absolute minimum. If they do not, you will have difficulty in expanding your company's revenue base; to do so you must incentivize them and communicate regularly with them about the good job they are doing.

B&P Initiation Form

B&P initiation date: _____   B&P internal tracking number: _____

Client: **FAA**
Procurement title: **Software engineering**
Division responsible for contract (if awarded): _____

Acquisition manager: _____
Proposal manager: **M. Hendrick**

Due date of proposal: _____
Prime: _____   Sub: _____
Teaming partners: _____
_____
_____

Location of performance contract: _____
Type of contract: _____
Expected period of performance: _____ (base and option years)
Persons/year staffing level: _____
Estimated contract dollar value: _____

Estimated B&P costs (please attach the direct labor analysis and ODC forms)
  Hours required: **175**
  Direct labor: **$4,925**
  Overhead: _____
  ODCs: **$825**
  Total: _____

Start date of B&P effort: **November 2012**   Ending date of B&P effort: **January 2013**

Signatures below indicate that the staff have (1) full awareness of this procurement, (2) have reviewed the items above for accuracy and completeness, and (3) accept the B&P hours estimate as reasonable for a procurement of this dollar and level of effort.

Signature lines: _____

Figure 16.1   B&P initiation form.

In recognition of the extended effort of your professional-level and support staff, your company should strongly consider developing and implementing a clearly defined business development bonus policy. The policy should be designed to provide incentives and extra monetary compensation for those employees who have provided outstanding support for proposals or business development. You certainly want to retain and motivate your technical and support talent base.

Date prepared: August 14, 2012								
Analyzed by: M. Hendrick, proposal manager								
Projected Spending								
Month	**November 2012**		**December 2012**		**January 2013**			
Employee Name	**Hours**	**Dollars**	**Hours**	**Dollars**	**Hours**	**Dollars**	**Total Hours**	**Total Dollars**
B. Frank	15	$525	35	$1,225	25	$875	75	$2,625
G. Sinclair	5	$125	45	$1,125	10	$250	60	$1,500
J. Landis	10	$200	25	$500	5	$100	40	$800
Monthly Total	30	$850	105	$2,850	40	$1,225	175	$4,925

Table 16.1   Direct Labor Analysis—Software Engineering Procurement for the FAA

Date prepared: August 14, 2012							
Analyzed by: M. Hendrick, proposal manager Include types of expenditures, such as documentation, travel, training, advertising, equipment purchases, lease agreements, supplies, software.							
Month Projected							
	Amount	**Amount**	**Amount**	**Amount**	**Amount**	**Amount**	**Total**
Type of expenditure	November	December	January				
Local travel	$75	$150	$50				$275
Position advertising	$550	0	0				$550
	$625	$150	$50				$825

Table 16.2   ODC Analysis—Software Engineering Procurement for the FAA

In a reward and motivational survey conducted by Jo W. Manson, then of the Andrulis Research Corporation in Arlington, Virginia, it was determined that during the actual proposal response life cycle, special meals were used as a motivator by 25% of the respondents. After a proposal had been submitted, expressions of appreciation, bonuses, and time off were used as motivational tools.[1] Ms. Manson reminds us that "we are in the people business and, no matter how automated and process driven we may become, we must still rely on well-motivated staff to produce our winning proposals."

According to research by Shari Caudron that appeared in *Industry Week* magazine, "[C]ompanies are starting to extend their incentive programs to nonsales employees with the hope of generating renewed enthusiasm and commitment" [1]. Incentives may take the form of select merchandise, travel, catalog merchandise, cash, jewelry, and honorary titles.

16.4 Stretching limited marketing funds

Most small companies face limited staff power for marketing and business development activities. One mechanism to augment and supplement your company's marketing staff is to use the services of one of a wide variety of marketing consulting firms, such as Deltek FedSources (http://www.deltek.com/services/fedsourcesconsulting/default/asp); INPUT Deltek Information Solutions, which has offices in Reston, Virginia, (http://www.input.com/corp/About/contact.cfm); and Centurion Research Solutions in Chantilly, Virginia (http://www.centurionresearch.com); and Environmental Information Ltd., headquartered in Edina, Minnesota (http://www.envirobiz.com). Consulting companies can provide market research and trend analyses, competitor analysis, marketing opportunity identification, procurement informational databases, intercompany information sharing, strategic planning support, and proposal planning and guidance. Spending dollars for specific, well-directed marketing and planning support from an outside source can help to stretch your company's internal resources and actually help them to be more efficient. Taking the marketing information from outside firms and assessing, distributing, and archiving it in an easily retrieved manner is critical in order to maximize its value to your company.

Let us consider several specific ways in which outside marketing consulting and research firms can assist your company. They can be used to identify and conduct initial screening of potential teaming partners for an important procurement. Such firms can also help validate the funding for a particular procurement. They can be employed to collect competitor

---

1   The survey was distributed to 400 members of the Association of Proposal Management Professionals (APMP) and resulted in a 25% response rate. Expressions of appreciation noted included letters, verbal praise, win parties, and publicity within the company.

bidding and pricing patterns. Often, these marketing research firms offer a basic suite of services such as a regularly updated automated database and hardcopy notebooks of marketing information. This standard suite is, in turn, augmented for additional costs with such services as on-demand telephone hotline support, Web-based information access, news release support and access, and senior-level consulting on a one-on-one, personal level.

Direct experience has shown that a company is well served to judiciously employ the services of several outside marketing consulting firms. Although there will be overlapping information provided, each firm contributes potentially important analysis and data that another may not.

Accurate, current marketing intelligence must be built into your company's proposal. We will now examine proposal writing techniques that are effective in incorporating that intelligence into a solutions-oriented, compliant set of knowledge-based sales documents that convey a compelling, client-focused story.

ENDNOTE

1. Caudron, Shari, "Spreading Out the Carrots," *Industry Week,* May 19, 1997, p. 20.

Chapter 17

Tried-and-true proposal writing and editing techniques

17.1 Proposals are knowledge-based sales documents

Accuracy, brevity, and clarity

The essence of effective proposal writing is responding to the RFP or RFS requirements while completing the process begun during marketing, namely, convincing the client that your team and approach are the most beneficial and cost-effective. Remember that proposals are, first and foremost, sales documents through which validated strengths to the government are conveyed in terms they view as important—quality, schedule, cost, and risk mitigation. They are not technical monographs, white or position papers, or user's manuals. Conceptualizing and developing the technical solution is an engineering or scientific issue. Packaging that solution in a combination of crisp, convincing narrative and high-impact graphics is a sales issue (see Figure 17.1).

Your company's proposal manager must articulate clearly to his or her technical writing team exactly what the expectations and acceptance criteria are. He or she must foster ongoing communication and feedback not only to himself but also among all of the writers. This will help to ensure a consistent approach and minimize rewriting.

Most proposals for a given procurement look and read essentially the same. The challenge is to incorporate well-substantiated information in your proposal that only your company can say. Identify precisely what will separate, or discriminate, your company from the competition. If your company is the incumbent contractor for a particular project and has performed favorably, use the names (and photos) of your incumbent staff people throughout your proposal. Reassure the client that they will be working again with the same competent technical staff who will be supervised by the same responsive management team they know and trust. Help the client understand that their investment in training and building intellectual capital will be retained. Write to a level of technical detail that exceeds what nonincumbents could gain from your project monthly reports (obtained through the FOIA),[1] published articles, and marketing

Figure 17.1
Packaging the
technical solution
is a sales problem.

---

1   FOIA requests should be made to the appropriate agencies in written form. Letters should contain only one specific request. The reason for this practice is that an agency could decline to process one item of a multi-item request, and then the entire request would be returned to the contractor and the process would have to begin again. It is suggested that you begin your request with, "Pursuant to the Freedom of Information Act, 5 U.S.C., Section 552 as amended, Company XYZ hereby requests a copy...." Keep an electronic log of each FOIA request, and place follow-up calls to the agencies after 2 weeks have elapsed.

conversations with government staff. Demonstrate that your company understands the technical and programmatic risks as well as the success criteria. Strive to have your proposals not be boring.

Contributors should keep in mind the following ABCs of proposal writing:

- *Accuracy:* It is not enough, for example, to tell your client that your company has saved time and money on projects of similar size, contract type, technical scope, and geographic area. Tell the client exactly how much time you have saved, how you accomplished this, precisely how much money over what period of time, and the reasons why. Authenticate your claims with concrete, accurate information. Quantify your claims whenever possible with reference to your company's ACASS, PPIRS, or CPARS (see Appendix D for full discussion of these terms) ratings, contractual evaluation reports prepared by your clients, or FASA-driven[2] client "report cards" for contracts in excess of $1 million.

- *Brevity:* Keep your writing crisp. Do not assume that volume will make up for quality. Too many times I have heard technical staff say, "Give them 50 pages, and they'll just assume the correct responses are in there." Guess what? No, they (the evaluators and their support staffs) will not. Unless your company demonstrates through subheadings, graphical pointers, volume-level or sectional tables of contents, and cross-reference matrices that it has responded completely and appropriately to all elements in Sections L, M, and C, you will not score the maximum points available.

- *Clarity:* Assist the client's evaluators to understand, for example, exactly how your company proposes to manage this new project, how you will integrate your subcontractor staff on the job, how your proposed project manager can access corporate resources quickly, and how you will manage tasks in geographically diverse locations. Amplify your crisp, direct narrative descriptions with clear, easily interpretable, and meaningful graphics.

Ten pages of thematically integrated, well-constructed, and compliant prose are much preferred to 50 pages that contain most every technical detail the writers happened to know. Technical "data dumps" glued together produce a very uneven and most likely noncompliant proposal.

---

2   As required by the FASA, a contractor's past performance in government contracts is considered a relevant factor in the award of future contracts.

Keep your ideas focused on the client's requirements as stated in the RFP, and keep your sentences short. This author has seen sentences in proposal narrative that have extended more than 80 words!

Focus on translating the features of your technical and management approaches and into benefits to the client and his project, his budget, his schedule, his career, and his organization's mission and business goals (see Figure 17.2). Demonstrate in clear terms that your company will help him succeed in his mission within his organization. This is an aspect of proposal writing that demands concrete, current, and in-depth marketing intelligence and sharing of this knowledge internally. Without this, your proposal will describe your staff, facilities, contractual experience, and technical capabilities in a vacuum. There will be little or no direct linkage of your company's capabilities and solutions with your client's perceived requirements and success criteria.

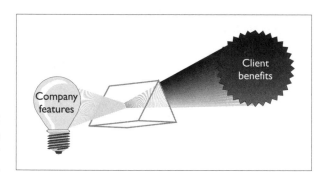

Figure 17.2
Translate features into benefits for your clients.

17.2 Active voice adds strength and saves space

Proposal writers should make every effort to employ the active voice: "We accomplished XYZ," not "XYZ was accomplished by us." The active voice adds strength to the proposal presentation and can save as much as 14% in terms of space as compared with passive voice depending upon the font that is used.

Contributors should attempt to vary sentence and paragraph structure. If you examine a proposal and most of the paragraphs on a page begin with "The" or your company's name, the narrative requires editing to infuse variety.

Writers should also try to employ strong and descriptive verbs, adjectives, and adverbs (see Figure 17.3), such as the following:

- Our staff of six seasoned engineering professionals on the ground today all exceed the stipulated experience level requirements.

High-impact descriptors

- Rigorous development approach
- Principled and fully engaged management
- Seasoned field technicians
- Innovative networking solutions
- Comprehensive community-relations plan
- Results-oriented project team
- Industry-standard sampling methodologies
- Demonstrated success in providing superior-quality engineering solutions
- Responsive organizational structure and seasoned program leadership
- Proven and externally certified business processes
- Technology-driven core competencies

Figure 17.3
High-impact
descriptors for
proposal text.

- Over the course of 3 years of successful enterprise IT service to the Air Force Space Command, our senior programmers developed and implemented effective and cost-efficient ...

- Our company offers field-tested prototyping experience supported by a local testbed laboratory.

- Our 15 analysts embody a knowledge base and legacy of experience that is unmatched.

- Key practices and lessons learned from award-winning performance-based IT support will be shared through established KM processes.

- We are a people-oriented firm with a very low turnover rate as measured against the industry standard in the Washington metropolitan area.

- We will deliver highly defensible results through the conduct of all activities in strict compliance with our sound, metrics-based QA-QC program.

- We will maintain full technical continuity of operations (COOP) and preserve intellectual capital on this important Department of State program through proactive incumbent hiring.

- Our technical understanding is greatly enhanced by our award-winning past performance on two critical contracts for the Office of Personnel Management.

- With an extensive IT portfolio that includes Dell Precision T5500 workstations to support off-site scientific data processing, our company ...

- Our company's 4 years of progressive support of the VA validates our commitment to ...

- We are committed to joining a working partnership with NOAA National Weather Service during the life of this contract.

17.3 Guide the client's evaluators through your proposal

Formulate ideas precisely, concretely, and simply. To include every technical detail each writer knows about a certain topic will probably not result in a successful proposal. This is where storyboards and bullet drafts as well as elevator speeches and pain tables come into play—to guide your writers in preparing a thematically consistent response of uniform technical depth. Proposals must appear as if written by a single, well-organized individual. Your proposal narrative must contribute to fast and easy comprehension by a variety of client evaluators who are reading your document with technical, contractual, and programmatic frames of reference. Use frequent subheadings or graphical icons to break up text and to facilitate the evaluation of your proposal.

Contributors should write from the general to the specific, from the easy-to-understand to the more difficult to comprehend. Proceed from an overview of each major topic to the finer grained technical and programmatic details. Always ask yourself the question: What's next? [1]. Writers should identify and discuss tangible benefits to the client of your company's technical, management, staffing, quality, and past performance approach, such as the following:

1. When we build and implement solutions, we offer value engineering recommendations that result in significant cost savings for our clients, including the DOE and GSA.

2. We have established clear lines of authority and channels of communication to ensure accountability for this important FAA program at all levels within our organization and to expedite decision making.

3. We will incorporate our formalized and widely deployed operating procedures along with automated applications into the operational environment to ensure that state-of-the-art services are being provided that meet the requirements of Department of Treasury end users.

4. Our company has been successful in transitioning five other projects by focusing on the prospective employees and their career goals, and by offering a superior benefits package.

5. Our single-vendor contract management approach will eliminate program accountability complexities, reduce costs, and minimize overall management risks.

6. Our demonstrated record of careful cost controls on Army and Air Force programs will result in best value support for the Navy throughout the life of this important contract.

7. With an established regional presence in Texas since 2008, we have performed 6 projects in the Dallas–Ft. Worth area in the past 4 years.

8. Complementing our presence in Connecticut and our technical knowledge base with Coast Guard programs is the collective technical, programmatic, and human talent of our two teaming partners.

9. To effectively manage and conduct technical work under each task order assigned, we have created the position of task leader. The task leader will serve as the single point of contact with the Department of Homeland Security.

10. Our outstanding and well-established lines of communication among our team and with the Air Combat Command will help to ensure rapid problem resolution.

There is a natural tendency to dwell on familiar ground. Often, this is of the least significance as far as the RFP requirements are concerned. Demonstrate how the features of your approach translate into performance, schedule, cost, risk mitigation, and business-level benefits. Use facts—support all statements with concrete, quantified (if possible) examples. Include the following:

- What your company will do for the client;
- How your staff will do it;
- Why you will do it that way;
- What you did in the past, that is, your previous or current contractual experience, highlighting the relevant lessons learned, key practices discovered, and quantified successes generated from similar contractual experience.

Summarize the content of each proposal section in the first paragraph of discussion. Write for a variety of readers, including the skim or executive-level reader. To be a winner, a proposal must contain concise, understandable, and closely related thoughts woven into a compelling story. Identify the critical technical areas. In discussing them, use a level of detail that exceeds what a nonincumbent could use, and do not drown the reader in jargon or equations. Your proposal should be built on solution-oriented writing. Write-ups should be risk-aware and solution-oriented and demonstrate an understanding of the evolutionary changes likely to occur over the life of the contract. This is particularly true with today's 5-, 7-, and 10-year contract vehicles.

Make your company's compliance with the requirements and responsiveness to your client's evolving needs apparent to the evaluator over and over again. Use RFP or RFS terminology exactly (or in shortened form) for your proposal headings and subheadings. Employ the RFP terminology as a point of departure for further original writing. Do not simply recite the RFP verbiage in the actual narrative of your proposal. A DoD COTR once told me that he felt personally insulted when contractors, both large and small, merely replaced the words "the contractor shall" that appear in the SOW, with "our company will." Such an approach demonstrates no technical understanding whatsoever. In a NASA RFQ from 2011, the government stipulated that "[s]tating that you understand and will comply with the specifications, or paraphrasing the specifications is inadequate, as are phrases such as 'standard procedures will be employed' and 'well known type techniques will be used.'"

Define acronyms and abbreviations the first time they are used in each major proposal section. Not all evaluators see the entire technical, management, and past performance proposal volumes, so redefinition of acronyms is certainly acceptable assuming page-count constraints allow. Avoid sectional or page references in the text because references must be changed each time the section or page numbers change. References such as "See Section 5.1.1 on page 5-34" should not be used. Let the compliance matrix and table of contents assist the evaluators in locating specific pages or sections. In addition, avoid fifth-order headings (for example, Section 4.3.1.3.1).

Proposal writers should attempt to think graphically as well as in written form (see Chapter 11). Every proposal section should have a figure or table associated with it that is referenced and discussed clearly in the text. Figure captions should appear centered beneath the appropriate figure. Table legends should appear centered above the appropriate table. Assuming the RFP permits, label all illustrations as "exhibits" to avoid confusion between what is a table and what is a figure.

17.4 **Action captions**

A great place to use theme statements is in the captions or legends for figures, tables, photographs, and other graphic presentations. Let's look at the difference between simply identifying what a graphic or photograph is, and using the caption as a forum to convey important sales messages that have been tailored to the specific procurement.

- Instead of "Project Organizational Chart," your caption might read "Our project team is proficient in each of the USACE technical requirement areas."

- Instead of "Map of Our Local Locations," your caption might read "The proximity of our offices to Fort McCloud will afford rapid response to changing requirements."

- Instead of "Capabilities Matrix," your caption might read "Each one of our four proposed senior technical staff holds an accredited degree in a relevant engineering and scientific discipline."

- Instead of "Our Laboratory Staff," your caption might read "Our well-trained laboratory staff are dedicated to and trained in quality-oriented procedures that ensure appropriate chain-of-custody handling."

- Instead of "Appropriate H/S Procedures," your caption might read "We actively practice a comprehensive health and safety program designed to meet the requirements of 29 CFR 1926.65 for hazardous waste site work."

- Instead of "Scope of Support Services," your caption might read "We provide cost-effective, innovative support services across a broad spectrum of financial regulatory acts."

In each one of these examples, we have taken a flat statement and added positive, dynamic sales messages. We have introduced benefits of your approach and capabilities to the client. These sales messages, or themes, should be developed early in the proposal response cycle so that the entire proposal writing team can incorporate them into their narrative and into the captions they develop for their graphics. Please note, however, that it is always critical to be totally compliant with the RFP. If a particular RFP stipulates that figure and tables shall be named in a particular manner, you must adhere to that guidance.

17.5 Methods of enhancing your proposal writing and editing

Toward the goal of keeping your proposal writing highly focused, consider the four following stages [2]:

1. Collect the technical and marketing intelligence information you need for your section(s). Focus on the basic features of those materials.

2. Identify the information in those materials that is relevant to the RFP requirements for your particular section and which supports the strategic win themes that have been noted for that section.

3. Extract, organize, and reduce the relevant information. Begin to compose the relevant information into sentence form in accordance with the proposal outline that was part of the Kickoff Package or proposal directive. Slant your writing toward your audience, that is, the client evaluators of the proposal. Be informative but brief. Be concise, exact, and unambiguous. Use short, complete sentences.

4. Refine, review, and edit the relevant information to ensure completeness, technical accuracy, and the inclusion of theme statements.

Importantly, one of the best ways to polish the writing in your company's proposals is to read it aloud to a colleague or yourself. Awkward sentence constructions quickly become obvious. The flow of the narrative can be smoothed and refined through this process of reading.

A longer-term key to effective proposal writing is reading many different types of materials across a variety of disciplines and media—such as professional and scholarly journal articles, public relations brochures, newspapers, textbooks, novels, and other works of literary fiction. An enhanced functional vocabulary is one result. Another is learning how to use the same word in a broad spectrum of contexts. Reading in this manner can also produce an appreciation of nuance, that is, using precisely the most appropriate word for the given application.

There are many courses available through local colleges and universities that can be of assistance in enhancing your staff's technical and business writing capabilities.

In terms of editing proposal narrative, the following checklist can prove very useful [3]:

1. Check for completeness.

2. Check for accuracy.

3. Check for unity and coherence.

4. Include effective transition statements.

5. Check for consistent point of view.

6. Emphasize main ideas.

7. Subordinate less important ideas.

8. Check for clarity.

9. Eliminate ambiguity.

10. Check for appropriate word choice.

11. Eliminate jargon and buzzwords.

12. Replace abstract words with concrete words.

13. Achieve conciseness.

14. Use the active voice as much as possible.

15. Check for parallel structure (for example, a list begins with all *-ing* or all *-ed* words).

16. Check sentence construction and achieve sentence variety.

17. Eliminate awkwardness.

18. Eliminate grammar problems.

19. Check for subject–verb agreement.

20. Check for proper case (such as upper case and initial caps).

21. Check for clear reference of pronouns.

22. Check for correct punctuation.

23. Check for correct spelling, abbreviations, acronym definitions, contractions (avoid them), italics, numbers, symbols, for example.

24. Check for correctness of format.

17.6 **The power of framing**

Frames offer proposal professionals a powerful tool for aligning proposal solutions with customers' preexisting sentiments and mental pictures. Try applying them on your next proposal. *They work.* Framing activates *existing* beliefs and thoughts, rather than adding *something new* to an individual's beliefs about a given issue [4]. It is helpful to present the story in a vessel familiar to most listeners (see Table 17.1) [5]. Frames exert their distinctive power through the *selective description* and *omission* of features of a situation [6]. Selecting appropriate frames will help your customer resonate with your solution.

One of the key questions that a company must ask itself when pursuing a bid opportunity to provide services, products, or knowledge sets to the U.S. federal government is: *Who must we be to win?* Initially, this question might appear confusing. So let's unravel it to see why it's so important.

There are many facets that make up the overall image of your company. Representative facets might include:

Why try to introduce the British ITIL quality standard for managing IT services to a customer who is already familiar with and using ISO 9001:2000 standards?
Why propose a Project Manager (PM), Deputy Project Manager, and three Task Leaders to manage a project on which the customer is used to interacting with one "working" PM and two "working" Task Leaders?
Why offer a monthly, paper-based performance satisfaction assessment program to a customer who is reticent to complete automated performance assessments on an annual basis?
Why introduce a six-company team to perform on a program that has been awarded historically to a contractor that offers a streamlined, two-vendor solution?
Why design and build your proposal documents in a manner that does not adhere to the structure, nomenclature, and sequence provided in Sections L, M, and C of the government's final Request for Proposal (RFP)—an RFP that the government spent months developing and reviewing?
Why frame the benefits of your organization's solution in terms of exacting schedule control when increased return on investment (ROI) and decreased total cost of ownership (TCO) are the critical customer success factors?

Table 17.1
Increased Proposal Success: Connecting with the "Known"

- Small business;
- Minority-owned business;
- *Woman-owned business;*
- *Financially stable firm;*
- Mission support contractor;
- Performance-based support contractor;
- Proven prime contractor;
- Core competency in information technology (IT);
- *Core competency in engineering;*
- *Core competency in telecommunications support;*
- Core competency in scientific support;
- ISO 9001:2008-certified organization;
- Established defense contractor;
- *Known NASA contractor;*
- Documented cyber security provider;
- Employee-focused culture.

For a given bid opportunity, *emphasizing* (that is, "giving salience," academically speaking) your organization's *woman-owned business status* and *core competency in telecommunications support* may well be the ideal picture you want to paint. On another bid opportunity, your firm's *financial stability, core competency in engineering,* and being a *known NASA contractor* may constitute the image that you want to frame, and then project to your customer at multiple points and in multiple ways (e.g., narrative, graphics, cover art) throughout your proposal.

Note that the majority of the descriptive elements that comprise your organization's overall image are *not* employed when answering the question: *Who must we be to win?* Most are, in fact, omitted. Deciding what information to *present* (in effect, "inclusion"), what points to *emphasize* ("salience"), and what information to *omit* ("exclusion") is a critical process in framing exactly what image of your company you want to project to your customer.

One other important step must be accomplished at this juncture as well. It is critical to *alter* the weight or importance value of particular elements. In the example just described, wherein your firm's financial stability, core competency in engineering, and being a known NASA contractor were the key elements in the image that you want to frame and project to your customer, it is also important to *weigh* one element as the most vital. It may be *financial stability*, given validated marketing intelligence that your Business Development staff uncovered that indicates the current incumbent contractor's difficulty in meeting payroll during contract startup or its inability to offer *prepaid* educational and training benefits to it employees. Frames lend additional weight to an already accessible concept by influencing its perceived relevance or importance [7].

To frame, therefore, is to select some aspects of a perceived reality and make them more salient in communicating text in such a way as to promote a particular problem definition, causal interpretation, and/or recommendation for the item described [8]. The same certainly applies to graphics as well.

A frame offers perspective by managing the alignment of the observer (federal government evaluator) in relation to an issue (your company's image or your proposed solution set). In addition, a frame directs the observer to focus on a feature of an issue within the frame, and then to disregard other features of the same issue that fall outside the frame. Finally, a frame influences subsequent judgment in that it organizes and tailors information to fit into it. It therefore not only contains, but also constrains [9]. In his ballad "Against the Wind," guitarist Bob Seeger sang about "What to leave in, what to leave out." These song lyrics are directly analogous to framing as it relates to proposals. We as proposal professionals have to make very conscious choices about what to leave in—that is, include within the frames that we present to the government—and what to leave out.

17.6.1 Grasping the highlights of framing theory

Cognitive consistency theory in psychology explains that a person is more likely to accept new claims if they are shown to be similar to already accepted ideas and practices. Advocates (proposal professionals) must attempt to construct frames that resonate with the broader understanding of customers [10]. Framing theory asserts that the way in which we receive information—indeed, how the story is told, begins to structure how we view what has transpired [11]. At its core, frame analysis is the study of how events in everyday life are organized or made sense of in coherent ways. "We react to things in the world based on the information coming to us through frames" [12].

17.6.2 Framing, photography, and proposaling

Frames refer to *lenses* that stakeholders (government evaluators) use to make sense [13]. These lenses can be applied selectively to frame customer requirements in such a way as to align with your company's solution sets. For example, your customer's requirements as presented in the Statement of Work (SOW) of the RFP or Statement of Objectives (SOO) in the RFS may focus on Tier 1 and Tier 2 help desk support. Your company may elect to frame your solution strictly in terms of help desk solutions and commercial-off-the-shelf (COTS) products such as IBM Tivoli, FrontRange HEAT, Numara FootPrints, and Applix. Alternatively, you might frame the customer's requirement in terms of enterprise-wide information cyber security governance, management, and architecture in accordance with the Federal Information Security Management Act (FISMA). Finally, your company might expand the ramifications of the basic task- and project-level help desk requirements to frame the ultimate requirement as helping the customer agency get to "green" on the Office of Management and Budget's (OMB) Exhibit 300s. The Exhibit 300s constitute part of the Executive Branch Management Scorecard. Precisely how you elect to frame the government's requirements will depend upon the marketing intelligence that you collect and validate. A very different picture emerges depending upon the lens you choose to use. Any event (or in this case, *solution*) can be framed in multiple ways [14].

17.6.3 Pictures, maps, and stories

American journalist and political commentator Walter Lippmann, who wrote the influential book *Public Opinion,* asserted that people act based on "'the pictures inside our heads'" rather than on objective reality [15]. University of California–Berkeley professor George Lakoff writes that we understand words on the basis of a "mental map" [16]. In general, people create stories to organize their experiences, create order, gain perspectives, and make evaluations [17].

Pictures. Maps. Stories.... A long way from logic, analysis, objectivity, metrics, and fact. Yet Stephen Denning, former World Bank knowledge management executive, says that: "'analysis might excite the mind, but it hardly offers a route to the heart'" [18]. The World Advertising Research Center finds that storytelling injects emotional value, thereby increasing the perceived value of the product (or proposal solution) and making it more attractive to buy [19], or select as part of the competitive bid process. Stories work because they are engaging, easy to remember, and nonadversarial [18]. Stories function as bridges [20], reaching across boundaries of culture, profession, and age [21]. Dr. Deborah Sole of Harvard University asserts that stories can convey one's trustworthiness, as well as signal one's trust in others [22]. Storytelling makes experience visible [23].

17.6.4 **Applying framing to your proposals**

So you're working on your next competitive proposal to provide support services for one of the major civilian agencies of the federal government. With the direction provided in the Federal Acquisition Streamlining Act, you already know that this contract you are pursuing *must* focus on meaningful and measurable cost, schedule, and performance goals. In addition, the "25 Point Implementation Plan to Reform Federal IT Management" also tells you that this civilian agency—like all other federal agencies—needs to adopt "light" technologies and shared solutions. Given this critical background information coupled with the project- and customer-specific marketing intelligence that your company has collected through business development activities and customer relationship management over the past 6 months, you might *frame* your management solution to include processes and tools that track, document, and provide near-real-time insight into quality, schedule, and cost performance. Furthermore, you might convey the strengths of your proposed key personnel in your staffing section through the "frame" of staff professionals committed to and experienced with performance-based contracts and cloud technologies ,and meeting the metrics associated with service level agreements (SLAs) and service level objectives (SLOs). Your past performance volume or section might be framed to highlight performance-based contracts, service delivery models of operation, and improved operational efficiencies in support of government business and mission goals. Additionally, your technical volume or section might include discrete subsections that focus on, in effect, *frame,* your solution set in terms of embracing metrics across the scope of the contractual work to be performed and reducing costs through efficiencies. "A frame is a central organizing idea for making sense of relevant events and *suggesting what is at issue*" [24]. Given this fact, your proposal can frame every aspect of your solution set for this civilian agency in terms of meaningful and measurable *results.*

By taking this approach, you are emphasizing specific aspects of your solution, presenting particular information and omitting other information, and aligning your solution with your civilian agency customer's preexisting vision (e.g., FASA, OMB 300s, performance-based contracting). It is important to note that page count restrictions contained in the RFP or RFS are not the primary drivers of what information to include or omit in your proposal. Rather, your solution and the frames in which that solution is constructed should drive these decisions.

17.7 Government-recognized writing standards

There are several writing, editorial, and proofreading standards recognized by the federal government. Among these are the 30th edition of the *United States Government Printing Office Style Manual 2008* (available online at http://www.gpoaccess.gov/stylemanual/browse.html); *Word Division: Supplement to United States Government Printing Office Style Manual* (1987); *The Gregg Reference Manual* by William A. Sabin, 11th ed. (2010) and *The Tongue and Quill* [Air Force Handbook (AFH) 33-337, August 1, 2004]. The consistent application of an appropriate standard is important to implement within your company's publication or editorial group. Pages 4 and 5 of the *GPO Style Manual 2008* provide a useful reference for proofreader's markings.

17.8 Additional sources of writing guidance

Judith A. Tarutz, *Technical Editing: The Practical Guide for Editors and Writers* (Hewlett-Packard Press, 1992); Philip R. Theibert, *Business Writing for Busy People* (Career Press, 1996); *The Chicago Manual of Style: The Essential Guide for Writers, Editors, and Publishers,* 16th ed. (University of Chicago Press, 2010), Edward T. Cremmins, *The Art of Abstracting,* 2nd ed. (Info Resources Press, 1996); Charles T. Brusaw, Gerald J. Alred, and Walter E. Oliu, *Handbook of Technical Writing,* 9th ed. (Bedford St. Martin's Press, 2008); Marjorie E. Skillin and Robert Malcom Gay, *Words Into Type,* 3rd ed. (Pearson, 1974); Robert A. Day, (ed.), *How to Write and Publish a Scientific Paper,* 6th ed. (Greenwood Press, 2006); and Herbert B. Michaelson, *How to Write and Publish Engineering Papers and Reports,* 3rd ed. (Oryx Press, 1990) each offer insight and direction for clearer and more concise writing. Edward Cremmins' work is exceptional in helping one to understand how to convey information accurately and robustly while simultaneously conserving the number of words used.

17.9 Storytelling as an art form

Storytelling as an art form—coupled with quantitative, scientific, technical, and business validation—constitutes an intensely powerful and highly cost-effective framework for developing and conveying proposal solutions, which can in turn lead to winning significantly more new and recompeted federal government contractual business. In addition, organizational performance as it relates to business development and the management of bid and proposal (B&P) dollars can be optimized.

Proposals are, in fact, complex contractual and legal entities. In addition, they can be perceived as "knowledge products," that is, the synthesis of technical, programmatic, past and present contractual performance, and pricing knowledge coupled with a detailed understanding of government customers, industry competitors, and current and emerging technologies. Furthermore, they can correctly be considered as "sales products"— focused on *completing* the sale to the government that began during the marketing phase of your small company's overall business development life cycle for a specific government procurement opportunity.

This is precisely where the art of fact-based storytelling becomes so important as the tool and framework by which to convey solution sets, in effect, knowledge and "sense." It is also precisely where the majority of companies—both small and large—fail in their capture management and proposal development strategies and efforts. Compliance-oriented and process-driven capture management and proposal development approaches alone cannot and will not produce winning proposal documents and stellar oral presentations on a sustainable basis. The oft-cited "answer the mail" model for responding to government RFPs and RFSs is necessary, but certainly not sufficient for long-term success in the federal marketplace.

Fact-based storytelling is the knowledge transfer and communications mechanism that constitutes the core of proposal solution development. Research suggests that sharing experiences through narrative (i.e., storytelling) "builds trust," "transfers tacit knowledge," and "generates emotional connections" [25]. Solution development, in turn, refers to the critical activity of building and articulating fact-based *storylines* or *story arcs* that convey your small business's specific approaches to providing meaningful, measurable, achievable, and risk-aware outcomes for your federal government customer. Robust solution sets must encompass such proposal areas as technical, program management, staffing, contract phase-in, and past/present contractual performance. The storylines must draw together such major elements as "Understanding the Customer Environment," "Technical and Programmatic Approach," and "Measurable Outcomes/Value Proposition" in a manner that ensures continuity of major sales messages or themes. More to the point, these storylines convey both sense and sensibility to the federal customer.

People buy from people, and people buy emotionally. Transactions are very personal. For these critical reasons, fact-based storytelling should be considered the central cornerstone of proposal development. To the detriment of countless small and large businesses, however, it is not afforded that keystone role at present.

The real-world implications of this approach for today's and tomorrow's high-velocity business environment are substantive and tangible. Small companies can optimize their valuable and perennially limited B&P dollars by employing the storytelling framework for successful capture management and proposal development. In today's extraordinarily competitive performance-based federal marketplace, the *delta*, or difference, between winning and coming in second borders on the microscopic. On a NASA Glenn Research Center proposal in 2011, the delta between first and second place was 9 points out of 1,000. Storytelling in the proposal process can help articulate and deliver meaningful and positive differences between one company and its competitors. Through well-articulated stories augmented by appropriate and quickly comprehensible graphics and photographic images, federal proposal evaluators as well as federal customers and stakeholders can come to understand "possible futures" [25] that include a given small company's suite of solutions being deployed to meet the government's set of technical and business requirements, and solve the government's challenges. This positive sentiment ("customer sentiment" is a term employed by proposal expert Hyman Silver) on the government's part will, in turn, contribute to increased proposal win rates, bookings, and revenue streams for the proposing small company.

The validity of this innovative fact-based storytelling approach for capture management and proposal development was well established empirically during the period of 1999–2007 with a small, minority-owned federal contracting company. Staffing levels increased by a factor of *14* to nearly 1,960 within that period, and revenues increased by a factor of *23.5* to $250 million. In addition, the scholarly literature also provides a defensible theoretical basis for the foundational planks of this storytelling approach.

We will look at the critical information management processes that link directly to business acquisition success.

ENDNOTES

1. Miner, Lynn E., and Jeremy T. Miner, *Proposal Planning and Writing*, 3rd ed., Westport, CT: Greenwood Press, 2003.

2. Adopted from Cremmins, Edward T., *The Art of Abstracting*, Philadelphia, PA: ISI Press, 1982, pp. 17, 73.

3. Adopted from Cremmins, Edward T., *The Art of Abstracting*, Philadelphia, PA: ISI Press, 1982, p. 85.

4. Nelson, Thomas E., Zoe M. Oxley, and Rosalee A. Clawson, "Toward a Psychology of Framing Effects," *Political Behavior,* Vol. 19, 1997, p. 236.

5. Ibarra, Herminia, and Kent Lineback, "What's Your Story?" *Harvard Business Review,* Vol. 83, January 2005, p. 70.

6. Entman, Robert M., "Framing: Toward Clarification of a Fractured Paradigm," *Journal of Communication,* Vol. 43, 1993, p. 54. See also Hallahan, Kirk, "Seven Models of Framing: Implications for Public Relations," *Journal of Public Relations Research,* Vol. 11, 1999, p. 207.

7. Nelson, Thomas E., Zoe M. Oxley, and Rosalee A. Clawson, "Toward a Psychology of Framing Effects," *Political Behavior,* Vol. 19, 1997, pp. 236–237.

8. Entman, Robert M., "Framing: Toward Clarification of a Fractured Paradigm," *Journal of Communication,* Vol. 43, 1993, p. 52.

9. Venter, David, "Framing—An Important Negotiation Tool," *The Negotiator Magazine*, October 2004, http://www.negotiatormagazine.com/article224_1.html.

10. Payne, Roger A., "Persuasion, Frames, and Norm Construction," *European Journal of International Relations,* Vol. 7, 2001, http://www.louisville.edu/a-s/polsci/payne/REVFRAME.doc.

11. Hayden, C. A., "Power in Media Frames: Thinking About Strategic Framing and Media System Dependency and the Events of September 11, 2001," 2003, p. 5, http://lass.calumet.purdue.edu/cca/gmj/fa03/graduatefa03/gmj-fa03-hayden.htm.

12. Stout, Daniel A., and Judith M. Buddenbaum, "Media, Religion, and 'Framing,'" *Journal of Media and Religion,* Vol. 2, 2003, p. 1.

13. Gray, B., "Strong Opposition: Frame-Based Resistance to Collaboration," *Journal of Community & Applied Social Psychology,* Vol. 14, 2004, p. 167.

14. Chyi, Hsiang I., and Maxwell McCombs, "Media Salience and the Process of Framing: Coverage of the Columbine School Shootings," *Journalism & Mass Communication Quarterly,* Vol. 81, Spring 2004, p. 30.

15. Hallahan, Kirk, "Seven Models of Framing: Implications for Public Relations," *Journal of Public Relations Research,* Vol. 11, 1999, p. 206.

16. Miller, Nora, "Thinking Inside the Frame," *ETC: A Review of General Semantics,* Vol. 62, No. 2, April 2005, p. 205.

17. Escalas, J. E., "Narrative Processing: Building Consumer Connections to Brands," *Journal of Consumer Psychology,* Vol. 14, 2004, p. 168.

18. "Why Denning Is Nuts About Stories," *New Zealand Management,* September 2004, p. 7.

19. Fonnesbaek, J., and M. M. Anderson, "Story Telling: How LEGO Told a Story and Sold a Toy," *Young Consumers,* 2005, Quarter 2, p. 33.

20. Hale, Charles R., "The Sales Power of Storytelling," *Advisor Today*, Vol. 50, July 2005.

21. Harris, J., and B. K. Barnes, "Leadership Storytelling," *Leadership Excellence,* Vol. 22, April 2005, p. 7.

22. Sole, Deborah, "Sharing Knowledge Through Storytelling," Learning Innovations Laboratories, Harvard University Graduate School of Education, April 2002, http://www.providersedge.com/docs/km_articles/Sharing_Knowledge_Through_Storytelling.pdf.

23. Johansson, Anders W., "Consulting as Story-Making," *The Journal of Management Development,* Vol. 23, 2004, p. 341.

24. Nelson, Thomas E., Zoe M. Oxley, and Rosalee A. Clawson, "Toward a Psychology of Framing Effects," *Political Behavior,* Vol. 19, 1997, p. 222.

25. Sole, Deborah, and Daniel G. Wilson, "Storytelling in Organizations: The Power and Traps of Using Stories to Share Knowledge in Organizations," http://lila.pz.harvard.edu/_upload/lib/ACF14F3.pdf.

Chapter 18

Packaging and managing proposal information and knowledge effectively

Overview

Proposals are authenticated information and knowledge in carefully packaged form. Organizing a centralized, fully operational, and scalable informational data system or knowledge base is imperative to your company's business development success. Maintaining frequently used proposal materials in compatible electronic formats as well as in easily accessible hardcopy form will help your proposal planning and preparation process significantly. These materials include résumés, project descriptions or summaries, proposal boilerplate or reuse material such as configuration management and health and safety plans, and previously submitted proposals. Proposal managers require ready access to the latest[1] company and marketing intelligence information. But be sure to store all company-sensitive marketing and proposal information in a secure physical area and within a secure partition of an electronic network.

18.2 The all-important résumés

Your company's human technical and programmatic talent is the basis for your success to date. Staff are a particularly important consideration in the case of support services contracts, because the client is, in effect, purchasing human expertise in, for example, pollution prevention, electrical engineering, systems design, network engineering, facilities management, applications development, green cloud computing, vitrual desktop infrastructure (VDI), or integrated logistics support (ILS). Indeed, a company's staff being presented in the best possible light is valid for every federal government procurement. This means that résumés have to be customized or tailored for each proposal. Tailoring is not altering or misrepresenting a person's experience or education in an unethical or illegal manner, but rather involves highlighting relevant experience, publications, certifications, and education to the exclusion of other information. Some RFPs or RFSs require that each person proposed sign a statement that the information contained in his or her résumé is accurate. Adequate time within the proposal response schedule needs to be built in to secure those requisite signatures. Smaller companies need stellar résumés; they function like name brands.

At times, the RFP will provide a very detailed résumé format, or indicate in narrative form how the issuing government agency wants to receive the résumés. When résumé format, content, or page count are stipulated, you must comply fully. However, many times you will have a degree of autonomy to structure the résumé.

A technique for helping evaluators quickly understand your staff's capabilities is to include a box entitled "Experience Summary," "Benefits to the Client," "Basis of Team Selection," or "Relevance to the Project" on the first page of each résumé required by the RFP. Within that summary box, highlight the particular individual's expertise and accomplishments

---

1 Ensuring that proposal managers are provided with the latest company information is an ongoing effort in configuration management. For example, a comprehensive written overview about your company that is used in most every proposal needs to contain the most up-to-date information on contract awards, company commendations and success stories, annual revenue, staff level, funded contract backlog, and corporate organizational structure and leadership. If this business overview is updated for a given proposal, the corporate library boilerplate file that contains this same overview must be revised as well.

relevant to the specific position description or technical requirements of the procurement—this might include education, management experience on specific contract types, number of staff managed, publications, certifications, professional society memberships, work on similar projects, innovations, relevant training, and years of successful experience in a given operational environment. Other items to consider include award/honors, knowledge of federal agency policies and directives, and skill sets mapped to relevant task areas. Three to four bulleted items are sufficient. If you do not use an "Experience Summary" box, you might consider including a "Benefits to the Project" section in each résumé. Do not assume that the evaluators will take the time to carefully review each résumé and extract the relevant details that correspond to the position description. If you make their job difficult, you simply cannot expect to receive the maximum points possible.

Résumés should focus on relevant technical and programmatic accomplishments and excellence. They should accentuate results—increased production rates, improved quality, on-schedule performance, cost savings or avoidance, meeting performance thresholds, and the implementation of innovative techniques and technologies. As appropriate, they should be client specific, site specific, and geography specific. Résumés should use transferable, action-oriented lead words to describe an individual's activities and contributions (see Figure 18.1). These types of words help the evaluators to understand the relevance of your staff's

---

Action-oriented words for staff résumés

• Manages	• Negotiates	• Leverages	• Brings	• Field-tests
• Performs	• Reviews	• Translates	• Provides	• Establishes
• Implements	• Writes	• Offers	• Facilitates	• Cocreates
• Conducts	• Designs	• Serves	• Enforces	• Assists
• Directs	• Supports	• Oversees	• Selects	• Plans
• Coordinates	• Builds	• Delivers	• Trains	• Employs
• Prepares	• Drives	• Ensures	• Operates	• Studies
• Initiates	• Leads	• Participates	• Troubleshoots	• Examines
• Develops	• Determines	• Maintains	• Audits	• Assesses
• Investigates	• Applies	• Practices	• Analyzes	• Consults
• Inspects	• Characterizes	• Deploys	• Compiles	• Surveys

Figure 18.1
Use action-oriented words to transfer capabilities from past contracts to the current opportunity.

current and past experience to the new project at hand. They facilitate the transfer of talent and capability from one project to another.

Review the following example.

- *Wrong way:* "Mr. Jones managed an investigation at Ft. Baltimore, Maryland."
- *Appropriate way:* "Mr. Jones managed a lead contamination groundwater investigation at Ft. Baltimore, Maryland. He negotiated technology-based cleanup criteria with the Maryland Department of the Environment in the decision document."

One of the most important information-management activities your company can undertake is to create, update, archive, and make available for retrieval a résumé for each member of your technical, management, and support staff. Use the same software application and version that you use to produce your proposals, and format each résumé in a style that will be compatible aesthetically with the rest of your proposal text. Store hardcopies of all résumés in alphabetical order in three-ring notebooks for ease of access. Establish an electronic subdirectory of all company résumés so that they might be searched (using infoRouter from Active Innovations, or SharePoint 2010, for example) for a combination of appropriate keywords based upon the position descriptions in the RFP. And you would be well served to generate and maintain a genuine database (using database software such as Microsoft Access) of résumé information to facilitate rapid searches to meet position description parameters or prepare tables and graphics providing information about your technical and professional staff. Many times RFPs will request the number of staff with specific degrees, certifications, or levels of experience. Appendix B of this book illustrates a form that can be used to capture the employee information used to populate the database.

Creating, word processing, editing, proofreading, and updating résumés is a time-consuming and ongoing task. But without résumés readily accessible, much of your proposal response time will be consumed preparing them. And having more information than is required by the average RFP—such as grade point average (NASA has required this information), name and address of high school, previous supervisors and telephones, security clearances, years of supervisory experience, and professional references (including telephone numbers and e-mail addresses)[2]—is always preferable to having to search for that information under the pressure of preparing a proposal.

18.3 Project descriptions (project summaries or project citations)

A cumulative, regularly updated hardcopy and electronic file copy of your company's contracts, both as prime and sub, is a vital building block in the knowledge foundation.

Create project descriptions at the time of contract award and update them at the completion of specific tasks, or semiannually, and then again at contract completion. As with résumés, storing hardcopies of each project description in a three-ring notebook allows ease of access. In the front of the binder, include a current list or matrix that includes all project description titles, contract and purchase order numbers, and client agencies in some logical order. It would be advisable to put your boilerplate project descriptions in the format required by your major client(s). One such format is presented in Figure 18.2. Specific information can always be added or removed in the tailoring process. Project or division managers should oversee and approve the updating process to ensure completeness and accuracy. As with the proposal response process, the updating of résumés and project summaries will require top-down management support, otherwise it will rarely be given the attention it deserves. Résumés and project summaries are a great activity on which to leverage freelance or part-time writing support.

Project descriptions or summaries should focus on project successes—cost savings to the client, schedule adherence, enhanced quality, awards (including repeat business from the same client), value-added service provided, conformance with performance metrics, and application of innovative technologies. Be specific, and be quantitative in your narrative

---

2   To this listing might be added date of hire, current approved job title, total years of professional experience, maximum number and type of staff supervised, technical publications written, knowledge of ISO and SEI CMMI® standards as well as industry-specific regulatory guidelines such as technology export compliance rules, experience working for or supporting specific federal agencies, general technical areas of expertise, and computer-related experience [subdivided to include such items as hardware; hardware operating systems; computer-aided software engineering (CASE) methodologies and products; application development tools and languages; communications protocols; communication controllers, hubs, and hardware; network operating systems; databases; system tools; software, and the real-time delivery of products, services, and solutions over the Internet through cloud computing].

Title of project:
Name of client:
Address of client:
Contract number:
Contract type:
Contract value (with options):
Period of performance (with options):
Place of performance (include OCONUS support locations):

Method of acquisition (competitive/noncompetitive):
Nature of award (initial/follow-on):

COTR:
Telephone:
Fax:
E-mail:

Contracting officer:
Telephone:
Fax:
E-mail:

Company point of contact (POC):
Subcontractors:

Overview of customer's mission and operational environment:
Brief description:
Detailed description:
Number of users served
Technical performance/accomplishments/innovations:
    Major functional areas of support
    Tools and technologies applied
Programmatic performance:
    Contract transition
    Business management
    Personnel management/staffing (capacity to meet fluctuating workloads)
    Reporting
    Schedule control
    Program management tools
    Application of ISO 9001: 2008, SEI CMMI®, ITIL v3, and Agile structured processes
    On-time rating and quality rating of deliverables
    Training/cross-training programs
Cost-price management history:
    Record of cost overruns/underuns
    Tools/processes used to ensure cost control, accurate and timely invoicing, and so forth.

Risk mitigation approach and supporting tools [e.g., Risk Radar Enterprise (RRE)]:
Performance metrics and service-level agreements (SLAs):
Award fee history:
Quality assurance/process improvement:
Lessons learned:
Key practices:

Client performance evaluation highlights (award fees, CPARS, PPIRS, customer-approval rating):
Average number of personnel utilized per contract year:
Percentage turnover:
Incumbent capture:
Incumbent retention rate:
Add-on/follow-on work:
Alliances with local colleges and universities:
Mentor-protégé programs:
Contact termination history:

Figure 18.2
Effective project
summary format.

descriptions. Highlight applicable key practices and lessons learned, such as the development of appropriate timesaving techniques or the application of certain automated project management or knowledge-sharing tools.

As client evaluation factors for award are weighted increasingly toward past performance, well-written and photodocumented project summaries become more and more valuable. Clients buy from companies that have performed similar work and can demonstrate and validate that fact effectively and appropriately in their proposals. You might consider investing in a digital camera to take client-approved photographs on site for your company's projects.

Sometimes in small businesses, because of the corporate culture or the pathway of company growth, one division may be reluctant to use staff and contractual experience from other divisions when responding to a procurement. This is one example of the change of thinking that needs to occur as a small business enters the competitive arena. Each division of your company must harness fully the collective human and contractual expertise and knowledge base resident in the entire firm.

One important caveat: Be certain to obtain your client's permission to prepare an in-depth project summary about your company's support for that client organization. In particular, private-sector clients, as well as federal law enforcement and intelligence agencies, can be extremely sensitive about having the scope of work and specific points of contact made public. It is always the best policy to confirm what you intend to do with your client point of contact.

18.4　Proposal boilerplate (canned or reuse material) as knowledge assets

Translate boilerplate into client-focused text.

As your company prepares more and more proposals, it is important to extract certain boilerplate sections from past proposal documents, copy the text and graphics (see Figure 18.3) from these sections, and archive them in a central corporate library, proposal data center, or knowledge base. Boilerplate must still be tailored for each application, but it represents a rich collection of fodder for the writers and planners of future proposals. Table 18.1 presents examples of boilerplate files, which are actually knowledge assets.

Proposal writers should not have to start from scratch on every proposal effort. You should create an electronic proposal toolbox or knowledge base so that proposal writers can consult the latest reuse

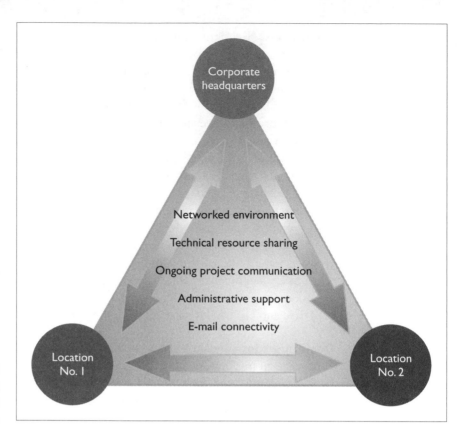

Figure 18.3
Integrated staffing and resource management.

Company Assets
Company core competencies (technical discussion)
Company bonding, registrations, and certifications
Licenses
Maps (office locations, project locations, number of projects by state or region)
Customer base
Patents
Trademarks
Company organizational charts
Company key practices
Industry certifications and accreditations [e.g., Software Engineering Institute (SEI) Capability Maturity Model Integration® (CMMI®), ISO 9001:2008, ITIL v3, and IEEE]
Facility and personnel security clearances

Table 18.1
Examples of Boilerplate Files

Industry and business community awards, commendations, and recognition (e.g., SBA Entrepreneur of the Year, Ernst & Young)

Customer endorsements and commendations

Small-minority-business involvement; HUBZone involvement

Corporate-sponsored community service and outreach activities

Company videos

Facilities diagrams

Best management practices (BMPs)

Technical and business articles and books authored by company staff

Interview guides

Vendor manuals

Contractual Resources

Project and product descriptions or summaries

Project performance metrics

Award fee statistics per project

Project success stories

Human Resources

Résumés

Personnel diversity data (minorities, women, veterans, handicapped individuals)

Incumbent capture rates

Employee turnover rates

Employee recruitment plan and metrics

Employee retention metrics

Staff by project, office, technical discipline, degree

Business Development and Proposal Development Assets

Strategic plans and benchmarking data

Market segmentation analyses

Competitor information

B&P spending patterns

Winning proposals

Table 18.1
(continued)

Multimedia presentations to clients

Teaming agreements

Teaming agreement SOWs

Proposal templates (e.g., executive summaries, cover letters)

Freedom of Information Act (FOIA) documents

Proposal lessons learned (from client debriefings)

Sales volumes by client sector, line of business (LOB), and geographic area

Tactical business plans

Corporate Infrastructure and Process Assets

Documentation capabilities

Business processes (procurement systems and mechanisms, financial systems, invoicing procedures, cost accounting, scheduling, automated tracking tools)

Project-Specific Assets

Customer evaluation reports [A/E Contract Appraisal System Support (ACASS), CPARS, and PPIRS ratings]

Contract deliverables

Earned value analysis (EVA) results by project

Work breakdown structures (WBSs)

Project management plans

Computer-Related Assets

Software development capabilities and practices

Software source code

Nonoperational hardware and software test-bed laboratory environments

Computer equipment and resources

Financial Assets

Budget forecasts

Capital expenses

Annual revenues

Table 18.1
(continued)

Relationship Assets

Cooperative agreements with colleges and universities, particularly HBCUs

Strategic business alliances (with organizations such as Microsoft, IBM, Dell, and Oracle)

Public Relations Assets

Ads placed in professional and trade journals

Trade show modules (text and graphics)

External news releases

Engineering and Manufacturing Assets

Engineering white papers (position papers)

Manufacturing defect rate data

Engineering drawings

Engineering change proposals (ECPs)

Test procedures

Requirements data

Policies and Plans

Make-or-buy policy

Management plans

Health and safety plans

Technology transfer plans

Professional compensation plans

Design control plans

Software quality assurance (SQA) plans

Phase in/phase out and transition plans

Subcontractor management plans

Table 18.1
(continued)

Configuration management (CM) plans

material under one electronic umbrella. Invest the time and resources early in your corporate life to develop these knowledge assets. They will be used again and again to develop your proposals.

18.5 Marketing targets

As your company grows, it will reach a point at which it needs a systematic, formalized mechanism to track its business opportunities. A variety of excellent data base software packages, such as Microsoft Access or IBM Lotus Notes [1], can be employed for this purpose. Database software allows for the generation of customized business reports and provides a quickly retrievable information source, for example, for planning and bid–no bid decisions. General access to the network drive on which marketing targets reside should be controlled carefully through password protection.

Other, more robust marketing opportunity tracking and customer relationship management (CRM) applications span: (1) Deltek GovWin CRM, (2) Salesforce.com and (3) Intuit QuickBase.

18.6 Corporate library

An important step in the transition from the 8(a) environment to the competitive world is to establish a centralized library, proposal data center, or knowledge base (electronic and hardcopy) in which previously submitted proposals and presentations, RFPs, proposal debriefings files, résumés, project summaries, technical materials, FOIA-requested materials (competitor proposals and monthly progress reports for specific projects), professional and trade journals, potential teaming partner information, public relations materials, and photographs reside. The library is best administered by the business development group.

Cataloging materials can be done using a variety of alphanumeric schemes that best fit your needs and uniquely identify each informational entity in the library. For example, all proposal documents could be catalogued with the prefix 1, followed by a two-digit calendar year designator, a three-digit federal agency code of your choosing, and so forth. Be prepared to dedicate at least one large, secure office with lateral and vertical file cabinets to your company's library. The volume of hardcopy information multiplies very rapidly. Using magnetic-backed drawer labels in the library is particularly advantageous. As your company's collection of materials increases in certain areas, the labels can be switched easily from drawer to drawer.

Personal experience has shown that storing a duplicate set of CD-ROM or tape copies in appropriate containers along with the paper copies of proposals and other library documents is very beneficial. The original storage medium for a given document can reside with the publications group, but the duplicate medium can be used for electronic searches to locate specific verbiage, numbers, for example, that would be difficult to find manually. And having a backup of electronic files is always a good idea. An alternative to a duplicate set of stored CD-ROMs or tapes is network storage, such as an intranet. Intranets allow companies to connect their own people as well as their vendors. "Participants using browsers inside and outside the company share a common interface and communications environment" [2]. All of a company's business processes can be executed online in a secure manner. Important intranet standards include TCP/IP and HTML. "[T]hink of the intranet's design just as you do the physical organization of your company. If there's a locked door in front of an office, lock that door to the virtual office. If you have a secretary acting as a gatekeeper in front of certain offices, require passwords to access those files in the virtual office. Model the virtual world on your real world" [3]. A significant advantage of an intranet is the "increased productivity that results from quick, companywide communications and data sharing.... Some of the many functions that intranets provide include repositories for volatile company information; easy access to company handbooks, guidelines, and forms of all kinds; and real-time calendaring and scheduling services" [4].

Data volumes of proposal-related files are increasing due to high-end desktop publishing software and the use of integrated text and graphics. With files such as style files, graphics files, text files, and mirror files, a midsized set of proposal volumes produced with desktop publishing software can range from 40 MB to more than 200 MB. Storage media are now more appropriately CDs, DVDs, USB drives, magnetic tape, and multigigabyte or terabyte external hard drives.

Effective information management is a critical factor in achieving marketing and proposal success. It is essential that this activity within your company receives the attention and support of senior management. Although it appears administrative and mundane, nothing could be farther from reality. Even very large companies have not done a good job in documenting and tracking their human and contractual talent and experience. Your company, being small at present, has the opportunity to start on the right footing. Build an appreciation for the integrated nature of externally directed business development, internal sales support, information management, knowledge management, and corporate image.

To be effective over time, the information management activity within your company must receive the support of senior management.

18.7 Proposal lessons-learned database

To ensure that your company will derive both short- and long-term benefits from both proposal successes as well as losses, it is advisable to develop and maintain an automated proposal lessons-learned database (see Table 18.2) using commercially available software applications such as IBM Lotus Notes or Microsoft Access. Capture managers should be responsible for providing the specific information for the lessons-learned database when proposals are won or lost. Once the data have been captured, they should be subject to senior-level review to help ensure impartiality.

By carefully tracking the reasons for wins and losses, you can begin to discern patterns in your business development performance with regard to specific client organizations, particular lines of business, certain types of contract vehicles, and proposal costing strategies. Are you consistently receiving low scores on ID-IQ contracts on which you submit proposals? Is your win percentage on Navy proposals particularly low in the Pacific Northwest? Does the lack of an established office near Wilmington, Delaware, seem to impact your chances of being selected for contract award for particular DuPont projects? Are your management plans missing the mark far too consistently? Those patterns must be discerned and communicated to appropriate business development and operations staff within your company, and then, most importantly, translated into prudent shifts in marketing, intelligence gathering, proposal development, and operational strategies and processes. In addition, through this database you can begin to generate a solid basis for estimating B&P costs for specific types and sizes of proposal efforts. This is critical for efficient staff and equipment resource planning and allocation, as well as more accurate B&P fiscal and resource projections.

It is worth noting that your company must strive—from the top downward—to develop a business culture that allows for appropriate and constructive introspection. The lessons-learned database will be most valuable when internal company politics do not skew the interpretation of the information that the database contains. For example, let's say that your company received a low score under the key staff evaluation factor because your proposed project manager had allowed a previous contract for the same client to run significantly over budget and behind schedule. Although

Client name

Brief scope of work

Place of project performance

Contract type (ID/IQ, CPFF, FFP, T&M)

Proposal due date

Internal proposal B&P number

Contract value to our company

Status of proposal (won or lost)

Capture manager/proposal manager and other key staff present

Was a debriefing conducted with the client organization?

Date of debriefing

Has our company worked for this client before? (yes or no)

What was our relationship with the client before the RFP was released?

Was our proposal determined by the client to be in the competitive range (shortlisted)?

Did we conduct advanced marketing with this client?

Winning contracting firms

Winning bid amounts ($)

Our bid ($)

B&P budget estimate versus actual direct labor and ODCs

Specific reasons why we were not selected (check all that apply):
❑ Technical approach
❑ Lack of understanding of client mission and requirements
❑ Past performance
❑ Contractual experience
❑ Staff qualifications
❑ Management approach
❑ Company size
❑ Financial condition
❑ Direct labor costs
❑ ODCs
❑ Subcontracting plan
❑ Teaming arrangements
❑ Geographic location of staff, projects, or offices
❑ Missing information
❑ Late delivery of proposal
❑ Noncompliance with RFP-driven proposal structure, format, or page count

Additional relevant information

Client's source of feedback

Table 18.2
Sample Information for a Proposal Lessons-Learned Database

this fact does not place this PM candidate in the best possible light, it is important to record the causes for your loss as completely and accurately as possible, and then act upon the patterns discerned in the causes. For example, management plans in your future proposals may have to emphasize specific strategies and tools that your firm has implemented and deployed to monitor and control costs and schedule effectively and successfully.

18.8 Applying IT solutions: scalable informational data systems

As your company grows, staff in various office locations need easily accessible and usable proposal-related information that can be modified to reflect local and regional requirements. Ongoing advances in information and communications technologies continue to facilitate data and information sharing across distributed locations and networks, and include scenarios such as virtual proposal centers.

18.8.1 IBM Lotus Notes scenarios

One powerful automated solution to this ever-growing requirement is an IBM Lotus Notes–based domain of information we will refer to as *proposal building blocks*. Lotus Notes groupware provides a searchable, sortable document storage and management system for group use. As illustrated in Figure 16.4, the proposal building blocks are represented by icons on a Lotus Notes screen on a PC. From their desktops and with no third-party interaction, your field office or corporate staff can click on these icons to access proposal guidelines and key internal points of contact for support along with sample outlines, résumés and project summaries, technical narrative, and standard graphics. Each icon should have a HELP function associated with it to further enhance this system's self-containment. The building blocks should be designed to guide proposal managers and technical staff through the proposal-building process.

Drawing on Lotus Notes' replication feature, electronic files can be updated, amended, or deleted from the proposal building blocks domain by a corporate-based systems administrator in a controlled manner and made available to your staff nationwide in real time. Everyone in the company will be able to access the latest materials. Such a system facilitates localized customization of proposals that are built upon a common, corporate-approved source domain of information. Distributed office locations can have access to the latest narrative on your company's business processes, résumés of recent new hires, key success stories from ongoing projects, and the most current letters of commendation from your clients.

18.8.2 Microsoft SharePoint 2010 scenarios

The SharePoint business collaboration platform allows you to manage and share documents with colleagues inside and outside of your oganization. Competition-sensitive information is protected through document-level permissions. See Figures 18.4(a) and 18.4(b) respectively for a sample proposal portal framework and key benefits and attributes of integrating SharePoint into your proposal development framework.

18.8.3 Intranet scenarios

An *intranet* is an internal information distribution system supported by a server or multiple servers that uses Web technology and graphical user interfaces. An intranet can be used to make the information depicted in Figure 18.5 available to your staff at multiple geographic and office locations. Search engine software such as infoRouter can be employed to find and filter relevant information on your company's intranet.

18.9 Small business KM success story—this stuff really works!

18.9.1 Small-scale, pilot KM initiatives applied to proposal development

Small-scale pilot KM initiatives are critical to launch and sustain, and then to leverage and propagate their success throughout your organization. Successful pilots become proofs of concept that can be transplanted and adopted in other parts of your organization. Most important, knowledge initiatives focused on measurable and achievable business benefits will have a higher probability of acceptance and sustained success.

My former employer, RS Information Systems, Inc. (RSIS), in McLean, Virginia, funded and proactively supported the RSIS Business Development Knowledge Base as an integral part of an enterprisewide KM initiative. This knowledge repository was a robust Web-based, password-protected interactive tool that RSIS staff professionals accessed remotely to qualify marketing opportunities and develop proposals and presentations. Approximately 50 RSIS staff had access to the knowledge

(a)

Figure 18.4 (a) SharePoint and other collaborative tools such as Privia and InfoRouter can increase your proposal organization's effectiveness and efficiency; (b) SharePoint allows proposal teams to manage their own content and collaboration sites with minimal reliance on IT operations.

base on PC workstations and laptop computers, although the system can serve more than 2,000 end users. Using the infoRouter search engine manufactured by Active Innovations in a secure networked Windows environment, company employees could browse thousands of indexed files or perform keyword searches to identify relevant files in multiple application formats, including MS Word, Corel WordPerfect, HTML, XML, RTF, and PowerPoint, as well as PDF (Adobe Acrobat), Excel, and

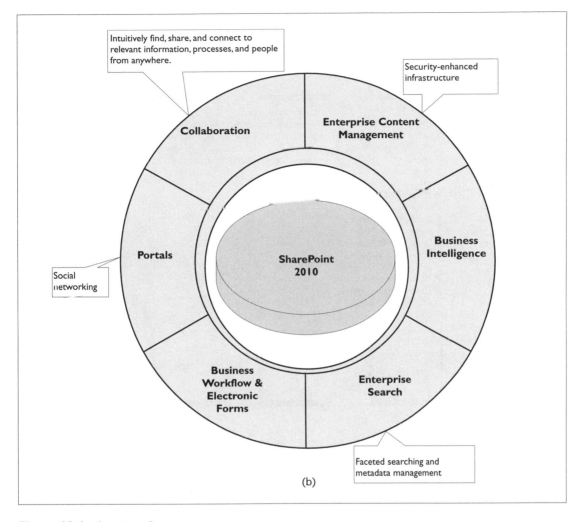

Figure 18.4 (continued)

MS Outlook e-mail files. Queries result in lists of files prioritized by relevance and presented to users in the familiar format of a Google or Yahoo search result. The RSIS knowledge base captured the staff's domain-specific technical knowledge, as well as its programmatic and client-specific expertise. In addition, the repository archives current best-of-breed proposal narrative, graphics, and oral presentation slides. Currency is a critical parameter of the knowledge base's validity and value.

The direct business development benefits of the Business Development Knowledge Base encompassed rapid proposal prototyping, as well as informed bid–no bid decision making. By leveraging the knowledge base, RSIS proposal managers could generate first-draft

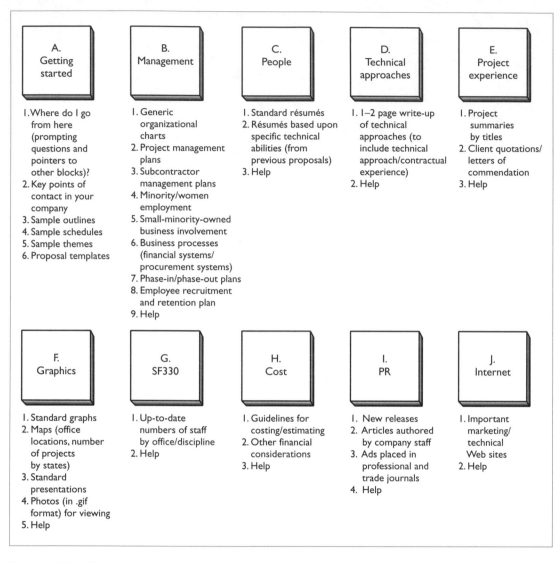

Figure 18.5 Guiding geographically distributed staff through the proposal building process—beginning your knowledge base.

proposal documents quickly with minimal B&P expenditure and little impact on billable technical staff. The proposal response life cycle could then be used to enhance and polish proposal documents, rather than expend time and resources tracking and locating résumés, project summaries, and other company information assets. We had progressed to the point where three people could and did develop a 50-page technical and management proposal, including résumés and project descriptions, to the National Oceanic and Atmospheric Administration's (NOAA) Geophysical Fluid Dynamics Laboratory (GFDL) at Princeton University within 24 hours from RFP release to client delivery! Without the knowledge base, it would have taken those same people at least a week to produce the proposal. RSIS marketing staff and capture managers also used the Business Development knowledge base to make informed decisions on the feasibility of pursuing a given procurement opportunity by assessing past and present contractual experience and technical skill sets of professional staff.

18.9.2 Balance of tools, disciplined methodologies, and a supportive business culture

Structured processes for knowledge transfer and capture ensure the sustained value and validity of the RSIS knowledge base. Key practices, lessons learned, client commendations and awards, performance metrics and standards, emerging technologies, staffing success stories, incumbent capture statistics, and information regarding rapid contract transitions were routinely funneled into the RSIS Proposal Development Department. Sources of this information spanned executive management, monthly technical progress reports for projects nationwide, division-level leadership, and direct interviews of select subject-matter experts and other technical staff. The knowledge transfer and sharing expertise and experience of RSIS professional staff were also captured annually as an integral part of the corporate résumé update process. All levels of management reinforced these knowledge transfer processes regularly. Successful KM at RSIS resulted from the dynamic integration of supportive, forward-looking executive leadership; a business culture of and organizational commitment to mutual trust and sharing; the passion of people at all levels of the organization; and technology-based, user-driven solutions and tools.

18.9.3 Development drivers and challenges

The RSIS Business Development Knowledge Base, and indeed the company's entire KM initiative, began late in 1998. Given the reality of 120 total company staff in 1998 and only two full-time professionals in proposal development at the time, the need to do more with limited resources was immediate and critical. We had no centralized, electronic repository of information. There were no institutionalized or even ad hoc processes in place to identify, audit, collect, archive, and leverage key knowledge within the company. On the other hand, we had a significant number of electronic directories and files of proposals, presentations, résumés, and project summaries. One individual prior to 1998 had actually attempted to extract, catalog, and organize proposal-related information into some semblance of order, but that initiative had never been completed. After having developed and received management buy-in for the architecture of the initial proposal system in mid-1999, one of my staff (a full-time proposal manager) and I began the arduous task of manually sorting through scores of proposal directories and hundreds of related files. This was done in addition to a full-time proposal development workload. Within 7 months, 5 years' worth of electronic files for proposals, presentations, résumés, project summaries, awards and commendations, white papers, public relations materials, and other information had been reviewed, purged as appropriate, and organized into the preapproved architecture. The initial search engine selected was dtSearch, manufactured by dtSearch Corporation, which is incorporated in Virginia. Unfortunately in late 1999, dtSearch required frequent, time-consuming, and manual indexing and reindexing. Server space demands were significant as the number of proposal modules increased. Search results were not as user-friendly as they needed to be for our requirements.

By mid-2000, one of my proposal managers, who was also our knowledge engineer, along with one Web developer and I migrated the prototype knowledge base from dtSearch to Microsoft Index Server. With this application, which was fed continuously by established knowledge transfer processes, the RSIS Business Development Knowledge Base was fielded in late 2000. Our KM specialist and one Web developer maintained the repository, which was migrated to infoRouter in November 2001. System maintenance requirements were modest. Incoming information was evaluated during the course of several days and then rapidly indexed into the knowledge base. As vice president of knowledge management for the firm, I provided both oversight for the KM initiative enterprisewide, as well as hands-on collection and analysis of various knowledge assets.

Concurrent with our efforts to architect and populate our fledgling knowledge base, I worked closely with RSIS executive management to secure their support to institute knowledge transfer and collection processes in a disciplined and repeatable manner nationwide. Monthly technical progress reports were sent to me, as well as to the technical managers. Those reports were then combed for relevant technical innovations, lessons learned, staffing successes, best practices, and so forth. Résumés are generated for every new hire, and annual résumé updates are linked to the performance appraisal process. Eventually, knowledge-sharing experience was a key element incorporated into each RSIS résumé for all staff nationwide. Project summaries were created according to a structured, consistent, and comprehensive template when contracts phased in. Summaries were updated when major new tasks are added and then again upon contract completion. On a regular basis during business development review meetings and strategic planning meetings, critical knowledge was shared from across the many defense, civilian, and law enforcement contracts that RSIS supported. The culture of knowledge sharing within the company extended to the establishment of technical Centers for Excellence (CFEs). Through these institutionalized programs, domain-specific technical knowledge and best practices were applied rapidly to provide our clients with proven solutions in near-real time. An important, relevant development in corporate communications and public relations was integrated directly into a civilian agency proposal within 1 hour of notification.

18.9.4   **Transferable lessons learned**

There were four key ingredients in the RSIS KM success story. The first was a KM champion, an individual who understood and articulated the tangible benefits of knowledge management to executive management, as well as business development and technical staff. The second comprised the executive leadership, support, and vision necessary to grasp the value of KM and then fund the processes and clear the internal impediments to knowledge sharing. The third entailed the disciplined and repeatable processes put in place enterprisewide within the company to funnel knowledge and information into one central point in near real time. And the fourth included the Web-based KM tools.

Experience has demonstrated the value of starting your own company's business development KM initiative as soon as possible in the corporate life of your firm. This approach does two things. One, there will be less raw information and data to review, purge, and categorize. And two, the sooner your staff develops and hones their knowledge-sharing skills and behaviors, the more quickly your firm will emerge as a learning organization—one that adapts and prospers in a business environment of fast-paced and unpredictable change.

18.10   Leveraging federal performance appraisal systems to your company's benefit

An important element of your company's proposal information repository is the evaluations and appraisals conducted by your clients about your project support. Make certain to request and archive the most recent appraisal results from the federal evaluation systems, as appropriate. Your company can certainly trumpet your excellent scores accrued under

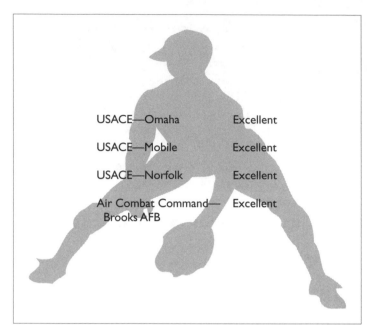

USACE—Omaha   Excellent

USACE—Mobile   Excellent

USACE—Norfolk   Excellent

Air Combat Command—   Excellent
Brooks AFB

Figure 18.6
Project
prowess—our
ACASS ratings are
consistently in the
strike zone.

these federal performance appraisal systems in your proposals, as shown in Figure 18.6.

18.11 ISO-driven proposal and business development excellence

The International Organization for Standardization, or ISO, is a network of national standards institutes from 147 countries working in partnership with international organizations, governments, industry, and business and consumer representatives. ISO 9001:2008 is one of the standards in the ISO 9008 family's core series on quality management systems (QMSs). *How do ISO 9001:2008 standards apply to the actual processes of proposal development and business development? And why do these disciplined processes contribute to the generation of excellent proposal end products?* To be clear, we will not be focusing on companywide or program-specific ISO certifications that are discussed and illustrated within management and technical proposals, as important as these are to a company's success. Rather, our emphasis will be on how ISO-driven standards are applied successfully to define, clarify, and enhance proposal development as well as business development processes.

18.11.1 **Small business success story**

Under forward-looking executive leadership, RS Information Systems, Inc. (RSIS), established a corporate-level Quality Improvement Office (QIO) to initiate and manage quality initiatives and certifications across the company and its federal contracts. The QIO implemented a Quality Management System (QMS) that was certified to the ISO 9001:2000 standard by an auditing firm approved by the American National Standards Institute (ANSI)/Registrar Accreditation Board. RSIS joined only 10% of U.S. service providers that had registered their QMS to ISO 9001:2000 (Certificate # US2195).

The QMS manual detailed the specific controls that were implemented at RSIS to ensure quality service, customer satisfaction, and continual improvement of all of the company's systems and processes from end to end. The QMS manual was divided into five sections modeled on the sectional organization of the ISO 9001:2008 standard. Importantly, RSIS exceeded ISO standards with the development of its QMS. The company proactively included all of its corporate infrastructure and program support processes such as proposal development, business development, contract management, human resources and recruiting, and finance and accounting. In addition, RSIS developed a methodology that enabled it to apply its QMS and ISO 9001:2008-certified processes to any contract for certification.

As part of RSIS' continuous improvement initiative, the company added a variety of programs into the scope of its QMS and had them audited for certification to the ISO 9001:2008 standard. A high-profile program with the Air Force Space Command (AFSPC) received a recommendation for ISO 9001:2008 certification. Of note is that the independent auditor determined that "RSIS' QMS has best in class processes for software design and development activities." RSIS' structured quality approach provided definitive quality assurance (QA) responsibility and accountability, coupled with an independent reporting tool to top management.

18.11.2 **Associated costs**

Up-front costs are associated with implementing an internal QMS. In RSIS' case, it was approximately $3,000. Once implemented and if working well, however, the QMS will *reduce* costs by:

- Making work processes more efficient and streamlined, thereby reducing complexity (without documented processes, most staff professionals perform work in their own unique way, which increases complexity and the potential for rework);

- Reducing rework and work product correction;
- Having core business processes documented, which aids in bringing new employees up to speed faster;
- Providing a management system that aids in disaster recovery should an unfortunate event occur;
- Providing a management system that enables management decisions based on validated performance data.

ISO certification of business processes helps a corporation meet customer requirements, achieve business goals and objectives, keep within budget guidelines, provide consistent services and products, train new employees on the appropriate way to perform tasks, and improve internal and external communications.

18.11.3 Methodologies, tools, and training

RSIS' Quality Operational Procedure (QOP) for "New Business Identification, Qualification, and Capture" stood among 26 other QOPs. The Business Development QOP is further decomposed into seven detailed work instructions (WIs). The entire body of QOPs, associated WIs, and standard forms was fully documented and available electronically to all company staff professionals via a secure intranet. In fact, staff understood that the most current version of all QOPs and WIs resides solely on the intranet. This site was built using Active Innovations Inc.'s commercial off-the-shelf (COTS) infoRouter tool, a powerful Web-based document management system (DMS) and search engine.

Of note is that all RSIS Business Development and Proposal Development Department staff completed a minimum of two internal training courses. These courses were entitled "Introduction to the ISO 9000 Process" and "Process Management and Procedure Development." In addition, as an entire department, mandatory interactive meetings were held every 6 months to provide an overview of the Business Development QOP and Business Development and Proposal Development WIs, to review forms and any changes to those forms, and to ensure that hand-off procedures were well understood. For example, proper hand-off procedures of proposal documents to the Finance and Contracts Department for cost reviews were emphasized. Appropriate, timely, and quality-conscious interaction at various connection points in the proposal and business development processes was an essential concern in the ISO paradigm.

As part of the ISO process, annual *internal* customer satisfaction audits were conducted of Proposal Development and Business

Development processes and level of support. Internal customers include, for example, representative leaders from the three RSIS operating divisions as well as from the Contracts and Finance Department. The audit scale ranges from 1 to 4, with 4 being a superior metric. When the audit data were collected and synthesized, an action plan is developed and implemented to ensure that any issues identified are addressed and fixed promptly.

18.11.4 Proposal development work instruction

The parent (or master) Business Development QOP presented a detailed and comprehensive flow diagram of all Business Development and Proposal Development processes. Decision points, end points, and connection points are identified in that flow diagram. Under this specific QOP is a WI entitled "Proposal Development and Review." The overarching *purpose* of this WI was to establish the processes for proposal development and review, including solution development; review team selection, scheduling, and conduct; and reporting of findings relating to business proposal content. The *scope* of this WI identified the dollar thresholds to which these processes apply under prime and subcontractor conditions. *Inputs,* in effect, triggers, for this WI include a "go" bid decision, B&P charge number assignment, and release of an RFP or RFS by the federal government.

Roles and responsibilities were delineated clearly in tabular form for all cognizant staff, including business development directors, capture managers, proposal managers, production managers, and proposal coordinators. *Outputs* of the WI spanned: (1) completed and delivered proposal documents and/or electronic files, (2) completed proposal approval forms, and (3) completed proposal delivery forms.

18.11.5 Case study insights

RSIS' ISO implementation process got under way in March 2003. Registration was achieved in December 2003—less than 9 months. Typically, ISO implementation takes 12 to 18 months within the industry. Visionary *strategic leadership* enabled implementation throughout all areas of the company from business development through service delivery. Having no gaps in process certification (in effect, no exclusions) ensured that service delivery is managed from end to end consistently with customer requirements always in the foreground.

Another key is to find an *auditing firm* that understands your corporation's primary business. RSIS interviewed many auditing firms, and determined that Intertek Testing Services, NA, Inc., had the closest understanding of our core business areas.

Finally, having an *executive champion* aided in RSIS' achievement of registration. In the case of RSIS, this was the company's executive vice president and chief operating officer. This executive champion helped to remove internal barriers, find alternate solutions, and speed the certification. It is also important to have an executive champion who is very cognizant of QMS implementation and certification activities.

18.11.6 Benefits of the ISO 9001-driven processes

RSIS' ISO 9001-driven proposal and business development approach resulted in important, tangible benefits:

- *Repeatable* proposal processes that leverage lessons learned;
- *Documented* processes that serve as excellent training tools for new staff;
- Built-in focus on *continuous process improvement,* a recent example of which was the incorporation of a Blue Team Review process for storyboard, storyline, and solution set assessment prior to any proposal text development. This has proven to be tremendously beneficial in terms of launching the proposal in the proper direction early in the process. It was directly related to RSIS winning a major $65 million procurement with NASA.
- Generation of a living *knowledge base* to retain intellectual capital as proposal staff transition to other positions, leave the company, or retire.

Endnotes

1. Elbert, Bruce, and Bobby Martyna, *Client/Server Computing: Architecture, Applications, and Distributed Systems Management,* Norwood, MA: Artech House, 1994.

2. Blankenhorn, Dana, "11 Lessons from Intranet Webmasters," *Netguide,* October 1996, p. 82.

3. Blankenhorn, Dana, "11 Lessons from Intranet Webmasters," *Netguide,* October 1996, p. 89.

4. Tittel, Ed, and James Michael Stewart, "The Intranet Means Business," *Netguide,* July 1996, p. 122.

Chapter 19

Building the cost/price volume[1]

A MONG THE KEYS to building compliant and robust cost/price proposals is to have a fundamental understanding of pricing terminology that appears in the Federal Acquisition Regulation (FAR), Cost Accounting Standards, and the role of the Defense Contract Audit Agency.

---

1   The content for this chapter was developed by Mr. Kevin M. McQuade, president and CEO of MSM Group, Inc., winner of the 2009 NASA Glenn Research Center Small Business Subcontractor of the Year. Founded in 1999, MSM Group's professionals possess over 50 years of combined experience in all areas of business management of government contracts. A veteran-owned small business based in Cleveland, Ohio, MSM specializes in accounting and information systems for small businesses performing government contracts. Mr. McQuade has presented seminars on DCAA-compliant accounting systems through NASA's Jet Propulsion Laboratory (JPL) in Pasadena, California.

19.1   Overview of the FAR

The FAR is the principal set of rules in the Federal Acquisition Regulation System. This system consists of sets of regulations issued by agencies[2] of the federal government of the United States to govern what is called the "acquisition process." This is the process through which the government purchases ("acquires") goods and services. It does not regulate the purchasing activities of private-sector firms, except to the extent that those parts of it are incorporated into government solicitations and contracts by reference. The purpose of the FAR is to provide uniform policies and procedures for acquisition. Among its guiding principles are: to have an acquisition system that satisfies customers' needs in terms of cost, quality, and timeliness; to minimize administrative operating costs; to conduct business with integrity, fairness, and openness; and to fulfill other public policy objectives. As a starting point for this chapter, let's ensure that we have factual understanding of important pricing terms and concepts.

19.1.1   Defining key pricing terminology

Cost objective

As defined in FAR 31.001, a *cost objective* is a function, organizational subdivision, contract, or other work unit for which cost data are desired and for which provision is made to accumulate and measure the cost of such elements as processes, products, jobs, and capitalized projects.

Final cost objective

A *final cost objective*, as defined in FAR 31.001, is a cost objective that has allocated to it both direct and indirect costs and, in the contractor's accumulation system, is one of the final accumulation points. *Cost accumulation* refers to the manner in which costs are collected and identified with specific customers, jobs, orders, departments, and processes.

Direct costs

As defined in FAR 31.202, *direct costs* are identifiable to a final cost objective (a particular contract) such as direct material and direct labor. All costs identified specifically with a specific contract are direct costs for that

---

2   Organizations such as the Central Intelligence Agency (CIA), United States Postal Service (USPS), U.S. Senate, and Tennessee Valley Authority (TVA) have their own acquisition regulations outside the FAR.

contract, and cannot legally be charged to another contract either directly or indirectly. No cost can be charged to a contract as a direct cost, if other costs incurred for the same purpose in like circumstances have been charged as an indirect cost.

Direct labor

Direct labor is the cost of all the time (hours) that people spend on a particular final cost objective that is directly related to the contract objectives. This direct labor cost is the number of hours spent by an individual on the job times the dollars per hour which that person is paid. Direct labor is the salary and wages of employees performing work identifiable to a final cost objective, such as a contract.

Labor categories

Labor categories and their descriptions identify the skills, knowledge, abilities, experience, training, and educational requirements of the labor to be provided on a contract. Contractors use these descriptions in developing their prices/costs for labor.

Other direct costs (ODCs)

ODCs are cost accumulation elements (other than labor and material) in the contractor's accounting system that can be specifically assigned to a contract or other final cost objective. ODCs are other costs charged directly to the government that have not been included in proposed material, direct labor, indirect costs, or any other category of cost. ODCs can include travel, expenses, computer time, special tooling, relocation expenses, preproduction and start-up costs, packaging and transportation costs, royalties, spoilage and rework, federal excise taxes, and reproduction costs, along with subcontracts and services.

Indirect costs

As defined in FAR 31.203, *indirect costs* are not directly identified with a single, final cost objective, but identified with two or more final cost objectives. After direct costs have been determined and charged directly to the contract or other work, indirect costs are those remaining to be allocated to intermediate or two or more final cost objectives. No final cost objective can have any cost allocated to it as an indirect cost, if other costs incurred for the same purpose in like circumstances have been included as a direct cost of that or any other final cost objective.

19.2 Typical basic indirect rate structure elements

19.2.1 Fringe benefits

In a separate indirect pool,[3] most government contractors accumulate the costs associated with three main components of benefits afforded to their employees, namely: (1) absences, (2) taxes, and (3) benefits. Absences include such paid time off as holiday, vacation, and sick leave. Taxes encompass statutory elements such as the Federal Insurance Contributions Act (FICA), the Federal Unemployment Tax Act (FUTA), and the State Unemployment Tax Act (SUTA). Employee benefits include medical, retirement, insurance, education, certification, and technical refresh.

19.2.2 Overhead (on-site versus off-site)

Overhead includes those costs *not* directly related to a final cost objective. These consist of indirect costs that are associated with the production of goods and services and that benefit more than one contract or cost objective. Examples of overhead encompass material handling and subcontract management.

19.2.3 Material handling and subcontract administration

Material handling costs are those costs related to acquiring, transporting, receiving, inspecting, handling, and storing materials. Subcontract administration relates to expenses associated with administering contracts and subcontracts.

19.2.4 General and administrative (G&A)

G&A expenses represent the cost of activities that are necessary to the overall operation of the business as a whole, but for which a direct relationship to any particular cost objective cannot be shown. Indirect G&A costs include the top management functions for executive control and direction over all personnel, departments, facilities, and activities of the contractor.

---

3   An "indirect cost pool" is a logical grouping of indirect costs with a similar relationship to the cost objectives. For example, engineering overhead pools include indirect costs that are associated with engineering efforts.

Typically, it includes human resources, accounting, finance, public relations, contract administration, and legal.

19.2.5 Fully burdened rate

A contractor's fully burdened rate (sometimes referred to as a "wrap rate") is the factor applied to direct labor to arrive at the total cost of labor. For example, if a contractor has direct labor of $10.00 and a fully burdened wrap rate of 1.65, then the total cost per labor hour would be $16.50. Wrap rate is the total multiplier (overhead, G&A, and fee) that is applied to an individual's hourly rate to get the rate that appears on an invoice.

19.2.6 Fee

Both the government and contractors recognize that profit (fee) is a motivator of efficient and effective contract performance. Negotiations aimed merely at reducing prices by reducing profit, without proper recognition of the function of profit, are not in the government's interest. When performing a profit analysis, the government will take into consideration factors such as performance risk, contract type risk, facilities capital employed, and cost efficiency.

19.3 Unallowable costs

Costs that are expressly unallowable or mutually agreed to be unallowable, including those that are mutually agreed to be unallowable directly associated costs, must be identified and excluded from any billing, claim, or proposal applicable to a government contract. A directly associated cost is any cost that is generated solely as a result of incurring another cost and that would not have been incurred had the other cost not been incurred. When an unallowable cost is incurred, its directly associated costs are also unallowable. Examples of FAR-defined unallowable costs include bad debts, contributions or donations, and entertainment.

19.4 Overview of Federal Travel Regulations (FTR)

FAR 31.205-46 states that costs for transportation, lodging, meals, and incidental expenses incurred on official company business are allowable contract costs provided that the method used results in a "reasonable" charge. These travel costs will be considered reasonable as long as they do not exceed the maximum per diem rates in effect as set forth in the Federal Travel Regulations (FTR) or the Joint Travel Regulations (JTR) for travel outside of the contiguous United States. The FTR and JTR policies and procedures ensure accountability of taxpayer's money. FTR is contained in the Code of Federal Regulations (CFR) chapters 300-304. The purpose of the FTR is to interpret policy requirements to ensure that official travel is conducted in a responsible, most cost-effective manner. It also strives to communicate the policies in a clear manner to federal agencies and employees.

19.5 Overview of the Cost Accounting Standards (CAS)

The Cost Accounting Standards (popularly known as CAS) are a set of 19 standards and rules promulgated by the United States government for use in determining costs on negotiated procurements. The purpose of the CAS is to achieve consistency and uniformity in cost accounting principles. These principles must be followed by contractors in the several phases of contract pricing, including estimating accumulating and reporting of costs.

The three areas of cost accounting (48 CFR 9903.302-1) include: (1) the measurement of cost, which involves the methods and techniques used in defining the components of cost, determining the basis of cost measurement, and establishing criteria for use of alternative cost measurement techniques; (2) assignment of cost to the cost accounting period, which refers to the method used in determining the amount of cost to be assigned to individual cost accounting periods (examples are the requirements for use of accrual basis or cash basis accounting); and (3) allocation of cost to cost objectives, which refers to the method of determining direct and indirect allocation of cost.

19.6 Overview of relevant Generally Accepted Accounting Principles (GAAP)

Generally Accepted Accounting Principles (GAAP) refer to the common set of accounting concepts, standards, and procedures that represent a general guide. GAAP principles are those that have substantial authoritative support or are based on accounting practices accepted over time by prevalent use by the Financial Accounting Standards Board (FASB), American Institute of Certified Public Accountants (AICPA), and Accounting

Principles Board (APB), among others. The end products of the accounting cycle, the financial statements (e.g., balance sheet and income statement) are prepared in accordance with GAAP.

19.7 Adequacy of contractor's internal accounting system

FAR 16.301-3 requires that a contractor's accounting system be adequate for determining costs applicable to the contract *prior* to the award of a cost-reimbursable contract, grant, Small Business Innovation Research (SBIR), or Broad Agency Announcement (BAA). An adequate accounting system is not an evaluation criterion. It is a basic contract requirement with a pass/fail determination. The FAR states that a contract vehicle may only be awarded to an offeror who is determined to have an adequate accounting system by the Defense Contract Audit Agency (DCAA).

So what is an adequate accounting system? An adequate accounting system is one that conforms with GAAP, produces equitable results and is verifiable, is applicable to the contemplated contract(s), and is capable of being consistently followed. DCAA will perform a Preaward Accounting Survey to determine accounting system adequacy. A preaward survey is an evaluation of a prospective contractor's ability to perform a proposed contract. In order to be determined to be adequate, your accounting system must have: (1) proper segregation of direct costs from indirect costs; (2) identification and accumulation of direct costs by contract; (3) a logical and consistent method for allocation of indirect costs to intermediate and final cost objectives; (4) accumulation of costs under general ledger control; (5) a timekeeping system that identifies employees' labor by intermediate or final cost objectives and a labor distribution system that charges direct and indirect labor to the appropriate cost objectives; (6) interim (at least monthly) determination of costs charged to a contract through routine posting to books of account; (7) exclusion from costs charged to government contracts of amounts that are not allowable pursuant to FAR Part 31, Contract Cost Principles and Procedures, or other contract provisions; (8) identification of costs by contract line item and units if required by the proposed contract; and (9) segregation of preproduction costs from production costs.

19.8 The Defense Contract Audit Agency (DCAA)

Organizations that wish to provide goods and series to the federal government must be prepared to comply with regulations promulgated by a host of government agencies. The DCAA is perhaps the most prominent governing agency in the government contracting arena. The DCAA provides standardized contract audit services for the Department of Defense, as well as accounting and financial advisory services regarding contracts and subcontracts responsible for procurement and contract administration. These services are provided in connection with negotiation, administration, and settlement of contracts and subcontracts. The DCAA also provides contract audit services to some other government agencies. Importantly, the DCAA follows generally acceptable government auditing standards (GAGAS) when conducting its audits.

The DCAA's major areas of emphasis include: (1) internal control systems, (2) management policies, (3) accuracy and reasonableness of cost representations, (4) adequacy and reliability of records and accounting systems, (5) financial capability, and (6) contractor compliance with contractual provisions having accounting or financial significance such as the Cost Principles (FAR Part 31), the "Cost Accounting Standards Clause" (FAR 52.230-2), and the clauses pertaining to the Truth in Negotiations Act of TINA (FAR 52.215-10, -11, -12, and -13).

The DCAA stands as a distinct agency within the DoD and reports directly to the Under Secretary of Defense (Comptroller). The agency is organized into five regions and a field detachment and has individual field audit offices (FAOs) and suboffices throughout the United States and overseas. The DCAA's main service is performing contract audits requested by representatives of various military and civilian acquisition organizations and by the Defense Contract Management Agency (DCMA). Each year, the DCAA audits about 9,000 contractors, using a risk-based approach to identify the highest priority audits. At the completion of an audit, an audit report is furnished to the requestor for use in negotiations and/or in determining current or future contractor costs. An audit report can also be used to determine compliance with existing regulations and contractual requirements.

19.9 RFP review

Production of the cost volume and pricing the proposal is an exercise that parallels the approach incorporated for the rest of the proposal response.

First, read the solicitation—all of it (even the boring parts). Then reread the solicitation—all of it—*again*. Section L instructs offerors how to respond and contains specific language pertaining to proposal preparation and adherence, provides an index of proposal contents and structure, identifies cost proposal evaluation factors, and is intended to correlate to Section M on one-to-one basis (note, however, that is sometimes not the case). If you have any questions, ask before the question-and-answer period for the given solicitation closes; do not assume that you have the correct understanding of the RFP instructions. Have someone (not the preparer) check the proposal against the solicitation requirements.

19.10 Importance of aligning the cost proposal with the technical and management proposals

Cost proposals should absolutely not be produced in a vacuum. While the technical volume (in a NASA proposal, this is called mission suitability) and the cost volume are separate factors in the evaluation, the proposed price and underlying rates may be considered by the government to be significant indicator of the offeror's understanding and ability to perform the Statement of Work (SOW), the Statement of Objectives (SOO), and other requirements of the RFP or RFS. It is therefore extremely important that that cost information be consistent with the technical and management approach. The programmatic schedule to perform the technical work must align precisely with the schedule used in developing cost information. The staffing levels must be consistent and the labor costs must link directly with the skill levels discussed in the technical proposal. The total price cost estimated must include the costs (labor or other) of all activities described in the technical approach. Likewise, the approach articulated in the management volume should also be clearly evident in the cost volume. Strategies and approaches for lines of authority, span of control, total compensation, and Project Management Office (PMO) responsibilities all must align with the pricing approach and resultant final cost volume methodologies. Because all portions of your response to an RFP will be used to evaluate your company's understanding of the services and products required, the government may adjust your overall technical score based upon the degree of realism in price.

19.11 Cost estimating methods

There are a number of important techniques that may be applied to estimate your proposed price, as shown in Table 19.1.

19.12 Example methodology for determining salary ranges

Salary ranges are determined by comprehensive market surveys according to skill, discipline, and level. In addition, actual salaries of current employees in similar roles may be incorporated. Also, in some cases, data supplied by the RFP may be used to determine salary ranges to be proposed.

Estimating method	Characteristics
Analogy	Estimate of costs based on historical data of a similar item. The analogy method compares a new or proposed system with one that is an analogous (i.e., similar) system and typically acquired in the recent past for which there is accurate cost and technical data. There must be a reasonable correlation between the proposed and "historical" system. The estimator makes a subjective evaluation of the differences between the new system of interest and the historical system. The analogy method is typically performed early in the cost estimating process, such as the pre-Milestone A and Milestone A stages of a program.
Engineering (bottom-up)	The most detailed of all the techniques and the most costly to implement. It reflects a detailed buildup of labor, material, and overhead costs.
Parametric (top-down)	A cost-estimating methodology using statistical relationships between historical costs and other program variables such as system physical or performance characteristics, contractor output measures, or staff power loading.
Actual costs	The actual cost method uses the actual cost of the previous production lot adjusted for inflation, labor saving, material cost, technology changes, and other factors. An actual cost is a cost sustained, in fact, on the basis of costs actually incurred and recorded in accomplishing the work performed within a given time period, as distinguished from forecasted or estimated costs.

Table 19.1 Spectrum of Cost Estimating Methodologies

Reputable sources for salary survey data include Washington Technical Personnel Forum (WTPF), Western Management Group Government Contractors Compensation Survey (WMG GCS), and Towers Watson Data Services.

19.13 Methodology for computing labor escalation

Providing local market-informed competitive compensation to employees is a critical component in retaining the current contract workforce. Direct labor escalation in the cost proposal is the year-to-year increase in the direct labor base resulting from merit increases, promotions, cost-of-living trends, movement within the company, and changes in the size and composition of the workforce. Direct labor escalation factors are often based on a number of sources including internal historical data, the Bureau of Labor Statistics, commercial databases such as Salary.com, and local salary survey data. When the correlation of labor rate data between multiple sources is strong and confidence level is high, the minimum and maximum salary ranges proposed will support the overall proposed price as well as provide documentation for the audit file.

19.14 Highlights of the process to calculate indirect costs

The development of indirect rates and resultant costs in pricing a proposal is a major step in the overall pricing process. The cost accounting structure for indirect rates should be suited to match a given business unit's operations, and the allocation base should be the best representation of the causal/beneficial relationship between costs and cost objectives. Indirect rate cost accounting structure should be designed for maximum cost recoverability and competiveness.

A well-written set of policies and procedures should be in place in your company that document estimating procedures; the DCAA auditors will look for consistency among estimating, accumulating, and reporting practices. Estimating indirect costs to be applied to a particular proposal starts with an understanding of the pools, bases, and resultant indirect rate. Pools are defined by placing costs in logical groupings (e.g., fringe costs, overhead costs, G&A costs, and unallowable). The "allocation base" is defined as some measure of cost that can be used to allocate the pool cost (e.g., direct labor hours, direct labor dollars, and machine hours).

19.15 Determining annual productive labor hours

Direct labor is estimated on the basis of productive effort. Productive effort is the estimated number of hours required to perform the work. Vacations, holidays, sick leave, and any other paid absences are not to be cited as direct labor, but must be separately identified and priced or included in indirect cost.

19.16 Methodology to compute fee

In determining the level of fee to propose, contractors need to consider a number of factors as described in FAR 19.905-1. These include contractor incentive, complexity of work, management effort, cost risk, capital investment, financing of operations, and past performance.

19.17 Cost volume narrative and production

In addition to responding to the requirements by including the detailed pricing in the proposal, the cost volume should include a narrative section that is compliant with the requirements of the RFP or RFS. The narrative should articulate all pricing and estimating techniques in detail, including projections, rates, ratios, percentages, and factors, as required. You should also provide a complete disclosure of the methods you used in determining the classifications of cost (direct versus indirect). Many contractors also furnish a synopsis of their accounting policies and procedures. The proposed overhead and G&A rates should be supported by forecasts, dollar values, factors, and substantiating rationale for each rate. A well-written, comprehensive, and logically connected narrative demonstrates competence and increases overall win probability. A competitive proposal is one that is compliant, credible, compelling, consistent, and cost-effective. Before submitting the proposal, be sure to: arrange for an independent edit of the final text, recheck the final against RFP requirements, include a compliance matrix in the submittal, prepare a cover letter for signature, refine the final graphics, test the print final version (even if delivering electronically), and arrange for delivery in exact accordance with the RFP instructions.

19.18 Audit files

Your company needs to build and maintain a complete, separate "audit file" during the proposal process. This will ensure that the DCAA auditor has all information necessary to conduct a comprehensive audit of the proposal. Supporting information encompasses:

- Evidence of consistency between your company's estimating and accounting systems;
- Documentation of cost presentation by cost element at the summary level;
- Subsidiary schedules that support summary-level costs;
- Adequate documentation readily traceable to estimates in detailed schedules and to summary level;
- Written rationale defining the basis for costs;
- Validation for basis of estimate (BOE) requirements;
- History of prior bid proposal audits;
- Schedules that are annotated with references to detailed support;
- Written estimating system methods/procedures.

19.19 Special topics

19.19.1 Uncompensated overtime

Uncompensated overtime is the unpaid hours worked over and above the standard 40 hours for exempt employees. The DCAA is concerned about how these hours are recorded because an inequity in the pricing and costing of government contracts could occur if uncompensated overtime is worked, but not accounted for, and more than one contract or project is worked on by the salaried employee. The lack of proper accounting for the overtime hours can create the potential for contractors to manipulate their labor accounting systems.

While contractors can choose from a number of different approaches for how to account for uncompensated overtime in pricing proposals, there is the concern that contractors might lower the effective labor rates by proposing uncompensated overtime. In order to satisfy the DCAA and

Risk in the Cost Volume	Risk Considerations
Price to win (PTW) risk	Is our PTW too high or too low? Will our price be subject to a cost reasonableness analysis performed by the government?
Performance risk	Can we perform the contract for the proposed price?
Cost accounting strategy risks	A cost-estimating methodology using statistical relationships between historical costs and other program variables such as system physical or performance characteristics, contractor output measures, or staff power loading.
Contract type risks	Cost type contracts shift cost growth risk to the government, while fixed price contracts shift cost growth risk to the contract.
Other risks	Ceilings on indirect rates can impact pricing risk decisions.

Table 19.2
Being aware of potential risks associated with the cost volume helps to avoid them.

ensure that your proposal demonstrates cost realism, the accounting practices you use to estimate uncompensated overtime must be consistent with your accounting practices that are used to accumulate and report uncompensated overtime hours. Companies should also include a copy of their uncompensated overtime policy in their proposal.

19.19.2 Addressing risk in the cost volume

While many RFP evaluation criteria place more emphasis on technical and past performance factors over price and the stated evaluation criteria may be "best value," more often than not, cost is a major deciding factor in federal contract awards. In other words, cost is incredibly important to win. The importance of cost on selection places tremendous importance on pricing strategies and the resultant risks associated with pricing the effort. Some of the critical risks to consider in pricing and the cost volume are shown in Table 19.2.

19.20 What is cost realism?

Cost realism takes into consideration reviewing and evaluating specific elements of each offeror's proposed cost estimate to determine whether the cost elements are realistic for the work to be performed, reflect a clear understanding of the requirements, and are consistent with the unique methods of performance and materials described in the offeror's technical proposal.

Cost realism is not considered in the evaluation of proposals for the award of a fixed-price contract, because these contracts place the risk of loss upon the contractor. However, when awarding a fixed-price contract, an agency may provide for a price realism analysis for the purpose of measuring a company's understanding of the solicitation requirements, or of assessing the risk inherent in an offeror's proposal.

19.21 What is cost reasonableness?

According to the FAR, a contract cost is reasonable if, in its nature and amount, it does not exceed that which would be incurred by a prudent person in the conduct of competitive business. In determining the reasonableness of a specific cost, the government will consider:

- Whether it is the type of cost generally recognized as ordinary and necessary for the conduct of the contractor's business or the contract performance;
- The restraints or requirements imposed by such factors as generally accepted sound business practices, arm's-length bargaining, federal and state laws and regulations, and contract terms and specifications;
- The action that a prudent businessperson, considering responsibilities to the owners of the business, employees, customers, the government, and the public at large, would take under the circumstances;
- Any significant deviations from the established practices of the contractor that may unjustifiably increase the contract costs.

19.22 What is cost or pricing data?

In accordance with FAR 15.406-2, federal agencies require cost or pricing data for contracts or subcontract actions where the negotiated values are likely to exceed specific dollar thresholds or meet other specific criteria. When cost or pricing data are required, the contracting officer will request that the offeror complete, execute, and submit to the contracting officer a certification that cost and pricing date are accurate, complete, and current as of a specified date.

Cost or pricing data are defined as all facts that, as of the date of price agreement, or, if applicable, an earlier date agreed upon between the parties that is as close as practicable to the date of agreement on price, prudent buyers and sellers would reasonably expect to affect price negotiations significantly. Cost or pricing data consists of more than historical accounting data—facts that can be reasonably expected to contribute to the soundness of estimates of future costs and validity of incurred costs. It includes such factors as vendor quotations, nonrecurring costs, information on changes in production methods and in production or purchasing volume, data supporting projections of business prospects and objectives and related operations costs, unit-cost trends such as those associated with labor efficiency, make-or-buy decisions, estimated resources to attain business goals, and information on management decisions that could have a significant bearing on costs.

19.23 Price to win

Price to win (PTW) is the proposed contract price which, when evaluated via the government's source selection process, will result in your proposal being selected for award. Together with technical and past performance, PTW must rank your proposal high enough, based on the objective and subjective assessments from the Source Selection Evaluation Board (SSEB) to guide the Source Selection Authority (SSA) to award the contract to your company.

The process used to determine the PTW is iterative. It is the responsibility of the capture manager and is designed to increase overall win probability. It cannot be overemphasized how critical PTW is as an overall component in bid/no bid decision. A thorough PTW analysis will take into consideration factors such as the customer's funding, should-cost, and rough order of magnitude, as well as the government's historical buying behavior and buying constraints for this specific opportunity. Likewise, PTW will consider the competition's likely win strategy, approach and teaming strategy, historical pricing behavior, and the competition's likely pricing behavior on the specific opportunity.

19.24 Common cost proposal problems

Considerable time, effort, and scarce resources are committed to submitting a quality proposal in an effort to secure a contract. You need to ensure that the cost proposal offers the best value to the government, is consistent with the other volumes, and does not contain glaring weaknesses. Some of the more common proposal problems/challenges are:

- Proposals with omissions or failure to follow the RFP or RFS;
- Lack of detail on overhead, G&A, and other indirect rates;
- Lack of narrative with supporting rationale;
- Inconsistent content within the proposal;
- Not using the government-provided pricing model;
- Not submitting the proposal on time;
- Not submitting the complete proposal (including subcontractors);
- Failure to propose correct wage determination minimum rate;
- Professional base rates that are too low or too high;
- Failure to identify uncompensated overtime, the definition: of which is hours worked by exempt employees in excess of 40 hours per week for no additional pay;
- Not changing overhead formulas when the base is other than that assumed by the government;
- Not using the latest DCAA-approved rates;
- Failure to use the correct government estimate for ODCs;
- Failure to report and provide a cost estimate for additional ODCs, if appropriate;
- Not submitting a total compensation plan when required.

19.25 Useful templates and worksheets

Several important cost-related documents include:

- Certificate of Cost or Pricing Data (Figure 19.1);
- SF 1408 (Figure 19.2).

CERTIFICATE OF CURRENT COST OR PRICING DATA (FAR 15.406-2)

(When cost or pricing data are required in accordance with FAR 15.406-2, the Contracting Officer will request that the offeror complete, execute, and submit to the Contracting Officer a certification in the format shown in the following Certificate of Current Cost or Pricing Data. The certification shall be submitted only at the time negotiations are concluded. Offerors should complete the certificate and return it when requested by the Contracting Officer.)

This is to certify that, to the best of my knowledge and belief, the cost or pricing data (as defined in section 15.401 of the Federal Acquisition Regulation (FAR) and required under FAR subsection 15.403-4) submitted, either actually or by specific identification in writing, to the Contracting Officer or to the Contracting Officer's representative in support of _____ * are accurate, complete, and current as of_____**.

This certification includes the cost or pricing data supporting any advance agreements and forward pricing rate agreements between the offeror and the Government that are part of the proposal.

Firm _____

Signature _____

Name _____

Title _____

Date of execution*** _____

*   *Identify the proposal, request for price adjustment, or other submission involved, giving the appropriate identifying number (e.g., RFP No.)*

**   *Insert the day, month, and year when price negotiations were concluded and price agreement was reached, or, if applicable, an earlier date agreed upon between the parties that is as close as practicable to the date of agreement on price.*

*** *Insert the day, month, and year of signing, which should be as close as practicable to the date when the price negotiations were concluded and the contract price was agreed to.*

(End of Certificate)

Figure 19.1   Certificate of Current Cost or Pricing Data.

PREAWARD SURVEY OF PROSPECTIVE CONTRACTOR ACCOUNTING SYSTEM

SERIAL NO. *(For surveying activity use)*

OMB No.:**9000-0011**
Expires: 10/31/97

PROSPECTIVE CONTRACTOR

Public reporting burden for this collection of information is estimated to average 24 hours per response, including the time for reviewing instructions, searching existing data sources, gathering and maintaining the data needed, and completing and reviewing the collection of information. Send comments regarding this burden estimate or any other aspect of this collection of information, including suggestions for reducing this burden, to FAR Secretariat (VRS), Office of Federal Acquisition and Regulatory Policy, GSA, Washington, DC 20405; and to the Office of Management and Budget, Paperwork Reduction Project (9000-0011), Washington, DC 20503.

SECTION I - RECOMMENDATION

1. PROSPECTIVE CONTRACTOR'S ACCOUNTING SYSTEM IS ACCEPTABLE FOR AWARD OF PROSPCTIVE CONTRACT

☐ YES   ☐ NO *(Explain in 2. NARRATIVE)*

☐ YES, WITH A RECOMMENDATION THAT A FOLLOW ON ACCOUNTING SYSTEM REVIEW BE PERFORMED AFTER CONTRACT AWARD
(Explain in 2. NARRATIVE)

2. NARRATIVE *(Clarification of deficiencies, and other pertinent comments,. If additional space is required, continue on plain sheets of paper.)*

IF CONTINUATION SHEETS
ATTACHED - MARK HERE ☐

	a. SIGNATURE AND OFFICE *(Include typed or printed name)*	b. TELEPHONE NO. *(include area code)*	c. DATE SIGNED
3. SURVEY MADE BY			
4. SURVEY REVIEWING OFFICIAL	a. SIGNATURE AND OFFICE *(Include typed or printed name)*	b. TELEPHONE NO. *(include area code)*	c. DATE REVIEWED

AUTHORIZED FOR LOCAL REPRODUCTION
Previous edition usable

STANDARD FORM 1408 (REV. 9-88)
Prescribed by GSA
FAR (48 CFR) 53.209-1(f)

Figure 19.2 Standard Form 1408: Preaward Survey of Prospective Contractor Accounting System.

SECTION II - EVALUATION CHECKLIST			
MARK"X" IN THE APPROPRIATE COLUMN *(Explain any deficiencies in SECTION I NARRATIVE)*	YES	NO	NOT APPLIC-CABLE
1. EXCEPT AS STATED IN SECTION I NARRATIVE, IS THE ACCOUNTING SYSTEM IN ACCORD WITH GENERALLY ACCEPTED ACCOUNTING PRINCIPLES APPLICABLE IN THE CIRCUMSTANCES?			
2. ACCOUNTING SYSTEM PROVIDES FOR:			
a. Proper segregation of direct costs from indirect costs.			
b. Identification and accumulation of direct costs by contract.			
c. A logical and consistent method for the allocation of indirect costs to intermediate and final cost objectives. (A contract is a final cost objective.)			
d. Accumlation of costs under general ledger control.			
e. A timekeeping system that identifies employees' labor by intermediate or final cost objectives.			
f. A labor distribution system that charges direct and indirect labor to the appropriate cost objectives.			
g. Interim (at least monthly) determination of costs charged to a contract through routine posting of books of account.			
h. Exclusion from costs charged to government contracts of amounts which are not allowable in terms of FAR 31, Contract Cost Principles and Procedures, or other contract provisions.			
i. Identification of costs by contract line item and by units (as if each unit or line item were a separate contract) if required by the proposed contract.			
j. Segregation of preproduction costs from production costs.			
3. ACCOUNTING SYSTEM PROVIDES FINANCIAL INFORMATION:			
a. Required by contract clauses concerning limitation of cost (FAR 52.232-20 and 21) or limitation on payments (FAR 52.216-16).			
b. Required to support requests for progress payments.			
4. IS THE ACCOUNTING SYSTEM DESIGNED, AND ARE THE RECORDS MAINTAINED IN SUCH A MANNER THAT ADEQUATE, RELIABLE DATA ARE DEVELOPED FOR USE IN PRICING FOLLOW-ON ACQUISITONS?			
5. IS THE ACCOUNTING SYSTEM CURRENTLY IN FULL OPERATION? (If not, describe in Section I Narrative which portions are (1) in operation, (2) set up, but not yet in operation, (3) anticipated, or (4) nonexistent.)			

GSA FORM 1408 (REV. 9-88) **BACK**

Figure 19.2 (continued)

Chapter 20

Leveraging business complexity in a knowledge-based economy

The competitiveness of SMEs [small and medium-sized enterprises] will depend increasingly on the quality of the knowledge they apply to their business processes and the amount which is embedded in their outputs. Essentially, prosperity in the twenty first century will be dependent on their ability to establish a mechanism that enables them to continuously acquire, share and apply knowledge.
—Kuan Yew Wong and Elaine Aspinwall, "Characterizing Knowledge Management in the Small Business Environment," *Journal of Knowledge Management* [1]

20.1 Turbulent transition toward knowledge-based business

In merely 50 years, "the transistor, whose modest role is to amplify electrical signals, has redefined the meaning of power, which today is based as much on the control and exchange of information as it is on iron or coal. The throbbing heart of this sweeping global transformation is in the tiny solid-state amplifier invented by [John] Bardeen, [Walter] Brattain, and [William] Schockley. The crystal fire they ignited during those anxious postwar (World War II) years has radically reshaped the world and the way in which its inhabitants now go about their daily lives" [2]. When processed individually and collectively, information is interpreted, congealed, repackaged, and produced into personal and organizational knowledge. And it is knowledge that rose to prominence as the currency of the global economy late in the twentieth century and continues today in 2012 and beyond. The timeworn aphorism that cash is king is undergoing emendation, and employees are being reconceptualized as knowledge or gold-collar workers who provide and possess valuable, strategically advantageous, and renewable intellectual capital. As British research associate Michael Lissack asserts, "In the future information will be the load-bearing structure of organizations." Economies of scale—bigness—are being replaced by economies of speed in this digital age. And Swedish Professor Johan Roos, formerly of the International Institute for Management Development (IMD) in Switzerland, speaks of the "knowledge economy" and "knowledge landscapes."

The transition from the money-capital and management skill-capital eras to the intellectual-capital era has been concretized by a host of discrete decisions and events, including the creation of careers based upon knowledge management, measurement of (metrics for) knowledge-creating processes and intangible assets, and implementation of knowledge-sharing business cultures. Noteworthy among these events was when Skandia Assurance & Financial Services (AFS)—a major Stockholm-based insurance company—appointed Lief Edvinsson as the corporate world's first director of intellectual capital in 1991. Other companies and organizations at the vanguard of recognizing and acting upon the reality, and the value, of intellectual capital and intangible assets (e.g., corporate brain power, organizational knowledge, client relationships, innovation ability, and employee morale) include the Canadian Imperial Bank of Commerce; Booz-Allen & Hamilton; PwC; DuPont; and Hughes Space & Telecommunications, which launched considerable efforts to understand and enhance intellectual capital management. In addition, Buckman Labs, a U.S.-based biotechnology firm, created a Knowledge Sharing

Department. Buckman Labs incentivizes those employees who contribute to its knowledge-sharing culture through financial rewards and management positions. Chevron engineered a best-practice database to capture and make available the company's collective experience with drilling conditions and innovative solutions to technical problems on site. Sweden's Celemì company published the world's first audit of intangible assets in its 1995 Annual Report. Celemì's Intangible Assets Monitor focuses on its customers (image-enhancing customers, from whom testimonials are valuable; brand names; trademarks); their internal organization (patents, computer systems, management infrastructure); and their staff (competencies, flexibility). Skandia published the first ever annual report supplement on intellectual capital. Pfizer of Switzerland created competence models for recruiting executives that include knowledge building and sharing as important criteria. WM-data of Sweden, a fast growing IT company, links nonfinancial indicators to strategy, and considers financial ratios of little use for management. The Swedish telecommunications company Telia has published its annual Statement of Human Resources for 10 years. This statement includes a profit-and-loss account that visualizes human resources costs and a balance sheet that shows investments in human resources [3].

During a speech before the American Accounting Association's annual meeting held in Dallas, Texas, in August 1997, Michael Sutton, Chief Accountant of the United States Securities and Exchange Commission (SEC), noted that "historically, accounting has been strongly influenced by the reporting needs of a manufacturing-based economy" [4]. In April 1996, the SEC had convened a symposium on intangible assets in Washington, D.C., during which invited participants from prestigious business, academic, and government organizations discussed issues related to the measurement of intangible assets by preparers of financial reports, concerns about disclosures related to intangible assets, and the experience of U.S. and overseas trendsetters with regard to the accounting and disclosure of intangible assets. The Sarbanes-Oxley Act of 2002 (P.L. 107-204) and Finance Accounting Standards Board (FASB)[1] Statement No. 141, *Business Combinations*, and Statement No. 142, *Goodwill and Other Intangible Assets*, converge with the trend of the increasing importance of intangibles to the value of a business. An Accenture survey found that 49% of companies said that they relied primarily on intangible

---

1   The FASB is the designated organization in the private sector for establishing standards of financial accounting that govern the preparation of financial reports by nongovernmental entities. These standards are officially recognized as authoritative by the Securities and Exchange Commission (SEC) and the American Institute of Certified Public Accountants (AICPA).

assets to create shareholder wealth, but only 5% had a robust system to measure and track the performance of intangible assets [5].

Converting human intellect into proposals, and ultimately into useful products and services, is becoming increasingly critical to any business' success [6]. "We now know where productivity—real and limitless productivity—comes from. It comes from challenged, empowered, excited, rewarded teams of people. It comes from engaging every mind in the organization" [7]. There is an accelerating recognition among corporations that their future profitability depends on intangible assets such as "creativity, flexibility and the speed with which they can share new ideas and information. In a literal sense, modern corporations *are what they know*" [8]. Major firms like Xerox, Hewlett-Packard, and Dow Chemical are spending significant resources on knowledge identification and management. Alan Webber, a founding editor of the Boston-based business magazine *Fast Company,* has noted that "[t]he world of business is realizing that ultimately, what matters is the quality of the people in the organization, and how they treat their customers and how creative they are in coming up with new products and new services" [9].

Another significant transition among such major corporations as Microsoft, Compaq, Sun Microsystems, and Hewlett-Packard is the paradigm shift away from business as a battlefield to that of business as a "complex ecosystem in which the company that wins is the one that is quickest to adapt. Employee individuality and diversity are honored and encouraged" [10]. To adapt to new market circumstances and translate them quickly into meaningful opportunities, employees simply cannot be viewed and treated as mere mindless troops, crank-turners, or line items on a traditional Excel or Lotus accounting spreadsheet. With small companies in particular, leveraging the collective intellect is integral to business development achievement and superlative, long-term client support. Providing work environments that are conducive to the generation, exchange, and respect of ideas will pay dividends in morale, employee retention, and financial revenue. Pleasant and secure physical facilities; progressive human resources policies; an open-door management culture; articulated, achievable proposal win and performance incentive programs; and so forth all participate in inspiring and harnessing the best in and from employees.

Small businesses hold several key advantages in KM implementation, as noted by Wong and Aspinwall [1] and presented in Table 20.1.

A comprehensive model of 11 critical success factors for implementing KM within small businesses includes: (1) management leadership and support; (2) organizational culture that defines core business beliefs, values, norms, and social customs (e.g., knowledge creation, sharing, and

Ownership and management	Decision-making and control are largely centralized. Owners can readily declare a need for KM and serve as the main driver for the KM initiative.
Organizational structure	Streamlined structure allows for rapid implementation of change. Shorter and more direct communication supports faster acceptance of KM initiative.
Business culture and behavior	Unified culture provides a strong foundation for change. Organic and fluid business dynamics fosters a knowledge-sharing culture.
Systems, processes, and procedures	People-dominated systems and flexible processes support agile implementation of new KM initiatives. The real benefit here is that the small business can emerge as an "adaptive enterprise" that can learn to deal with uncertainty [11].
Human resources	Having fewer employees means faster alignment with change initiatives as well as more robust collaboration.
Direct pathway for acquisition of customer knowledge	Managers and employees in small firms tend to have close and direct contact with customers ("customer intimacy") and may know them personally or socially. A stronger knowledge channel can be fostered to improve the firm's capacity to capture customer knowledge in areas related to needs and preferences, which should be leveraged to support capture management and proposal development activities.

Table 20.1
Small Businesses Enjoy Important Advantages in Terms of KM Implementation Versus Larger Corporations

application); (3) information technology as an enabler for implementing KM; (4) clear and well-planned strategy and purpose for the KM initiative; (5) measurement to determine and quantify the benefits and effectiveness of KM; (6) organizational infrastructure that defines and established role and teams to perform knowledge-related tasks; (7) processes and activities that span knowledge creations, storage, retrieval, transfer, and application; (8) motivational aids, such as incentives and rewards for knowledge sharing and collaboration; (9) resources to coordinate and manage the KM implementation process as well as to shoulder knowledge-related roles; (10) training and education to build a common language of KM, to help staff understand their new roles in the knowledge-sharing enterprise, as well as to use the KM system and other tools; and (11) human resources management (HRM)—managing knowledge is managing people, as Thomas Davenport and Sven Völpel have observed [12].

20.2 How to communicate effectively on your knowledge landscape

The command-and-control model ... remains part of the baggage carried by many of our best executives.
—The PeopleWise Organization, Kepner-Tregoe

Profound redefinition of the images we hold and the language we use to define ourselves as well as our companies, product lines, colleagues, competitors, proposals, business processes, and the entire economic spectrum is required to generate and sustain business health within our increasingly knowledge-based economy. Metaphors and language directly influence the manners in which corporate and project managers perceive the world and, consequently, the approaches by which they manage their companies, projects, and proposals. Transformed iconography, or "word pictures," can expand the domain of possible and realizable interactions and approaches. Business metaphors that include concepts of war, a race, survival of the fittest, or a jungle and machine- and clock-like images (e.g., go full steam on a project; crank up the pace of activity; C^3 or command, control, and coordinate; and reengineering) will do little to enhance the fitness of American companies on a worldwide knowledge landscape that is subject to nondeterministic change, plateaus of relative stability, and coevolution. Open, complex systems such as company organizations demand concomitant open, flexible architectures of understanding and interaction that have matured far beyond the linear, top-down paradigms that served to generate business success from the Industrial Revolution to the mid-twentieth century. Frederick Taylor's enduring principles of scientific management no longer provide valuable enhancement of human productivity.[2]

"Metaphors allow the transfer of bands of information where other means only transfer smaller bits" [13]. In effect, new words and metaphors

---

2 Frederick Winslow Taylor, M.E., ScD. (1856–1915), conceptualized a system that he termed *scientific management* to address "the great loss which the whole country is suffering through inefficiency in almost all of our daily acts." In his work *The Principles of Scientific Management* (1911), Taylor asserted that "the remedy for this inefficiency lies in systematic management, rather than in searching for some unusual or extraordinary man." Taylor's form of industrial engineering established the organization of work on Henry Ford's assembly lines in Michigan, which were the pride of the industrialized world at that time. However, many of Frederick Taylor's principles were misinterpreted or misapplied, and too often were translated into time-and-motion studies to extract more work from people for less pay. The migration away from labor-intensive mass production operations in American business and manufacturing has neutralized the effectiveness and applicability of Taylor's principles.

constitute new linguistic domains. These new domains promote the conceptualization of avant-garde models and discourse that in turn can guide business decision making on an economic landscape contoured functionally and in real time by human thoughts and ideas. Johan Roos and David Oliver assert that contemporary management issues will increasingly be hindered by the lack of appropriate language to describe emerging organizational phenomena. This is precisely the point at which complexity theory may, in fact, offer senior managers and project managers a robust, multidimensional mode of understanding and decision making.

Within a complexity framework, a company might be conceptualized as a complex adaptive organization, a shifting constellation (à la Henry Mintzberg) with independent and semiautonomous organizations. Machine-like, linear, cause-and-effect must be transformed to the nonlinear ecological interconnectedness of living organisms. Rather than being fiscal liabilities, employees might be perceived to provide valuable intellectual capital and intangible assets within a structured organization and environment. The complex role of management then shifts to visualizing, articulating, measuring, leveraging, expanding, and creating options for the knowledge resources of the firm. Dr. Touraj Nasseri, a consultant and strategist for industry and government, suggests that mapping a company's intellectual capital and employing it productively to achieve strategic objectives are valuable initiatives for senior management to pursue [14]. Nasseri goes on to say that "[t]he potential inherent in well managed intellectual capital extends its impact well into the future as it adapts, renews, and replaces capabilities so that strategies remain responsive to rapid change and much uncertainty" [15]. "Management needs to develop systematic processes that stimulate languaging throughout the company so that, over time, an internal lexicon is formed that can provide the foundation for an effective corporate identity" [16]. *Languaging*, according to Professor Johan Roos, is the art of word choice. And Karl Sveiby introduces the term knowledge management, "the art of creating value from an organization's Intangible Assets." Traditional command-and-control management functions must now give way to mapping and acquiring intellectual capital, communicating a clear vision for the firm, developing and implementing a business lexicon with shared meanings and nuances to foster generalized understanding of strategic goals, and facilitating the rapid assessment and multidirectional flow of knowledge throughout the organization and with external entities. Caveats and pronouncements issued from senior management will not be internalized throughout the knowledge organization.

In the knowledge economy, companies should focus on adapting, recognizing patterns, and building ecological webs to amplify positive feedback rather than trying to achieve optimal performance. Managers should attempt to discern interrelationships and recognize patterns rather than conduct forecasting based upon rationalist (read: Tayloresque) causes and effects. Hierarchical management schemas that rely heavily upon the paternalistic authority that marked the Industrial Era are best transformed into partnership models for the Knowledge Era that incorporate values such as cooperation, caring, creativity, empathy, connectedness, mutualism, and compassion. A sustainable competitive advantage is now maintained on a nonlinear, unpredictable economic landscape (i.e., a rugged knowledge terrain) through leveraging the collective knowledge base of a company and fostering an agile learning organization rather than simply effecting financial capital investment in infrastructure and institutional legacy systems.

At a practical level, sustainability in 2012 and beyond follows from nurturing a business culture, infrastructure, and managerial approaches that encourage *self-organization.* (Biologists use the term self-organization to describe organisms that continually adapt to their environment without losing their basic identity.) Fundamentally, there are no accurate predictions that pertain to a business landscape that is subject to multidimensional, emergent change and on which companies coevolve, that is, mutually affect the development and direction of each other.

Michael Lissack correctly and profoundly observes that "[t]he descriptive metaphor that everything is changing and thus an organization must be poised to adapt to change says nothing about what to do next or about how to convert conflict into cooperation" [12]. What does the "everything is changing" metaphor mean at the level of hour-by-hour, day-to-day managerial decision making? Functionally, very little, according to this author's observation during the course of the past 25 years in the aerospace, defense, IT, and environmental marketplaces. Many American companies continue to operate according to a cluster of timeworn nineteenth-century paradigms, superimposed with a smattering of late twentieth-century management metaphors and buzzwords such as value innovation, total quality management (TQM), business process reengineering (BPR), continuous process improvement (CPI), and quality circles. The parental, autocratic, or mechanistic models of management, inextricably coupled with and often driven by manufacturing-related paradigms of accounting and asset evaluation, remain deeply entrenched and closely guarded. Business performance is still measured largely in financial terms, rather than collectively from a knowledge development perspective, infrastructure perspective, and customer perspective, as well as a financial perspective [17]. However, this situation presents the opportunity to think, and therefore act, in fundamentally different ways. Collectively, American companies are fully capable of inspired vision.

20.3 Envisioning supple business models

Creating open-architecture business models that can function effectively (i.e., converge on reality rather than diverge from real-world data and experience) and evolve within a knowledge-based economy will involve a shift in approach that spans several orders of magnitude. With information and knowledge becoming the currency of American business, the organizations that can share this new currency "ecologically" in an effort to arrive at effective and appropriate solutions for both their external and internal clients in the shortest possible time and with the least amount of resources expended will be those firms that occupy positions, or *optima*, above the knowledge landscape. From these vantages, companies will be less likely to be displaced by new technologies, reconfigured marketing paradigms, social and demographic shifts, and political and legislative climate changes.

Let us reconsider the notion of clients, for example. Within a traditional company, clients are perceived as the buyers or procurers of products or services being offered. In a knowledge-oriented company, clients include both external elements such as buyers, key subcontractors, regulatory agencies, and government institutions, as well as internal clients. The latter might include professional, project management, and support staff; operational units; sales and marketing as well as proposal development elements; financial and accounting modules; senior management; and so forth. The currency of knowledge must flow in meaningful, multidirectional pathways among all of these clients. Each client is critical to the sustainability and performance (i.e., positive energetics) of the company, and each requires, and in turn provides, vital information and knowledge to the other much as enzymes are shared within a living cell to perform a host of vital maintenance, replicative, and growth functions.

The traditional organizational diagram that most American companies use to illustrate internal structure has little applicability in the knowledge-based economy. Organizational charts are by nature highly linear, pyramidal, and top-down in direction. As Figure 20.1 depicts, however, businesses in 2012 and beyond should strongly consider an ecological model with knowledge constituting the currency or fuel that is transferred among clusters of entities we will call clients, business process and metaprocesses, employees, and finances. Table 20.2 suggests how traditional line and staff organizations can be reconceptualized according to this new model.

In this model, every cluster and module within the learning organization is afforded a pivotal complex of roles in ensuring the sustainability of the company. Everyone is involved with and contributes to the new currency—knowledge, which is quite unlike the traditional paradigm wherein any element not involved in the most linear manner with generating cash is perceived as a "leech on the corporate purse." In fact, within a knowledge-based and forward-looking organization, intangible assets are considered quantitatively along with such tangible assets as cash, accounts receivable, computers and other amortizable equipment, facilities, and inventories.

20.4 Sample application: tracing complexity and KM through the proposal development process

Technically, a proposal is an offer prepared by a contractor (such as your company) to perform a service, supply a product, or a combination of both in response to an RFP or RFS document by a procuring organization within government or private industry. Proposals are legal documents, often incorporated by reference into the final contract. That means that they must be factual and accurate—including information provided in

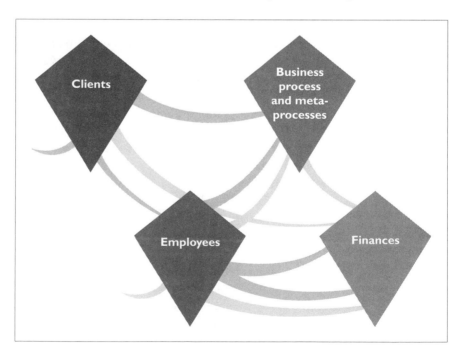

Figure 20.1
Knowledge fuels complex, ecological business interactions.

Traditional Organizational Element/Function	Reconceptualized Cluster in a Complex, Learning Organization	Reconceptualized Functions/Comments
Chairman of the Board Chief Executive Officer President	Metaprocesses	Map intellectual capital, communicate a clear vision for the firm, develop and implement a shared business lexicon to foster generalized understanding of strategic goals, and facilitate the rapid assessment and multidirectional diffusion of knowledge throughout the organization. In effect, senior management must leverage and manage the intellectual capital of the company, as well as conduct strategic planning activities.
Risk Management	Business Processes	Develop business continuation strategies that permit the transfer of core business-specific knowledge to a new management team.
Operations/Manufacturing	Business Processes (called Process Owners)	Leverage and empower the intellectual capital of knowledge workers to generate localized, real-time solutions that can then be cataloged and transferred to other operational modules within your company.
Finance, Procurement, Travel, and Facilities	Finances	Assess and report intellectual and structural capital in monetary terms. As Dr. Nasseri notes, "physical assets owe most of their value to intellectual capital" [18].
Human Resources	Business Processes (called Human Capital Development)	Acquire, train, retain, foster continuing education for, and incentivize human intellectual capital. Develop compensation policies appropriate for knowledge workers. Ensure that employees are always climbing a learning curve.*

* Far from being a detriment, a learning curve within a learning organization is a prerequisite to continued sustainability.

Table 20.2   Reconceptualizing organizational elements toward a knowledge-based framework

Traditional Organizational Element/Function	Reconceptualized Cluster in a Complex, Learning Organization	Reconceptualized Functions/Comments
Information Services (IS)	Business Processes	Facilitate the rapid assessment and multidirectional flow of knowledge throughout the organization via data warehousing, data mining, and data filtering supplemented by ongoing training.
Sales and Marketing Secondary Marketing Business Development Advanced Planning	Business Processes	Assess and communicate the economic landscape, develop and share knowledge of clients, conduct benchmarking[†] and competitor assessments, define client and product lines (congealed knowledge), and design and develop proposals.
Legal Support (contracts, insurance, litigation, compliance and regulatory support) Auditing	Business Processes	Congeal intellectual capital as patents, software source code, published papers and books, marketable user manuals, research papers, productizable business processes and protocols.
Project Management[‡]	Business Processes (called Knowledge Integrators or Knowledge Managers rather than Project Managers)	Serve external and internal clients; implement client-focused vision; empower staff for success; and foster accountability, commitment, and ownership. Serving external clients extends to assembling appropriate knowledge sources from within the organization and matching those sources to external client requirements on budget and within the required time frame. Internal client servicing includes reporting requirements.

[†] Benchmarking is a rigorous process for linking competitive analysis to your company's strategy development. Benchmarking is a method that measures the performance of your best-in-class competitors relative to your industry's key success factors. It also is a mechanism for determining how the best-in-class achieve those performance levels and competitor assessments, define client and product lines (congealed knowledge), and design and develop proposals.

[‡] Too often in American business, the functional reality is that project managers are technical staff who also happen to sign time sheets. Their focus is on technical nuts-and-bolts, frequently to the exclusion of client interaction, staff empowerment, knowledge sharing, and so forth.

Table 20.2   (continued)

Traditional Organizational Element/Function	Reconceptualized Cluster in a Complex, Learning Organization	Reconceptualized Functions/Comments
Administrative Support	Business Processes	Produce congealed knowledge products in the form of proposals, contract deliverable reports, marketing presentations, annual and other SEC-required reports, client correspondence.
Internal Research and Development (IR&D) Product Development	Business Processes	Innovation in a company is nourished and driven by knowledge-based capabilities and by management systems that leverage the capabilities [15].
Health and Safety Quality Control/Quality Assurance	Business Processes	

Table 20.2   (continued)

résumés and project summaries, which summarize applicable contractual experience. In actuality, résumés and project summaries reflect a significant percentage of intellectual capital of a service organization. Relevant knowledge resident in the employees of the company as gained through education, training, technical refresh, and professional experience coupled with initiative, dedication, and innovation should be highlighted in each résumé. Similarly, to be effective, project summaries must reflect the organizational knowledge of the firm from technical, managerial, and geographic perspectives, to name but several.

Proposals are, first and foremost, sales-oriented knowledge products that include a host of marketing, technical, programmatic, institutional, pricing, and certification information. Through a choreographed process of knowledge generation, transfer, and congealment, a proposal is designed to sell both technical and managerial capabilities of a company to accomplish all required activities on time and at a reasonable cost. Your company's proposal document(s) is scored, literally, by the client's evaluators against formalized, specific standards in a process analogous to pattern recognition. A proposal is the tangible result of knowledge-building processes, supported in turn by hard and directed work and buoyed by a positive collective attitude within your company's proposal team of knowledge workers.

Crucial to proposal success both as a process and a product is the transfer of relevant marketing information to appropriate members of the capture and proposal team. From there, that information must be interpreted, assigned value, and translated into knowledge that will ultimately be congealed into the actual proposal documents—into narrative, theme statements, graphics, captions, compliance matrices, tabs, oral presentation slides, and so forth. If marketing data and information do not find their way into the knowledge product called a proposal, then a company's proposal will not receive the maximal point score. Therefore, the marketing data are valueless. In effect, if intellectual capital measured in client, project, competitor, technological programmatic, and political knowledge is not transferred to appropriate staff (knowledge workers) and converted efficiently into hardcopy or electronic proposal documents via established, articulated business processes, your company's proposal win ratios in terms of dollars (x dollars of contracts awarded for every $100 of contract value pursued) and number (x number of proposals won) will be suboptimal.

20.5 Summation

Evidence "suggests that the business world may be a complex system poised at the edge of chaos" [19]. If we grant that such is the case, then we who are an integral part of this world must leverage the complexity with which we are faced every day into optima (that is, business processes, business thinking, and the like) that lift us above the unpredictable knowledge landscape and ensure business sustainability. Implementing business processes that actively promote knowledge valuation, development, transfer, management, and congealment will help American companies maximize both intellectual and structural capital as we enter the twenty-first century.

We now turn our attention to a specific type of contracting with the federal government—the important SF330 solicitation process. These solicitations are presented in the Federal Acquisition Regulations (FAR) at Part 53.236-2, Architect-engineer services. SF330 documents are prepared for business opportunities with the federal government as well as states, municipalities, and quasigovernmental agencies such as port and transit authorities.

ENDNOTES

1. Wong, Kuan Yew, and Elaine Aspinwall, "Characterizing Knowledge Management in the Small Business Environment," *Journal of Knowledge Management*, Vol. 8, No. 3, 2004, pp. 52–53.

2. Riordan, John, and Lillian Hoddeson, *Crystal Fire: The Birth of the Information Age*, New York: W. W. Norton & Co., 1997, p. 10.

3. Information in this paragraph was drawn from Karl E. Svieby, "What Is Knowledge Management?" pp. 5–6, http://www.sveiby.com/articles/KnowledgeManagement.html, April 2001, as well as Sacha Cohen, "Knowledge Management's Killer App," http://www.astd.org/magazine/current/cohen.htm, and Laton McCartney, "Getting Smart About Knowledge Management," *Industry Week*, May 4, 1998, p. 32.

   See also Karl E. Sveiby, "The Intangible Assets Monitor," http://www.sveiby.com/articles/IntangAss/CompanyMonitor.html, December 20, 1997. Celemì employs metrics such as efficiency (sales per customer, staff turnover), stability (repeat orders, growth in sales per administrative staff), and growth and renewal (average years of professional competence). Celemì is headquartered in Malmö, Sweden, and is dedicated to creating processes that help companies leverage the power of learning.

   Sacha Cohen notes that Hewlett-Packard employs a Web-based system called Connex to help identify subject experts in specific geographic locations. Also, Booz Allen uses a best-practice application on its intranet, Knowledge On Line (KOL), an automated knowledge repository in which that firm's collective knowledge and expertise are captured, classified, and quantified.

4. Sutton, Michael H., "Dangerous Ideas: A Sequel," Remarks delivered during the American Accounting Association 1997 Annual Meeting in Dallas, Texas, on August 18, 1997, p. 3; http://www.corpforms99.com/83.html.

5. Banham, Russ, "Valuing IP Post-Sarbanes-Oxley," *Journal of Accounting*, November 2005, http://www.jounalofaccounting.com/Issues/2005/Nov/ValuingIpPostSarbanesOxley/htm.

6. Quinn, James Brian, Philip Anderson, and Sydney Finkelstein, "Managing Professional Intellect: Making the Most of the Best," *Harvard Business Review*, March/April 1996.

7. Quinn, Judy, "The Welch Way: General Electric CEO Jack Welch Brings Employee Empowerment to Light," *Incentive*, September 1994, p. 50.

8. Hamilton, Martha A., "Managing the Company Mind: Firms Try New Ways to Tap Intangible Assets Such as Creativity, Knowledge," *Washington Post*, August 18, 1996, p. H1.

9. Hamilton, Martha A., "Managing the Company Mind: Firms Try New Ways to Tap Intangible Assets Such as Creativity, Knowledge," *Washington Post*, August 18, 1996, p. H5.

10. James, Geoffrey, "It's Time to Free Dilbert," *New York Times*, September 1, 1996, p. F-11.

11. Chesebrough, David, E. "Knowledge Management: A Tool for SMEs to Enhance Competitiveness," *CACCI Journal*, Vol. 1, 2006, p. 11. *See also*, Haeckel, Stephan H., *Adaptive Enterprise: Creating and Leading Sense-and-Respond Organizations*, Cambridge: Harvard Business School Press, 1999.

12. Wong, Kuan Yew, "Critical Success Factors for Implementing Knowledge Management in Small and Medium Enterprises," *Industrial Management & Data Systems*, Vol. 105, No. 3, 2005, pp. 266–273.

13. Lissack, Michael R., "Complexity Metaphors and the Management of a Knowledge Based Enterprise: An Exploration of Discovery," http://www.lissack.com/writings/proposal.htm.

14. Nasseri, Touraj, "Knowledge Leverage: The Ultimate Advantage," *Kognos: The E-Journal of Knowledge Issues*, Summer 1996, p. 4.

15. Nasseri, Touraj, "Knowledge Leverage: The Ultimate Advantage," *Kognos: The E-Journal of Knowledge Issues*, Summer 1996, p. 2.

16. Roos, Johan, and Georg von Krogh, "What You See Depends on Who You Are," *Perspectives for Managers*, No. 7, September 1995, p. 2.

17. Roos, Johan, "Intellectual Performance: Exploring an Intellectual Capital System in Small Companies," October 30, 1996, pp. 4, 9.

18. Nasseri, Touraj, "Knowledge Leverage: The Ultimate Advantage," *Kognos: The E-Journal of Knowledge Issues*, Summer 1996, p. 1.

19. Phelan, Steven E., "From Chaos to Complexity in Strategic Planning," Presented at the 55th Annual Meeting of the Academy of Management, Vancouver, British Columbia, August 6–9, 1995, p. 7; http://www.aom.pace.edu/bps/Papers/chaos.html.

Chapter 21

Planning and producing SF330 responses for architect-engineer services

Architectural, engineering, and construction procurements are frequently presented to industry in the form of a request for Standard Form 330. On the FedBizOpps opportunity portal in 2011, SF 330 Qualification Forms were being requested by the U.S. Department of Agriculture, Department of the Interior, Department of Labor, and the National Institutes of Health, among other federal agencies.

21.1 SF330 and the FAR

The FAR at Part 53.236-2(b), Architect-engineer (A-E) services, describes a special type of solicitation that has broad-based applicability at the federal, state, municipality, and quasigovernmental levels such as port authorities and transit authorities. This type of solicitation is called an SF330. Architectural and engineering firms of all sizes submit this document routinely to establish their credentials with client organizations as diverse as the U.S. Coast Guard (USCG), U.S. Army Corps of Engineers (USACE), U.S. Navy, U.S. Department of Agriculture (USDA), the National Forest Service, and Harford County, Maryland.

SF330, the Architect-Engineer Qualifications form, was developed to replace the long-standing SF254 and SS255. SF254, Architect-Engineer and Related Services Questionnaire, and SF255, Architect-Engineer and Related Services Questionnaire for Specific Projects, had been largely unchanged since their introduction in 1975. The A-E industry, however, has changed substantially and the requirements of federal agencies have evolved considerably. In response to these changes, the SF330 was developed by an interagency committee, submitted to industry and government for comment through the *Federal Register*, and fielded.

SF330 reflects current A-E practices and provides the essential information agencies need for the selection of A-E firms in a streamlined format. SF330 is a two-part form (see Figure 21.1). Part I, Contract-Specific Qualifications, replaces SF255. Part II, General Qualifications, replaces SF254. SF254 is now essentially used as an appendix to SF255 and is rarely used alone. Hence, SF330 was designed as a single two-part form. Similar to SF254, Part II of SF330 can still be separately submitted to agencies to be maintained in their A-E qualification data files.

The objectives of the SF330 are as follows:

- Merge SF254 and SF255 into a single streamlined form;
- Expand essential information about qualifications and experience;
- Reflect current A-E disciplines, experience types, and technology;
- Eliminate duplicate information;
- Eliminate information of marginal value;
- Facilitate electronic usage.

Presented in Figure 21.1 are the forms and formats in which the government wants to receive the specific information regarding, for example, contractor personnel, office locations, and contract experience.

ARCHITECT - ENGINEER QUALIFICATIONS

PART I - CONTRACT-SPECIFIC QUALIFICATIONS

A. CONTRACT INFORMATION

1. TITLE AND LOCATION *(City and State)*

2. PUBLIC NOTICE DATE

3. SOLICITATION OR PROJECT NUMBER

B. ARCHITECT-ENGINEER POINT OF CONTACT

4. NAME AND TITLE

5. NAME OF FIRM

6. TELEPHONE NUMBER

7. FAX NUMBER

8. E-MAIL ADDRESS

C. PROPOSED TEAM
(Complete this section for the prime contractor and all key subcontractors.)

(Check) PRIME / J-V PARTNER / SUBCONTRACTOR	9. FIRM NAME	10. ADDRESS	11. ROLE IN THIS CONTRACT
a.	CHECK IF BRANCH OFFICE		
b.	CHECK IF BRANCH OFFICE		
c.	CHECK IF BRANCH OFFICE		
d.	CHECK IF BRANCH OFFICE		
e.	CHECK IF BRANCH OFFICE		
f.	CHECK IF BRANCH OFFICE		

D. ORGANIZATIONAL CHART OF PROPOSED TEAM ☐ *(Attached)*

AUTHORIZED FOR LOCAL REPRODUCTION

STANDARD FORM 330 (6/2004) PAGE 1

Figure 21.1   SF330.

E. RESUMES OF KEY PERSONNEL PROPOSED FOR THIS CONTRACT
(Complete one Section E for each key person.)

12. NAME	13. ROLE IN THIS CONTRACT	14. YEARS EXPERIENCE	
		a. TOTAL	b. WITH CURRENT FIRM

15. FIRM NAME AND LOCATION *(City and State)*

16. EDUCATION *(DEGREE AND SPECIALIZATION)*	17. CURRENT PROFESSIONAL REGISTRATION *(STATE AND DISCIPLINE)*

18. OTHER PROFESSIONAL QUALIFICATIONS *(Publications, Organizations, Training, Awards, etc.)*

19. RELEVANT PROJECTS

a.

(1) TITLE AND LOCATION *(City and State)*	(2) YEAR COMPLETED	
	PROFESSIONAL SERVICES	CONSTRUCTION *(If applicable)*
(3) BRIEF DESCRIPTION *(Brief scope, size, cost, etc.)* AND SPECIFIC ROLE	☐ Check if project performed with current firm	

b.

(1) TITLE AND LOCATION *(City and State)*	(2) YEAR COMPLETED	
	PROFESSIONAL SERVICES	CONSTRUCTION *(If applicable)*
(3) BRIEF DESCRIPTION *(Brief scope, size, cost, etc.)* AND SPECIFIC ROLE	☐ Check if project performed with current firm	

c.

(1) TITLE AND LOCATION *(City and State)*	(2) YEAR COMPLETED	
	PROFESSIONAL SERVICES	CONSTRUCTION *(If applicable)*
(3) BRIEF DESCRIPTION *(Brief scope, size, cost, etc.)* AND SPECIFIC ROLE	☐ Check if project performed with current firm	

d.

(1) TITLE AND LOCATION *(City and State)*	(2) YEAR COMPLETED	
	PROFESSIONAL SERVICES	CONSTRUCTION *(If applicable)*
(3) BRIEF DESCRIPTION *(Brief scope, size, cost, etc.)* AND SPECIFIC ROLE	☐ Check if project performed with current firm	

e.

(1) TITLE AND LOCATION *(City and State)*	(2) YEAR COMPLETED	
	PROFESSIONAL SERVICES	CONSTRUCTION *(If applicable)*
(3) BRIEF DESCRIPTION *(Brief scope, size, cost, etc.)* AND SPECIFIC ROLE	☐ Check if project performed with current firm	

STANDARD FORM 330 (6 2004) **PAGE 2**

Figure 21.1 (continued)

F. EXAMPLE PROJECTS WHICH BEST ILLUSTRATE PROPOSED TEAM'S QUALIFICATIONS FOR THIS CONTRACT *(Present as many projects as requested by the agency, or 10 projects, if not specified. Complete one Section F for each project.)*		20. EXAMPLE PROJECT KEY NUMBER

21. TITLE AND LOCATION *(City and State)*	22. YEAR COMPLETED	
	PROFESSIONAL SERVICES	CONSTRUCTION *(If applicable)*

23. PROJECT OWNER'S INFORMATION

a. PROJECT OWNER	b. POINT OF CONTACT NAME	c. POINT OF CONTACT TELEPHONE NUMBER

24. BRIEF DESCRIPTION OF PROJECT AND RELEVANCE TO THIS CONTRACT *(Include scope, size, and cost)*

25. FIRMS FROM SECTION C INVOLVED WITH THIS PROJECT

	(1) FIRM NAME	(2) FIRM LOCATION *(City and State)*	(3) ROLE
a.			
b.			
c.			
d.			
e.			
f.			

STANDARD FORM 330 (6/2004) **PAGE 3**

Figure 21.1 (continued)

G. KEY PERSONNEL PARTICIPATION IN EXAMPLE PROJECTS

26. NAMES OF KEY PERSONNEL (From Section E, Block 12)	27. ROLE IN THIS CONTRACT (From Section E, Block 13)	28. EXAMPLE PROJECTS LISTED IN SECTION F (Fill in "Example Projects Key" section below before completing table. Place "X" under project key number for participation in same or similar role.)									
		1	2	3	4	5	6	7	8	9	10

29. EXAMPLE PROJECTS KEY

NO.	TITLE OF EXAMPLE PROJECT (FROM SECTION F)	NO.	TITLE OF EXAMPLE PROJECT (FROM SECTION F)
1		6	
2		7	
3		8	
4		9	
5		10	

STANDARD FORM 330 (6/2004) PAGE 4

Figure 21.1   (continued)

H. ADDITIONAL INFORMATION

30. PROVIDE ANY ADDITIONAL INFORMATION REQUESTED BY THE AGENCY. ATTACH ADDITIONAL SHEETS AS NEEDED.

I. AUTHORIZED REPRESENTATIVE

The foregoing is a statement of facts.

31. SIGNATURE

32. DATE

33. NAME AND TITLE

STANDARD FORM 330 (6/2004) PAGE 5

Figure 21.1   (continued)

ARCHITECT-ENGINEER QUALIFICATIONS	1. SOLICITATION NUMBER *(If any)*

PART II - GENERAL QUALIFICATIONS
(If a firm has branch offices, complete for each specific branch office seeking work.)

2a. FIRM (OR BRANCH OFFICE) NAME			3. YEAR ESTABLISHED	4. DUNS NUMBER
2b. STREET			**5. OWNERSHIP**	
			a. TYPE	
2c. CITY	2d. STATE	2e. ZIP CODE		
			b. SMALL BUSINESS STATUS	
6a. POINT OF CONTACT NAME AND TITLE			7. NAME OF FIRM *(If block 2a is a branch office)*	
6b. TELEPHONE NUMBER	6c. E-MAIL ADDRESS			

8a. FORMER FIRM NAME(S) *(If any)*	8b. YR. ESTABLISHED	8c. DUNS NUMBER

9. EMPLOYEES BY DISCIPLINE				10. PROFILE OF FIRM'S EXPERIENCE AND ANNUAL AVERAGE REVENUE FOR LAST 5 YEARS		
a. Function Code	b. Discipline	c. No. of Employees (1) FIRM	(2) BRANCH	a. Profile Code	b. Experience	c. Revenue Index Number *(see below)*
	Other Employees					
	Total					

11. ANNUAL AVERAGE PROFESSIONAL SERVICES REVENUES OF FIRM FOR LAST 3 YEARS
(Insert revenue index number shown at right)

a. Federal Work	
b. Non-Federal Work	
c. Total Work	

PROFESSIONAL SERVICES REVENUE INDEX NUMBER

1. Less than $100,000
2. $100,00 to less than $250,000
3. $250,000 to less than $500,000
4. $500,000 to less than $1 million
5. $1 million to less than $2 million
6. $2 million to less than $5 million
7. $5 million to less than $10 million
8. $10 million to less than $25 million
9. $25 million to less than $50 million
10. $50 million or greater

12. AUTHORIZED REPRESENTATIVE
The foregoing is a statement of facts.

a. SIGNATURE	b. DATE
c. NAME AND TITLE	

AUTHORIZED FOR LOCAL REPRODUCTION

STANDARD FORM 330 (6/2004) **PAGE 6**

Figure 21.1 (continued)

464

SF330 is available on the Web at http://www.gsa.gov/portal/forms/
download/21DBF5BF7E860FC185256E13005C6AA6.

21.2 Understanding the required structure of the response

SF 330 submittals are prepared in response to synopses for A-E services
that appear on FedBizOpps. Although generally prepared for federal
government agencies such as the USACE, USCG, U.S. Army, or specific
Air Force bases, SF330s or modified versions of this form can be required
submittals for states and municipalities as well. One major difference in
contractor response to a government RFP versus an SF330 synopsis is that
labor rates and other direct costs are included with a proposal but are not
part of an SF330 response.

21.3 Overall strategy of response

The SF330, Part I, submittal consists essentially of a series of nine major
elements. As with response to RFPs, you should follow the guidance provided in the FedBizOpps synopsis very carefully.

When strategizing your response to an SF330 opportunity, focus on
Section E, Résumés of Key Personnel Proposed for This Contract, first.
During the prekickoff planning phase, reach a consensus regarding the
personnel you will be proposing and exactly what position on the project
organizational chart they will occupy. Particularly critical to decide on are
the program/project manager and the delivery/task order managers.
Attempt to structure the project organizational chart in accordance with
the government agency's organization and in compliance with the technical
subareas named in the FedBizOpps synopsis. If, for example, the
government agency is divided into three primary elements, then your
company's project organization might reflect three similarly named
elements as well. Your marketing intelligence should indicate the
appropriate number of delivery or task order managers to propose. Does
the particular government agency want streamlined contractor project
management structures? In that case, one or two delivery or task order
managers for each major organizational element might be appropriate.
When selecting personnel for Section E, keep in mind that these staff
should have been integrally involved in the projects that you will select in
Section F, Example Projects Which Best Illustrate Proposed Team's
Qualifications for This Contract. Section G, Key Personnel Participation

in Example Projects, requires this involvement. The government wants to be assured that the staff your company is proposing have actually worked on the contracts that you are presenting as similar technical or programmatic experience in Section F.

Once the project organizational chart has been constructed for Section D, Organizational Chart of Proposed Team, your next step is to identify 10 relevant projects for inclusion in Section F. Most government agencies limit the number of projects to 10, although there are occasional exceptions.[1] When the applicable projects have been identified, your proposal manager can then turn his or her attention to Section H, Additional Information. Most companies and individual proposal managers make the mistake of beginning their response to an SF330 with Section H because this is the technical heart of the document. However, it is extremely difficult to design a successful SF330 response without first having made the pivotal decisions regarding Sections E and F. Remember that evaluators are reviewing 30 to 50 SF330s for even small procurements. They may spend only 30 minutes on any one proposal during their preliminary evaluation sequence. That is all the time your company will get to make a positive, lasting impression.

21.4 Section F: selling your project experience

In selecting the 10 projects for Section F, you might apply the following criteria to determine their relevancy to the particular procurement.

- Same client (USACE, Portland District);
- Same agency (USACE);
- Same technical work (landfill closure);
- Same geographic location (Pacific Northwest);
- Same type of contract vehicle [Indefinite Delivery/Indefinite Quantity (ID-IQ)].

---

1   In one SF254/255 solicitation, Tinker Air Force Base in Oklahoma allowed up to 50 projects in Block 8, which is analogous to Section F of the SF330!

21.5 Section H: structure according to the evaluation criteria

Your company's response to the technical requirements and evaluation criteria found in the FedBizOpps synopsis is the foundation of Section H. Ensure that each of the technical areas in the synopsis is addressed in your response. Use the wording of the particular synopsis to build the headings and subheadings of Section H. In responses that are not page limited, Section H affords an opportunity to present additional project-specific experience to amplify and expand that which was provided in Section F. There is one caveat, however: As with all proposal writing, keep the narrative in Section H crisp and focused on the requirements and how your company can meet them fully.

Section H also includes your company's project management plan. Link this narrative to the staff proposed in Section E. Highlight the advantages of selecting your company at the conclusion of Section H. Provide authenticated benefits of your technical and management approach to the client. In addition, Section H should include the specific rationales for why your company has teamed with other firms (if this is the case) in order to propose on this procurement.

21.6 Section H outlining

Let us suppose that the USACE, Savannah District, your client, has released a synopsis in FedBizOpps for miscellaneous environmental services. The weighted evaluation criteria are: (1) technical excellence, (2) prior experience and past performance, (3) management capabilities, (4) personnel qualifications, and (5) computer capabilities. How should you outline Section H?

Build the Section H outline around these stated evaluation criteria, making sure to include subheadings for each one of the points stated under a given evaluation criterion. For example, you might consider outlining this section as shown in Table 21.1, if the management capabilities criterion (3) reads as follows:

(3) Management capabilities (23%) as demonstrated by internal quality control and quality assurance procedures used to ensure the technical accuracy and the coordination of disciplines, the structure of the firm as it relates to the overall approach to project management, capability to perform work in house, and ability to manage fluctuating workload.

H.3	Management Capabilities (Evaluation Criterion 3)	
	H.3.1	Overview
	H.3.2	Management of Projects of Similar Size and Scope
		• Cost-Effective Strategies
		• Time-Efficient Strategies
	H.3.3	Structure of the Firm
	H.3.4	Project Execution Strategies
		H.3.4.1 Project Initiation and Kickoff
		H.3.4.2 Internal QC-QA Procedures
		• QC-QA Metrics for Deliverables
		H.3.4.3 Ability to Manage Fluctuating Workloads
		H.3.4.4 Cost and Schedule Control Approaches
		H.3.4.5 Performance Measurement and Control Systems
	H.3.5	In-House Capabilities
	H.3.6	Project Leadership
		• Project Manager's Role and Span of Authority
		• USACE-Company Interfaces
		• Monthly Reporting
	H.3.7	Subcontractor Management

Table 21.1
Section H:
management
section outline

Consider building and maintaining an electronic subdirectory of high-impact client quotations to authenticate your proposals and SF330s.

21.7   Subcontractor participation

During the prekickoff planning phase of the SF330 process, ensure that written teaming agreements are in place with all of your subcontractors. Call on them during the writing phase to provide résumés for Section E, project summaries for Section F, a company overview and technical information for Section H, any appropriate letters of commendation, and a letter of commitment from the president of the subcontracting firm to your company's president or senior vice president. (See Table 21.2 for a comprehensive list of materials required and guidelines for submittal.) Include résumés and project summaries from your subcontractors in accordance

A. Software Application Requirements

    1. Submit all text in Microsoft Word 2010.

    2. Submit all line-art graphics as CorelDRAW files or Windows metafiles.

    3. Any photos, submit as tiff or jpeg files.

    4. All text and graphics provided in electronic form MUST be provided through the virtual private network or on DVD, not via e-mail.

    5. No graphics from the Internet may be submitted. We need 200-dpi-resolution photos or images.

B. Formatting Requirements

    1. Use as few formatting commands (e.g., **bold**, <u>underline</u>, *italic*, centering, indenting) as possible in creating your text. Make text flush left, and separate paragraphs with hard returns.

C. Required Materials from Each Teaming Partner

    1. Signed, original letters of commitment on company letterhead

    2. Tailored résumés, including all relevant professional certifications and registrations, along with associated dates and states

    3. Tailored project summaries

    4. Overview of company history and relevant technical, programmatic, and contractual capabilities

    5. Statement of financial strength and solvency

    6. High-resolution company logos

    7. Project-specific photos and identifying captions

    8. Relevant client references, along with full title, name, address, telephone, fax, and e-mail

    9. Recent Architect/Engineer Contract Administration Support System (ACASS) performance ratings

    10. Office locations map

    11. Total number of projects performed for the client organization

    12. Mileage from nearest office locations to client HQ

    13. Specific numbers of personnel by discipline in the relevant geographic area

    14. Relevant client commendation letters or awards

Table 21.2
Comprehensive guidelines for teaming partners

with the percentage of the contract that is being subcontracted. In effect, if only 15% of the contract will be performed by the subcontractors, then one or two project summaries should be from the subcontractors.

Your subcontractors can also be used in a review capacity for the SF330s. As with responses to RFPs and RFSs, your SF330s should also undergo internal reviews and quality checking throughout the response life cycle. SF330s have specific due date and times, just like formal RFPs. Ensure that your company receives a time- and date-stamped receipt for your submittal.

21.8 Building teaming agreements

Teaming agreements between your company and other organizations are established for several important reasons. Many times, FedBizOpps synopses for SF330s (and RFPs as well) stipulate that a certain percentage of the contract must be performed, for example, by SDBs, WOBs, and historically black colleges and universities (HBCUs). Depending on its size and spectrum of specific competencies, your company may need to enter into teaming agreements with these organizations to fulfill these stipulated contractual requirements. It is beneficial to build a database of potential teaming partners that fall into these categories and have been prequalified with the particular client agency, if necessary. Your company can and should also consult the Central Contractor Registration (CCR) database (http://www.bpn.gov/ccr/default.aspx) for small business partners. You can use the Dynamic Small Business Search feature of CCR.

Another common reason for entering into a teaming agreement is that each company will benefit from the other's technical expertise, contractual experience, programmatic strength, geographic proximity to the government site, and number and diversity of professional staff. For example, perhaps your company offers many important and relevant environmental services, but the FedBizOpps synopsis for a specific USCG project also requires support in the areas of unexploded ordnance (UXO) and noise reduction. Under these circumstances, teaming is essential in order to meet the USCG's technical needs completely.

Teaming agreements are formal documents that define the specific association of companies and other entities, and which offer the basis for legal action if they are violated. In actual practice, they are not infallible but do articulate the basis of mutual interaction for the purpose of acquiring business. Agreements may be exclusive, or nonexclusive, depending upon the procurement. In effect, a given company may elect to join several teams to heighten its chances of winning a portion of the contract work. When

---

Potential Teaming Agreement Topics

1. Mutual support during the entire preproposal, proposal, and postproposal life cycle, including negotiations.

   Timely submission of all proposal materials, including tehcnical content, résumes, past performance, and cost/pricing data.

   Availability of qualified staff to assist in developing the proposal or SF330, as well as In conducting discussions and negotiations with the government.

2. Prime contractor's right to include additional subcontractors on the team.

3. Prime and subcontractor may share costs for document formatting, artwork, printing, binding, and delivery of the proposal.

4. Prime will have sole right to decide the form and content of all documents submitted to the government.

5. Prime will make every reasonable effort to subcontract to the sub that portion of the work stipulated in a statement of work (attached to the teaming agreement).

6. Any news releases, public announcements, advertisement, or publicity released by either party concerning the agreement, any proposals, or any resulting contracts or subcontracts will be subject to the prior approval of the other party.

7. Nondisclosure and protection of proprietary data and information.

   Each party will hold the other party's Information confidential, unless such information becomes part of the public domain or unless subject to lawful demand (e.g., subpoena).

8. Duration or term of the agreement.

   Termination of the agreement.

9. Noncompete clause.

10. Percentage of the contract to be allocated to the subcontractor.

11. Interfaces with the government.

12. Patentable inventions and software developed pursuant to the work performed as a result of the agreement.

13. Nonproselytizing clause.

    Neither party shall solicit for employment any employee(s) of the other party to work on the project contemplated in the agreement.

14. Conditions and mechanisms for amending, modifying, or extending the agreement.

15. Communication between the two parties.

16. Authorized signatures from both parties with witness.

17. Date of execution.

18. Agreement shall be enforced and interpreted under applicable state laws.

Figure 21.2
Potential topics for teaming agreements.

your company serves as the prime contractor, your goal will be to secure exclusive teaming agreements with your subcontractors. This helps to eliminate the possibility of company-sensitive or procurement-sensitive information leaking to your competitors.[2]

The language of teaming agreements varies depending upon the procurement, the exact nature of the working relationship, and the business culture of the companies involved. Articles and elements that might be built into a teaming agreement include: (1) the particular purpose of the agreement, (2) the relationship of the parties involved, (3) scope of services to be performed upon contract award, (4) costs incurred, (5) the process for executing contracts, (6) termination procedures, (7) notices (i.e., points of contact in each party), (8) nondisclosure of proprietary information, and (9) grounds for and limits of any liability. Presented in Figure 21.2 are topics that your company may want to consider including in your teaming agreements when you serve as the prime contractor. It is advisable to include a specific list of proposal-related information and materials (as presented previously in Table 21.2) as an attachment to your formal teaming agreement. Too often, proposal-related requirements and the specific process of information exchange are poorly defined and result in production challenges and delays throughout the proposal response life cycle. These topics include those for SF330s as well as RFPs and international procurements.

It is strongly suggested that your company's legal counsel review the terms and conditions of all teaming agreements into which you enter.

---

2 I have had the experience of coordinating a major IRS proposal effort that involved a team of companies, some of which were important members of competitor proposal teams. The logistics of conducting effective strategy meetings and comprehensive review sessions were quite challenging.

Chapter 22

Pursuing international business and structuring international proposals

The time and space buffers that used to limit a company's exposure to changes are gone. Business now is vulnerable to anything that happens anywhere instantly.
—Marc J. Wallace, Jr., Center for Workforce Effectiveness,
    quoted in *Industry Week*

22.1 Overview

The benefits of doing business in the international market can be substantial; however, "[c]ompanies that want to operate globally must have a global mind-set" [1]. In 2012 and beyond, your firm's business opportunities will probably be linked very closely to unfamiliar cultures and customs. Advances in information and telecommunication technology have intensified competition in product and financial markets during the past 20 years, as noted by Marina Whitman and Rosabeth Moss Kanter [2]. And new and different trade, economic, and business models are likely to become necessary to understand and implement within your own company. Professor Vijay Govindarajan of Dartmouth College's Amos Tuck School of Business Administration suggests that "companies must open themselves to cultural diversity and be ready to adopt best practices and good ideas regardless of their country of origin" [1]. Pulitzer Prize winner Thomas L. Friedman argues that the competitive playing fields between industrialized and emerging market nations are leveling, and indeed "flattening." Friedman's book, *The World Is Flat 3.0: A Brief History of the Twenty-First Century,* (2007) is important reading for any company planning international expansion.

Many large U.S. high-tech firms have doubled their size in the global marketplace. And the Peoples' Republic of China, the Republic of Korea (South Korea), and Mexico are assuming leading economic roles, according to Franklin Root, author of *Entry Strategies for International Markets* [3]. *The Economist* (September 10, 2011, p. 86) has projected China and India to be among the countries with the greatest share of world Gross Domestic Product (GPD), trade, and net captial exports by 2030. Indeed, the United States is predicted to be number two in the world in terms of these measures. Root sees the transformation of the international economy as "a geographical extension of the industrial revolution that started in Great Britain more than two centuries ago" [3]. He asserts that "[t]o survive and prosper..., companies will need to develop new strategies. For the truth is that today all business firms—small or large, domestic or international—must strive for profits and growth in an international economy that features enormous flows of products, technology, intellectual and financial capital, and enterprise among countries. In this economy, no market is forever safe from foreign competition. And so even when companies stay at home, sooner or later they learn from hard experience that there are no domestic markets, only global markets" [4].

The losses associated with international business, however, can be devastating. Contract awards can actually result in severe financial losses and liabilities for the selling firm, depending upon the type of the contract and terms and conditions of that contract. Time delays in RFP or tender release dates are frequent, so booking and sales projections should be conservative [5]. A significant challenge associated with conducting international business in many countries (particularly developing nations) is supplying the technical and programmatic expertise, as well as the funding—all as a package to the host country. Two examples of funding sources are the World Bank, headquartered in Washington, D.C., and the Asian Development Bank, centered in Manila in the Philippines. The

World Bank receives its resources from industrialized nations and from tapping the world's financial capital markets. Projects funded by the World Bank are not limited geographically, whereas the Asian Development Bank is a lending institution serving only the Pacific Rim [6].

22.2 Where in the world to begin?

As a small U.S. business, the international marketing arena can certainly appear overwhelming. There are, however, several important starting points that can maximize your time and energy when preparing to market your company's goods, services, and knowledge overseas. Among the U.S. small businesses with successful penetration of the international marketspace are S3 International of Milwaukee, Wisconsin; JQ American Corp. of Hayward, California; and PRTech LLC of Honolulu, Hawaii. And keep in mind that according to the U.S. Department of Commerce in 2008, 42% of all U.S. exporters had fewer than 19 employees.[1]

- *Export.gov,* the U.S. government's export portal (http://export.gov). The Export.gov community is comprised of federal government organizations involved in opening foreign markets and promoting the export of U.S. products and services. The Export.gov Website is the gateway for the U.S. public to access a broad range of export assistance, export finance, training, market research, and trade advocacy services.

  The U.S. Department of Commerce and SBA launched an online tool in 2010 to help small businesses interested in exporting to tap into global marketplace (see http://www.export.gov/begin). This is part of the National Export Initiative (NEI) launched by President Obama through Executive Order in March 2010.

- *Featured U.S. Exporter (FUSE)* is a directory of U.S. products featured on U.S. Commerical Service's Websites around the world. FUSE gives your company the opportunity to target specific markets in the local language of business.

- *Export Yellow Pages* (http://www.exportyellowpages.com) is a public-private partnership of the U.S. Department of Commerce and Global Publishers LLC. The primary objective is to introduce U.S. companies and their products and services to the global marketplace.

---

[1] According to the April 2011 *Trade and Economy: A Small Business Report,* 97% of identified U.S. exporters were small businesses. A total of 281,668 small businesses exported from the United States in 2008.

- *Small Business Exporting Association of the United States* (SBEA; http://www.sbea.org), the largest nonprofit association representing small-business exporters. SBEA also provides its members with networking opportunities and cost-saving tools.

- *BuyUSA.gov* (http://www.buyusa.gov/home/). The U.S. Commercial Service helps U.S. companies find new international business partners in worldwide markets.

- *The Trade Americas* (http://export.gov/tradeamericas/index.asp). The Trade Americas Web site brings together the resources of U.S. Commercial Service offices in 16 countries and State Department sections at U.S. Embassies in 8 additional markets, providing your company with a single point of access to regional trade events, their extensive services, and research covering markets throughout the region. The Trade Americas site also provides information on the existing and proposed free-trade agreements throughout the region, market research, best prospects in the region, trade event lists, industry-specific information, business service providers, useful links, and key contacts.

- *The Economist Intelligence Unit (EIU)* (http://www.eiu.com). The Economist Intelligence Unit is a leading provider of country, industry, and management analysis. Its mission is to provide timely and reliable analyses for making successful global decisions.

  The U.S. SBA maintains an Office of International Trade (OIT; http://www.sba.gov/about-offices-content/1/2889). A good place to begin is the SBA publication *Breaking into the Trade Game: A Small Business Guide to Exporting, Third Edition,* (http://archive. sba.gov/idc/groups/public/documents/sba_homepage/ serve_entire.pdf).

- *Trade.gov* (http://trade.gov/). This is the Web site of the International Trade Administration (ITA) of the Department of Commerce. ITA's mission is to strengthen the competitiveness of U.S. industry, promote trade and investment, and ensure fair trade and compliance with trade laws and agreements. Trade.gov provides your business with access to ITA's information and services regarding U.S. international trade policy.

- *A Basic Guide to Exporting 10th Edition (2008)* (http://unzco.com/ regre/eireg.htm#basic). This 2008 publication of the U.S. Department of Commerce was created in cooperation with Unz & Co., Inc, and costs $18.

22.3 The importance of the World Bank Group

The World Bank is not a "bank" in the common sense, but rather is one of the United Nations' specialized agencies. The World Bank centers its efforts on reaching the eight Millennium Development Goals (MDGs), which were agreed to by UN members in 2000 and are aimed at sustainable poverty reduction.

With more than $20 billion in new loans each year, the World Bank is the largest global provider and coordinator of developmental and infrastructure assistance, which takes a financial, as well as technical, form. The World Bank is owned by its 187 member countries, with the largest industrialized nations—the Group of Seven or G7[2]—controlling about 45% of the Bank's shares. The board of governors and the Washington-based, 24 full-time-member board of directors of the World Bank, however, represent all member countries. Of note is that a central tenant of the evolving role of the World Bank is to build it into a world-class knowledge bank. In FY1998, prototype knowledge management systems (country-specific best practices, lessons learned, success stories) in education and health were established under the direction of the bank's then president, James D. Wolfensohn[3] [7]. The bank's current and proactive Knowledge for Development (K4D) program is a vital case in point. It aims to enhance the capacity of development-oriented organizations in client countries to achieve greater impact through the application of knowledge management tools and practices. The World Bank finances more than 300 new projects each year, which involve nearly 30,000 individual contracts. Projects financed span AIDS testing in Ukraine, job skills in Afghanistan's urban growth centers for girls and young women, education of girls in Bangladesh, basic health care delivery in Mexico, and helping Timor-Leste rebuild following independence. Specific projects include the African Virtual University (AVU), which became an intergovernmental organization; the Millennium Science Initiative in Chile, designed to boost Chile's science sector; and the SEECALINE community-based nutritional program in Madagascar. Together, the International Bank for Reconstruction and Development (IBRD), the International Development Association (IDA), and the

---

2   The G7 members are Canada, France, Germany, Italy, Japan, the United Kingdom, and the United States. The addition of Russia led to the emergence of the G8. These countries meet annually to address major economic and political issues facing their domestic societies as well as the international community as a whole. The 38th annual summit was scheduled to be held in Chicago in 2012.

3   Robert B. Zoellick is the current president of the World Bank.

Multilateral Investment Guarantee Agency (MIGA) comprise the World Bank Group, which also works closely with the International Finance Corporation (IFC) which is headquartered in Washington, D.C.

The publication called *UN Development Business* (UNDB), which is released by the United Nations (UN) Department of Public Information and sells for $590 per year (print) and $550 (online), contains comprehensive World Bank and UN procurement information. (See http://www.devbusiness.com.) The paper version is printed and mailed twice monthly. The online version is updated several times a week. This publication includes invitations to bid on World Bank and UN projects as well as information about projects financed by the African, Asian, Caribbean, and Inter-American Development Banks; the European Bank for Reconstruction and Development; and the North American Development Bank. [Established in 1959, the Inter-American Development Bank (IDB) is an international financial institution that finances economic and social development in Latin America and the Caribbean. Its loans exceeded $12.1 billion in 2010.]

UN Development Business provides a monthly operational summary report listing all of the projects being considered for financing by the World Bank; general and specific procurement notices to supply the products and services required to carry out World Bank–financed projects; and contract awards for major projects. General Procurement Notices (GPNs) alert potential bidders to the overall types of goods and services needed for a project and invite firms to express interest in being placed on lists to receive further announcements. Specific Procurement Notices (SPNs) identify the specific goods and services needed for a project including how to obtain bidding documents, their cost, and the bid deadline date. Your company can subscribe to this important publication at:

> http://www.devbusiness.com
> Tel. (212)963-1516
> Fax (212)963-1381
> E-mail: dbsubscribe@un.org

The UN Business Directory (http://www.devbusiness.com/directory.asp) lists Web sites of companies and consulting firms involved in international business. This list can be used for advertising products and services and for locating partners already doing business overseas.

The International Bank for Reconstruction and Development and the International Development Association provide average annual lending commitments for investment projects of $10 billion to $15 billion a year. These funds are used by recipient countries to purchase goods and equipment, construct civil works, and obtain the consulting services needed to implement these projects. Each project may involve many separate contracts and business opportunities for suppliers, contractors, and consultants worldwide. Companies, academic institutions, nongovernmental organizations (NGOs), and individuals from member countries of the World Bank are eligible to compete for these business opportunities. Within any given project, there can be literally hundreds of business opportunities varying in size from as little as a few thousand dollars to as large as tens of millions of dollars.

When pursuing business opportunities in projects financed by the World Bank, it is essential to understand that *the implementing agency in the recipient country is responsible for procurement.* All contracts are between the borrower (usually the government department that is its implementing agency) and the supplier, contractor, or consultant. The World Bank's role is to make sure that the borrower's work is done properly; that the agreed procurement procedures are observed; and that the entire process is conducted with efficiency, fairness, transparency, and impartiality.

More information on this process can be found in the *Guidelines: Procurement of Goods, Works, and Non-Consulting Services under IBRD Loans and IDA Credits and Grants,* dated January 2011 (http://web. worldbank.org/WBSITE/EXTERNAL/PROJECTS/PROCUREMENT/ 0,,contentMDK:20060840~pagePK:84269~piPK:60001558~theSitePK:8 4266,00.html]. For comprehensive guidance, you should refer to the *Resource Guide to Consulting, Supply and Contracting Opportunities in Projects Financed by the World Bank* (http://web.worldbank.org/ WBSITE/EXTERNAL/PROJECTS/PROCUREMENT/0,,contentMDK: 20109705~pagePK:84269~piPK:60001558~theSitePK:84266,00.html).

eConsultant2 is the World Bank Group's portal to enable your participation in solicitations for consulting opportunities on Bank Group Operations for both individual consultants and firms. (http://web. worldbank.org/WBSITE/EXTERNAL/OPPORTUNITIES/EXTCORP PROCUREMENT/0,,contentMDK:2589227~menuPK:7092717~pagePK :64147231~piPK:64147158~theSitePK:84266,00.html).

World Bank borrowers are required to submit timely notification of bidding opportunities and to advertise these opportunities and expressions of interest. Invitations to bid or express interest for contracts under World Bank-financed projects can be found at the Development Gateway Market (http://www.dgmarket.com/). Currently, dgMarket publishes tender notices for projects funded by the African Development Bank, the Asian Development Bank, Europe Aid, European Commission, North American Development Bank, United States Agency for International Development

(USAID), Canadian International Development Agency (CIDA), and the World Bank among others. Current tenders are categorized into topic areas such as information and communications, transport, energy, services, finance, urban development, and agriculture and food.

To assess the qualifications of firms and to assist in-country borrowers who are trying to establish a short list of potential contractors, the World Bank and Inter-American Development Bank maintain an automated database of consulting firms interested in doing business on World Bank–financed projects. This database is called the Data on Consulting Firms (DACON) system at http://www.dgmarket.com/dacon.

Of note is that a private company cannot approach the World Bank directly to request financial assistance for a project in which it and the host country government are interested. Only the government of an eligible World Bank member can request such financing.

22.4 Your company's participation in United Nations procurements

The United Nations (UN), which follows U.S. government procurement methods and is very professional and methodical, is comprised of a variety of organizational entities such as agencies, organizations, commissions, programs, and funds. Each entity has a distinct mandate that addresses political, economic, social, scientific, or technical fields. Although each organization is responsible for its own procurement requirements, there are many commonalities in the procurement processes across the UN system. As part of fomer Secretary-General Kofi Annan's[4] reform of the United Nations, the procurement activities of the UN system underwent considerable change. *Why?* To make the process more efficient and cost-effective, as well as to maximize equity, openness, and integrity. To this end, a single portal, the United Nations Global Marketplace (UNGM), http://www.ungm.org, has been established to link all of the Web sites of all participating UN organizations. The United Nations, including its 18 UN-affiliated organizations, represents a global market of approximately $10 billion annually for all types of goods and services. The UNGM acts as a single portal through which the business community may register with the UN system, providing an excellent springboard to introduce your goods and services to many UN organizations, countries, and regions. The database facilitates the interchange of supplier information within the UN

---

4   The current Secretary-General is Ban Ki-Moon from the Republic of Korea.

system as information is made available to all UN organizations, and it acts as a procurement tool to shortlist suppliers for competitive bidding.

Also, the Inter-Agency Procurement Service Office (IAPSO) has developed booklets with practical tips on how to do business with the United Nations. *The General Business Guide, 20th Edition,* 2006 (http://www.iapso.org/pdf/gbg_ master.pdf) for potential suppliers of goods and services is a 139-page booklet that describes the procurement needs and procedures of all UN organizations (with mailing addresses, phone/fax numbers, and e-mail addresses) and indicates the dollar value of goods and services purchased during the year. *Doing Business with the UN System* can be downloaded at http://www.iapso.org/ pdf/ tips.pdf. *Doing Business with the United Nations Secretariat* is available at http://www.un.org/depts/ptd/pdf/pd_brochure.pdf.

In addition, the UN Procurement Division posts its current year acquisition plan at http://www.un.org/Depts/ptd/acquisition.htm. This plan offers a projection of requirements from offices and departments at UN Headquarters and offices away from Headquarters.

IAPSO was established by the United Nations Development Program (UNDP) in 1978 to assist its partner organizations within the UN system in the most economical acquisition of essential equipment and supplies. Originally based in New York, and designated the Interagency Procurement Services Unit (IAPSU), it moved to Geneva in 1982. In July 1989, the office was relocated to Copenhagen and renamed the Interagency Procurement Services Office (IAPSO). In January 2008, UNDP and IAPSO consolidated their business operations to strengthen the procurement capacities of the UN system.

22.5 European Bank for Reconstruction and Development (EBRD)

Established in 1991, the European Bank for Reconstruction and Development (EBRD; http://www.ebrd.com) assists 29 countries in central and eastern Europe and central Asia with privatization and entrepreneurship efforts and promotes structural and sectoral economic reforms. The EBRD encourages cofinancing and foreign direct investment from both the private and public sectors. The mandate of the EBRD stipulates that it must only work in countries that are committed to democratic principles. The EBRD's *Procurement Policies and Rules* (revised May 2010)—derived from Standard Bidding Documents (SBDs) developed and in use by the World Bank, the Asian Development Bank, and the Inter-American Development Bank—articulates the procurement guidelines to be followed in

EBRD-financed operations and establishes tendering procedures for use by clients when procuring goods and services following open tendering in operations financed by the EBRD. In addition, the EBRD *Procurement Policies and Rules* outlines how tenders are received, opened, and evaluated under open-tendering procedures for contracts financed by the European Bank for Reconstruction and Development. Invitations to tender, expressions of interest, contract award information, and other essential information regarding EBRD-funded contracts is available on the Bank's Web site at http://www.ebrd.com/saf/search.html?type=procurement_notice.

The term *EU* denotes the European Union (http://www.europa.eu.int), which now consists of 27 member nations that include Austria, Belgium, Bulgaria, Czech Republic, Denmark, Estonia, Finland, France, Germany, Greece, Hungary, Ireland, Italy, Latvia, Lithuania, Luxembourg, the Netherlands, Poland, Portugal, Romania, Spain, Sweden, and the United Kingdom. This group of European countries has decided to collaborate on a variety of significant areas that encompass a single economic market as well as a common foreign policy and legislative and judicial policies. The European Union came into existence as a result of the ratification of the Maastricht Treaty in November 1993; however, its roots can be traced back to the Treaty of Paris in 1951 and the Treaty of Rome in 1957. The EU consisted of three pillars: the European Parliament, the Council of the European Union, and the European Commission. The Treaty of Lisbon entered into force in December 2009, allowing the EU to address issues beyond the economic realm to include globalization, climatic and demographic changes, security, and energy. The European Investment Bank (EIB) serves as the European Union's financing institution.

Official Journal of the European Union

The *Official Journal of the European Union* (OJEU; http://eur-lex.europa.eu/JOIndex.do) provides a gateway to specialized resources for purchasers who wish to publish tender notices in the S series of the OJEC and suppliers who wish to search for business opportunities. The *Official Journal of the European Union* is the only periodical published every working day in all 23 official languages of the European Union. It consists of two related series (the L series for legislation and C series for information and notices) and a supplement (the S series for public tenders). Approximately 160,000 invitations to tender are published each year.

The MyTenders Web site (http://www.mytenders.org/?source=OJEC) is a tender publication and management service that enables suppliers to access high-value tenders that are listed by purchases in the OJEU), Tenders Direct (http://www.tendersdirect.com) by Millstream Associates Limited in Aberdeen, UK, provides access to more current government and utility company contracts in the United Kingdom and Europe. Tenders Direct is provided on a subscription basis; 24 business and support categories can be searched.

22.6 Asian Development Bank (ADB)

The Asian Development Bank (ADB), a multilateral development finance institution whose capital stock is owned by 67 member countries including the United States, is engaged in promoting the economic and social progress of its developing member countries in the Asia-Pacific region. Since the ADB began operations in December 1966, it has been a catalyst in promoting the development of one of the most populous and fastest growing regions in the world. ADB makes loans and equity investments, and provides technical assistance grants for the preparation and execution of development projects and programs, and also for advisory purposes. It promotes investment of public and private capital for development purposes. You can visit ADB on the Web at http://www.adb.org. Headquartered in Manila, Philippines, the ADB is led by a board of governors and board of directors. At the time of this writing, Haruhiko Kuroda was serving as the bank's eighth president, a seat he has held since 2005.

Like the World Bank, ADB's mandate to assist developing member countries in the Asia-Pacific region has resulted in the need to maintain an inventory of suitably qualified firms or organizations from its member countries that could act as consultants to provide services required for various projects assisted by the bank. The ADB's *Procurement Guidelines* (April 2010) for goods, works, and services can be downloaded in English at http://www.adb.org/Documents/Guildlines/Procurement/Guidelines-Procurcment.pdf. ADB's information on the capabilities and experience of firms or organizations is maintained in the ADB DACON system, the acronym for Data on Consultants. It is a computer inventory used by ADB to record the eligibility of such firms for possible engagement as well as their experience and qualifications for easy retrieval by ADB when needed. Procurement notices for ADB are found by country at http://www.adb.org/documents/adbbo/procurement.asp.

22.7 International market planning

In developing international marketing entry and marketing plans, keep in mind that your company is entering both a new country and a new market [8]. The entry mode (export, contractual, or investment) determines the amount of a company's control over the marketing program in the target country. For example, indirect exporting and pure licensing allow little or no control over the marketing program. Your company's international marketing plan should include objectives for sales volumes, market share, profits, and return on investment as well as resource allocations and a time schedule [9].

The U.S. Commercial Service, the trade promotion arm of the U.S. Department of Commerce, provides market research that is available free of charge to U.S. citizens and U.S. companies. Market research publications are available online at http://trade.gov/publications/.

- *International Trade Update:* A monthly newsletter on new trade opportunities and partnerships.
- *National Export Strategy,* 2011 Edition: Focuses on methods of implementing 70 recommendations made to President Obama regarding the National Export Initiative (NEI).

The Economist Intelligence Unit (EIU) out of London, England, publishes special reports on specific international marketing topics [10]. The EIU, http://www.eiu.com/public, is an information provider for companies establishing and managing operations across national borders anywhere in the world. Established 65 years ago in London, the organization now has a worldwide network of offices in London, New York, Hong Kong, Vienna, Singapore, and Tokyo. The EIU produces analyses and forecasts of the business and political environments in more than 200 countries. The EIU's new Industry Forecasts are 5-year economic forecasts for eight key industries. The service covers the world's 60 major economies, which account for more than 95% of global output and trade. The EIU is part of the Economist Group, which also publishes *The Economist* magazine.

Many small companies simply do not have the staff to dedicate to the time-consuming task of international marketing. There are local and regional trade programs designed to assist small businesses with identifying international markets. One such organization is the South-West Texas Border Small Business Development Center (SBDC) Network, which provides consulting and technical assistance to the small business community in the area of international trade, among others. Another example is the California Centers for International Trade Development (CITD). And in Virginia, there is the Virginia Economic Development Partnership (VEDP), which makes available 45 international trade consultants who can provide in-country market research and matchmaking with potential customers. Additionally, Pennsylvania's World Trade PA programs help companies in the Commonwealth to find new markets in other countries.

Because of the critical shortages of resources in small companies, international business must be a carefully planned and orchestrated process. Small companies successful in this field often have foreign shareholders who know the local environment and its pitfalls and processes. International market entry must become part of your strategic plan and marketing plan if it is to be pursued with the diligence that successful international business requires.

22.8 In-country partnerships

Creating ongoing business partnerships with the host country's key decision makers is essential to long-term marketing, proposal, and contractual success. Partnerships can be strengthened through scheduled in-country visits [be sure to work around major holidays and holy days such as Ramadan in Islamic countries, Setsubun in Japan, Carnival in Brazil, and Spring Festival (Chinese New Year)] that include social and community activities, reciprocal invitations to the United States, and establishment of offices in country. Well-managed representatives, agents, or distributors who understand the language, culture, and procurement laws and processes and are sensitive to the in-country political directions can be invaluable to your company's success. Cross-cultural considerations must be taken into account, so it is suggested that these representatives be employees or consultants of the buying country's nationality. Also, do not try to cover the whole world—develop a profitable beachhead in a country that your company knows already.

In-country partnerships can result in your company defining the technical requirements that will appear ultimately in the RFP or tender.

Your company might also consider establishing formal business partnerships with several select consulting firms in strategically important countries throughout the world. These firms can then function as in-country partners, providing important and personalized local support as well as facilitating worldwide coverage for your multinational clients.

22.9 Host country procurement environments

As in domestic U.S. business development efforts, long-term marketing and relationship building on a global scale are critical to your company's contract award success and long-term profitability. Understanding your international client includes his technical expectations, procurement and source selection cycle, business decision-making processes and framework, import-export regulations, cultural environment, language requirements, and political agenda. Detailed understanding extends to potential tax exposure, countertrade requirements, work visas required, host country law, U.S. treaties with the host country, quality assurance parameters, delivery and acceptance restrictions, payment parameters, currency restrictions [11], and U.S. Department of State trade controls, such as the International Traffic in Arms Regulations (ITAR) 2011. In certain countries (e.g., Brazil) and on specific types of procurements, your competitors will have the opportunity to openly and thoroughly review your proposal documents for the purpose of attempting to disqualify your submittal on technical grounds or procedural or administrative technicalities.

22.10 Import-export considerations and technology transfer

Time must be allocated in delivery schedules for any necessary U.S. Department of State approval or Department of Commerce licensing, such as in the case of advanced electronic equipment. "The international customer community wants to obtain as much technology from U.S. corporations as possible" [12].

The United States has export controls for two primary reasons: (1) national security (terrorism and weapons control) and (2) trade protection (supply shortages and crime control). The U.S. Directorate of Defense Trade Controls (DDTC), Bureau of Political-Military Affairs, in accordance with 22 U.S.C. 2778-2780 of the Arms Export Control Act (AECA) and the International Traffic in Arms Regulations (ITAR) (22 C.F.R. Parts 120-130), is charged with controlling the export and temporary import of defense articles and defense services covered by the United States Munitions List (USML). It has among its primary missions: (1) taking final action on license applications for defense trade exports, and (2) handling matters related to defense trade compliance, enforcement, and reporting. ITAR regulations prohibit the export of military articles and information as well as defense services to countries such as Iran, Iraq, Libya, North Korea, Syria, and Belarus.

22.11 Risk assessment

Your company may want to consider establishing a separate legal entity for the purpose of minimizing corporate exposure in the international arena. Carefully consider the following: taxes and duties, import-export quotas, host country legislation and regulations, language, host country culture, quality and audit standards, countertrade requirements, packaging or labeling standards, political issues and stability, currency exchange rates, foreign direct investment, customs paperwork and protocol, weather, religion, inspection and acceptance guidelines, in-country banking restrictions, and host country law.

22.12 Terms and conditions

Developing restrictive, risk-aware terms and conditions (Ts & Cs) is absolutely vital for international proposals. There are many challenges associated with resolving legal problems at an international level. Questions arise as to where geographically to try a particular case, which law should apply, and how to apply foreign laws. To help mitigate the problems inherent in such issues, include clauses in your Ts & Cs that address in detail which specific laws will obtain in any contractual disputes [13].

There are certainly risks associated with international payments, two of which are nonpayment and variations in the foreign exchange rate [14]. Such risk can be mitigated by stipulating cash in advance or an irrevocable confirmed letter of credit. This letter of credit is issued by the importer's bank and then confirmed by a bank in the exporter's (your company) country. Thus, your company does not have to depend on the importer for payment [15]. Be aware, however, that your competitors may be offering easier, more flexible, and therefore more attractive payment terms. U.S. exporters can obtain export credit insurance that protects against the risks of nonpayment for both commercial and political reasons from the FCIA Management Company, Inc. (FCIA), a wholly owned subsidiary of the Great American Insurance Company. Having this insurance can allow your company to extend credit on more favorable terms to overseas buyers and thus be more competitive.

Ts & Cs will vary depending on the product or service being provided to the host country or industry. A listing of frequently used line items found in Ts & Cs includes the following:

- Warranty terms, such as commencement of warranty and warranty for replacement parts;

- Warranty exclusions (for example, improper unpacking, installation, or treatment of equipment or unauthorized attempts to repair, reconfigure, or modify equipment);
- Extended warranty and maintenance;
- Limitations on liability;
- *Force majeure* (protects supplier from causality or cause beyond reasonable control, such as strikes, floods, riots, acts of governments, and war);
- Pricing for tasks beyond scope of work;
- U.S. government approvals;
- Taxes and duties;
- Dispute resolution [for example, arbitration under the Rules of Procedure of the International Chamber of Commerce (ICC), Paris, France];
- Excusable delays;
- Shipping and insurance;
- Contract termination;
- Acceptance criteria;
- Payment terms, schedule, and currency;
- Training;
- Documentation (it is critical to specify the language and dialect in which training manuals will be provided).

22.13 Ex-Im Bank of the United States assists small businesses

The Export-Import Bank of the United States (Ex-Im Bank; http://www.exim.gov) is the official export credit agency of the United States. With more than 77 years of experience, the Ex-Im Bank has supported more than $456 billion of U.S. exports, primarily to developing markets worldwide. The bank's mission is to assist in financing the export of U.S. goods and services to international markets. Led by Fred P. Hochberg, president and chairman, the Ex-Im Bank enables U.S. companies—large and small—to turn export opportunities into real sales that help to maintain and create U.S. jobs and contribute to a stronger national economy. In the period fiscal year 2005–2010, the Ex-Im Bank authorized financing to support $65.5 billion of U.S. exports worldwide. More than

$5 billion of this financing supported U.S. small business exports in FY2010 alone.

Global access for small business has become a top priority for the Ex-Im Bank as part of the National Export Initiative. The bank has a business development team dedicated to veteran-, women-, and minority-owned businesses.

The Ex-Im Bank does not compete with private-sector lenders but provides export financing products that fill gaps in trade financing. It assumes credit and country risks that the private sector is unable or unwilling to accept. The bank also helps to level the playing field for U.S. exporters by matching the financing that other governments provide to their exporters.

Ex-Im Bank provides working capital loan guarantees (pre-export financing), export credit insurance (postexport financing), and loan guarantees and direct loans (buyer financing). No transaction is too large or too small. On average, 87% of the bank's transactions directly benefitted U.S. small businesses in FY2010.

Importantly, there are U.S. Export Assistance Centers (EACs) located in major metropolitan areas throughout the United States. These centers serve as one-stop shops that are ready to provide your small- or medium-sized business with local export assistance. You can receive personalized assistance by professionals from the SBA, the U.S. Department of Commerce, the Ex-Im Bank, and other public and private organizations. For a listing of Export Assistance Centers near you, visit http://export.gov/eac.

General export information and development assistance are located on the SBA's Web site (http://www.sba.gov/about-offices-content/1/2889). A good place to begin is the SBA publication *Breaking into the Trade Game: A Small Business Guide to Exporting, Third Edition,* (http://archive.sba.gov/idc/groups/public/documents/sba_homepage/serve_entire.pdf).

22.14 Helpful Web-based resources and in-country support infrastructures for small businesses

The Web provides small businesses with a host of business development sites to support international marketing initiatives.

State Trade and Export Program (STEP)

http://www.sba.gov/content/state-trade-and-export-promotion-step-fact-sheet. This 3-year pilot trade and export initiative was authorized by the Small Business Jobs Act of 2010, and is funded by federal grants and matching state-level funds.

MERX: Canada's national electronic tendering service

http://www.merx.com. MERX is the most complete source of Canadian public tenders, private tenders, and U.S. tenders available in Canada. This Internet-based electronic tendering system was established and launched in 1997 by Cebra, the Bank of Montreal's electronic commerce company. The service is designed to improve access, increase competition, and provide a level playing field for small businesses competing for bidding opportunities within the public sector in Canada. At the present time, MERX provides the opportunity to bid on most Canadian federal government contracts. The system also posts opportunities for provincial governments: Ontario, New Brunswick, Nova Scotia, Manitoba, Prince Edward Island, Newfoundland and Labrador, Alberta, Saskatchewan, and Nunavut. MERX replaced Canada's existing Open Bidding System in October 1997.

e-Tendering.com (Hong Kong and Asia Pacific)

This Web site is mainly designed for displaying tender notices, contract award notices, and general terms and conditions for tenders. By subscribing to e-Tendering.com, you can log onto the system and enjoy additional functions such as quickly searching for tenders and awards, receiving automatic and personalized e-mail notifications, obtaining industry news and information, and submitting tender offers.

European Tenders Direct Procurement Gateway

The subscription-based Tenders Direct service (http://www.tendersdirect.co.uk) has been supplying information on UK tenders and contracts to companies since 1992. Twenty-four predefined categories help users quickly find relevant tenders. Keyword searching is also available.

European Commission Network Enterprise (Europe)

http://www.enterprise-europe-network.ec.europa.eu/index_en.htm. The Enterprise Europe Network brings together business support organizations from 49 countries and 580 member organizations. The European Commission launched a new strategy called Small Business, Big World, in 2011 to support small and medium-sized enterprises (SMEs) expand their businesses outside the European Union.

Middle East Association

Established in 1961, the Middle East Association (http://www.the-mea.co.uk/) is the United Kingdom's premier organization to promote trade and investment in the Middle East and North Africa, on behalf of its members. This independent, nonprofit association maintains close relations with British government departments, particularly the Foreign and Commonwealth office and UK Trade and Investment. In addition, the London-basd association has connections with overseas government ministries and departments and other official bodies as well as links with businesses and business organizations in the region.

Implementation of the new definition of small firms within the European Union (EU)

Micro, small, and medium-sized enterprises (SMEs) are very socially and economically important, because they represent 99% of the estimaged 19.3 million enterprises in the EU, based upon a World Bank report. These firms also provide approximately 65 million jobs and contribute to entrepreneurship and innovation. However, they faced particular difficulties that the EU and national legislation try to redress by granting various advantages to SMEs. A legally secure and user-friendly definition was necessary in order to avoid distortions in the single market. A single market is a customs union with common policies on product regulation and freedom of movement of all the factors of production (goods, services, capital, and labor). Examples of single markets include the European Union and the European Economic Area (EEA).

In May 2003, the European Commission adopted a new definition of micro as well as SMEs. This definition was aimed at promoting entrepreneurship, investment, and growth; facilitating access to venture capital; cutting administrative burdens; and increasing legal certainty. This definition was shaped by two rounds of extensive public consultation in 2001 and 2002. It maintains the different staff thresholds that define the categories of micro and SMEs. However, it provides for a substantial increase of the financial ceilings (turnover or balance sheet total), in particular as a result of inflation and productivity increases since 1996, the date of the first European Community SME definition.

Various provisions mean that the benefit of access to national SME support mechanisms and European programs supporting SMEs is reserved exclusively for those enterprises that have the characteristics of real SMEs (without the economic strength of larger groupings). To allow a smooth transition at EU and national level, the new definition will be used as of January 1, 2005. This modernization of the SME definition will have an impact on promoting growth, entrepreneurship, investments, and innovation. It will favor cooperation and clustering of independent enterprises. A July 2009 European Commission Assessment concluded that the SME definition has been applied throughout EU member states "without any notable difficulty."

At the EU level, almost every policy has an SME dimension. SMEs' special needs and concerns are incorporated into most EU policies and programs. The EU's Sixth Framework Programme for Research, Technological Development and Demonstration included more than € 2.1 billion to support SMEs' research and innovation efforts.

The revision ensures that enterprises that are part of a larger grouping—and could therefore benefit from a stronger economic backing than genuine SMEs—do not benefit from SME support schemes. The increase of the financial ceilings is designed to take into account subsequent price and productivity increases since 1996, however the head count ceilings remain fixed (see Table 22.1).

The European Charter for Small Enterprises was approved by EU leaders at the Feira European Council in June 2000. The charter calls on Member States and the commission to take action to support and

Enterprise Category	Headcount	Annual Turnover or Annual Balance Sheet Total	
Medium-sized	< 250	≤ € 50 million	≤ € 43 million
Small	< 50	≤ € 10 million	≤ € 10 million
Micro	< 10	≤ € 2 million	≤ € 2 million

Table 22.1 Categorization of Small and Medium-Sized Businesses within the European Union

encourage small enterprises in 10 key areas, which are still valid and applicable today:

1. Education and training for entrepreneurship;

2. Cheaper and faster start-up;

3. Better legislation and regulation;

4. Availability of skills;

5. Improving online access;

6. Getting more out of the Single Market;

7. Taxation and financial matters;

8. Strengthening the technological capacity of small enterprises;

9. Making use of successful e-business models and developing top-class small business support;

10. Developing stronger, more effective representation of small enterprises' interests at European Union and national levels.

UK Trade & Investment (UKTI)

UK Trade & Investment (http://www.tradepartners.gov.uk) is the British government organization that supports both companies in the United Kingdom trading internationally and overseas enterprises seeking to locate in the United Kingdom. This organization's trade services offer support to companies based in the United Kingdom to achieve their export potential. For those firms exporting for the first time or businesses experienced in international trade expanding into new markets, this organization can help develop export capabilities and provide expert advice, reliable data, and professional research. Its international trade teams are active in more than 200 posts worldwide and are available in more than 45 U.K. offices. UK Trade & Investment works closely with the English regional development agencies and the national development agencies in Scotland, Wales, and Northern Ireland.

SIMAP—Information Systems for European Public Procurement

http://simap.europa.eu/index_en.htm. The SIMAP portal provides access to the most important information about public procurement in Europe.

Irish Government eTenders Public Procurement

This site at http://www.e-tenders.gov.ie has been developed as part of the Irish government's strategy for the Implementation of eProcurement in the Irish public sector. The site is designed to be a central facility for all public-sector contracting authorities to advertise procurement opportunities and award notices. The site is managed by the National Public Procurement Policy Unit (NPPPU) of the Department of Finance.

On a daily basis, the site displays all public-sector procurement opportunities currently being advertised in the *Official Journal of the European Union* (OJEU), as well as other opportunities directly uploaded to the site from awarding authorities. At any given time, it will contain all open opportunities in the form of tender notices, prior indicative notices (PINs), and contract award notices (CANs). It also provides associated tender documents (where available) that can be downloaded from the site. Awarding authorities are encouraged to publish information on opportunities not currently being advertised in other media. In addition, the site has the functionality to allow awarding authorities to publish notices on the site that will then be sent to the OJEU automatically. The http://www.etenders.gov.ie site also provides background information on procurement rules and guidelines. These include European Directives and National Guidelines on the Public Procurement Process. The site offers the opportunity to widen the net of potential suppliers to the Irish public sector. There is no charge to contracting authorities for this service; the site is also freely available for use by the public.

The public-sector tender market in Ireland is worth about €14 billion annually. All of the procurement opportunities advertised in this market by Central and Local Government in Ireland (North and South) are published on the Tenders Ireland Web site (http://www.tendersireland.com).

THEMiS: The EC Procurement Legislation Guidance System

Public and utility procurement in the European Union is subject to regulation that articulates detailed procedures for awarding contracts. Achilles Information Ltd. is a specialist in this area of procurement, and provides both consultancy and software to help purchasers meet their commercial needs while complying with the legislation. Because of the complexity of the requirements of the EU procurement legislation, Achilles developed THEMiS (http://www.achilles.com/en/uk), a Web-based system designed by experts in the field of European Community procurement legislation to provide the tools to comply with the legislation easily and with minimum cost. The system also gives access to the latest news and information in the

United Kingdom, Europe, and beyond, where legislation on public procurement is becoming increasingly important.

Global Tenders

http://www.globaltenders.com/index.htm is a large database of international and national tenders and competitive bids from around the world. Full access is subscription based.

Tenders India

http://tenders.gov.in/innerpage.asp?choice=ot4 is the Indian government tenders information system.

Confederation of German trade fair and exhibition industries

For more than 100 years, the Association of the German Trade Fair Industry (AUMA; http://www. auma.de) has represented the interests of the trade fair industry on a national and international level in dealing with Parliament ministries, and authorities. AUMA, in close cooperation with the German Federal Ministry of Economics and Tchnology and also the Ministry of Food, Agriculture, and Consumer Protection prepares the official German trade fair program abroad. Within the framework of this program, the German federal government provides financial assistance for German companies' joint participation at foreign events, as well as for independent presentations by German industry abroad. AUMA's members include the central associations of German business (industry, trade, skilled trades), trade associations of the exhibiting and visiting industries, and the German trade fair and exhibition organizers, as well as the companies organizing foreign fair participation.

Germany is a leading site for international trade fairs. German trade fair organizers planned to hold 275 trade fairs in 37 countries in 2012. More than 150 major international trade fairs and exhibitions attracted 10 million visitors in 2010. For German companies, trade fairs constitute a vital vehicle for business-to-business communication.

UBIFRANCE—The French Trade Commission Portal

UBIFRANCE, the French agency for international business development, is directed by France's Ministry for the Economy, Industry & Employment. With 64 trade commissions in 44 countries, UBIFRANCE provides business information, consultancy, and promotional operations to assist French-based companies in their development of export markets (http://www.ubifrance.com).

Japan External Trade Organization

Japan External Trade Organization (JETRO; http://www.jetro.go.jp) is a nonprofit, Japanese government–related organization dedicated to promoting mutually beneficial trade and invesetment between Japan and other nations around the globe. Established in 1958 to promote Japanese exports abroad, JETRO's focus in the twenty-first centry has shifted towards promoting foreign direct investment (FDI) into Japan, and helping small to medium size Japanese firms to maximize their global export potential.

Backed by a worldwide network comprising JETRO Headquarters Tokyo, JETRO Osaka, (IDE), 36 branches throughout Japan, and 77 overseas, JETRO is helping Japanese enterprises, particularly small and medium-sized enterprises, build stronger business ties in the Association of Southeast Asian Nations (ASEAN) countries and the rest of East Asia, thereby stimulating the Japanese economy.

JETRO focuses on promoting foreign direct investment in Japan— including greater inflows of capital, technologies, know-how, and intellectual assets—to stimulate the Japanese economy, increase employment, and enable Japan to continue demonstrating leadership in the global economy. This organization also assists Japanese small and medium-sized enterprises in the export of high-quality products, technologies, and designs to the global market.

In addition, JETRO continues to carry out economic research overseas and collects extensive information for dissemination to business circles. JETRO also provides a variety of other valuable services and support, including the organization of exhibitions and trade fairs and the dispatch of international trade and investment missions. At the JETRO Web site, users can locate the Trade Tie-up Promotion Program (TTPP), an online service that helps companies find each other for international business tie-ups.

Asia-Pacific Economic Cooperation

The Asia-Pacific Economic Cooperation (APEC; http://www.apecsec.org.sg) was established in 1989 in response to the growing interdependence among Asia-Pacific economies. Begun as an informal dialogue group, APEC has since become the primary regional vehicle for facilitating economic growth, cooperation, trade, and investment in the Pacific Rim.

Its 21 member nations include the Philippines, Australia, New Zealand, Peru, Japan, Hong Kong, Singapore, Canada, the United States, Mexico, People's Republic of China, Taiwan, Russia, and Vietnam. The goals of this cooperative, multilateral economic and trade forum are to advance trade and investment liberalization, business facilitation, and economic and technical cooperation. As of 2010, APEC's member economies bring a combined 54% of world gross domestic product and account for 44% of global trade. Ambassador Muhamad Noor Yacob from Malaysia is the 2011 executive director of the APEC Secretariat. SMEs account for more than 90% of the business in the APEC region, and employ up to 80% of the workforce.

Tender.Net—Australia

Since its conception in 1989, Information Network Fully Online (I.N.F.O.; http://www.tenders.net.au/), an Australian organization, has been a world leader in electronic tendering and procurement systems. Tenders.Net offers a complete tendering and procurement system for firms seeking to purchase goods and services in Australia, New Zealand, and the Pacific Islands. In addition, the site offers a thorough information and submission service for firms seeking to supply goods and services. AusTENDER (https://www.tenders.gov.au) is the site for the Australian Government's tender system.

Australian Trade Commission (Austrade)

Established in 1985, the Australian Trade Commission (Austrade; http://www.austrade. gov.au) is the Australian government agency that helps Australian companies win overseas business for their products and services by reducing the time, cost, and risk involved in selecting, entering, and developing international markets. Operating an international network of offices in 102 locations in 55 countries (per the Australian Trade Commission Annual Reprot 2010–11), Austrade is able to identify potential buyers, accurately match Australian suppliers with interested overseas contacts, and arrange introductions. Austrade maintains an export hotline, provides export consulting services, coordinates Australian stands at more than 100 international trade fairs annually, and also offers financial assistance to Australian exporters.

GeBIZ—Singapore Govenment

http://www.gebiz.gov.sg is the Singapore government's one-stop e-procurement portal.

22.15 British-American Business Council

An association of British-American chambers of commerce and business associations, the British-American Business Council [BABC; http://www.babc.org/; 52 Vanderbilt Avenue, 20th Floor, New York, NY 10017; tel. (212)661-4060; fax (212)661-4074] is based in major cities throughout North America and the United Kingdom. It is the largest transatlantic business organization, representing more than 2,500 companies. The BABC's objectives are to support the unique business partnership between the United States and the United Kingdom and to ensure its continuing vitality; to help its member associations provide business development and business intelligence services to their member companies; and to provide a broader, transatlantic business network for these member companies. Founded in 1993, the BABC now includes two associate organizations in Canada and Mexico. The commercial interactions between the United States and United Kingdom represent the most substantial business relationship between any two countries in the world. The United Kingdom is the largest overseas investor in the United States with $57 billion invested in 2008, according to the Organization for International Investment's *Foreign Direct Investment in the United States* (March 18, 2009). U.S. companies provide employment for about a million people in the United Kingdom, and U.K. companies employ about a million people in the United States.

The BABC is governed by a board of directors, on which all its member associations are represented, and an executive committee. The BABC's Chief Executive Secretariat are based in New York.

22.16 U.S. Trade and Development Agency

The U.S. Trade and Development Agency [USTDA; http://www.tda.gov; 1000 Wilson Boulevard, Suite 1600, Arlington, VA 22209; tel. (703)875-4357; fax (703)875-4009] assists in the creation of jobs for Americans by helping U.S. companies pursue overseas business opportunities. The hallmark of USTDA assistance is establishing links between U.S. companies and overseas project sponsors. In 2008, USTDA awarded 94% of all FAR-governed contracts to small businesses. Through the funding of feasibility studies, orientation visits, specialized training grants, business workshops, and various forms of technical assistance, TDA enables American businesses to compete for infrastructure and industrial projects in middle-income and developing countries. Procurement notices for USTDA direct contracts, such as definitional missions, can be accessed through the Federal Business Opportunities Web site (http://www.fbo. gov). Small and minority-owned U.S. firms that wish to be included in USTDA's consultant database and considered for future Desk Study and Definitional Mission solicitations should register online at https://www.tda.gov/consultantdb/.

22.17 U.S. Agency for International Development

Established in 1961 by President John F. Kennedy, the United States Agency for International Development (USAID; http://www.usaid.gov) is the independent government agency that provides economic development and humanitarian assistance to advance U.S. economic and political interests overseas. The Office of Small and Disadvantaged Business Utilization and Minority Resource Center (OSDBU/MRC) is the initial point of contact at USAID for U.S. small businesses, small disadvantaged businesses, women-owned small businesses, HUBZone small businesses, and service-disabled veteran-owned small businesses. OSDBU/MRC is a small business advocacy and advisory office with the responsibility for ensuring that these enterprises receive access to USAID programs. The office serves as an information clearinghouse for U.S. small businesses, counsels small businesses on how to do business with USAID, and examines USAID buying needs for possible set-asides for 8(a) and other small businesses prior to publication on the FedBizOpps Web site. In addition, OSDBU/MRC reviews all prime contracts to identify subcontracting opportunities for small businesses.

An Office of Small and Disadvantaged Business Utilization exists in all U.S. federal agencies in accordance with Public Laws 95-507 and 100-656 to ensure the participation of U.S. small businesses, small disadvantaged businesses, women-owned small businesses, HUBZone small businesses, and service-disabled veteran-owned small businesses in federal procurement opportunities.

The USAID business site (http://www.usaid.gov/business/) is your one-stop place for finding important information to get you started. Contracts are awarded primarily for technical assistance but also for commodities and/or equipment, transportation services, and occasionally construction. Grants are awarded for a variety of programs—some recurring (e.g., Food for Peace grants and other grant programs exclusively for Private Voluntary Organizations)—and some for unique nonrecurring programs. All contracts and grants issued ultimately support objectives of that part of the U.S. foreign assistance program managed by USAID.

Established in 1994 as a U.S. Agency for International Development program (it is now a part of the U.S. Commerical Service of the Department of Commerce), the Global Trade Network (GTN; http://www. usgtn.net/) has worked to facilitate sustainable economic growth in developing countries and emerging markets through business links and technology transfer. In 2002, GTN launched an Internet-based trade facilitation platform to further spur trade between companies located in the United States and developing nations. Since that time, the GTN trade platform has become a leading worldwide provider of international trade lead services. GTN's trade services include trade and investment business matching services, technology transfer, trade lead follow-up services, trade financing referrals, and market information. Since 2002, GTN has achieved successes, including these:

- Facilitated more than $345 million in potential transactions;
- Generated more than 4,000 trade and investment leads;
- Assisted with more than 350,000 matches.

International business planning resources for small companies in the United States include the Federation of International Trade Associations (FITA), founded in 1984 and located in Reston, Virginia (http://www.fita. org). This site has links to more than 8,000 international trade and import-export Web sites.

United States International Trade Commission

The United States International Trade Commission (USITC; http://www. usitc.gov) is an independent, nonpartisan, quasijudicial federal agency, with broad investigative responsibilities on matters of trade that provides objective trade expertise to both the legislative and executive branches of government, determines the impact of imports on U.S. industries, and directs actions against certain unfair trade practices, such as patent, trade-mark, and copyright infringement. USITC analysts and economists investigate and publish reports on U.S. industries and the global trends that affect them.

International Trade Administration

The International Trade Administration (ITA; http://trade.gov), which is an organization within the U.S. Department of Commerce, helps U.S. businesses participate fully in the growing global marketplace. ITA provides practical information to help you select your markets and products. It also ensures that you have access to international markets as required by U.S. trade agreements.

Guidelines on international business

Take full advantage of the numerous free or modestly priced exporter training and mentoring conferences that are held across the United States. Several examples include:

- Asia/Pacific Business Outlook Conference, sponsored by the University of Southern California (USC);
- National Export Conference, sponsored by the Capital Region of the Maryland Small Business Development Center;
- Small-Business Export Conferences, such as the one in 2011 sponsored by United States Representative Bill Cassidy in Louisiana;
- Export Matchmaker Trade Fair & Conference series held in Tampa, Florida, and sponsored by the U.S. Department of Commerce Commercial Services;
- STEP Export Assistance for Small Business program, sponsored by the Minnesota Trade Office;
- Alabama International Trade Center programs convened through the University of Alabama;
- U.S. Small Business Administration's "Export 101" workshops (e.g., Aberdeen, Maryland).

Organizations such as the Colorado Office of Economic Development and International Trade sponsor incoming foreign buyer delegations to meet with Colorado-based businesses.

When conducting international business, get paid in U.S. dollars, free of local taxes and other withholding. Try to avoid filing a tax return in the country in which you are doing business. Ensure that all terms and conditions are clearly stipulated in the contract. One area that requires special attention is maintenance of equipment over time. The "boundary conditions," that is, who is responsible for what service and under what particular conditions (e.g., virtual, in-person), must be articulated for your financial protection.

We now turn our attention in the next chapter to preparing for graduation form the SBA 8(a) program.

ENDNOTES

1. From "Test Your Global Mindset," *Industry Week*, November 2, 1998, p. 12.

2. Whitman, Marina, and Rosabeth Moss Kanter, "A Third Way? Globalization and the Social Role of the American Firm," *Washington Quarterly*, Spring 1999.

3. Root, Franklin R., *Entry Strategies for International Markets*, revised and expanded, New York: Lexington Books, 1994, p. 1.

4. Root, Franklin R., *Entry Strategies for International Markets*, revised and expanded, New York: Lexington Books, 1994, p. 19.

5. Flagler, Carolynn, "The ANY Aspects of International Proposals," *Contract Management*, March 1995, p. 13.
   Franklin Root suggests that "[f]or most companies the entry strategy time horizon is from three to five years, because it will take that long to achieve enduring market performance." Root, Franklin R., *Entry Strategies for International Markets*, revised and expanded, New York: Lexington Books, 1994, p. 22.

6. Conceived in 1944 at the United Nations Monetary and Financial Conference held in the United States, the World Bank is a multilateral development institution whose purpose is to assist its developing member countries further their economic and social progress. The term *World Bank* refers to two legally and financially distinct entities: the International Bank for Reconstruction and Development (IBRD) and the International Development Association (IDA). The IBRD and IDA have three related functions: to lend funds, to provide economic advice and technical assistance, and to serve as a catalyst to investment by others. The IBRD finances its lending operations primarily from borrowing in the world capital markets. IDA extends assistance to the poorest countries on easier terms, largely from resources provided by its wealthier members. (See *The World Bank Annual Report 1994*, Washington, D.C.: The World Bank.)

7. *The World Bank Annual Report 1998*, Washington, D.C.: The World Bank; http://www.worldbank.org/html/extpb/annrep98/overview.htm.

8. Root, Franklin R., *Entry Strategies for International Markets*, revised and expanded, New York: Lexington Books, 1994, pp. 25–26.

9. Root, Franklin R., *Entry Strategies for International Markets*, revised and expanded, New York: Lexington Books, 1994, pp. 41–42, 44.
   An entry mode is "an institutional arrangement that makes possible the entry of a company's products, technology, human skills, management

or other resources into a foreign country." Root, Franklin R., *Foreign Market Entry Strategies*, New York: AMACOM, 1987, p. 5. See also Erramilli, M. Krishna, and C. P. Rao, "Choice of Foreign Market Entry Modes by Service Firms: Role of Market Knowledge," *Management International Review*, Vol. 30, 1990, pp. 135–150.

10. Douglas, Susan P., C. Samuel Craig, and Warren J. Keegan, "Approaches to Assessing International Marketing Opportunities for Small- and Medium-Sized Companies," *Columbia Journal of World Business*, 1982, p. 27.

11. Flagler, Carloynn, "The ANY Aspects of International Proposals," *Contract Management*, March 1995, pp. 14, 16, 19.

    A common area of tax liability exposure relates to sending technical staff into the buying country to provide technical support and training. This type of technical support is often subject to taxes. *Countertrade* refers to a mandated purchase requirement imposed on the foreign seller by the buying community or its government.

12. Flagler, Carolynn, "The ANY Aspects of International Proposals," *Contract Management*, March 1995, p. 17.

13. See McCubbins, Tipton F., "Three Legal Traps for Small Businesses Engaged in International Commerce," *Journal of Small Business Management*, Vol. 32, July 1994, pp. 95–103.

14. Root, Franklin R., *Entry Strategies for International Markets*, revised and expanded, New York: Lexington Books, 1994, p. 97.

15. Root, Franklin R., *Entry Strategies for International Markets*, revised and expanded, New York: Lexington Books, 1994, p. 98.

Chapter **23**

Preparing for graduation from the 8(a) program

Planning, positioning, and preparing for successful transition out of the U.S. Small Business Administration's (SBA) 8(a) program must begin years in advance of your small business's actual date of 8(a) graduation. "The day you go into the 8(a) program is the day you have to start thinking about putting things in place and supporting yourself once you get out," said Amos Otis, chief executive officer of SoBran, Inc., a successful 8(a) graduate located in Fairfax, Virginia [1]. The decisions that you as a business leader make regarding the following aspects of your company can have profound impact on your long-term success as an organization.

- *Adding the right key staff:* Be willing to invest in key staff with proven records of professional results within specific areas of competence, and who are ready, willing, and able to be both "thinkers" and "doers." My direct experience suggests that you will want to strongly consider key staff who are "player-coaches," that is, who have a big-picture business view with an over-the-horizon perspective coupled with a can-do, hands-on, results-driven work ethic. Strongly consider investing in, developing, and honing the competitive business skills necessary for your success in the full-and-open competitive arena. Building marketing and proposal development infrastructures and staffing them with seasoned, proven performers are pivotal steps in that process.

Be aware, however, that the people whom you bring into your organization early in your company's tenure in the 8(a) program may or may not be the right staff for success in the full-and-open competitive marketspace. Preparation for 8(a) graduation might well necessitate a change in people assets.

- *Implementing a forward-looking incentive program:* Early in your company's corporate life, establish and continuously upgrade a straightforward, well-documented, and well-communicated incentive program for staff professionals in all areas of your organization, including business development, operations, and infrastructure. Everyone has customers for whom they must provide exemplary customer care, whether those customers are internal (within your company) or external (government agencies, teaming partners, vendors, banking institutions, and auditing entities, for example). Serving those customers in such a manner as to generate and sustain genuine customer enthusiasm should be incentivized in a meaningful and tangible manner. Be forward-looking with your incentive program. Make it as aggressive as possible to retain staff who deliver important business results on an ongoing basis.

  Two other critical areas to incentivize are *knowledge-sharing* and *innovative thinking and results.* Harvard University's Michael Porter asserts that innovation is the most critical driver and determinant of sustainable competitive advantage. Also, your company will need to generate sustainable competitive advantage both during and following your participation in the 8(a) program.

- *Building a knowledge-sharing culture:* Establish and propagate a business culture in which trust-based knowledge-sharing is encouraged, institutionalized, and rewarded. That sharing should span a knowledge of customers, competitors, market trends, current and emerging technologies, business processes, company contractual performance, and staff capabilities, among many others. In our increasingly globalized knowledge economy, organizations that can harness and leverage their resident knowledge for near-real-time decision support, agile positioning in the marketplace, and continuous process improvement will have a greater likelihood of long-term business success. Knowledge-sharing allows your company to function as a learning organization, in the words of Peter Senge, and as an ambidextrous organization, as articulated by Michael L. Tushman and Charles A. O'Reilly in the *Harvard Business Review*.

Regular "Lunch-n-Learn" or brown-bag seminars are of direct benefit to share information across traditional boundaries, such as business development and operations. You might have BD staff give a 15-minute overview of the importance and business value of an upcoming opportunity. Operations managers and select staff might present a 15-minute overview of an emerging technology area, such as green cloud computing or virtual desktop infrastructure (VDI).

- *Ensuring that everyone is a marketeer:* Instill in each and every staff person in your company that they have a critical marketing role—from the receptionist to the on-site project manager to the recruiter and the folks in proposal development. Your receptionist imparts the first impression of your company to government staff, large business prime contractors, subcontractors, banking institutions, and so forth. Your on-site project manager is the day-to-day "face" of your company to the customer and also must build cohesion and company loyalty among your staff on the customer's site. Your recruiter is in the business of attracting human talent into your organization. He or she is also accountable for filling open positions on contracts as quickly as possible with highly qualified staff to meet performance metrics and to ensure full customer satisfaction with your organization's capacity to meet workload fluctuations. Your recruiter also helps the project team to deliver full continuity of operations. Also, proposal professionals have the key role of telling fact-based stories about your company in written and presentation format that sell your human talent and contractual experience.

- *Building your company into your customer's decision pathways:* Through a sustained and carefully targeted corporate communications program, articulate and disseminate your company's brand and value proposition. This should be done at both the business development and day-to-day operations level.

- *Pursuing and implementing industry-standard certifications, accreditations, and processes:* The simple fact is that the federal government is placing increasing emphasis upon such certifications, accreditations, and industry-leading processes as ISO 9001:2008, SEI CMMI® Maturity Level (ML), ITIL (ISO 20000, the codification of ITIL as a standard), Six Sigma, Lean, IEEE, Earned Value

Management (EVM), Project Management Professional (PMP) and emerging Agile project management methodologies[1], DCAA-approved cost accounting systems, and Cost Accounting Standards (CAS)-compliant procurement systems. More and more RFPs and RFSs have requirements for these and related value-added recognitions and processes. To prepare to compete effectively in the full-and-open marketspace, it is prudent to pursue relevant certifications and appraisals as soon as possible in your company's life cycle.

- *Pursue full-and-open contractual opportunities:* From a business development and company valuation perspective, it is also important to pursue non-8(a) contract opportunities several years in advance of graduation from the program. Winning full-and-open competitions is critical to your company's confidence in itself as well as the confidence of teaming partners and banking institutions in your company.

- *Letting loose of the corporate reins:* Delegation of authority inside your company is an important step to put in place. As the entrepreneur, you should not become a "chokepoint" for decisions and approvals. Additionally, and this is very difficult for entrepreneurs to accept, you as the founder or one of the founders of a small business should come to recognize that the very same business behaviors and approaches that helped make you so successful early in your company's life may not be applicable in the full-and-open world. What this means from a functional standpoint is that as the entrepreneur, you need to continue to paint an actionable vision of your company's future, but you may be well served to distance yourself from the day-to-day decisions and actions in business development, operations, and infrastructure. Hire and empower staff professionals with the big-business leadership skills and functional competencies to be accountable for daily, monthly, quarterly, and annual success. You provide encouragement, insight, incentives, and passion, and break down any barriers to success.

Success stories

Graduation from the 8(a) Program does not need to mean "plateauing" of revenues in the hyper-competitive full-and-open marketspace. Nor does

---

1   The Project Management Institute (PMI) has built a new certification (in pilot mode) called the PMP Agile Certified Practitioner. COBIT (Control Objectives for Information Technology) is gaining ground as an IT governance framework. Among the range of ISO standards is ISO 27000 for security.

transition out of 8(a) status necessarily result in the sale of the small organization. Three examples of prominent success stories come to mind immediately: (1) Stinger Ghaffarian Technologies (SGT) of Greenbelt, Maryland; (2) NCI Information Systems (NCI) headquartered in Reston, Virginia; and (3) STG, Inc. of Reston, Virginia. SGT opened its doors in 1994, and now has more than 1,500 employees serving federal government customers such as NASA, NOAA, and DoD. The company entered the 8(a) Program in 1996, and graduated in August 2005. Notably, SGT is the second-largest service provider in NASA. In 2010, it began a strong GWAC focus as part of a diversification strategy.

Founded in 1989, NCI now has annual revenues above $580 million, and 2,800 employees worldwide in more than 100 locations. The company provides IT, engineering, and professional services to the federal govenment. Finally, STG, established in 1986, is on target to reach $1 billion in revenues by 2016. The company delivers enterprise network operations, cyber security, financial services, systems engineering and integration, and software engineering support for civilian and defense agencies.

ENDNOTE

1. Hayes, Heather B., "Ensuring a Smooth Exit. Planning Is the Key to Successfully Graduating from the 8(a) Program," *Washington Technology*, Vol. 22, No. 18, October 1, 2007.

Chapter 24

Small business entrepreneurs in the federal marketspace: leader self-efficacy and resource allocation decisions

24.1 Small businesses in context

We know that small businesses are vital to the near- and long-term success of America's economy. The statistical facts to validate this assertion are impressive. Indeed, the United States Small Business Administration's (SBA) Office of Advocacy reports that small businesses represent 99.7% of all employer firms in this country, employ nearly half of all private-sector employees, have generated 65% of net new jobs over the past 17 years, hire 43% of high-tech workers (e.g., scientists, engineers, and computer programmers), comprised 97.5% of all identified United States exporters, and produced 31% of export value in Fiscal Year (FY) 2008 (http://www.sba.gov/sites/default/files/sbfaq.pdf). The problem, however, is that many United States small businesses do not survive or prosper.

> Small business leaders should be aware of decision bias. Consider forming a small and empowered executive management team.

24.2 Building the "business case" for this study

Because small business leaders are the primary decision makers within their respective organizations, and decision making is related to small business performance [1], further understanding the influences on leaders' resource allocation decisions contributes to the success of both industry and government. Decisions about the acquisition and distribution of organizational resources are of particular importance for such businesses because they generally have fewer of them. Within small services-oriented companies that contractually support the United States federal government, the largest marketplace in the world [3] in terms of contractual dollars, the allocation of limited human talent and financial assets is most often decided by the business leader who founded, owns, and operates the company.

These resource allocation decisions do not always align with current or forecasted business requirements or market conditions, nor do they necessarily result in sustained competitive advantage [3] for the small businesses. Indeed, many small businesses do not survive, and economic sustainability is a very real challenge for small business leaders. Data from the United States Small Business Administration's *Small Business Economy Report to the President* (2009, p. 108) [4] indicate that in the period 1995–2006, there were more than 500,000 small business "deaths" each year. In 2009, that number stood at more than 660,900. It is the leader (generally, the entrepreneur) who is central to the strategies developed and decisions made within small business concerns [5]. Gray [5] suggested that decision making is positively correlated with small business performance. Decision making within small businesses in particular is focused largely on the allocation of scarce organizational resources such as human talent and financial assets. Allocation decisions have cognitive antecedents. It is precisely these antecedents associated within small business leaders and entrepreneurs that this study explored.

Notwithstanding a centuries-old lineage, entrepreneurship as a disciplinary research field is less than 30 years old. It is a young and primarily descriptive field. There are no overarching and tightly integrated theories established to explain and predict entrepreneurial behaviors and decisions and their relationship to resources and business outcomes. Much of the published work on entrepreneurship has focused on the personality traits of business leaders rather than on their decisions and actions. In addition, entrepreneurship is largely overlooked or played down within mainstream economic theory. What we do learn from entrepreneurship research, however, is that entrepreneurs allocate resources to various alternative uses [6].

A pivotal question emerged, namely: Do small business leaders have a tendency to invest resources in business support function (infrastructure) areas that favor their own self-assessed strengths? In effect, do small business leaders put their money and their staff resources into the infrastructure area they know best? In addition, do small business leaders invest resources in the business infrastructure area that they believe is most important to their success?

As an integral part of this author's Doctor of Management (DM) earned in 2009 through the University of Maryland University College, an empirical effort was undertaken to learn more about the factors that determine how small business leaders whose firms provide support services on a contractual basis to the United States federal government make decisions about allocating their scarce organizational resources. The question examined was whether small business leaders tend to invest resources in infrastructure areas that favor their own strengths (i.e., self-efficacy). The theory tested and assessed was that small business leaders tend to allocate resources with a bias [2] toward areas in which they have greater knowledge and self-perceived competence.

This study saw small business entrepreneurs as thinking agents whose cognitive reflections about their own competencies are related to the strategic and tactical decisions they make in the business setting. In this case, the business setting is the federal government marketspace. These decisions, in turn, have been shown to affect the performance of the business. Given that financial assets and human talent are scarce organizational resources in small businesses, the decisions that entrepreneurs make regarding their arrangement, allocation, and organization will have a major impact on such business performance indicators as bookings and annual revenues [7]. Strategic outcomes follow directly from "[h]ow resources are actually allocated and used" [8].

24.3 Conceptual framework

This conceptual framework is founded on the following key planks:

- Organizational resources are necessarily constrained within a small business.

- Self-efficacy and resource decision making were studied in an entrepreneurial setting because there is a stronger nexus between the leader's decisions and the small business's actions than exists in established firms, where formal processes and other actors mediate the influence of managerial bias on firm action [9].

- The entrepreneurial setting is characterized by uncertainty, which is associated with an increased prevalence of personal beliefs (e.g., self-efficacy) in decision making [10].

- We would expect that an entrepreneur's self-efficacy will play a role in his or her decisions, including those involving the allocation of resources.

- Decision making plays a central role in small business performance.

The thesis of this study was: What leaders think they are good at, in effect, self-efficacy, will influence their decisions about allocation of resources within their small organizations. In particular, the focus was on leader decisions regarding allocation of people and financial assets within infrastructure functions of their organizations.

Currently, there are gaps in the management literature regarding small businesses and the government marketspace. Furthermore, there is uncharted theoretical and empirical territory that encompasses the domain of leader decision making during a small business's entire life cycle—well beyond the prenascent and initiation stages of the venture (Figure 24.1). In addition, there has been inadequate quantitative substantiation of the associations between self-efficacy and small business leader behavior.

24.4 Characterizing the quantitative research

Cross-sectional quantitative research involving a Web-based survey instrument was conducted, using the individual small business leader as the "unit of analysis." This unit of analysis included small business leaders with the title and/or function of entrepreneur, owner, president, chief executive officer (CEO), principal, executive, chairman, and founder. The population consisted of the approximately 50,000 leaders in small businesses

Figure 24.1
The focus was on "operating" leaders [11] whose small businesses provide support services to the United States federal government.

(less than 1,500 employees or less than $27 million annual revenues), including minorities, women, veterans and service-disabled veterans, founders/owners of historically underutilized business zone (HUBZone) companies, and handicapped individuals. All firms provided support services to the United States federal government on a contractual basis, either directly, or as a subcontractor through a major government prime contractor (e.g., SAIC, HP, Northrop Grumman, Lockheed, General Dynamics, and Boeing).

The independent variable (IV) in this study was the level of self-efficacy among leaders of small businesses that provide support services to the federal government. The dependent variable (DV)—the one that was expected to change—was the allocation of infrastructure resources, as measured in terms of staff and monetary investment. The allocation of infrastructure resources was examined both in terms of people and dollars, the two principal "buckets" or categories of resources that small business leaders tend to consider. In turn, the allocation of people included study of full-time, part-time, and freelance/consultant staff. The allocation of dollars focused specifically on overhead (OH), that is, general ledger operating expenses that cannot be charged directly to contracts. Resource allocation types were considered separately as well as in select pairs based upon direct experience. In particular, overhead allocation for 2008 and 2009 were considered separately as well as in combination. Full-time and freelance/consultants were also examined separately as well as in combination. Experience suggests that consultants often fulfill roles in support of small business leaders that extend far beyond specific job descriptions. In this regard, they align closely with full-time management and infrastructure staff. Finally, allocation of part-time resources was considered separately. Generally, part-time staff provide very prescribed, time-bounded support to an organization, and thus are functionally distinct from full-time staff and consultants.

Figures 24.2 and 24.3 depict the major steps involved in the research methodology. In addition, L.I.S.T., Inc., a business-to-business (B2B) e-mail broker located in Armonk, New York, was contacted. For a fee, this organization provided access to opt-in e-mail lists maintained by Carroll Publishing, Inc., and Washington Techway. A total of 20,000 e-mails were sent through this firm to small business owners and leaders, appropriately delimited by annual revenues, employee number, and North American Industrial Classification System (NAICS) codes of the respective small companies. The survey questionnaire was presented through the Web to the participating leaders, who answered questions about themselves, their

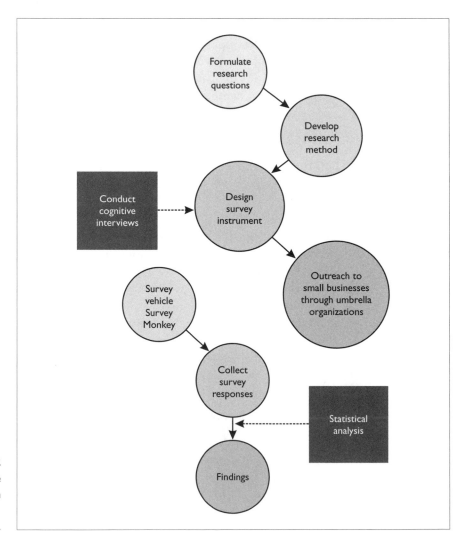

Figure 24.2
Major steps in the research methodology (view 1).

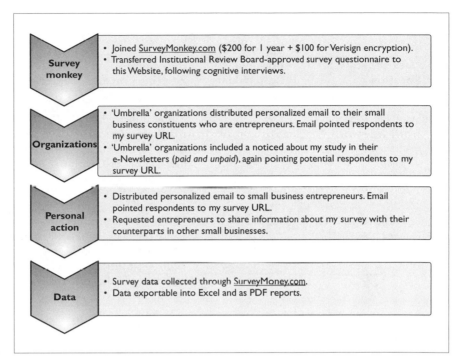

Figure 24.3
Major steps in
the research
process
(view 2).

organizations, their areas of perceived business strengths, and the infrastructure areas of their businesses that received the greatest allocation of people and dollars.

24.5 Sources of data

Sources of data for this research study (see Table 24.1) included individual small business leaders and owners who were contacted via broadcast and narrow-cast e-mail, e-newsletter, and/or print newsletter through such "umbrella" organizations as the Professional Services Council (PSC) and INPUT, Inc., and then pointed to the survey on the Web. These sources were coupled with B2B specific e-mail listings from Carroll Publishing, Inc., and Washington Techway. Working with L.I.S.T., Inc., leaders' e-mails were down-selected from Carroll Publishing, Inc.'s database of federal contractors by numbers of employees (less than 999 staff), sales (less than $27 million per year), and NAICS code (54—professional, scientific, and technical services; and 561—administrative and support services) as well as owner (president, CEO, principal, entrepreneur). With Washington Techway, business owners' e-mails were selected from the database by specific and relevant industry type: aerospace/defense, consulting/

Data Source/ Location	Superset of Potential Respondents	Relevancy/ Filtering Process	Distribution Mechanism
Input, Inc. (research firm in federal marketspace), Reston, Virginia	1,059	Master database of constituents filtered by annual revenues of less than $27 million; presidents, CEOs, owners only	Personal e-mail from senior vice-president
Professional Services Council (PSC), Arlington, Virginia	150	Constituents filtered by annual revenues less than $27 million and less than 1,500 employees; presidents, CEOs, owners only	Announcement in e-newsletter
Business Research Services, Inc. (BRS), Bethesda, Maryland	8,500	Federally certified minority- and women-owned businesses	*Set-Aside Alert* e-newsletter
Small Business and Enterpreneurship (SBE) Council (national, nonpartisan advocacy organization), Oakton, Virginia	70,000	Small business enterpreneurs	*The Weekly Brief* eNews, personal e-mail from the president and CEO of the SBE Council, Web site
Southern Illinois Entrepreneurship Center, Carbondale, Illinois	Less than 30	Small business entrepreneurs in the federal space	Personal e-mail from the director
Association of Proposal Management Professionals (APMP), Dana Point, California	270	The criteria for distribution was member self-identification containing one of the following terms: founder, president, COO, owner, chief, chair, principal	E-mail announcement with statement validating approval by APMP board of directors

Table 24.1 Sources of data.

Fedmarket, Inc., Bethesda, Maryland	17,000 (narrow-cast)	Broadcast target was small businesses; narrow-cast target was veteran-owned and service disabled-veteran-owned small businesses	Broadcast and narrow-cast e-mails
Researcher's personal contacts	80	Small business entrepreneurs	Personal e-mail
MIT Entrepreneurship Center, Cambridge, Massachusetts	Less than 100	Small business entrepreneurs	E-mail
Kansas Women's Business Center, Lenexa, KS	Less than 50	Small business entrepreneurs	E-mail
Illinois Procurement Technical Assistance Center (PTAC), Carterville, Illinois	30	Small business entrepreneurs	Personal e-mail
Small business entrepreneurs forwarding notice about survey to their peers	Unknown	Small business entrepreneurs	E-mail

Table 24.1 (continued)

professional services, system integrator/value-added reseller (VAR), and telecommunications. The particular job title was executive management.

As shown in Table 24.2, the average total years of entrepreneurial experience among the 577 survey respondents was 13.78, and the average years of service with the current organization was 9.92. Descriptive statistics for both of these variables are reported in Table 24.2. For both of these variables, the mean is greater than the median, which indicates positive or right skewness. Nearly half (48.7%) of the sample population of small business leaders had 11 or fewer total years of entrepreneurial experience. Slightly more than half (51.6%) had 8 or fewer years of

Descriptive Statistics	Total Years of Entrepreneurial Experience	Years of Entrepreneurial Experience with the Current Organization
Arithmetic mean	13.78	9.92
Median	12.00	8.00
Mode	10	5
Standard deviation	9.586	7.373
Skewness	1.113	0.994
Range	1–55	0–35

Table 24.2
Descriptive Statistics for Sample (n = 577)

entrepreneurial experience with their current firm. Frequencies histograms responses are found in Figures 24.4, 24.5, and 24.6.

When asked about the area of their greatest personal expertise, 45.7% of respondents selected business development and marketing (see Figure 24.7). These specific infrastructure areas were also identified as being most important for business success in the federal marketspace for this population (46.5%) (see Figure 24.8).

24.6 Analysis of our results

Annual revenues (in dollars) for 64.2% of the companies owned by those who responded to the survey was less than $3 million in the year ending December 31, 2008 (see Figure 24.9). This meets the threshold for a very small business.

The mean staffing level reported by respondents was nearly 45 people (44.76), with a standard deviation of 106.104 and a skewness of 6.428. The mode for staffing level among respondents was 1, with approximately 32% having four people or less in their companies. This aligns roughly with the most recent data available from the United States Small Business Administration Office of Advocacy (http://www.sba.gov/advo/research/us_06ss.pdf) that shows 47.7% of the

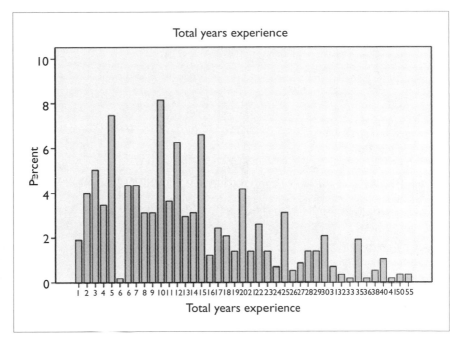

Figure 24.4
Histogram illustrating the percentage associated with each one of the values for total years of entrepreneurial experience.

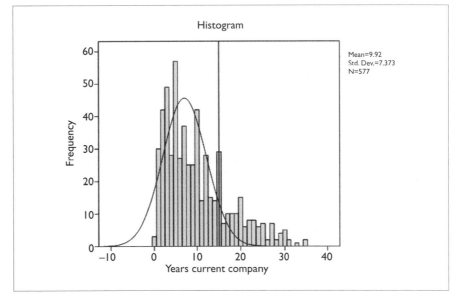

Figure 24.5
Frequency histogram for years of entrepreneurial experience with the current company.

total population of United States small businesses have four or fewer people. Fully 41.0% of those responding to this survey reported annual revenues of less than $1 million (Figure 24.10). This is not unexpected, given that 78.9% of the total population of United States small businesses have annual revenues ("receipt size of firm") less than $1 million based

Figure 24.6
Histogram illustrating the percentage associated with each one of the values for years of entrepreneurial experience with the current company.

Figure 24.7
Most small business leaders perceived themselves to have specific self-efficacy in business development and marketing among the business infrastructure areas presented for consideration.

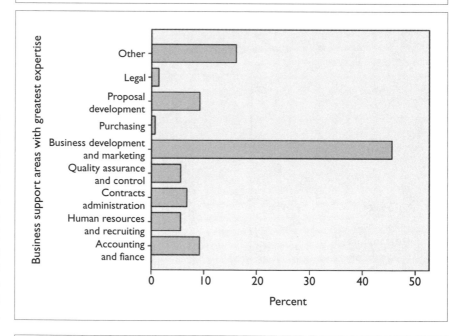

Work in a close, trust-based partnership with mentors and experts to ensure that investment dollars and staff resources are allocated in infrastructure areas that are most beneficial to organizational success, given current and projected market conditions.

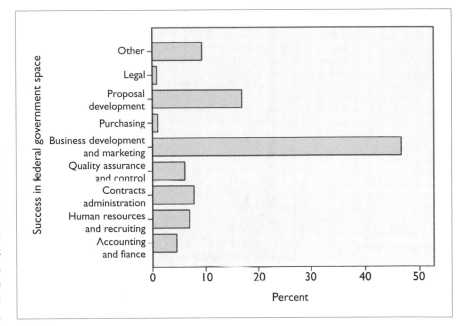

Figure 24.8
Most small business leaders believed business development and marketing was the most important infrastructure area for success in the federal marketspace.

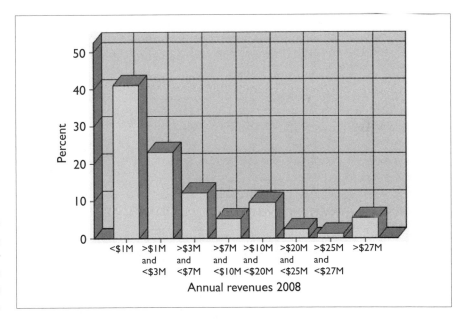

Figure 24.9
Annual revenues in dollars in 2008 for the small business organizations surveyed.

upon Office of Advocacy data as well (http://www.sba.gov/advo/research/us_rec_mi.pdf).

The business infrastructure function to which this sample of 577 small business leaders allocated the greatest percentage of overhead (OII) dollars in 2008 was business development and marketing (30.8%) as shown in

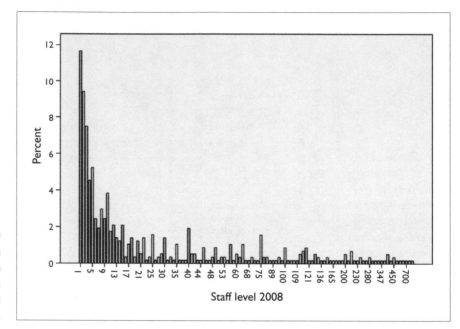

Figure 24.10
Histogram of the percentage associated with each staff level value.

Figure 24.11. The business infrastructure function to which this sample of small business leaders plans to allocate the greatest percentage of overhead (OH) dollars in 2009 is also business development and marketing (40.0%), as shown in Figure 24.12.

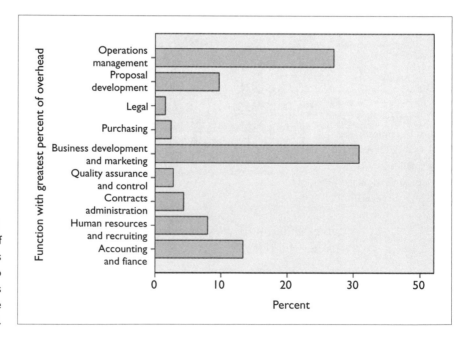

Figure 24.11
Percentage of overhead dollars allocated to specific business infrastructure functions in 2008.

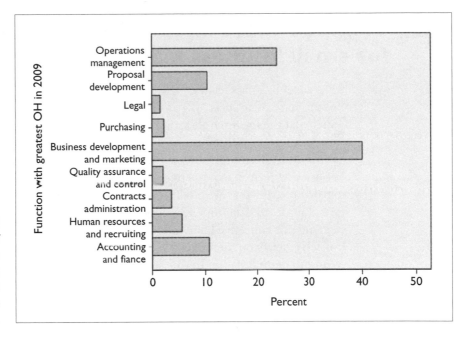

Figure 24.12
Percentage of overhead dollars allocated to specific business infrastructure functions in 2009.

Descriptive and nonparametric (chi-square and uncertainty coefficient) statistical analyses conducted on the 577 survey responses indicate that knowing a business owner's perceived area of self-efficacy improves ability to predict the owner's allocation of resources. Results of this study form the first preliminary steps toward developing a decision-making model.

Three key findings include:

1. At a statistically meaningful level, knowing a business owner's perceived area of self-efficacy in the sample obtained (n = 577) improves our ability to predict that owner's allocation of full-time equivalents (FTEs), part-time and freelance staff, and overhead dollars to the corresponding business infrastructure area.

2. Small business owners' resource allocation decisions were related to their level of general self-efficacy as well as their self-efficacy in a specific business infrastructure area.

3. Knowing a small business leader's perceived area of expertise (self-efficacy) would help to predict the business infrastructure area that he or she deems most important, over against random chance.

24.7 What do these findings and results suggest for small business leaders?

For small business leaders, this research suggests that they should be aware of this particular "bias" [2]. They might form small management teams such that the resource allocation decisions that may derive from the leader's specific self-efficacy are balanced with other viewpoints. Small business leaders might also work in a trust-based partnership with seasoned and proven experts to ensure that resources are allocated in infrastructure areas that are most beneficial to organizational success.

Empirical data from 577 operating small businesses across the country extend our collective knowledge of small business leaders and the influence of self-efficacy on their decision making beyond prenascent and nascent entrepreneurial stages. In this sample population, small business leaders' perceived self-efficacy in a given area of business made them more likely to allocate resources to that particular area. The level of general self-efficacy is positively associated with allocation of full-time staff in the infrastructure area they perceive as being their personal strength. In addition, knowing a business leader's perceived area of self-efficacy improves the ability to predict the area deemed most important by that leader, as compared to random chance. These results contribute empirical insight into an arena that is dominated by popular literature that offers many divergent guidelines and ostensibly "ideal" actions that a small business leader should do or not do to be successful. For example, many popular magazine and newspaper articles suggest that one can do little to prepare to become a better entrepreneur because entrepreneurship is portrayed as being an in-born set of traits [13]. Importantly, the current study supports the notion that small business leaders can make choices to improve their performance and that of their organization.

Findings indicate that for the sample obtained, knowing a business leader's perceived area of self-efficacy improves the ability to predict that leader's allocation of full-time equivalents (FTEs), part-time and freelance staff/consultants, and overhead dollars to the corresponding business infrastructure area. Because the survey data were categorical, specific correlations cannot be established to generalize to the larger population of small business leaders. Nonetheless, there exists strong alignment with what would be predicted from established entrepreneurial, self-efficacy, decision-making, and resource allocation theory. Results indicate that small business leaders in this sample with high general self-efficacy have a stronger association between their perceived expertise in a specific business infrastructure area and their allocation of FTEs in that infrastructure area than do individuals with low self-efficacy. Small business leaders' resource allocation decisions were related to their level of general self-efficacy as well as their self-efficacy in a specific business infrastructure area. This aligns well with Albert Bandura's self-efficacy mechanism of personal agency and decision making [14].

In addition, the findings indicate that for this sampling frame, knowing a small business leader's perceived area of expertise (self-efficacy) would help to predict the business support area that he or she deems most important as compared to random chance. There are no known antecedents in the academic or business literature that discuss this linkage between what business function a leader perceives to be his or her strength and the business function those same leaders see as being most critical to success in the government marketspace.

Knowing what small business leaders think they know was shown to be related to the infrastructure area in which they invest the most people and overhead (indirect) dollars. This insight is applicable across the small business community, government, business schools, venture capital firms (investors), and consultants. For small business leaders themselves, this research suggests that they should be aware of the propensity to have their resource allocation decisions influenced by their own self-perceived strengths. One possibility is that they might consider forming an executive management team so that resource-allocation decisions that derive from the small business leader's specific self-efficacy are balanced with other points of view.

Alternatively, small business leaders might work in a close, trust-based partnership with mentors to ensure that allocation of resources for business support functions is most beneficial to organizational success. This type of partnership would apply to small businesses operating in the federal government marketspace as well as state and local government markets.

To return to small business leaders in particular, results of this study suggest the value of developing a "working," very practical decision-making model (see Figure 24.13). For example, business development/marketing self-efficacy is shown to be related to the allocation of infrastructure resources into business development and marketing. Further consideration might be given to proposal development in order to support the marketing opportunities that are identified and qualified. Additional people and dollars might also be allocated to the firm's recruiting function in order to staff contracts that are awarded. This model might be employed for a spectrum of key business decisions including hiring, budgeting, staff-power forecasting, controlling general and administrative (G&A) costs, and outsourcing decisions.

A key consideration is for leaders in small companies to learn to rely on others with proven expertise and hands-on experience in business areas outside of their particular sphere of self-perceived expertise. One corollary

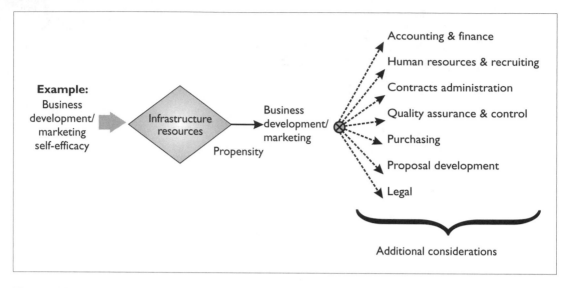

Figure 24.13 Moving toward a balanced organization.

would be to develop balanced management support expertise in the organization that includes a breadth of business infrastructure knowledge across the management team. A second corollary would be to pursue and engage in a formal mentor-protégé program.

ENDNOTES

1. Jung, Dong I., et al., "Entrepreneurial Self-Efficacy and Its Relationship to Entrepreneurial Action: A Comparative Study Between the US and Korea," *Management International*, Vol. 6, No. 1, Fall 2001, pp. 41--53.

2. Bazerman, Max H., and Don Moore, *Judgment in Managerial Decision Making*, 7th ed., Hoboken, NJ: John Wiley & Sons, 2009, p. 1.

3. Mick, Todd D., and Patricia G. Greene, "Minority and Women Entrepreneurs Contracting with the Federal Government," *Journal of Small Business Strategy*, Vol. 15, No. 1, Spring 2004, pp. 33–48.

4. Porter, Michael, *Competitive Advantage: Creating and Sustaining Superior Performance*, New York: Free Press, 1985.

5. Gray, Judy, "A New Measure of Entrepreneurial Decision-Making Style," *Academy of Entrepreneurship Journal*, Vol. 7, No. 2, 2001, pp. 1–15.

6. Cuervo, Ávaro, Domingo Ribeiro, and Salvador Roig, (eds.), *Entrepreneurship: Concepts, Theory and Perspective*, Berlin, Germany: Springer-Verlag, 2007.

7. Baum, J. Robert, and Edwin A. Locke, "The Relationship of Entrepreneurial Traits, Skill, and Motivation to Subsequent Venture Growth," *Journal of Applied Psychology*, Vol. 89, No. 4, August 2004, p. 589.

8. Bower, Joseph L., Yves L. Doz, and Clark G. Gilbert, "Linking Resource Allocation to Strategy," in Joseph L. Bower and Clark G. Gilbert, (eds.), *From Resource Allocation to Strategy*, New York: Oxford University Press, 2007, p. 12.

9. Simon, Mark, Susan M. Houghton, and Sonja Savelli, "Out of the Frying Pan…? Why Small Business Managers Introduce High-Risk Products," *Journal of Business Venturing*, Vol. 18, No. 3, May 2003, pp. 419–440.

10. Busenitz, Lowell W., and Jay B. Barney, "Differences Between Entrepreneurs and Managers in Large Organizations: Biases and Heuristics in Decision-Making," *Journal of Business Venturing*, Vol. 12, No. 1, January 1997, pp. 9–30.

11. Cassar, Gavin, and Henry Friedman, "Does Self-Efficacy Affect Entrepreneurial Investment?" May 15, 2009. Retrieved June 28, 2009, from Social Science Research Network (SSRN), http://papers.ssrn.com/sol3/papers.cfm?abstract_id=1405426.

12. Bazerman, Max H., and Don Moore, *Judgment in Managerial Decision Making*, 7th ed., Hoboken, NJ: John Wiley & Sons, 2009, p. 1.

13. Shane, Scott A., *The Illusions of Entrepreneurship: The Costly Myths That Entrepreneurs, Investors, and Policy Makers Live By*, New Haven, CT: Yale University Press, 2008.

14. Bandura, Albert, "Human Agency in Social Cognitive Theory," *American Psychologist*, Vol. 44, No. 9, September 1989, pp. 1175–1184.

Epilogue

Thinking to win small-business competitive proposals

The magic is in the people. And so are the results.
—The PeopleWise Organization, Kepner-Tregoe

Succeeding in the world of *very* small businesses

EFFECTIVE SEPTEMBER 29, 2005, the U.S. Small Business Administration amended its regulations to remove provisions relating to the Very Small Business Program (VSB). The agency no longer has statutory authority to provide assistance under this program. Nonetheless, very small businesses—generally considered to be entities with 15 staff people or less—can and should continue to pursue work with the U.S. federal government. Support can be obtained at the local and state levels, such as the Greater Reston Chamber of Commerce (Virginia) (http://www.restonchamber.org/), Virginia Business Incubation Association (http://www.vbia.org/), Business 1ne Stop in Virginia (http://bos.virginia.gov), Maryland Business Incubation Association (http://www.mdbusinessincubation.org/), and Central Valley Business Incubator (http://cvbi.org).

Having worked with very small businesses in a consulting capacity, I am acutely aware of the many challenges that they face on an hour-to-hour and day-to-day basis. One of the most significant challenges is optimizing productivity per unit time. Despite working 18-hour days, an entrepreneur and her small staff have only so much time for business development, proposal development, customer operations, development of reports and deliverables, accounting, human resources/recruiting, procurement, office management, information technology infrastructure support, and so forth. Thus, highly effective and efficient *time management* takes on an accentuated importance as a competency among all of the members of the organization. It is critical to master the art and science of multitasking. Productivity and time management can be enhanced through the select application of tools and technologies such as calendaring software, personal digital assistants (PDAs), laptop computers, cellular telephones, and conferencing tools. Prioritization among competing requirements and demands is also pivotal in achieving effective time management. More importantly, staff professionals must stay focused in the present. They need to avoid the propensity to multitask at the expense of contributing to and staying engaged with the meeting at hand, the project now underway, and the conversation that is transpiring right now.

Another key competency is clear and accurate *communication* among each member of your company. You simply cannot afford to duplicate effort, work at cross-purposes, or allow an important action item to go undone. Communication also extends to idea- and knowledge-sharing. It is absolutely critical for each member of a very small business to voice and consider ideas from every other person in the firm. Linked directly with knowledge sharing is the need to optimize the subject matter expertise of each company member. People will, by necessity, have to shoulder multiple responsibilities and areas of accountability.

A third vital competency is *risk-taking*, that is, being opportunity-driven and willing to make a key new hire, pursue a business program with a new customer, or invest in a seasoned business development consultant. The point is to foster the capacity to take selective, bold steps based on business acumen and experience. As a very small business, you will want to avoid "analysis paralysis" and "overthinking the issue." Conversely, you avoid "analysis paralysis" and "overthinking the issue." Conversely, you will have to balance risk-taking with fiscal prudence. The critical ingredient here is *balance*.

Within a very small business, it is highly advisable to build a *culture of teamwork* and collegial interaction. Drive the accountability for decision making and problem solving throughout your small organization. With accountability needs to come responsibility and tangible *incentives* for success. Entrepreneurs of very small businesses must ensure that their teams of dedicated staff share in the rewards of success as that unfolds. Staff having "skin in the game" is critical for sustained success and business growth.

A business culture of teamwork and positive interaction is built in large part on mutual trust. Ideas and knowledge are shared much more fluidly in environments in which folks trust each other and are focused on common goals and objectives.

As a very small business, you will want and need to get *outside support* as necessary and appropriate. Some small businesses' back-office infrastructures (accounting, human resources, recruiting, procurement, and so forth) are comprised almost entirely of part-time and/or freelance staff. While not an ideal situation in terms of continuity, it can be a viable alternative to hiring full-time staff at a stage in the business life cycle at which such investment is not possible or justifiable from a business perspective.

Capture and document information about your very small business, your customers, technical and programmatic "success stories," subject matter expertise among your staff professionals, core competencies, and business processes very early in your organizational life. This will be extremely valuable as you move forward responding to federal government proposals because you will need elements of this information in each and every proposal.

Finally, know what your organizational strengths are and focus on pursuing contractual work that leverages those strengths. There is a tremendous temptation to respond to a broad cross-section of requests for proposal or requests for solution. However, as a very small business, it is imperative to focus your extremely limited resources on high-probability business opportunities that align well with your strengths and competencies. A proven method for staying focused on your core competencies is the *strategic planning process*. However, strategic planning must be accompanied closely with the *managerial discipline* to prioritize and say no to ancillary or tangential marketing targets that emerge.

Small business strengths—making the most of them

Fundamentally, very small businesses need to hire and retain highly qualified people, apply structured and disciplined business development processes, share and communicate the entire team's collective knowledge in a trust-based environment, and leverage appropriate tools and technologies to support time management and maximize productivity. Small firms are in the enviable position of being able to respond rapidly to changing business environments. As a key builder of your company's business future, you should maximize your agility as a small contracting firm and establish as soon as possible in your corporate history appropriate internal and external business development and knowledge management processes and patterns of thinking and behavior that will facilitate winning proposals in the federal, private-sector, and international marketplace. Genuine teamwork is a critical element of success in the contracting arena. Proposalmanship is a capability that needs to be cultivated throughout the levels of your organization in order to fully harness the talent and energy resident there. Many companies struggle because only a few of their staff are trained and experienced in proposal management, design, and development. And often, business development and knowledge management are ill-defined and poorly implemented.

Ongoing, positive communication throughout your company is another measure of your successful business culture. That multidirectional communication extends among the acquisition/capture team and the proposal team, business development staff and technical operations staff, business development staff and your client, proposal manager and senior management, proposal manager and capture manager, proposal manager and proposal writers, and proposal manager and publications staff.

Management support must necessarily assume many different forms. But it must be manifested clearly in order to be fully effective. That support should be present in ensuring that efforts to build appropriate résumé and project summary files (part of an overall knowledge base) on your company's staff and contractual history are met with complete and timely support throughout the technical and programmatic (operations) ranks. Management support should take the shape of assisting the proposal manager in enforcing the proposal milestone schedule and of empowering the proposal manager to meet the challenges of a given proposal effort. Ensure qualified leadership with the authority to do the job. And management involvement and support also lie in committing the resources—such as human, financial, time, equipment, and floor space—to make every proposal your company elects to pursue a superior, client-centered sales document that tells a compelling story, which is validated by facts. Support for an apprentice system for proposal managers would be well-targeted energy.

As a leader, you are able to infuse an ethos of rational and formal planning into your company's business development and proposal development infrastructure. Expend the time and effort early in your firm's history to develop a mission statement and strategic plan. Generate and have all of your management team follow written, albeit revisable, business development and knowledge management protocol and processes. This applies particularly to bid–no bid decision making. Too many times, small and large businesses dilute their collective resources in pursuing marketing opportunities that do not support their primary lines of business. Planning also extends to developing the proposal directive or capture plan prior to conducting the formal kickoff meeting. Up-front planning, analysis, and decision making yield significant dividends downstream in the proposal and oral presentation processes.

And finally, recognition and reward. People need to know in a variety of ways that they are meeting your company's business and proposal development expectations. They need to be recognized when they contribute in any one of several ways to a proposal victory. Senior management should develop and implement a definitive recognition and incentive plan that is documented and communicated clearly to everyone in your company. Success should be noted in a big way. Those people in your firm who are thinking to win should be recognized and should receive tangible benefits. Remember that your people and their knowledge are the most important ingredients in your company's success in establishing and sustaining a recognizable and sustainable brand of excellence in the marketplace.

Appendix A

Sample proposal kickoff package

A well-prepared proposal kickoff package or proposal directive—which includes important components such as a milestone schedule, annotated outline, page allocations, and key person contact list—is a valuable tool for proposal managers to maximize the value of bringing staff together for the formal kickoff meeting. The kickoff package also serves as a helpful, easy-to-follow reference tool for proposal writers, contracts staff, teaming partners, production staff, and senior management throughout the proposal response life cycle.

KICKOFF PACKAGE
GROUNDWATER TREATMENT SYSTEM
for
Any County, Virginia

Prepared by:

Acquisition Team
XYZ, Inc.

Proposal #:
Department Code:
_____

COMPETITION–SENSITIVE
INFORMATION

Agenda

1. Proposal Summary

2. Schedule for Technical and Business Management Volumes

3. Volume Responsibilities

4. Evaluation Factors for Award

5. Technical Outline and Writing Assignments

a. Themes and Critical Issues

b. Page Allocations

c. Proposal Writing Guidelines

6. Business Management Writing Assignments

7. Action Items

8. Items for Management Approval

9. Telephone List

10. Proposal Security

Proposal Summary Sheet

Title:	Groundwater Treatment System
Solicitation Number:	
Client:	Any County, Virginia
1. Proposal Due Date and Time:	Technical proposals and bids are due by 5 P.M. on Monday, in Virginia
2. Client Name (Point of Contact): Telephone #:	Contract Specialist
3. Period of Performance:	25 weeks + 1 month O&M
4. Copies to Client:	3 copies of the proposal and 1 copy of the bid (p. 8)[1]

---

1   Page number references are from the RFP.

Proposal Team
Procurement Name

Proposal Manager:

Proposal Team Members:

Technical:

Program Management:

Cost:

Legal:

QA:

Evaluation Factors for Award
Procurement Name

The evaluation factors are listed below:

(1)	Project Organization	15
(2)	Project Execution	25
(3)	Schedule	15
(4)	Qualifications and Experience	30
(5)	Health and Safety	5
(6)	SB, SDB, or WOB	5
(7)	Financial Resources	5
	Total	100

Proposal Milestone Schedule

Day 1 Analyze final solicitation documents. Meeting to discuss the contract scope and proposal team membership.	**Day 2** Develop Kickoff Package that includes a milestone schedule and detailed outline.	**Day 3** Develop Kickoff Package that includes a milestone schedule and detailed outline. Convene Proposal Kickoff meeting.	**Day 4** Conduct technical and programmatic solution development sessions, including development of key graphics concepts.	**Day 5** Conduct technical and programmatic solution development sessions, including development of key graphics concepts.	**Day 6** Convene cost/pricing solution development session.	**Day 7** Generate Blue Team work products, to include elevator speeches, pain tables, process flow diagrams, key graphics concepts, and past performance validation.
Day 8 Generate Blue Team work products, to include elevator speeches, pain tables, process flow diagrams, key graphics concepts, and past performance validation.	**Day 9** Review Blue Team work products; sign off on Blue Team work products.	**Day 10** Proposal writing and interactive, informal, near-real-time cyclical reviews.	**Day 11** Proposal writing and interactive, informal, near-real-time cyclical reviews.	**Day 12** Proposal writing and interactive, informal, near-real-time cyclical reviews.	**Day 13** Proposal writing and interactive, informal, near-real-time cyclical reviews.	**Day 14** Generate and produce Pink Team draft (narrative and graphics).
Day 15 Review Pink Team draft including cost/price.	**Day 16** Pink Team Recovery and interactive, informal, near-real-time cyclical reviews.	**Day 17** Pink Team Recovery and interactive, informal, near-real-time cyclical reviews.	**Day 18** Pink Team Recovery and interactive, informal, near-real-time cyclical reviews.	**Day 19** Generate and produce Red Team draft, with edited narrative and mature graphics.	**Day 20** Generate and produce Red Team draft, with edited narrative and mature graphics.	**Day 21** Review Red Team draft, including cost/price.
Day 22 Review Red Team draft, including cost/price.	**Day 23** Red Team recovery.	**Day 24** Red Team recovery.	**Day 25** Red Team recovery.	**Day 26** Generate and produce Gold Team draft, all volumes.	**Day 27** Conduct Gold Team review. Address Gold Team recommendations.	**Day 28** Produce, edit, quality check, photocopy, and package all volumes.
Day 29 Deliver final proposal volumes to Virginia by 1 p.m.	**Day 30**					

Technical Proposal Outline

Prepared by Proposal Manager

EXECUTIVE SUMMARY

1. PROJECT ORGANIZATION   10 pages

1.1   Project Management (include an organizational chart)

1.2   Key Personnel Résumés

Project Manager
            Construction Superintendent
            Health and Safety Representative
            Quality Control Manager
            Field Engineering Staff

2. PROJECT EXECUTION   20 pages

2.1   Construction Operations Work Plan

2.1.1   Civil Works and Building Installation

Understanding the Work
            Approach to Ensuring Quality

2.1.2   Equipment Purchasing

Understanding the Work
            Approach to Ensuring Quality

2.1.3   Mechanical Work

Understanding the Work
            Approach to Ensuring Quality

2.1.3.1   Piping

2.1.3.2   Electrical Conduit

2.1.3.3   Termination Control and Field Instruments

2.1.4   Functional Testing and Start-up

Understanding the Work
        Approach to Ensuring Quality

2.2   Community Relations Plan

2.3   Subcontractors

2.3.1   Scope Items and Approximate Dollar Amount

2.3.2   Use of SB, SDB, or WOB

3. SCHEDULE   5 pages

3.1   Capacity to Accomplish Work in Required Time Frame
        (includes a Critical Path Method diagrams that shows critical
        equipment purchases)

3.1.1   Staff Time Commitments

3.1.2   Equipment Commitments

3.1.3   Strategies for Resolving Competing Demands

4. QUALIFICATIONS AND EXPERIENCE   15 pages

4.1   Institutional Overview
        Number of years in business
        Superfund and hazardous waste site work experience, by
        number of years and specific role
        Annual Experience Modification Rating (EMR)
        OSHA violations
        Construction Equipment

Workforce Questionnaire for an IT Firm

Employee ID No:
Division:
Current job title:

Software applications experience:
Adobe Acrobat X Pro
Adobe ColdFusion 9 (for building enterprise-ready Internet applications)
Adobe Dreamweaver Creative Suite (CS) 5.5
Adobe Flash Player-cross-platform, browser-based application
Adobe Illustrator CS5
Adobe Pagemaker 7.0
Adobe Photoshop CS5
C# 4.0 (C Sharp programming language)
C++ (C plus plus programming language)
CA Unicenter Service Desk
Corel Quattro Pro spreadsheet application
Corel WordPerfect Office X5
FileMaker Pro 11
FORTRAN 2008 programming language
HEAT help desk software (FrontRange Solutions)
Hyena v8.x total system administration tool
IBM Lotus 1-2-3 Release 9.8 (part of the Lotus SmartSuite)
IBM Rational ClearCase software configuration management
IBM Rational DOORS (requirements management solution)
IBM Rational Rose—modeling and development tool
IBM Tivoli—manages infrastructure services
ISS RealSecure (IBM Internet Security Systems)
Java 7 (Oracle)
Java Platform, Enterprise Edition 6
MATLAB high-level technical computer language (Mathworks)
Microsoft Access 2010 (Office Suite)
Microsoft Excel 2010 (Office Suite)
Microsoft PowerPoint 2010 (Office Suite
Microsoft Project Professional 2010

Microsoft Project Server 2010

Microsoft SharePoint 2010

Microsoft Visual BASIC 2010

Microsoft Windows

Microsoft Word 2003 and 2007

Opentext ECM Suite 2010 (enterprise content management)

Oracle database 11g Release 2

Perl 5.14.2—high-level, dynamic programming language

RAZOR—cross-platform configuration management tool (Visible Systems)

Red Hat Enterprise Linux

Remedy IT Service Management (BMC Software Inc.—software-as-a-service (SaaS) or Premises software

Samba 3.6.0

SAS/STAT Statistical Analysis Software - data analysis

TCP/IP (Transmission Control Protocol/Internet Protocol)

UML (Unified Modeling Language)

UNIX (The Open Group)

VRML (Virtual Reality Modeling Language)

XML (Extensible Markup Language)

Hardware experience:

Supercomputers (e.g., Cray Jaguar, IBM Blue Gene, Hitachi SR 11000)

Mainframes (IBM System z10 Enterprise Class mainframes)

Workstations (e.g., Apple, Dell, Toshiba, HP, Acer, and Lenovo)

Database experience:

IBM Informix

Microsoft Access 2010

Microsoft SQL server

Oracle Database 11g Release 2

SAP Sybase database management software technologies

Experience supporting or working for government organizations:

Department of Agriculture (USDA)

Department of Defense (DoD)

Army

DISA
DLA
Navy
Marine Corps.
NAVAIR
NAVSEA
Office of Naval Research (ONR)
SPAWAR
Office of the Secretary of Defense (OSD)
Department of Energy (DOE)
Department of Homeland Security (DHS)
Department of Justice (DOJ)
Department of Transportation (DOT)
General Services Administration (GSA)
NASA HQ and NASA Centers
Treasury
IRS

Technical areas of expertise:
Acquisition planning and support
Applications development
Business intelligence (BI)
Business process management
CASE tools
Cloud computing
Configuration management (CM)
Data analytics
Database Administration
Data analysis and planning
Data quality engineering
Data systems modeling
Enterprise architecture (EA)
Geographic Information Systems (GIS)
Graphical user interface (GUI)
Green IT
Help desk support and end-user support (service desk)

Information Assurance (IA)/cyber security

Integration and test (I&T)

Independent verification & validation (IV & V)

IT Management:

IT Service Operations

Knowledge Management (KM)

Managed services/seat management

Modeling and simulation

Multimedia/graphics/documentation support

Network engineering/management

Numerical analysis

Program management and control

Requirements analysis

Risk assessment and management

Scientific computing

Scientific support services

Service oriented architecture (SOA)

Software quality assurance (SQA)

Software engineering

Software development

Systems engineering and integration

Telecommunications

Total quality management (TQM)

Training

Web design and maintenance

Project or program management or technical leadership experience:

Maximum number of staff supervised:

Levels and labor categories of staff supervised:

Publications: Yes

Knowledge of and experience with industry standards (ISO 9001:2008, IEEE, SEI, CMMI®, ITIL v3 Foundation/Expert, COBIT): Yes

Security clearance [Confidential, Secret, Top Secret, Sensitive Compartmented Information (SCI), DOE, Q, L (DOE and Nuclear Regulatory Commission), DHS Background Investigation (BI), and so forth]:

Appendix C

Marketing information and intelligence sources: federal, international, and private sector

THERE ARE THREE MAJOR information sources for federal competitive procurements: (1) publicly available information, (2) client-derived information, and (3) community-derived information. The latter refers to friends, competitors, seminars, subcontractors, vendors, and published scientific or conference reports.

Sources of federal marketing leads and information

Acquisition or Procurement forecasts

Public Law 100-656, the Business Opportunity Development Reform Act of 1988, amended the Small Business Act to place new emphasis on acquisition planning. The law requires agencies to annually compile and make available 1-year projections of contracting opportunities that small and small disadvantaged companies can perform. The NASA Acquisition Forecast (http://prod.nais.nasa.gov/cgi-bin/nais/forecast.cgi), for example, includes projections of all anticipated contract actions above $100,000 that small and small disadvantaged businesses can perform under direct contracts with the government or as part of a subcontract arrangement. NASA's Acquisition Forecast is divided into sections for Headquarters in Washington, D.C., and for each Center (Goddard, Marshall, Ames, Glenn, and so forth). Retain these forecasts in your company's proposal data center or library for 3 to 5 years in order to track contracts as they become available for recompetition. Examples of online agency acquisition forecasts include the following:

U.S. Environmental Protection Agency (EPA)

http://yosemite1.epa.gov/oarm/oam/forecastdatabase.nsf

U.S. Army

http://www.sellingtoarmy.info/User/ShowSpecialPage.aspx?PageID=350

NASA Dryden Flight Research Center (DFRC)

http://www.nasa.gov/centers/dryden/pdf/599491main_DFRC_Acqfor12-01.pdf

NASA Glenn Research Center (GRC)

http://www.grc.nasa.gov/WWW/Procure/Acquisition_Forecast.xls

Department of Education

http://www2.ed.gov/fund/contract/find/forecast.html

Department of Energy (DOE) e-Center

http://www.pr.doe.gov

Department of Homeland Security (DHS)

http://www.dhs.gov/xopnbiz/gc_1300288340710.shtm

Nuclear Regulatory Commission (NRC)

http://www.nrc.gov/about-nrc/contracting/forecast.html

Department of Transportation (DOT)

http://osdbuweb.dot.gov/procurement/index.cfm

Department of Treasury

http://www.treasury.gov/resource-center/sb-programs/pages/dcfo-osdbu-mp-forecast.aspx

Department of Veterans Affairs (VA)

http://www.venderportal.ecms.va.gov/eVP/fco/FCO.aspk

U.S. Department of Agriculture (USDA)

http://www.pforecast.net/

Additional resources

Aerospace Daily & Defense Report (AviationWeek) [International Standard Serial Number (ISSN) 0193-4546/90]

http://www.Aviationweek.com/aw/generic/channel_.jps?channel
=aerospacedaily#

Aviation Week & Space Technology (AW&ST)

Part of the Aviation Week Intelligence Network
http://www.aviationweek.com/aw/generic/channel_.jsp?channel=awst

Baltimore Business Journal (newspaper)

American City Business Journals, Inc. (Baltimore)
1 East Pratt Street #205
Baltimore, MD 21202
(410)576-1161
Editor, Joanna Sullivan
Circ.: 66,000
http://baltimore.bizjournals.com/baltimore

Business Credit (journal)

National Association of Credit Management (NACM)
8840 Columbia 100 Parkway
Columbia, MD 21045-2158
(410)740-5560
http://www.nacm.org/business-credit-magazine.html

Competitors' newsletters and annual reports

These can be obtained via the Web or by contacting public relations departments. You may need an outsider such as a college student or consultant to do this.

Contractual exposure

When your company's personnel are on the client's site to perform existing work, they can certainly ask questions.

Defense Technical Information Center (DTIC)

8725 John J. Kingman Road
Ft. Belvoir, VA 22060-6218
(800)225-3842
http://www.dtic.mil/dtic/index.html
DTIC is the central point within the DoD for acquiring, storing, retrieving, and disseminating scientific and technical information to support the management and conduct of DoD research, development, engineering, and studies programs. DTIC services are available to DoD and its contractors, and to other U.S. government organizations and their contractors.

Defense Procurement and Acquisition Policy (DPAP)

DPAP is responsible for all contracting and procurement policy matters including e-business within the DoD.
3060 Defense Pentagon
Room 3B855
Washington, D.C. 20301-3060
http://www.acq.osd.mil/dpap

DIALOG (ProQuest)

Corporate Headquarters
2250 Perimeter Park Drive
Suite 300

Morrisville, NC 27560
(800)3 DIALOG (North America)
http://www.dialog.com
The online service called DIALOG is available for use in gathering marketing intelligence. DIALOG can be used to query any of 900 business and commercial, defense, aerospace, academic, career placement, *Federal Register*—File 180, Federal Research in Progress (FEDRIP)—File 266, Foundation Grants Index—File 27, and other databases. The cost for this service is determined by method of access, access time, specific database being used, and method of downloading the data. Searches can be performed, for example, on public or private companies, specific market segments, general subject areas, government policy and research forecasts, competitor acquisitions and contract award history, and general fiscal trends.

Federal Business Council, Inc. (FBC)

(A nonprofit association)
8975 Henkels Lane
Suite 700
Annapolis Junction, MD 20701
(800)878-2940; (301)206-2940
http://www.fbcinc.com
The Federal Business Council sponsors a variety expos, conferences, and business seminars to give your company procurement direction, contacts, and specific knowledge regarding the federal marketplace. For example, in 2012, the FBC was scheduled to sponsor an event on cloud computing during which small businesses with cloud computing technology were invited to share information about their companies and how their solutions might be leveraged by the Federal Bureau of Investigation (FBI).

Federal Computer Week (FCW)

3141 Fairview Park Drive
Suite 777
Falls Church, VA 22042
(703)876-5100
Circ.: 110,049
http://www.fcw.com
Published 40 times per year, *Federal Computer Week* provides practical news, analysis, and insight on how to buy, build, and manage technology across all segments of federal, state, and local government. Also available online through http://www.fcw.com.

FedMarket DBA FedMarket

Wood River Technologies, Inc.
191 Sun Valley Road
Suite 202
Ketchum, ID 83340
(888)661-4094
Fax: (208)726-5590
http://www.fedmarket.com

FedMarket provides assistance to companies in marketing and selling products and services to the federal government as well as state and local governments and international governments and organizations.

FedMarket assists companies in the process of becoming a GSA-approved vendor and also offers software templates to support the proposal writing process. The company helps to identify appropriate points of contact within customer organizations to assist in the business development and marketing intelligence-gathering processes. FedMarket's *Bidengine* search engine locates proposal opportunities posted by international, federal, state, local, and county governments along with universities, school districts, and public buying cooperatives. The company's Federal Sales Academy assists organizations in learning how to become successful federal government contractors. Finally, FedMarket also provides business development and market intelligence reports for selling to the U.S. government.

Federal Register [Published by the Office of the Federal Register, National Archives and Records Administration (NARA)]

http://www.gpoaccess.gov/fr/

Official daily newspaper for rules, proposed rules, and notices of federal agencies and organizations, as well as executive orders and other presidential documents. It is in the *Federal Register* that the FAR receives its official publication. Changes to the FAR are published as *Federal Acquisition Circulars* (FACs). Careful attention to the *Federal Register* will help to identify program changes and new priorities.

Federal Yellow Book Winter 2011 (ISSN 0145-6202)

Leadership Directories, Inc. (LDI)
1001 G Street, NW
Suite 200 East
Washington, D.C. 20001
(202)347-7757
Fax: (202)628-3430

http://www.leadershipdirectories.com/Products/
LeadershipPrintDirectories/Government/FederalYellowBook.aspx
The *Federal Yellow Book* is an organizational directory of 85 departments
and agencies of the executive branch of the federal government. It provides
organizational position, address, and telephone number for more than
45,000 senior people. The *Federal Yellow Book* is also available online.

Freedom of Information requests

Freedom of Information Act (5 U.S.C. § 552). Consider asking for only
one item per written request to avoid delay if a particular item undergoes
further legal review or is denied.

GovCon (Web site)

http://www.govcon.com
This site offers market research reports, proposal-related books, and a free
consultant locator service.

Government Information Quarterly: An International Journal of Information Technology, Management, Policies, and Practices (ISSN 0740-624X)

A cross-disciplinary and refereed journal that covers information and telecommunications policy, information management, information technology
planning and management, and e-government practices, policies, and
issues. Published by Elsevier.
http://www.elsevier.com/government-information-quarterly

Journal of Contract Management

National Contract Management Association (NCMA)
21740 Beaumeade Circle
Suite 125
Ashburn, VA 20147
(800)344-8096
http://www.ncmahq.org/News/publications/

Minority business associations (for example, Women's Business Center of Northern Virginia; http://www.wbcnova.org)

The Nash & Cibinic Report (ISSN 0891-9291)

A monthly report of analysis and advice on U.S. government contracts prepared by Professor Ralph C. Nash, Jr. of George Washington University[1]. Published by Federal Publications, Inc.

National Technical Information Service (NTIS)

5301 Shawnee Road
Alexandria, VA 22312
(703)605-6585
http://www.ntis.gov
NTIS is a part of the U.S. Department of Commerce Technology Administration and is an excellent source (3 million) for U.S. and foreign government-sponsored research and development (R&D) results, business information, engineering solutions, and marketing reports. Complete technical reports for most government-sponsored R&D and engineering activities are provided through NTIS. The Service also makes available U.S. Army and Air Force manuals and regulations as well as a wide variety of software, data files, and databases, and information on federal laboratory inventions and technologies.

SBA's Office of Women's Business Ownership (OWBO)

Small Business Administration
409 Third Street SW
Washington, D.C. 20416
(800)827-5722
http://www.sba.gov/about-offices-content/1/2895

Trade association meetings

Trade association meetings are announced in trade journals and newsletters as well as on the Internet.

U.S. General Services Administration (GSA) Next Generation Federal Procurement Data System (FPDS-NG)

https://www.fpds.gov
FPDS-NG is a congressional database established to collect historical and statistical information about the federal governement's procurements.

---

1   John Cibinic, Jr., Professor Emeritus at George Washington University, passed away in 2005.

Once registered at www.fpds.gov, you will have access to all actions that have been submitted to FPDS-NG from across the government. There are 27 standard reports available to the public.

Washington Business Journal (ISSN 0737-3147)

Washington Business Journal
1555 Wilson Blvd., Suite 400
Arlington, VA 22209-2405
(202)258-0800
Circ: ~18,000
http://washington.bizjournals.com/washington

Washington Technology (ISSN 1058-9163) 1105 Government Information Group

8609 Westwood Center Drive
Suite 500
Vienna, VA 22182-2215
(703)876-5100
http://www.washingtontechnology.com/Home.aspx
Washington Technology is published semimonthly. Importantly, *Washington Technology* provides annual rankings of the top 100 federal prime contractors, top 25 small business 8(a) contractors, and Fast 50 government contractors. These are great resources for small businesses seeking a large business mentor or prime. The *Washington Technology* Web site offers a wealth of up-to-date information on contract awards, small business topics, and emerging technologies, among many other subject areas.

Sources of international marketing leads and information

From the U.S. federal government

- Export.gov; http://export.gov;
- U.S. Agency for International Development (U.S. AID); Washington, D.C.; http://www.usaid.gov;
- U.S. Environmental Protection Agency (U.S. EPA); Washington, D.C.; http://www.epa.gov;
- U.S. Trade and Development Agency (USTDA); Washington, D.C.; http://www.ustda.gov.

From state-level organizations (example for Maryland)

- Department of Business & Economic Development (http://www. choosemaryland.org/businessinmd/international/pages/ marylandinternationalbusinesscenter.aspx);
- World Trade Center Institute; Baltimore, Maryland (http://www. wtci.org);
- Maryland Sister States Program; Baltimore, Maryland (http://www. sos.state.md.us/international/MSSP.aspx).

From other organizations and media

- Multilateral Banks: World Bank, Asian Development Bank (ADB), and Inter-American Development Bank (IDB); Washington, D.C.;
- Border Environmental Cooperation Commission (BECC), head-quartered in Chihuahua, Mexico (http://www.cocef.org/english/ index.html);
- Canada-China Business Association (CCBA), headquartered in Calgary, Alberta (http://www.chinacanada.com/);
- Maryland/Israel Development Center, Baltimore, Maryland (http://www.marylandisrael.org);
- Canada China Business Council (CCBC) (http://www.ccbc.com);
- U.S.-China Business Council, Washington, D.C., Beijing, Shang-hai, (http://www.uschina.org);
- *The China Business Review* (*CBR;* http://www.chinabusinessreview. com); official magazine of the U.S.-China Business Council pub-lished in Washington, D.C.;
- *China Daily,* published in the Peoples' Republic of China, distrib-uted from New York, is the only national English-language newspa-per in China (http://www.chinadaily.com.cn);
- *Diario Oficial de la Federación*, Mexico City, Mexico (Mexico's Federal Official Journal); contains information about bidding opportunities in Mexico;
- World Bank Monthly Operational Summary (MOS), Washington, D.C. (http://www.web.worldbank.org);
- *The Economist*, London, United Kingdom;
- The Economist Intelligence Unit (EIU), London—leading provider of country-specific market trends and business strategies, spanning 200 countries and 8 key industries (http://www.eiu.com).

Sources of U.S. private-sector marketing leads and information

EI Hazardous Waste Digest

8525 Arjons Drive
Suite H
San Diego, CA 92126
(858)695-0050
http://www.envirobiz.com/EI-hazardous-waste-digest.html
The *EI Hazardous Waste Digest* subscription-based research service is an excellent source of business research focusing on the management of hazardous waste and toxic substances.

is the "owner" for A-76 studies, as per the May 2003 revision to the circular. The roots of Circular A-76 can be traced from the former Bureau of the Budget's Bulletin 55-4 (issued January 15, 1955), which stated that the federal government would "not start or carry on any commercial activity" that the private sector could do. Revisions have been made periodically ever since. A-76 is a federal government management tool. The A-76 competition provides an opportunity for government managers to streamline organization, implement best business practices, increase productivity, enhance quality, increase efficiency of operations, lower operational costs, and adjust IT initiatives to new regulatory drivers such as the President's Management Agenda. The A-76 study process focuses on:

- Government/customer requirements;
- Organizational structure;
- Work processes;
- Defined outcomes;
- Competition.

Historically, the government wins 50% to 84% of competitions. But regardless of who wins, 30% to more than 40% savings are achieved.

Action caption or title   Figure or exhibit caption that conveys a validated sales message with a customer benefit. Captions should emphasize themes. Example: Well-Defined Interfaces at the Project Manager/COTR Level Will Ensure Mutual Understanding of Changing Requirements.

Architect-Engineer Contract Administration Support System (ACASS)   ACASS is a database of selected information on architect-engineering (A-E) firms. ACASS provides required information for DoD and federal government selection committees to aid them in their process of awarding A-E contracts. It is maintained by the Portland, Oregon, office of the U.S. Army Corps of Engineers (USACE). It contains detailed Standard Form 330 and historical SF254/255 data on contractors, DoD awards, and past performance evaluations for the last 6 years of A-E services contracts. For more information on ACASS, go to https://www.nwp.usace.army.mil/ct/I/welcome.htm.

ACASS provides an efficient and economical automated database system by which to adhere to these requirements. The use of ACASS for past performance history is mandated for all DoD agencies in the Defense Federal Acquisition Regulation Supplement (DFARS). For the Corps of Engineers, ACASS eliminated the need for 43 district offices to disseminate performance evaluations among each other and to maintain copies of

SF254s. ACASS is a catalyst for overall improvement in performance of the A-E community. If the performance evaluation is to be rated "below average" or "poor," the A-E firm will receive notification of such prior to the evaluation being signed by the reviewing official. The firm then has 15 days to appeal the proposed rating.

Armed Services Procurement Act (ASPA)   Along with FPASA, this act covered most areas of government procurement (10 U.S.C. § 2301 et seq, 1948).

Base year   The first year of a given contract.

Basis of estimate (BOE)   The basic purpose of the BOE is to sell your company's technical approach, staffing level, skill mix, and cost to the client. The BOE is a nontechnical communication mechanism to present an argument in favor of expending a stated quantity of resources to accomplish a given task. It is documentation of how your estimate was developed and includes your company's assumptions that impact cost, a description of the methodology used in developing the estimate, and justification for using a particular methodology. BOEs must reflect an internal consistency among the Technical, Management, and Cost Volumes of your proposal. And BOEs must be traceable to task descriptions, the SOW, and the WBS. BOEs are most appropriate when the government has not specified hours or any quantitative level of effort (LOE).

Instead of merely stating that Task A will require 5 staff-months of Labor Category 1 personnel and 8 staff-months of Labor Category 4 personnel, a BOE-based approach might build on the following:

Task A requires 5 staff-months of Labor Category 1 personnel and 8 staff-months of Labor Category 4 personnel because, on a similar task performed in 2010 under our XYZ-11 contract with Marshall Space Flight Center, this ratio of senior to junior labor proved to be extremely effective in bringing the work to a successful, on-budget conclusion. Such a labor mix will meet all task requirements as discussed in our Technical Approach section of this proposal.

BOEs may be substantiated by historical or current corporate contractual or commercial work, trade-off studies (particularly in the case of design-oriented procurements), vendor quotes, purchase orders, and so forth. Show your calculations, as you would on a math test, and document your references, as you would in a technical or scientific paper. Your client's source selection board needs quantifiable data to evaluate your proposal. Make sure that you would buy your products or services based on

Capability Maturity Model Integration® (CMMI®)   CMMI® is a comprehensive process improvement approach that combines the Capability Maturity Model® (CMM®) for software with broader disciplines in systems engineering and product development. CMMI® best practices enable organizations to more explicitly link management and engineering activities to business objectives. See http://www.sei.cmu.edu/cmmi.

Capture plan (or strategy)   Formalized, documented sequence of activities that includes the formation of an Acquisition/Capture Team, the generation of a call plan, and actual proposal design and development. A capture plan is directed to the acquisition of a specific business target. Prepared early in the proposal life cycle, the capture plan should include a call plan to define and orchestrate frequent contact with the customer at all levels, and include executive management to business development to all appropriate technical ranks. Specifically, the call plan is designed to gather intelligence about the customer, the particular procurement, and the competition. Information collected must then be analyzed by members of the acquisition team, built into the proposal directive, and eventually factored into your company's proposal where appropriate.

Central Contractor Registration   The Central Contractor Registration (CCR) site (http://www.bpn.gov/ccr) is the primary vendor database for the U.S. federal government. The CCR collects, validates, stores, and disseminates data in support of agency acquisition missions. Both current and potential federal government vendors are required to register with CCR in order to be awarded contracts by the U.S. government. The CCR Web portal is also valuable for searching for small business sources.

Clarifications   Limited exchanges between the government and offerors that may occur when award without discussions is contemplated.

Clinger-Cohen Act (CCA) of 1996   Public Law 104-106, signed into law on February 10, 1996, and also known as the Clinger-Cohen Act, was driven by the federal government's growing reliance on information technology (IT) and the resulting increased attention and oversight on its acquisition, management, and use. Building on FASA, the Clinger-Cohen Act provided the statutory foundation to streamline IT acquisitions and minimize layered approvals. The act emphasized accountability, outcomes-based performance, and results-based IT management. It promoted the improved performance of the civilian agency acquisition workforce. And it allowed contracting officers to select competitive contractors more efficiently. In addition, Clinger-Cohen required federal agencies to use a disciplined capital planning and investment control (CPIC) process to acquire, use, maintain, and dispose of information technology. The use of commercial-off-the-shelf (COTS) products was to be maximized. The Federal Acquisition Reform Act (FARA) and the Information Technology Management Reform Act (ITMRA) are parts of the Clinger-Cohen Act.

The Clinger-Cohen Act rescinded the Brooks Act (Public Law 92-582), also known as Qualifications Based Selection (QBS), which was enacted on October 18, 1972. This 1972 act had established the procurement process by which architects and engineers (A-Es) were selected for design contracts with federal design and construction agencies. The Brooks Act had also established a qualifications-based selection process, in which contracts for A-Es were negotiated on the basis of demonstrated competence and qualification for the type of professional services required at a fair and reasonable price.

Cloud computing　Delivery of hosted information technology services on a shared platform over the Internet. A "cloud" can be private, public or a hybrid model.

Commercial and government entity (CAGE)　A five-character code used to support a variety of automated systems throughout the government. The Defense Logistics Information Service (DLIS) Center in Battle Creek, Michigan, is the only source for assignment and maintenance of CAGE codes. To receive a CAGE code, you must apply online at the Central Contractor Registration Web site (http://www.bpn.gov/ccr).

Communications　Exchanges between the government and offerors, after receipt of proposals, leading to the establishment of competitive range.

Competition in Contracting Act (1984)　CICA, P.L. 98-369, July 18, 1984. This act provides for increased use of competitive procedures in contracting for procurement. CICA modified both FPASA (1949) and ASPA (1947). (Cibinic, John, and Ralph C. Nash, *Formation of Government Contracts*, 2nd ed., Washington D.C.: George Washington University, 1986, pp. 13–14, 287.)

Competitive range　FAR 15.306(c) Proposals deemed within the competitive range are technically sufficient and exhibit a reasonable relationship between cost or price and the product or service to be procured. Proposals with a reasonable chance of being selected for contract award are deemed within the competitive range. The competitive range consists of the most highly rated proposals.

Consolidated contracting initiative (CCI)   A management process that emphasizes developing, using, and sharing contract resources to meet government agency objectives. CCI emphasizes development of contracts that can be used by other government procurement offices and agencies. The goals of CCI are to reduce government contracting staff's time spent on acquisition-related tasks, shorten acquisition lead times, minimize redundant contracts, and improve cooperation with other government agencies.

Contracting officer (CO)   The contracting officer is the federal government person with authority to enter into, administer, and/or terminate contracts and make related determinations and findings. The term includes certain authorized representatives of the contracting officer operating within the limits of their authority as delegated by the contracting officer.

Contractor Performance Assessment Reporting System (CPARS)   A Web-enabled application that collects and manages the library of automated CPARS. CPARS is for unclassified use only. Classified information is not to be entered into this system. A CPARS report assesses a contractor's performance and provides a record, both positive and negative, on a given contract during a specific period of time. Each assessment is based on objective facts and supported by program and contract management data, such as cost performance reports, customer comments, quality reviews, technical interchange meetings, financial solvency assessments, construction and production management reviews, contractor operations reviews, functional performance evaluations, and earned contract incentives.

Cost analysis   Cost analysis is the review and evaluation of the separate cost elements and profit/fee in an offeror's proposal (including cost or pricing data or information other than cost or pricing data). Cost analysis is also determining how well the proposed costs represent what the cost of the contract should be, assuming reasonable economy and efficiency.

Cost realism analysis   Cost realism is the process of the government independently reviewing and evaluating specific elements of each offeror's proposed cost estimate to determine if the estimated proposed cost elements are realistic for the work to be performed, reflect a clear understanding of the requirements, and are consistent with the unique methods of performance described in the offeror's technical proposal.

Data Universal Numbering System (DUNS)   A unique nine-digit identification sequence that is now standard for all U.S. federal government e-commerce transactions. It is the principal contractor identification code. To apply for a DUNS number, visit Dun & Bradstreet online at http://www.dnb.com.

DD Form 254   Department of Defense Contract Security Classification Specification. (Last updated December 1999.)

Defense Contract Audit Agency (DCAA)   Performs contract audit functions required by the DoD and many civilian agencies. Determines the suitability of contractor accounting systems for government work, evaluates the validity of proposed costs, and also reviews the efficiency of contractor operations. Negotiated solicitations contain a clause that authorizes the government Contracting Officer (CO) or his representative to examine the contractor's records under circumstances prescribed in FAR 52.215-2. The DCAA auditor is generally the CO's representative. (See McVay, Barry L., *Proposals That Win Federal Contracts: How to Plan, Price, Write, and Negotiate to Get Your Fair Share of Government Business,* Woodbridge, VA: Panoptic Enterprises, 1989, p. 16.)

Deficiency   Material failure of a proposal to meet a government requirement or a combination of significant weakness in a proposal that increases the risk of unsuccessful contract performance to an unacceptable level. (see FAR 15.001.)

Desktop publishing (DTP)   Desktop publishing refers to a method by which text and graphic materials of publishable quality are produced under author control (as opposed to outside printing company control) at relatively low cost. DTP can introduce higher quality, more professional documentation in your company's publication group. Desktop publishing software applications include Corel Ventura and Adobe PageMaker.

Discriminators   Authenticated, conclusive statements that demonstrate clearly the positive differences between your company and the competition, and demonstrate the benefits of those differences to your client in terms that are meaingful to them, such as quality, schedule, cost, and risk mitigation. Also known as competitive or unique themes.

Discussions   Negotiations conducted in a competitive acquisition. Discussions take place after establishment of the competitve range.

Electronic commerce (EC) or e-commerce   The paperless exchange of business information over the Internet, using electronic data interchange

(EDI), electronic mail, electronic fund transfer (EFT), File Transfer Protocol (FTP), and other related technologies.

Electronic Government (E-Government) Act of 2002   Public Law 107-347, 44 U.S.C. Ch. 36, the Electronic Government Act, was signed into law December 17, 2002. This act, which advocates a more citizen-focused approach to current governmentwide IT policies and programs, was designed in part to institutionalize the President's Management Agenda (PMA). This law requires federal agencies to develop performance measures for implementing e-government. This act also requires agencies to conduct governmentwide e-government initiatives and to leverage cross-agency opportunities to leverage e-government. The Federal CIO Council, originally established in 1996 by Executive Order 13011, was codified under the E-Government Act. Lead by Steven Van Roekel, this council is comprised of the CIOs of 28 federal agencies as well as representatives from the Office of Management and Budget. Its charter is to implement elements of GPRA, FISMA, and ITMRA. The Federal CIO Council is the principal interagency forum to support President Obama's goals of greater transparency, accountability, and public participation in government through the innovative use of IT.

Evaluation Notice (EN)   The procurement contracting officer's (PCO) written notification to the offeror for the purpose of clarifications, communications, or in support of discussions.

E-Verify   Internet-based system operated by the Department of Homeland Security (DHS) and U.S. Citizenship and Immigration Service (USCIS) that allows employers to validate the employment eligibility of their employees, regardless of citizenship. When a contractor wins the bid on a federal contract that contains the FAR E-Verify clause, the contractor must enroll in the E-Verify program within 30 days of award.

Excluded parties list (EPLS)   List of parties excluded from participating in federal procurement programs.

Export Working Capital Program (EWCP)   A joint SBA and Export-Import Bank of the United States program that provides short-term, transaction-specific financing for certain loans.

Federal Acquisition Reform Act (FARA) of 1996   FARA (Division D of P.L. 104-106; 40 U.S.C. 1401) was signed into law on February 10, 1996. This act enabled the federal procurement system to emulate many of the most successful buying practices used in the commercial marketplace. FARA focused on reforming the way in which the federal government makes larger dollar purchases and acquires IT. FARA increased the discretion of federal contracting officers in making competitive range determinations and lowered the approval levels for justification and approvals resulting in efficient competition. FARA also permitted the use of SAP in the acquisition of commercial items up to $5 million.

Federal Acquisition Regulations System Established for the codification and publication of uniform policies and procedures for acquisition by all executive agencies. The Federal Acquisition Regulations System consists of the FAR, which is the primary document, and agency acquisition regulations that implement or supplement the FAR. The FAR System is articulated in Title 48 of the CFR. The FAR is organized into Subchapters a–h, Parts (of which there are 53), Subparts, Sections, and Subsections. Example: 25.108-2, Part 25, Subpart 1, Section 08, and Subsection 2. The FAR is published by the GSA FAR Secretariat and maintained by the DoD, the General Services Administration (GSA), and NASA under several statutory authorities of those agencies. Any critical understanding of the FAR must include the protest decisions of the Comptroller General and the General Services Board of Contract Appeals (GSBCA). The FAR is available online at http://www.gsa.gov/portal/content/101126.

Federal Acquisition Streamlining Act (FASA) of 1994 FASA (Title V, FASA VP.L. 103-355) was signed into law October 13, 1994. It required federal agencies to establish cost, schedule, and measurable performance goals for all major acquisition programs and to achieve, on average, 90% of those goals. FASA focused largely on the purchase of commercial items and smaller dollar buys (those under $100,000). Importantly, the act exempted commercial items from many unique government requirements. Acquisitions of more than $2,500 but not exceeding $100,000 were reserved for small businesses. Under FASA, contracting officers were encouraged to use approaches in awarding contracts that leveraged SAP. In addition, FASA gave agencies statutory authority to access the computer records of contractors doing business with the federal government. The act also placed greater emphasis on the use of past performance when selecting a contractor. Finally, FASA encouraged the use of electronic commerce and established the statutory framework for task- and delivery-order contracting.

Federal Activities Inventory Reform Act (FAIR) of 1998 Legislation that requires federal government agencies to identify functions that could be performed by the private sector.

Federal Business Opportunities (FedBizOpps)   http://www.fbo.gov is the single point-of-entry portal for federal government procurement opportunities of more than $25,000. Government buyers are able to publicize their business opportunities by posting information directly to FedBizOpps via the Internet. Through one portal—FedBizOpps— commercial vendors seeking federal markets for their products and services can search, monitor, and retrieve opportunities solicited by the entire federal contracting community.

Federal Enterprise Architecture (FEA)   To facilitate efforts to transform the federal government into one that is citizen centered, results oriented, and market based, the Office of Management and Budget (OMB) is developing the Federal Enterprise Architecture (FEA), a business-driven and performance-based framework and planning and management tool to support cross-agency collaboration, transformation, and governmentwide improvement. Begun on February 6, 2002, the FEA was constructed through a collection of five interrelated "reference models" (business, performance, data and information, service component, and techncial reference models) designed to facilitate cross-agency analysis and the identification of duplicative investments, gaps, and opportunities for collaboration within and across federal agencies. FEA provides OMB and other federal agencies with a common language for describing, analyzing, and improving the federal government and its ability to serve the American citizen. The outcome of this effort will be a more citizen-centered, customer-focused government that maximizes and shares technology investments to better achieve mission outcomes. OMB Circular A-11 requies that federal agencies and departments demonstrate that their IT investments align with FEA standards and guidelines in order to receive OMB approval.

Federal Information Resources Management Regulation (FIRMR)
Governmentwide regulations that govern the purchase of computer goods and services (41 CFR Chapter 201).

Federal Information Processing Standards Publications (FIPS)
FIPS199 are the standards for categorizing federal agency information systems based on the objectives of providing appropriate levels of information security according to a range of risk levels. FIPS 200 are the minimum security requirements for information and information systems supporting executive branch agencies of the federal government and a risk-based process for selecting security controls to meet requirements.

Federal Property and Administrative Services Act (FPASA)   This act covered most areas of government procurement along with the Armed Services Procurement Act (41 U.S.C. § 252; 1949).

Federal Stock Number (FSN)   A code used to identify documents sold by the U.S. Government Printing Office, Superintendent of Documents.

Federal Supply Schedules   Under the Schedule program, GSA enters into indefinite-delivery, indefinite-quantity contracts with commercial firms to provide commercial goods and services governmentwide at stated prices for given periods of time. Authorized buyers at agencies place separate orders for individual requirements that specify the quantity and delivery terms associated with each order, and the contractor delivers products or services directly to the agency. The program is designed to provide federal agencies with a simplified process for obtaining millions of commonly used commercial supplies and services at prices associated with volume buying. The program consists of single award Schedules, in which GSA awards contracts to multiple companies supplying comparable services and products, often at varying prices. When agency requirements are to be satisfied through the use of multiple award schedules, the small business provisions (such as the exclusive reservation for small businesses for contracts over $2,500 up to $100,000) of the FAR do not apply.

Federal Supply Service (FSS)   An organization within the U.S. General Services Administration.

Fee determination official (FDO)   A government official who determines amount of award fee on a contract based upon contractor performance.

File Transfer Protocol (FTP)   A method of transferring files to and from remote locations.

Foldout page   An 11 × 17–inch double page, usually graphical in nature. Certain RFPs limit the number of foldout pages in a proposal. Foldouts can be important space-savers for page-limited proposals.

Freedom of Information Act (FOIA)   Enacted in 1966 and last amended in 2002, this act provides that select government information is to be made available to the public either by publication in the *Federal Register*, providing an opportunity to read or copy records, or providing copies of records (5 U.S.C. 552). FOIA also identifies nine exceptions that allow the government to withhold information in responding to public requests.

Full-and-Open Competition   All responsible sources are eligible to compete.

Fully loaded labor rates or fully burdened labor rates   *Fully loaded* or *fully burdened* labor rates refer to the full combination of all costs, including but not limited to any combination of benefits, G&A, fee, profit, incentives, bonuses, and other fees or costs included with direct labor. Direct labor rates are the hourly rates of pay actually paid to employees.

G-2   Intelligence; information on competitors, contracts, and so forth.

Gantt chart   A bar chart named after American engineer Henry L. Gantt who devised such a presentation in 1917. Sometimes referred to as project time lines, Gantt charts are commonly used scheduling charts. Gantt charts ordinarily have a list of tasks down the left side (vertical axis). A bar or line on the horizontal axis shows the date when each task begins and ends. Gantt charts are useful for envisioning an entire project over time.

Ghosting   Lines of argumentation used in proposal text to discredit or play down the competitor's strong points or emphasize weak areas. For example, suppose your competitor has demonstrated an inability to deliver technical progress reports in a timely manner. In your proposal—*without naming the competitor*—you would emphasize your commitment to and success with *on-time deliverables*.

Government Information Security Reform Act (GISRA) of 2000
This act brought together existing IT security requirements from the Paperwork Reduction Act of 1995 and the Clinger-Cohen Act of 1996. GISRA also codified existing OMB IT security policies found in OMB Circular A-130 and IT security budget guidance in OMB Circular A-11, "Preparation, Submission, and Execution of the Budget." Specifically, GISRA directed agency CIOs to conduct annual IT security reviews of their systems and programs. Review results are to be reported to OMB. After GISRA expired in November 2002, the Federal Information Security Management Act (FISMA) was signed into law by President George W. Bush as Title III, part of the Electronic Government Act of 2002. FISMA permanently reauthorized the framework established by GISRA.

Government Performance and Results Act (GPRA)　This act holds federal agencies accountable for achieving performance results. Enacted in 1993, it legislates that federal agencies are to be more responsive and accountable to the public/customers relative to achieving program results. GPRA requires that agencies develop comprehensive strategic, business, and performance plans documenting the organizational objectives, goals, strategies, and measures for determining results. The organizational plans and measures for achieving the goals are key elements in determining an agency's need for services (P.L. 103-62, 1993).

Government Wide Acquisition Contract (GWAC)　Defined in Part 2.101 of the Federal Acquisition Regulation, GWACs are critical federal contractual vehicles for small, midsized, and large businesses. They are becoming the vehicle of choice for many government agencies. Much of the procurement paperwork, price justifications, and contractor selections can be done up front in the GWAC procurement process. Individual purchases can then be made from a small cadre of qualified vendors quickly through the use of a task order competition or purchase order. Examples of important current and upcoming GWAC vehicles include GSA STARS II, GSA Alliant Small Business, NIH CIO—SP23, Veterans Technology Services (VETS), and NASA SEWP IV.

Greening　Insertion of junior-level staff in the labor mix over time to reduce life cycle costs in close coordination with the introduction of business processes that increase effectiveness and efficiency.

Homeland Security Presidential Directive 12 (HSPD-12)　Critical mandate that charged federal agencies with developing secure and reliable forms of identification that verify an individual's identity, are resistant to identification fraud, and can be authenticated electronically. HSPD-12 addresses both physical access to federally controlled facilites, and logicial access to federally controlled information systems.

HUBZone　The Small Business Administration (SBA) Historically Underutilized Business Zone (HUBZone) Empowerment Contracting Program (http://www.sba.gov/hubzone) provides federal contracting assistance for HUBZone-certified small business concerns located in qualified business communities in an effort to increase employment opportunities, investment, and economic development. The program provides for set-asides, sole-source awards, and price evaluation preferences for HUBZone small business concerns. In order to be considered for a contract award, the small business concern must be certified by the SBA as a HUBZone small business concern and appear on the SBA list of HUBZone small business concerns. Nationally, HUBZones are located in more than 7,000 urban census tracts, in 900 rural counties, and on every federally recognized Native American reservation.

The HUBZone Empowerment Contracting Program refers to Historically Underutilized Business Zones and was created in 1997 as a result of legislation sponsored by Senator Christopher "Kit" Bond, the ranking member of the Senate Small Business Committee. The federal government has a 3% goal of channeling federal contracts through the HUBZone program, which equated to about $11.97 billion in FY2010.

For a small business to be HUBZone certified, its principal office must be located in a HUBZone and at least 35% of its employees must reside in one of these specially designated areas. In addition, the firm must be owned and controlled by U.S. citizens, a community development company, or Indian tribe. Participants in the program can receive contracts through competition limited to qualified HUBZone firms or on a sole-source basis. HUBZone firms are also given a price preference in bidding during full and open competition over non-HUBZone large firms.

Hypermedia   Richly formatted documents that contain a variety of information types, such as textual, image, movie, and audio.

Hypertext Markup Language (HTML)   Coding mechanism used to author Web pages. HTML is a subset of SGML.

Hypertext Transport Protocol (HTTP)   The protocol, or planned method, for exchanging text, graphic images, sound, video, and other multimedia files used by Web servers.

Incumbent   The contractor or contractor team that is currently performing on a contract that is approaching recompetition.

Indefinite-delivery, indefinite-quantity contract   This type of contract provides for an indefinite quantity, within stated limits, of goods and services during a fixed period of time. Agencies place separate task or delivery orders for individual requirements that specify the quantity and delivery terms associated with each order. The Federal Acquisition Regulation (FAR) expresses a preference for multiple awards of these contracts, which allows orders to be placed using a streamlined, commercial style selection process where consideration is limited to the contract awardees. The competition between the multiple awardees is designed to encourage better prices and responses than if the agency were negotiating with a single contractor. Contractors are to be afforded a fair opportunity to be considered for award of task and delivery orders but cannot generally protest the award of such orders. Indefinite-delivery, indefinite-quantity contracts—such as Network-Centric Solutions-2 (NETCENTS2), Army Information Technology Enterprise Solutions-2 (ITES-2), and the Marine Corps Commerical Enterprise Omnibus Support Services (CEOSS) contract—include GWACs and GSA Federal Supply Schedule contracts.

Information Technology Management Reform Act (ITMRA)
IMTRA (Division E of P.L. 104-106) was signed into law on February 10, 1996. This act enables the federal procurement system to emulate many of the most successful buying practices used in the commercial marketplace. It is focused on reforming the way in which the federal government makes larger dollar purchases and acquires IT, and it establishes the role, duties, and qualifications of the chief information officer within federal agencies.

IT Infrastructure Library (ITIL)   ITIL is a series of documents used to aid in the implementation of a framework for IT service management. It is the most widely accepted approach to IT service management (ITSM) in the world. Created by the U.K. government, ITIL helps to align IT with the business needs of an organization. See http://www.itil-officialsite.com. Also known as ISO 20000.

Javits-Wagner-O'Day (JWOD) Act   The JWOD program—now called AbilityOne (http://abilityone.org)—creates employment and training opportunities for people who are blind or have other severe disabilities and, whenever possible, prepares them for competitive jobs. Under the JWOD Program, government employees are required to buy selected supplies and services from nonprofit agencies employing such persons. As a result, federal customers obtain quality products and services at reasonable prices, while JWOD employees are able to lead more productive, independent lives. The Committee for Purchase from People Who Are Blind or Severely Disabled is the federal agency that administers the JWOD Program and maintains a Procurement List of mandatory source items. Two national organizations, NIB (National Industries for the Blind) and NISH (serving people with a range of disabilities), have been designated to provide technical and financial support to more than 600 nonprofit agencies participating in the AbilityOne Program. The Federal Acquisition Streamlining Act of 1994 continues the legal requirement to buy JWOD items.

Joint Photographic Experts Group (JPEG)   A method of compressing and storing an image in digital format.

Knowledge Management   The enterprisewide application of intellectual capital to achieve organizational mission and business goals.

Labor surplus area (LSA)   A federal program to set aside certain contracts to businesses located in areas with high unemployment.

Lean Six Sigma (LSS)   Business improvement methodology that combines tools from both Lean Manufacturing and Six Sigma. Lean Manufacturing focuses on speed, and Six Sigma focuses on quality.

Lowest Price Technically Acceptable (LPTA)   Process used in competitive negotiated contracting wherein the best balue is expected to result from selection of technically acceptable proposal with the lowest evaluated price. See FAR 15.101-2.

Matrix management   Management configuration in which staff are assigned to support a program or project manager outside their own line organizations or groups.

Micropurchase   A subcategory of simplified acquisitions that refers to purchases of less than $25,000.

Minority On-Line Information Service (MOLIS)   An online database maintained by iAM Solutions in Silver Springs, Maryland, that provides information on Historically Black Colleges and Universities (HBCUs) and Minority Institutions (MIs) to government and private industry to foster partnerships. This online database of more than 260 minority institutions that is used by government agencies, the private sector, and other organizations and institutions to develop partnerships with minority institutions. MOLIS is also used by government agencies to identify possible faculty at minority institutions to serve as peer reviewers.

MOLIS is a one-stop source of in-depth information about the research and educational capabilities of participating Hispanic-serving institutions (HSIs), historically black colleges and universities (HBCUs), tribal colleges and universities (TCUs), and minority postsecondary institutions (MPIs). MOLIS provides information on the minority institutions' research centers, research interests and capabilities, facilities, equipment, faculty profiles, statistics on the number of degrees awarded and enrollment figures, scholarship and fellowship information, and federal opportunity information.

MOLIS has complete searching capabilities, file transfer/document delivery, and multiple access methods, including an 800 number for minority institutions. Key federal agencies support MOLIS under a cooperative agreement from the Department of Defense, including the National Aeronautics and Space Administration, the Department of Defense (OSDBU), the U.S. Department of Agriculture, and the Agency for International Development. These agencies use MOLIS to identify potential beneficiaries of available federal resources. See http://www.molis.us.

Minority-owned business   A business that is at least 51% owned by one or more individuals classified by the U.S. government as socially and economically disadvantaged and whose management and daily business operations are controlled by one or more such individuals. Socially or economically disadvantaged individuals, by government classification, include Black Americans, Hispanic Americans, Native Americans (includes Eskimos, Aleuts, and native Hawaiians), Asian-Pacific Americans, and Asian-Indian Americans.

Modular   A proposal volume format in which each section strictly adheres to a page allocation that contains facing text and art pages, usually one page of each per section.

Modular contracting   Type of contracting that provides for the delivery, implementation, and testing of a workable IT system or solution in discrete increments, or modules. Modular contracting is one of many approaches that can be used by federal agencies to acquire major IT systems. It may be achieved by a single procurement, or multiple procurements, but is intended to ensure that the government is not obligated to purchase more than one module at a time. Modular contracting is intended to balance the government's need for fast access to rapidly changing technology and incentivized contractor performance, with stability in program management, contract performance, and risk management.

To help improve federal agencies' acquisition and management of major IT systems, Congress passed, and the president signed, the Information Technology Management Reform Act (ITMRA, P.L. 104-106, February 1996; also known as the Clinger-Cohen Act). Section 5202 of this law directs federal agencies to use modular contracting, to the maximum extent practicable, for the acquisition of major IT systems. Following the ITMRA, the president issued Executive Order No. 13011, which instructs agencies to apply modular contracting "where appropriate" and "to the maximum extent practicable."

Note that one of great enablers of modular contracting is the ready availability of task order, multiagency, and Governmentwide Acquisition Contracts (GWACs). With these tools, program managers have access to many major IT service and product providers through these contracts. In some cases, task orders can be in place within 60 days of the initial request. This allows program managers to compete modular tasks quickly and easily.

Modular contracting is one of the federal government's strategies that moves the acquisition strategy from a traditional grand design to a more manageable incremental approach. A significant benefit offered by modular contracting is its potential to refocus acquisition management attention and strategies to a more responsive and realistic systems development acquisition model.

National Stock Number (NSN)   A unique number assigned by the General Services Administration that catalogs a wide range of items by commodity, group, and class.

North American Industry Classification System   NAICS (pronounced "nakes"), which replaced the Standard Industrial Classification (SIC) code system, was developed jointly by the United States, Canada, and Mexico to provide comparable statistics about business activity across North America's three NAFTA trading partners. NAICS makes it easier to compare North American business data with the International Standard Industrial Classification System (ISIC), developed and maintained by the United Nations. The *NAICS Manual* is available through the National Technical Information Service (NTIS) at (800) 553-6847 or on the Web at http://www.ntis.gov/products/naics.asp.

Office of Small and Disadvantaged Business Utilization (OSDBU)   An office within federal agencies that provides procurement assistance to small, disadvantaged, minority-8(a), HUBZone, veteran-owned, service-disabled-owned, and woman-owned businesses. The Small Business Act as amended by P.L. 95-507 established the OSDBU. The OSDBU in federal agencies acts as an advocate for small businesses.

Option years   Additional years available on a given contract if the government elects to exercise its option to renew that contract.

Oral presentation   An oral examination in which an offeror submits information bearing on its capability and proposed solution to a panel of government source selection officials. This information may include, for example, a description of, and justification for, the offeror's performance policies, processes, and plans. The oral presentation is distinct from the offer (i.e., the proposal) in that it is not itself an offer or part of an offer, and does not become a part of any resultant contract. However, the government may include the results of its assessment of oral presentations in its overall technical or management evaluation. The source selection panel uses the oral information to determine the offeror's understanding of the prospective work and, thus, its capability to perform successfully. Oral presentations may be audio or videotaped for subsequent government review.

Out years   The final years exercised on a given contract.

Past Performance Information Retrieval System (PPIRS)   The PPIRS database (http://www.ppirs.gov/) is available to all source selection officials across the entire federal government. Its purpose is to assist federal acquisition officials in purchasing goods and services that represent the best value for the federal government. Contractor access to PPIRS is gained through the Central Contractor Registration (CCR) (http://www.bpn.gov/ccr) process. A contractor must be registered in CCR and must have created a Marketing Partner Identification Number (MPIN) in the CCR profile to access their PPIRS information.

Formerly called the Past Performance Automated Information System (PPAIS), the federal PPIRS database is a Web-enabled application that allows the retrieval of contractor past performance information. It is also a central warehouse used to retrieve performance assessment reports received from the recognized federal report card collection systems.

Performance-based acquisition (PBA)   The term *performance-based acquisition* (PBA) has replaced *performance-based contracting* (PBC). Performance-based acquisition is a major trend within federal procurement. The Services Acquisition Reform Act (SARA), which was included in the National Defense Authorization Act of 2004 (P.L. 108-136), provides incentives for performance-based services acquisitions in a manner similar to what the Federal Acquisition Streamlining Act (FASA) and the Clinger-Cohen Act did with regard to federal hardware procurement.

The principal objective of PBA is to express government needs in terms of required and measurable performance objectives, outcomes, and/or results, rather than the method of performance. This approach is to encourage industry-driven, competitive solutions and commercial best practices. The overarching focus is on the *results,* not the processes used to deliver those results. Either a performance work statement (PWS) or statement of objectives (SOO) may be used for performance-based service acquisition (PBSA). Performance-based Requests for Solutions (RFSs) describe how the contractor's performance will be evaluated in a quality assurance surveillance plan (QASP). Positive and negative incentives are identified as appropriate.

The PWS is a statement within the solicitation that identifies the technical, functional, and performance characteristics of the agency's requirements. The SOO is an alternative to the PWS. It is a summary of key agency goals and outcomes. The QASP is a plan for assessing contractor performance in order to ensure accomplishment of the government's objectives. The level of surveillance is linked to contract dollar amount, risk, and complexity of the requirement.

Performance-based service contracting (PBSC)   PBSC is the process of contracting for services by using mission-related, outcome-oriented statements of work [performance work statements (PWSs)] and quality assurance performance measures. PBSC focuses on the desired outcome and its quality measures rather than on the how of providing the required services. A PWS is the basic document used in PBSC that describes the specific requirements the contractor must meet in performance of the contract in terms of output and a measurable standard for the output.

Performance confidence assessment   Evaluation of the likelihood (or government's confidence) that the offeror will successufly perform the solicitation's requirements. The evaluation is based upon past performance information.

Performance risk   Performance risks are those risks that are associated with an offeror's likelihood of success in performing the solicitation's requirements as indicated by that offeror's record of current or past performance.

Performance Work Statement (PWS)   A statement in a solicitation that identifies the technical, functional, and performance characteristics of the agency's requirements.

PERT chart   The Arrow Diagram Method (ADM)/PERT, or Program Evaluation and Review Technique, is a "flow diagram showing the sequence of ... various activities and their interdependence in terms of completion dates. In a sense it is a road map to a destination to show the intermediate points and distances between them. Activities are sequenced from left to right." (See Krathwohl, Dave R., *How to Prepare a Research Proposal: Guidelines for Funding and Dissertations in the Social and Behavioral Sciences,* 3rd ed., Syracuse, NY: Syracuse University Press, 1988, p. 75.) Developed initially by the U.S. Navy, Lockheed, and Booz Allen Hamilton in the 1950s, PERT charts are used in project management and project planning activities and are useful because task dependencies are illustrated. Tasks are scheduled, organized, and coordinated. Critical Path Method (CPM) has become synonymous with the PERT technique.

Portrait versus landscape pages   *Portrait* refers to pages of a document oriented such that the vertical dimension is 11 inches and the horizontal dimension is 8.5 inches. (This page is in portrait format.) *Landscape* refers to pages oriented such that the vertical dimension is 8.5 inches and the horizontal dimension is 11 inches. Landscape pages are often used for full-page graphics or tables.

Preinvitation notice (PIN)   A summary of a solicitation package sent to prospective bidders, who may then request the entire solicitation package.

Preproposal conference   A face-to-face meeting between the government technical and contractual contacts and the potential bidders from industry. Attendance is very important as it goes directly to your company's interest in the given procurement. Many times, the major technical requirements will be reviewed in a briefing format. A site visit may be included with the proposal conference.

Price analysis   The process of examining and evaluating an offeror's proposed price to determine if it is fair and reasonable, without evaluating its separate cost elements and proposed profit.

Procurement Technical Assistance Centers (PTACs)   Government and privately funded organizations dedicated to helping small companies do business with the federal government.

Profit center   The smallest organizationally independent segment of a company charged by that company's management with profit and loss (P&L) responsibilities.

Proposal   An offer prepared by a contractor to perform a service or supply a product (or a combination of both) in response to an RFP or RFS issued by a procuring agency. A proposal is a sales document, knowledge product, and legal document.

Proposal Directive   The Proposal Directive is a carefully structured "living document" that serves as the "encyclopedia" of a win for a given procurement opportunity. During the course of the acquisition/capture and proposal process, the Proposal Directive may undergo 10 or more iterations as new intelligence about the competition, for example, is uncovered and other information (e.g., win themes, technical solutions, management solutions) is further refined. The Proposal Directive is the repository that contains all of the relevant information about the customer organization, competition, specific program/project, and relevant technologies and best practices. It contains the call plan reports from customer visits; a synopsis of the hopes, fears, biases, success criteria, and critical issues of key government decision makers; the win strategy white paper for your company along with the proposal outlines for each volume; win themes and discriminators; proposal response milestone schedule; and specific proposal-related action items. Thus, the *marketing intelligence* that the Business Development staff gather is collected in the Proposal Directive. The *solution sets* that the Acquisition/Capture Team develops based on the marketing intelligence are documented in the Proposal Directive. And the *proposal development work products*—schedules, outlines, action items, and so on—are also included within the Proposal Directive. Note that the Proposal Directive is a highly competition-sensitive document and, therefore, must be safeguarded very carefully.

Proposal risk   Proposal risks are those risks associated with the likelihood that an offeror's proposed approach will meet the requirements of the solicitation. Proposal risk is different from project-level risk.

Provisional rate   A temporary rate established for a future prospective period of time to permit budgeting, obligations, and payment of funds by awarding federal government agencies until such time as the actual indirect costs can be determined and a final rate is established. A provisional rate is a type of *indirect rate*.

Quality assurance surveillance plan (QASP)   A plan for assessing contractor performance in order to ensure accomplishment of the government's performance objectives stated in the contract and compliance with the appropriate inspection clauses. The level of surveillance should be commensurate with the dollar amount, risk, and complexity of the requirement. Contractors may be required to generate DRAFT QASPs as part of the proposal

Recency   As it pertains to past performance information, it is a measure of the time that has elapsed since the past performance reference has occured. Recency is generally expressed as a time period during which past performance references are considered relevant.

Relevancy   As it pertains to past performance information, is a measure of the extent of similarity between the service/support effort, complexity, dollar value, contract type, and subcontract/teaming or other comparable attributes of past performance exmples and the source solicitation requirements. Relevancy is a measure of the likelihood that the past performance is an indicator of future performance.

Risk   As it pertains to source selection, is the potential for unsuccessful contract performance. The consideration of risk assesses the degree to which an offeror's proposed approach may involve risk of disruption of schedule, increased cost or the degradation of performance, the need for increased government oversight, and the likelihood of unsuccessful contract performance.

Risk-sharing method   Also known as share-in-savings, shared-savings, value-based, transaction-based, and shared-benefits contracting, the risk-sharing method calls for vendors and contractors to cover the up-front funding of a project in return for the promise of a share of the savings or additional benefits that result downstream. In addition to reducing costs and relieving government agencies of capital funding expenditures or major investments, share-in-savings acquisition has significant potential both to improve the performance of agency programs and to infuse new technology and new methods of doing business. Shared-savings approaches are a significant shift away from the way federal agencies traditionally have bought services: by closely specifying the how and what of each contract and paying contractors to enact their plans. Slowly, federal agencies are moving toward performance-based contracting—specifying only results, leaving companies free to devise the solutions to achieve them while closely measuring performance and basing rewards on meeting outcome goals. By adding fiscal incentives for performance exceeding what is expected and penalties for falling short, federal agencies are shifting even more risk to vendors and contractors. But shared-savings deals can also extend to reserving payment until the contractor produces tangible results.

Writing in *Government Executive* magazine, Anne Laurent notes that perhaps the best-known example of benefits-sharing contracting in government is operated by the Department of Energy to help agencies install energy-saving devices. DOE's Federal Energy Management Program (FEMP) has crafted energy-savings performance contracts under which energy service companies absorb all the up-front costs of identifying a facility's energy needs and then buying, installing, operating, and maintaining energy-efficient equipment to cut energy bills. In return, companies get a share of the energy savings generated by improvements made during the contracts, which can last as long as 25 years.

A cogent example of risk sharing was found in the major RFP released by the Department of Veterans. In Section C of the RFP, Partnering Services, it was stipulated that the prime shall construct a flexible arrangement with the VA Austin Automation Center (AAC) that focuses on a long-term partnership instead of a project-by-project relationship. The partnership goals include supporting AAC in marketing, business planning, solution development, proposal preparation, and systems implementation services. AAC desires that the contractor invest in the business relationship and assume a portion of the business risks involved with implementing new services and maintaining existing services. The RFP continued by stating that a partnership agreement shall be developed by the contractor and mutually agreed to by the government. AAC anticipated that the partnership agreement would provide for: (1) agreement that each party will assume its portion of the business risk associated with the partnership, and (2) share business risks and rewards in implementing new services and maintaining existing services.

Sealed bidding   A method of contracting that employs competitive bids, public bid openings, and awards. Award is made to the responsible bidder whose bid, conforming to the invitation for bids (IFB), will be most advantageous to the government considering only price and price-related factors included in the invitation.

Services Acquisition Reform Act (SARA) of 2003   SARA (P.L. 108-136; Title 14 of the FY2004 National Defense Authorization Act) provides incentives for use of performance-based contracting for services.

Set aside   A kind or class of procurement reserved for contenders who fit a certain category, for example, business size, region, or minority status (see FAR 19.501).

SF33   Solicitation offer and award. SF 33 is prescribed for use in soliciting bids for supplies or services and for awarding contracts that result from bids.

SF330   SF330, Architect-Engineer Qualifications form, was developed to replace the long-standing SF254 and SF255. SF254, Architect-Engineer and Related Services Questionnaire, and SF255, Architect-Engineer and Related Services Questionnaire for Specific Projects, had been largely unchanged since their introduction in 1975. The A-E industry, however, has changed substantially and the requirements of federal agencies have evolved considerably. In response to these changes, SF330 was developed by an interagency committee, submitted to industry and government for comment through the *Federal Register*, and fielded.

SF330 reflects current A-E practices and provides the essential information agencies need for the selection of A-E firms in a streamlined format. The SF330 is a two-part form. Part I, Contract-Specific Qualifications, replaces SF255. Part II, General Qualifications, replaces SF254. SF254 is now essentially used as an appendix to SF255 and is rarely used alone. Hence, SF330 was designed as a single two-part form. Similar to SF254, SF330 Part II can still be separately submitted to agencies to be maintained in their A-E qualification data files.

The objectives of the SF330 are as follows:

- Merge the SF254 and SF255 into a single streamlined form.
- Expand essential information about qualifications and experience.
- Reflect current A-E disciplines, experience types, and technology.
- Eliminate duplicate information.
- Eliminate information of marginal value.
- Facilitate electronic usage.

SF 1411   Contract Pricing Cover Sheet.

Simplified acquisition procedures (SAPs)   Streamlined techniques and guiding principles designed to reduce the administrative burden of awarding the lower dollar value procurements that account for the vast majority of DoD acquisition. They allow for informal quoting and competition procedures, encourage accepting oral quotes versus written quotations, prefer comparing quoted prices versus conducting negotiations, and provide streamlined clauses to support the award document. Saving money, improving opportunity and efficiency, and avoiding administrative burden are at the core of the SAP program. The Federal Acquisition Streamlining Act and the Federal Acquisition Reform Act were integral in the creation of simplified acquisitions and the simplified acquisition threshold of $100,000.

Size standard   A size standard, usually stated in terms of number of employees or average annual receipts, represents the largest size that a business (including its subsidiaries and affiliates) may be to remain classified as a small business for SBA and federal contracting programs.

Six Sigma   A statistical and business process improvement method focusing on quality from a customer's point of view. The goal of Six Sigma is to increase profits by eliminating process output variability, defects, and waste that undermine customer loyalty. Six Sigma is a federally registered service mark and trademark of Motorola. See http://www.isixsigma.com.

Small business   A business that is independently owned and operated and is not dominant in its field; a business concern meeting government size standards for its own particular industry type. A small business in the manufacturing field normally employs, with its affiliates, not more than 500 persons. In the services arena (e.g., NAICS Section 54—Professional, Scientific, and Technical Services), small businesses are usually defined as businesses that generate less than $7 million in gross annual receipts.

Small Business Act (SBA)   This 1953 act established the U.S. Small Business Administration. Public Law 95-507, enacted in October 1978, made major revisions to strengthen the SBA.

Small Business Administration (SBA)   The federal government agency whose function is to aid, counsel, provide financial assistance to, and protect the interests of the small business community (from McVay, *Proposals That Win Federal Contracts,* p. 324). The U.S. SBA has the responsibility of making certain that small business obtains a fair share of government contracts and subcontracts. Their mission is articulated in the Small Business Act of 1953, which established that organization.

Small Business High Technology Institute (SBHTI)   SBHTI fosters the development of R&D-based small businesses.

Small Business Innovation Research (SBIR) program   SBIR is a highly competitive SBA program that encourages small businesses to explore their technological potential and provides the incentive to profit from its commercialization. Under this program, federal agencies with large R&D budgets must direct designated amounts of their R&D contracts to small businesses. Small businesses must be American-owned and independently operated, for-profit, principal researcher employed by the business, and have no more than 500 employees. Federal agencies that participate in the SBIR Program include the DoD, USDA, DOC, DOE, DHHS, DOT, EPA, NASA, NRC, NSF, and the Department of Education. These agencies designate R&D topics and accept proposals for a three-phase program. Phase I (feasibility studies) has awards up to $100,000 for 6 months, and Phase II (full-scale research) has awards up to $750,000 for up to 2 years. Phase III (commercialization) is the period during which the Phase II innovation moves from the laboratory into the marketplace. No SBIR funds support this phase. The small business must find the funding in the private sector or non-SBIR federal agency. The U.S. SBA serves as the coordinating agency and information link for SBIR. Examples of successful SBIR proposals include thin-film optical filters for intense laser light, membrane-based process for debittering citrus juice, and neonatal/infant/ fetal pump-oxygenator system. Since the inception of the SBIR Program in 1983, nearly $4 billion in competitive federal R&D awards have been made to qualified small business concerns under the program. Only Phase I winners may submit Phase II proposals.

Software Engineering Institute (SEI) The Software Engineering Institute is a federally funded research and development center sponsored by the U.S. Department of Defense and operated by Carnegie Mellon University. SEI is the current "steward" of the CMMI® model.

Sole source acquisition A contract for the purchase of supplies or services that is entered into or proposed to be entered into by the contracting officer of an agency after soliciting and negotiating with only one source (vendor, contractor). This is done on the grounds that only that one source is capable of satisfying the government's requirements.

Special Drawing Rights (SDR) An international currency unit set up by the International Monetary Fund.

Standard form (SF) SFs and optional forms may be obtained from the Superintendent of Documents, Government Printing Office (GPO), Washington, D.C., 20402, the prescribing agency (see FAR 53.107), or most easily, at the GSA Forms Library at http://www.gsa.gov/portal/forms/download/21DBF5BF7E860FC185256E13005C6AA6.

Standard International Trade Classification (SITC) A classification system devised by the United Nations for commodities used in international trade.

Statement of Objectives (SOO) An alternative to a performance work statement (PWS); it is a summary of key agency goals, outcomes, or both that is incorporated into performance-based service acquisitions in order that competitors may propose their solutions, including a technical approach, performance standards, and a quality assurance surveillance plan based on commercial business practices.

Statement of Work (SOW)   A statement that defines the government's requirements in clear, concise language identifying specific work to be accomplished.

Stet   Literally, "let it stand"; a proofreader's notation meaning that the indicated change should not be made.

Storyboarding   Storyboarding (the associated work products are also referred to as *scenarios* and *scribble sheets*) is a critical management process that focuses on building a coherent, consistent, and compelling proposal story. Building on the marketing intelligence and solution sets for a given procurement, key stakeholders in the proposal process (your capture manager, proposal manager, business development staff, subject matter experts, and so on) meet in a series of brainstorming sessions and generate the following critical work products: (1) annotated outline for each major section of the proposal that provides an expanded architecture for each proposal section; (2) "elevator speeches" that tell the overarching story for each section; and (3) populated "pain tables" that illustrate your company's understanding of the customer's "pain points" and major issues, your approach/solution, and your company's value proposition. Your value proposition includes the tangible and intangible benefits that your solution will bring to the customer organization.

Storyboarding allows your company and your proposal and capture teams to achieve the "right dive angle off the board." Just as a championship diver cannot adjust her position relative to the water when she's a mere foot above the surface, neither can a proposal team move in a fundamentally different direction when deep into the proposal response life cycle—at least not without a lot of depleted morale, extremely long hours, wasted resources, and interpersonal challenges across the team.

Coming out of the storyboarding process, one should be able to review the elevator speeches from end to end and grasp the entire fact-based storyline of the proposal response.

Strawman RFP or proposal   Mock, simulated, or preliminary RFP or proposal.

Strength   An aspect of an offeror's proposal that has merit or exceeds performance or capability requirements in a way that will be advantageous to the government during contract performance. Any aspect of a proposal that, when judged against stated evaluation criteria, enhances the merit of the proposal or increases the probability of successful performance on the contract.

Tag Image File Format (TIFF)   A file format used to store image files.

Technical leveling   The elimination of differences between competitors by repeated discussions and exchange of information. It is inappropriate for the government to assist offerors by suggesting modifications that improve their proposals [FAR 15.610(d)(1)]. (Cibinic, John, and Ralph C. Nash, *Formation of Government Contracts*, 2nd ed., Washington, D.C.: George Washington University, 1986, pp. 529, 625.)

Technical transfusion   The transfer of one competitor's ideas to another competitor during the course of discussions with the government. (Cibinic, John, and Ralph C. Nash, *Formation of Government Contracts*, 2nd ed., Washington, D.C.: George Washington University, 1986, pp. 529, 622.)

Themes   Authenticated, substantiated statements that clearly articulate why the client should select your company over your competition. Examples include common themes, unique themes (discriminators), competitive themes. Themes are supported claims, platforms, and sound arguments.

Tiger Team   Specialized working group generally assigned to track and address one particular aspect of a proposal effort, such as cost strategy.

Trade-off process   The process that permits trade-offs among cost/price and noncost factors and allows the government to accept other than the lowest priced proposal. Specific information on the relative strengths and weaknesses of a proposal is the basis of trade-off analysis.

Transmission Control Protocol/Internet Protocol (TCP/IP)   A set of rules that establish the method by which data are transmitted over the Internet between computers.

Uniform resource locator (URL)   A path or pointer for locating files and sites on the Web.

Walsh-Healey Act   Enacted in 1936, "41 U.S.C. §§ 35–45, requires that, for contracts exceeding $10,000, the contractor be a 'manufacturer of' or a 'regular dealer in the materials, supplies, articles, or equipment to be manufactured or used in the performance of a contract.' " (Cibinic, John, and Ralph C. Nash, *Formation of Government Contracts*, 2nd ed., Washington, D.C.: George Washington University, 1986, p. 226.)

War room   A facility or portion of a facility dedicated to proposal operations, planning, writing, and review. The walls of a war room are often used to display proposal (and RFP) sections for review and comment. Seeing specific proposal sections in the context of other sections aids in overall continuity and flow, as well as helps eliminate unnecessary redundancy. A war room should be a highly secure area because of the open display of proposal materials.

Weakness   A flaw in a proposal that increases the risk of unsuccessful contract performance. See FAR 15.001.

Woman-owned business (WOB)   A business that is at least 51% owned, controlled, and operated by a woman or women. "Control" is defined as exercising the power to make policy decisions, and "operate" is defined as actively involved in day-to-day management.

World Wide Web (WWW; W3; the Web)   A distributed hypertext-based information system conceived at CERN to provide its user community with an easy way to access global information. The Web allows for the presentation and linkage of information dispersed across the Internet in an easily accessible way. The Internet 2 is projected to be 100 times faster than the Internet. More than 206 U.S. colleges and universities are participating in the upgrade process. The Internet is an international computer network of networks that connect government, academic, and business institutions. See http://www.internet2.edu.

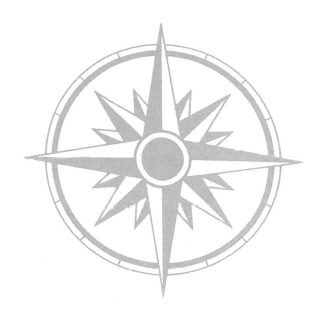

Selected list of acronyms and abbreviations

AAMB	American Association of Minority Businesses
AAP	acquisition analysis process
AAR	after action review
AAWBOA	African American Women Business Owners Association
ABC	activity-based costing
ABELS	Automated Business Enterprise Locator System (former online listing of minority-owned firms, maintained by the Minority Business Development Agency; now called Phoenix database)
ACA	after contract award
ACASS	architect-engineer contract administration support system

ACE	American Council on Education; Acquisition Committee for eGovernment
ACEC	American Consulting Engineers Council
ACH	Automated Clearing House
ACO	administrative contracting officer
ACOP	Acquisition Center Business Opportunity (U.S. Army CECOM)
ACRI	acquisition cost reduction initiatives
ACT	American Council for Technology
ACWP	actual cost of work performed
ADA	Americans with Disabilities Act (Section 508)
ADB	Asian Development Bank; African Development Bank
ADP	automated (or automatic) data processing
ADPE	automatic data processing equipment
ADR	administrative dispute resolution; alternative dispute resolution
A-E	architect-engineer
A/E/C	Architect/Engineer/Construction
AECA	U.S. Arms Export Control Act
AEP	Asian Environmental Partnership
AES	advanced encryption standard
AF	Air Force; award fee
AFAA	Air Force Audit Agency
AFARS	Army Federal Acquisition Regulation Supplement
AFB	Air Force base
AFBOP	Air Force Business Opportunities Page
AFCEE	Air Force Center for Engineering and the Environment (formerly Air Force Center for Environmental Excellence)
AFFARS	Air Force Federal Acquisition Regulation Supplement
AFH	Air Force Handbook
AFI	Air Force Instruction (e.g., AFI 32-4002, "Hazardous Materials Emergency Planning and Response Compliance")
AFMC	Air Force Material Command

AFMPCOE	Air Force Mentor-Protégé Center of Excellence
AFOPO	Air Force Outreach Program Office
AFR	Air Force Regulation
AFRL	Air Force Research Laboratory
AFSPC	Air Force Space Command
AICPA	American Institute of Certified Public Accountants
AID	Agency for International Development (http://www.usaid.gov)
AIS	Automated information system
AISB	American Institute of Small Business (http://www.aisb.biz)
AKO	Army Knowledge Online
ALC	additional labor categories
ALN	asynchronous learning network
AMC	Army Material Command
AMD	Acquisition Management Directorate (DCAA)
AMS	Acquisition Management System; Advisory Multi-Step Acquisition (Army)
AMSDL	acquisition management source data list
ANC	Alaska Native Corporation
ANSI	American National Standards Institute
AOL	America Online
APB	Acquisition Program Baseline; Accounting Principles Board
APEC	Asia-Pacific Economic Cooperation
API	application programming interface
APMP	Association of Proposal Management Professionals (http://www.apmp.org)
APR	agency procurement request
AQL	acceptable quality level
AR	Army regulation; acquisition reform
ARDEC	Armament Research, Development and Engineering Center
ARNet	Acquisition Reform Network
ARO	after receipt of order

ARRA	American Recovery and Reinvestment Act (2009); P.L. 111-5
ARRT	Acquisition Reengineering and Realignment Task Force
ASBA	American Small Business Association [Rock City, IL; (800)942-2722]
ASBCA	Armed Services Board of Contract Appeals
ASBCD	Association of Small Business Development Centers
ASC	Accredited Standards Committee (ANSI); Aeronautical Systems Center (WPAFB)
ASCII	American Standard Code for Information Exchange
ASEAN	Association of Southeast Asian Nations
ASFI	Army Single Face to Industry (acquisition Web site)
ASPA	Armed Services Procurement Act (1948, 10 U.S.C. § 2301 et seq.)
ASPM	Armed Services Pricing Manual
ASPR	Armed Services Procurement Regulation
ASSIST	Acquisition Streamlining and Standardization Information System
ATO	authority of operate
ATP	Advanced Technology Program (NIST)
ATR	assistant technical representative
ATRB	Award-Term Review Board
AVU	African Virtual University
AWBC	Association of Women's Business Centers
B&P	bid and proposal
B2B	business-to-business
B2G	business-to-government
BA	basic agreement; budget authority; budget activity
BAA	broad agency announcement; Buy American Act (41 U.S.C. 10a)
BABC	British-American Business Council
BAFO	best and final offer (replaced by FPR)
BARBB	Missile Defense Agency Business Acquisition Reporting Bulletin Board
BARFO	best and revised final offer
BBS	bulletin board system

BCA	Board of Contract Appeals
BCWP	budgeted cost for work performed
BCWS	budgeted cost for work scheduled
BDG	business development group
BDO	blanket delivery order
BECC	Border Environmental Cooperation Commission
BI	SBA's Office of Business Initiatives; business intelligence; background investigation
BIC	business information center
B/L	bill of lading
BLS	Bureau of Labor Statistics, U.S. Department of Labor
BMP	best management practices
BOA	basic ordering agreement
BOD	bid opening date
BOE	basis of estimate
BOM	bill of materials
BOS	business opportunity specialist (SBA)
BOTB	British Overseas Trade Board
BPA	blanket purchase agreement
BPCR	breakout procurement center representative
BPO	blanket purchase order
BPR	business process reengineering
BRAC	Base Realignment and Closure
BRC	business resource center
BRM	Business Reference Model
BSC	Balanced Score Card
BSO	business support centers (Japan)
BT	British Telecom
BusinessLINC	Business Learning, Information, Networking, and Collaboration
BVA	best value analysis

BVS	best value selection
BY	budget year
C&A	certification and accreditation
C2	command and control
C3I	command, control, communications, and intelligence
C4	command, control, communications, and computers
C4I	command, control, communications, computers, and intelligence
CAAC	Civilian Agency Acquisition Council
CAAS	contract for advisory and assistance services
CAC	common access card
CACES	computer-aided cost estimation system
CACO	corporate administrative contracting officer
CAD	computer-aided design
CAE	computer-aided engineering
CAF	contract administration fee; contract access fee
CAGE	commercial and government entity
CAIP	community adjustment and investment program
CAIV	cost as an independent variable
CALS	computer-aided acquisition and logistics support
CAM	Contract Audit Manual (DCAA)
CAN	contract award notice
CANDI	commercial and nondevelopmental item
CAO	chief acquisition officer (government position); chief administrative officer
CAP	contractor-acquired property
CAR	commerce acquisition regulation
CARE	Cooperative for Assistance and Relief Everywhere, Inc.
CAS	Cost Accounting Standards (enumerated at FAR 30); contract administration services
CASB	Cost Accounting Standards Board
CASE	computer-aided software engineering

CBA	collective bargaining agreement; cost benefit analysis; component-based architecture
CBD	*Commerce Business Daily* (now defunct, replaced by FedBizOpps)
CBR	*China Business Review*
CBO	Congressional Budget Office
CBSC	Canada Business Service Center
CCA	Clinger-Cohen Act of 1996 (P.L. 104-106; also includes FARA and ITMRA)
CCASS	construction contract appraisal support system
CCB	configuration control board
CCBA	Canada-China Business Association
CCBC	Canada China Business Council
CCF	Contract Cases Federal
CCH	Commerce Clearing House
CCI	consolidated contracting initiative
CCL	Commerce Control List (15 C.F.R. § 774, Suppl. 1)
CCN	Cooperating Country Nationals; contract change notice; configuration change notice
CCP	current cost or pricing
CCR	Central Contractor Registration (Columbus, Ohio, and Ogden, Utah; an electronic database of government vendor firms that is maintained by the DoD; http://www.bpn.gov/ccr/default.aspx); Central Consultancy Register (Brussels, Belgium)
CDA	Contract Disputes Act (1978)
CDC	certified development company
CDL	contract data list
CDRD	contract data requirements document
CDRL	contract data requirements list; contractor establishment code
CEB	cost element breakdown
CEC	Center for Electronic Commerce; contract establishment code
CECOM	U.S. Army's Communications-Electronics Command

CEEBIC	Central & Eastern Europe Business Information Center (now defunct)
CEI	contract end item
CENDI	Commerce, Energy, NASA, and Defense Information
CEO	chief executive officer
CEOss	Commercial Enterprise Omnibus Support Services contract (Marine Corps)
CER	cost estimating relationship
CERN	Conseil European pour la Recherche Nucleaire (European Organization for Nuclear Research; originators of HTTP and HTML)
CEU	continuing education unit
CFE	contractor-furnished equipment; centers for excellence
CFME	Committee for External Economic Events (France)
CFO	chief financial officer
CFP	customer-furnished property
CFR	Code of Federal Regulations (e.g., Title 41, Public Contracts)
CGLI	comprehensive general liability insurance
CI	configuration item; contractor inquiry
CIA	Central Intelligence Agency
CICA	Competition in Contracting Act of 1984 (P.L. 98-369, 98 Stat. 1175)
CID	commercial item description
CIDA	Canadian International Development Agency
CIF	cost, insurance, freight
CIO	chief information officer
CIP	critical infrastructure protection
CIS	capability/interest survey; Commonwealth of Independent States (former Soviet Union)
CISO	chief information security officer
CIT	Center for Information Technology (NIH)
CITD	Center for International Trade Development (California)
CITEC	Centers for Industrial and Technological Cooperation

CITI	Center for Information Technology Innovation
CKA	chief knowledge architect
CKO	chief knowledge officer
CLIN	contractor line item
CLS	contractor logistics support
CM	configuration management; contract management; continuous monitoring
CMM®	Capability Maturity Model® (Software Engineering Institute)
CMMI®	Capability Maturity Model Integration® (Software Engineering Institute)
CMO	chief management officer
CMP	configuration management plan
CMU	Carnegie Mellon University
CO	contracting officer
COA	chart of accounts
COB	close of business
COBIT	Control Objectives for Information Technology (framework for IT governance and control)
COC	certificate of competency (issued by SBA)
COCO	contractor owned, contractor operated; Chief of the Contracting Office (DOT)
COD	cash on delivery
CODSIA	Council of Defense and Space Industries Associates
COE	common operating environment; center of excellence
COFC	Court of Federal Claims
COG	continuity of government
COI	conflict of interest
COMSEC	communications security
CONAHEC	Consortium for North American Higher Education Collaboration
CONOPS	concept of operations
CONUS	continental (or contiguous) United States
COO	chief operating officer

COOP	continuity of operations plan
COP	communities of practice
COR	contracting officer's representative
CORBA	Common Object Request Broker Architecture
CORDUS	Community R&D Information Service (Europe)
COTR	contracting officer's technical representative
COTS	commercial-off-the-shelf
CP	cost plus
CPA	certified public accountant
CPAF	cost plus award fee
CPARS	contractor performance assessment reporting system
CPD	comptroller's procurement decisions
CPFF	cost plus fixed fee
CPI	consumer price index; continuous process improvement
CPIC	capital planning and investment control
CPIF	cost plus incentive fee
CPM	critical path method
CPMO	Contractor Performance Measurement Organization
CPNF	cost plus no fee
CPO	chief performance officer; chief privacy officer
CPPF	cost plus percentage fee
CPRS	contractor purchasing system review
CPU	central processing unit; corporate qualification package
CQP	corporate qualification package
CR	clarification request; continuing resolution
CRA	continuing resolution authority
CRADA	cooperative research and development agreement
CRM	customer relationship management
CRS	Catholic Relief Services

C/SCSC	cost/schedule control system criteria
CSO	cheif security officer
CSP	cloud service provider
CSR	commercial market representative; corporate social responsibility
CTO	chief technology officer
CTW	Contracts and Tenders Worldwide (White Plains, New York, and London)
CWBS	contract work breakdown structure
CY	calendar year
D&B	Dun & Bradstreet
D&F	determinations and findings
DAA	designated approving authority
DABBS	Defense Communications Agency's Acquisition Bulletin Board System
DACON	Data on Consulting Firms (automated World Bank and Inter-American Development Bank systems)
DAPS	Defense Automated Printing Service (Philadelphia)
DAR	Defense Acquisition Regulation
DARC	Defense Acquisition Regulatory Council
DARO	days after receipt of order
DARPA	Defense Advanced Research Projects Agency
DARS	Defense Acquisition Regulations System
DAU	Defense Acquisition University
DBA	Davis-Bacon Act (1931); doing business as; database administrator
DBE	disadvantaged business enterprise
DBMS	database management system
DCA	delegation of contracting authority
DCAA	Defense Contract Audit Agency
DCAAM	Defense Contract Audit Agency Manual
DCADS	Defense Contract Action Data System
DCAS	Defense Contract Administration Service, Defense Logistics Agency

DCI	data collection instrument
DCMA	Defense Contract Management Agency
DCMC	Defense Contract Management Command
DCSC	Defense Construction Supply Center
DDTC	U.S. Directorate of Defense Trade Controls
DEARS	Department of Energy FAR Supplement
DELTA	Defense Loan and Technical Assistance
DESC	Defense Electronics Supply Center
DFAR	Defense Federal Acquisition Regulations (also called DAR)
DFARS	Defense Federal Acquisition Regulation Supplement
DFAS	Defense Finance and Accounting Service
DGR	designated government representative
DGSC	Defense General Supply Center
DHHS	Department of Health and Human Services
DHS	Department of Homeland Security
DIACAP	Department of Defense Information Assurance Certification and Accreditation Process (DoD Instruction 8510.01 and 8510.02)
DICON	Data on Individual Consultants (automated Asian Development Bank system)
DID	data item description
DII	Defense Industry Initiative
DIRMM	DOT's IRM Manual
DISA	Defense Information Systems Agency; Data Interchange Standards Association
DITSCAP	Department of Defense Information Technology Security Certification and Accreditation Program (replaced by DIACAP)
DISC	Defense Industrial Supply Center
DLA	Defense Logistics Agency; Direct Labor Analysis
DLIS	Defense Logistics Information Service
DLSC	Defense Logistics Services Center (now called DLIS)
DM	division manager

DMAIC	define-measure-analyze-improve-control (Six Sigma)
DMS	document management system
DN	deficiency notice
DNI	Director of National Intelligence
D.O.	delivery order
DOC	Department of Commerce
DoD	Department of Defense
DoDAF	Department of Defense Architecture Framework (version 1.0 released in August 2003, version 2.0 released in May 2009)
DODD	Department of Defense Directive (e.g., DODD 5000.1)
DODI	Department of Defense Instruction (e.g., DODI 5000.2)
DODISS	Department of Defense Index of Specifications and Standards
DODSSP	Department of Defense Single Stock Point for Specifications and Standards
DOE	Department of Energy
DoED	Department of Education
DOI	department operating instruction; Department of the Interior
DOJ	Department of Justice
DOL	Department of Labor
DoN	Department of the Navy
DOS	Department of State
DOSAR	Department of State Acquisition Regulation
DOSC	delivery order selection criteria
DOT	Department of Transportation
DPA	Delegation of Procurement Authority
DPAP	Defense Procurement and Acquisition Policy
DPAS	Defense Priorities and Allocations System
DPLH	direct productive labor hour
DPO	downselect package to offerors
DR	deficiency report; disaster recovery

DRD	data requirements document
DRFP	draft request for proposal
DRL	data requirements list
DRM	Federal Data Reference Model
DROLS	Defense Research Development, Test, and Evaluation On-Line System
DRP	disaster recovery plan
DSARC	Defense Systems Acquisition Review Council
DSBS	Dynamic Small Business Search
DSP	Defense Standardization Program
DTC	design to cost
DT&E	development, test, and evaluation
DTI	Department of Trade and Industry (United Kingdom)
DTIC	Defense Technical Information Center
DTP	desktop publishing
DTS	Defense Travel System
DUAP	Dual-Use Applications Program (DoD)
DUNS	Data Universal Numbering System
DVBE	Disabled Veteran Business Enterprise
DWCF	Defense Working Capital Fund
E&MD	engineering and manufacturing development
EA	enterprise architecture
EAC	estimate at completion (cost); Export Assistance Center
EAGLE	Enterprise Acquisition Gateway for Leading Edge Solutions (DHS contract)
EAI	enterprise application integration
EAMMF	Enterprise Architecture Management Maturity Framework
EAR	Export Administration Regulations (15 C.F.R. § 730-774)
eB	electronic business
EBIDTA	earnings before interest, taxes, depreciation, and amortization
EBRD	European Bank for Reconstruction and Development

EBS	electronic bid set
EC	electronic commerce; European Community; European Commission
ECAPMO	Electronic Commerce Acquisition Program Management Office
ECI	electronic commerce infrastructure
ECIC	Electronic Commerce Information Center
ECIP	electronic commerce interoperability process
ECM	enterprise content management
ECP	engineering change proposal
ECPN	electronic commerce processing node
ECPO	Electronic Commerce Program Office
ECRC	Electronic Commerce Resource Center
ECU	European currency unit
ED	Department of Education
EDF	European Development Fund
EDI	electronic data interchange
EDIFACT	EDI for Administration, Commerce and Transport (Europe and Asia)
EDWOSB	Economically Disadvantaged Women-Owned Small Business
EEA	European Economic Area (Norway)
EELV	evolved expendable launch vehicle
EEO	Equal Employment Opportunity
EEOC	Equal Employment Opportunity Commission
EFT	electronic funds transfer
EIB	European Investment Bank
EIC	Euro Information Centre(s)
EIN	employer identification number
EIT	electronic and information technology
EIU	Economist Intelligence Unit (London)
ELA	enterprise license agreement
ELAN	Export Legal Assistance Network

EN	evaluation notice
EO	executive order
EOI	expression of interest
EOL	end of life (product life cycle)
EOM	end of month
EOY	end of year
EPA	Environmental Protection Agency
EPAAR	Environmental Protection Agency Acquisition Regulations
EPIC	Electronic Processes Initiatives Committee
EPIN	European Procurement Information Network
EPLS	excluded parties list
EPS	equipment performance specification; electronic publishing system; electronic proposal submission; Electronic Posting System (replaced by FedBizOpps); encapsulated postscript
EPTF	Electronic Procurement Task Force (APMP)
ERM	electronic records management; enterprise risk management
ERP	enterprise resource planning
ESS	electronic source selection
eSRS	Electronic Subcontract Reporting System
E-TAP	Export Trade Association Partnership
ETC	estimate to complete
ETS	Electronic Tendering System (Hong Kong)
ETTAP	Entrepreneurial Training and Technical Assistance Program
EU	European Union
E-Verify	DHS Employment Eligibility Verification
EVA	earned value analysis
EVM	earned value management
EVMS	earned value management system
EWCP	Export Working Capital Program
F&O	full and open

F3I	form, fit, function, and interface
FAA	Federal Aviation Administration
FAC	Federal Acquisition Circular
FACNET	Federal Acquisition Computer Network (now defunct)
FAI	Federal Acquisition Institute
FAIR	Federal Activities Inventory Reform Act of 1998
FAO	Field Audit Office (DCAA)
FAPIIS	Federal Awardee Performance and Integrity Information System
FAQ	frequently asked questions
FAR	Federal Acquisition Regulation
FARA	Federal Acquisition Reform Act (included in the 1996 Defense Authorization Act, Clinger-Cohen Act)
FAS	free along side
FASA	Federal Acquisition Streamlining Act (October 1994) (P.L. 103-355)
FASB	Finance Accounting Standards Board
FAST	Federal and State Technology Partnership Program
FAT	factory acceptance test; first article testing (when DoD buys certain goods, they may perform extensive tests on the first item delivered)
FBC	faster, better, cheaper
FBI	Federal Bureau of Investigation
FCCM	facilities capital cost of money
FCIA	Foreign Credit Insurance Association
FCL	facility security clearance
FCR	federal contracts report
FCRA	Fair Credit Reporting Act
FCW	*Federal Computer Week*
FDCC	Federal Desktop Core Configuration
FDCCI	Federal Data Center Consolidation Initiative
FDI	foreign direct investment
FDIC	Federal Deposit Insurance Corporation

FDO	fee determination official
FEA	Federal Enterprise Architecture
FEAF	Federal Enterprise Architecture Framework (published in September 1999 by the Federal CIO Council)
FedBizOpps	Federal Business Opportunities
FedRAMP	Federal Risk and Authorization Management Program
FEDRIP	Federal Research in Progress (database)
FEDSIM	Federal Systems Integration and Management
FED-STD	federal standard
FEDSTRIP	Federal Standard Requisitioning & Issue Procedures
FedTeDS	Federal Technical Data Solution
FEMA	Federal Emergency Management Agency
FEMP	Federal Energy Management Program
FESMCC	Federal EDI Standards Management Coordinating Committee
FFP	firm-fixed price
FFRDC	Federally Funded Research and Development Center
FFS	fee for service
FFWA	Florida Freelance Writers Association
FHWA	Federal Highway Administration
FICA	Federal Insurance Contributions Act
FIND	Federal Information & News Dispatch
FIP	Federal Information Processing
FIPS	Federal Information Processing Standards (developed by NIST and approved by the Department of Commerce)
FIRMR	Federal Information Resources Management Regulation (41 CFR Chapter 201)
FISMA	Federal Information Security Management Act of 2002
FITA	Federation of International Trade Associations
FLC	Federal Laboratory Consortium
FLSA	Fair Labor Standards Act

FMMI	Federal Management Modernization Initiative
FMS	foreign military sales
FMSS	Financial Management Systems Software
FMV	fair market value
FNS	Food and Nutrition Service (USDA)
FOB	free on board
FOCI	foreign ownership, control, or influence
FOIA	Freedom of Information Act
FOIR	Freedom of Information Request
FOUO	for official use only
FP	fixed price
FP-EPA	fixed price with economic price adjustment
FPASA	Federal Property and Administrative Services Act (1949, 41 U.S.C. § 251 et seq.)
FPDC	Federal Procurement Data Center
FPDS	Federal Procurement Data System
FPDS-NG	Federal Procurement Data System–Next Generation
FPI	fixed-price incentive
FPIF	fixed-price incentive fee
FPLE	fixed-price level of effort
FPLH	fixed-price labor hour
FPLOE	fix-price level of effort
FPMR	Federal Property Management Regulations
FPO	for position only (used in reference to graphics or photos)
FPR	Federal Procurement Regulations; fixed price with redetermination; final proposal revision
FPRA	forward pricing rate agreement
FR	Federal Register
FSC	Federal Supply Classification (or Class) (associated with SAACONS Vendor Information Program)

FSN	Federal Stock Number
FSS	Federal Supply Service
FSSI	Federal Strategic Sourcing Initiative
FTE	full-time equivalent
FTP	File Transfer Protocol
FTR	Federal Travel Regulations
FUSE	Featured U.S. Exporters (directory)
FUTA	Federal Unemployment Tax Act
FY	fiscal year
FYDP	five-year defense plan or program; future years defense program
G&A	general and administrative
G/L	general ledger
GAAP	generally accepted accounting principles
GAGAS	generally accepted government auditing standards
GAAS	generally accepted auditing standards
GAO	Government Accountability Office
GATT	General Agreement on Tariffs and Trade
GBL	government bill of lading
GCA	Government Contractors Association
GDP	gross domestic product
GEF	Global Environmental Fund (World Bank)
GEMPC	Government Estimate of Most Probable Cost
GEMS	Australian Government Electronic Marketplace Service
GFDL	Geophysical Fluid Dynamics Laboratory (NOAA)
GFE	government-furnished equipment
GFF	government-furnished facilities
GFM	government-furnished material
GFP	government-furnished property
GFS	government-furnished software

GFY	government fiscal year
GIF	Graphics Interchange Format
GIG	Global Information Grid
GIS	geographic information system
GISRA	Government Information Security Reform Act of 2000
GISS	Goddard Institute for Space Studies (New York)
GMSS	guaranteed maximum shared saving
GOCO	government owned, contractor operated
GOGO	government owned, government operated
GPA	grade point average
GPC	Government Purchase Card
GPE	governmentwide point of entry
GPEA	Government Paperwork Elimination Act
GPN	General Procurement Notice (*UN Development Business*)
GPO	Government Printing Office
GPRA	Government Performance and Results Act (P.L. 103-62, 1993)
GRA&I	Government Reports Announcements and Index
GRC	NASA Glenn Research Center
GSA	General Services Administration
GSBCA	General Services Board of Contract Appeals
GSD	Government Supplies Department (Hong Kong, China)
GSFC	Goddard Space Flight Center
GST	goods and services tax (Canada)
GTN	Global Technology Network
GWAC	governmentwide acquisition contract
H&S	health and safety
HBCU	historically black colleges and universities
HC	human capital
HCA	head of contracting activity

HHS	Health and Human Services
HIA	high-impact agencies
HMSO	Her Majesty's Supply Office (United Kingdom)
HOA	head of the operating administration
HPO	high performing organization
HRIS	Human Resource Information System
HRM	Human Resources Management
HS	harmonized system (international trade)
HSARPA	DHS Homeland Security Advanced Research Projects Agency
HSI	Hispanic-serving institution
HSPD	Homeland Security Presidential Directive
HTML	Hypertext Markup Language
HTRW	hazardous, toxic, and radioactive waste
HTTP	Hypertext Transport Protocol
HUBZone	historically underutilized business zone
HUD	Department of Housing and Urban Development
I&T	integration and test
IA	information assurance
IAC	Industry Advisory Council (Fairfax, VA)
IACWBE	Interagency Committee on Women's Business Enterprises
IAE	Integrated Acquisition Environment
IAPSO	Interagency Procurement Services Office (United Nations)
IAW	in accordance with
IBRD	International Bank for Reconstruction and Development (part of the World Bank Group)
ICAR	Individual Contract Action Report (Standard Form 279)
ICB	international competitive bidding
ICC	International Chamber of Commerce
ICE	independent cost estimate
ICR	intelligent character recognition (scanning technology)

ICSB	International Council for Small Business (http://www.icsb.org)
ICSID	International Center for Settlement of Investment Disputes (part of the World Bank Group)
IDA	International Development Agency (part of the World Bank Group)
IDB	Inter-American Development Bank; Industrial Development Board
IDC	indefinite delivery contract
IDDQ	indefinite delivery definite quantity
IDE	Institute of Developing Economies (Japan); integrated development environment
IDEA-EC	Interior Department Electronic Acquisition System-Electronic Commerce
ID-IQ	indefinite delivery/indefinite quantity (contract type, examples of which are the Air Force's Desktop V and the Army's Small Multiuser Computer Contracts)
IE	individual experience (SF254, Block 11)
IEC	International Electrotechnical Commission
IEEE	Institute of Electrical and Electronics Engineers
IEI	invitation for expression of interest
IESC	International Executive Service Corps
IEW	intelligence and electronic warfare
IFB	invitation for bid
IFC	International Finance Corporation (part of the World Bank Group)
IFN	item for negotiation
IG	inspector general
IGCE	independent government cost estimate
IK	Indigenous Knowledge (World Bank initiative)
ILA	integrated logistics assessment
ILS	integrated logistics support
IMAS	International Marketing Assistance Service (SUNY-Albany program)
IMC	International Medical Corps
IMD	International Institute for Management Development (in Switzerland)
IMF	International Monetary Fund (World Bank)

I.N.F.O.	Information Network Fully Online
INFOSEC	information security
INGO	international nongovernmental organization
IOC	initial operating capability
IOT&E	initial operational test and evaluation
IP	Internet Protocol; intellectual property
IPD	integrated logistics assessment
IPPA	Integrated Public Procurement Association (Europe)
IPPD	integrated product and process development
IPT	integrated product team; integrated project team
IQC	indefinite quantity contract
IR&D	internal (independent) research and development
IRAD	independent research and development
IRM	information resources management
IRS	Internal Revenue Service
ISBC	International Small Business Consortium (Norman, Oklahoma; http://www.isbc.com/); International Small Business Congress (http://www.isbc.or.jp)
ISDN	Integrated services digital network (128 Kbps)
ISIC	International Standard Industrial Classification system
ISM	Institute for Supply Management
ISO	International Organization for Standardization
ISP	Internet service provider (current top commercial ISPs are Comcast, Time Warner Cable, AT&T, Cox, Optimum, Charter, Verizon, CenturyLink, Suddenlink, and EarthLink)
ISSA	Interservice Support Agreement; Information Systems Security Association
ISSAA	Information Systems Selection and Acquisition Agency (U.S. Army)
ISSN	International Standard Serial Number
ISSO	information system security officer
IT	information technology

ITA	International Trade Administration
ITAR	International Traffic in Arms Regulations (22 C.F.R. Parts 120–130)
ITES	Information Technology Enterprise Solutions
ITIL	Information Technology Infrastructure Library (British standards for managing information technology services)
ITL	International Trade Law
ITMRA	Information Technology Management Reform Act (Clinger-Cohen Act of 1996)
ITOP	Information Technology Omnibus Procurement (GWAC)
ITSM	IT Service Management (ITIL)
ITT	invitation(s) to tender
IV&V	independent verification and validation
J&A	justification and approval
JCALS	Joint Computer-Aided Acquisition and Logistics Support
JDAM	Joint Direct Attack Munition
JECPO	Joint Electronic Commerce Program Office
JETRO	Japanese Government Procurement Database (Japan External Trade Organization)
JFTR	Joint Federal Travel Regulations
JIT	just in time
JN	job number
JOFOC	justification for other than full-and-open competition
JPEG	Joint Photographic Experts Group
JSC	Johnson Space Center
JTR	Joint Travel Regulations (Department of Defense)
JV	joint venture
JWOD Act	Javits-Wagner-O'Day Act
K4D	Knowledge for Development Program (World Bank)
Kbps	kilobits per second
KISS	keep it short and simple

KM	knowledge management
KME	knowledge management environment
KO	contracting officer
KPA	key process area
KPI	key performance indicator; key process indicator
KSC	Kennedy Space Center
LAN	local-area network
LBC	large business corporation
LCC	life-cycle costs
LCOTR	lead COTR
LCV	lifetime contract value
LEDU	Local Enterprise Development Unit (Northern Ireland)
LEED	Leadership in Energy and Environmental Design (third-party rating system and certification program developed by the U.S. Green Building Council)
L-H	labor-hour
LIB	limited international bidding
LLC	limited liability company
LLNL	Lawrence Livermore National Laboratory
LLP	limited liability partnership
LNGO	local nongovernmental organization
LOB	line of business
LOE	level of effort
LOI	letter of interest (Canadian equivalent of RFI); letter of intent (e.g., to pursue a merger or acquisition); letter of inquiry (often part of grant proposal process)
LOO	letter of obligation
LOSP	Liaison Outreach and Services Program (DOT)
LPO	local project overhead
LPTA	lowest price, technically acceptable (source selection process described at FAR 15.101-2)

LRAE	long-range acquisition estimate (Air Force)
LS	lump sum
LSA	labor surplus area
LSI	lead system integrator (e.g., Northrop Grumman, EDS an HP company, CSC, and Lockheed Martin)
LSS	Lean Six Sigma
LTOP	lease-to-ownership program
LWOP	lease with option to purchase; leave without pay
M&H	material and handling
MAC	multiple award contract; multiagency contract; mandatory access control
MACOM	Major Army Command
MA/IDIQ	multiple award/indefinite delivery, indefinite quantity
MAJcom	Major Command (Air Force)
MAN	metropolitan area network
MAS	Multiple Award Schedule (GSA)
MBDA	Minority Business Development Agency (U.S. Department of Commerce)
MBDC	Minority Business Development Center (DOT)
MBE	minority business enterprise
MBIRD	Minority Business Information Resources Directory
MBOC	Minority Business Opportunity Committee
Mbps	megabits per second
MBRC	Minority Business Resource Center
MCTL	Military Critical Technology List
MDA	Missile Defense Agency; Multilateral Development Agencies
MDG	Millennium Development Goal (World Bank)
MED	Minority-/female-/disabled-owned business; Minority Enterprise Development
MEGA	Minority Enterprise Growth Assistance
MEO	most efficient organization
MERX	Internet-based national electronic tendering service (Canada)

MESBIC	Minority Enterprise Small Business Investment Company
MI	minority institutions
M&IE	meals and incidental expenses
MIGA	Multilateral Investment Guarantee Agency (part of the World Bank Group; established in 1988)
MIL-HBK	Military Handbook
MILSPEC	Military Specification
MIL-STD	Military Standard
MILSTRIP	Military Standard Requisitioning & Issue Procedures
MIS	management information system
ML	Maturity Level (SEI CMMI®)
MMO	Materials Management Office
MNC	multinational corporation
M&O	maintenance and operations
MOA	memorandum of agreement
MOLIS	Minority On-Line Information Service
MOS	monthly operational summary (World Bank)
MOU	memorandum of understanding
MP	Mentor-Protégé (DoD, NASA, SBA, and so forth)
MPC	most probable cost
MPCG	most probable cost to the government
MPI	minority postsecondary institution
MPIN	marketing password identification numbers
MPJV	Mentor-Protégé Joint Venture
MPT	modular proposal technique
MR	modification request
MRO	maintenance, repair, and operating supplies
MSE	major source of employment
MSFC	Marshall Space Flight Center
MTBF	mean time between failures

MTTF	mean time to failure
MYP	multiyear procurement
NABDC	Native American Business Development Center
NACA	Native American Contractors Association
NACM	National Association of Credit Management
NAF	nonappropriated fund
NAFE	National Association of Female Executives
NAFTA	North American Free Trade Agreement
NAICS	North American Industry Classification System (NAFTA, 1997) (pronounced "nakes")
NAIS	NASA Acquisition Internet Service
NAPM	National Association of Purchasing Management
NARA	National Archives and Records Administration
NAPS	Navy Acquisition Procedures Supplement
NARA	National Archives and Records Administration
NASA	National Aeronautics and Space Administration
NASAPR	NASA Procurement Regulation
NAVSEA	Naval Sea Systems Command
NAVSUP	Naval Supply Systems Command
NAWBO	National Association of Women Business Owners
NBA	National Business Association
NCAIED	National Center for American Indian Enterprise Development
NCB	national competitive bidding
NCMA	National Contract Management Association
NCMB	National Coalition of Minority Businesses
NCR	National Capital Region
NCSA	National Center for Supercomputing Applications (at the University of Illinois, Urbana-Champaign)
NDI	nondevelopmental items
N.E.C.	not elsewhere classified (related to SIC codes)

NECO	Navy's Electronic Commerce Online
NEH	National Endowment for the Humanities
NEI	National Export Initiative
NEP	network entry point (EC/EDI; two NEPs in Ohio and Utah)
NETCENTS	Network-centric Solutions (Air Force GWAC contract)
NFAR	NASA Federal Acquisition Regulations
NFIB	National Federation of Independent Businesses
NFS	NASA FAR Supplement
NFWBO	Now called, the Center for Women's Business Research (CFWBR), Washington, D.C.; http://www.cfwbr.org (Formerly the National Foundation for Women Business Owners)
NGLCC	National Gay & Lesbian Chamber of Commerce
NGO	nongovernmental organization
NHB	NASA Handbook
NIB	National Industries for the Blind
NIC	newly industrializing countries
NICRA	Negotiated Indirect Cost Rate Agreement
NIGP	National Institute of Governmental Purchasing (Canada)
NIH	National Institutes of Health
NIS	New Independent States (of the former Soviet Union)
NIST	National Institute of Standards and Technology
NITAAC	National Information Technology Acquisitions and Assessment Center
NLT	no later than
NMBC	National Minority Business Council (http://www.nmbc.org)
NMCARS	Navy Marine Corps Acquisition Regulation Supplement
NMI	NASA Management Instruction
NMSDC	National Minority Supplier Development Council
NMSO	National Master Standing Offers (Canada)
NMVC	New Market Venture Capital program (SBA)
NNSA	National Nuclear Security Administration (DOE)

NOAA	National Oceanic and Atmospheric Administration
NORAD	Norwegian Agency for Development Cooperation; North American Aerospace Defense Command (Colorado)
NPA	nonprofit agency
NPP	notice of proposed procurement
NPPPU	National Public Procurement Policy Unit (Ireland)
NPR	National Partnership for Reinventing Government (formerly National Performance Review)
NRA	NASA Research Announcement
NRC	Nuclear Regulatory Commission
NSA	National Security Agency
NSBU	National Small Business United
NSF	National Science Foundation
NSN	National Stock Number
NSNA	no stock number assigned
NSP	not separately priced
NSS	National Security Systems
NTDB	National Trade Data Bank
NTE	not to exceed
NTIS	National Technical Information Service
NTP	notice to proceed
NWBC	National Women's Business Council
NWBOC	National Women Business Owners Corporation
o/a	on or about
O&M	operations and maintenance
O&S	operations and support
OA	office automation
OBE	overcome by events
OBS	organizational breakdown structure; Open Bidding Service (Canada)
OCI	organizational conflict of interest

OCIO	Office of the Chief Information Officer
OCR	optical character recognition (scanning technology)
ODC	other direct cost
ODMA	Open Document Management API
OEM	original equipment manufacturer
OFCC	Office of Federal Contract Compliance
OFPP	Office of Federal Procurement Policy
OGAS	other government agency system
O/H	overhead
OIB	Office of International Business (Maryland)
OICC	officer in charge of construction
OIG	Office of the Inspector General
OIRM	Office of Information Resources Management
OJ or OJEC	*Official Journal of the European Community* (changed to OJEU)
OJEU	*Official Journal of the European Union*
OLAP	online analytical processing
OLE	object linking and embedding
OMB	Office of Management and Budget
OMG	object management group
OPBA	Ontario Public Buyers Association (Canada)
OPIC	overseas private investment corporation
OPM	Office of Personnel Management
OPW	Office of Public Works (Ireland)
OSCS	One Stop Capital Shop
OSD	Office of the Secretary of Defense
OSDBU	Office of Small and Disadvantaged Business Utilization
OSHA	Occupational Safety and Health Administration (established in 1970)
OSINT	open source intelligence
OSR	order size representation

OSTA	Optical Storage Technology Association (Santa Barbara, California)
OTA	Office of Technology Assessment
OT&E	operational test and evaluation
OTS	off-the-shelf; Overseas Trade Services
OUPMA	Ontario University Purchasing Management Association
P&L	profit and loss
P&S	product and service code
P³I	preplanned product improvement
PAD	Project Approval Document (part of NASA acquisition process)
PALT	procurement administrative lead time
PAO	public affairs office; public affairs officer
PAR	proposal analysis report
PARC	principal assistant responsible for contracting
PASS	procurement automated source system (now defunct; replaced by PRO-*Net* and then by the CCR)
PAT	Process Action Team (DoD)
PBA	performance-based acquisition
PBBE	performance-based business environment
PBC	performance-based contracting (now called PBA)
PBO	performance-based organization
PBSA	performance-based service acquisition
PBSC	performance-based service contracting
PBWS	performance-based work statement
PC	personal computer
PCO	procuring (or procurement or principal) contracting officer
PCL	personal security clearance
PCP	Potential Contractor Program (DTIC)
PCR	procurement center representative
PDF	personnel data form; Portable Document Format (.pdf)
PEA	Procurement Executives Association

PEAG	proposal evaluation analysis (or advisory) group
PEB	performance evaluation board
PEDS	program element descriptive summary
PEN	program element number
PEO	program executive officer
PEP	project execution plan; performance evaluation plan
PER	proposal evaluation report
PERT	program evaluation and review techniques (diagrams)
PFPA	Pentagon Force Protection Agency
PI	principal investigator
PID	procurement initiation document (German procurement law)
PII	personally identifiable information
PIID	procurement instrument identifier (required of all U.S. federal agencies by FAC 2001–16; each procurement must have a unique identifier)
PIIN	procurement instrument identification number
PIN	preinvitation notice; prior indicative notice
PIO	procurement information online
PIP	procurement improvement plan
PIXS	Preaward Information Exchange System (Wright-Patterson AFB)
PKI	public key infrastructure
PL	public law
PLI	professional liability insurance
PM	project manager, program manager
PMA	President's Management Agenda (2001)
PMBOK	Project Management Body of Knowledge
PMC	Procurement Management Council (within DOT)
PMI	Project Management Institute
PMO	Program Management Office
PMP	Project Management Professional
P/N	part number

PN	procurement notice
PO	purchase order
POA	plan of action
POA&M	plan of action and milestones
POC	point of contact
POG	paperless order generator
PON	program opportunity notice
POP	period of performance
PP&E	property, plant, and equipment
PPAIS	DoD Past Performance Automated Information System (now PPIRS)
PPB&E	planning, programming, budget, and execution
PPBS	planning, programming, and budgeting system (obsolete, now PPBE)
PPI	proposal preparation instruction; pixels per inch; past performance information
PPIMS	Past Performance Information Management System (U.S. Army)
PPIRS	Past Performance Information Retrieval System
PPM	principal period of maintenance
PPT	performance-price trade-off (U.S. Air Force evaluation strategy); past performance tool (U.S. Army)
PQ²D	price quantity quality delivery
PQS	personnel qualification sheet
PR	purchase request or public relations
PRA	Paperwork Reduction Act of 1995
PRAG	Performance Risk Assessment Group (government evaluators)
PRDA	program R&D announcements
PRO-*Net*	Procurement Marketing and Access Network (now CCR)
PROCNET	Procurement Network (ARDEC)
PSA	Presolicitation Announcement (for SBIR and STTR opportunities, published quarterly by SBA); professional services agreement
PSC	product service code

PSD	private sector development
PSPQ	potential supplier profile questionnaire
PTAC	Procurement Technical Assistance Center
PVO	private voluntary organizations
PWBS	program (or project) work breakdown structure
PWS	performance work statement
QA	quality assurance
QAP	quality assurance plan
QASP	quality assurance surveillance plan
QBL	qualified bidders list
QBS	qualifications-based selection
QC	quality control
QCBS	quality- and cost-based selection
QCI	quality conformance inspection
QDR	Quadrennial Defense Review
QML	qualified manufacturers list
QPL	qualified products list
QSL	qualified suppliers list
QVL	qualified vendors list
R&D	research and development
RAFV	risk adjusted functional value
RAM	random access memory; reliability, availability, and maintainability
RAM-D	reliability, availability, maintainability, or durability
RCAS	Reserve Component Automation System
RDF	resource description framework (semantic Web)
RDT&E	research, development, test, and evaluation
RFA	request for application (grants); request for assistance
RFB	request for bid
RFC	request for comment

RFI	request for information
RFO	request for offer
RFP	request for proposal
RFQ	request for quotation [normally prepared on Standard Form 18, FAR 53.301-18. Unlike bids or proposals following an IFB or RFP, quotations submitted in response to an RFQ are not considered to be offers. Standing alone, a quotation cannot be accepted by the government to form a contract for goods or services. (Cibinic, John, and Ralph C. Nash, *Formation of Government Contracts*, 2nd ed., Washington D.C.: George Washington University, 1986, p. 158.)]; request for qualifications
RFS	request for solution
RFT	request for tender
RFTP	request for technical proposals
RIF	reduction in force
RIP	raster image processing
RM	risk management
RM&S	reliability, maintainability, and supportability
RMP	risk management plan
ROI	return on investment
ROICC	resident officer in charge of construction
ROM	rough order of magnitude (cost)
ROS	return on sales
RRE	Risk Radar Enterprise (American Systems' Web-based risk management application)
RTF	Rich Text Format
RTN	routing and transfer number (electronic payments)
RTO	representative task order
SA	supplemental agreement
SAACONS	Standard Army Automated Contracting System
SaaS	software as a service
SADBUS	small and disadvantaged business utilization specialist

SAME	Society of American Military Engineers
SAN	storage area network
SAP	Simplified Acquisition Procedures (FAR Part 13)
SAR	DoD Selected Acquisition Report
SARA	Service Acquisition Reform Act of 2003
SAT	Simplified Acquisition Threshold
SBA	Small Business Administration
SBANC	Small Business Advancement National Center (University of Central Arkansas; http://sbaer.uca.edu)
SBC	small business concern; small business corporation
SBD	Standard Bidding Documents (e.g., the World Bank)
SBDC	Small Business Development Center (there are 58 SBDCs)
SBE	small business enterprise
SBEA	Small Business Exporters Association of the United States
SBHTI	Small Business High Technology Institute
SBIC	Small Business Investment Company
SBIR	Small Business Innovation Research program
SBLO	small business liaison officer
SBS	Small Business Service (United Kingdom)
SBSA	small business set aside
SBTT	small business technology transfer
SBU	sensitive but unclassified
SCA	Service Contract Act
SCAP	security content automation protocol
SCAMPI	Standard CMMI® Appraisal Method for Process Improvement
SBTC	Small Business Technology Coalition
SCORE	Service Corps of Retired Executives (SBA program with more than 360 chapters)
SCI	sensitive compartmentalized information
SDB	small and disadvantaged business

SDLC	system development life cycle
SDR	Special Drawing Rights
SDRL	subcontract data requirements list
SDVOB	service disabled, veteran owned business
SEB	Source Evaluation Board
SEC	Securities and Exchange Commission
SECDEF	U.S. Secretary of Defense
SEDB	Socially and Economically Disadvantaged Business
SEED	Support for East European Democracy
SEI	Software Engineering Institute (Carnegie Mellon University, Pittsburgh, Pennsylvania)
SEMP	system engineering management plan
SES	senior executive service
SETA	systems engineering and technical assistance
SEWP	Solutions for Enterprise-wide Procurement (NASA GWAC)
SF	standard form
SFAS	Statement of Financial Accounting Standards
SGML	Standard Generalized Markup Language
SI	systems integrator
SIC	Standard Industrial Classification (replaced by NAICS codes)
SIG	special interest group
SIMAP	Système d'Information pour les Marchés Public (European Commission)
SIR	screening information request
SITC	Standard International Trade Classification
SLA	service-level agreement
SLIN	subcontractor line item
SLO	service level objective
SMC	Space and Missile Systems Center (Air Force)
SMDC	U.S. Army's Space and Missile Defense Command

SME	small and medium-sized enterprises (European Commission); subject matter expert
SML	solicitation mailing list
SOA	service-oriented architecture
SOC	statement of capability; security operation center
SOFA	Status of Forces Agreement (between the United States and Iraq)
SOHO	small office, home office
Sol.	solicitation
SON	statement of need (equivalent of SOW)
SOO	statement of objectives
SOQ	statement of qualifications
SOW	statement of work
SP&BDG	Strategic Planning and Business Development Group
SPE	senior procurement executive (government position)
SPI	single process initiative
SPN	Specific Procurement Notice (*UN Development Business*)
SQA	software quality assurance
SQL	structured query language
SRD	system requirements document
SSA	source selection authority; Social Security Administration
SSAC	Source Selection Advisory Council
SSBIC	Specialized Small Business Investment Company
SSC	Source Selection Committee
SSCASS	Service and Supply Contract Appraisal Support System
SSDD	source selection decision document
SSEB	Source Selection Evaluation Board
SSET	source selection evaluation team
SSF	source selection facility
SSN	sources sought notice; Social Security number
SSO	source selection official; source selection organization; single sign on

SSP	source selection plan
SSQAAP	Small Supplier Quality Assurance Assistance Program
SST	source selection team
STARS	Streamlined Technology Acquisition Resources for Services (GSA GWAC)
STEP	State Trade and Export Program
STOP	sequential thematic organization of proposals (technique developed at Hughes Ground Systems)
STR	senior technical review; senior technical representative
STRICOM	U.S. Army Simulation Training and Instrumentation Command
STTR	Small Business Technology Transfer Pilot Program
SUNY	State University of New York
SUTA	State Unemployment Tax Act
SWOT	Strengths, Weaknesses, Opportunities, and Threats
T4	Transformation Twenty-One Technology (Department of Veterans Affairs)
Ts & Cs	terms and conditions
T&E	test and evaluation
TABD	Transatlantic Business Dialogue
TAC	Transportation Acquisition Circular; Technology Assistance Centers
TADSBAT	Training and Development of Small Businesses in Advanced Technologies (OSDBU program under NASA)
TAM	Transportation Acquisition Manual
TAR	Transportation Acquisition Regulation
TARP	Troubled Asset Relief Program
TASBI	Transatlantic Small Business Initiative (United States and European Union)
TBD	to be determined
TBIC	Tribal Business Information Center
TBN	to be negotiated
TBP	to be proposed

TCN	Third County Nationals
TCO	termination contracting officer; total cost of ownership
TCP/IP	Transmission Control Protocol/Internet Protocol
TCS	Technical Consulting Services (part of USAID)
TCU	tribal college and university
TD	task description
TDA	U.S. Trade and Development Agency
TDI	technical data interchange
TDO	term-determining official
TDP	technical data packages (U.S. Army)
TDY	temporary duty
TED	*Tenders Electronic Daily*
TEP	total evaluated price
TEV	total evaluated value
TFC	termination for cause (of a contract)
TIFF	Tag Image File Format
TILO	Technical Industrial Liaison Office (Army)
TIN	Taxpayer Identification Number; contact the IRS to obtain a TIN
TINA	Truth in Negotiations Act [P.L. 87-653 (1962); extended in 1984]
T&M	time and materials
TM	technical monitor
TM Online	Trade Mission Online
TMIS	technical management information system
T.O.	task order
TOA	total obligation authority
TOPS	Total Operating Paperless System (Army CECOM)
TOR	technical officer's representative; task order request
TORFP	task order RFP
TPCC	Trade Promotion Coordinating Committee

TPCR	traditional procurement center representatives
TPIN	trading partner identification number
TQM	total quality management
TRCO	technical representative of the contracting officer
TRD	technical requirement document
TRM	technical reference model
TTPP	Trade Tie-up Promotion Program (Japan)
TVA	Tennessee Valley Authority
U2	unclassified/unlimited
UAT	user acceptance testing or test
UCA	undefinitized contract action
UCC	uniform commercial code
UCF	uniform contract format
UCLINS	uniform contract line item numbering system
UKTI	United Kingdom Trade & Investment
UN	United Nations
UNCITRL	United Nations Commission on International Trade Law
UNCSD	United Nations Common Supply Database
UNDB	*UN Development Business*
UNDP	United Nations Development Program
UNGM	United Nations Global Marketplace
URL	uniform resource locator
URN	unique reference number
USACE	United States Army Corps of Engineers
USAFE	United States Air Force–Europe
USAID	United States Agency for International Development
USAREU	United States Army–Europe
USASBE	U.S. Association for Small Business and Entrepreneurship
USB	universal serial bus

U.S.C.	United States Code
US-CERT	United States Computer Emergency Readiness Team
USCG	U.S. Coast Guard (part of DHS)
USCIS	U.S. Citizenship and Immigration Service (part of DHS)
USDA	U.S. Department of Agriculture
USEAC	U.S. Export Assistance Centers (SBA is a key partner)
USEPA	U.S. Environmental Protection Agency
USGCB	U.S. Government Configuration Baseline
USGS	U.S. Geological Survey
USITC	U.S. International Trade Commission
USML	United States Munitions List
USPAACC	U.S. Pan Asian American Chamber of Commerce
USPS	U.S. Postal Service
USTDA	U.S. Trade and Development Agency
UXO	unexploded ordnance
V&V	verification and validation
VA	Department of Veterans Affairs
VAAR	Veterans Administration Acquisition Regulation
VAN	value-added network
VAR	value-added reseller
VAS	value-added service
VDI	virtual desktop infrastructure
VE	value engineering
VECP	value engineering change proposal
VEDP	Virginia Economic Development Partnership
VEP	value engineering proposal
VETS	Veterans Technology Services (VETS)
VGA	video graphics adapter
VIBES	virtual international business and economic sources

VMM	value measuring methodology
VoIP	Voice over Internet Protocol
VP	vice president
VPC	virtual proposal center
VPN	virtual private network
VPO	virtual procurement office
VSB	very small business
VTC	video teleconference
VUSME	Virtual University for Small and Medium-Sized Enterprises
W2W	Work to Welfare Program
WAIS	Wide Area Information Server (a database)
WASME	World Association of Small and Medium-Sized Enterprises
WBE	woman-owned business enterprise
WBENC	Women's Business Enterprise National Council
WBS	work breakdown structure
WEIC	Wales Euro Info Centre
WinPET	Windows proposal evaluation tool
WISBIS	Women in Small Business Information Site
WISE	Web-integrated solicitation elements
WMDVBE	Women, Minority, and Disabled-Veteran Business Enterprise
WMG GCS	Western Management Group Government Contractors Compensation
WNET	Women's Network for Entrepreneurial Training
WOA	Web-oriented architecture
WOB	woman-owned business
WOBREP	women-owned business representative (federal agencies such as the Department of Agriculture, Commerce, Defense, Education, and Veterans' Affairs have WOBREPs)
WTO	World Trade Organization
WTO GPA	World Trade Organization Agreement on Government Procurement
WTPF	Washington Technical Personnel Forum

WWW	World Wide Web
WYE	work year equivalent
XML	Extensible Markup Language
YTD	year to date
ZUI	zooming user interface

Selected bibliography

Abramson, Neil R., and Janet X. Ai, "You Get What You Expect in China," *Business Quarterly*, Winter 1996, pp. 37–44.

Anderson, Tania, "8(a) Companies Learn the Secret of Partnering," *Washington Technology*, Vol. 10, October 1996, p. 22.

Angus, Jeff, Jeetu Patel, and Jennifer Harty, "Knowledge Management: Great Concept . . . But What Is It?" *Information Week*, Vol. 673, March 16, 1998, pp. 58–70.

Anthes, Gary H., "Procurement Horror Stories Draw Feds' Scrutiny," *Computerworld*, February 21, 1994.

Banham, Russ, "Valuing IP Post-Sarbanes-Oxley," *Journal of Accounting*, November 2005, http://www.journalofaccounting.com/Issues/2005/Nov/ValuingIPPostSarbanesOxley.htm.

Barquin, Ramon C., Alex Bennett, and Shereen G. Remez, (eds.), *Knowledge Management: The Catalyst for Electronic Government,* Vienna, VA: Management Concepts, Inc., 2001.

Beazley, Hamilton, Jeremiah Boenisch, and David Harden, *Continuity Management: Preserving Corporate Knowledge and Productivity When Employees Leave,* New York: John Wiley, 2002.

Becerra-Fernandez, Irma, Avelino Gonzalez, and Rajiv Sabherwal, *Knowledge Management: Challenges, Solutions, and Technologies*, Upper Saddle River, NJ: Prentice-Hall, 2003.

Becerra-Fernandez, Irma, and Rajiv Sabherwal, *Knowledge Management: Sysetms and Processes,* Armonk, NY: M.F. Sharpe, 2010.

Beveridge, James M., and Edward J. Velton, *Positioning to Win: Planning and Executing the Superior Proposal,* Radnor, PA: Chilton Book Company, 1982.

Blankenhorn, Dana, "11 Lessons from Intranet Webmasters," *Netguide,* October 1996, pp. 82–90.

BMRA Procurement Alert Notice, Fairfax, VA: Business Management Research Associates, Inc., Vol. 8, No. 3, Fall 2003.

Bounds, Andy, *The Jelly Effect,* Chichester, U.K.: Capstone, 2007.

Bowman, Joel P., and Bernadine P. Branchaw, *How to Write Proposals That Produce*, Phoenix, AZ: Oryx Press, 1992.

Brockmeier, Dave, "Help Shape Federal Acquisition Regulations," *Business Credit*, Vol. 97, March 1995, pp. 40–42.

Brusaw, Charles T., Gerald J. Alred, and Walter E. Oliu, *Handbook of Technical Writing*, New York: St. Martin's Press, 1976.

Caudron, Shari, "Spreading Out the Carrots," *Industry Week,* May 19, 1997, pp. 20, 22, 24.

Cavill, Peter, "COTS: The Reality," *Military & Aerospace Electronics*, June 2005, p. 13.

Chesebrough, David E., "Knowledge Management: A Tool for SMEs," *CACCI Journal,* Vol. 1, 2006, pp. 1–12.

The Chicago Manual of Style, 16th ed., Chicago, IL: The University of Chicago Press, 2010.

Chyi, Hsiang I., and Maxwell McCombs, "Media Salience and the Process of Framing: Coverage of the Columbine School Shootings," *Journalism & Mass Communication Quarterly,* Vol. 81, Spring 2004, p. 30.

Cibinic, John, and Ralph C. Nash, *Formation of Government Contracts*, 2nd ed., Washington, D.C.: George Washington University, 1986.

Cibinic, John, Ralph C. Nash, and James F. Nagle, *Administration of Government Contracts*, 4th ed., New York: Wolters Kluwer Law & Business, 2006.

Clemons, Erid K., and Bruce W. Weber, "Using Information Technology to Manage Customer Relationships: Lessons for Marketing in Diverse Industries," *Proceedings of 26th Hawaii International Conference on System Sciences,* January 1993.

Clipsham, Neil B., "Appraising Performance Appraisal Systems," *The Military Engineer,* No. 591, April–May 1998, pp. 31–32.

Cohen, Sacha, "Knowledge Management's Killer App," *The Knowledge Management Yearbook 1999–2000,* James W. Cortada and John A. Woods, (eds.), Boston, MA: Butterworth-Heinemann, 1999, pp. 394–403.

"Community KM Glossary," http://knowledgecreators.com/km/kes/glossary.htm.

"Complying with the Anti-Kickback Act," *Developments in Government Contract Law*, No. 10, September 1990.

Cranston, H. S., and Eric G. Flamholtz, "The Problems of Success," *Management Decision*, Vol. 26, September 1988, p. 17.

Cremmins, Edward T., *The Art of Abstracting*, Philadelphia, PA: ISI Press, 1982.

Dale, Charles V., *Minority Contracting and Affirmative Action for Disadvantaged Small Businesses: Legal Issues,* CRS Report for Congress, February 24, 2006 [Order Code RL 33284].

Daum, Juergen H., *Intangible Assets and Value Creation,* New York: John Wiley, 2002.

Davenport, Thomas H., and Laurence Prusak, *Working Knowledge: How Organizations Manage What They Know,* Boston, MA: Harvard Business School Press, 1997.

Davenport, Tom, and Larry Prusak, "Know What You Know," http://www.brint.com/km/davenport/cio/know.htm, 2000.

Davidson, Paul, "U.S. Air Force SMC Innovations in Electronic Procurement," *APMP Perspective*, Vol. I, July/August 1996, pp. 7, 12, 13, 15.

Day, Robert A., *How to Write and Publish a Scientific Paper*, Philadelphia, PA: ISI Press, 1979.

December, John, and Neil Randall, *The World Wide Web Unleashed*, 2nd ed., Indianapolis, IN: Samsnet, 1995.

Delphos, William A., *Inside the World Bank Group: The Practical Guide for International Business Executives*, Washington, D.C.: Delphos International, 1997.

Denning, Stephen, *The Leader's Guide to Storytelling: Mastering the Art and Discipline of Business Narrative*, San Francisco, CA: Jossey-Bass, 2011.

Desktop Guide to Basic Contracting Terms, 2nd ed., Vienna, VA: National Contract Management Association, 1990, 1989.

DiGiacomo, John, and James Klekner, *Win Government Contracts for Your Small Business*, Riverwoods, IL: CCH, 2001.

"Disadvantaged Firms to Get Edge in Bids for Federal Contracts," *Baltimore Sun*, June 25, 1998, p. 2A.

"DOD Acquisition Chief Pushes COTS/Dual-Use, Wants More Suppliers," *Technology Transfer Week*, Vol. 30, April 1996.

"DOD's Airborne Recon Plan Pushes Sensors, Image Recognition," *Sensor Business News*, May 8, 1996.

Doebler, Paul D., "Who's the Boss? Sorting Out Staffing and Workflow Issues," *EP&P*, April 1988, pp. 21–26.

Do-It-Yourself Proposal Plan, TRW Space & Defense Proposal Operations, Rev. 3, February 1989.

Douglas, Susan P., C. Samuel Craig, and Warren J. Keegan, "Approaches to Assessing International Marketing Opportunities for Small- and Medium-Sized Companies," *Columbia Journal of World Business*, Fall 1982, pp. 26–32.

Edvinsson, Leif, and Michael S. Malone, *Intellectual Capital: Realizing Your Company's True Value by Finding Its Hidden Brainpower*, New York: HarperBusiness, 1997.

Edwards, Vernon J., *Competitive Proposals Contracting*, Falls Church, VA: Educational Services Institute, 1989 (in association with The George Washington University School of Government and Business Management).

Edwards, Vernon J., *Federal Contracting Basics*, Falls Church, VA: Educational Services Institute, 1990 (in association with The George Washington University School of Government and Business Management).

Edwards, Vernon, J., *Source Selection Answer Book*, 2nd ed., Vienna, VA: Management Concepts, 2006.

Elbert, Bruce, and Bobby Martyna, *Client/Server Computing: Architecture, Applications, and Distribution Systems Management*, Norwood, MA: Artech House, 1994.

Entman, Robert M., "Framing: Toward Clarification of a Fractured Paradigm," *Journal of Communication*, Vol. 43, 1993, p. 52.

Erramilli, M. Krishna, and C. P. Rao, "Choice of Foreign Market Entry Modes by Service Firms: Role of Market Knowledge," *Management International Review*, Vol. 30, 1990, pp. 135–150.

Escalas, Jennifer E., "Narrative Processing: Building Consumer Connections to Brands," *Journal of Consumer Psychology*, Vol. 14, 2004, p. 168.

Farrell, Michael, "Many Firms Want to Do Business Internationally But Lack the Wherewithal," *Capital District Business Review*, Vol. 22, September 1995, p. 15.

"Federal Acquisition Streamlining Act Enacted," *Business Credit*, Vol. 97, March 1995, p. 6.

Flading, Jeffrey L., "Certifications and the Contracting Community," *Contract Management*, Vol. 47, No. 7, July 2007, pp. 18–22.

Flagler, Carolynn, "The ANY Aspects of International Proposals," *Contract Management*, March 1995, pp. 11–19.

Fleming, Quentin W., and Joel M. Koppleman, *Earned Value Project Management,* 4th ed., Newtown Square, PA: Project Management Institute, 2010.

Fonnesbaek, J., and M. M. Anderson, "Storytelling: How LEGO Told a Story and Sold a Toy," *Young Consumers,* Quarter 2, 2005, p. 33 [World Advertising Research Center (WARC)].

Fox, Harold W., "Strategic Superiorities of Small Size," *Advanced Management Journal,* Vol. 51, 1986, p. 14.

Frank, C., "Uncle Sam Helps Business Get High Tech to Market," *Missouri Tech Net News,* November 4, 1997; http://www.umr.edu/~tscsbdc/sbirsumm.html.

Freed, Richard C., Shervin Freed, and Joe Romano, *Writing Winning Business Proposals: Your Guide to Landing the Client, Making the Sale, and Persuading the Boss*, New York: McGraw-Hill, 1995.

Frey, Robert S., "Beyond Compliance: Toward Solution and Storyline Development as Valuable Proposal Management Core Competencies," *Journal of the Association of Proposal Management Professionals,* Spring/Summer 2003, pp. 8–11.

Frey, Robert S., "Build Tangible and Intangible Benefits into Your Proposals," *Kansas City Small Business Monthly*, February 2001, pp. 34, 39.

Frey, Robert S., "Contracting with the Federal Government," *St. Louis Small Business Monthly*, Vol. 15, Issue VI, July 2002, pp. 1, 3.

Frey, Robert S., "Contracting with Uncle Sam: Preparing Early and Paying Attention to Some Key Issues Will Help Build Success," *Kansas City Small Business Monthly,* April 2005, Vol. 14, No. 4, p. 25.

Frey, Robert S., "Effective Small Business Response Strategies to Federal Government Competitive Procurements," *The Journal of Business and Management,* Vol. 4, No. 1, Summer 1997, pp. 40–74.

Frey, Robert S., "Envisioning Your Future Contracting with the Federal Government," *Kansas City Small Business Monthly*, March 2002, pp. 19, 47.

Frey, Robert S., "Federal Contracting and Small Business," *Kansas City Small Business Monthly*, Vol. 13, Issue 2, February 2004, p. 21.

Frey, Robert S., "Federal Performance-Based Contracting: What Is It, and What Does It Mean for Your Small Business," *Corporate Corridors*, Vol. 2, No. 3, July/August 2003, pp. 60–61.

Frey, Robert S., "Federal Procurement Policies: Making Sense of Important Federal Acquisition Laws and Directives," *Kansas City Small Business Monthly,* January 2005, Vol. 14, No. 1, p. 19.

Frey, Robert S., "ISO-Driven Proposal and Business Development Excellence," *APMP Perspective*, Vol. 13, No. 4, Fall 2003, pp. 3–6.

Frey, Robert S., "Knowledge Management Benefits Federal Contracting Initiatives," *Kansas City Small Business Monthly*, April 2002, pp. 21, 47.

Frey, Robert S., "Knowledge Management, Proposal Development, and Small Business," *Journal of Management Development,* Vol. 20, No. 1, 2001, pp. 38–54.

Frey, Robert S., "Leveraging Business Complexity in a Knowledge Economy," *Journal of Business,* Vol. XI, Spring 1999, pp. 4–21.

Frey, Robert S., "Making Sense of Important Federal Acquisition Laws and Directives," *Corporate Corridors,* February/March 2005, Vol. 4, No. 1, pp. 60–61.

Frey, Robert S., "Making the Leap: Graduating Successfully from the U.S. SBA 8(a) Program," *Corporate Corridors*, Vol. 1, No. 8, November 2002, pp. 54–55.

Frey, Robert S., "Mentor-Protégé Programs Can Benefit Your Small Business," *Kansas City Small Business Monthly,* September 2004, Vol. 13, No. 9, p. 18.

Frey, Robert S., "Once-Upon-a-Time Proposals: Winning New Government Contracts Through the Art of Customer-Focused, Fact-Based Storytelling," *Kansas City Small Business Monthly*, Vol. 13, Issue 7, July 2004, p. 21.

Frey, Robert S., "Past Performance: It's More Important Than You Think!" *Corporate Corridors*, Vol. 3, No. 1, February 2004, pp. 60–61.

Frey, Robert S., "Performance-Based Contracting: What Does It Mean for Small Business?" *Kansas City Small Business Monthly*, Vol. 12, Issue 2, February 2003, pp. 21, 43.

Frey, Robert S., "Proactive Strategic Partnering and Subcontracting Initiatives," *Corporate Corridors*, Vol. 2, No. 1, January/February 2003, pp. 54–55.

Frey, Robert S., "Resources for International Success: Information and Partnerships Can Jumpstart Global Business Opportunities," *St. Louis Small Business Monthly*, Vol. 16, Issue X, November 2003, p. 10.

Frey, Robert S., "Small Business Knowledge Management Success Story—*This Stuff Really Works!*" *Knowledge and Process Management: The Journal of Corporate Transformation*, Vol. 9, No. 3, July–September 2002, pp. 172–177.

Frey, Robert S., "Stop Selling Your Product! Build Tangible and Intangible Benefits Into Your Proposals," *Texas Small Business News*, Vol. 4, Issues 6/7, June/July 2002, pp. 7–8.

Frey, Robert S., "Strategic Partnering and Subcontracting," *Kansas City Small Business Monthly*, June 2001, pp. 34, 39.

Frey, Robert S., "Submitting Successful Private-Sector Proposals," *Kansas City Small Business Monthly Entrepreneur's Guide*, 2003–2004, p. 72.

Frey, Robert S., "Understanding and Responding to a Request for Proposal (RFP)," *Kansas City Small Business Monthly*, Vol. 11, Issue 8, August 2002.

Frey, Robert S., "Winning Federal Government Contracts Through Fact-Based Storytelling," *Journal of the Association of Proposal Management Professionals (APMP)*, Spring/Summer 2005, pp. 50–59.

Frey, Robert S., "Winning New Government Contracts Through the Art of Customer-Focused, Fact-Based Storytelling," *Corporate Corridors (Annual Government Contracting Issue)*, 2004, Vol. 3, No. 2, pp. 61–62.

Frey, Robert S., "Your Company's Federal Report Card," *Corporate Corridors*, Vol. 2, No. 2, April/May 2003, pp. 60–61.

Gibson, Diane L., Dennis R. Goldenson, and Keith Kost, "Performance Results of CMMI®-Based Process Improvement," Carnegie Mellon Software Engineering Institute, CMU/SEI-2006-TR-004, August 2006.

Gibson, Rowan, (ed.), *Rethinking the Future: Rethinking Business, Principles, Competition, Control, Leadership, Markets and the World*, London, England: Nicholas Brealey Publishing, 1997.

Godin, Seth, *All Marketers ~~are Liars~~ Tell Stories: The Underground Classic That Explains How Marketing Really Works—And Why Authenticity Is the Best Marketing of All,* New York: Penguin Group, 2009.

Goldberg, Mim, "Listen to Me," *Selling Power,* July/August 1998, pp. 58–59.

Goretsky, M. Edward, "When to Bid for Government Contracts," *Industrial Marketing Management,* Vol. 16, February 1987, p. 25.

Gouillart, Francis J., and Frederick D. Sturdivant, "Spend a Day in the Life of Your Customers," *Harvard Business Review,* January/February 1994.

Graham, John R., "Getting to the Top, and Staying There," *The New Daily Record,* Baltimore, MD, July 26, 1997, pp. 7A–7B.

Gray, Barbara, "Strong Opposition: Frame-Based Resistance to Collaboration," *Journal of Community & Applied Social Psychology,* Vol. 14, 2004, p. 167.

Grundstein, Michel, "Companies & Executives in Knowledge Management," http://www.brint.com/km/cko.htm.

Guide to Doing Business in All 50 States for A/E/P and Environmental Consulting Firms, Natick, MA: Zweig White and Associates, 1998.

A Guide for Preparing BOEs (Basis of Estimates), TRW Space & Defense Sector, 1989.

Gurak, Laura J., *Oral Presentations for Technical Communications,* Boston, MA: Allyn and Bacon, 2000.

Hackeman, Calvin L., "Best Value Procurements: Hitting the Moving Target," McLean, VA: Grant Thornton, 1993 (a white paper prepared in connection with Grant Thornton's Government Contractor Industry Roundtables).

Haeckel, Stephen H., *Adaptive Enterprise: Creating and Leading Sense-and-Respond Organizations,* Cambridge, MA: Harvard Business School Press, 1999.

Hager, Peter J., and Howard J. Scheiber, *Designing & Delivering, Scientific, Technical, and Managerial Presentations,* New York: John Wiley & Sons, 1997.

Hale, Charles R., "The Sales Power of Storytelling," *Advisor Today,* Vol. 50, July 2005.

Hall, Dane, "Electronic Proposal Evaluation: How One U.S. Government Agency Does It," *The Executive Summary: The Journal of the APMP's National Capital Area Chapter,* June 1996, pp. 6, 8–9.

Hallahan, Kirk, "Seven Models of Framing: Implications for Public Relations," *Journal of Publications Research,* Vol. 11, 1999, pp. 206, 207.

Hamilton, Martha A., "Managing the Company Mind: Firms Try New Ways to Tap Intangible Assets Such as Creativity, Knowledge," *Washington Post,* August 18, 1996, pp. H1, H5.

Hand, John R. M., and Baruch Lev, *Intangible Assets: Values, Measures, and Risks,* New York: Oxford University Press, 2003.

Hardy, Michael, David Hubler, and Matthew Weigelt, "Experts Nitpick SARA Panel Proposals," *Federal Computer Week.com,* January 8, 2007, http://www.fcw.com/article97283-01-08-07-Print.

Harris, Jack, and B. Kim Barnes, "Leadership Storytelling," *Leadership Excellence,* Vol. 22, April 2005, p. 7.

Hartman, Curtis, and Steven Pearlstein, "The Joy of Working," *INC.,* November 1987, pp. 61–71.

Hayden, Craig A., "Power in Media Frames: Thinking About Strategic Framing and Media System Dependency and the Events of September 11, 2001," 2003, p. 5, http://lass.calument.purdue.edu/cca/gmj/fa03/graduatef03/gmj-fa03-hayden.htm.

Heiman, Stephen E., and Diane Sanchez, *The New Strategic Selling, Revised and Updated for the 21st Century,* New York: Warner Books, 1998.

Heisse, John R., " 'Best Value' Procurement: How Federal and State Governments Are Changing the Bidding Process," April 29, 2002, http://www.constructionweblinks.com/Resources/Industry_Reports_Newsletters/April_29_2002/best_value_procurement.htm.

Helgeson, Donald V., *Engineer's and Manager's Guide to Winning Proposals,* Norwood, MA: Artech House, 1994.

Henry, Shannon, "The 8(a) Dating Game: Primes and Small Business Find Each Other Through Hard Work and Happenstance," *Washington Technology*, Vol. 12, September 1996, p. 24.

Hesselbein, Frances, Marshall Goldsmith, and Richard Beckhard, (eds.), *The Organization of the Future*, San Francisco, CA: Jossey-Bass Publishers, 1997.

Hevenor, Keith, "Storage Product Buyers Guide," *Electronic Publishing*, August 1, 1996, p. 10.

Hewitt, Tom, "Preparing Winning Proposals and Bids," Virginia: Federal Sources.

Hill, James W., and Timothy Whalen, (eds.), *How to Create and Present Successful Government Proposals: Techniques for Today's Tough Economy*, New York: IEEE Press, 1993.

Hinton, Henry L., *Federal Acquisition: Trends, Reforms, and Challenges*, Washington, D.C.: United States General Accounting Office, March 16, 2000. Testimony before the Subcommittee on Government Management, Information, and Technology, House Committee on Government Reform, GAO/T-OGC-007.

History at NASA [NASA HHR-50], Washington, D.C.: NASA Headquarters, 1986.

Hoft, Nancy L., *International Technical Communication: How to Export Information About High Technology*, New York: John Wiley & Sons, 1995.

Holtz, Herman, *Proven Proposal Strategies to Win More Business*, Chicago, IL: Upstart Publishing Co., 1997.

Holtz, Herman, and Terry Schmidt, *The Winning Proposal: How to Write It*, New York: McGraw-Hill, 1981.

"How the Pros See the Global Business Scene," *Rochester Business Journal*, Vol. 12, June 21, 1996, p. 10.

Howard, James S., and John Emery, "Strategic Planning Keeps You Ahead of the Pack," *D & B Reports*, Vol. 33, March/April 1985, p. 18.

Hoyle, David, *ISO 9000 Quality Systems Handbook: Updated for the ISO 9001:2008 Standard*, 6th ed., Oxford, UK: Butterworth-Heinemann, 2009.

Hoyt, Brad, "What Is KM?" *Knowledge Management News,* 1998; http://www.kmnews.com/Editorial/whatkm.htm.

Hubler, David, "Federal Contract Spending Slowdown Just Beginning, OMB Official Says," *Washington Technology,* February 18, 2011.

Hunt, Rodney, "8(a) Grads Face a Daunting Future," *Washington Technology,* Vol. 21, No. 17, September 4, 2006.

Huseman, Richard C., and Jon P. Goodman, "Realm of the Red Queen: The Impact of Change on Corporate Education, and the Emergence of Knowledge Organizations," The Corporate Knowledge Center @ EC^2, Annenberg Center for Communications, University of Southern California, 1998.

Ibarra, Herminia, and Kent Linebeck, "What's Your Story?" *Harvard Business Review,* Vol. 83, January 2005, p. 70.

"IBM, U.S. Chamber of Commerce Announce Results of New Study on U.S. Small Business and Technology," http://216.239.39.104/search?q=cache:v86sqMvVWmQJ:americanbusinessplans.com/1.pdf+%22IBM,+U.S.+Chamber+of+Commerce+Announce+Results%22hl=en.

"Information Warfighter: Leveraging Commercial Internet Protocol Technology," *Military Information Technology*, Vol. 10, Issue 7, August 2006, pp. 33–34.

Ingram, Thomas N., Thomas R. Day, and George H. Lucas, "Dealing with Global Intermediaries: Guidelines for Sales Managers," *Journal of Global Marketing*, Vol. 5, 1992.

Ink, Dwight, "Does Reinventing Government Have an Achilles Heel?" *The Public Manager: The New Bureaucrat*, Vol. 24, Winter 1995, p. 27.

Introduction to the Federal Acquisition Regulation Training Course, Vienna, VA: Management Concepts, Inc.

Ireland, Lewis, R., *Quality Management for Projects and Programs,* Newtown Square, PA: Project Management Institute, 2007.

Jain, Subash C., *International Marketing Management*, Boston, MA: Kent Publishing Company, 1993.

James, Geoffrey, "It's Time to Free Dilbert," *New York Times*, September 1, 1996, p. F-11.

Jennings, Robert W., *Make It Big in the $100 Billion Outsource Contracting Industry,* Westminster, CO: Westfield Press, 1997.

Johansson, A. W., "Consulting as Story-Making," *The Journal of Management Development,* Vol. 23, 2004, p. 341.

Jones, Stephen, "Navigating the Federal Bureaucracy Labyrinth," *Computerworld,* November 14, 1988, p. 145.

Joss, Molly W., "Authoring Alchemy: Ingredients for Brewing Up a Multimedia Masterpiece," *Desktop Publishers,* January 1996, pp. 56–65.

Kasse, Tim, *Practical Insight into CMMI,* 2nd ed., Norwood, MA: Artech House, 2008.

Kasser, Joe, *Applying Total Quality Management to Systems Engineering,* Norwood, MA: Artech House, 1995.

Keller, John, "Could RoHS Mean the End of COTS as We Know It?" *Military & Aerospace Electronics,* Vol. 17, No. 7, July 2006, p. 1.

Kelman, Steven, "Remaking Federal Procurement," Working Paper No. 3, The John F. Kennedy School of Government Visions of Governance in the 21st Century, January 3, 2002, http://www.ksg.harvard.edu/visions/ publication/kelman.pdf.

Keninitz, Donald, "The Government Contractor's Dictionary: A Guide to Terms You Should Know," http://www.kcilink.com/govcon/ contractor/gcterms.html.

Kerzner, Harold, *A Systems Approach to Planning, Scheduling, and Controlling,* New York: John Wiley & Sons, 2006.

Kerzner, Harold, *Project Management Workbook and PMP/CAPM Exam Study Guide,* New York: John Wiley & Sons, 2006.

"Knowledge Management: Collaborating on the Competitive Edge," *CIO White Paper Library,* 2000; http://www.cio.com/sponsors/0600_km.

Knudsen, Dag, "The Proposal Game: Two Strikes and You're Out," *American Consulting Engineer,* May/June 1998, p. 13.

The 2011 KPMG Federal Word Book: A Directory of Federal Financial Management and IT Acronyms, Laws and Regulations, Terms and Agencies and URLs, The KPMG Government Institute; kpmginstitutes.com/ government-institute.

Krathwohl, David R., *How to Prepare a Research Proposal: Guidelines for Funding and Dissertations in the Social and Behavioral Sciences*, 3rd ed., Syracuse, NY: Syracuse University Press, 1988.

LaFlash, Judson, "The Target Proposal Seminar," Woodland Hills, CA: Government Marketing Consultants, June 1981.

Laurent, Anne, "Shifting the Risk," *Government Executive Magazine*, August 30, 1999; http://www.govexec.com/features/99top/08a99s1.htm.

League, V. C., and Odessa Bertha, (eds.), *The Proposal Writer's Workshop: A Guide to Help You Write Winning Proposals*, Sacramento, CA: Curry-Co Publishing, 1998.

Leibfried, Kate H. J., and Joe Oebbecke, "Benchmarking: Gaining a New Perspective on How You Are Doing," *Enterprise Integration Services Supplement*, October 1994, pp. 8–9.

Lev, Baruch, "Accounting Needs New Standards for Capitalizing Intangibles," *ASAP: Forbes Supplement on the Information Age*, April 7, 1997; http://www.forbes.com/asap/97/0407/034.htm.

Lev, Baruch, *Intangibles: Management, Measurement, and Reporting*, Washington, D.C.: Brookings Institution, 2001.

Letavec, Craig J., *The Program Management Office: Establishing, Managing and Growing the Value of a PMO*, Ft. Lauderdale, FL: J. Ross Publishing, 2006.

Letavec, Craig, J., and Denis Bolles, (eds.), *The PMOSIG Program Management Office Handbook: Strategic and Tactical Insights for Improving Results*, Ft. Lauderdale, FL: J. Ross Publishing, 2011.

Lingguang, Song, *Earned Value Management: A Global and Cross Industry Perspective on Current EVM Practice*, Newtown Square, PA: Project Management Institute, 2010.

Lissack, Michael R., "Complexity Metaphors and the Management of a Knowledge Based Enterprise: An Exploration of Discovery," http://www.lissack.com/writings/proposal.htm.

Loring, Roy, and Harold Kerzner, *Proposal Preparation and Management Handbook*, New York: Van Nostrand Reinhold, 1982.

Maher, Michael C., "The DOD COTS Directive—What About Radiation Hardness?" *Defense Electronics*, Vol. 26, October 1994, pp. 29–33.

Malone, Thomas W., and John K. Rockart, "Computers, Networks, and the Corporation," *Scientific American,* September 1991, pp. 128–136.

Mariotti, John, "Nursery-Rhyme Management," *Industry Week,* May 5, 1997, p. 19.

Markie, Tracy, and Mark Tapscott, "COTS: The Key to a Tougher Military Marketplace," *Defense Electronics*, Vol. 25, November 1993, pp. 29–33.

Marshall, Colin, "Competing on Customer Service: An Interview with British Airways' Sir Colin Marshall," *Harvard Business Review,* November/December 1995.

Martin, James A., "Team Work: 10 Steps for Managing the Changing Roles in Your Desktop Publishing Work Group," *Publish!*, December 1988, pp. 38–43.

McCartney, Laton, "Getting Smart About Knowledge Management," *Industry Week,* May 4, 1998, pp. 30, 32, 36–37.

McConnaghy, Kevin V., and Robert J. Whitehead, "RFPs: Winning Proposals," *Environmental Lab*, May/June 1995, pp. 14–19.

McCubbins, Tipton F., "Three Legal Traps for Small Businesses Engaged in International Commerce," *Journal of Small Business Management*, Vol. 32, July 1994, p. 95–103.

McVay, Barry L., *Proposals That Win Federal Contracts: How to Plan, Price, Write, and Negotiate to Get Your Fair Share of Government Business*, Woodbridge, VA: Panoptic Enterprises, 1989 (Panoptic Federal Contracting Series).

McVey, Thomas W., "The Proposal Specialist as Change Agent," *APMP Perspective,* May/June 1997, pp. 1, 3, 13.

Meador, Roy, *Guidelines for Preparing Proposals: A Manual on How to Organize Winning Proposals for Grants, Venture Capital, R&D Projects, and Other Proposals,* Chelsea, MI: Lewis Publishers, 1985.

Michaelson, Herbert B., *How to Write and Publish Engineering Papers and Reports*, Philadelphia, PA: ISI Press, 1982.

Miller, Jason, "OMB Puts Pressure on Agencies to Boost Use of Performance-Based Acquisition," *Government Leader,* August 11, 2006.

Pine, B. Joseph, *Mass Customization: The New Frontier in Business Competition News,* Boston, MA: Harvard Business School Press, 1993.

Piper, Thomas S., "A Corporate Strategic Plan for General Sciences Corporation," Spring 1989 (unpublished).

Porter, Kent, "Usage of the Passive Voice," *Technical Communication,* First Quarter 1991, pp. 87–88.

Porter-Roth, Bud, *Proposal Development: How to Respond and Win the Bid,* Central Point, OR: Oasis Press/PSI Research, 1998.

Potter, Robert A., *Winning in the Invisible Market: A Guide to Selling Professional Services in Turbulent Times,* self-published, 2003.

Preparing Winning Proposals and Bids, U.S. Professional Development Institute (USPDI), Washington, D.C., September 16–17, 1987.

"Presenting Your Proposal Orally and Loving It!" TRW, 1979.

Proposal Preparation Manual, 2 vols., Covina, CA: Procurement Associates, 1989 (revised).

Prusak, Laurence, (ed.), *Knowledge in Organizations,* Boston, MA: Butterworth-Heinemann, 1997.

Quinn, James Brian, Philip Anderson, and Sydney Finkelstein, "Managing Professional Intellect: Making the Most of the Best," *Harvard Business Review*, March/April 1996.

Quinn, Judy, "The Welch Way: General Electric CEO Jack Welch Brings Employee Empowerment to Light," *Incentive*, September 1994, pp. 50–52, 54, 56.

Ramsey, Leslie A., and Phale D. Hale, *Winning Federal Grants: A Guide to the Government's Grantmaking Process,* Alexandria, VA: Capital Publications, 1996.

Ray, Dana, "Filling Your Funnel: Six Steps to Effective Prospecting and Customer Retention," *Selling Power*, July/August 1998, pp. 44–45.

Reis, Al, and Jack Trout, *The 22 Immutable Laws of Marketing: Violate Them at Your Own Risk,* New York: HarperBusiness, 1994.

Reyonlds, Garr, *Presentation Zen: Simple Ideas on Presentation, Design and Delivery,* Berkeley, CA: New Riders, 2008.

Ricks, David A., *Blunders in International Business*, Cambridge, MA: Blackwell Publishers, 1993.

Rifkin, Jeremy, *The End of Work: The Decline of the Global Labor Force and the Dawn of the Post-Market Era,* New York: G.P. Putnam and Sons, 1995.

Riordan, John, and Lillian Hoddeson, *Crystal Fire: The Birth of the Information Age,* New York: W. W. Norton & Co., 1997.

Roam, Dan, *The Back of the Napkin: Solving Problems and Selling Ideas with Pictures,* New York: Penguin Group, 2009.

Roberts, J. B., *The Art of Winning Contracts: Proposal Development for Government Contractors,* Ridgecrest, CA: J. Melvin Storm Co., 1995.

Roos, Johan, "Intellectual Performance: Exploring an Intellectual Capital System in Small Companies," October 30, 1996, pp. 4, 9.

Roos, Johan, and Georg von Krogh, "What You See Depends on Who You Are," *Perspectives for Managers,* No. 7, September 1995.

Root, Franklin R., *Entry Strategies for International Markets*, revised and expanded, New York: Lexington Books, 1994.

Root, Franklin R., *Foreign Market Entry Strategies*, New York: AMACOM, 1987.

Ruggles, Rudy L., *Knowledge Management Tools,* Boston, MA: Butterworth-Heinemann, 1997.

Sabherwal, Rajiv, and Irma Becerra-Fernandez, *Business Intelligence,* New York: Wiley, 2010.

Sabo, Bill, "Orals: Your Worst Nightmare or Your Greatest Competitive Advantage?" *APMP Perspective*, September/October 1996, pp. 1, 11.

Safford, Dan, *Proposals: On Target, On Time,* Washington, D.C.: American Consulting Engineers Council, 1997.

SBA Budget Request & Performance Plan, FY2007 Congressional Submission, February 10, 2007, pp. 2, 3.

Scarborough, Norman M., and Thomas W. Zimmerer, "Strategic Planning for Small Business," *Business*, Vol. 37, April/June 1987, p. 11.

Schillaci, William C., "A Management Approach to Placing Articles in Engineering Trade Journals," *Journal of Management in Engineering*, September/October 1995, pp. 17–20.

Schwalbe, Kathy, *Information Technology Projecct Management,* 6th ed., MA: Boston Course Technology, 2009.

Schultz, Benjamin, "Business Documents Don't Have to Be Boring," *Business Communications Quarterly,* Vol. 64, No. 4, December 2006, pp. 407–409.

"Selected Viewgraphs from Judson LaFlash Seminars on Government Marketing and Proposals," *Government Marketing Consultants,* July 1980.

Selling to the Military, DOD 4205.1-M, Washington, D.C.: Department of Defense.

Shuman, Jeffrey C., and John A. Seeger, "The Theory and Practice of Strategic Planning in Smaller Rapid Growth Firms," *American Journal of Small Business*, Vol. 11, 1986, p. 7.

Slaughter, Jeff, "New Way of Doing Business with Uncle Sam: Electronic Commerce/Electronic Data Interchange," *Mississippi Business Journal,* Vol. 18, February 1996, p. 10.

Small Business Administration—FY2007 Budget Request and Performance Plan, p. 40, http://www.sba.gov/idc/groups/public/ documents/sba_homepage/serv_abf_budget_1.pdf.

Small Business Notes, Release Number 06-52, September 1, 2006, http://www.smallbusinessnotes.com/federalgovernment/sba/sbanews/ sbanews090106.html.

The Small Business Economy: A Report to the President, Washington, D.C.: United States Government Printing Office, 2010.

Smith, P. R., and Dave Chaffey, *eMarketing eXcellence: The Heart of eBusiness,* Oxford, England: Butterworth-Heinemann, 2003.

Soat, Douglas M., *Managing Engineers and Technical Employees: How to Attract, Motivate, and Retain Excellent People*, Norwood, MA: Artech House, 1996.

Sole, Deborah, "Sharing Knowledge Through Storytelling," Learning Innovations Laboratories, Harvard University Graduate School of Education, April 2002, http://www.providersedge.com/docs/km_articles/ sharing_knowledge_throughstorytelling.pdf.

Sole, Deborah, and Daniel G. Wilson, "Storytelling in Organizations: The Power and Traps of Using Stories to Share Knowledge in Organizations;" http://lila.pz.harvard.edu/_upload/lib/ACF14F3.pdf.

Solomon, Robert, "International Effects of the Euro," Brookings Institution Policy Brief #42, Washington, D.C.: The Brookings Institution, 1999.

Source Evaluation and Selection, Vienna, VA: Management Concepts, Inc.

Source Selection: Greatest Value Approach, Document #KMP-92-5-P, Washington, D.C.: U.S. General Services Administration, May 1995.

Stanberry, Scott A., *Federal Contracting Made Easy*, Vienna, VA: Management Concepts, Inc., 2001.

Standard Industrial Classification Manual, Executive Office of the President, Office of Management and Budget, 1987.

Statements of Work Handbook [NHB 5600.2], Washington, D.C.: Government Printing Office, February 1975.

Steiner, Richard, *Total Proposal Building: An Expert System Dedicated to One Result: Winning Grants & Contracts from Government, Corporations & Foundations*, 2nd ed., Albany, NY: Trestleetree Publications, 1988.

Stewart, Rodney D., and Ann L. Stewart, *Proposal Preparation*, New York: John Wiley & Sons, 1984.

Stewart, Thomas A., *Intellectual Capital: The New Wealth of Organizations*, New York: Doubleday, 1997.

Stewart, Thomas A., "Mapping Corporate Brainpower," *Fortune*, Vol. 132, No. 9, 1995, p. 209.

Stout, D. A., and J. M. Buddenbaum, "Media, Religion and 'Framing,'" *Journal of Media & Religion*, Vol. 2, 2003, pp. 1–3.

Sullivan, Robert, *United States Government New Customers Step by Step Guide*, Information International, 1997.

Sutton, Michael H., "Dangerous Ideas: A Sequel," Remarks delivered during the American Accounting Association 1997 Annual Meeting in Dallas, Texas, August 18, 1997, p. 3, http://www.corpforms99.com/83.html.

Sveiby, Karl E., "The Intangible Assets Monitor," http://www.sveiby.com/articles/IntangAss/CompanyMonitor.html, December 20, 1997.

Sveiby, Karl E., "What Is Knowledge Management?" http:www.sveiby.com/articles/KnowledgeManagement.html, April 2001.

Tapscott, Mark, "COTS Regulation Reforms Sought by Industry Coalition," *Defense Electronics*, Vol. 25, October 1993, pp. 8–11.

Taylor, Leslie, "Number of Small Businesses Reaches All-Time High," Inc.com, December 22, 2006, http://www.inc.com/criticalnews/Articles/200612/sba.html.

Ten Steps to a Successful BOE: Basis of Estimate Estimator's Checklist, TRW Space & Defense Sector, 1987.

Tepper, Ron, *How to Write Winning Proposals for Your Company or Client*, New York: John Wiley & Sons, 1990, 1989.

Terpstra, Vern, *International Marketing*, 4th ed., New York: The Dryden Press, 1987.

"Test Your Global Mindset," *Industry Week*, November 2, 1998, p. 12.

Thompson, Arthur A., and A. J. Strickland, *Strategy Formulation and Implementation: Tasks of the General Manager*, 4th ed., Homewood, IL and Boston, MA: BPI/IRWIN, 1989.

"Thriving on Order" (an interview of Steve Bostic), *INC.*, December 1989, pp. 47–62.

Training and Validation in Basis of Estimates, TRW Space & Defense Sector, 1987 [vugraphs].

Twitchell, James B., *AdcultUSA: The Triumph of Advertising in American Culture*, New York: Columbia University Press, 1996.

Unisys Defense Systems Proposal Development Digest, McLean, VA: Unisys, 1989.

Ursey, Nancy J., *Insider's Guide to SF254/255 Preparation*, 2nd ed., Natick, MA: Zweig White & Associates, 1996.

U.S. Small Business Administration, "BSA Streamlines 8(a) Contracting," Press Release Number 98-24, June 4, 1998; http://www.sba.gov/news/current98-24.html.

U.S. Small Business Administration, "Lockheed Martin Division, Nova Group Earn SBA's Top Awards for Subcontracting," Press Release Number 98-43, June 4, 1998; http://www.sba.gov/news/current98-43.html.

U.S. Small Business Administration, "Vice President and SBA Administrator Announce Pact with Big Three Automakers," Press Release Number 98-09, February 19, 1998; http://www.sba.gov/news/current98-09.html.

U.S. Small Business Administration, "Vice President Gore Praises SBA for Expanding Economic Opportunity: Congratulates Agency on 45th Birthday," Press Release Number 98-68, July 30, 1998; http://www.sba.gov/news.

Venter, David, "Framing—An Important Negotiation Tool," *The Negotiator Magazine,* October 2004, http://www.negotiatormagazine.com/article224_1.html.

Verespej, Michael A., "Drucker Sours on Terms," *Industry Week,* April 6, 1998, p. 16.

Verespej, Michael A., "The Old Workforce Won't Work," *Industry Week,* September 21, 1998, pp. 53, 54, 58, 60, 62.

Verespej, Michael A., "Only the CEO Can Make Employees King," *Industry Week,* November 16, 1998, p. 22.

Vivian, Kaye, *Winning Proposals: A Step-by-Step Guide to the Proposal Process,* Jersey City, NJ: American Institute of Certified Public Accountants, 1993.

Wall, Richard J., and Carolyn M. Jones, "Navigating the Rugged Terrain of Government Contracts," *Internal Auditor,* April 1995, pp. 32–36.

Weil, Ben H., I. Zarember, and H. Owen, "Technical-Abstracting Fundamentals," *Journal of Chemical Documentation,* Vol. 3, 1963, pp. 132–136.

Whitely, Richard, and Diane Hessan, *Customer-Centered Growth: Five Proven Strategies for Building Competitive Advantage,* Reading, MA: Addison-Wesley, 1996.

Whitman, Marina, and Rosabeth Moss Kanter, "A Third Way? Globalization and the Social Role of the American Firm," *Washington Quarterly,* Spring 1999.

"Why Denning Is Nuts About Stories," *New Zealand Management*, September 2004, p. 7.

Wodaski, Ron, "Planning and Buying for Multimedia: Effective Multimedia for the Small Office," *Technique: How-To Guide to Business Communication*, October 1995, pp. 16–25.

Wong, Kuan Yew, "Critical Success Factors for Implementing Knowledge Management in Small and Medium Enterprises," *Industrial Management & Data Systems,* Vol. 105, No. 3, 2005, pp. 261–279.

Wong, Kuan Yew, and Elaine Aspinwall, "Characterizing Knowledge Management in the Small Business Environment," *Journal of Knowledge Management*, Vol. 8, No. 3, 2004, pp. 44–61.

Words into Type, 3rd ed., Englewood Cliffs, NJ: Prentice-Hall, 1974.

The World Bank Annual Report, Washington, D.C.: The World Bank, 1994.

Worthington, Margaret, "The Ever Changing Definition of Allowable Costs," *Government Accountants Journal*, Vol. 35, Spring 1986, p. 52.

Worthington, Margaret M., Louis P. Goldsman, and Frank M. contra Alston, *Contracting with the Federal Government,* 4th ed., New York: John Wiley & Sons, 1988.

Writing Winning Proposals, Farmington, UT: Shipley Associates, 1988.

Wysocki, Robert K., *Effective Project Management: Traditional, Agile, Extreme,* 6th ed., New York: Wiley, 2011.

Zimmerman, Jan, *Doing Business with the Government Using EDI: A Guide for Small Businesses,* New York: Van Nostrand Reinhold, 1996.

Zuckman, Saul, "Is There Life After 8(a)?" *The Columbia (Md.) Business Monthly*, October 1994, p. 37.

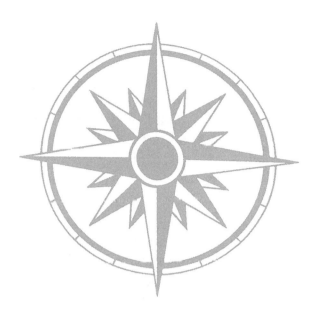

About the author

ROBERT S. FREY is a principal in the northern Virginia–based consultancy Successful Proposal Strategies, LLC (http://www.proposal23.com). In this capacity, he has been instrumental in supporting customers attain $3.359 billion in contract awards. He brings the insights, key practices, and lessons learned of 25 years of sustained proposal development excellence. He has successfully performed proposal solution development and management; end-to-end proposal development, design, and production; capture management; and business planning and development. That deep experience base is coupled with more than 30 years of writing and publication-related activities. Dr. Frey has conceptualized and established effective proposal development infrastructures for six federal contracting firms in Virginia and Maryland. Five of those firms were small businesses operating under the Small Business Administration's 8(a) program. In addition, he has provided end-to-end proposal development, design, and production support for more than 3,000 government, private-sector, and international proposals.

He has coordinated all phases of up to 12 scientific and engineering proposals concurrently.

Of particular note is Dr. Frey's hands-on experience with most facets of proposal development. In the process of establishing and implementing proposal infrastructures for various companies, he has actually performed the myriad tasks associated with responding to government, private-sector, and international requests for proposals and tenders, including graphics conceptualization, electronic-text editing, computer troubleshooting, and photocopying, along with solution development, original writing, and detailed review. During various periods, he was the only full-time staff person in a business-development capacity. He has developed a very thorough understanding of both the big picture and the day-to-day, hour-to-hour logistical, organizational, and interpersonal activities and processes associated with successful proposalmanship.

Dr. Frey also develops and presents innovative proposal training curricula and has delivered numerous interactive seminars nationwide to businesses and academe. These seminars have included a 2-day short course at the University of California at Los Angeles (UCLA), a daylong seminar for Microsoft Corporation in Redmond, Washington, the University of Texas-Pan American, the Eighth, Ninth, and Tenth NASA Mentor-Protégé Program Conferences, Department of Commerce Minority Business Development Agency (MBDA), U.S. Department of Energy 7th Annual Small Business Conference, George Washington University, and a workshop at Gallaudet University in Washington, D.C., sponsored by the Deaf and Hard of Hearing Entrepreneurship Council. He possesses a detailed understanding of marketing-intelligence resources, as well as collection and analysis techniques. Dr. Frey participates in business strategizing and planning for numerous federal, civilian, defense, law enforcement, and intelligence agencies under a broad umbrella of acquisition vehicles, such as governmentwide agency contracts (GWACs), ID-IQs, and cost-reimbursable, firm-fixed-price, and time and materials contracts.

He has prepared proposals for defense, civilian, law enforcement, and intelligence agencies, including the U.S. Army Corps of Engineers; Air Force Center for Environmental Excellence; U.S. Army and Navy; NASA; National Oceanic and Atmospheric Administration; Air Force Space Command; Environmental Protection Agency; Department of Transportation; Department of Energy; National Institutes of Health; Department of Veterans Affairs; Department of the Treasury; Bureau of Alcohol, Tobacco, and Firearms; Department of Education; Defense Logistics Agency; Department of Homeland Security; Federal Aviation Administration; Department of State; and the Defense Information Systems Agency.

Dr. Frey is an active member in the international Association of Proposal Management Professionals (APMP, http://www.apmp.org), serving as a member of the editorial review board for the *APMP Professional Journal: Journal of the Association of Proposal Management Professionals*. He was selected as an APMP Fellow in 2006. He delivered a presentation titled "Getting Your Story Straight: The Path to Blue Team," at the APMP annual conference held in Savannah, Georgia, in 2007. In addition, Dr. Frey published an article entitled "Effective Small Business Response Strategies to Federal Government Competitive Procurements" in the Summer 1997 issue of *The Journal of Business and Management* (Western Decision Sciences Institute/California State University, Dominguez Hills).

Successful Proposal Strategies for Small Businesses: Using Knowledge Management to Win Government, Private-Sector, and International Contracts, Sixth Edition, is the ninth book that Dr. Frey has written since 1985. He holds three master's degrees, including an M.B.A. and master of science in management (MSM) with a focus in marketing from the University of Maryland University College. He earned his Doctor of Management (DM) degree at Maryland in 2009. His dissertation, for which he collected data from 577 small business leaders nationwide, focused on how operating small business leaders supporting the federal government make decisions about the allocation of scarce organizational resources in their small firms. In 2012, Dr. Frey began a Master of Applied Science degree from The University of Denver. The focus of this degree is information and communications technology. For 9 years, Dr. Frey served as senior vice president of knowledge management and proposal development for RS Information Systems (RSIS), a highly successful midtier federal systems integrator with core competencies in information technology, engineering, telecommunications, and scientific consulting, headquartered in McLean, Virginia. RSIS graduated from the SBA's 8(a) program and grew to stand among the 50 largest federal IT contractors in the United States. The company sustained an incredible 9-year proposal win rate of 67%. It was aquired by Wyle Information Systems in 2008.

You can contact Dr. Frey at rfrey@proposal23.com or by calling (410) 812-1177. He can also be reached by U.S. mail at 11017 Devenish Drive, Oakton, VA 22124.

Planning and Design for High-Tech Web-Based Training, David E. Stone and
   Constance L. Koskinen

A Practical Guide to Managing Information Security, Steve Purser

Preparing and Delivering Effective Technical Presentations, Second Edition,
   David Adamy

Reengineering Yourself and Your Company: From Engineer to Manager to Leader,
   Howard Eisner

The Requirements Engineering Handbook, Ralph R. Young

Running the Successful Hi-Tech Project Office, Eduardo Miranda

Successful Marketing Strategy for High-Tech Firms, Second Edition, Eric Viardot

*Successful Proposal Strategies for Small Businesses: Using Knowledge Management
   to Win Government, Private-Sector, and International Contracts, Sixth Edition*,
   Robert S. Frey

Systems Approach to Engineering Design, Peter H. Sydenham

Systems Engineering Principles and Practice, H. Robert Westerman

Systems Reliability and Failure Prevention, Herbert Hecht

Team Development for High-Tech Project Managers, James Williams

For further information on these and other Artech House titles, including
previously considered out-of-print books now available through our
In-Print-Forever® (IPF®) program, contact:

Artech House
685 Canton Street
Norwood, MA 02062
Phone: 781-769-9750
Fax: 781-769-6334
e-mail: artech@artechhouse.com

Artech House
16 Sussex Street
London SW1V HRW UK
Phone: +44 (0)20 7596-8750
Fax: +44 (0)20 7630 0166
e-mail: artech-uk@artechhouse.com

Find us on the World Wide Web at: www.artechhouse.com